D0022580

Teaching Today's Health in Middle and Secondary Schools

David J. Anspaugh

Memphis State University

Gene Ezell

University of Tennessee—Chattanooga

LB 1588 .U6 A84 1994
Anspaugh, David J.
Teaching today's health in
middle and secondary

PITTS LIBRARY
BALDWIN WALLACE COLLEGE
WITHDRAWN

Merrill, an imprint of
Macmillan College Publishing Company
New York

Maxwell Macmillan Canada
Toronto

Maxwell Macmillan International
New York   Oxford   Singapore   Sydney

Cover photo: Ron Rovtar
Editor: Ann Castel Davis
Production Editor: Julie Anderson Tober
Art Coordinator: Ruth Kimpel
Photo Editor: Anne Vega
Cover Designer: Cathleen Norz
Production Buyer: Pamela D. Bennett

This book was set in Garamond by Carlisle Communications, Ltd. and was printed and bound by Book Press, Inc., a Quebecor America Book Company. The cover was printed by Phoenix Color Corp.

Copyright © 1994 by Macmillan College Publishing Company, Inc. Merrill is an imprint of Macmillan Publishing Company.

Printed in the United States of America

All rights reserved. No part of this book may be reproduced or transmitted in any form or by any means, electronic or mechanical, including photocopy, recording, or any information storage and retrieval system, without permission in writing from the Publisher.

Macmillan College Publishing Company
866 Third Avenue
New York, NY 10022

Macmillan College Publishing Company is part of the Maxwell Communication Group of Companies.

Maxwell Macmillan Canada, Inc.
1200 Eglinton Avenue East, Suite 200
Don Mills, Ontario M3C 3N1

Library of Congress Cataloging-in-Publication Data
Anspaugh, David J.
    Teaching today's health in middle and secondary schools / David J. Anspaugh, Gene Ezell.
        p.   cm.
    Includes bibliographical references and index.
    ISBN 0-02-303562-5
    1. Health education (Elementary)—United States. 2. Health education (Secondary)—United States. I. Ezell, Gene. II. Title.
LB1588.U6A84 1994
372.3'7044'0973—dc20   93-30752
                                                                 CIP

Printing: 1 2 3 4 5 6 7 8 9   Year: 4 5 6 7

Photo Credits: Centers for Disease Control, p. 304; Cleo, pp. 180, 191; Robert Finken, 103; Kevin Fitzsimmons/Macmillan, pp. 88; Mary Hagler/Macmillan, p. 37; Jean-Claude Lejeune, pp. 24, 110, 115, 322, 432; Photo Researchers, p. 266; Barbara Schwartz/Macmillan, pp. 68, 78, 248; Michael Siluk, pp. 60, 144, 156, 204, 214, 328, 360, 374, 392, 401, 458; Courtesy U.S. Health Corp., p. 442; Anne Vega/Macmillan, pp. 0, 9, 54; Allan Zak/Macmillan, p. 294.

Permission to include information from the book *Students Speak* © 1984 Comprehensive Health Education Foundation (C.H.E.F.®) was granted from C.H.E.F.®, Seattle, WA. All rights reserved.

Cindy and Megan Ezell—
  "They are the wind beneath my wings."

Aimee, Jay, Susan and my students—
  "My points of light."

Preface

For health education in the middle and secondary schools to be successful, the effort must begin in the elementary school and continue throughout the student's educational experience. This effort can only be successful if parents, administrators, and school board members support and promote quality health education. Imperative to this process are quality teachers who are prepared to teach health, who are assertive in their promotion of health education, and who can develop and implement comprehensive health-education programs.

Part of what we as health educators must develop is a "marketing mentality" to educate, inform, and promote health education at all levels of government. All potential sources of support must be gathered for this effort, including professional health associations such as the Association for the Advancement of Health Education (AAHE), the American School Health Association (ASHA), voluntary health organizations, foundations, and business-corporate agencies.

The need for health education is paramount. A number of health problems represent a threat to the nation and its youth. HIV infection, drug abuse, sexually transmitted diseases, and teenage pregnancies are just a few of the problems facing our youth and our nation. The Healthy People 2000—National Health Promotion and Disease Prevention Objectives can serve as the basis for our health education efforts. To truly educate, however, we must develop not only a comprehensive approach, but we must accept the challenge for our own well-being and seek to carry out health-enhancing behaviors as opposed to health-deterring behaviors. As educators, we must provide a solid cognitive base along with ample opportunities for students to personalize and assimilate information into their personal value systems. Helping our students see the importance of health information will encourage them to act in a positive fashion. Also of concern are the special needs of disabled, poor, and minority youth. To be successful health educators, we must give special attention to the needs of these students.

We hope that this text will allow students to acquire some of the skills, knowledge, and philosophy necessary to become health educators. We hope the information provided will serve as a conceptual framework for a comprehensive school health program. Our emphasis is upon the classroom and curricular programs that will enable students to achieve high-level health and wellness. These concepts are based upon our experiences as teachers, consultants, in-service trainers, and as participants in curricular projects at local, regional, and national levels and active members in professional organizations. We hope that the years of experience we bring to this project will help students become better, more enthusiastic teachers and spokespersons for health education. We are in a helping profession where our most important product is the student we serve. We must provide quality opportunities for our students to become more healthy, productive, and worthwhile citizens.

We wish to thank all those who helped make this book possible. A special thanks to Ann Castel Davis for her guidance and support throughout the project; to Carol Walls for keeping us on task, organized and informed; to Julie Tober for her management of the project and to Megan Rowe for her editing of the manuscript; and to the reviewers who provided helpful input and suggestions: E. Jean Denney, California State University, Chico; Onie Grosshans, University of Utah; L. Mike Morris, Idaho State University; and Barbara Wilks, University of Georgia. Finally, we wish to thank our students for giving us the desire and inspiration to do this project.

David Anspaugh
Gene Ezell

Contents

Chapter 3
Meeting the Needs of the Learner   54

Chapter 4
Strategies for Implementing Health Instruction   68

Chapter 7
Substance Use and Abuse   144

Alcohol and Tobacco   180

    Alcohol   182
            Effects of Alcohol   182
            Who Drinks?   183
            Why Do People Begin Drinking?   183
            Consequences of Alcohol Use   185
            Drinking and Accidents   185
            Alcoholism and Alcohol-Related Problems   186
            Treatment of Alcoholism   187
            Objectives for Reducing Alcohol-Related Problems   188
    Tobacco   188
            Effects of Tobacco Smoking   190
            Why People Smoke   192
            Second-Hand and Sidestream Smoke   193
            Reducing the Hazards of Smoking   194
            Smokeless Tobacco   194
            Preventing and/or Reducing Tobacco Use   195
    Student Concerns: Alcohol and Tobacco   196
    Summary   197
    Discussion Questions   197
    Activities for Teaching About Alcohol and Tobacco   197
    References   203

Chapter 9

Human Sexuality and Family-Life Education   204

    Program Goals   205
    Social Aspects of Sexuality and Family Living   206
            Types of Families   206
            The Changing Nature of the U.S. Family   206
    Mate Selection   207
            Love and Intimacy   207
            Why People Marry   209
            Dating and Courtship   209
            Choosing a Partner   209
            Marriage   211
            Parenthood   212
            Divorce   213
    Psychological Aspects of Sexuality and Family Living   214
            Gender Development   215
            Sex Roles   215
            Developing Sexuality   215

Chapter 10
Nutrition   248

Chapter 11
Concepts for Teaching Communicable Disease   294

Chapter 14

Concepts for Teaching Environmental Health   392

Chapter 15

Aging, Dying, and Death   432

CHAPTER 1

Comprehensive School Health

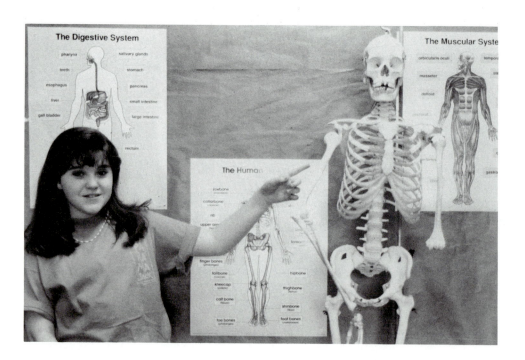

Health and intellect are the two blessings of life.

OBJECTIVES

After reading this chapter, you should be able to

- Define health, wellness, health promotion, and health education
- Describe the health-related problems facing youth today
- Identify the Healthy Nation 2000 Objectives
- Describe the comprehensive school health program
- Describe how to select content for health education instruction

U.S. public schools have long included health as part of the curriculum. Beginning with the earliest U.S. history and continuing through the present day and the Healthy Nation 2000 Objectives, health has been an integral part of public school education. Today's educators cannot ignore the fact that they must teach youth the importance of making sound, positive health decisions to maximize their quality of life.

DEFINING HEALTH

Health education has come a long way since its early history. Today, the challenge for a teacher is to motivate students to improve their own health status through positive self-direction. Health education offers students an opportunity for personal growth and enhancement that is not duplicated anywhere else in the school curriculum. Therefore, it is vital to the development of a total, positive lifestyle.

It is interesting to note that, since the 1970s, death rates among Americans have declined significantly. This decline reflects a decrease in deaths due to cardiovascular disease. It also coincides with the declining use of tobacco and intake of dietary fats and cholesterol and the increase in exercise among adults. Today, lifestyle, more than medicine, can lead to decreases in death rates. Health is uppermost in the minds of many Americans today. It is probably most visible in the wellness movement, which stresses personal responsibility for one's health.

But what is **health**? The World Health Organization (WHO) in 1947 defined health as having three dimensions. WHO defined health as "A state of complete physical, mental, and social well-being and not merely the absence of disease and infirmity" (World Health Organization, 1947, p. 3). This particular definition is quite positive and serves to point out the multifaceted nature of health. In an attempt to expand on this concept, Hoyman (1975) stated that the concept of health had several dimensions, each with its own continuum. Each continuum ranges from desirable to undesirable, as illustrated in Figure 1.1. The model portrays health not as a state but as a continually evolving process that is a result of behavior. The individual's ability

Figure 1.1   The health/wellness
continuum

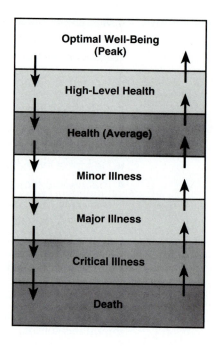

to make decisions and to interact socially, psychologically, and physically with others determines the quality of health.

Halbert Dunn (1961, 1977) developed a conceptualization of health and expanded on the definition. Because he believed that the term health was so distorted, he coined the term **high-level wellness**. Dunn stated that optimal health or high-level wellness is "an integrated method of functioning which is oriented toward maximizing the potential of which the individual is capable. It requires that the individual maintain a continuum of balance and purposeful direction within the environment where he or she is functioning" (p. 15). Today, health is composed of many elements. High-level health requires a balance among all of the factors that contribute to these elements.

A key in Dunn's definition is the "method of functioning" that maximizes potential. Dunn's definition suggests activity rather than passive behavior; it implies taking charge and accepting responsibility for our own quality of life.

The components that must be balanced to achieve high-level wellness are spiritual, intellectual, emotional, social, and physical. Briefly, each component can be viewed as follows:

Spiritual: This component provides meaning and direction in life. It includes a person's own morals, values, and ethics. Optimal spirituality is a person's ability to discover, articulate, and act on his/her basic purpose in life (Chapman, 1987).

Social: The ability to develop and maintain intimacy with others and respect/ tolerance for those with different opinions from our own.

Emotional: The ability to recognize and accept feelings and express them appropriately, to deal effectively with setbacks/failures, and to control stress.

Intellectual: The ability to learn and use information for personal growth and development. Intellectual wellness means striving for continued growth and being able to learn to deal with new challenges.

Physical: Developing cardiovascular fitness, maintaining proper nutrition, and refraining from using drugs, alcohol, and tobacco products.

Based on these definitions, total health (wellness) is a combination of the physical, intellectual, emotional, social, and spiritual components of life, balanced in a way that produces individual satisfaction and happiness. To accomplish this goal, an individual must engage in wellness activities such as maintaining proper nutrition, not smoking, exercising regularly, abstaining from substance abuse, and effectively dealing with stress. To achieve high-level wellness, each person must foster attitudes that improve the quality of life and expand the human potential. The earlier students begin the lifelong process of becoming healthy, the likelier is their success in achieving high-level wellness.

WHAT IS HEALTH EDUCATION?

Teachers must recognize that students bring to school many values and behaviors. These values represent both the positive and the negative aspects of each student's lifestyle. At the same time, teachers should be aware of their powerful influence on their students' lives. Consequently, a teacher who exemplifies a lifestyle conducive to high-level wellness, who exhibits a style of living that is physically, socially, and psychologically healthy, enhances the probability that his students will attempt to adopt such behavior in their own lives.

Like the definition of health, the meaning of **health education** has evolved over the years. Although health education has many definitions, the one used by the National Education Association (NEA) (Wilson, 1971) provides a framework for understanding what health education is. According to the NEA definition, health education is "the process of providing learning experiences which favorably influence understanding, attitudes, and conduct relating to individual and community health" (p. 2). To help understand and amplify how this process is to be accomplished it is necessary to understand several additional terms. The following definitions are taken from the Report of the 1990 Joint Committee on Health Education Terminology (1991).

Health Education Field. The health education field is that multidisciplinary practice which is concerned with designing, implementing, and evaluating educational programs that enable individuals, families, groups, organizations, and communities to play active roles in achieving, protecting, and sustaining health.

Health Education Program. A health education program is a planned combination of activities developed with the involvement of specific populations and based on a needs assessment, sound principles of education, and periodic evaluation using a clear set of goals and objectives.

Health Education Process. The health education process is that continuum of learning which enables people, as individuals and as members of social structures, to voluntarily make decisions, modify behaviors, and change social conditions in ways which are health enhancing (p. 7).

From the teacher's perspective, health education is the process of developing and providing planned learning experiences in such a way as to supply information, change attitudes, and influence behavior. In theory, this process results in the student taking personal responsibility in health-care issues, which leads to health enhancement, or high-level wellness. All this is accomplished through the teacher creating and facilitating learning experiences that develop decision-making ability. Good decision-making skills will help students make better choices about the personal, family, peer, and societal factors that influence their quality of life.

Health education is a lifelong process. As a person develops awareness of the many components of health and incorporates them into her own life, she

- Assumes responsibility for personal health and health care and participates in the decision-making process
- Respects the benefits of medical technology but is not in awe of medical equipment and tests
- Seeks information regarding health matters
- Tries new behaviors and modifies others
- Is an active partner with the physician in the decision-making process
- Is skeptical of health fads and trends
- Asks questions, seeks evidence, and evaluates information
- Strives for self-reliance in personal health matters
- Voluntarily adopts practices consistent with a healthy lifestyle

Accomplishing Health Education

Health education that is relevant and that motivates students requires careful planning. The quality of health instruction depends on the amount of teacher planning and organization. While health education can take many approaches, each teacher must be sure to create and facilitate direct instruction in health and incorporate relevant health-related topics whenever the opportunity arises. Only in this way can health become a meaningful part of each student's learning experience. *Meaningful* health education is education that influences decision-making. Thus, health instruction must blend information with attitudinal experiences. Brown (1974) describes this balance of information and attitude assessment as **confluent education**, which he defines as "the integration of cognitive learning with affective learning" (p. 4). In short, a student will be better able to make personal decisions concerning health behavior if the teacher has provided cognitive and affective opportunities for growth.

Presenting factual information alone—that is, addressing the cognitive aspect of health education—is not enough. Knowledge of facts alone does not lead to changes in behavior. The failure of so many cognitive drug-education programs in the past is evidence of this. Knowledge must become personalized for it to have an effect. This personalization is the affective aspect of health education. Strategies for accomplishing this are presented throughout the text.

HEALTH HIGHLIGHT
What Health Education Is and Is Not

What Health Education Is Today

Health education is an applied science basic to the general education of all children and youth. Its body of knowledge represents a synthesis of facts, principles, and concepts drawn from biological, behavioral, sociological, and health sciences, but interpreted in terms of human needs, human values, and human potential. Acquisition of information is a desired purpose but not the primary goal of instruction.

Growth in critical thinking ability and problem-solving skills is both the process and the product of instruction. Information can be quickly outdated, but cognitive skills remain an always dependable means of discovering fresh data when they are needed. The ultimate goal of health education is the development of an adult whose lifestyle reflects actions that tend to promote his or her own health as well as that of family and the community.

What Health Education Is Not

Sometimes objects or phenomena of any kind are defined as effectively by explaining what they are not as by describing what they are. Health education is not simply a minor aspect of physical education nor is it hygiene with a new name. It is not a program in physical fitness, although physical fitness surely is one of its goals. It is not the inculcation of health habits. It is not watered-down anatomy, physiology, biology or any combination of these sciences. It is not one or two short units specific to certain health concerns and temporarily hosted by another course as a means of satisfying state requirements or local concerns with the health crisis of the month or year. It most certainly is not an assembly lecture program, a rainy day activity, or incidental teaching in response to momentary health problems or concerns.

Source: "Health Education: The Basic of the Basics" by M. Pollock and M. Hamburg, April 1984. Paper presented at Delbert Oberteuffer Centennial Symposium, Atlanta. Reprinted by permission of the American Alliance for Health, Physical Education, Recreation and Dance, 1900 Association Drive, Reston, Virginia 22091.

To be efficient, health instruction must be:

1. *Sequential:* Health should be taught from kindergarten through twelfth grade, in a sequence that introduces concepts at appropriate learning levels. The curriculum at each grade should build on what has been learned in previous years and should be the basis for curricula in future years.
2. *Planned:* Health instruction should have stated goals, objectives, activities, and evaluation criteria. It should be given scheduled time within the total curriculum, not taught sporadically or used as a substitute for other subjects.
3. *Comprehensive:* Instruction in only one or several health topics (e.g., drugs, nutrition, or sexuality) is not adequate for an understanding of health. A comprehensive health curriculum includes instruction in growth and development, mental and emotional health, personal and family lifestyles, nutrition, disease prevention and control, safety, drug use and abuse, and consumer and community health. More important than the individual subjects, however, is a study of how all subjects are interrelated and how all affect the quality of life.

4. *Taught by qualified health teachers:* A teacher requires training to teach health concepts and to relate these to the wellness of the students. Junior and senior high school teachers and school health coordinators should be professionally prepared health educators. State departments of education have information regarding certification requirements in each state. Also, it is important to remember that in the last 20 years topics such as drug abuse, smoking, heart disease prevention, teenage pregnancy, adolescent suicide, stress control, incest, child abuse, AIDS, and CPR have been added to an already long list of topics such as nutrition, disease, mental health, sexuality, personal health, environmental health, first aid, and quackery. (Purdy & Tritsch, 1985, p. 185)

Why Health Education?

Perhaps the best argument for teaching health is that health behaviors are the most important determinant of health status. Because health-related behaviors are both learned and amenable to change, health education has the potential to help students avoid many of the pitfalls of a negative lifestyle. This potential becomes increasingly important with mounting evidence that most health problems result from smoking,

HEALTH HIGHLIGHT
Adolescents' Health Knowledge, Attitudes, and Behaviors

The need for a comprehensive health education program in the secondary school can be seen when viewing a survey recently taken. The survey was titled the *National Adolescent Student Health Survey* (NASHS). Published in 1988, the research was the first survey in more than 20 years to determine the knowledge, attitudes, and behavior of the nation's youth. NASHS questioned over 11,000 eighth and tenth graders on eight topics: AIDS, injury prevention, violence, suicide, alcohol, drug and tobacco use, sexually transmitted diseases, consumer health, and nutrition. Some of the highlights of the survey are listed for each content area.

- 94% of the students surveyed know there is an increased risk of AIDS from having intercourse with someone who has the AIDS virus.
- 91% know there is an increased risk of AIDS by sharing drug needles.
- 82% know there is an increased risk of AIDS by having more than one sex partner.
- 86% know that condoms are an effective way to reduce the risk of being infected with the AIDS virus.
- 91% agree that people their age should use condoms if they have sex.
- 71% mistakenly believe that blood transfusions are a common way to get AIDS today.
- 47% mistakenly believe that there is an increased risk of contracting AIDS when donating blood.
- 51% are either unsure or mistakenly believe that washing one's genitals after sex reduces one's chances of being infected with the AIDS virus.
- 94% of the girls and 76% of the boys believe it is acceptable to "say no" to having sex.
- 18% of the boys and 4% of the girls believe it is acceptable for people their age to have sex with several different people.

Source: "National Adolescent Student Health Survey," August/September 1988, *19, Health Education,* pp. 4–8. Used with permission of the Association for the Advancement of Health Education (AAHE).

poor nutrition, excess weight, lack of exercise, stress, abuse of drugs and alcohol, and unsafe personal behavior (O'Rourke, 1985).

Unfortunately, health education still suffers from a lack of respect in the school curriculum and a lack of adequately trained teachers. If we wish to help prevent many of the conditions that are now the leading causes of death (cardiovascular disease, cancer, accidents, and so on), then we must emphasize prevention in our educational efforts. Students receive nearly 12,000 hours of education in kindergarten through grade 12, yet less than 3% of that time is in health (Educational Research Service, 1983). America has only one qualified health educator per 21,500 students, or one for every 50 schools (National Center for Educational Statistics, 1984).

Following are some of the health problems faced by adolescents. According to *Healthy People 2000* (1990), these problems fall into two major areas: injuries and violent acts, and lifestyles that affect health in both the short and long term.

Causes of Death. About half of all deaths among people 15 to 24 years of age result from unintentional injuries, with 75% of these deaths involving motor vehicles. Again, lifestyle factors enter into the problem, since more than half of all motor vehicle accidents involve alcohol. In the school setting, accidents happen more often to males than to females. For example, in the 1985–1986 school year, for every 100 males of school age there were 51 injuries and 50 lost days from school, whereas for every 100 females there were 29 injuries and 22 lost days. Most school injuries occurred during physical education class or interscholastic sports.

Perhaps even more alarming are the rates of homicide and suicide. Homicide is the second leading cause of death among males in the 15- to 24-year-old age group. It is the number one cause of death among African-American males in this age range. Alcohol is associated with half of all homicides. Nationwide, 10% of all homicides are associated with drugs, although this figure is much higher in most cities. Suicide rates in this age group are continuing to climb. The rate of increase is most alarming, particularly among young white men 15 to 24 years old. From 1950 to 1987, the death rate from suicide rose from 7% to almost 23% per 100,000 population. The rates of suicide among African-American adolescents and young adults is half that of whites. In general, suicides have decreased among older youth and have increased in the earlier teenage years. (*Healthy People 2000,* 1990).

Nutrition. Nutritional problems, although they have changed in nature, continue to exist. The Metropolitan Life Foundation (1991) conducted a study of the health status of American youth. The study reported that most students knew that a nutritious diet leads to good health; however, only 21% said they thought about whether the food they chose to consume was good for them.

Many said they buy candy (65%), potato chips (44%), soda (44%), gum (27%), and cake and cookies (19%). These eating habits set the stage for many chronic diseases. The typical American diet consists of more than 36% fat, is too high in sodium and simple carbohydrates, and lacks in fiber. This type of diet is associated with cardiovascular disease, hypertension, diabetes, and certain types of cancer.

Health Concerns. When more than 3,000 high school students were surveyed to determine health needs with which they might want help, the top five were acne, sex education, depression, weight control, and relationships with their parents.

Smoking. Young people, especially teenage girls, are taking up smoking at earlier ages. Three-fourths of high school seniors who smoke reported that they smoked their first cigarette by grade 9. The use of snuff and chewing tobacco has increased dramatically among teenage boys. Between 1970 and 1986, snuff use increased 15-fold and chewing tobacco use increased 4-fold. In 1987, nearly 9% of young men used smokeless tobacco.

Alcohol. Alcohol remains a significant problem. In 1989, about 60% of high school seniors reported drinking alcohol in the previous month, with 33% reporting heavy drinking—five or more drinks on one occasion within a two-week period. Alcohol use is also prevalent in middle school/junior high school. Twenty-eight percent of eighth graders reported occasions of heavy drinking.

Drugs. On a positive note, efforts at drug education seem to be affecting drug use. Illicit drug use reached a record low of about 20% in 1989. This reflected a 50% drop over the last decade. In 1989, marijuana use was 17% for high school seniors. Only 3% of the class of 1989 reported using cocaine at least once in the month preceding the survey, and 1.4% reported using crack cocaine. This represents a significant drop of more than 20% from the figures reported in 1988. On the other hand, illicit drug experimentation still seems to start early. A survey of eighth and tenth graders reported that 6% of the eighth graders and 10% of the tenth graders had used cocaine in the month before the survey was taken (NASHS, 1988).

Sexual Activity. In the area of sexual behavior, an estimated 78% of adolescent girls and 86% of adolescent boys have engaged in sexual intercourse by age 20 (Sonnenstein, Pleck, & Ku, 1992, p. 154). Approximately 1.1 million girls aged 15 through 19 become pregnant each year. In addition, there is the obvious risk of sexually transmitted diseases.

In 1987, an update of the health problems that U.S. students face appeared in *Why School Health* (American Association of School Administrators, 1987, p. 1). Some of the findings were as follows:

1. At least one third and perhaps as many as 60% of American youth already exhibit at least one of the primary risk factors for heart disease, the nation's primary killer.
2. In the past 20 years, the incidence of obesity among teenagers has increased 39%.
3. In that same period of time, the incidence of anorexia nervosa has doubled.
4. Only 36% of American young people aged 6 to 17 meet the standard for "average fitness."
5. Of the 29 million adolescents over age 12, about 12 million are sexually active.
6. Seventy-five percent of all sexually transmitted diseases are found in the 15 to 24 age group.
7. Each day, 3,000 girls in the United States become pregnant. Four out of 10 teenage girls will become pregnant sometime before they reach the age of 20, and 50% of teenage mothers drop out of school.
8. Nearly 25% of young people between the ages of 12 and 17 have a serious drinking problem. More than half of all teenage deaths are related to the use of alcohol or other drugs.
9. The leading causes of death among Americans including heart disease, high blood pressure, and cancer are at least partly related to factors that individuals can learn to control, such as smoking, diet, weight, and stress.

10. The American Medical Association found that two thirds of all students have used an illegal drug before they leave high school; 1 in 16 uses alcohol daily.
11. Both drug use and sexual activity place adolescents at greater risk for developing AIDS and other sexually transmitted diseases.

This list does not touch on every area of concern in a comprehensive health-education program. But it is hoped that the pressing need for health education has been established. The scope of health education is broad: We must effectively address personal, family, and community problems if we are to have personally and socially satisfying lives.

Many educators share this philosophy. They know that a comprehensive health-education program can provide both immediate and long-term benefits for both our physical and fiscal well-being. Americans spent an average of $1,100 per person per year on health care in 1988, or about 11.1% of the country's Gross National Product (GNP). Today, estimates indicate that 16% of the GNP is spent on health care and health-care services, and that percentage continues to rise.

More tragic is the loss in human potential. Today, the diseases that are killing Americans are chronic diseases such as cancer and heart disease. Many of these deaths could be prevented by helping people alter their lifestyles through improved eating habits, regular exercise, and not smoking. Decreasing the incidence of these

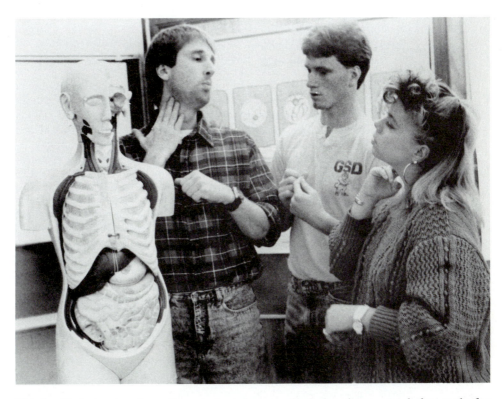

This health instructor shows these students how to check their heart rates before and after aerobic activity.

diseases depends not on additional medical care or expenditures but on educating people to live healthy lives and thereby prevent disease. As a nation, we must invest our resources in helping people take control of their lives.

Health Objectives for the Year 2000

The United States Department of Health and Human Services (1990), through the Public Health Service, issued a statement listing the Nation's Health Objectives for the year 2000. The statement, *Healthy People 2000—National Health Promotion and Disease Prevention Objectives,* listed the opportunities for improving the quality of life for U.S. citizens. The purpose of these objectives is to commit the nation to attainment of three broad goals: (1) increase the span of healthy life for Americans, (2) reduce health disparities among Americans, and (3) achieve access to preventive services for all Americans (*Healthy People 2000,* p. 6).

The objectives designed to accomplish these goals by the year 2000 fall into 22 priority areas. The first 21 of these areas are grouped into three broad categories

---

HEALTH HIGHLIGHT
Healthy People 2000

Healthy People 2000: National Health Promotion and Disease Prevention Objectives, released in September 1990, offers a vision for the new century, characterized by significant reductions in preventable death and disability, enhanced quality of life, and greatly reduced disparities in the health status of populations within our society.

Healthy People 2000 does not reflect the policies or opinions of any one individual or any one organization, including the federal government. It is the product of a national effort, involving professionals and citizens, private organizations, and public agencies from every part of the country. It is deliberately comprehensive in addressing health promotion and disease prevention opportunities to allow local communities and states to choose from among its recommendations to address their own highest priority needs.

Schools offer the most systematic and efficient means available to improve the health of youth and enable young people to avoid health risks. They provide an avenue for reaching more than 46 million students each year, as well as over 5 million instructional and noninstructional staff. The American Public Health Association noted that the school, as a social structure, provides an educational setting in which the total health of the child during the impressionable years is a priority concern. No other community setting even approximates the magnitude of the grades K–12 school education enterprise; thus, it seems that the school should be regarded as a focal point to which health planning for all other community settings should relate.

Planned and sequential quality school health education programs help young people at each appropriate grade to develop increasingly complex knowledge and skills they will need to avoid important health risks, and to maintain their own health, the health of the families for which they will become responsible, and the health of communities in which they will reside.

Source: *Healthy people 2000—National Health Promotion and Disease Prevention Objectives.* (1990). (conference ed.). U.S. Department of Health & Human Services: Washington D.C.

consisting of health promotion, health protection, and preventive services. **Health-promotion strategies** are related to individual lifestyle—personal choices made in a social context that can have a powerful influence over quality of life. Priorities under this heading include physical activity and fitness, nutrition, tobacco, alcohol and drugs, family planning, mental health and mental disorders, and violent and abusive behavior. **Health-protection strategies** are related to environmental or regulatory measures that protect U.S. citizens. The areas of concern include unintentional injuries, occupational safety and health, environmental health, food and drug safety, and oral health. **Preventive services** include counseling, screening, immunization, or chemoprophylactic intervention for individuals in clinical settings. Some of the areas of prevention included are heart disease and stroke, cancer, HIV infections, and sexually transmitted diseases. Figure 1.2 summarizes these areas of concern for the Nation's Health Objectives.

Many of the objectives listed under each of these headings relate directly to a comprehensive school health-instructional plan. The American School Health Asso-

Figure 1.2 *Healthy People 2000* priority areas

Health Promotion

1. Physical Activity and Fitness
2. Nutrition
3. Tobacco
4. Alcohol and Other Drugs
5. Family Planning
6. Mental Health and Mental Disorders
7. Violent and Abusive Behavior
8. Educational and Community-Based Programs

Health Protection

9. Unintentional Injuries
10. Occupational Safety and Health
11. Environmental Health
12. Food and Drug Safety
13. Oral Health

Preventive Services

14. Maternal and Infant Health
15. Heart Disease and Stroke
16. Cancer
17. Diabetes and Chronic Disabling Conditions
18. HIV Infection
19. Sexually Transmitted Diseases
20. Immunization and Infectious Diseases
21. Clinical Preventive Services

Surveillance and Data Systems

22. Surveillance and Data Systems

ciation (ASHA) identified the following areas related to the 22 priorities: (1) school health education, (2) healthy school foodservices, (3) physical education, (4) a healthy school environment, (5) school health services, (6) counseling and school psychology, (7) integrated school and community health-promotion efforts, and (8) school-site health promotions for faculty and staff. ASHA's recommendations for these areas appear in Figure 1.3.

The basic responsibility for a student's health is with the parents, but the school plays an important role—sometimes primary, sometimes secondary—in maintaining the health of each student.

All teachers should be concerned with student health, as any deviation from normal health is a possible deterrent to the ability to learn effectively. Even minor disturbances such as a cold or stomachache can impair a student's ability to concentrate and, therefore, to learn. The teacher's primary role in this part of the health program is in observation, record keeping, referral, and follow-up. Teachers can also become involved in screening students for various health-related functions, such as vision and hearing. Teachers should also prepare students for any screening examination they might be taking in the near future. This preparation serves two purposes. First, it reduces student anxiety regarding the testing because it removes fear of the unknown. Second, it turns the screening exam into a learning experience in health education for the students. The school nurse should supervise the actual screening examination. The classroom teacher and school nurse should cooperate in all three areas of the comprehensive school health program. These two professionals can form a vital team in promoting student health in grades 7 through 12.

THE SCHOOL NURSE

In a comprehensive school-health plan, the school nurse is most visible in the health-services area. Unfortunately, many school districts have been forced to cut back the role of school nurses by assigning each nurse to several schools. This does not allow sufficient time to develop the health service completely for a given school. In other communities, parents, school secretaries, or some other undertrained individuals perform health services.

The services that school nurses provide are extremely important to students' welfare. Most frequently, they provide direct care to students who are sick or injured. They also gather information through assessment of the students and do record keeping. Assessments should help ensure appropriate follow-up care and aid in interpreting conditions for parents.

Nurses are excellent resources. They should be included on any health-education curriculum-planning committee and involved in planning the education of special students. Since passage of Public Law 94–142, the Individuals with Disabilities Education Act, the nurse has become increasingly involved in planning educational programs for disabled students. Nurses can assist these students in becoming self-sufficient in the classroom and help alleviate teachers' fears and concerns. Finally, the nurse should help develop emergency procedures for injuries, accidents, and sickness because the school faces obvious legal concerns when administering

Figure 1.3   Recommendations for health education

School Health Education

1. Increase to at least 75 percent the proportion of the nation's schools that provide nutrition education from preschool through 12th grade, preferably as part of quality school health education.
2. Increase the proportion of high school seniors who perceive social disapproval associated with the heavy use of alcohol, occasional use of marijuana, and experimentation with cocaine.
3. Increase the proportion of high school seniors who associate risk of physical or psychological harm with the heavy use of alcohol, regular use of marijuana, and experimentation with cocaine.
4. Provide to children in all school districts and private schools primary and secondary school educational programs on alcohol and other drugs, preferably as part of quality school health education.
5. Increase to at least 85 percent the proportion of people aged 10 through 18 who have discussed human sexuality, including values surrounding sexuality, with their parents and/or have received information through another parentally endorsed source, such as youth, school, or religious programs.
6. Increase to at least 50 percent the proportion of elementary and secondary schools that teach nonviolent conflict resolution skills, preferably as a part of quality school health education.
7. Increase to at least 75 percent the proportion of the nation's elementary and secondary schools that provide planned and sequential kindergarten-through-grade-12 quality school health education.
8. Provide academic instruction on injury prevention and control, preferably as part of quality school health education, in at least 50 percent of public school systems (grades K through 12).
9. Increase to at least 95 percent the proportion of schools that have age-appropriate HIV education curricula for students in 4th through 12th grade, preferably as part of quality school health education.
10. Include instruction in sexually transmitted disease transmission prevention in the curricula of all middle and secondary schools, preferably as part of quality school health education.

Healthy School Foodservices

1. Increase to at least 90 percent the proportion of school lunch and breakfast services and child care food services with menus that are consistent with the nutrition principles in the *Dietary Guidelines for Americans*.

School Physical Education

1. Increase to at least 50 percent the proportion of children and adolescents in 1st through 12th grade who participate in daily school physical education.
2. Increase to at least 50 percent the proportion of school physical education class time that students spend being physically active, preferably engaged in lifetime physical activities.

Healthy School Environment

1. Establish tobacco-free environments and include tobacco-use prevention in the curricula of all elementary, middle, and secondary schools, preferably as part of quality school health education.
2. Extend requirement of the use of effective head, face, eye, and mouth protection to all organizations, agencies, and institutions sponsoring sporting and recreation events that pose risks of injury.

School Health Services

1. Increase to at least 90 percent the proportion of all children entering school programs for the first time who have received an oral health screening, referral, and follow-up for necessary diagnostic, preventive, and treatment services.
2. Increase immunization levels as follows:
   Basic immunization series among children under age 2: at least 90 percent.
   Basic immunization series among children in licensed child care facilities and kindergarten through post-secondary education institutions: at least 95 percent.

Areas six (counseling and school psychology), seven (integrated school and community health promotions efforts) and eight (school-site health promotion for faculty and staff) all can be influenced in important ways by schools, but these efforts are outside the scope of this text. See *Healthy People 2000* (1990) and disease prevention objectives for suggestions.

Source: *Healthy People 2000—Nation's Health Promotion and Disease Prevention Objectives.* (1990). (conference ed.). U.S. Department of Health & Human Services: Washington D.C. Identified by ASHA's *Selected School Health Support Statements,* Sept. 1991, Kent, Ohio.

aid in any of these situations. The nurse can help ensure proper care will be given by helping to develop emergency guidelines and workshops for teachers, aides, and office personnel. In addition, every teacher should find the time to take a basic first aid course, learn CPR, and follow the emergency procedures established by the school district and the nurse.

THE TEACHER'S COOPERATION WITH OTHER SCHOOL PROFESSIONALS

The health teacher can be of special assistance in working with the school guidance counselor or the school nurse in a number of ways.

Observation. The teacher should look for any deviation in verbal and nonverbal behavior that might indicate a health problem. Has a normally outgoing student become withdrawn? Does a student strain to see what is written on the chalkboard? Does a student show undue irritability, aggressiveness, or apathy? These are all signs of possible health problems, either physical, psychological, or social.

Teachers are in an excellent position to appraise their students' health. They see the student each day in a variety of situations in the classroom, in the cafeteria, and in the gymnasium. Teachers familiar with the expected growth and development patterns of students are more likely to be objective in their appraisal than someone more closely identified with a student, such as a parent.

When a student poses a possible threat to the health of the other students—for example, because of a contagious upper respiratory infection—the teacher must take appropriate steps to remove that individual from the class.

Record Keeping. The teacher should keep an individual card file for each student. This file can be used as a referral source and can also be useful when discussing specific behaviors with parents or other members of the school health team. Objectivity should be the goal when making card file notes. The teacher should refrain from making value judgments about a student's behavior or condition and should avoid attempts at diagnosing the student's condition, since that is the responsibility of others on the health team. A teacher may, however, refer to school health records for each student, because this information could be valuable in understanding the student's behavior. Health records can also familiarize the teacher with any specific condition, such as diabetes or epilepsy, that might require emergency care in the classroom. All school personnel must remember that information contained in a student's health records is confidential and should not be discussed in the teacher's lounge.

Referral. Upon noticing any detrimental change in a student's health or behavior, the teacher should place the student under his/her care. If a school nurse is not immediately available, the teacher should notify the appropriate member of the administrative staff. The classroom teacher should be able to help the school nurse, physician, or counselor understand the everyday behavior of the individual. For instance, whereas the physician might see the student in an isolated situation, a teacher can supply a history of that student's behavior and explain whether the current behavior is typical or represents a drastic change.

Teachers should also be familiar with health-related agencies in the community that can provide assistance for specific health problems. This knowledge could be valuable to parents in getting help if they cannot afford the services of a private physician.

Follow-up. A dedicated teacher will continue to follow the student's case, even after observation and referral. If the student is absent from school for any time, checking with parents or the proper school official concerning that student's health is appropriate. When the student returns to the classroom, the teacher should resume careful observation to aid in recovery.

A good example of employing observation, record keeping, referral, and follow-up is the instance when a teacher observed that a student had recurring injuries on various parts of his body. The teacher carefully noted the injuries in her personal card file on the student. After several weeks of observation, she referred the case to the school guidance counselor. The teacher, nurse, and guidance counselor met with the parents, who described the child as "accident-prone." As part of the follow-up, the school nurse and guidance counselor reviewed the teacher's anecdotal records on the student. In turn, the physician submitted his findings to juvenile authorities, who tried and prosecuted the parents for child abuse. This dedicated teacher, operating within the school health team, played a significant part in promoting the health of her student in a difficult situation. She was careful not to make any diagnosis, nor to accuse the parents of any wrongdoing, but she did keep an accurate file on the student, referred the situation to the proper individuals, and followed up the case to its conclusion.

THE COMPREHENSIVE SCHOOL-HEALTH PROGRAM

A total school-health program is needed for the school to promote high-level wellness effectively. A comprehensive school-health program includes eight components: (1) school health services, (2) healthful school environment, (3) school health instruction, (4) school physical education, (5) school nutrition and foodservices, (6) school based counseling, (7) school-site health promotion, and (8) school, family, and community health promotion partnerships (see Figure 1.4). Each component involves planning, administration, and evaluation. Adequate planning for all eight components ensures their comprehensiveness. Effective leadership coordinates the components and ensures proper staffing, budgeting, policy fulfillment, and evaluation.

School Health Services

These programs seek to promote students' health through screening, intervention, and remediation of various health conditions. The school nurse most often coordinates and provides the services for this component. Health services include dental, visual, auditory, and scoliosis screenings, first aid procedures, illness protocol, and services for the disabled. Professionals who make up the school health services team include the school physician, dentist, social worker, speech pathologist, and nurse.

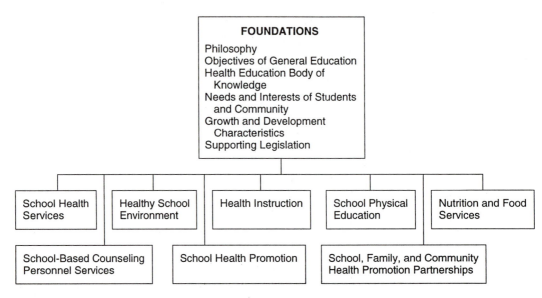

Figure 1.4   The comprehensive school-health program

Healthy School Environment

This aspect of the school health program includes the physical and psychological environment in which students and faculty exist. Issues addressed include the emotional and social environment of the classroom; the development of self-worth and self-esteem; and the fostering of positive relationships for students and school personnel. In addition, safety hazards on the school grounds and within the physical plant are of concern. This includes chemical agents, temperature, humidity, noise, lighting, and radiation found within the building and classroom. Few teachers are fortunate enough to be able to work in ideal situations. They should strive for an ideal, however. The classroom should be physically adequate, pleasant, attractive, and comfortable for students. When the classroom setting is bright, lively, and dynamic, morale is improved.

Teachers should require a quality working environment. This is important not only for the teaching/learning process, but also for teacher and student morale. Whenever possible, teachers should volunteer as consultants in planning and maintaining the school site and surroundings. Fostering a cooperative relationship with the custodial staff, lunchroom staff, and administrators in charge of the various aspects of the environment is beneficial. Working with the custodians by keeping the classroom sanitary and by diplomatically suggesting improvements can enhance the environment significantly.

The psychological setting is just as important as the physical one, and the teacher is responsible for establishing the emotional tone within the classroom. The overall atmosphere should be one of acceptance, one in which the teacher knows the students well and is sensitive to their individual needs. The classroom should be nonthreatening.

Stress is reduced when the teacher takes a relaxed approach to instruction, one that de-emphasizes competition that pits student against student. Students should feel free to express their feelings honestly without fear of ridicule or rebuke. They should also feel free to fail occasionally without punishment. A teacher can promote students' well-being by being kind but fair in promoting teacher-student relationships, setting reasonable goals for each student, praising positive behavior, challenging students within their capabilities, and tolerating occasional frustration. Allowing students to assist in planning health learning opportunities is also very important. If they are involved in planning, they will become more interested in the subject matter. When students are interested, discipline is less likely to become a problem.

Although this section has emphasized the classroom environment, other considerations are part of the healthy school environment. An issue of particular importance is the safety of students when transported on school buses. Guidelines are needed for daily riding of buses, as well as for special occasions such as field trips or extracurricular events. Safety in the classroom, the cafeteria, and the gymnasium and within the general school physical plant is an important aspect of a healthy school environment.

School Health Instruction

The third area of the school-health program is instruction that presents information to students in a way that fosters desirable health knowledge, attitudes, and practices. Strategies, information, and methods concerning this aspect of a comprehensive school-health program are described later in the text.

School Physical Education

A comprehensive physical education program offers a daily program of activities. These programs should be based upon developing cardiovascular fitness, strength, flexibility, and agility. A sound program can help reduce stress and promote social development.

School Nutrition and Foodservice

This component involves training for food preparation personnel and the development of nutritionally sound food programs for the school. Part of this component is helping students to select nutritionally balanced meals and ensuring that food served in the school cafeteria is nutritional, attractive, and palatable.

School-Based Counseling and Personnel Support

This aspect of the comprehensive health program seeks to meet students' needs by providing services such as assertiveness training, problem-solving training, and self-esteem training. Services also are provided by school psychologists for students who are mentally retarded or have behavioral problems.

School-Site Health Promotion

Programs for faculty and staff can reduce health care costs, improve morale, and increase productivity of the faculty and staff. Health promotion programs are a natural for the school, since facilities and personnel for conducting programs are already present. Health educators, physical educators, nurses, counselors, and nutritionists are available to aid in program development.

School, Family, and Community Health Promotion Partnerships

An effective strategy for promoting the health of school-age students is the development of collaborative efforts between community agencies and the school. These coalitions can coordinate and advocate improving the various aspects of the comprehensive school-health program.

Health educators should consider themselves part of a team whose main mission is to provide optimal conditions to enhance each student's wellness. Each member of the health team has a particular role to play. Like a chain, the health team is only as strong as its weakest link. Everyone involved with the health of students (including the students themselves) must take that personal responsibility seriously. Each member must cooperate with other members to reach the ultimate goal of total health.

CONTENT AREAS FOR HEALTH EDUCATION

Teaching health education, like teaching any subject, requires careful planning. Teachers must know what to teach, when to teach, and how to teach for the content to have meaning for students. Virtually every state department of education has a state curriculum guide for health education, and these frameworks contain a variety of content areas. Although state guidelines vary, generally the following content areas are appropriate: mental/emotional health; physical fitness; nutrition; family life; alcohol, drugs, and tobacco; safety and first aid; personal health; consumer health; chronic and communicable diseases; environmental health; and community health.

Determining What to Teach

Pollock and Middleton (1989) list a number of questions to consider when determining what content to teach in health education. They include:

- Who is to be educated?
- What does that person need and want to know about health?
- What are the important ideas that health-education authorities believe are representative of its body of knowledge?
- How can these ideas become a functional part of the learner's personal framework of knowledge? (p. 70)

Students' interest in certain health topics varies according to their age, maturity, socioeconomic background, and intelligence. Questionnaires, checklists, and direct questioning all can aid in determining student interests. Professional literature on the subject can also indicate what subjects would be appropriate for each grade level.

All secondary students have certain basic health needs. These include the need for love, nurturing, and intellectual stimulation. In addition, they need information concerning good nutrition, dental care, safer sex, drugs, and sound health decision making, among other things. These needs may vary from community to community; for example, inner-city students may need to discuss different types of personal-safety issues from a student living in a rural setting.

In addition to students' health needs and interests, other factors, such as the community's social mores, community needs, national health and education goals, and available textbooks and courses of study, must be considered.

Social Mores

Health-education content must be acceptable to the community in which the school is located. Ascertaining the social mores of the community demands careful judgment. Teachers have an advantage if they are well acquainted with the community. Even then, they may have trouble assessing feelings within the community about how best to teach certain health topics, such as substance abuse or family-life education. The teaching of controversial topics will be discussed in a later chapter.

Special-interest groups also influence curriculum development. These local, state, or national groups want to promote or protect their own philosophy or special interests. Most of these groups are sincere about bringing beneficial services to the student, but such groups can limit curricular content. For example, groups that form to stop family-life education can be formidable opponents to development of a comprehensive health-education program.

Community Needs

Community needs are essential considerations when developing a curriculum. What unique and specific characteristics of the community would influence content? Pollution, substance abuse, poor nutrition, and smoking are possible areas of concern.

Several good sources can help identify local concerns. Newspapers provide information about a wealth of problems and trends with implications for health teaching. Local morbidity and mortality statistics may indicate needs that are specific to a community or neighborhood. These statistics are available through local health departments. When using such information as morbidity statistics, the health educator needs to be sensitive to the values, philosophy, and moral and ethical forces within the community. Certain groups may wish to prohibit teaching about some health problems; for example, the rates for sexually transmitted diseases, pregnancy, and HIV infection.

National Health and Education Goals

The goals of *Healthy People 2000* (1990) mentioned earlier in the chapter contain a multitude of implications for teaching health education in secondary schools. These goals, which emphasize self-responsibility for health and safety, must receive high priority in our schools. Any content decisions should consider the 15 priority areas addressed in the *Healthy People 2000* framework.

Textbooks and Courses of Study

Most secondary textbooks contain detailed suggestions for developing curricular content. The teacher's editions of texts provide outlines and units for teaching health and identify major concepts to be taught at given grade levels. Like state health guidelines, textbooks cannot tailor a course of study to a specific community or specific classroom. Because textbooks are developed for use nationally, they may lack sufficient depth of coverage on topics of particular relevance to a local community.

To supplement the textbook, a plethora of education materials are available from health-related agencies, including pamphlets, filmstrips, teaching modules, and so on. All these materials should be reviewed to determine their appropriateness for a particular situation.

SUMMARY

Quality of life for each individual depends in part on the health decisions the person makes. Our health is continually evolving and changing as a result of our behavior and decisions. Health is not a state but a process through which we seek to feel at ease with our social, emotional, and physical environment. To achieve health, many complicated, interrelated components must be balanced. This integrated approach to health has led to the term *high-level wellness,* which is the individual's accepting responsibility for her/his quality of life.

Health education is the process of developing and providing planned learning experiences that encourage effective decision making. The process must provide a balance between cognitive and affective educational experiences. This balance, sometimes referred to as *confluent education,* is important for presentation of knowledge. Factual information does not ensure behavioral change, however. Learning opportunities must provide for discussion to personalize the information.

The need for health education is great. Many lifestyle-related illnesses, such as cardiovascular diseases, could be significantly reduced by a successful, comprehensive health-education program. Mental illness, alcoholism, drug abuse, sexually transmitted diseases, and teenage pregnancy rates also might decline with better health education. Nutrition, dental health, and physical fitness can also benefit from early health education. To help meet the challenges facing the United States, the Nation's Health Objectives were formulated for this decade. Many of these objectives have direct implications for teaching health in the schools.

An effective school-health program has eight components: (1) health services, (2) a healthful school environment, (3) an emphasis on health instruction as part of a comprehensive approach to health education, (4) school physical education, (5) nutrition and foodservices, (6) counseling and personnel services, (7) school health promotion, and (8) school, family and community health promotion partnerships. One of the primary considerations in health education is the correct determination of content. Possible content areas include mental/emotional health; physical fitness; nutrition; family life; alcohol, drugs, and tobacco; safety and first aid; personal health; consumer health; chronic and communicable diseases; environmental health; and community health. Factors to consider when determining what to teach include community social mores, student interests and health needs, community needs, national health and education goals, and the textbooks and courses of study available. In developing content, teachers must also consider who they are teaching, what their concerns are, and what health-education authorities deem important.

DISCUSSION QUESTIONS

1. Why is health a difficult concept to define?
2. What is meant by the term *high-level wellness?*
3. Why is prevention the best approach to improving the quality of health in the United States?
4. What is health education?
5. Discuss why self-responsibility is so important to promote health education.
6. Why are the Nation's Health Objectives important to teaching health in the schools?
7. Discuss the importance of each of the three elements of a comprehensive school-health program.
8. What are some of the roles of the school nurse?
9. How can the classroom teacher aid the school nurse in developing a healthy school environment?
10. Discuss how a negative classroom environment might affect the student.
11. How can the teacher exemplify good health in the learning environment?
12. What questions or factors should be considered in determining content?

REFERENCES

Accident facts. (1988). Chicago: National Safety Council.

Allensworth, D. D., & Kolbe, L. J. (1987). The comprehensive school health program: Exploring an expanded concept. *Journal of School Health, 57,* 409–412.

American Association of School Administrators. (1987). *Why school health.* Arlington, VA: Author.

American School Health Association. (1983). *Selected school health support statements.* Kent, OH: Author.

Brown, G. I. (1974). *Human teaching for human learning: An introduction to confluent education.* New York: Viking.

Chapman, L. S. (1987). Developing a useful perspective on spiritual health: Love, joy, peace, and fulfillment. *American Journal of Health Promotion 2*(22), 12–17.

Constitution of the World Health Organization. (1947). In *Chronicle of the WHO.* Geneva: World Health Organization.

Dunn, H. L. (1961). *High-level wellness.* Arlington, VA: Beatty.

Dunn, H. L. (1977). What high-level wellness means: Healthy values. *Achieving High-Level Wellness, 1,* 9–16.

Educational Research Service. (1983). Local school district budget items by type of community. *Spec-trum: Journal of School Research and Information, 1* (3), 16.

Focus on alcohol and drug issues. Muncie, IN: *Eta Sigma Gamma, 3* (1).

Frederick, C. J. (1977). Suicide in the United States. *Health Education, 8* (6), 17–22.

Garn, S., & Clark, D. (1976). Trends in fatness and the organs of obesity. *Pediatrics, 57* (4), 443–456.

Hanson, W. (1977). Even moderate drinking may be hazardous to maturing fetus. *Journal of the American Medical Association, 237* (24), 2585–2587.

Healthy people 2000—National health promotion and disease prevention objectives (Conference ed.). (1990). Washington, DC: U.S. Department of Health & Human Services.

Healthy people 2000—National health promotion and disease prevention objectives and healthy schools (1991). *Journal of School Health, 61* (7), 298–328.

Hoyman, H. S. (1975). Rethinking an ecologic-system model of man's health, disease, aging, and death. *Journal of School Health, 45* (9), 509–518.

Metropolitan Life Foundation. (1991). *Health you've got to be taught—an evaluation of comprehensive health education in American public schools.* New York: Louis Harris & Associates, Inc.

National Adolescent Student Survey. (1988, August/September). *Health Education, 19,* 4–8.

National Center for Educational Statistics. (1984). *The condition of education.* NCES Pub. No. 84 401. Washington, DC: U.S. Government Printing Office.

O'Rourke, T. W. (1985). *Why school health education? The economic point of view.* Presentation at Why school health education? Delbert Oberteuffer Centennial Symposium, Atlanta. Cosponsored by Association for the Advancement of Health Education and the Office of Disease Prevention and Health Promotion.

Purdy, C., & Tritsch, L. (1985). *Why health education? The practical point of view.* Presentation at Why school health education? Delbert Oberteuffer Centennial Symposium, Atlanta. Cosponsored by the Association for the Advancement of Health Education and the Office of Disease Prevention and Health Promotion.

Pollock, M., & Middleton, M. (1989). *Elementary school health instruction* (2nd ed.). St. Louis: Times Mirror/Mosby College.

Report of the 1990 Joint Committee on Health Terminology. (1991). *Journal of Health Education, 22,* 97–108.

Sonnenstein, F. L., Pleck, J. H., and Ku, L. C. (1992). Sexual activity, condom use, and AIDS awareness among adolescent males. *Family planning perspective 21* (4), 152–158.

Why health education in your school? (1982). Chicago: American Medical Association.

Wilson, C. C. (Ed.). (1971). *School health services.* Washington, DC: National Education Association.

World Health Organization. (1947). Constitution of the World Health Organization. *World Health Organization, 1,* 2–43.

CHAPTER 2

Teaching Health Education

Walking into a classroom at any level without having first planned the day's objectives is like beginning an automobile trip with an empty gas tank.   Donald A. Read & Walter H. Greene, *Creative Teaching in Health*

OBJECTIVES
After reading this chapter, you should be able to

- List the content areas of health education
- Describe the scope and sequence of health education
- Discuss the factors that influence what is taught in health education
- Identify the variety of curricular approaches used in school-health education
- Design an effective lesson plan
- Identify agencies for health-education resources
- Compare the various classifications of objectives
- Write instructional objectives
- Discuss how to plan and teach controversial health-education topics

Teaching health education, like teaching any subject, requires careful planning. Teachers must know what to teach, when to teach it, and how to teach it so that students internalize the content. Health instruction at each grade level must be tailored to students' maturational, intellectual, and interest levels.

Virtually every state department of education has a health-education syllabus that can be used as a guide for curriculum planning. It contains a recommended list of topics to be presented at each grade level. Effective planning takes far more than just reading the state health-education guide, however. As Willgoose (1974) puts it:

> Good planning for creative and innovative classwork requires long hours of reading about what others have accomplished; visiting other schools; participating in curriculum development; attending health workshops; evaluating new methodologies; working with school health services personnel; previewing films, slides, filmstrips, cassettes and video tapes; and preparing demonstration materials and displays. These are tasks that take considerable time primarily because health topics and health education methods are so multidisciplinary and multidimensional. (p. 439)

Various health-education authorities cite from 10 to 20 different content areas, depending on how areas are grouped or separated. Most health educators agree on the following content areas for secondary health instruction: mental/emotional health; physical fitness; nutrition; family life; alcohol, drugs, and tobacco; safety and first aid; personal health; consumer health; chronic and communicable diseases; environmental health; and community health.

Each of these content areas covers dozens of topics. For example, personal health encompasses dental care, personal care, exercise, rest, and physical fitness, to name just a few topics. Content emphasis also changes to reflect current knowledge and health concerns. Community mores also determine content areas. Some communities consider family-life education a vital part of health education; many other communities do not consider it appropriate.

GRADE PLACEMENT FOR HEALTH-EDUCATION TOPICS

Once basic content areas have been charted, the teacher must determine how much emphasis to place on each area at each grade level. Emphasis should reflect students' developmental level, health needs, and interests. A planned cycle for presenting content areas ensures that necessary topics will be included and will receive appropriate emphasis at each grade level. An example of a cycle plan based on developmental needs is shown in Table 2.1.

A cycle plan helps eliminate useless repetition and ensures that topics are covered to the depth necessary for a particular grade. A cycle plan helps the teacher plan for each grade level by determining what to emphasize for a given year. Any plan must be flexible enough to address needs that may arise, of course. For example, the pressing need to educate students concerning HIV infection could not have been anticipated a decade ago.

DEVELOPING SCOPE AND SEQUENCE

Content areas must not only be identified; they must also be ordered and organized. That is, the scope and sequence of the health-education curriculum must be determined. **Scope** refers to the depth or difficulty of the material. **Sequence** refers to

Table 2.1   Cycle Plan for Teaching Health, Grades 7 Through 12

Content area	Grade					
	7	8	9	10	11	12
Mental/emotional health	E	R	E	R	E	E
Physical fitness	R	R	O	R	O	R
Nutrition	R	E	R	E	R	E
Family life	E	R	E	R	E	E
Alcohol, drugs and tobacco	E	R	E	E	E	E
Safety and first aid	R	R	R	E	R	R
Personal health	E	R	E	R	E	R
Consumer health	R	E	R	E	R	R
Chronic and communicable diseases (Includes STDs and HIV)	E	R	E	R	E	R
Environmental health	R	E	E	R	R	E
Community health	E	R	R	R	R	E

Key: E = Emphasis at grade level   R = Review at grade level   O = Omit at grade level

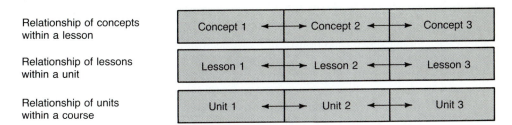

Figure 2.1 Horizontal organization of the health curriculum

Source: *Teaching Today's Health,* 3rd ed., by David J. Anspaugh and Gene Ezell, 1990, New York: Merrill/Macmillan.

the order in which the material is to be covered and when to teach it. Here, again, the state department of education health guide can be of great use. Such guides usually spell out the scope and sequence of health education for each grade level. They may also indicate expected student competencies following the course of study.

Planned health instruction should attempt to ensure that each previous learning experience provides the basis for new learning. Topics should build on one another and not be presented as discrete bits of information. Concepts within each lesson should relate to each other, lessons within a unit should relate to each other, and units within the course should relate to each other. This will help students to see health education as a whole rather than as seemingly unrelated fragments. This unity of relationships, as conceptualized by Fodor and Dalis (1989), is referred to as **horizontal organization**, and is shown in Figure 2.1

Vertical organization refers to the arrangement of the curriculum from kindergarten through senior high school. As such, it serves as a reminder that everything done in the classroom should be built on what has been previously accomplished so that initial learning becomes the basis for subsequent learning. This relationship is shown in Figure 2.2 (Fodor & Dalis, 1989).

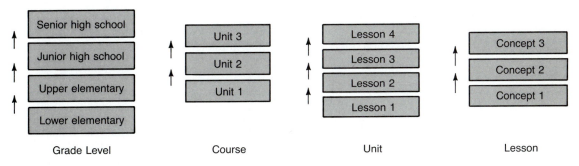

Figure 2.2 Vertical organization

Source: *Teaching Today's Health,* 3rd ed., by David J. Anspaugh and Gene Ezell, New York: Merrill/Macmillan.

TEACHING FOR VALUES

Values give direction to life and determine behavior. Members of our society share many of the same values. Each community, family, and individual has a more specific set of values, however. Values are closely linked with personal feelings and must be carefully considered when planning health instruction. Failure to do so can result both in the blocking of effective learning and opposition from parents and community organizations. Values are learned through a variety of experiences and interactions with the environment. The family, peer group, school, church, and media all influence personal value formation. In other words, value formation is a continual process, yet many parents become concerned when schools get involved in values-related teaching. Many parents fear that the school will promote values contrary to their own. In some cases, parents interpret any recommendation or point of emphasis by a teacher as an imposition of values. At the other extreme, they may see a teacher who takes no stand at all as encouraging an anything-goes attitude.

Therefore, in planning health instruction, the role of values in teaching must be clear. A teacher's job is not to impose her values; it is to help students develop their own values by making wise decisions about health-related matters. Students will form values with or without their teacher's assistance, but their teacher can help them make positive decisions that will lead to high-level wellness by providing factual knowledge about health and by allowing students to clarify their own feelings.

Attitudes and behavior are intertwined. To achieve a balance between knowledge and attitudes toward health education, teaching must address student feelings. In other words, the study of health must be personalized to have an impact. By providing opportunities for students to identify feelings and personalize health information, teachers can help them understand how information, attitudes, and behavior affect their quality of life. This knowledge better prepares students to deal with peer pressure, communicate more effectively, and develop sound decision-making skills.

Each person must weigh the importance or value of a decision against perceived rewards and costs involved. To brush one's teeth regularly, to smoke, to have regular physical examinations, and to experiment with drugs are all examples of decisions that affect health. Teachers must make a planned effort to help students think through the possible consequences of health-related decisions.

CURRICULUM APPROACHES

Beginning teachers will probably find many resources to help them plan a course of health education for the class. As noted, these resources include the state health-education guidelines, commercial health-education textbook series, and materials from government and private health-related agencies. None of these, however, constitutes a complete health-education curriculum.

A comprehensive health curriculum includes a detailed plan for teaching health. Later in the chapter, an overview of this process is presented. Rather than developing an entirely new curriculum plan, teachers often can adopt an existing one.

School Health Education Study (SHES)

The School Health Education Study (SHES) is a comprehensive K–12 health-education curriculum that was developed in the 1960s. The project developers visualized health as having physical, mental, and social dimensions, as shown in Figure 2.3. In this conceptual model, health is seen as "dynamic interaction and interdependence among the individual's physical well-being, his mental and emotional reactions, and the social complex in which he exists" (School Health Education Study, 1967). SHES is mentioned because it holds historical significance and serves as a reference for several curriculum projects. Although dated, it still reflects an excellent conceptualization of health education.

The curriculum's interaction and interdependence are reflected in the key concepts shown in the model: growing and developing, interacting, and decision making. Growing and developing are defined as a dynamic life process whereby the individual is in some ways like all individuals, in some ways like some individuals, and in some ways like no other individual. Interacting is an ongoing process in which the individual is affected by and, in turn, affects certain biological, social, psychological, economic, and physical forces in the environment. Decision making is a uniquely human process of consciously opting to take or not to take an action or of choosing one alternative over another.

The scope of the SHES curriculum is embodied in the 10 concept statements shown in Figure 2.3 as C1, C2, and so on. These statements are as follows:

1. Growth and development influences and is influenced by the structure and functioning of the individual.
2. Growing and developing follows a predictable sequence, yet is unique for each individual.
3. Protection and promotion of health is an individual, community, and international responsibility.
4. The potential for hazards and accidents exists, whatever the environment.
5. There are reciprocal relationships involving man, disease, and environment.
6. The family serves to perpetuate man and to fulfill certain health needs.
7. Personal health practices are affected by a complexity of forces, often conflicting.
8. Utilization of health information, products, and services is guided by values and perceptions.
9. Use of substances that modify mood and behavior arises from a variety of motivations.
10. Food selection and eating patterns are determined by physical, social, mental, economic, and cultural factors. (pp. 21–23)

Subconcepts of these 10 conceptual areas serve as guides in the selection and ordering of subject mater, as well as in the development of appropriate instructional or behavioral objectives. Each subconcept is viewed through physical, mental, and social dimensions. For each of the concepts, long-range goals are stated in terms of

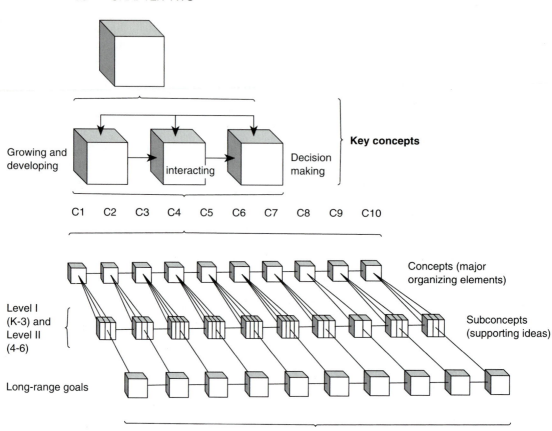

Figure 2.3   Conceptual model of the SHES curriculum

Source: School Health Education Study in *Health Education: A Conceptual Approach to Curriculum Design,* 1967, St. Paul, MN: 3M Education Press.

behavioral objectives. These goals represent desired student outcomes for the total sequential curriculum.

The SHES curriculum marked an important breakthrough in comprehensive K–12 health education. The emphasis is on the conceptualization of concepts rather than on facts, because facts become dated and require constant revision.

Health Skills for Life

Health Skills for Life is a relatively new approach to health education. The emphasis is on skill acquisition rather than knowledge acquisition. Ten major health content areas consisting of 118 units are used in a comprehensive K–12 curriculum. The 10 content areas include:

1. Health Services and Consumer Health (6 units)
2. Fitness (2 units)

3. Dental Health (4 units)
4. Environmental Health (4 units)
5. Disease Prevention (9 units)
6. Growth and Development (12 units)
7. Nutrition (12 units)
8. Substance Use and Abuse (9 units)
9. Safety and First Aid (27 units)
10. Mental Health, Family Life, and Human Sexuality (33 units)

Each unit is independent of the other units in the curriculum. Any teaching aids needed for the program can be found locally. Units are bound in three-ring binders to facilitate revisions to the various units. Evaluation plans and tests for pretesting and posttesting, as well as skill tests, are included. An administrative guide is also included. A section of each unit includes the sequence for teaching, goals, performance indicators, estimated teaching time, content, student handouts, preparations needed, and integration with other subjects. The developers of the curriculum offer training to school districts that purchase the materials. The entire program was certified by the Oregon State Department of Education in 1982. The program is offered, either in parts or in its entirety, in many states. Figure 2.4 outlines the scope and sequence of the various units in grades 7, 8, and 9–12.

Growing Healthy

The Growing Healthy program has undergone several name changes over the years, but like other curriculum models, it seeks to provide children with the skills and information needed to live healthy, productive lives. Hundreds of school districts in more than 40 states have used the program.

What sets Growing Healthy apart from other programs is the variety of methods it employs. It is a multimedia, multidimensional, and multimethodological plan designed to be integrated with other subject areas. It also can be adopted to local needs and circumstances.

The curriculum seeks to provide a comprehensive sequence of courses for kindergarten through seventh grade in all aspects of health. Each grade level has a theme: Happiness Is Being Healthy (kindergarten), Super Me (grade 1), Sight and Sounds (grade 2), The Body—Its Framework and Movement (grade 3), Our Digestion, Our Nutrition, Our Health (grade 4), About Our Lungs and Our Health (grade 5), Our Health and Our Hearts (grade 6), and Living Well with Our Nervous System (grade 7).

Instead of textbooks, the program uses films, slides, pamphlets, records, cassettes, books, and resource people to supply information. Children receive hands-on learning experiences in small groups at learning centers located around the classroom. They investigate, share, teach, and learn from one another, and they are encouraged to express their ideas and share feelings about their experiences.

Before school districts use the Growing Healthy program, workshops train teachers to use it; those teachers then train others. The success of the program seems to depend on proper training of the teachers.

Figure 2.4   Scope and sequence of unit titles for Health Skills for Life

Grade 7

1. Observing Warning Signs for Physical and Emotional Health
2. Signs and Symptoms of, and Health Services for S.T.D.s
3. Prevention of Chronic Disease
4. Body System Interrelationships
5. Using Nutrient Charts and Food Labels
6. Making Decisions About Drugs/Alcohol
7. Personal Safety - Risk Profile
8. Home Fire Escape Techniques
9. Coping with Personal Losses
10. Techniques for Resolving Conflicts

Grade 8

1. Consumer Health Decision Making
2. Altering the Environment
3. Living with Chronic Disease and Physical Disabilities
4. Pregnancy & Birth
5. Conserving Food for Hungry People
6. Making Decisions about Drugs
7. Deciding on Over-the-Counter Drugs
8. Drug Crisis Skills & Services
9. Coping Skills for Dating & Sexuality
10. Selecting Appropriate Contraceptives
11. Plans for Improving Holistic Health

Grades 9–12

1. Seeking Medical Help
2. Selecting Qualified Health Professionals and Reputable Resources
3. Planning Lifetime Physical Fitness
4. Current Methods in Dental Health
5. Global Environmental Health
6. Medical Self-Care

7. Preventing Sexually Transmitted Disease
8. Food Handling, Cooking, Storage and Selection
9. Changes within the Life Cycle
10. Evaluating Nutrient Adequacy of Meals
11. Menu for a Week
12. Vegetarian Menu Planning
13. Weight Maintenance
14. Drug Decisions
15. Crisis Intervention for Poisoning & Drug Overdose
16. First Aid for Broken Bones & Transporting Victims
17. Insect Stings & Snake Bites
18. CPR
19. Altering Behavior to Promote Personal Safety
20. Planning for Community Safety
21. Clarifying Beliefs, Attitudes & Values on Sex Related Issues
22. Dealing with Teenage Pregnancy
23. Responsible Intimate Relationships
24. Effective Parenting Techniques
25. Risks with Early Marriage
26. Genetic Defects & Counseling
27. Reducing the Risks of Birth Defects
28. Selecting Social Living Units
29. Prenatal Care
30. Postnatal Care
31. Supporting People Experiencing Climacteric and Menopause
32. Prevention & Early Intervention for Sexuality Related Health Problems
33. Effective Interpersonal Communication Techniques
34. Coping with Stress
35. Plans to Holistic Health

Other Teaching Materials

Agencies such as the American Cancer Society, American Heart Association, March of Dimes, American Red Cross, American Dental Association, and American Dairy Association provide free and inexpensive materials through their local affiliates. Table 2.2 lists titles of free and inexpensive health education materials available from these agencies.

Table 2.2 Sample Listing of Curricular Health-Education Materials from Voluntary Health Organizations, by Grade

Association	Program	Suggested Grade Level/Age
American Cancer Society	Health Myself	7–9
American Dairy Association	Smart Moves	7–12
(National Dairy Board)	Food Power: Coaches' Guide	11–12
	You Booklet: Food, Nutrition, Exercise	11–12
American Dental Association	Learning about Oral Health (Lev. III)	7–9
	Learning about Oral Health (Lev. IV)	10–12
American Heart Association	Heart Decisions	7–9
	Heart Challenges:	10–12
	■ Lesson Plans, Test	
	■ Nutrition and the Athlete	
	■ Taking Charge	
	■ Smoking	
American Lung Association	Growing Healthy	7–12
American Red Cross	Babysitting	Ages 11 and older
	CPR/First Aid	Ages 8 to adult

DEVELOPING A HEALTH CURRICULUM

A health curriculum is a comprehensive K–12 plan designed to encompass pertinent health concerns and provide learning experiences throughout the school years. Such a plan should help promote responsible decisions and practices regarding personal, family, and community health. A comprehensive school health-education plan should be prepared for each local school district and then for the individual schools within the district. Although a district may elect to use a state-developed or other existing curriculum, in some cases it may choose to develop a new curriculum approach.

Designing and implementing a comprehensive program require a great deal of expertise, time, and effort in addition to input from community leaders, parents, teachers, students, and administrators. It cannot be developed in a summer or even a year. After determining students' needs, interests, and comprehension abilities, teachers must take the following steps:

1. Development and writing of the first draft by grade-level experts, who coordinate the lessons and units for scope and sequence
2. Evaluation and rewriting of the first draft
3. Field testing of the second draft in representative schools
4. Evaluation and rewriting of the second draft
5. Printing and distribution of the final draft for classroom use
6. Workshops and in-service training sessions to make the most effective use of the developed curriculum
7. Ongoing evaluation.

RITTER LIBRARY
BALDWIN-WALLACE COLLEGE

Resource Units

Most curriculum plans are not intended to substitute for commercially prepared textbooks. Rather, they represent a series of resource units based on the major concepts that should be taught at each grade level. A **resource unit** is a plan that teachers can use to present topics in an effective scope and sequence. It is strictly an aid for planning, not a teaching unit.

A resource unit contains general objectives, content suggestions, suggestions for learning experiences, evaluation procedures, and appropriate references for the teacher and the students. Because of its general nature, a resource unit is adaptable to a wide range of learning situations. Many resource units are divided by grade level, giving planning suggestions for K–3, 4–6, 7–9 and 10–12. With the aid of a resource unit, the teacher can then develop actual teaching units.

Teaching Units

A **teaching unit** is an organized method for developing lesson plans for a particular group of students; it can be tailored to each classroom. The resource unit serves as a guide, whereas the teaching unit is the plan for student learning. Unlike the resource unit, which a curriculum committee prepares, the classroom teacher develops the teaching unit. It is specific, whereas the resource unit is general. The teacher selects the specific concepts to be studied as well as the objectives, content, learning experiences, evaluation methods, and references that the class will use. Given a well-developed resource unit that identifies major concepts, creating a teaching unit is fairly easy. In addition to the resource unit, the state health-education guidelines, the teacher's edition of the classroom textbook, and various materials from health-related agencies can all be used to develop the teaching unit.

A teaching unit can follow a variety of formats, depending on individual preference. Regardless of format employed, the teaching unit should contain the following components: title of unit, grade level, conceptual statement, and objectives.

Title of Unit

The title of a teaching unit should describe what the unit is actually about. It should also serve as a motivational tool and suggest what direction the teaching will take. Examples of effective titles include "Keeping Our Environment Healthy," "Good Foods for Good Health," and "Exercising for Good Health."

Grade Level

The grade level for which the unit is intended should be clearly identified. Some teachers even indicate the room and school year in which the unit will be used. Such a record can be valuable when units are revised for use with other classes.

Conceptual Statement

This section of the teaching unit defines the major concepts emphasized in the unit. The conceptual statement serves as a general information organizer and is rather abstract. That is, it does not contain facts about the unit, but acts instead as a focal point for instruction. The conceptual statement is also a guide to the competencies that students should be able to demonstrate upon completion of the unit. Every conceptual statement should have a main theme, a consequent behavior, and a future ramification, as in the following examples:

1. It is essential to conserve (theme) our existing natural resources (consequent behavior) if we are to maintain a high-quality lifestyle (ramifications).
2. Friendships (theme) provide an important avenue for dealing with our emotions (consequent behavior) and developing a positive self-image (ramifications).
3. Sports activities (theme) help us develop many attributes and skills (consequent behavior) that are useful throughout life (ramifications).

Objectives

An objective should describe what the student will be able to do after completing the unit. Several types of objectives will be discussed in greater detail later in this chapter. Objectives add direction to the conceptual statement by indicating what content should be taught and how it should be taught. The appropriate type of evaluation can also be determined in a properly stated objective.

Content

The content portion of a teaching unit should summarize the facts needed to teach the unit. Content, which must be appropriate to the students' age, is based on the conceptual statement and the objectives for the unit. The statement of content should also provide clear direction for the teacher, as in Figure 2.5, an example from a family-life teaching unit for grade 9.

Learning Activities

Learning activities are experiences that help students internalize content and form concepts. They provide the spark for discovery and examination of new ideas. Without effective learning activities, the best concepts, objectives, and content have little impact. Because activities represent the point at which students come in contact with the actual curriculum, no unit can be effective if the learning activities are poorly planned or inappropriate.

Most resource units contain several suggestions for teaching the content. Each teacher should select activities that she believes will work best in her own class. She must also feel comfortable using a particular methodology for the learning experience to be effective. For example, teachers who have never used values clarification activities should become familiar with such activities in another setting before presenting them in their own classrooms.

In learning activities, an adequate description of what the class should do is important. The thoroughness of description tends to vary from one resource guide to the next, but it should be detailed enough that another teacher reading the unit would know exactly what to do. Even if no one but the regular teacher ever reads the

One learning activity required students to research healthy eating habits and bring resources to class. Articles in these magazines prompted discussion.

description, sufficient detail will help ensure that an activity is carried out correctly. For example, how would the following strategy be handled based on this description?

> Discuss consumer products that do not measure up to advertised claims.

A more detailed description is far more useful in conducting a successful learning activity. For example:

> Examine the various advertising techniques used to promote consumer products. Note such approaches as testimonials, scientific, medical, or band-wagon. How do these techniques exaggerate a product's worth? Select representative advertisements and describe how they might depict the product more accurately.

Evaluation

Evaluation has two purposes: (1) to determine whether a student has developed the skill or assimilated the concepts of the unit, and (2) to enable the teacher to assess her own teaching effectiveness. Resource units usually contain several suggestions for evaluating their main objectives.

References

The teaching unit should list two types of references. Student references are books, pamphlets, magazines, or chapters from texts that students can use to increase their understanding of the topic. Teacher references should help develop greater understanding and insight into content and methodology for teaching the unit.

LESSON PLANNING

Once the teaching unit has been developed, the teacher plans how to teach the unit. This is done by creating daily lesson plans that provide for a logical progression of the unit from start to finish. Each lesson plan must be based on concepts taught in previous lessons so that learning builds on the established base.

In a daily lesson plan, each learning activity should precede an evaluation activity. Through this activity, the teacher will get some idea of how well students have learned the concept presented. Because the activity is a performance, it also indicates how well it has achieved its objectives.

Following the daily lesson, teachers should also evaluate their own performance. How well did they present the content? How effective were the activities? Were the instructional objectives fulfilled? Such evaluation can help teachers improve their teaching skills and thus better satisfy students' needs. See Figure 2.5 for an example of a lesson plan.

TEACHING THE CONTROVERSIAL ISSUES: SEXUALITY, FAMILY LIFE, AIDS, AND DRUGS

Teaching in content areas such as family life, drugs, and AIDS can be a difficult task, since these areas always seem to generate controversy. Disagreements center on religious beliefs, public versus private morality, and control of the school curriculum. Moreover, people bring deeply rooted personal values and attitudes to any discussion of these topics.

Teachers can avoid many problems by carefully planning the process that precedes actual teaching. Initial efforts should involve formation of a community advisory committee consisting of leaders from the local community, parent-teacher organizations, religious groups, and the medical field. Committee members can serve as consultants, evaluators, and spokespersons for the curriculum. The more community input, the less the fear of what is going to be taught and the greater the sense of cooperation. No curriculum for teaching controversial topics should be developed without this broad base of community input and support.

Schiller (1973) lists 11 steps for gaining support for a family-life program. These steps are appropriate guidelines for teaching any controversial area:

1. A proposed program must first gain support from the highest authority within the school organization. Administrators and parent leaders alike must provide backing.
2. A small committee is then formed to determine the receptiveness of parents and other appropriate individuals. If strong opposition is likely from some individu-

Figure 2.5   New lesson plan

Unit title: *Consumer Health—The Effects of Advertising on Selecting*   **Date:** *February 19*
Health-Related Products   **Teacher:** *Hunter Smith*
Conceptual statement: *Advertising plays an important role in*   **Grade:** *Nine*
determining what health care products are used.
Objectives: *The learner will define what is meant by health-related products and be able to*
identify at least five types of techniques used to sell these products.
Teacher needs: *Index cards, advertisements from magazines, poster board, thick ink marker pen*
Introductory statements: *(Warm-up, establish psychological set/direction of lesson) Q.1) How*
many of you know what the term health-related product means? Q.2) How many of you purchase
health-related products? Q.3) Are all of those products useful? Q.4) What types of products do
you purchase? Q.5) What persuaded you to purchase these products?
Transition statement: *"Today we are going to define what is meant by health-related products*
and examine some of the mechanisms used to convince us we should use them."

Content (Outline)	*Learning Strategies*	*Evaluation*

I. Define consumer
   health products
   A. Useful
      products
      1. toothpaste
      2. dental floss
      3. deodorant
   B. Useless or
      questionable
      products
      1. skin cleaners
      2. laxatives
      3. eyewash

1. Define and discuss what health-related
   products are.
2. List on board the definition of HRP: Health
   products that people purchase and use in the
   desire to affect their physical, social, or mental
   health.

II. Techniques for
    promoting
    A. Glamour/
       elegance
    B. Sex/love
    C. Macho image
    D. Slogans
    E. Testimonials
    F. Bandwagon

1. Quiz over definition of these products.
2. Observe if students distinguish the techniques
   utilized. Can the claims be recognized and the
   misconceptions pointed out?
3. Discuss the various techniques used to promote
   these products and techniques of advertising.
4. Provide examples of health-related
   advertisements. Have students determine what
   technique was being used to sell the products.
5. Have students develop an advertisement for a
   product (teacher assigned) that would reflect
   truthfulness in promoting the product. Compare
   the difference with above advertisements.

Teacher Evaluation
1. Keep the lesson as taught?   3. What I need to improve: _____
   _____ yes   _____
   _____ no   4. Strengths of lesson: _____
2. Next time make sure: _____   _____
   _____
   _____

als, informed professionals should meet with these individuals to answer questions and lessen anxieties.

3. An advisory committee representative of appropriate community components should be formed. Chaired by an influential leader, this committee should advise and support professional personnel on overall policy concerning the nature of the program and its philosophy, concepts, and approaches.
4. The advisory committee spearheads parent meetings to describe what family-life education is and why it should be taught. Such meetings should give attendees a chance to meet in small groups to discuss their feelings.
5. After the meetings, parents should answer a questionnaire to determine their feelings about family-life education. They should be asked about content, approaches, and desired qualifications for those running the program.
6. Technical experts should help in developing a curriculum for family-life education.
7. Educators should be trained through in-service programs, workshops, college courses, or other practical means.
8. Educators ought to be volunteers and should be carefully screened for their attitudes, values, and ability to relate to students, parents, and other involved individuals.
9. The initial program should be small to allow for pilot testing and evaluation. The school should meet with the advisory committee frequently and consultants should be used.
10. If the program is successful, it should be revised and broadened to improve it. This helps keep everyone involved and facilitates program understanding. If the program is unsuccessful, alternate approaches should be considered.
11. Parallel to the basic program should be parent education or education for other significant groups.

Once the community support system is in place, the following steps are useful for developing the actual curriculum:

- *Needs assessment:* Need and justification for the content area are determined. Student needs and interests are assessed, and society's needs and priorities are considered.
- *Statement of problems:* Results of the needs assessment are translated into statements for the curriculum planners to address. Statements developed at this point should include the amount of community support, the amount of administrative support, the philosophy of the proposed curriculum, the emphasis to be placed on cognitive and affective education, and the expectations for accomplishing the goals and objectives.
- *Curriculum design:* An organizational framework is established for developing the curriculum.
- *Formulation of goals:* Broad statements are developed to give direction to instructional efforts at each grade level. These statements should also express the nature of change the educational effort will attempt to effect.
- *Formulation of objectives:* Program and behavioral objectives are determined; they will serve as the basis for individual lesson objectives.
- *Selection of subject matter:* Content is based on the established objectives and the grade level.

- *Strategy selection:* The planned learning opportunities, experiences, and activities are selected that will help students accomplish specific objectives. Selected strategies should help the content come alive and help the student internalize the concepts and evaluate the information.
- *Selection of resources:* Personnel and material resources are chosen that can be used to support the school's teaching function. Media, guest speakers, and volunteer or professional sources should be considered.
- *Evaluation component:* Methods are devised for determining whether objectives have been accomplished.

Teacher Sensitivity to Controversial Issues

Teachers must be sensitive to their qualifications and must prepare themselves thoroughly before attempting to teach a controversial subject area. They must always present accurate, factual information. This involves obtaining materials for teaching from professional sources, not being embarrassed when teaching sexually related material, and presenting a balanced viewpoint on controversial issues. For example, abortion, premarital sex, or religious doctrine should be presented carefully, giving one viewpoint no more emphasis than another. In essence, the teacher should seek to "educate, not indoctrinate; teach fact, not fallacies; formulate a code of ethics, not preach strict self-denial; be objective, not subjective; be democratic, not autocratic, and seek knowledge, not emotionally biased constructs" (McCary, 1982).

Suggested Topics for Teaching Controversial Issues

Suggested Topics for Drug Education in Junior High and High School
The U.S. Department of Education has published suggested topics for drug education (U.S. Department of Education, 1986). Suggestions included the following:

- Stress: how the body responds to stress; how drugs increase stress
- The chemical properties of drugs
- The effects of drugs on the circulatory, digestive, nervous, reproductive, and respiratory systems, as well as the effects of drugs on adolescent development
- Patterns of substance abuse; the progressive effects of drugs on the body and mind
- The drug problem at school, among teenagers, and in society
- Student responsibility in promoting a drug-free school
- Local, state, and federal laws on controlled substances; why these laws exist and how they are enforced
- Legal and social consequences of drug use; penalties for driving under the influence of alcohol or drugs; the relationship between drugs and other crimes
- The influence of popular culture on behavior
- The influence of peers, parents, and other important individuals on a student's behavior; how the need to feel accepted by others influences behavior
- Ways to make responsible decisions and deal constructively with disagreeable moments and pressures

HEALTH HIGHLIGHT
Signs of Drug Use

Changing patterns of performance, appearance, and behavior may signal use of drugs. The items in the first category listed below provide direct evidence of drug use; the items in the other categories offer signs that may indicate drug use. For this reason, adults should look for extreme changes in adolescents' behavior, changes that together form a pattern associated with drug use.

Signs of Drugs and Drug Paraphernalia
- Possession of drug-related paraphernalia such as pipes, rolling papers, small decongestant bottles, or small butane torches
- Possession of drugs or evidence of drugs, peculiar plants; butts, seeds, or leaves in ashtrays or clothing pockets
- Odor of drugs, smell of incense or other "cover-up" scents

Identification with Drug Culture
- Drug-related magazines, slogans on clothing
- Conversation and jokes that are preoccupied with drugs
- Hostility in discussing drugs

Signs of Physical Deterioration
- Memory lapses, short attention span, difficulty in concentration
- Poor physical coordination; slurred or incoherent speech
- Unhealthy appearance; indifference to hygiene and grooming

Dramatic Changes in School Performance
- Distinct downward turns in student's grades - not just from Cs to Fs, but from As to Bs and Cs; assignments not completed
- Increased absenteeism or tardiness

Changes in Behavior
- Chronic dishonesty (lying, stealing, cheating); trouble with the police
- Changes in friends, evasiveness in talking about new ones
- Possession of large amounts of money
- Increasing and inappropriate anger, hostility, irritability, secretiveness
- Reduced motivation, energy, self-discipline, self-esteem
- Diminished interest in extracurricular activities and hobbies

- Reasons for not taking drugs
- Situations where students may be pressured into using drugs
- Ways of resisting pressure to use drugs; benefits of resisting pressure to use drugs

Suggested Topics for AIDS Education
AIDS education in the middle, junior high, and high school should be designed to reduce excessive fear of the disease. Concepts to be taught include the following

HEALTH HIGHLIGHT
Guidelines for Family-Life Education

To those groups responsible for developing school and community programs in family life, we suggest the following guidelines:

1. Such education should strive to create understanding and conviction that decisions about sexual behavior must be based on moral and ethical values, as well as on considerations of physical and emotional health, fear, pleasure, practical consequences, or concepts of personality development.
2. Such education must respect the cultural, familial and religious backgrounds and beliefs of individuals and must teach that the sexual development and behavior of each individual cannot take place in a vacuum, but are instead related to the other aspects of his life and to his moral, ethical and religious codes.
3. It should point out how sex is distorted and exploited in our society and how this places heavy responsibility upon the individual, the family and institutions to cope in a constructive manner with the problems thus created.
4. It must recognize that in school, family life, insofar as it relates to moral and religious beliefs and values, complements the education conveyed through the family, the church or the synagogue. Family life in the schools must proceed constructively with understanding, tolerance and acceptance of differences.
5. It must stress the many points of harmony between moral values and beliefs about what is right and wrong that are held in common by the major religions on the one hand and generally accepted legal, social, psychological, medical and other values held in common by service professions and society generally.
6. Where strong differences of opinion exist on what is right and wrong sexual behavior, objective, informed and dignified discussion of both sides of such questions should be encouraged. However, in such cases, neither the sponsors of an educational program nor the teachers should attempt to give definite answers or to represent their personal, moral and religious beliefs as the consensus of the major religions or of society generally.
7. Throughout such education human values and human dignity must be stressed as major bases for right and wrong; attitudes that build such respect should be encouraged as right, and those that tear down such respect should be condemned as wrong.
8. Such education should teach that sexuality is a part of the whole person and an aspect of his dignity as a human being.
9. It should teach that people who love each other try not to do anything that will harm each other.
10. It should teach that sexual intercourse within marriage offers the greatest possibility for personal fulfillment and social growth.
11. Finally, such a program of education must be based on sound content and must employ sound methods; it must be conducted by teachers and leaders qualified to do so by training and temperament.

Source: List quoted from a statement on family life by the National Council of Churches, the Synagogue of America, and the United States Catholic Conference.

(*Guidelines for Effective School Health Education,* 1988). General concepts for the middle school include:

1. Viruses are living organisms too small to be seen by the unaided eye.
2. Viruses can be transmitted from an infected person to an uninfected person through various means.
3. Some viruses cause disease among people.
4. People who are infected with some viruses that cause disease may not have any signs or symptoms of disease.
5. AIDS (an abbreviation for acquired immunodeficiency syndrome) is caused by a virus that weakens the ability of infected individuals to fight off disease.
6. People who have AIDS often develop a rare type of severe pneumonia, a cancer called Kaposi's sarcoma, and certain other diseases that healthy people normally do not get.
7. About 1 to 1.5 million of the total population of approximately 240 million Americans currently are infected with the AIDS virus and, consequently, are capable of infecting others.
8. People who are infected with the AIDS virus live in every state in the United States and in most other countries of the world. Infected people live in cities as well as in suburbs, small towns, and rural areas. Although most infected people are adults, teenagers can also become infected. Females, as well as males, are infected. People of every race are infected, including whites, blacks, Hispanics, Native Americans, and Asians or Pacific Islanders.
9. The AIDS virus can be transmitted by sexual contact with an infected person, by use of needles and other injection equipment that an infected person has used, and from an infected mother to her infant before or during birth.
10. A small number of doctors, nurses, and other medical personnel have been infected when they were directly exposed to infected blood.
11. It sometimes takes several years after becoming infected with the AIDS virus before symptoms of the disease appear. Thus, people who are infected with the virus can infect other people even though the people who transmit the infection do not feel or look sick.
12. Most infected people who develop symptoms of AIDS only live about 2 years after their symptoms are diagnosed.
13. The AIDS virus cannot be caught by touching someone who is infected, by being in the same room with an infected person, or by donating blood. (p. 6)

Education about AIDS for students in senior high school grades should be developed and presented taking into consideration the following information from *Guidelines for Effective School Health Education* (1988):

1. The virus that causes AIDS and other health problems is called human immunodeficiency virus (HIV).
2. The risk of becoming infected with HIV can be virtually eliminated by not engaging in sexual activities and by not using illegal intravenous drugs.
3. Sexual transmission of HIV is not a threat to those uninfected individuals who engage in mutually monogamous sexual relations.
4. HIV may be transmitted in any of the following ways: a) by sexual contact with an infected person (penis/vagina, penis/rectum, mouth/vagina, mouth/penis,

mouth/rectum); b) by using needles or other injection equipment that an infected person has used; c) from an infected mother to her infant before or during birth.

5. A small number of doctors, nurses, and other medical personnel have been infected when they were directly exposed to infected blood.

6. The following are at increased risk of having the virus that causes AIDS and consequently of being infectious: a) persons with clinical or laboratory evidence of infection; b) males who have had sexual intercourse with other males; c) persons who have injected illegal drugs; d) persons who have had numerous sexual partners, including male or female prostitutes; e) persons who received blood clotting products before 1985; f) sex partners of infected persons or persons at increased risk; and g) infants born to infected mothers.

7. The risk of becoming infected is increased by having a sexual partner who is at increased risk of having contracted the AIDS virus (as identified previously), practicing sexual behavior that results in the exchange of body fluids (i.e., semen, vaginal secretions, blood), and using unsterile needles or paraphernalia to inject drugs.

8. Although no transmission from deep, open-mouth (i.e., "French") kissing has been documented, such kissing theoretically could transmit HIV from an infected to an uninfected person through direct exposure of mucous membranes to infected blood or saliva.

9. In the past, medical use of blood, such as transfusing blood and treating hemophiliacs with blood clotting products, has caused some people to become infected with HIV. However, since 1985 all donated blood has been tested to determine whether it is infected with HIV; moreover, all blood clotting products have been made from screened plasma and have been heated to destroy any HIV that might remain in the concentrate. Thus the risk of becoming infected with HIV from blood transfusions and from blood clotting products has been virtually eliminated.

10. Persons who continue to engage in sexual intercourse with persons who are at increased risk or whose infection status is unknown should use a latex condom (not natural membrane) to reduce the likelihood of becoming infected. The latex condom must be applied properly and used from start to finish for every sexual act. Although a latex condom does not provide 100% protection—because it is possible for the condom to leak, break, or slip off—it provides the best protection for people who do not maintain a mutually monogamous relationship with an uninfected partner. Additional protection may be obtained by using spermicides that seem active against HIV and other sexually transmitted organisms in conjunction with condoms.

11. Behavior that prevents exposure to HIV also may prevent unintended pregnancies and exposure to the organisms that cause chlamydia infection, gonorrhea, herpes, human papilloma virus, and syphilis.

12. Persons who believe they may be infected with the AIDS virus should take precautions not to infect others and to seek counseling and antibody testing to determine whether they are infected. If persons are not infected, counseling and testing can relieve unnecessary anxiety and reinforce the need to adopt or continue practices that reduce the risk of infection. If persons are infected, they should: a) take precautions to protect sexual partners from becoming infected; b) advise previous and current sexual or drug-use partners to receive counseling and testing; c) take precautions against becoming pregnant; and d) seek medical care and counseling about other medical problems that may result from a weakened immunologic system. (pp. 8–9)

Suggestions for Family-Life Education

It is difficult to determine what to teach at the junior high and high school level in family-life education. Each school district should review and approve the content and strategies for the curriculum.

Topics to be considered for grades 7 through 9 might include:

1. Overview of biological materials (reviews of what has been previously covered).
2. More detail on birth control:
   - how various methods work
   - research in contraception
3. Intimate sexual behavior:
   - how far to go
   - why individuals feel the way they do
   - why people behave sexually the way they do
4. Dating and interpersonal relationships:
   - what to expect from a date (both the person and the experience)
   - why people date; why some do not date
5. Variations in sexual behavior:
   - homosexuality
   - voyeurism
   - transvestism
   - transsexualism
   - exhibitionism

Issues to be covered in upper secondary grades include:

1. Birth control research and detail:
   - population dynamics
   - abortion
2. Dating decisions:
   - dating standards and regulations
   - premarital sexual behavior
   - communication
3. Contemporary marriage patterns:
   - companionship and patriarchal structures
   - communes and group marriages
   - three-way marriages
   - living together
   - contract marriages
4. Sexual myths
5. Moral decisions
6. Control of sex drive
7. Parenthood
   - childbirth
   - childrearing
   - sex education of children
8. Masculinity and femininity

9. Research in sexuality:
   - human sexual response
   - sexual dysfunction
   - sterility
   - pornography
10. Sexuality and legality:
    - personal behavior
    - treatment and information
    - sex education
11. Historical and social factors affecting sexuality:
    - selected historical and social factors affecting sexuality
    - cultural aspects of sexuality
12. Sexuality and advertising

DEVELOPING OBJECTIVES

The terms *goals, behavioral objectives,* and *instructional objectives* are not synonymous. A **goal** is a statement of instructional intent. Goals give direction and purpose to educational efforts. Goals are long-range and may take years to accomplish. They are useful in developing long-term objectives for curriculum and grade-level expectations. **Behavioral objectives** extend beyond one lesson and involve a number of lessons or units. They do not tell the teacher what or how to teach, but they do provide a framework for selecting appropriate content, learning activities, and evaluation procedures. **Instructional objectives** indicate the learning or behavior that a particular lesson should generate. An instructional objective, which is specific and short-term, falls within the framework of each health class. If the time required to teach the objective is longer than one class period, it begins to resemble a behavioral objective (see Table 2.3).

The explicit task called for in the objective must be stated in measurable, action-oriented form (Kibler, Cegala, Barker, & Miles, 1974). Instructional objectives are used as a basis for selecting content and learning activities and in planning evaluation. Objectives must be based on students' developmental level and on concepts appropriate to that developmental level. Properly constructed objectives will increase the ability to focus on what needs to be accomplished. They also provide accountability to administrators, parents, and students. All instructional effort should be based on the objectives for the particular lesson or unit.

Classification of Objectives

With the foregoing criteria in mind, instructional objectives in three areas should be developed. These areas are the cognitive, the affective, and the action domains. As defined by Bloom (1956), the cognitive domain centers around knowledge; the affective domain emphasizes skills and attitudes; and the action, or psychomotor, domain focuses on skills and behavior.

Cognitive Domain

Bloom describes the cognitive domain as "those objectives which deal with recall or recognition of knowledge and the development of intellectual abilities, skills" (p. 8).

Table 2.3   How Goals and Objectives Lead to Comprehensive Health-Education Experiences

Comprehensive Health Education	*based on* →	Learner Characteristics	→ Process →	Evaluation
(Grades 7–12)		Needs Interests Developmental Level ■ Social ■ Emotional ■ Psychological ■ Physical		1. Determines the degree that program, behavior, and instructional objectives have been achieved 2. Teacher effectiveness in educational process

Goals —— *based on* ——→ **Learner Characteristics**
(philosophical/curricular)   that contribute to ⌐
For high-level wellness; learner
  based
                                          ↓

Objectives —— *types* ——→ **Cognitive** (knowledge) ——→
■ Program (annual)   **Affective** (attitude)
■ Behavioral (units/modules)   **Psychomotor** (behavior)
                                Personalizing Experiences
                                  (Confluent education)
                                  ■ Knowledge base for decision making

Curriculum ——————→   **(Methods)** ——→
■ Content for grade level   **(Strategies)**
■ Personalizing experiences   ■ Learning/personalizing
■ Organization and Curriculum   experiences
  design

The six progressive levels of development in the cognitive domain range from simple to complex. These levels fall into two divisions, low and high.

Low-level stages of development include:

1. Knowledge: Recognizing and recalling information, terms, classes, procedures, theories, and structures. Some terms indicative of knowledge-level objectives are *define, recall, describe, identify, list, match, name,* and *recite.*
2. Comprehension: Interpreting what has been learned, changing knowledge to another form, or predicting outcomes and effects. Terms indicative of a comprehensive objective are *explain, summarize, interpret, rewrite, estimate, convert, infer, translate, rearrange,* and *paraphrase.*

High-level stages of development include:

3. Application: Use of knowledge in new situations. Terms used to construct this level of objective are *change, compute, demonstrate, operate, show, use,* and *solve.*

4. Analysis: Breaking whole units into regulated parts (deduction), understanding the organization and the relationship of its parts, noting similarities and differences. Terms used are *outline, break down, subdivide, discriminate, diagram, order, categorize,* and *distinguish.*
5. Synthesis: Combining elements into new wholes (induction) or integrating information and concepts. Terms used for constructing synthesis-level objectives include *combine, compile, compose, create, design, rearrange, plan,* and *produce.*
6. Evaluation: Judging materials and methods, using standards or criteria to make a quantitative or qualitative judgment. Terms used to construct this level of objective are *justify, appraise, criticize, compare, support, conclude,* and *contrast.*

Most instructional objectives in the cognitive domain require low-level development. However, teachers must also promote higher-level objectives for students to progress beyond simple recall. High-level objectives help promote decision making and the personalizing of health information. Closely examining the nature of the four high-level areas of the cognitive domain will help the teacher better plan activities that will promote higher levels of cognitive development.

Affective Domain

The affective domain emphasizes the emotional processes of feelings, attitudes, values, and judgments. Development in this domain also ranges from the simple to the complex, with low-level and high-level divisions. The five stages of affective development, as described by Krathwohl, Bloom, and Masia (1964), are as follows.
Low-level stages include

1. Receiving: Passive attention to stimuli (sensory inputs)
2. Responding: Reacting to stimuli (complying, volunteering, and so on)

High-level stages include

3. Valuing: Taking action consistent with a belief or value
4. Organizing: Commitment to a set of values (formulating values)
5. Characterizing: Total behavior conforming to internalized values and the integration of beliefs and attitudes into a philosophy of life

Objectives in the affective domain must be prepared in order to personalize the teacher's instruction for students. As Harbeck (1970) points out, instructional objectives that assess student attitudes and feelings are needed:

> The affective domain is central to every part of the learning and evaluation process. Awareness initiates learning. Willingness to respond is the basis for psychomotor responses and value systems provide the motivation for continued learning and for most of the individual's overt behavior. (p. 150)

One way to prepare affective objectives is to ask students to weigh the advantages and disadvantages, or possible rewards and penalties, of a health-related act. As with cognitive objectives, it is easier to prepare low-level affective objectives than higher level ones. Still, you should do all you can to assist students in developing affectively from lower to higher levels.

Measuring the results of affective objectives is difficult. You must rely largely on observation. Checklists and attitude scales are also of some help. However, children may respond to such devices with "approved" or teacher-advocated answers without adopting the actual value or behavior.

Action Domain

The action domain deals with what the student actually does. Instructional objectives for health in this domain concern the health practices and behavior that students will exhibit immediately or in the future.

Three action behaviors described by the School Health Education Study (1967) are useful in preparing instructional objectives in this domain: observable health behaviors, nonobservable health behaviors, and delayed behaviors.

1. **Observable health behaviors** are those that can be seen and evaluated to some extent in the school equipment. Examples include observations of a student's relationships with others, activities on the playground or in the classroom, personal appearance and grooming, and food selection in the school cafeteria.
2. **Nonobservable health behaviors** cannot be systematically observed in the school setting. Teachers can obtain information about such behaviors by questioning the student and others aware of the student's health practices. Areas for questioning include nutritional practices, safety practices, social conduct, sleep habits, and exercise patterns. Substance abuse and family relationships are also important areas in this domain, but teachers must take care to avoid invading the privacy of students or parents.
3. **Delayed behaviors** are health behaviors that the student will not or cannot practice in daily life before reaching adulthood, being confronted with the problem, or being in a position to assume greater responsibility for personal behavior. Examples of such behavior include maintaining a desirable weight, getting regular medical and dental checkups, and using community health services. In this area of the action domain, the teacher can lay the groundwork for much positive behavior.

Obviously, the three domains have a great deal of overlap. For example, behaviors in the highest-level affective domain are similar to behaviors in the action domain. Measuring the higher levels of all three domains is difficult. What, then, should be the goal in evaluating the effectiveness of instructional objectives? Emphasizing only what can be measured trivializes instruction. Further, it is unrealistic to expect the student to receive information, process it, and incorporate it in every instance. Well-planned objectives can ensure exposure to all three domains so that students make decisions that will enhance the overall quality of their own wellness throughout life. Internalizing information helps them make decisions that lead to positive health behavior.

Writing Instructional Objectives

At first, writing instructional objectives may seem difficult; however, step-by-step procedures can help teachers develop proficiency. Writing low-level objectives is easiest. In time, writing effective higher level objectives should also grow easier.

An instructional objective should contain five components. Following are definitions and examples of these components.

1. *Who:* The student or the one who is to exhibit the behavior. Usual terms used are *student, pupil,* or *learner.*
2. *Behavior expected:* What the student will do to show that learning has taken place.
3. *Learning requirement:* What the student will know, feel, or do when the unit or lesson is complete. For example, the student will define the terms, label the diagram, or demonstrate bandaging. The verb in this statement must be action oriented rather than abstract. Use verbs such as *write, construct, label, name, count, categorize,* and *organize.* Where possible, avoid vague terms such as *know, think, master, learn, grasp,* and *believe.* Such terms are difficult to evaluate and are open to broad interpretation.
4. *Conditions:* The specific conditions under which the student will be expected to do the activity; for example, *on a test, orally,* or *working in pairs.*
5. *Standard of performance:* The minimum level of achievement, either quantitative or qualitative, that will be accepted as meeting the objective; for example, *80% correct, four out of five times, within six months,* or *as judged acceptable by a panel.*

Instructional objectives must contain at least the first three components. Behavioral and program objectives should contain all five components. The following example illustrates how the five components are developed in an objective:

The student (*who*) will demonstrate (*behavior expected*) correct CPR technique (*learning required*) utilizing Resuscitation Annie (*conditions*) for 2 minutes with 100% accuracy (*standard of performance*).

Limitations of Objectives

To be effective, objectives must be stated as precisely as possible. Properly developed, objectives clarify communication and help establish expectations for the learner. As Zais (1986) points out, however, objectives also have limitations and drawbacks. First, he notes, objectives are practical only for specifying the lowest levels of learning. Higher-level aspects of the three domains are difficult or even impossible to measure. Blind reliance on objectives can lead to only the trivial (quantifiable) aspects of instruction being measured and considered important.

Second, objectives tend to limit or restrict definitions of learning. For example, an objective may define the measurement of physical strength as the ability to do 20 pushups or to lift a 50-pound weight. However, many other indicators of strength exist. By its very precision and criterion of measurable performance, an objective can obscure other valid indicators of a skill or ability.

Third, judgments about abstract qualities, such as personal concern or appreciation, are based on subjective, indirect measures or observations. Zais convincingly argues that objectives cannot be developed to measure such qualities adequately.

Although these limitations do not detract from the general usefulness of objectives, teachers should always keep them in mind to avoid misusing objectives. Objectives should be seen as starting points, only one part of quality education. They should not be used to stipulate behavior in advance. The student exhibiting an alternate behavior at the end of instruction may be an equally valid indicator that learning has taken place.

SUMMARY

The key to effective curriculum construction is good planning, which requires thorough investigation of the literature and review of health-education materials. To be effective, content areas in health education must be organized to ensure comprehensive coverage of grades kindergarten through 12. Health topics should be based on students' needs, interests, and comprehension level as well as community mores. A comprehensive health-education program should also consider scope and sequence by development of a cycle plan that focuses on the concept necessary for the students to understand at that point in their lives.

Effective health education requires a balance between the factual portion and the attitude or valuing portion of a curriculum. Students must have adequate time to examine their feelings and internalize the information under consideration. This allows them to develop decision-making skills. Presentation of *facts* alone does not ensure learning, but teaching *concepts* promotes long-term use of basic information.

Many useful commercial health-education programs represent innovations in health education. Most states have resource guides that teachers may use to develop teaching units. Each teaching unit should follow a prescribed format and be designed for a particular grade and group. This unit then determines lesson plans for daily activities.

An area of concern for a health educator is how to develop a sound approach to teaching controversial health topics. Community leaders, parents, administrators, teachers, and students should be part of the planning process.

Objectives are precise statements of intended learning outcomes. When stated properly, they facilitate communication and help focus the content, learning activities, and evaluation procedures. There are three types of objectives: cognitive, affective, and action. An objective should contain five different components: who, the behavioral task, the product of the behavior, conditions under which the student performs, and the standard of performance.

DISCUSSION QUESTIONS

1. What are the advantages of sound planning?
2. Define *vertical organization* and *horizontal organization* and discuss their implications for health educators.
3. What criteria should curriculum developers consider when planning the various health content areas?
4. What types of materials can agencies provide for teaching health?
5. What are values and how are they learned? What are the implications for values in teaching health?
6. What are the differences between a resource unit and a teaching unit?
7. What purposes do well-developed objectives serve?
8. What are some guidelines for teaching family-life education?

9. What are some topics that should be included in AIDS education for the middle school student? For the high school student?
10. Why is it important to state objectives as precisely as possible?
11. What is the difference between a high-level and a low-level objective?

REFERENCES

Bloom, B. S. (1956). *Taxonomy of educational objectives, handbook I: Cognitive domain.* New York: McKay.

Guidelines for effective school health education to prevent the spread of AIDS. (1988). *Morbidity & Mortality Weekly Report Supplement, 37*(2).

Kibler, R. J., Cegala, D. J., Barker, L. L., & Miles, D. T. (1974): *Objectives for instruction and evaluation.* Boston: Allyn & Bacon.

McCary, J. L., & McCary, S. P. (1982). *McCary's human sexuality.* Belmont, CA: Wadsworth.

Schiller, P. (1973). *Creative approach to sex education and counseling.* New York: Association Press.

School Health Education Study. (1967). In *Health education: A conceptual approach to curriculum design.* St. Paul, MN: 3M Education Press.

U.S. Department of Education. (1986). *What works: Schools without drugs.* Washington, DC: Author.

Willgoose, C. E. (1974). *Health education in the elementary school.* Philadelphia: Saunders.

Zais, R. S. (1986). *Curriculum principles and foundations.* New York: Crowell.

CHAPTER 3

Meeting the Needs of the Learner

My guess is that when schools focus on what really matters in life, the cognitive ends we now pursue so painfully and artificially will be achieved somewhat more naturally. . . . It is obvious that students will work harder and do things for people they love and trust.
Nel Noddings, *Caring: A Feminine Approach to Ethics and Moral Education*

OBJECTIVES

After reading this chapter, you should be able to

- Describe the associative theory of learning as espoused by Thorndike and Skinner
- Explain the cognitive theory of learning
- Discuss the three phases of the Health Belief Model
- Relate the theories of learning to the behavior change process
- Explain how to educate students who are disabled most effectively
- Describe the importance of preparing teachers to teach students from various cultures
- Discuss the value and the content of individualized education programs

LEARNING THEORIES

No discussion concerning the nature of the secondary school student would be complete without at least a brief description of how students learn. Learning, after all, is what teachers are mainly concerned with and address day in and day out. A teacher who is knowledgeable about both student development and learning theory can better select instructional activities that capture the attention and fascination of students at a given level. In addition to helping choose activities, an awareness of the major principles of learning theory should enhance the teacher's ability to present these experiences in challenging, stimulating ways.

No one knows exactly how learning takes place. It is obvious that students learn in a variety of ways and from diverse experiences and opportunities. Learning itself is the lifelong process of accumulating, internalizing, and applying information to beliefs, attitudes, and practices. Learning allows people to achieve personal goals and interests and effects cognitive, affective, and behavioral changes that mature and broaden the individual.

Many theories about learning have sprung from well-researched and documented facts and observations. The theories generally fall into two major categories: **associative theories** and **cognitive** or **field theories**. The associative theories of learning originated from Aristotle's perception that ideas become associated with one another based on their similarity or difference. More modern psychological thought presented the concept, now known as **behaviorism**, that says behavior is learned as a result of associating experiences with either pleasure or pain. Cognitive or field theories, on the other hand, grew out of the Gestalt movement that began in the early 1900s in Germany. These theories state that behavior is learned through studying the whole pattern of behavior instead of analyzing it as separate elements, since the whole is more than the sum of its parts. (Bedworth & Bedworth, 1992).

Associative Theories

The chief associative theories of learning are **connectionism**, developed by Edward L. Thorndike, and **operant conditioning**, an outgrowth of **classical conditioning** theory, developed by B. F. Skinner. Connectionism is the cornerstone of the associative theories and is based on Thorndike's work of more than 50 years in educational psychology. Thorndike argued that every general principle of teaching must be applied with the particular person in mind. People respond differently to stimuli, he asserted, because of their individual capacities, interests, and previous learning. On the basis of his detailed observation of animals, Thorndike concluded that learning is a trial-and-error process in which random choices or selections are made in response to a given problem or situation until the "correct" response is discovered. When placed in the same situation or faced with a similar problem, experimental animals repeat that response until it becomes a habit. According to Thorndike, this habit develops as a result of a connection, or bond, that forms as part of a neurophysiological reaction. Thorndike visualized a hierarchy of these stimulus-response behaviors making up what he called his law of effect; that is, learning depends on the number of synaptic connections or associations that have been established (i.e., the previous experiences of the learner) (Fodor & Dalis, 1989).

Based on Thorndike's work, as well as Pavlov's famous experiments with dogs using classical conditioning (conditioned response), B. F. Skinner proposed that an organism is rewarded or punished for its behavior. In other words, learning takes place when positive reinforcement of and immediate information about one's actions or behaviors are provided. Therefore, a behavior is learned not because of a neurophysiological reaction, but because of positive reinforcement that follows it. Meaningful reinforcement and feedback can thus change undesirable behavior. Skinner called his theory **operant conditioning** and believed that only positive reinforcers promote learning (Bedworth & Bedworth, 1992).

Thorndike's and Skinner's theories have both been used by educators, either consciously or unconsciously, for years. Instructional methods that emphasize drills, repeated practice of a skill, rote memory lessons, and programmed instruction incorporate the ideas of associative learning with some degree of success for most students.

Cognitive or Field Theories

The cognitive or field theories of learning most frequently noted are those of Jean Piaget, John Dewey, Carl Rogers, and Abraham Maslow. The Swiss psychologist Jean Piaget believed that the individual gathers knowledge about the world to adapt to it through a progression of emphasis from motor activities to perceptions to conceptualization. He hypothesized that the first stage of learning reflects childhood learning experiences (Bedworth & Bedworth, 1992). At the preschool level, students explore the world mainly through their perceptions and finally develop a logical, conceptual, cognitive framework for learning and behavior during middle to late childhood by viewing the total world (situation) with reason, using all stages as a reference.

The philosopher John Dewey suggested that problem solving occurs through **pragmatic education**; that is, students need opportunities to experience solving the problems of life and need to learn how to become better-functioning members of society (Lumpkin, 1986). Dewey believed that students develop judgment and reason only if they are placed in surroundings that allow them to make judgments. Dewey was also concerned that the problem solving and learning that take place in schools may not readily apply to real-life situations and surroundings.

The movement commonly known as **humanism** approaches learning from the standpoint that we must view students first as human beings and not students. The writings of psychologists Carl Rogers and Abraham Maslow, in particular, emphasize that personality formation and learning ability depend on meeting the biological and emotional needs of students. Rogers and Maslow are sometimes referred to as phenomenological psychologists because they believe that personal experience, not a standard human experience, is the basis for problem solving and decision making and therefore is relative to individual feelings and perceptions. The total of one's experiences—not isolated pieces of information or situations—produces patterns of learning and behaving (Mouley, 1973).

Like the principles of learning hypothesized by the associative theories of Thorndike and Skinner, educators have used those proposed by cognitive theorists such as Piaget, Rogers, and Maslow as the foundation for curricular decisions in schools all over the country, because these ideas have proved effective. On the other hand, U.S. educators have only recently accepted the suggestions of John Dewey. When he proposed major educational revisions at the turn of the century, many considered him both a revolutionary and a charlatan, because unlike the other theorists, he did not test his ideas. Today, Dewey's principles are widely acknowledged and accepted, however. In addition, the humanistic approach to learning that Rogers and Maslow postulated in the early 1960s seems to have gained a solid foothold within the U.S. educational system, even though it has drawn criticism from those who favor a more traditional approach to learning.

HEALTH BELIEF MODEL

The connectionist and cognitive theories have implications for the field of health education. The **health belief model** (Ross & Mico, 1980) represents the most extensive effort thus far in developing a theory and a science of health behavior change. According to this theory, motivation is very important to learning, and learning involves changes in both cognition (knowledge) structure and motivation. The health belief model contains three distinct phases leading up to a health action: individual perception, modifying factors, and likelihood of action.

HEALTH HIGHLIGHT
Youth Risk Behavior Survey—Centers for Disease Control

The Centers for Disease Control (CDC) established a Youth Risk Behavior Surveillance System to monitor the prevalence of youth behaviors that most influence health. The following data describe the results from the 1990 survey:

- Among those aged 1–24 in the U.S., nearly 70% of all deaths were due to four causes: motor vehicle crashes (33%), other unintentional injuries (15%), homicides (10%), and suicides (10%).
- Alcohol and drug abuse was associated with these four causes of death and with many social problems that were not reflected in health statistics.
- 800,000 unintended pregnancies occurred among teenagers every year—this contributed to the high rate of infant mortality in the U.S.
- There were 2.5 million cases of increasingly serious sexually transmitted diseases among teens every year.
- One out of every five cases of AIDS in the U.S. occurred among those who were 20–29 years old. Given the average incubation period between contracting the AIDS-causing virus and the onset of AIDS, most of these were infected as teens.
- More than one-third of all students in the survey reported tobacco use during the 30 days preceding the survey—the prevalence of tobacco use was significantly greater among male students than among female students.
- 27.3% of all students in grades 9–12 reported that they had thought seriously about attempting suicide—16.3% had made a specific plan to attempt suicide—8.3% had actually attempted suicide.
- 88.1% of all students in grades 9–12 had consumed alcohol in their lifetime—58.6% reported having at least one drink of alcohol within 30 days of the survey—36.9% reported having five or more drinks on one occasion.
- 12% reported using marijuana at least once.
- 2% reported using any form of cocaine.
- Male students were significantly more likely to consider themselves either the right weight (68.8%) or underweight (16.5%) than were female students; black students were significantly less likely to consider themselves overweight than were white and Hispanic students.
- Female students were more likely to report currently trying to lose weight than were male students—27.4% of females who considered themselves the right weight reported currently trying to lose weight—females were significantly more likely than males to report having taken diet pills or induced vomiting for weight management.
- Of students in grades 9–12, 54.2% reported ever having had sexual intercourse—39.4% reported having had sexual intercourse during the 3 months preceding the survey.
- Male students were significantly more likely than female students to have ever had sexual intercourse—black students were significantly more likely than white or Hispanic students to ever have had sexual intercourse—the percentage of students ever having had sexual intercourse and having had sexual intercourse during the 3 months preceding the survey increased significantly by grade of student from 9th through 12th grade.
- 37% of students grades 9–12 reported being vigorously physically active three or more times per week—vigorous activity was significantly less common among female students than among males—vigorous activity was significantly less common among black students than among white or Hispanic students and less common among female students in grades 11 and 12 than among those in grade 9.

Source: *1990 Youth Risk Behavior Surveillance System,* U.S. Department of Health and Human Services, (1990), Atlanta: Centers for Disease Control.

Individual Perceptions

According to the health belief model, a person's behavior will be influenced away from a negative health behavior or will continue a positive health behavior if the person perceives the effects of the negative behavior as a serious threat to health and perceives that conditions resulting from the negative behavior are very serious. In addition, the person must perceive the negative health behavior as greatly increasing the likelihood of developing a disease. These two perceptions—personal susceptibility to a disease and the severity or seriousness of disease as a personal threat—are interacting perceptions that are necessary for modifying the negative behavior or maintaining the positive behavior.

Modifying Factors

Assuming that the foregoing perceptions or conditions are present, the ultimate decision by the individual to change or maintain his or her behavior depends, to a great extent, on the modifying factors present in the person's situation. For example, if the person's peers and parents model exemplary health behavior, that greatly enhances the prospects of changing a negative behavior to a positive behavior or of continuing a positive behavior. If this person is a student who has just learned in a health class about the hazardous effects of a negative behavior, that learning adds an important influence on behavior change. The combined influence of the home, peer group pressure, and health knowledge gained at school modifies the person's negative behavior or reinforces the continuation of positive behavior.

These perceptions also influence interpretation of the mass media and other sources. If the cues from these sources encourage negative behavior, the individual is more likely to reject them because they are inconsistent with the major predisposing forces identified in this situation. Positive media presentations and similar advice from friends and respected adults, on the other hand, are interpreted as consistent with the many other factors that support the positive behavior.

Likelihood of Action

According to the health belief model, individual action depends on the balance or imbalance between perceived positive and negative forces affecting an individual's health behavior. In the preceding example, positive behavior wins approval for the individual from family and friends. This action also is consistent with the knowledge (cognitive structure) that the individual has acquired in the school health course.

Admittedly, this example illustrates a situation in which all of the psychological forces favor the positive behavior. Another example might show the major forces in the student's life as encouraging continuation or initiation of a negative behavior. A more true-to-life example would show both negative and positive values, some favoring and some opposing negative behaviors, that combine to pose a genuine dilemma for an individual. In this situation the student's health education experiences can play a major role in decision making. Obviously, the quality of this instruction, the preparation of the teacher, and the teacher's sensitivities to the student's dilemma are of critical importance (Creswell & Newman, 1989).

When positive health behavior is reinforced by peers, the individual is likely to continue the behavior.

Theory of Learning and Behavior Change Process

Rabinowitz points out that health education programs have for years been dominated by what he calls a **pedagogic model** that has strongly stereotyped a teacher-student relationship as consisting of a one-way flow of information in which the teacher is the dispenser and the student is the passive recipient. A true teaching-learning situation is one in which a reciprocal effect or information exchange takes place between the teacher and the student (Rubinson & Alles, 1984).

Examination of health programs reveals wide use of a knowledge-attitude-behavior consistency model. Undoubtedly, the early work of Hochbaum, Rosenstock, and others in developing the health belief model, which draws heavily on communication theory, as well as the research of Katz and Lazarsfeld in diffusion theory, have had a major influence on the field. If teachers want to change behavior, they should focus on increasing knowledge or changing attitudes, and that will ultimately lead to a change in behavior. This idea, used in mass communication media, should work in the health education classroom, too. Although lacking in the technical skills and the resources available in mass communication, the health educator does have other advantages, such as additional opportunities and time to clarify and to reinforce the health message through close personal contact and sharing information with students. In fact, experience and research have demonstrated the superiority of person-to-person communication over that of impersonal mass media methods (Rubinson & Alles, 1984).

Social learning theory (SLT) is relatively new, but it has developed into what is currently perhaps the most influential approach to both personality development and general learning theory. This theory focuses intensely on people as opposed to ideas or objects. SLT deals with complex behavior, such as eating or exercise habits. It provides a framework for the self-regulation of behavior; this is quite compatible with the health educator's ideal of "voluntary adaptations of behavior conducive to health." In addition to these features, SLT also incorporates a number of natural, common sense-type concepts and strategies into its theoretical framework. At its most basic level, SLT reflects the following phenomenon: If people are asked how they learned to prepare a meal, comb their hair, throw a ball, or do any of a multitude of similar tasks, often they say they simply observed someone else doing that task. In other words, they learned by observing a model. And while the most obvious examples involve behavior with a skill component, for example, *how to* comb one's hair, the process can easily extend to attitudinal or motivational aspects of behavior; for example, *why* the hair should be combed or *why* seat belts should be worn. When health educators emphasize why something should be done and neglect to teach how to do it, at least two types of problems may result. First and most obvious are possible adverse consequences for one's health. If, for instance, we teach people about the detrimental consequences of cholesterol without also teaching them how to select low-fat foods, we may find that some of them eat the wrong foods because they think the foods are low in fat. In other words, the learners are motivated, but lack the skills to correctly apply the information (Greene & Simons-Morton, 1984).

EDUCATING STUDENTS WITH DISABILITIES

Incidence

Because of advances in medical technology and health care, many students with genetic defects, who years ago would have had shorter lives, are now surviving birth and living longer. Formerly segregated into separate schools or classrooms, these students are now in mainstream classrooms. Although the number of students with disabilities in the public schools is not known, some educators believe that the estimates of students who need assistance through special education are unrealistically low.

Approximately 40 million school students are enrolled in 87,000 schools across the country. These students are served by an estimated 30,000 school health nurses and an unknown number of school health aides. Within this population some 4 million students have specific disabilities. For these 4 million people Congress passed PL 94-142, the Education for All Handicapped Children Act, in November 1975. The principal intent of this legislation is to do the following:

1. Guarantee free, appropriate public education at no cost to the parents of all handicapped students 3 to 21 years of age.
2. Identify, locate, and evaluate all handicapped students regardless of the severity of their disabilities.

3. Evaluate yearly each handicapped student and develop an individualized education plan.
4. Provide educational services in the *least restrictive environment,* a process that often has been referred to as **mainstreaming**.
5. Ensure for parents a clear role as participants in the identification, evaluation, and placement of students.
6. Ensure that students who are placed in private schools or special schools receive special education services at no cost to the parents; also that these students receive the same rights and programs as students enrolled in public education institutions.
7. Provide in-service training for all teachers and support staff.
8. Develop and implement public awareness programs to ensure greater sensitivity to and understanding of handicapped students. (Creswell & Newman, 1989)

Public Law 94-142, the Education for All Handicapped Children Act, and **PL 93-112** (The Rehabilitation Act of 1973—see the following Health Highlight) stated that students with disabilities have the same rights to equal participation as all other students and that these students must be educated in the least restrictive environment. Special needs may qualify a student for special education considerations. For example, short-term illnesses, injuries, accidents, respiratory tract diseases, paralysis, orthopedic disorders, hearing defects, speech defects, and heart disease also represent special conditions.

These laws were amended by the passing of **PL 99-457** (the Education of the Handicapped Amendments Act of 1986) and **PL 101-476** (Individuals with Disabilities Education Act). **PL 99-457** amended **PL 94-142** to include a wider age range of students (infants and toddlers) and their parents. PL 101-476 replaced the term *handicapped* with the term *disability.* As a result of these laws, infants and toddlers with disabilities and their parents receive early intervention services. Parents play a significant part in the delivery of the services to the student, and schools cooperate with other community agencies in delivering appropriate programs to the students. Schools and parents develop an individualized family service plan (IFSP) for each student and family that is designed to meet the student's developmental needs (Dunn, 1991).

Who Are Students with Disabilities?

Students with disabilities include, among others, those who are mentally retarded, orthopedically impaired, deaf or hearing impaired, autistic, blind or partially sighted, and speech impaired. Disability is, however, a relative term. Some persons with disabilities are trained to assemble complex electronic components, perform stunts, entertain as actors and singers, and serve as administrators in large companies. Each of these people has some type of disability, yet in other important ways each is not at all disabled.

The **Rehabilitation, Comprehensive Service, and Developmental Disabilities Amendment of 1978** defines a developmental disability as a severe chronic disability of a person that:

■ Is attributable to a mental or physical impairment or combination of mental and physical impairments

HEALTH HIGHLIGHT
Legislation Related to Education of Students with Disabilities

1975: PL 94-142: The Education for All Handicapped Children Act of 1975

PL 94-142 is the landmark legislation and principal referent for policies that provide free and appropriate education, including physical education, for all eligible children between 3-21. (Initially, the age range was 3-18, implemented in Fall, 1978. It was later mandated for ages 3-21 by September 1, 1980.) The law is also known as the Education for the Handicapped Act-Part B (EHA-Part B).

1983: PL 98-199: Education of the Handicapped Act Amendments of 1983

PL 98-199 expanded funds and provided incentives for states to plan, develop, and implement an early intervention system for children with disabilities from birth to age five.

1986: PL 99-457: Education of the Handicapped Act Amendments of 1986

Part B of PL 99-457 required states to provide services for all eligible preschoolers, 3-5 years, or lose some federal funding. Part H of PL 99-457 authorized funds to states to develop and implement a statewide, comprehensive, coordinated, multidisciplinary, interagency program of early intervention services for infants and toddlers with disabilities and their families.

1990: PL 101-476: Individuals with Disabilities Education Act (IDEA)

PL 101-476 resulted in several significant changes. The Education of the Handicapped Act (EHA) was renamed Individuals with Disabilities Education ACT (IDEA); thus, the term "handicapped" is replaced by the term "disability." For future reference, the Office of Special Education and Rehabilitative Services now recommends that IDEA rather than EHA be used in all references. The Infants and Toddlers with Disabilities Program, which was enacted as part of PL 99-457, is now Part H of the IDEA. The Preschool Program, which also was enacted as part of PL 99-457, is included in Section 619 of Part B of the IDEA.

Source: "Legislative Terminology Affecting Adapted Physical Education" by J. Cowden & R. L. Eason. This article is reprinted with permission from the *JOPERD* (*Journal of Physical Education, Recreation & Dance*), August 1991, p. 34. JOPERD is a publication of the American Alliance for Health, Physical Education, Recreation and Dance, 1900 Association Drive, Reston, VA 22091-1599.

- Is manifested before the person attains age 22
- Is likely to continue indefinitely
- Results in substantial functional limitations in three or more of the following areas of major life activity: self-care, receptive and expressive language, learning, mobility, self-direction, capacity for independent living, and economic self-sufficiency
- Reflects the person's need for a combination and sequence of special, interdisciplinary, or generic care, treatment, or other services that are lifelong or of extended duration and are individually planned and coordinated (Auxter & Pyfer, 1985)

Accommodating Students with Disabilities in Integrated Settings

Many argue that teaching students with different learning characteristics is too difficult, but many educators take exception to that position. Teachers must use innovative ways to accommodate individual differences. Successful teaching of individuals with disabilities in regular classes requires individualized teaching skills. It also requires teachers who can modify rules, environments, and tasks to promote meaningful play among those with and without disabilities.

Mainstreaming and the Least Restrictive Environment

Current federal and state legislation uses the term *least restrictive environment* to suggest that the regular class offers fewer restrictions on learning opportunities. *Mainstreaming,* often used concurrently with least restrictive environment, is the practice of providing persons with disabilities the best education possible in an integrated setting with other students. This means that individuals, regardless of type or severity of their disability, should participate in activities with other students whenever possible. Students should be moved from more to less restrictive environments as their needs warrant. An individualized education program should improve the skills of students with disabilities and should help them achieve advanced placement on the continuum. Advancing students on a continuum of least restrictive alternatives requires (1) periodic review of educational progress, (2) frequent assessment of what least restrictive environment means for a particular student at a particular time, and (3) possible modifications in the services that may produce optimum progress in the future.

Successful mainstreaming depends on two factors: (1) the teacher's attitude toward the student, and (2) the teacher's ability to teach the student. Awareness sessions, including actual contact with individuals with disabilities, are necessary for teachers to overcome their natural fears and misconceptions about the disabled. All undergraduate health education majors should participate in awareness sessions. This must also be a priority for in-service and retraining experiences for already certified health educators (Eichstaedt & Kalakian, 1987, pp. 40–41).

The Individualized Education Program

The individualized education program (IEP) required by PL 94-142 represents the culmination of a long-standing position in American education. IEPs may be viewed as a set of statements guiding instructional strategies. The varied needs of students with disabilities make individualization of instruction a necessity. The focus of special education has moved to designing instruction for each student regardless of disability or categorical designation (Auxter & Pyfer, 1985).

Value of IEPs

IEPs are useful to students with disabilities, parents, teachers, and society in the following ways:

> *Students with disabilities:* IEPs are personal and fair. Students with disabilities are neither entirely like others nor entirely different. The IEP acknowledges special needs and ensures that no part of education will be neglected.
>
> *Parents:* An IEP ensures the parents a voice in planning services and instructional content.

Society: An IEP is a useful document for ensuring to the greatest extent possible that education contributes to students' self-sufficiency.

Teachers: An IEP provides accessible and current data; it is a tool that links supportive expertise. The IEP is the basis for day-to-day lesson planning. It keeps student and teacher on target because the predicted outcome is clear to both. The IEP also helps teachers tailor the instructional plan (Auxter & Pyfer, 1985).

Content of the IEP

Public policy requires that the IEP include: (1) annual goals, (2) short-term instructional objectives, (3) present levels of educational performance, (4) specific educational services, (5) extent to which each student will be able to participate in regular education programs, (6) projected date for initiation and anticipated duration of such services, and (7) criteria and evaluation procedures for determining whether instructional objectives are being achieved.

Short-term instructional objectives are "measurable intermediate steps between present levels of educational performance and the annual goals" (Auxter & Pyfer, 1985). Because present levels of performance are observable and measurable and all components of the IEP instructional process are related, goals and objectives also should be observable and measurable.

Objectives occur at different levels of curricular development and must be appropriate for the ability level of a specifically diagnosed individual. They require assessment of the learner's capabilities. In the event that mastery of a specific behavior is not possible, the question is asked: What prerequisites does this individual need to master this task? This question, once answered, is restated until the student's present performance level and the appropriate instructional objectives are determined. A sequence of prerequisite activities thus provides a chain of instructional events that leads the learner from lower to higher levels of mastery. The use of this instructional process requires keeping detailed records on each learner to determine the student's position in a learning activity sequence. The mastery of one objective is the prerequisite that gives rise to a more complex objective, making development progressive.

The instructional objective must incorporate four concepts: (1) it must possess an action; (2) it must establish conditions under which actions occur; (3) it must establish a criterion for mastery of a specific task; and (4) it must lie outside the child's present level of educational performance. (Auxter & Pyfer, 1985).

The Teacher's Responsibility in Educating Students with Disabilities

Teacher Qualities

Teachers should possess a variety of skills to accommodate individual differences when teaching specific content. Teacher attitudes toward having students with disabilities in their class and their ability to accommodate students with disabilities are also important considerations. Research shows that the majority of teachers believe that they are not equipped to deal with students with special needs. Studies also indicate that teachers harbor generally negative attitudes toward students with disabilities whose ability levels and needs are different from those of most students. It is therefore extremely important that the teacher become knowledgeable about students with disabilities. Teachers should establish a close working relationship with the special educator who has been trained and will be able to answer questions about most disabling conditions. The special educator should act as a consultant when specific information about a student is required.

As a teacher, you must stress to all of your students that they each are unique and should strive to coexist with each other regardless of differences. Emphasize what they can do rather than what they cannot do. Search for opportunities for students to cooperate with others and to display their talents to the group. These positive actions will both help special students adjust to the regular classroom, and encourage the other students to accept them (Eichstaedt & Kalakian, 1987).

Multicultural Education

The classroom is changing in many ways. It is estimated that, by the year 2020, higher birth rates among minority populations and changing immigration patterns will result in nearly half of all school-aged children being nonwhite. These minority youth are chronically the worst educated in our society. To meet the needs of all learners, teachers must be prepared for the growing diversity of a multicultural student population.

Students also represent diverse family structures and economic status. Twelve per cent of children born today are born out of wedlock, and 40% are born to parents who divorce before the child is 18. The numbers of children born outside of marriage and born to teenaged mothers are increasing.

For health education to be truly effective, all students should have the chance to achieve their educational capacity. Teacher-training programs must focus on preparing teachers for culturally diverse classrooms, including concepts of health and disease that apply to various cultures. A comprehensive school health-education program must allow for differences in cultural beliefs and attitudes.

Recent studies reveal that a disproportionately small number of minorities are receiving degrees in health education or are involved in professional teacher-training programs. National professional organizations, educational agencies, and governmental agencies must combine their efforts to correct this shortage. Until then, these agencies must ensure that teachers (those in the profession currently as well as those in training) are prepared to promote a learning environment that is equitable for all students (Association for the Advancement of Health Education, 1992).

SUMMARY

Associative and cognitive (field) learning theories have influenced the way we teach today. Some of these theories have helped to shape the health belief model, which helps to explain how knowledge and values determine behaviors.

Teaching students with special needs is a challenge for all educators, including health educators. Several laws dictate how schools must provide education for students with disabilities; teachers must also develop their skills in dealing with all types of students.

DISCUSSION QUESTIONS

1. Differentiate between the associative and cognitive theories of learning.
2. Compare the health belief model with other theories of learning.
3. Discuss how the theories of learning relate to how individuals change their health behavior.
4. Discuss the importance of mainstreaming students with disabilities and placing them in the least restrictive education environment.
5. Discuss the laws that require appropriate education for students with disabilities.
6. Discuss how the U.S. classroom is changing to reflect a more culturally diverse society.

REFERENCES

Association for the Advancement of Health Education. (1992). *Cultural awareness and sensitivity: A crucial component to the success of school health education* (executive summary). Unpublished manuscript. AAHE: Reston, VA.

Auxter, D., & Pyfer, J. (1985). *Principles and methods of adapted physical education and recreation.* St. Louis: Times Mirror/Mosby College Publishing.

Bedworth, A. E., & Bedworth, D. A. (1992). *The profession and practice of health education.* Dubuque, IA: Wm. C. Brown.

Cowden, J., & Eason, R. L. (1991). "Legislative terminology affecting adapted physical education," *Journal of Physical Education, Recreation & Dance, 62,* 34.

Creswell, W. H., Jr., & Newman, I. M. (1989). *School health practice.* St. Louis: Mosby.

Dunn, J. M. (1991). "PL 99-457: Challenges and opportunities for physical education," *Journal of Physical Education, Recreation & Dance, 62,* 33–34.

Eichstaedt, C. B., & Kalakian, L. H. (1987). *Developmental/adapted physical education: Making ability count* (2nd ed). New York: Macmillan.

Fodor, J. T., & Dalis, G. T. (1989). *Health instruction: Theory and application* (4th ed.). Philadelphia: Lea & Febiger.

Greene, W. H., & Simons-Morton, B. G. (1984). *Introduction to health education.* New York: Macmillan.

Ross, H. S., & Mico, P. R. (1980). *Theory and practice in health education.* Palo Alto, CA: Mayfield.

Rubinson, L. & Alles, W. F. (1984). *Health education: Foundations for the future.* St. Louis: Times Mirror/Mosby College Publishing.

CHAPTER 4

Strategies for Implementing Health Instruction

Teaching is both a science and an art. . . . The effective blending of these into an educational recipe to ensure continuing progress of [students] toward optimal well-being and more abundant living is an art.   S. Bender and W. Sorochan, *Teaching Elementary Health Science,* 3rd ed.

OBJECTIVES

After reading this chapter, you should be able to

- List the factors that affect teaching strategy selection
- Discuss criteria and salient points of using values clarification strategies
- Describe effective use of decision stories in the classroom
- Explain the importance of using verbal strategies to implement health instruction
- Identify the elements necessary to prepare for discussion
- List action-oriented strategies used in health instruction
- Describe the different ways to use the computer in the classroom
- Describe the use of media in the classroom
- Describe the use of interactive video in health education

THE RELATIONSHIP OF STRATEGIES TO LEARNING

Any teaching or learning strategy focuses on the learner. **Teaching strategies** are planned approaches used to maximize learners' comprehension of a new situation or to increase their comprehension of a familiar situation. A teaching strategy is any activity or experience that the teacher uses to interpret, illustrate, or facilitate learning. To maximize learning, you should seek strategies that are student-centered and provide for group involvement. You also should use more than one strategy or activity for each major concept so that your instruction more fully encompasses the variety of student abilities and aptitudes. **Learning methods** are procedures that the learners use to give them greater insight into a new or familiar situation. **Learning strategies** are methods that make content and objectives come alive. This enlivening involves strategies and techniques that make learning exciting and motivating. Carrying this out is the direct responsibility of the teacher who, having established a working knowledge of the many strategies available in health education, is limited only by her own creativity (Bedworth & Bedworth, 1992).

The teacher must remember that selecting a variety of strategies does not ensure learning. Several other factors influence effective learning and must be considered, such as a relationship with the students that is conducive to learning. Treating students fairly is an important step in facilitating learning and creating a proper classroom atmosphere. Many techniques can help promote creative learning.

Regardless of the type of teaching strategy used in health education, the information must be clearly communicated. For communication to be effective, the student must perceive that the teacher is a credible source and must find the message meaningful (Rubinson & Alles, 1988).

Communicating health information to students should also involve the five senses. Typically, the more senses that can be stimulated and the more often the senses are stimulated through the teaching strategy, the more the student will learn and retain the information (Bender & Sorochan, 1989).

FACTORS AFFECTING STRATEGY SELECTION

Many variables affect selection and use of strategies in teaching health education. Greene and Simons-Morton (1984) provide a general background for selecting health-education strategies:

1. Because health education is multidisciplinary, strategies for teaching health follow many theoretical approaches. Some strategies are appropriate for cognitive and affective approaches, such as **values clarification, decision making, lecturing,** and **guided discovery.** In some settings with older students, social learning strategies such as goal setting, reinforcement, and feedback can be used effectively.

2. People of different ages learn different ways and at different paces. Learners represent a range of backgrounds, abilities, and interests. The typical way to deal with this situation is to adopt a variety of strategies that will help every learner at least some of the time. Another approach is to provide alternative learning experiences for some students.

3. Sometimes, teaching strategies depend on the nature of the subject to be covered. Factual information is best taught through lectures and printed materials. Skills, on the other hand, are usually taught through demonstration and feedback.

4. Many teaching strategies are available for use in health education (many of them are described in this chapter). Strategies may be active or passive, teacher-centered or learner-centered, media-dominated or activity-dominated. Teachers should keep a readily available file of strategies that they can pair with the specific objectives of a lesson.

5. Learners are often a good source of ideas for teaching strategies. When allowed to select the type of strategy to be used in a lesson, learners have a sense of ownership, which usually makes them more involved and more interested. Then, they are apt to learn more.

6. Many teaching strategies exist, and new ones are rarely developed. The health educator must read new information about a topic and decide the best way to teach it to students. Teachers can choose the appropriate strategies by developing a thorough understanding of the various ways of looking at health behavior. They should know the literature and think in terms of educational objectives and learning activities.

The two most important individuals in the teaching-learning process are the teacher and the student. The teacher can positively influence this process by choosing and implementing the appropriate strategy (as just described). Some other teacher characteristics and skills—while they may not seem directly involved in the teaching process—can be a positive or negative influence.

The Teacher's Personality. Charisma will engage students more than a dour, negative or sarcastic personality. A teacher's personality often determines a positive or negative emotional environment in the classroom. A consistent positive attitude toward students is very significant.

Behavior. Mannerisms that suggest the teacher is open and accepting of all students can enhance a teacher's effectiveness.

Voice and Diction. Lively use of voice and proper diction hold the students' attention better than a monotonous delivery.

Classroom Management. Personal interaction (e.g., eye contact) with students and movement around the room help remove physical barriers between the students and teacher.

Use of Materials to Supplement a Lecture. Regardless of how well a teacher can describe something in words, many students are visual learners. They benefit from seeing drawings and words on the board and audiovisual enhancement of the material to be learned.

The learner is the other partner in the teaching-learning process. Ultimately, the student is responsible for what is learned. Students must be receptive to learning new material, and they must be motivated (or willing to be motivated) to learn. Students' motivation depends on their interest in the material, and the perceived importance of the material to them.

Students also learn in a variety of ways. Some people can grasp abstract concepts with ease, while others are concrete-sequential learners and need to see, touch, or feel the material to internalize the information.

Obviously, the teacher can help make the most of these behaviors. For example, students typically learn better when they know what is expected; therefore, the teacher can be very specific in conveying what she expects from the class. Other aspects, however, such as students' physical, emotional, and intellectual readiness, are beyond the teacher's control. Teachers can try to reach each student at his or her own level, but this is very difficult with a very heterogeneous group of learners.

Selecting and using appropriate learning experiences is an art—a prescriptive, judgmental phase of teaching much like the physician's approach to selecting and prescribing a course of treatment for a patient.

APPLICATION OF STRATEGIES

Learning experiences are the means by which students learn both the content and the process of health science. Students acquire understanding, attitudes, and habits that help them to develop and maintain their quality of life. The teacher should use a wide variety of learning experiences to help students accomplish these purposes.

Many teachers should take care to choose activities carefully and avoid using more than necessary. Sometimes one activity is enough, but a difficult or abstract concept may require more than one activity to be understood. Using too many activities, on the other hand, will cause students to lose interest (Bender & Sorochan, 1989, pp. 148–149).

In selecting strategies to provide learning experiences, keep the following criteria in mind:

Select strategies that contribute to total learning. Some activities lend themselves to acquiring knowledge, whereas others are better suited to assessing attitudes and making decisions. Ideally, the strategies selected should help the student develop the ability to reason and to assess the information being presented. Any strategy selected should involve the students as participants in the activity.

The more complex the concept, the more activities needed to develop the concept. As a general rule, two strategies or activities should be employed for each concept. If the material being studied is difficult, more than two strategies or activities should be used. Another reason for using more than one strategy is that students learn in a variety of ways and through different means. Thus, a variety of strategies will help ensure that all students grasp the concept under examination.

The strategies selected should begin with the simple and move to the more complex. Once you have prepared the class for the activity through a proper introduction, students should become part of the learning activity. With simple activities, students should be able to learn through group involvement, self-assessment, and class-teacher interaction. As students become better able to deal with more difficult topics, more complex strategies can be used that require self-discovery or analysis of materials and conclusions.

Audiovisual aids should be included whenever possible. These can include models, classroom exhibits, films, filmstrips, and so forth. Audiovisual aids add another dimension to teaching concepts and are excellent for reinforcing learning.

Strategies fall into many different categories. Some authorities distinguish among strategies, media, and instructional materials, whereas others group all three into one category. For example, some divide strategies into didactic and interactive methods (Rubinson & Alles, 1988). **Didactic methods** include information dissemination such as lectures. These methods have proven to be effective when students demonstrate unhealthy behaviors because they lack information. These methods have limitations, however; namely, they typically do not involve the learner in the learning. Also, a person may have adequate knowledge about a health behavior, but values, desires or other factors cause the person to choose unhealthy behavior.

Interactive strategies of teaching emphasize that knowledge alone is not sufficient, that the student must be actively involved in the learning process. By becoming involved, the learner brings feelings and attitudes into the process, and compares them with others' feelings and attitudes.

Classifying teaching strategies is less important than understanding the strengths and weaknesses of each available technique. Your objective should be to select strategies that are most appropriate and effective with your class. The rest of this chapter is devoted to examining some of the many strategies that can be used in health education.

TYPES OF STRATEGIES

Values Clarification Strategies

Health education is unique in that strategies emphasizing the cognitive aspects alone are not effective. For example, a student may score 100% on a quiz about nutritional concepts, yet that same student may demonstrate unhealthy nutrition attitudes and behavior. Therefore, strategies in health education need to bridge the gap between knowledge and behavior. Students must be able to participate in affective activities that allow them to personalize the health concepts.

An excellent strategy for bridging this gap is to use values clarification activities. Examining and clarifying values assists students in fostering positive health behavior. As mentioned earlier, however, some controversy surrounds the use of values clarification techniques. Values cannot and should not be avoided when teaching health education, but the teacher must be prepared to do the job right.

Begin by recognizing that values are relative, personal, and often situational. You should not attempt to teach your personal values or the "correct" values; instead, your goal should be to assist students in assessing and developing their own values so that these values lead to positive health behavior. Students must make any value judgment through their own cognitive process. In order for students to benefit fully from a values clarification strategy, they must feel some ownership in the activity—that is, they must perceive that the issue being discussed is relevant to them and that the issue is serious enough to be considered. The teacher should present several options as viable solutions along with the possible consequences for each of the options that could be chosen.

Students also must be prepared in order to succeed at values clarification. Greenberg (1989) outlines the following requisites to such learner-centered instruction:

1. Familiarity with and trust of other program participants (students)
2. Friendship with at least one other participant
3. Listening skills
4. Knowledge of and experience with roles assumed by members and leaders of groups
5. Knowledge of and experience with the decision-making process
6. Cooperation and participation among all members of the program
7. An understanding and appreciation of both one's own feelings and the feelings of others
8. Open communication among disagreeing factions and empathy with those of opposing viewpoints
9. Recognition of unfulfilled needs of program participants and means of satisfying those needs
10. Appreciation of individual differences and unique potential (p. 43)

When engaging in any values clarification activity, the teacher must give students sufficient time to assess their own feelings about the issue under examination. Students must also feel free to assess their values without fear of ridicule or being forced to pay lip service to the opinions of others, including the teacher. Keep these points in mind:

■ Values clarification activities do not yield one "correct" solution to a problem; they are open ended. These activities are designed to open the doors to additional assessment.

- As a teacher, you act as a participant in the activities and as a role model for the students by accepting various viewpoints.
- Every student has the right to decline to speak without having to give a reason for declining. Respect individual feelings and keep the activity nonthreatening.

One of the basic tenets of values clarification strategies is to present all sides of the issue without bias. In keeping with that tenet, the criticisms of this learning approach should be discussed. Many criticize values clarification because it gives the student no guidance from the teacher. Of course, this same criticism is used to praise this strategy. Without guidance from the teacher, these critics charge, students (especially younger students) are left to determine their own moral standards without the benefit of adult input—and independent of the parents' or society's standards. This approach thus may create conflict between students and their families.

Another criticism of the values clarification approach concerns the teacher's objectivity. Some claim that teachers have trouble being truly unbiased in each situation. For example, a teacher might have had a relative killed by a drunk driver, and may thus have difficulty being objective when teaching about responsible uses of alcohol. Even if a teacher sounds objective, she may demonstrate a bias toward or against one value in nonverbal behavior. For example, the teacher might unknowingly become more animated and enthusiastic when describing the value she believes in and may present opposing values with less enthusiasm. Also, some teachers may show a bias toward a particular value by spending more time on it than on another.

Many instructional devices can incorporate values clarification activities into the health curriculum. The ones that you choose should be appropriate for students' developmental level. As already discussed, some students are not capable of dealing with highly abstract issues. Further, some do not have the experiential background to understand topics far removed from their everyday world. Therefore, grappling with such values-related issues as euthanasia or world hunger may not be realistic with some students.

Sentence Completion

Asking students to complete open ended statements is a simple values-related activity. This kind of activity is appropriate for students at a slightly higher developmental level. Examples of typical open ended statements include the following:

I think that smoking is: _____

_____ .

If my friend did something wrong, I would: _____

_____

_____ .

VERBAL AND DISCUSSION-ORIENTED STRATEGIES

Values clarification activities rely to a large extent on discussion, as do many other classroom strategies. Discussion is a useful technique, but it must be structured. Always keep in mind your objectives in employing any particular discussion strategy so that you do not lose the focus. Following are several other discussion-oriented strategies that have proven effective in health instruction.

Brainstorming

Like values clarification activities, brainstorming can help improve decision-making skills by having students generate many possible ideas concerning an issue. Brainstorming also encourages freedom of expression and creativity. Possible topics for brainstorming sessions include:

- How can you get students to follow driving safety rules?
- How can students be encouraged to eat nutritious snacks instead of junk food?
- How can we make our physical environment healthier and more pleasant?

In conducting a brainstorming session, it is very important to follow these four rules:

1. The problem to be brainstormed must be well defined.
2. Any and all ideas must be accepted and recorded.
3. Criticism of any idea put forth is not allowed.
4. All ideas should be evaluated objectively when the session is over.

Brainstorming can be used effectively in the secondary grades for problem solving. The biggest drawback is that in a large class not every student will get to express his thoughts; nonetheless, the activity can be quite productive. Encouraging and accepting all opinions may reveal new or novel possible solutions to a problem. Even impractical suggestions can lead to new ways of thinking about an issue.

Follow-up is important. In the follow-up session, ask students to elaborate on their ideas. Present additional information that will help make suggestions seem more practical or realistic. Doing so will emphasize to the class how the freewheeling brainstorming session produced many approaches to the problem.

Buzz Groups

Similar to brainstorming, buzz groups are an effective strategy for allowing students to express opinions, but not necessarily for devising creative solutions to problems. Generally, this technique is productive if students are mature enough to use the format. It allows for student participation in an atmosphere conducive to discussion. The buzz group strategy should not be overused, however, because too much small-group work can lessen student enthusiasm.

To use this approach, divide the class into groups of from three to five students. Have each group focus on a specific problem that you have introduced and discussed to give them a knowledge base for their discussion. Each group should choose a chairperson and a recording secretary. The chairperson must keep the discussion focused on the topic, and the secretary records important points.

Allow 3 to 15 minutes for buzz group discussion. Suitable topics for this strategy include the following:

- How should an accident victim be handled?
- How can students get along better with their peers?

- What can be done to educate students about the dangers of smoking?
- What can be done about vandalism?

When the discussion time is over, ask each group's recording secretary to present the results of that group's discussion. The more controversial the topic, the likelier that many diverse opinions will be aired. In the summary discussion, encourage objective consideration of all approaches put forth.

Case Studies

Case studies are actual events that you can use in class for discussion. The decision story format lends itself well to the case study strategy. Just substitute the actual event for the hypothetical one. The teacher can have students identify with one of the characters in the case study and determine how they would react in the situation. Also, students can discuss the conflicting views that arise from some case studies. Several stories—such as those about Ryan White, who contracted HIV/AIDS through a blood transfusion, and Karen Ann Quinlan, whose parents sued to remove her from a life support machine—serve as excellent case studies for discussions on health issues. Good sources for case study materials are health journals, newspapers, news magazines, and television programs.

Debate

Debate focuses on the merits and problems associated with a proposed solution to a problem. This technique ensures that both sides of an issue are presented. This strategy is more effective with older students, who are more articulate and better able to organize their thoughts for oral presentation. Students must also be able to work individually, cooperatively, and in groups.

Topics suitable for debate include protecting the environment versus creating jobs, the supposed merits of organic versus regular produce, and the pro-life versus pro-choice stands on abortion.

Thorough preparation for a debate is essential. Students who volunteer to be part of a debate team should have ample time to learn about the issue they will discuss. You should engage the whole class in this preparation so that students not on the debate teams are prepared to deal with the pros and cons of the arguments objectively.

In selecting students for debate teams, be sure to balance the sides in ability. The teacher, as moderator, should keep both teams on the topic and also guard against emotions building up during and after the debate. Remind the students that they may disagree with a person's philosophy, but not verbally attack the other person.

Committee Work

This technique allows small groups of students to research a topic of interest. Each group member has an opportunity to do in-depth research on the topic. Each member of the group must contribute to the project for it to succeed. The tendency in committees is for one or two members of the group to do the majority of the work, while the others won't or can't contribute.

Projects that lend themselves well to committee work include the following:

- Investigating different types of pollution
- Collecting newspaper and magazine articles on a recent medical discovery or health approach
- Researching types of foods that different cultures use as sources of essential nutrients

Committees present their results orally. The teacher should encourage committee members to use exhibits and audiovisual aids to reinforce their presentations. This strategy can also be used on an individual basis, with each student presenting his own research.

Lecture, Group, and Panel Discussion

Discussion is probably the most common technique used in education. While lecture discussion usually means a lecture delivered by the teacher, this strategy should not be limited to one-way communication. Lecture discussion can be from teacher to student, student to teacher, or student to student.

For group discussion to be effective, the teacher must develop an atmosphere of openness and acceptance in the classroom; otherwise, students will not state their true feelings. The teacher also needs to keep the discussion on course. Especially when discussing sensitive or controversial topics, the teacher and students should agree on certain guidelines, such as the following:

- Just as in debates, students may disagree with an opinion but may not attack the person who presents the opinion.
- Every student has the right to present a personal opinion without being ridiculed.
- The discussion should use proper terminology. If a slang term is used accidentally or otherwise, the teacher should substitute the correct term, and ask students to use the correct term in future discussion.

Panel discussion allows three to five students to investigate and report on a particular health topic. This strategy is similar to committee work, but it allows more give-and-take among participating students. Usually 15 minutes or less is sufficient time for a panel discussion. Adjust the time allotted to the class' attention span and developmental level. When using this strategy, panel members should have a precise theme to explore. A prepared outline is also necessary to organize the presentation.

All three of these discussion techniques encourage students to exchange information and ideas. This exchange involves students in the teaching-learning process. Discussion techniques also help students develop respect and understanding for others' feelings and opinions. To ensure a successful discussion, students should help choose a topic that they find interesting and relevant. Guide the students' preparation for the activity by providing them with sample issues and questions regarding the chosen topic. The teacher should moderate the panel discussion to keep the panelists focused on the topic. Especially if the topic is controversial, let the students actively participate in a summary activity that will help them form their own conclusions about the topic.

Resource Speakers

Resource speakers can be very instructive, especially if students are properly prepared and the speaker uses visual aids to keep their interest. Possible resource speakers include physicians, dentists, nurses, police and fire department personnel, nutritionists, and health researchers.

When contacting a resource speaker, be sure to provide information about your class, including grade and developmental level, so the speaker will be less likely to talk down to or over the heads of the students. You should also politely request that the speaker stick to a specific topic, because some speakers may digress to a favorite concern or endorsement of a product or political cause. Suggest audiovisual aids, if appropriate; this will heighten student interest. Also, ask the speaker to allow time for a question-and-answer session.

Before the speaker addresses the class, be sure that students have received adequate instruction so they are not introduced to the topic cold. Also, provide information about the position and background of the resource speaker. For example, what exactly is a nutritionist? What does a nutritionist do, and where does he or she work?

This police officer was invited to speak to this group about accident prevention, safety hazards, and first aid.

Action-Oriented Strategies

A variety of action-oriented or student-centered strategies can enliven health instruction. These range from seatwork activities to field trips. Whenever possible, any strategy selected should help students discover concepts through action-oriented means. Strategies that incorporate at least two of the senses can greatly facilitate learning. Listening is fine, but listening plus seeing, tasting, smelling, touching, feeling, and doing is better.

Dramatizations

Plays and skits, role playing, and puppet shows are all effective dramatization techniques. Each of these strategies is an excellent way of allowing students to express their feelings. Thorough preparation and follow-up are essential, however, lest students see these activities merely as fun and miss the point of the exercise.

Presenting a play can involve use of a script and props. You can use a commercial script or have students write their own. A skit is much more informal. Only an outline for the story needs to be prepared, not an actual script. Each character speaks extemporaneously, and props are not required. Nonetheless, plays and skits are both quite time-consuming.

Role playing, or sociodrama, is a technique whereby students act out roles chosen by you or by them. Each student receives a basic description of the role and the situation. Little or no rehearsal precedes the actual role playing. A typical sociodrama should last from 1 to 3 minutes and be followed by class discussion. Questions can include: Why did the role require the person to react to the situation in a particular way? What solutions suggest themselves from the sociodrama? Are these the only possible alternatives? If time permits, have students switch roles, or allow different students to play the same role.

Crossword Puzzles

Crossword puzzles are useful devices for building vocabulary and reinforcing concepts. The teacher, the students themselves, or a computer-generated program can develop puzzles, or commercial materials can be used.

Demonstrations and Experiments

Demonstrations and experiments help make verbal explanations more meaningful to students. In a demonstration, the outcome should always be the same; in an experiment, the predicted outcome may vary. These techniques are especially good because they usually involve the senses of sight, touch, and hearing, and sometimes other senses. Students are always interested in demonstrations and experiments because they help clarify what has been learned.

Careful planning is essential to make sure that a demonstration or an experiment will actually work. All equipment should be set up ahead of time, and a rehearsal before the class actually views the procedure is a good idea.

Appropriate areas for demonstrations and experiments include

- Typing blood or taking blood pressures
- Examining the effects of various pollutants on plants
- Determining the carbohydrate content of food
- Determining the effects of aerobic exercise on fitness levels

Introduce the procedure to the class and explain what you plan to do. All students should be able to see the activity. Encourage them to ask questions as you go, and be sure to explain what is happening at each stage. After the activity, reinforce the learning by writing important points on the chalkboard.

Exhibits

Exhibits allow students to view, examine, and touch health-related materials. Exhibits are most effective when students help in their design and construction. Careful planning is essential, as is a central theme. Always ask yourself: What is the point of the proposed exhibit? Your answer will provide a focus question for the students, too.

Examples of appropriate exhibits include X-ray plates of broken and healed bones, safety equipment used in different types of sports, dental instruments, and samples of raw foods. If actual objects are unavailable or impractical for classroom display, pictures can be substituted, although they are not as effective.

Everything in an exhibit should be clearly labeled. Sound and motion will make an exhibit more appealing. Use your imagination to make the exhibit as visually interesting as possible.

Many cities have health-education teaching centers that already include many exhibits. Often these exhibits are the best way to demonstrate health concepts.

Models and Specimens

Like exhibits, models and specimens offer students a multisensory approach to health-related topics. The value of models and specimens lies in their accuracy. Many excellent commercial models of body parts are available, including models of the human eye, heart, lungs, and other organs. Resuscitation Annie or functional mannequins used to teach mouth-to-mouth resuscitation, cardiopulmonary resuscitation, and other first aid procedures are also useful.

Specimens can be obtained from biological supply houses. These include tissue samples, animal eyes, and so forth. Commercial slaughterhouses can also supply some of these items. Exercise discretion in the use of specimens: For some students, such exhibits can be too grisly, and models are better employed.

Field Trips

Field trips can provide rich learning experiences. This strategy must be used sparingly, however, because field trips are time-consuming and often expensive. Many schools limit the number of field trips because of the expense. Also, some trips by teachers and students turn out to be nothing more than pleasure trips. Parents and administrators must give their approval for any activity outside the school, and liability must be considered.

A field trip should always be a culminating activity rather than an introductory one. Prior classroom instruction should prepare students for the experience. If the field trip is to be of value, the students must be able to understand what they will be seeing.

Good places for health-related field trips away from the school include the local health department, a dairy farm, a food processing plant, or a sewage treatment facility. Some field trips do not require leaving the school area. Although the places themselves are familiar, you can add a new dimension by explaining the structure and planning behind them. Examples of such on-site field trips include visits to the school cafeteria, to a crosswalk area, or to the playground. For instance, at the crosswalk area you can ask students how the crosswalk is planned for safety. Are school speed limit signs present to slow traffic during school hours? Are crosswalk lines painted on the street? Do crossing guards supervise the crossing? These and other questions will help students see the area in a new light.

Games

Games can stimulate interest while providing a review of concepts learned through other strategies. Sometimes they also provide welcome relief from the normal classroom routine. In addition, games especially help students understand the important of following rules and provide useful experience in socialization. Many commercially available games such as Bingo can be adapted to health-related topics. You may wish to develop your own games, if you have the time.

When using games as part of health instruction, be sure that the fun of the activity does not overshadow its health-related content. Also, keep the game from becoming too competitive so that no player feels inferior.

USING EDUCATIONAL MEDIA IN HEALTH INSTRUCTION

Educational media include everything from textbooks to videotape to computer-assisted instruction. For the present purposes, the term will be defined as any nonprint vehicle used for instructional intent. Such media include computers, television and videotape, films, filmstrips, slides, overhead transparencies, and recordings.

Computers and Computer-Assisted Instruction

The computer holds great potential as a motivational device and as a tool for allowing the student to apply knowledge to hypothetical problems. The first attempts to employ computers in the classroom occurred in the 1960s. A programmed instructional format was generally used—that is, the computer provided instructional information in small increments. By responding to questions the computer asked about the material, the student learned the material and received immediate reinforcement. Programmed instruction, with or without the computer as a vehicle, can be an effective educational tool, but rigid structure and format often lead to student boredom. (This is exactly what happened in the 1960s.) Additionally, the computers of that time were too expensive and impractical for common classroom use.

Development of microcomputers and video disks in the last few years has boosted use of computers in the classroom. In fact, in many students' homes, personal computers serve a variety of purposes, from preparing business records to playing video games. In the years ahead, use of computers in health instruction will no doubt grow.

By the 1980s, many health-education computer applications were being developed for microcomputers. In 1983, the National Health Information Clearinghouse produced the first information package on computer applications in health education (Gold, 1991, p. 20). In that same year, an entire edition of *Health Education* (number 6) was devoted to the topic of microcomputer applications in health education. Computers can be used to transmit information, complete personal and community health assessments, motivate appropriate health decisions, and as a management tool.

Gold (1991) notes that the traditional taxonomy of computer-assisted instructional applications includes the following five formats:

Drill and Practice. In health education, drill and practice may help in reinforcing material learned in such areas as terminology.

HEALTH HIGHLIGHT
Microcomputer Software: The Hard Part

Software programs are among the most critical components of any computer system, whether for small desktop microcomputers or for large mainframe operations. It is these programs that enable the hardware, such as the computers, printers, and other related devices, to carry out their major functions. Without software, computer systems are relegated to little more than collecting dust.

If the microcomputer is to become a more important part of the health educator's arsenal, there is a need for health educators to understand the role played by software. This means knowing how to find the necessary software programs. It also means knowing what software can be used to do, how it can be integrated into health education activities, and how to assess its quality. The issue of software quality and program evaluation is a significant issue in its own right, and one that merits serious examination.

Finding good software is, and for some time to come will probably continue to be, a formidable task. The volatility of the software market, and the promise of abundant software that will create a glut of choices, will make finding software increasingly difficult. Innovative solutions will be needed. Even more crucial will be the need for health educators to become involved in the use, development, and evaluation of the software. . . . Unless this is done, the quality and availability of health education software will likely be decided by default.

Source: "Microcomputer Software: The Hard Part" by Richard A. Sager, 1987, *Health Education, 18,* pp. 52–56. Reprinted by permission of AAHE/AAHPERD.

Tutorial. Such applications include all the necessary instruction and they usually allow the learner to ask for help, examples, rules, and review. An example of a health-related tutorial might be a program that teaches the concepts of excess risk from epidemiology.

Problem-Solving. A problem-solving program might take the previous example on excess risk one step further. By providing mathematical problems and allowing a learner to calculate risk of disease based on varying exposure levels, it can help improve a students' understanding of the concepts.

Simulations. These programs let learners make decisions on health issues and allow them to observe the resulting outcomes. In health education, a simulation program might be used to test a variety of ways to minimize the problems associated with the spread of a disease in a community. For example, a student might vary the number of people immunized against a disease and examine how immunization influences the subsequent cases of the disease.

Games. In games, learners make decisions and then must react to the consequences of those decisions. The challenge of winning points, or operating against a clock, often provides added enjoyment.

HEALTH HIGHLIGHT
Interactive Video Discs in Education

Every age has its own peculiar set of interesting issues and ideas. Today, in our computer-enhanced, video-saturated society, the use of interactive video discs has surfaced as a very significant one. This involves the use of laser discs acted on by powerful person-scale computers. Connected into interactive networks, these learning stations create a new model for health education. Interactive video discs help the student visualize information and access libraries of text.

According to the proponents of IVSs, it will not be long before students' access to computer-based video systems is as widespread as their use of the VCR. Students can learn health education from an interactive video system by completing a scenario in which they define their own role and can influence the outcome of the situation.

The video discs can be programmed for each student so that no subject is beyond a student's ability. An IVS lets the user be the boss and it responds almost immediately to the user's instructions. The student's actions cause the system to respond with a multiplicity of visual, auditory, and text-based messages. Some IVSs may partially direct the user's activity while others may be completely open-ended.

IVSs provide an automated system of instruction that truly encourages inquiry-oriented learning. At their best, IVSs will provide an environment in which students can learn to learn in an active, self-directed way. IVSs operate on the premise that the richer and more comprehensive the interactive environment, the greater the resulting learning.

Reprinted by permission of the publisher from McClintock, Robert O., ed., COMPUTING & EDUCATION: THE SECOND FRONTIER. (New York: Teachers College Press, © 1988 by Teachers College, Columbia University. All rights reserved.) 'Interactive Video Systems: Their Promise and Educational Potential,' by Carla Seal-Wanner, pages 22–32.

Television and Videotape

Most school systems have access to television receivers. Both the Public Broadcasting Service (PBS) and National Educational Television (NET) regularly provide programs that can be used in health education. The commercial networks also occasionally produce suitable programs. In addition to scheduled broadcasts, public and commercial agencies make many programs available on film or videotape.

Making your own videotapes for health instruction is also a useful approach, although an expensive one because of the equipment involved. If your school has the equipment, however, you should consider using it. Record class plays, skits, and sociodramas. Also, suggest that students produce their own health public service messages or "commercials" for use in conjunction with consumer health discussions.

Films

Most films used in the classroom are 16 mm, although 8 mm films conveniently spooled on cassettes are also available. A special projector is necessary for their use, but they have two advantages: students can view them with limited teacher supervision, and a larger number of students can view a screen versus a television monitor. Standard 16 mm films use a regular 16 mm projector, a piece of equipment to which virtually every school has access. When using a film, or any other audiovisual presentation, make sure that the material is age/grade-appropriate, that it will be interesting to the students, and that it blends with the objectives for the unit being discussed.

Before showing a film, the teacher should preview it and make a list of terms that students may not understand. This list of terms could be taught as a vocabulary list before the film is shown. Also, before the film is shown, the teacher should prompt the students to watch for specific things during the film (e.g., make a list of the nonverbal behaviors Sherry used in trying to convince Bob to do something he did not want to do). The teacher may wish to stop the film periodically to allow students to discuss significant events as they occur. This process is more effective than showing the entire film, since the students may become overwhelmed with all the important points.

In considering films as instructional devices, keep in mind that they should not serve as the sole basis of instruction and you must carefully choose and preview every film. Also, keep a file of all audiovisual materials you preview. Such record keeping will help you build an index of especially useful films and will alert you and your colleagues to inappropriate ones.

Filmstrips are continuous strips of 35 mm pictures. Captions or an accompanying sound track on a tape cassette provide the narrative. Filmstrips are colorful, relatively inexpensive, easy to use, and easy to store because they take up little space. The same criteria for selecting films should be used with filmstrips.

Slides

Another inexpensive medium is 35 mm slides. These can be purchased from commercial sources, or you can make them yourself if you have a 35 mm camera and a bit of photographic skill. Like filmstrips, slides are colorful and easy to store. Depending on the kind of projector system you have, one slide tray will hold from 40 to more than 100 two-by-two-inch slides.

If you make your own slides, the subject matter can include class activities and field trips, health fairs, environmental problems in the community, and class projects. An advantage to using slides is that you can delete or add slides to the sequence as you desire. In this way, you can keep your slide collection current.

Transparencies

Used with an overhead projector, transparencies are extremely popular as teaching tools. A transparency consists of a 10-by-10-inch sheet of transparent acetate, usually mounted in a thin cardboard frame. You can purchase prepared transparencies or you can make your own, either by using special transparency masters or by simply drawing on the acetate with felt-tipped pens. Both permanent and erasable inks are available.

One unique feature of a transparency is its ability to show a progression by using a series of overlays. Overlays can also be employed to show the position of organs within the body or to add or remove captions for informal quizzes. Another advantage to using transparencies is that the classroom does not need to be entirely darkened, as in the case of films or filmstrips.

Records and Tape Recordings

Selectively used, recordings can be valuable teaching tools. Both are inexpensive and can be stopped as needed for discussion. Finding useful records may take some work on your part, however, because relatively few are available that relate directly to health instruction.

Tape recordings are in some ways more versatile. You can easily make recordings of radio and television programs, for example, or of interviews with health officials, classroom guest speakers, and so forth. Recording commercials for the classroom can be useful when teaching consumer health. Tape cassettes are more portable than records and have the advantage of being scratchproof.

SELECTING APPROPRIATE MEDIA

Which of the many available media should you use for a particular instructional situation? How should you prepare yourself and your students for the medium that you have chosen? These are important questions that you must ask yourself before using television, films, tape cassettes, or any other instructional medium.

Media can have a positive or negative influence on instruction, depending on how the teacher uses them. The teacher must keep the objectives for the specific lesson in mind. After determining objectives, the teacher will have a better idea as to the type of instructional materials that should be chosen. Remember, media materials should not be used just to entertain or to take up class time.

The teacher must preview instructional media prior to using them with the class. Sometimes, study guides and/or manuals accompany the media materials. By previewing material, the teacher can best decide when in the lesson the media materials can be used most effectively.

Before using media materials in the classroom, the teacher should set the lesson up for students. When they are prepared prior to using instructional materials, students will assimilate the information much more readily. Students should be made aware of the objectives to be taught by the materials, just as in any other lesson plan. The teacher should prompt students for significant points in the materials to look for before using the media materials. Any new words, phrases, or symbols should be introduced to the students beforehand.

Before using the materials, the teacher should make sure all equipment and media are ready and in good working order. Backup equipment should be available in case of breakdown. The teacher should practice using the equipment beforehand to be sure she knows how to operate the equipment easily. Setting up the room ahead of time will ensure that the equipment, screen, and students are placed most effectively. Also, practice will help the teacher control the light and the sound properly.

To optimize the students' learning when using instructional media, make sure to involve them. Activities can be planned to prepare students before the media are shown and during presentation of the media. Some media, such as videotapes, can be stopped at critical points during the presentation so the class can discuss critical issues at optimal times. Of course, the degree of participation will depend on the students' age.

After using the instructional media, activities should be planned to help the students bring closure and/or to summarize the lesson taught by the media. Younger groups might need to have the media repeated for optimum effect. Older students could be tested on the material.

Finally, the teacher should evaluate the effectiveness of any instructional media used. Such an appraisal will help other teachers who are determining whether or not to use the media with their students. Evaluation should also include a determination of the ages and grade levels that could best benefit from the materials.

SUMMARY

Teaching strategies are planned approaches that are used to most effectively influence the learners' comprehension of a new situation or to further influence their comprehension of a familiar situation. Learning strategies are methods that make content and objectives more meaningful. Several factors affect the selection of teaching strategies in health education: Health education is multidisciplinary; students of different ages learn in different ways and at a different pace; the proper teaching methods depend on the nature of the subject to be covered (i.e., facts vs. skills; passive, teacher-centered, or learner-centered strategies); and learners are often a good source of ideas for teaching strategies.

Values clarification techniques are useful for helping students examine their feelings concerning health issues. The goal of values clarification is to provide the time and the setting for students to examine their own values; such activities should not be used for indoctrination.

Some educators criticize values clarification techniques because they allow younger students to determine their own moral standards, and because some teachers may show a bias toward one value or another during instruction. One example of a values clarification strategy is unfinished sentences.

Other effective strategies used in health education include brainstorming; buzz groups; case studies; debates; storytelling; lecture, group, and panel discussions; and committee work. All these employ discussion to some degree. More action-oriented strategies include dramatizations, crossword puzzles, demonstrations and experiments, exhibits, models and specimens, field trips, and games.

Instructional media are not strategies in themselves, but they serve as valuable approaches for involving students in the learning process and for enriching the classroom. Examples of media include computers, television, films, filmstrips, transparencies, and recordings. Interactive video discs are also becoming a popular form of instructional media.

The choice of a particular strategy should depend on how effective you believe it will be in facilitating learning. Other relevant considerations include appropriateness, amount of time and expense involved, and practicality. Finally, a strategy or medium should be chosen because it offers some teaching advantage, not simply novelty.

DISCUSSION QUESTIONS

1. What factors should you keep in mind when selecting strategies for classroom use?
2. Discuss the strengths and criticisms of values clarification techniques.
3. Select three types of discussion-oriented strategies, such as brainstorming and debate, and discuss the strengths and weaknesses of each approach.
4. Select three types of action-oriented strategies, such as dramatizations and field trips, and discuss the strengths and weaknesses of each.
5. What are the criteria for selecting films or filmstrips for the classroom?
6. Describe and discuss the considerations when selecting media for instructional use.
7. Select three types of media, such as computers and interactive video discs, and discuss the strengths and weaknesses of each.
8. Discuss the use of interactive video as a teaching strategy in health education.

REFERENCES

Bedworth, A., & Bedworth, D. (1992). *The profession and practice of health education*. Dubuque, IA: Wm. C. Brown.

Bender, S., & Sorochan, W. (1989). *Teaching elementary health science* (3rd ed.). Boston: Jones and Bartlett.

Gold, R. (1991). *Microcomputer applications in health education*. Dubuque, IA: Wm C. Brown.

Greenberg, J. S. (1989). *Health education: Learner-centered instructional strategies*. Dubuque, IA: Wm. C. Brown.

Greene, W., & Simons-Morton, B. (1984). *Introduction to health education*. New York: Macmillan.

Rubinson, L., & Alles, W. (1988). *Health education: Foundations for the future*. Prospect Heights, IL: Waveland Press.

CHAPTER 5

Measurement and Evaluation of Health Education

As you study the wide array of evaluation procedures used in schools, it is easy to view evaluation as simply a collection of techniques. Instead, evaluation should be seen as an integrated process for determining the nature and extent of pupil learning and development. Norman E. Gronlund and Robert L. Linn, *Measurement and Evaluation in Teaching*

OBJECTIVES

After reading this chapter, you should be able to

- Define measurement
- Explain evaluation
- List the teacher skills needed to be competent in measuring and evaluating student progress
- Identify the criteria for developing a teacher-made test
- List the advantages and disadvantages of the types of test items
- Identify means of measuring attitudes
- Identify alternative methods of assessing behavior (i.e., observation and anecdotal records)

MEASUREMENT AND EVALUATION

Every instructional effort should be evaluated to determine its success in promoting both student learning and teacher effectiveness. The emphasis in recent years on teacher accountability has made evaluation more important than ever.

Measurement can be defined as the process of obtaining a numerical description of the degree to which an individual possesses a particular characteristic (Gronlund & Linn, 1990). Measurement generally results in quantitative data in numerical form. The various tests, rating scales, attitude scales, checklists, and observation techniques used in schools are all forms of measurement. The resulting raw data, however, must be evaluated before the effectiveness of the instruction can be assessed. Data are not information; they are only the basis for information.

Evaluation is the process of collecting, analyzing, and interpreting information to determine the extent to which students are achieving instructional objectives (Gronlund & Linn, 1990). It determines the current status of the object of evaluation (Gay, 1985). Evaluation can be either objective or subjective. It is a judgment of what the numerical measurement data actually mean. For example, if all the students in a class get a perfect score on a test, has the instruction been successful? Perhaps not. The test might have simply measured what the students already knew before any instruction. Or the test might have been so poorly constructed that the correct answers were obvious, regardless of whether instruction had been provided.

Specifically, the purposes of measurement and evaluation are as follows:

To Assess the Effectiveness of the Learning Activities. Measurement and evaluation will help determine whether learning activities have increased knowledge, helped clarify values or determine attitudes, and promoted decision-making skills. If not, the activities must be revised or replaced.

To Motivate the Student. Tests help students recognize how much learning has taken place. Pretests are useful for introducing the scope of a topic and making students aware of the material that will be covered. Posttests then are used to chart actual student progress.

To Help Develop the Scope and Sequence of Teaching. Measurement and evaluation can help determine the level of teaching and the order in which it should occur. For example, if the knowledge level of a class is high, students may need only a simple review of the factual material before moving on to new subject matter. Or, if the factual material is known, the class may work on developing attitudes toward this knowledge.

Teacher Skills Needed for Competent Measurement and Evaluation

Competence in measurement and evaluation does not happen overnight. You are developing the needed skills now in methods classes, in educational psychology classes, and during student teaching. As professional teaching experience increases, these skills will be sharpened. To be competent at measuring and evaluating, the National Council on Measurement in Education (1990) notes that a teacher should be skilled in:

Choosing Assessment Methods Appropriate for Instructional Decisions. Criteria that should be considered include convenience and fairness. A variety of methods should be used and a teacher should know where to obtain information about them.

Developing Assessment Methods Appropriate for Instructional Decisions. If high-quality commercial methods are not available, teachers must create them. Methods include classroom tests, oral exams, rating scales, performance assessment, observation schedules, and questionnaires.

Administering, Scoring, and Interpreting the Results of Both Commercially Produced and Teacher Produced Assessment Methods. Knowledge about the common methods of expressing assessments is essential. Many quantitative concepts need to be assimilated (e.g., descriptive statistical methods, reliability, validity, etc.).

Using Assessment Results in Making Decisions about Individual Students, Planning Instruction, in Developing Curricula, and in School Improvement. Assessments are valueless unless they are applied at both group and individual levels. Planning is a vital part of the education process.

Developing Student Grading Procedures That Use Student Assessments. Grades and marks should be data-based. Grading, although subjective to a great extent, can be rational, justifiable, and fair. The rules must be the same for everyone.

Communicating Assessment Results to Students, Parents, Other Lay Audiences, and Educators. Effective communication should include not only the facts but an indication of the limitations and implications as well. In addition, everyone involved must use terminology in the same way.

Recognizing and Having Knowledge about Unethical, Illegal, and Inappropriate Assessment. Potential dangers of invasion of privacy and discrimination exist, and these—together with legal and professional ethics—should always be considered when planning and implementing assessment tasks.

Health education cannot limit measurement and evaluation to the cognitive domain; they must also determine the formation of attitudes and behavior patterns among students. Testing instruments emphasize quantitative measures, but these measures can also offer insight into qualitative areas. Selection of an instrument is not simply a matter of locating a test on a specific content. It is important to select the best test available; "best" meaning most appropriate for specific objectives and students. If a test fails to measure what the teacher wants, another one should be developed.

Generally, evaluation follows three general approaches that are expressed in terms of levels. Presented in Figure 5.1, these include process, impact, and outcome evaluation (Green, 1980). Most classroom teachers address the impact level. Process and outcome evaluation are important concerns, but, because of lack of time, are usually not assessed. For purposes of this text, impact evaluation will receive the major emphasis, since classroom health educators must deal daily with this type of assessment.

Tests of knowledge, attitudes, and practices can assess the impact on students. These tests fall into two general categories: **standardized tests** and **teacher-made tests**. Each type has advantages and disadvantages, which must be weighed when determining testing needs.

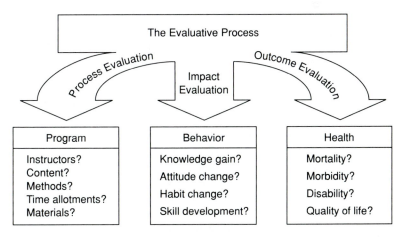

Figure 5.1   Three approaches to evaluation

Standardized Tests

One obvious advantage to using standardized tests is that they are already prepared. More important, such tests are usually carefully developed and refined before publication. Companies develop standardized tests by administering prototypes to large numbers of students. The developers cull poorly worded or misunderstood questions, then administer a second, third, or fourth version of the test to a sample population of students.

The results are analyzed statistically to determine whether the test actually measures what it is supposed to measure. This is termed **validity**. The **reliability** of the test must also be determined. Reliability means that using the test with different groups of the target population will produce similar results. The higher the reliability of a test, the more likely that the test will accurately gauge student learning.

Standardized tests are best used for pretesting and posttesting. A teacher administers a test before instruction takes place to measure current knowledge and attitudes. After instruction, students complete the same test again. Comparing the two scores shows growth or change in student knowledge and attitudes.

Solleder (1979) has described a number of standardized tests that can be used in health education. Some have been developed by commercial testing services and others by university researchers.

Teacher-Made Tests

Although standardized tests have the advantage of established validity and reliability, they also have certain disadvantages. First, such tests may not include items that a particular teacher has provided instruction about or they may include subject matter that has not been covered. Second, their readability levels may be too high or too low for a specific class. Third, they may have been normed with a target population different from the makeup of the class being tested.

The main advantage of teacher-made tests is that they can be tailored to specific purposes and groups of students. Teacher-made tests may lack validity and reliability, however, but with experience, they should become increasingly better indicators of student learning and change.

In constructing tests, teachers must consider validity, reliability, objectivity, discrimination, comprehensiveness, administration, and scoring.

Validity. Does the test measure what it is supposed to measure? If the teacher wants to determine changes in student attitudes, for example, a test that asks them for factual information will not fulfill this goal. Validity is a matter of degree, not a characteristic that is absent or present. In addition, a test that is currently valid may not necessarily be so in the future. Because tests are designed for a variety of purposes, and because validity can be viewed only in terms of a test's purpose, it is not surprising to find several types of validity. **Content validity** is defined as the degree to which a test measures an intended content area. **Construct validity** is the degree to which a test measures a hypothetical construct. Intelligence would be an example. **Concurrent validity** is the degree to which the scores on a given test are related to the scores on another test. **Predictive validity** is the degree to which a test can predict how well a student will do in a particular situation.

Reliability. Does the test measure accurately and consistently? A test that gives consistent results is said to be reliable. For example, if a class takes the same test two different days, the scores obtained should be about the same. A reliable test will yield data that are stable, repeatable, and precise (Hastad & Lacy, 1989). Comparing test results with classroom observations offers an intuitive idea of an instrument's reliability. Hopkins and Antes (1985) report that, in general, reliability will be greater for:

- A long test than for a short one
- A test over homogeneous content rather than heterogeneous content
- A set of scores from a group of examinees with a wide ability range rather than from a group which has members much alike
- A test composed of well-written and appropriate items
- Measures with few scoring errors than for measures which vary from test to test or paper to paper because of scoring procedures
- Test scores obtained by proper conditions for testing and students with optimum motivation (p. 292)

Other factors that can affect the reliability of a test include inappropriate test items, the way the test is administered to the students, how the test is scored and interpreted, and the physical condition of the test environment.

Objectivity. Is the test fair to the students? For example, if the readability level is too high, students may be unable to supply correct answers even if they understand the concept being tested. If more than one possible answer is correct, students should not be penalized for providing reasonable alternatives.

Discrimination. Does the test differentiate between good and poor students?

Comprehensiveness. Is the test long enough to cover the material? Keep in mind that a 50-item test may be no more comprehensive than a 10-item test if the items tap only certain areas while neglecting others.

Administration and Scoring. Is the test easy to give, use, and score? Keep in mind that the easiest test to administer and score may not be the best test for assessing the area. For example, an essay test, which is more difficult to score, may better measure learning of certain concepts than an easier-to-score true/false test.

DEVELOPING TESTS

Developing good tests is difficult. The starting point is to establish a table of specifications. This table serves as the blueprint for the test. Its purpose is to ensure that a test covers all the objectives for a unit or lesson. By developing the table, the teacher can ensure that test items for various objectives appear in proportion to their emphasis (see Table 5.1). The teacher follows these steps:

1. Prepare the table of specifications based on the unit objectives.
2. Draft the test items.

Table 5.1   Specifications for Unit on Substance Abuse

Objective: The learner will . . .	Content	% of items
Define what constitutes substance abuse	What substance abuse is; what abuse causes; what some symptoms are	15%
List the various substances that can be abused	Depressants (types); cocaine; marijuana; designer drugs; hallucinogens	35%
Discuss why people use drugs	Reasons for drug use	15%
List where to get help for substance abuse	Agencies; organizations; professionals	10%
Develop techniques for avoiding substance abuse	How to say no to substance abuse	25%

3. Decide on the length of the test.
4. Select and edit the final items.
5. Rate the items in terms of difficulty.
6. Arrange the items in order of difficulty from easiest to most difficult.
7. Prepare the instructions for the test.
8. Prepare the answer key and decide the rules for scoring.
9. Produce the test.

Paper-and-pencil tests are best suited for measuring student progress in the cognitive domain.

The next area of concern is developing the various types of test items. The following represent some of the advantages/disadvantages and rules for developing each type of item.

Several types of test items can be used for assessment. Some teachers may wish to use a variety of types, while others may prefer one or two. Employing at least two types of test items is advisable, since some students don't always do well on a particular type of test item. For example, some students do well on essay tests, while others do better on multiple choice types.

Another important consideration is the order in which the test items appear. Most important, all items should be grouped together. This helps simplify directions, helps students maintain the same psychological set throughout each section, and makes the scoring of the test easier. Test items should proceed from the simpler items to more complex ones. The following order is suggested for sections of test items:

1. True/False
2. Matching
3. Multiple choice
4. Short-answer questions
5. Essay questions

Regardless of the type of item employed, the effectiveness of each should be evaluated (Gronlund & Linn, 1990). The teacher should ask the following questions about each item and the test as a whole:

Is the item format appropriate for the learning outcome being measured? The action verb in the statement of each specific learning outcome (e.g., *defines, describes, identifies*) indicates which item format is more appropriate.

Does the knowledge, understanding, or thinking skill that the item requires match the specific learning outcome and subject-matter content being measured? The response to an item should agree with the purpose for which the item is to be used.

Is the point of the item clear? Each item should be so clearly worded that all students understand the task. A correct response should reflect their knowledge of what is being measured.

Is the item free from excessive verbiage? Items generally are more effective when the problem is stated as concisely as possible. If students can disregard any elements and still respond correctly, those elements probably should be removed.

Is the item of appropriate difficulty? The best judgment about item difficulty (unless item analysis data are available), should be based on the nature of the test and the educational background of the pupils.

Does the item have an answer that experts would agree upon? Do not include items that require students to endorse someone's unsupported opinion (even if it happens to be yours).

Is the item free from technical errors and irrelevant clues? An irrelevant clue is any element that gives away the correct answer and thereby prevents the item from functioning as intended.

Is the item free from racial, ethnic, and gender bias? Judicious, balanced use of different roles for minorities and males and females should contribute to more effective testing.

True/False Tests

A true/false test consists of declaratory statements that are either true or false. Students must consider each test item and answer accordingly.

Advantages of the true/false test are listed below. The true/false test

- Is familiar to students because it is so widely used
- Is easy to construct, which is one reason it is used extensively
- Can be used to sample a wide range of subject matter—the items can be answered in a short time, so a large number can be included on a single test
- Is easy to score, and the score is objective
- Can be used effectively as an instructional test to promote interest and introduce discussion points
- Is versatile and can be employed for short quizzes, lesson reviews, and end-of-chapter tests
- Can have items constructed either as simple factual statements or as questions that require reasoning
- Can have items that are especially useful when an issue has only two options

Disadvantages of the true/false test are as follows:

- A simple true/false item is of doubtful value for measuring achievement.
- The true/false test encourages guessing. Even without any knowledge of the subject matter, a student can pick many correct answers by random choice.
- Constructing items that are completely true or completely false without making the correct response choice obvious can be difficult.
- Avoiding ambiguities, irrelevant details, and clues is difficult.
- Unless the test consists of a large number of items, reliability is likely to be low.
- Items that test for minor details receive as much credit as items that test for major points.
- If the material is in any way controversial, true/false items are difficult to construct. For example, the following statement, although false, can give students a wrong perception: "Marijuana is not a harmful drug."
- Sometimes the relative degree of truth in an item is debatable. Such items should be avoided because students will try to guess what is in the teacher's mind instead of making their own decisions.

As long as the disadvantages of true/false tests are kept in mind, such tests can be helpful for assessing student performance. The teacher should follow these guidelines when constructing true/false tests:

- Approximately 60% of the items on a true/false test should be true.
- The method for indicating responses should be as simple as possible. Usually, a blank to the left of the item is the best format.
- Write original items. Do not lift statements directly from the textbook. (Using sample test questions from the teacher's guide is acceptable, however.)
- True statements should not be consistently longer than false statements, as this provides an obvious clue.
- Avoid ambiguous terms and qualifiers in the items, such as *many* and *few.*
- Use specific determiners carefully. Whenever such terms as *no, never, always, may, should, all,* and *only* are used, they should not make the correct answer obvious.
- Avoid using negatively stated items. For example, "Not eating balanced meals is not good for your health" is a confusing statement at best. Further, the second "not" can easily be overlooked in a quick reading.
- The items need to be clear so that the student has no doubt about what items seek to measure. One way to ensure clarity of purpose is to include the critical element of the item at the end of the statement. Underlining the crucial element is another way to achieve this end, but too much underlining can be distracting and may signal which statements are obviously true or false.
- Avoid trick or catch questions. Such items are poor measures of achievement and are not fair to the student. They measure general intelligence and alertness, not understanding of the concept. For example, "Coffee contains a drug called codeine" is a trick question. The student may know that the substance in coffee is caffeine, but may read caffeine for codeine.

Following are examples of properly developed true/false items:

_____ 1. Drugs are harmful if they are abused.
_____ 2. Regular check-ups are the best way to prevent tooth decay.
_____ 3. Meat is a good source of amino acids.
_____ 4. The heart and circulatory system move blood to all parts of the body.
_____ 5. A burn on the skin should be bandaged tightly.

Multiple-Choice Tests

Multiple-choice tests require the student to recognize which of several suggested responses is the best answer. This kind of test provides an opportunity to develop thought-provoking questions while covering a great deal of material. It is considered the best short-answer test format.

Advantages of the multiple-choice test are

- Items can be written to measure inference, discrimination, and judgment.
- Items can be constructed to measure recall as well as recognition.
- Guessing is minimized when three or four alternate choices are available.
- Sampling of material covered can be extensive. Many questions can be included on a test because a response can be made quickly.
- Scoring is objective. In a properly constructed item, only one possible response is correct.
- Scoring is rapid.

Disadvantages of the multiple-choice test are

- Developing a multiple-choice test is time-consuming.
- Items are too often factually based, unduly stressing memory.
- More than one response may be correct or nearly correct.
- It is difficult to exclude clues about the correct response.
- Incorrect, but plausible, alternative answers are often difficult to develop.
- Items can take up a considerable amount of space.
- The student must do a lot of reading.
- The format does not allow students to express their own thoughts.

Use the following guidelines when developing multiple-choice tests:

- Express each item as clearly as possible, using words with precise meanings and avoiding excess verbiage.
- All choices should be plausible. Including obviously incorrect options reduces the need to think accordingly.
- Only one response option should be clearly the correct or best response.
- The choices should be kept short whenever possible.
- The correct choice should be about the same length as the incorrect alternatives, not consistently longer or shorter.
- Parallel construction needs to be used in developing choices. This means all answers should be plausible and grammatically correct. Confusing and ungrammatical items such as this one should be avoided:

Shock can cause a person to pass out because not enough blood goes to:
a. the brain
b. is being pumped to the heart
c. the lungs slow down
d. stomach

Instead, grammatical construction should be consistent. A better example is the following:

Shock can cause a person to pass out because not enough blood goes to the:
a. stomach
b. brain
c. heart
d. lungs

- The position of the correct choices should be varied to avoid any set pattern.
- Negatively worded items need to be avoided. If negatives must be included, it is best to underline them so that they will not be missed.
- Use of "all of the above" and "none of the above" should be avoided.

Following are examples of properly developed multiple-choice items:

1. Which of these nutrients helps to repair the body?
   a. carbohydrates
   b. fats
   c. proteins
   d. vitamins
2. Which of these characteristics is not "an inherited trait"?
   a. shape of nose
   b. tooth decay
   c. blood type
   d. skin color

Matching Tests

Matching tests call for pairing answers in one column with the correct item in another column. This kind of test is, in effect, a form of multiple-choice test, except that the number of choices is compounded.

The advantages of the matching test are that such a test:

- Is adaptable to many subject areas
- Is especially useful for maps, charts, or pictorial representations
- Can be developed quickly
- Has a format that uses space economically
- Is easy to score

The disadvantages of the matching test are that such a test:

- Does not assess the extent to which meaning has been grasped
- Increases in difficulty as the number of items to be matched increases

- Tests only factual information
- Permits guessing
- Is likely to include clues to the correct answers

Use the following guidelines when developing matching test items:

- The test should cover only one subject area or topic.
- For older students, 15 items should be the maximum.
- The right column should be used for the response list.
- Only one possible correct response can be allotted for each item.
- Responses need to be in random order.
- All items and responses should be on a single page.
- More response options than terms to be matched can be included.
- Each response option is to be clearly, precisely worded.
- Avoid providing clues to the correct matches.

Figure 5.2 shows an example of a properly developed matching test.

Completion Tests

Completion item (or fill-in) tests consist of a number of statements with certain key words or phrases omitted. This type of test measures the student's ability to select a word or phrase that is consistent in logic and style with the other elements in the statement. If students understand the implications of the sentence, they should be able to provide the answer that best fulfills the intent of the item.

Advantages of the completion test are that it:

- Is easy to construct
- Has wide applications to testing situations presented in the form of charts or diagrams
- Minimizes guessing because the answer must come from the student
- Does not generally require student writing ability
- Allows for objective, quick scoring

Figure 5.2   Example of a matching test

_____ 1. Compensation	a. Refusal to recognize reality
_____ 2. Rationalization	b. Covering up faults by trying to excel in other areas
_____ 3. Regression	c. Making an excuse for a mistake or failure
_____ 4. Denial	d. Admiring someone to the point of seeing that person as perfect
_____ 5. Idealization	e. Creating make-believe events
	f. Acting in an immature way
	g. Shifting the expression of feeling about one person onto another person

Disadvantages of the completion test are as follows:

- This type of test stresses factual information. The result may be a collection of items calling for unrelated facts or isolated bits of information.
- It places a premium on rote memory rather than on real understanding.
- Phrasing an item so that only one correct response is elicited is often difficult. Alternative answers provided by students may be very close to correct, making scoring problematic.
- A poorly formatted completion test may scatter answers all over the page, as on a diagram, making scoring time-consuming.
- Clues within an item can allow students to respond correctly without understanding the concept being assessed.

Use the following guidelines when constructing completion test items:

- Phrase the items in language appropriate to the students' reading level.
- Items should not be lifted directly from the text with blanks inserted for key words or phrases. Original items should be created, to minimize students' reliance on rote memory.
- Reserve blanks for significant words and phrases rather than for minor details.
- The number of words needed for the correct response should be indicated, with spaces between the blanks.
- Avoid placing *A* or *an* before a blank.
- Items should not begin with a blank, if possible.
- A high ratio of words supplied to words called for should be allotted.
- When more than one correct answer is possible, alternatives in the scoring key must be provided, if hand scoring is not being used.

Following are examples of properly developed completion test items:

1. Light enters your eyeball through a clear tissue called the _____ .
2. The eyeball is filled with a fluid called _____ .
3. The iris controls the amount of _____ going to the lens behind it.

Essay Tests

The essay test requires the student to organize information systematically. Use of the essay question gives the teacher insight into the amount of understanding students have developed from instruction.

Advantages of the essay question test are as follows:

- This type of test is relatively easy to prepare.
- Essay questions can be written on the chalkboard or even dictated, thus eliminating the expense of duplicating materials.
- Essays encourage originality and creativity on the part of the student.
- Essay questions stimulate students to organize their thinking.
- Chances of cheating are minimized because of the amount of writing involved.

- Answers to essay questions help reveal students' individuality. Questions can invoke a variety of responses that reflect personal attitudes, values, habits, and differences.
- Guessing at answers is minimized.
- Essay questions are the best-known way of evaluating an individual student's ability to express himself.

Among the disadvantages of the essay-question test are the following:

- Determining reliability is difficult because different teachers score essay answers in different ways.
- Scoring is subjective and often reflects such factors as legibility, neatness, grammar, spelling, word choice, and bluffing.
- Scoring is time-consuming.
- Students with poor writing skills are at a disadvantage.
- Writing essay answers is time-consuming, and students may feel pressured by this type of test. Slow writers are not necessarily slow thinkers, but this may be the impression given.
- An essay test can sample only a limited amount of the material covered.

Teachers can use the following guidelines when preparing an essay test:

- Develop questions that will help assess critical thinking skills rather than retention of facts.
- Begin with relatively easy questions. Difficult items at the beginning of the test discourage less able students.
- Phrase the questions specifically enough so that students understand what kind of response is needed. Conversely, avoid focusing so narrowly that students merely list facts.
- Limit the number of questions so that students do not feel overly pressured and have adequate time to complete each answer.
- Write model answers and decide how incorrect responses will be handled.

MEASURING HEALTH ATTITUDES

The need to measure attitudes is probably greater in health education than in any other subject area. Remmers, Gage, and Rummel (1965) define attitude as "an emotionalized tendency, organized through experience, to react positively or negatively toward a psychological object" (p. 308). Attitudes have also been defined as "descriptions of how people typically feel about or react to other people, places, things or ideas" (Kubiszygn & Borich, 1990, p. 156). In other words, an attitude involves feelings, values, and appreciations. An attitude can also be described as a predisposition to actions. Because one of the goals in teaching health is developing positive health attitudes, teachers must assess student attitudes.

This is no easy matter, because attitudes are not within the cognitive domain and are not thus readily tapped by most kinds of tests. Even tests that are designed for this purpose often lack validity, as students may respond with answers they think the teacher will favor rather than by stating their true feelings or predispositions. Thus, the teacher must supplement such testing instruments with other means of assessment, such as observation, informal conferences, and anecdotal record keeping. With these limitations in mind, we now examine some of the more common written measures for assessing student attitudes.

Attitude Scales

A scale is a testing instrument that requires the student to choose between alternatives on a continuum. Only two polar choices—such as yes/no or agree/disagree—may be offered, or a range of choices may be provided.

The major disadvantage of the forced-choice scale is that students can readily perceive what the "correct" response should be. They will respond accordingly, even if the answer does not reflect their actual attitude toward the issue. This problem can be overcome to a certain degree by establishing an atmosphere in the classroom of warmth, trust, and rapport.

A **Likert scale** is a more sophisticated attitude scale that provides a range of choices for each issue. The more choices offered, the more discrimination a student must have to complete the scale. Figure 5.3 provides an example of a Likert scale.

Likert scales can be scored in a variety of ways, depending on how the statements in the scale are phrased. For example, the continuum of responses may be weighted

Figure 5.3   A Likert scale with a five-choice spread

Feelings About Exercise	Strongly Agree	Agree	Not Sure	Disagree	Strongly Disagree
1. Exercise is healthy for a person.	___	___	___	___	___
2. I like to run and jump.	___	___	___	___	___
3. I would rather watch TV than engage in exercise.	___	___	___	___	___
4. I feel relaxed after exercising.	___	___	___	___	___
5. Playing sports is fun.	___	___	___	___	___
6. I cannot work on exercise.	___	___	___	___	___
7. Playing sports and games is too much work to program into my daily schedule.	___	___	___	___	___
8. I would rather watch sports than play them.	___	___	___	___	___
9. Exercise helps keep me healthy.	___	___	___	___	___

from 1 to 5, with the lowest score for a "strongly disagree" statement and the highest score for a "strongly agree" statement. Thus, if a student checks "strongly agree" about the statement "Being stoned all the time is no way to live," the score would be a 5. An undecided response would rate a 3, and a "strongly disagree" would rate a 1. Note that the scoring rank must be reversed for oppositely worded statements, such as "Experimenting with drugs is not really very risky." In this case, a "strongly disagree" response would score as a 5.

The total numerical score derived from adding the individual response scores indicates how strongly students feel about the issues examined in the scale. This measure, however, despite its seeming quantitative preciseness, is only a rough indicator of attitude. Bear in mind that the scoring system is arbitrary; that even with five options, students are still making forced choices; and that students may respond with "correct" answers that do not reflect their true attitudes. Attitude assessment instruments should not be used for grading, because this will further bias the students' responses.

Observation and Anecdotal Record Keeping

As mentioned earlier, attitude scales have limitations in assessing student feelings and values. The results of such scales are often inconclusive. Teachers should

Anecdotal record keeping goes hand in hand with observation.

augment scales or other measurement devices, such as checklists or student surveys, with other techniques, including observation and anecdotal record keeping.

Observation is an excellent way of assessing behavior, especially when other school personnel and parents are brought into the process. Because observation can be done on an ongoing, daily basis, it can provide important clues as to attitudes and predispositions to actions. Unfortunately, observation is time consuming. Further, the observer must exercise discretion to avoid violating student and parent privacy.

Anecdotal record keeping goes hand in hand with observation. As with that technique, a disadvantage is the time that it requires. In addition, both observation and record keeping are subjective techniques. Evaluation can easily be based on biases or expectations. Cultural differences can also slant conclusions. In preparing to do anecdotal records, Mehrens and Lehmann (1984) make the following suggestions:*

1. The teacher should restrict her observations to those behaviors that cannot be evaluated by other means. Anecdotal records should be restricted to those situations from which it is possible to obtain data on how the pupil behaves in a natural situation.
2. Records should be complete. There are several different styles of anecdotal records. All, however, contain the following parts: (a) identifying information: pupil's name, grade, school, and class; (b) date of the observation; (c) the setting; (d) the incident; and (e) the signature of the observer. Some contain a section for the interpretation and recommendation for action.
3. Anecdotal records should be kept by all teachers and not be restricted to only the student's homeroom teacher. The validity of the anecdotal record will be enhanced with a variety of common information gathered from different sources.
4. The behavioral incident or action should be recorded as soon as possible after it has happened. It should be remembered that any lapse of time places heavy reliance on the teacher's memory, which may become blurred if too much time elapses.
5. Keep the anecdote specific. Just as too little information does not help much in having a better understanding of a pupil's behavior, too much information can cloud the real issue.
6. Keep the recording process simple.
7. Keep the anecdote objective.
8. Anecdotal records can be compiled on slips of paper, cards, or any material readily handy. It is recommended that some standard form be used for filing. Also, try to avoid using slips of paper, since they can be easily lost or misplaced. A large sheet of paper is preferred because it permits the teacher to write her interpretation on the same sheet as the description of the setting and incident.
9. Anecdotes should have interpretive value. A jumbled collection of anecdotes is of little value. They must be collated, summarized, and interpreted. If, for example, Ilene has only one record of aggressiveness, this is inconsequential. On the other hand, if Ilene has been observed to display aggressive behavior on 9/6, 9/14, 10/12,

---

*Excerpt from MEASUREMENT AND EVALUATION IN EDUCATION AND PSYCHOLOGY (third edition) by William A. Mehrens and Irvin J. Lehman, copyright © 1984 by Holt, Rinehart and Winston, Inc., reprinted by permission of the publisher. Sensitivity to the behaviors typical of a given age group is important for fair measurement and evaluation.

10/13, and 11/21, in a variety of different settings, this behavioral pattern does become significant.

10. Anecdotal records must be available to specified school personnel. We have already indicated that we feel strongly that the anecdotal record should be shared with other teaches and especially with the school counselor, if there is one. Also, this material should be incorporated in the student's folder with other test information. We also believe that a general summary should be shared with the parents, and with the pupil, if he is old enough to understand it. Other than for school personnel, parents, and the students, the anecdotal record should be considered as confidential information.

11. Anecdotal records as an educational resource should be emphasized. Because anecdotal records depend so heavily on the willingness of teachers to do a good job, it is essential that teachers develop an appreciation for the value of anecdotal records in helping them obtain a better understanding of their pupils. (Indirectly, this should result in the development of better-adjusted students.)

12. Anecdotal records should not be confined to recording negative behavior patterns. In fact, the anecdotal record should record significant behaviors regardless of their direction. Only in this way can the teacher obtain a valid composite picture of the student.

13. As in writing good test items, the teacher should have practice and training in making observations and writing anecdotal records.

When assessing student health attitudes, the teacher should try to remain neutral in observations. Variations in personal health attitudes and behaviors are not necessarily a cause for concern. Students are still forming their attitudes about health-related issues. They should not be expected to have completely made up their minds about health practices. If they have, there would be far less point to the job of teaching.

Further, attitude formation is a gradual process; instant changes in behavior patterns are unlikely. The teacher's efforts can make a difference. With these thoughts in mind, one method to use in assessing attitudes is the checklist. The checklist allows the observer to note quickly and effectively whether a trait or characteristic is present. Checklists can be useful in evaluating learning activities or some aspects of personal-social interaction.

As noted, measuring attitudes is difficult. Any technique used to measure and evaluate attitudes or health practices should not be used for grading, since that would make students even less likely to reveal their true feelings or their actual practices. Instead, the evaluation can be used to plan for future instruction and to help students understand their current development level. The more aware students become about themselves, the more likely they are to use this awareness to make conscious decisions about future behavior.

GRADING

Grades inform students, parents, teachers, and administrators about the progress and work efficiency of the student. Ideally, grades should not be an end in themselves. Instead, they should act as motivators for students to do their best and as guides to future courses of study. For parents, grades identify the student's strengths and weaknesses and also help clarify the goals of the school. If grades offer parents insight into what the school is attempting to accomplish, they will be in a better position to cooperate with the teacher in enhancing the student's education. Administrators can use grades to see how effective the curriculum is and to step in to provide extra help for students who need it through special programs, counseling, and so forth.

Each school district has its own approach to grading. The teacher's task is to become familiar with the system used in her district so that the standards can be applied objectively and fairly. Two traditional grading methods widely used are the percentage method and the A to F combination method.

The Percentage Method

This grading method is based on 100%. It assumes more preciseness than can actually exist and essentially reduces the range of scores from 70 to 100. Any student falling below 70% of correct responses on a given test fails. Most school districts that employ this method use a scale similar to the following:

93%–100% = A
85%–92% = B
78%–84% = C
70%–77% = D
Below 70% = F

The A to F Combination Method

This system of grading is a combination of the percentage method and other descriptors that indicate student performance. This method rates students according to both the group norm and personal development. The A to F combination method

HEALTH HIGHLIGHT
Guidelines for Effective Grading

1. Describe your grading procedures to students at the beginning of instruction.
2. Make clear to students that the course grade will be based on achievement only.
3. Explain how other elements (effort, work habits, personal-social characteristics) will be reported.
4. Relate the grading procedures to the intended learning outcomes (i.e., instructional objectives).
5. Obtain valid evidence (e.g., tests, reports, ratings) as a basis for assigning grades.
6. Take precautions to prevent cheating on tests, reports, and other types of evaluation.
7. Return and review all test results (and other evaluation data) as soon as possible.
8. Properly weight the various types of achievement included in the grade.
9. Do *not* lower an achievement grade because of tardiness, weak effort, or misbehavior.
10. Be fair. Avoid bias, and when in doubt (as with a borderline score), review the evidence. If still in doubt, assign the higher grade.

better informs students and parents whether learning and work are being accomplished at peak capacity. For example, it is possible for students to make a C grade and still have them appreciate that they are working near maximum effort. A typical example of how this method is structured is as follows:

A = Doing excellent work and working at or near capacity; 95%–100%
B = Good work and working at or near capacity; 85%–94%
C = Average work or all that should be expected; 77%–84%
D = Much less than should be expected; 70%–76%
F = No noticeable progress; less than 70%

The following numbers can be used in conjunction with letter grades to indicate where students are performing within their grade:

1 = Above grade level
2 = At grade level
3 = Below grade level

A student who receives a grade of B-2, for example, is performing near capacity at grade level, whereas one who receives a grade of B-3 is performing near capacity, but below grade level.

Other Grading Procedures

Some school districts use symbols for giving grades in health education. Most of the symbols are used to indicate a level of achievement. Students and parents may have trouble interpreting what the level of achievement indicates unless it is explained (Mehrens & Lehmann, 1984). Some of the symbols used to indicate achievement are O, S, and U for *outstanding, satisfactory,* and *unsatisfactory.* The symbols P and F are also used to indicate *pass* or *fail,* whereas others may use E, S, N, or U for *excellent, satisfactory, not satisfactory,* and *unsatisfactory.*

Unfortunately, any course using these symbols may be viewed as less important than those courses receiving more traditional grades. Certainly, this connotation must be avoided, because the knowledge, attitudes, and behaviors developed in health education have the potential to be life-enhancing, and, in some cases, life-saving.

Choosing a grading system is not simple. The best method is really a combination of systems. Each teacher and school system must weigh the advantages of each type of grading and select the one that best informs students and parents of progress.

Grade Inflation

In recent years, a great deal of discussion has concerned teachers assigning higher grades than did teachers in the past. This perceived phenomenon has prompted greater scrutiny of grades. Adherence to an acceptable grading policy and appropriate measurement/evaluation techniques are thus especially important.

The grade assigned should depend on how well the student has performed compared with pre-established standards. Remember, grades provide feedback about academic achievement only and are not based on popularity, attitude, potential, or how hard the student worked.

SUMMARY

The purpose of measurement and evaluation is to assess student progress, to determine whether instructional objectives have been fulfilled, and to show where changes should occur in the teaching process. Measurement involves the construction, administration, and scoring of tests. Evaluation is the process of interpreting, analyzing, and assessing the data gathered during the measurement phase.

Teachers must be able to develop, administer, score, and interpret valid and reliable tests. Test instruments are best suited for measuring in the cognitive domain, but attitudes and actions must also be assessed. Either standardized or teacher-made tests can be used for measurement. Both have their advantages and disadvantages. The biggest advantage of standardized tests is that they have been carefully developed and normed, ensuring a high degree of validity and reliability.

Teacher-made tests, on the other hand, often are more useful for day-to-day measurement. Among the types of teacher-made tests are true/false, matching, completion, and essay. Each has its own strengths and weaknesses, which the teacher must weigh.

Measurement and evaluation of attitudes are difficult. Attitude scales, checklists, and student surveys are of some help, but these methods should be supplemented by observation and anecdotal record keeping. The biggest problem in using any sort of attitude scale is that students may not reveal their true attitudes, even if an atmosphere of trust and rapport has been established.

Grading can take many forms. Traditional techniques are the percentage method and the A to F combination method. Pass-fail or satisfactory-unsatisfactory marks may also be used.

DISCUSSION QUESTIONS

1. Differentiate between measurement and evaluation.
2. Discuss the purposes of measurement and evaluation and explain how you can achieve these purposes.
3. What are some of the shortcomings of standardized tests?
4. Why is a table of specifications necessary when developing a test?
5. What are some of the shortcomings of teacher-made tests? Give specific examples from various types of teacher-made tests.
6. What characteristics should a good cognitive test have?
7. Discuss some of the techniques used to assess attitudes in health education. What are the shortcomings of these techniques?
8. What purposes does grading serve in health education?
9. Discuss the most common methods of grading used in the secondary school. Explain the details of each method.

REFERENCES

Gay, L. R. (1985). *Educational evaluation and measurement competencies for analysis and application*. New York: Merrill/Macmillan.

Green, W. H., & Simons-Morton, B. G. (1990). *Introduction to health eduction*. Prospect Heights, IL: Waveland.

Gronlund, N. E., & Linn, R. L. (1990). *Measurement and evaluation in teaching*. New York: Macmillan.

Hastad, D. N., & Lacy, A. C. (1989). *Measurement and evaluation in contemporary physical education*. Scottsdale, AZ: Gorsuch Scarisbrick.

Hopkins, C. D., & Antes, R. L. (1985). *Classroom measurement and evaluation*. Itasca, IL: Peacock.

Kubiszyn, T., & Borich, G. (1990). *Educational testing and measurement—classroom application and procedure*. New York: HarperCollins.

Mehrens, W. A., & Lehmann, I. J. (1984). *Measurement and evaluation*. New York: Holt, Rinehart & Winston.

National Council on Measurement in Education. (1990). *Standards for teacher competence in educational assessment of students*. Washington DC: NCME.

Remmers, H. H., Gage, N. L., & Rummel, J. F. (1965). *A practical introduction to measurement and evaluation*. New York: Harper & Row.

CHAPTER 6

Mental Health and Stress Reduction

Life is 10 percent what you make it and 90 percent how you take it.   Anonymous

OBJECTIVES
After reading this chapter, you should be able to

- Define mental health
- Identify the characteristics of mental health
- Describe how psychosocial factors contribute to mental health
- Define the terms *stress* and *stressor*
- Describe the detrimental health effects of prolonged stress
- Discuss the problems of depression and suicide in the school-age population
- Identify the mental health and stress-related concerns of middle and secondary school students
- Identify strategies for dealing with the concepts *mental health* and *stress*
- Briefly discuss each of the rules for fostering good mental health
- Discuss the role of the family in maintaining a child's emotional health

THE IMPORTANCE OF MENTAL HEALTH

Probably no area is more vital than helping students develop sound mental health practices. We need only look at the rates of alcohol and drug use among our nation's youth, the suicide rates for adolescents, the reported depression among youth, or the number of youth who run away from home each year to realize the importance of helping students achieve and maintain good mental and emotional health.

Without the sense of inner peace and balance that comes with good mental health, no individual can be considered completely healthy. The links between mental and physical health are clear. Yet good mental health is in many ways more elusive than good physical health. An individual who gets proper nutrition, exercises on a regular basis, gets plenty of relaxation and sleep, and follows good personal health practices has a high probability of remaining physically fit. Unfortunately, no such easy prescription exists for good mental health. People who are mentally healthy do exhibit certain characteristics, however. Hales (1992) defines **mental health** as the ability to perceive reality as it is, to respond to its challenges, and to develop rational strategies for living. A component of mental health is **emotional health**, the ability to deal constructively with reality, regardless of whether the situation is good or bad (Greenberg & Dintiman, 1992). Implied in these two definitions is the concept that an emotionally healthy person is in touch with her feelings and can express those feelings appropriately. This chapter provides information about mental health principles that will help your students develop sound mental health. Topics discussed include human needs and the development of

111

self-esteem, behavior and the expression of emotions, stress and its relationship to mental health, values and patterns of decision making, the role of the family in the development of mental health, and ways to avoid the pitfalls associated with prolonged stress.

Characteristics of the Emotionally Healthy

If mental health is defined as the ability to perceive reality and to respond to the challenges of life, then how do we recognize an emotionally healthy individual? Shapiro (1983) lists some of these qualities as points of reference to use in determining one's personal status:

- Determination and effort to be healthy
- Flexibility and adaptability to a variety of circumstances
- Development of a sense of meaning and affirmation of life
- An understanding that the self is not the center of the universe
- Compassion for others
- The ability to be unselfish in serving or relating to others
- Increased depth and satisfaction in intimate relationships
- A sense of control over the mind and body that enables the person to make health-enhancing choices and decisions

Emotional health has no one definition. Certainly the lack of any one characteristic does not indicate an emotionally unhealthy person, but these characteristics can provide a benchmark on how well we are achieving or moving toward emotional health.

Self-Esteem and the Development of Emotional Health

Self-esteem can be defined as how worthy and valuable a person considers herself. A positive self-image is critical to emotional health. Development of positive emotional health requires an open, nonthreatening environment that nurtures and supports feelings of self-worth and security. All human beings, young or old, have the same basic needs. Apart from the physical needs of water, food, clothing, shelter, and personal safety, we all need to receive love and affection. Everyone needs to feel a sense of acceptance and importance from others.

Self-esteem is necessary for developing self-expression and independence. A person with a feeling of self-worth is also better equipped emotionally to show concern for others. As the individual begins to develop meaningful relationships with others who recognize and reward her unique qualities of expression, independent thinking flourishes. A strong sense of self-worth permits open, honest communication with others, because fears of rejection or disapproval are not seen as great risks, as they are to someone with less ego strength.

Fulfillment of basic emotional needs like love, affection, acceptance, and a feeling of importance thus helps firmly establish a person's self-identity and self-esteem. This increases the person's potential for successfully interacting with others, meeting individual needs for independence and self-expression, and resolving personal and

Figure 6.1   Maslow's hierarchy of basic human needs

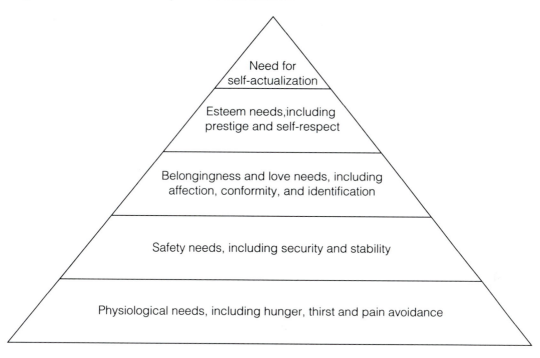

social conflicts. Improved self-esteem promotes a much more emotionally healthy resolution of such conflicts because of self-confidence in making life adjustments. The person is thus freer to pursue higher human goals, culminating with what Maslow calls self-actualization needs (Hamrick, Anspaugh, & Ezell, 1986). Maslow's hierarchy of human needs is shown in Figure 6.1.

The fulfillment of basic human needs and the establishment of self-esteem are lifelong processes. Their consistent reinforcement is essential to maintaining good mental health. This lifelong quest is more easily attainable if emotional and social well-being have been nurtured in infancy and childhood, thus promoting a sense of security, identity, autonomy, and intimacy early in life.

VALUES AND PATTERNS OF DECISION MAKING

Central to the establishment of self-esteem, the expression of emotions and resulting behavior, and the ability to cope effectively with distress are the decision-making patterns that each individual adopts in order to make life adjustments in harmony with her value system. When decisions about a particular issue involve actions and attitudes that reflect strongly held values, a person remains intact emotionally because behaviors and values are compatible. Decisions that produce behaviors contradicting a person's value system, conversely, diminish self-esteem; unhealthy emotions result from lack of resolution over inner conflicts, and distress increases. Decision-making patterns can serve as valuable clues to the way individuals perceive themselves, their relationships with others, and the world around them. An individual's actions tell much about her underlying value system, which in turn mediates many of the decisions made about life adjustments. Learning to make decisions following clarification and consideration of one's values can help one sustain and enhance the emotional balance crucial to good mental health.

BEHAVIOR AND THE EXPRESSION OF EMOTIONS

The most obvious indicator of a person's emotional health status is behavior. Psychologists say that behavior always has a reason. While the reasons may not be immediately apparent either to the individual or to others, all behavior has underlying motives. Much of an individual's behavior, both conscious and subconscious, involves fulfilling basic emotional needs. Such behavior patterns often depend on how these needs were satisfied or reinforced early in life. The individual may need to learn new, perhaps healthier, ways of fulfilling basic needs. Everyone experiences feelings of sadness, anger, joy, fear, depression and apprehension, but how these emotions are expressed varies from individual to individual. The expression of these feelings is usually labeled the individual's "behavior." Therefore, a better understanding of emotions may lead to greater understanding of human behavior and overall emotional health.

How a person expresses her feelings largely depends on how she perceives, either consciously or subconsciously, the situation that triggers the feeling. In other words, two people who are exposed to the same situation—say, disagreement with a teacher over an answer to a test question—may react very differently, based on their individual assessments of the situation. Such assessments are based in part on how the situation affects fulfillment of basic needs or efforts aimed at attaining autonomy, identity, or other personal goals. In many cases, the situation is perceived as having little impact and therefore elicits minimal emotional expression. Situations that are perceived as having great influence tend to elicit stronger, more overt expression. Thus, emotions are displayed in varying modes of expression as well as varying degrees of intensity. A person is considered more emotionally healthy when emotions are exhibited in a positive way and with an intensity proportional to the situation's impact. Individuals who consistently display either minimal emotional expression about circumstances generally viewed as having major importance (intimacy with others, successful completion of a difficult task, attainment of career goals, death of a family member) or intense emotional expression about events that are not generally viewed as having major importance (having to redo a homework assignment, misplacing an article of clothing, losing a school football game) are considered less emotionally well-adjusted.

It is not the emotion itself that determines mentally healthy or unhealthy behavior, but rather the degree and frequency of the emotion expressed. All of us

*Much of an individual's behavior,
both conscious and subconscious,
involves fulfilling basic emotional
needs.*

have on occasion allowed our emotions to run out of control or have expressed
them in ways that may not have been appropriate. This type of behavior is a
problem only when it becomes a consistent pattern. Often, a pattern of such
emotional outbursts indicates inner anxiety over conflicts between unconscious
drives or needs and conscious values. A feeling or emotion is neither inherently
"good" nor "bad," but can be expressed in ways that either promote well-being or
detract from it. Mentally healthy behavior largely stems from an individual's ability to
recognize, analyze, interpret, and communicate feelings in a consistent, balanced,
and positive manner.

DEFENSE MECHANISMS

A **defense mechanism** is any behavior a person uses to avoid confronting a situation
or problem. Although defense mechanisms can be helpful in dealing with the
stresses of life, some people take them to extremes. Used inappropriately, defense
mechanisms can impair one's emotional health. Table 6.1 lists examples of common
defense mechanisms.

Table 6.1 Common Defense Mechanisms

Defense mechanism	Definition
Compensation	Making up for weakness in one area by emphasizing strengths in another area. *Example:* An individual is unsuccessful as an athlete but is a good musician; consequently, emphasis is placed on music.
Daydreaming	Escaping from frustrations, boredom, or unpleasant situations through fantasy. *Example:* Faced with a break-up in a relationship, a person creates a mental image of the perfect relationship.
Displacement	Transferring feelings concerning one situation or person to another object, situation, or person. *Example:* Unable to respond to anger toward a coworker, an individual goes home and becomes angry with her spouse.
Idealization	Holding someone or something in such high esteem that the person or thing becomes perfect or godlike in the eyes of the beholder. *Example:* A star athlete is held in such high regard that his human characteristics or shortcomings are overlooked.
Identification	Assuming the characteristics of someone who is admired. *Example:* Performers are often so admired that people attempt to talk, walk, and act as they perceive their idol does.
Projection	Shifting responsibility for one's behavior onto someone else. *Example:* Blaming the teacher for a poor test grade rather than accepting responsibility for not studying sufficiently.
Rationalization	Providing plausible reasons for behavior that are not the real reasons. *Example:* A person declines an invitation to a social function stating she doesn't like parties when she really just feels insecure.
Reaction Formation	Reacting in a way opposite to the way one actually feels. *Example:* A student pretends it is not important when a fellow student receives an award that she does not, when she really believes she should have received it.
Regression	Childish, inappropriate behavior by an adult or a return to former, less mature behavior when under stress. *Example:* Becoming extremely angry when unable to attend a movie or social event. A regressive response may be to cry or throw something.
Repression	Attempting to bury or repress unpleasant or upsetting thoughts. *Example:* Having been in an automobile accident and being unable to recall the event.
Sublimation	Turning unacceptable thought or actions into socially acceptable behaviors. *Example:* Since breaking dishes is not an acceptable way to release anger, an individual may become feverishly involved in exercising to ease tension.
Substitution	Replacing a nonattainable goal with one that is attainable. *Example:* Unable to make the baseball team, an individual can become a student manager so she can still be part of the team.

ANXIETY DISORDERS

Negative emotional health results in anxiety. Individuals may attempt to cope in a variety of ways, many of which are subconscious and not emotionally healthy. All people deal with emotions and situations to some degree by exhibiting anxiety disorders. Like any emotion or action associated with behavior, the degree and frequency of anxiety disorders generally indicate the individual's level of emotional wellness. People who display anxiety disorders infrequently are considered to be emotionally healthier than are those who rely on these behaviors until they become a constant mode of expression.

Recognizing one's adoption of certain behaviors—and trying to reduce the degree and frequency of reliance on these behaviors to deal with emotions or situations—can foster more realistic, positive, and healthy emotional reactions. The most common anxiety disorders are anxiety reactions, obsessive-compulsive behaviors, phobias, hypochondria and hysterical conversions, and depressive disorders.

Anxiety Reactions

Anxiety reactions are characterized by physical symptoms that include a rapid and pounding heartbeat, feelings of faintness or dizziness, shortness of breath, extreme agitation or nervousness, sweating, dry mouth, nausea, and diarrhea. The attacks sometimes appear without apparent cause, are sudden, and may last as long as 20 to 30 minutes. General anxiety symptoms can appear in children and teenagers, but usually appear in people in their twenties and thirties. Men and women are affected equally.

Obsessive-Compulsive Behaviors

Obsessive-compulsive behaviors arise when an unwanted thought (the obsession) or action (the compulsion) or both continually intrude on and interrupt conscious functioning. Mild obsessive-compulsive behaviors include constantly looking at one's watch or being preoccupied by the thought of something not particularly important or pleasant. Occasionally, however, some people demonstrate more pronounced obsessive-compulsive behaviors that disrupt their normal daily living. For example, a person might become so obsessed with being on time for certain events that she does not take time to develop relationships with her peers.

Phobias

Like obsessive-compulsive behaviors, **phobias** are anxiety behaviors that can intrude on normal functioning if they become extreme. Phobias are unrealistic fears of animals, objects, or situations that produce an overwhelming desire to avoid what is feared. Common phobias include unrealistic fear of snakes, spiders, heights, elevators, and wide-open spaces. The causes of phobias are unclear, but underlying anxiety is usually at the root. Trauma or repressed sexual or aggressive impulses may also be responsible.

Hypochondria and Hysterical Conversions

Hypochondria is a constant concern about the possibility of contracting numerous ailments or illnesses. Like other anxiety disorders, hypochondria can be mild or severe. **Hysterical conversions** are the manifestations of physical disabilities that have no identifiable physiological basis. Examples include hysterical blindness, deafness, and paralysis.

Depressive Disorders

Depression, the most frequently occurring emotional disorder, is characterized by loss of interest in daily living and feelings of extreme or overwhelming sorrow, sadness, and debility. Depression is a symptom of underlying conflict, tension, or anxiety that may occur in varying degrees for varying lengths of time.

The Causes of Depression

Most experts now believe depression has multiple causes. According to the *Mayo Clinic Health Letter* (1989), some possible factors include:

Heredity. Studies show some depressive disorders are hereditary. For example, manic-depression has been linked, in some cases, to a genetic defect.

Environment. Environment can also contribute to the onset of a depressive disorder. Research has shown that stressful life events, especially those involving a loss or threatened loss, often precede episodes of depressive illness. Examples include: the death of a loved one, a divorce, the loss of a job, a move to a new home, physical illness, the breakup of an important relationship, or financial problems. In most instances the loss induces feelings of sadness and anxiety and often guilt or shame. Less commonly, depression follows the achievement of a desired position—the so called "success depression." In this case, the "loss" typically associated with depression is the loss of a future goal.

Background and Personality. People with certain psychological backgrounds or personality characteristics appear to be more vulnerable to depression. Many specialists believe that some depressive disorders can be traced to a troubled childhood; they attach particular importance to disturbed relationships between a child and his or her parents. Also, people who have low self-esteem, who consistently view themselves and the world with pessimism, or who become easily overwhelmed by stress tend to be more prone to depression.

Biochemical Factors. Some types of depression may result from abnormal chemical activity within the brain. These chemicals play a role in the transmission of electrical impulses from one nerve cell (neuron) to another. These chemical "messengers," called neurotransmitters, set in motion the complex interactions that control moods, feelings and behaviors. They also regulate pain, learning, and memory, as well as the desire to eat, drink and sleep. Three neurotransmitters—dopamine, norepinephrine and serotonin—have been associated with depressive illnesses. Research suggests that episodes of depression or mania may be related to an improper balance of neurotransmitters. Do biochemical factors cause depression or does depression cause the biochemical disturbance? No one knows with certainty. Some experts theorize that a genetic vulnerability combined with prolonged stress, physical illness or some other environmental condition or event, may bring about the chemical imbalance that results in depression.

Physical Illness. People with chronic medical illnesses are at high risk of psychiatric illness, especially depression. Some diseases, such as hypothyroidism (underactive thyroid gland) or arthritis can bring on a depressive reaction. Depression also may follow a heart attack or stroke. It may be an early sign of a serious underlying disease such as cancer of the pancreas, a brain tumor, parkinsonism, multiple sclerosis or Cushing's disease, among others. Also, depression can be an undesirable side effect of certain prescription medications—especially steroids (cortisone-like drugs), some antihypertensive medicines, antiparkinsonian agents and, less commonly, oral contraceptives.

Women frequently experience depressive symptoms with varying levels of severity preceding their menstrual periods (premenstrual syndrome), following childbirth (postpartum depression), or during menopause. Many specialists suggest there may be hormonal causes, but the biological mechanisms involving hormones and depression have yet to be discovered. (pp. 4–5)

Suicide and Adolescents

Each year more than 5,000 young people between the ages of 15 and 24 kill themselves. Each day more than 1,000 people in this age group attempt suicide. For every individual who commits suicide, 100 more will attempt the act and fail (Grollman, 1988). People who commit suicide feel cut off, alienated, and isolated. They truly believe that living is useless and more than they can tolerate.

Although the overall rate of suicide in the United States has remained fairly constant in recent years, the rate of suicide among young people has increased. The numbers might even be higher if the current social stigma against suicide did not cause many adolescent suicide cases to go unreported. Ten percent of the students in any public classroom may be considered suicidal (DeSpelder & Strickland, 1987).

Adolescents are most likely to commit suicide when they experience over-crowded conditions, a broken family, or feelings of rejection, hopelessness, and loss.

HEALTH HIGHLIGHT
Teenage Suicide Often Linked to Depression

In the last 25 years the rate of suicide among teenagers in the United States has increased dramatically. Today suicide accounts for more than 5,000 deaths annually among youths ages 15–24. Teenage suicide often is linked to depression, according to several recent medical studies. Tragically, parents and other adults can overlook teen depression because they expect adolescence to be a time of emotional turmoil.

Underlying causes that frequently lead to suicide attempts by teens: the experience of a significant loss (the breakup of a close relationship with a girlfriend or boyfriend); feelings of rejection or failure (failure to achieve a valued position associated with school or to get good grades); or feelings of falling short of parental expectations—all of which can harm self-esteem.

Other risk factors: a previous suicide attempt; a family history of major depression or alcoholism; constant family turmoil; having been physically or sexually abused; having a chronic or debilitating physical or psychiatric illness; and alcohol or substance abuse.

Source: "Depression," 1989, *Mayo Clinic Health Letter, 7*, p. 4.

Some wish to escape from a difficult situation, gain attention, or punish persons who caused them to have negative feelings. Further, an adolescent is at higher risk for suicide when her significant adult role models attempt or commit suicide or if violence is commonplace in her environment, either in the home or through the media (DeSpelder & Strickland, 1987).

Most adolescent suicides follow changes in behavior, some subtle and some more overt. A child may lose interest in school and friends, experience more frequent illness, become very sad for growing periods of time, and stop eating or sleeping well. Other observable signs of suicidal behavior include

- Giving away prized objects
- Lacking direction or goal-setting behavior
- Exhibiting depression, withdrawal, weight loss or apathy
- Showing a sudden lack of academic progress
- Communication of feelings of hopelessness
- Increased drug and alcohol use
- A withdrawal from friends, family and normal activities
- A radical personality change
- Violent, hostile or rebellious behavior
- A school composition revealing a preoccupation with death

RULES FOR DEVELOPING AND MAINTAINING MENTAL HEALTH

Adolescents should be encouraged to practice positive mental health habits in the same way they are taught to practice sound personal health habits. Just as people can take responsibility for their own physical well-being by following health "rules," they can also foster high levels of emotional well-being by following similar mental health rules. By internalizing certain guidelines and incorporating them into daily living, each individual can promote good mental health and effective life adjustment. Here are 10 "rules" that can help people achieve this goal:

1. Like yourself. Discover your unique qualities, skills, and talents and be proud of who you are.
2. Be good to yourself. Reward yourself with "strokes"—emotional or material favors—periodically.
3. Learn to be introspective, to examine motives for behavior, and to be insightful about your own conduct.
4. Accept your own limitations. Think in terms of competency levels rather than in terms of "success" or "failure."
5. Deal with a problem or crisis as it arises rather than allowing pressures to mount by worrying about "what ifs."
6. Establish realistic goals, both short-term and long-term, and work toward accomplishing them.
7. Express your emotions in terms of how the emotion makes you feel rather than in terms of how the person makes you feel. "I feel angry for having to do a homework assignment over the weekend" is healthier than "Mr. Barnes, you

make me angry. You shouldn't assign a homework assignment over the weekend."

8. Involve yourself in diversified activities and cultivate many interests. Do not center your life around one person, place, or activity.
9. Develop a sense of humor. Learn to laugh and enjoy life.
10. Be optimistic.

The Teacher's Role in Promoting Mental Health

The teacher can promote positive emotional characteristics in a number of ways. First, the teacher should treat each student as a unique individual. It is important for the teacher to offer personal observations or words of praise to let students know they are performing well on a given task or are progressing well. Teachers should encourage students to hone their individual talents by providing opportunities for them to do so during the normal course of classroom activity. The chance to work on a special project of personal interest or to contribute ideas and opinions without being ridiculed or rejected may enhance autonomy and initiative. Learning experiences that both challenge and provide success will reinforce students' feelings of competency and mastery.

Teachers can provide activities that help students consider how they want to live their lives and what their goals should be. For example, a teacher can ask them to write down things they hope to accomplish in the near and distant future, and he can help them develop ways of achieving these goals. This method of clarifying important goals will help students keep minor problems in perspective (Olsen, Redican, & Baffi, 1986). Teachers also need to help students place their inability to meet a goal in the proper perspective to avoid feelings of doubt, embarrassment, or inadequacy.

A teacher needs to become an effective listener and a skilled observer. Students regularly need opportunities to express their feelings and thoughts openly. A teacher can become an active listener by verbally paraphrasing the student's comments to let the student know that he understood the message. Such active listening will demonstrate to students that the teacher genuinely cares about them.

The role of the teacher in promoting student mental health is crucial. The attitudes that teachers demonstrate during their daily interaction with students affect the emotional climate of the classroom. One of the best things a teacher can do to promote emotional health in students is to help them learn to accept responsibility for their own behavior. A common mistake we all make is to try to shift the blame for something we did onto someone else. Students must learn that a crucial element of emotional development is the ability to accept responsibility for and live with mistakes. Further, the rapport established between teacher and student influences students' perceptions about acceptance, trust, support, self-esteem, competency, and independence.

The Family's Role in Developing Emotional Health

The foundations of positive mental health are first learned and cultivated within the family. As a result, all teachers should have some notion of how family structure, interaction, and values influence the behavior and attitudes of students.

Today's proliferation of single-parent households, for example, has an influence on many adolescents' views of themselves as well as the world in general. Some students also are part of two different family structures with stepparents and stepsiblings. Therefore, teachers must be sensitive to these differences in living arrangements and family structure.

Family interaction also influences the development of children's mental health. Communication patterns between parents, between parents and their children, and between siblings are all important factors. Communication should allow for intimacy, that is, a sharing of one's innermost fears and concerns, without worry about reprisal or rejection. Interactions among family members set the tone for all other social interaction. It is within the family that children develop a sense about what they can accomplish, what their roles in life should be, and what types of behaviors are appropriate, acceptable, and desirable. Children learn criteria for sharing, completing expected tasks, being praised or punished, and many other things according to family modeling and values. The family sets guidelines for all behavior by means ranging from various types of discipline to ways of expressing love and affection. As a result, a child's attitudes, habits, and emotions reflect family attitudes, habits, and emotions.

STRESS AND ITS RELATIONSHIP TO MENTAL HEALTH

Because of its influence on behavior and the expression of emotions that may result, stress should be included in any discussion of mental health. Everyone, young and old alike, encounters daily stress that must be accommodated to ensure emotional stability. Therefore, people of all ages need to realize that many situations produce feelings of anxiety or apprehension. The key is learning to reduce these feelings as they arise and thus better manage levels of stress.

Stress is the body's nonspecific response to an unanticipated or stimulating event, either pleasant or unpleasant. Hans Selye (1975) described stress resulting from a pleasant event as **eustress**. This type of stress comes from events such as an engagement, getting a new car or graduating from school. Although it produces anxiety, this type of stress helps us to be more effective in physical, social, and psychological functioning. **Distress** is generated by a negative or unpleasant event. Prolonged distress can undermine physical and mental health, since it interferes with physiological and psychological functioning (Selye, 1975).

Anything that elicits a stress response is called a **stressor** (see Figure 6.2). A stressor can be any event or situation. What one person may perceive as stress may be totally nonstressful to someone else. For example, skydiving would be terrifying for many people, yet others view it as a relaxing recreational activity.

A stress-free environment is both impossible and undesirable. Stress does occur and cannot be totally avoided. From a positive perspective, stress can enhance ability, act as a motivator and be a means of self-protection. Learning to reduce or effectively manage the stressors that create distress is the key.

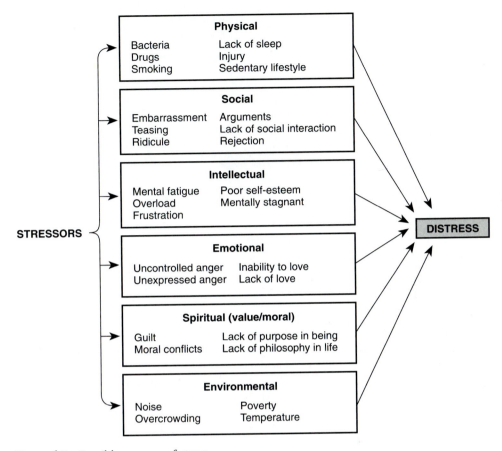

Figure 6.2 Possible sources of stress

The General Adaptation Syndrome

Any event or circumstance that upsets the body's physiological balance is a stressor. The body is constantly striving to maintain a physiological balance, called **homeostasis**. Regardless of whether the stress is positive or negative, when an individual perceives a stressor, her body automatically responds with a three-stage process known as the **general adaptation syndrome (GAS)** (Selye, 1975) (see Figure 6.3).

The first phase of the general adaptation syndrome is referred to as the *alarm* phase. The brain interprets an event or situation as a stressor and immediately prepares the body to deal with it. Sometimes this initial response is called the *fight or flight syndrome* because the body literally reacts as if it is either going to stand and fight or run away. The emotional response causes physical reactions such as muscle tension, increased heart rate, dry mouth, or sweaty palms.

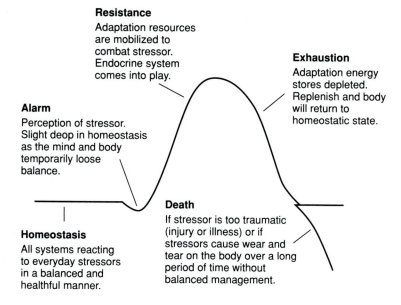

Figure 6.3 The General Adaptation Syndrome (GAS)

Resistance
Adaptation resources are mobilized to combat stressor. Endocrine system comes into play.

Exhaustion
Adaptation energy stores depleted. Replenish and body will return to homeostatic state.

Alarm
Perception of stressor. Slight deop in homeostasis as the mind and body temporarily loose balance.

Homeostasis
All systems reacting to everyday stressors in a balanced and healthful manner.

Death
If stressor is too traumatic (injury or illness) or if stressors cause wear and tear on the body over a long period of time without balanced management.

The second stage of the GAS is *resistance*. During this phase, the body deals with the perceived stressor through increased strength and sensory capacity. Only after meeting the demands of the stressful event can the body return to normal.

When stress is chronic, pervasive, or traumatic enough, the body reaches the third stage, *exhaustion*. At this point, the body must restore itself and rest to avoid serious health problems. Mismanaged long-term stress can cause heart and digestive problems; hypertension; sore, aching muscles and joints; and more.

All the stages in the GAS are the result of chemical messages in the form of hormones. During the alarm phase, for example, the pituitary gland releases the adrenocorticotropic hormone (ACTH), which stimulates other endocrine glands to also release hormones, resulting in the fight or flight response. Hormonal messages are sent that increase blood volume and blood pressure. The two hormones epinephrine and norepinephrine initiate a variety of physiological responses including increased heart rate and metabolic rate. They also stimulate the release of other hormones, called endorphins, that diminish pain.

Obviously, the continual hormonal stimulation that chronic stress causes doesn't allow the body to return to homeostasis. Fortunately, the effects of most stressors can be partially or completely reversed with adequate stress management techniques.

Effects of Chronic Stress

Chronic stress can cause problems in several areas of a student's life. Psychosomatic illness, such as headaches and physical injuries, may result from an abnormal response to stress. A student may withdraw emotionally from others and experience feelings of worthlessness, apathy, loneliness, anger, hostility, and low self-esteem. Behavioral problems like hyperactivity, accident susceptibility, truancy, substance abuse, and low academic achievement may also result from stress. Low self-esteem and anxiety may lead to a lack of concentration and a disrupted capacity to process information (Jones, 1985).

Other behaviors that could indicate that a person is under too much stress are

Frequent headaches	Back-and-forth rocking
Sighing	Depression
Diarrhea/constipation	Anger
Nausea	Continual boredom
Faintness	Lip biting
Hair twirling	Crying
Clenched fists	Proneness to errors
Nervous cough	Nightmares
Too much/too fast talking	Persistent (compulsive) itching
Fingernail biting	

Dealing with Distress

It is important to determine which sources of stress have intrinsic stimuli, such as being inwardly driven to reach a deadline, and which have extrinsic stimuli, such as pressure from a teacher to turn in a homework assignment.

Determining whether the source of stress is regular, routine, or consistent (e.g., a daily conflict or being self-conscious with peers) or if it is more sudden (e.g., the death of a family member) also is a good idea. Regular, routine, or consistent stressors generally have more potential for creating long-term negative effects if left unchecked, because they wear on the individual constantly and may therefore demand more time to resolve. Sudden, isolated sources of stress tend to be crisis situations that first require an initial return to some degree of normalcy and may later involve a more lengthy process of conflict resolution.

Putting the stress-producing situation in realistic perspective is helpful in objectively evaluating its impact. To do this, a person should mentally classify events as they arise. The individual must decide which situations can be personally handled with relative ease after careful consideration of the possible alternatives. Events involving either deeper inner conflict or interaction with others may require the assistance of a third party or outside expert. After putting the cause of the stress into perspective and outlining several courses of action, the individual should select the course of action that seems likely to produce the most healthy, positive, or desirable results based on personal values, goals, and conscience. The person should then carry out the course of action and evaluate its effectiveness to determine whether similar courses of action should be repeated for similar circumstances or whether modifications need to be considered.

Stress Management and Stress Reduction Techniques

Stress management and reduction skills can help individuals cope and increase their potential for reaching and maintaining high levels of emotional health throughout life. People can reduce the adverse effects of stress in a variety of healthy ways.

Examples include exercise and relaxation techniques. Some people use hobbies, arts and crafts, reading, and watching sports activities as alternative stress reducers.

Exercise

One of the most natural methods of relieving the effects of stress is exercise. Aerobic exercise activates the hormones, fatigues tense muscles, and allows the stressed individual to return to a pleasantly tired, but relaxed, state. Activities such as walking, jogging, cycling, and swimming all directly reduce adverse symptoms of stress.

Relaxation Techniques

Several kinds of relaxation techniques can combat the ill effects of stress. These techniques include but are not limited to progressive relaxation, deep-breathing exercises, meditation, and creative visualization. A person who is able to relax under very trying circumstances will experience fewer of the physical symptoms associated with stress.

Progressive relaxation is one method that is especially useful for individuals who experience muscle tension in response to stress. Progressive relaxation requires a quiet room and a comfortable position on a couch, chair, or bed. Instructions can be given on an audiotape or verbally by a teacher/facilitator in a group situation. The key to progressive relaxation is to tense each muscle group as the command is given (typically for about 10 to 15 seconds), then relax that muscle group immediately and completely at the signal (for approximately 10 to 15 seconds). This is a procedure that needs to be practiced, but once the method is learned, it can greatly reduce stress.

Deep-breathing exercises are very similar to natural relaxation. In fact, deep breathing uses the body's natural relaxation response. Students can be reminded that they often unconsciously use deep breathing (sighing) when under stress. Deep-breathing exercises done in regular patterns can further help the student relax when experiencing stress.

Meditation can be approached from several perspectives. The purpose of the technique is to help temporarily "tune out" the world while evoking the relaxation response. During a meditation session, a word or phrase is concentrated on to help eliminate all outside distractions. While in a comfortable position on a couch, chair or bed, the participant breathes deeply, slowly inhaling and exhaling. The word or phrase is focused on with each breath. This format can best be learned from an instructor or tape.

Visualization (creative imagery) is a form of relaxation that uses the imagination. In this technique, the individual assumes a comfortable position, closes her eyes, and takes several deep breaths. Several variations of visualization are possible. For example, a tranquil scene such as a beach or forest can serve as the focal point for the visualization. Visualization can be used to envision a goal or behavior change. A variety of tapes can aid in learning this technique.

Biofeedback is based on scientific principles designed to enhance awareness of body functioning. Sensory equipment is used to create awareness of subtle body changes such as increases or decreases in body temperature, muscle contractions, or brain wave variations. As people become more sensitive to fluctuations in functioning, they can learn to evoke the relaxation response by countering their automatic stress response as it occurs. A few sessions are usually required to recognize differences and then to alter physiological responses. The equipment used to learn this procedure ranges from relatively inexpensive to quite costly.

Other Relaxation Techniques

Areas that require no special equipment nor training but that help dissipate stress symptoms are humor, music, and effective time management.

Humor. Laughing is a powerful stress-reducing agent. Laughing or humor helps us: (1) realize that life is seldom perfect, (2) keep things in perspective, and (3) maintain a positive attitude. Blood pressure and heart rate can actually drop after a good laugh. Laughing or even smiling are excellent ways to alter a negative mood.

Music. Quiet music soothes the autonomic nervous system by easing tensions and lessening strong emotions. Obviously, it is difficult to invoke the relaxation response if the music is inappropriate or irritating to the listener.

Time Management. A perceived or actual lack of time is a major contributor to stress. Effective use of time can eliminate a great deal of stress. Some suggestions for effective time management include:

- Don't procrastinate.
- Set realistic goals.
- Establish priorities and write them down.
- Learn to say "no" when needed.
- Build in relaxation time every day.
- Visualize yourself completing your priorities.

HEALTH HIGHLIGHT
The Power of Positive Thinking

Our society promotes negative or self-defeating thoughts through "shoulds" and "should nots," which can lead to "I can'ts" and "I'm nots." These thoughts hinder progress toward goal achievement. A necessary step to developing good emotional health involves the positive belief by students that changes can be made and integrated into their lifestyles.

One way to counter negative thoughts is by altering one's "self-talk." Such mind/body communication plays a significant role in affecting health and well-being. Beliefs or thoughts held in the mind on a conscious or subconscious level cause the body to respond physiologically or behaviorally. Positive self-communication provides a key to effecting a healthy lifestyle. With practice and the use of self-suggestions, individuals can learn to increase their positive self-talk.

Source: Based on "Stop the Negative, Accentuate the Positive," by C. Chandler and C. Kolander, 1988, *Journal of School Health, 58.* pp. 295–297.

The Role of Effective Communication in Reducing Stress

People often experience considerable stress when they think others are controlling their lives. Anxiety results when a person feels exploited, humiliated, and/or not respected. A change in attitude toward oneself and use of effective communication skills can reduce this anxiety and stress.

Many times stress results from a person's inability to express feelings to others honestly. Individuals often refuse to express their feelings to others because they want to avoid a confrontation or because they do not feel as important as the other person. Some do not wish to hurt anyone's feelings, yet this type of passive behavior causes a person to think less of herself and to be angry at the other person. Such a lack of respect for self increases stress, because the person tends to store the anger internally. Conversely, aggressive behavior—whereby a person physically abuses, insults, or criticizes another—can ruin relationships and also increase stress.

Assertive communication, the type that communicates a respect for self as well as the other person, permits individuals to stand up for their rights without ignoring others' rights. An important part of assertive behavior is a healthy self-concept whereby persons believe they are worthy individuals, capable of having their own feelings and beliefs. It also implies that a person has a right to speak up if she has been treated unfairly and has a right to say no. Assertiveness involves making *I* statements; for example, *I feel . . . I think . . .,* which imply that a person takes full responsibility for her feelings. An assertive person is able clearly and confidently to say no and tell others what she thinks and feels without hurting others or putting them down. Many organizations offer assertiveness training, which teaches people to become more objective and less emotional in response to others' behavior, to speak with positive verbal and body language, and to cope with offensive people. Such communication is very effective in improving self-image and relationships with others and in dealing with stress.

Emotionally intimate communication with others also helps lessen the effects of life's stressors. This type of communication is more than just discussing the weather or other superficial topics. Such communication involves sharing one's innermost feelings with another person. Most people are afraid to share such feelings with others for fear of being rejected. If a person bares her soul to another person, there is a risk that the other person will not empathize with the situation and therefore, not provide emotional support. If the other person demonstrates through words or behavior an unwillingness to give any emotional support, that response can result in anxiety, loneliness, and rejection. If a person is willing to share such intimacies, however, it can strengthen some relationships. Such intimate relationships improve the quality of life, whereas the lack of such relationships contributes to discontentment, anxiety, and stress.

■ ■ ■   *STUDENT CONCERNS:* MENTAL HEALTH AND STRESS

As students move through grades 7 through 12, they encounter many issues of concern in the mental health and stress areas. The following statements reflecting the various grades are from *Students Speak—A Survey of Health Interests and Concerns: Kindergarten Through Twelfth Grade* (Trucano, 1984):

Grades 7 and 8

- Why do people have so many fears and worries?
- What should you do if you are considering suicide?
- Why do I sometimes feel high and other times feel depressed?
- Why do you hurt people's feelings when you don't mean to?
- How do you deal with stress?
- How do you handle, "Everyone does it; it's no big deal"?
- I would like to know how much everyone has in common including some reasons for fear, worries, and stress.
- How do you get more self-confidence?

Grades 9 and 10

- How can you tell what normal behavior is for someone?
- Are the people who commit suicide mentally ill or under a lot of stress?
- How do you make good, responsible decisions?
- Can you help people who don't like themselves?
- What are ways to help depression?
- How do you distinguish real values in yourself from what you are wishing them to be?
- How can you prevent sexual abuse and how do you deal with it?
- How can I have higher self-esteem?
- How do you relate to and get along with others?

Grades 11 and 12

- I think you should give out information about what to do or where to go if you're abused or thinking of suicide.
- How does your home life affect your mental health?
- How do you keep from being stressed?
- How do you learn to really like yourself?
- What makes people get upset over things that don't have to do with them?
- How do different attitudes affect other people?

SUMMARY

Mental health is, at times, a most elusive concept. No easy prescription guarantees good mental health, but several characteristics have been identified. An important aspect of sound emotional health is the fostering of positive self-esteem. A person with high self-esteem has a sense of self-worth, can better demonstrate concern for others, can better develop meaningful relationships; and can make decisions more easily.

Emotional reactions vary from person to person, depending on how the individual perceives the situation. When emotions are expressed in positive, appropriate ways that result from consideration of the feeling and how best to express it, behavior is much less likely to be impulsive. Unexpressed emotions and feelings, on the other hand, can lead to frustration, hostility, or resentment. Defense mechanisms, used to help deal with or even avoid confronting a situation, include compensation, daydreaming, idealization, projection, rationalization, regression, and substitution.

Sometimes certain neurotic behaviors can develop in attempts to cope with problems. Common neurotic behaviors are anxiety reactions, obsessive-compulsive behaviors, phobias, hypochondria/hysterical conversions, and depressions. Of these, depression is the most frequently occurring emotional disorder. Like all neurotic behaviors, depression is a symptom of underlying conflict or tension. Depression has multiple causes, including heredity, environment and personality, biochemical factors, and physical illness. Unrecognized depression is often the major reason for adolescent suicide. Rules for avoiding depression and developing positive emotional/mental health include liking oneself, being good to oneself, learning to be introspective, accepting personal limitations, dealing with problems, establishing realistic goals, expressing emotions appropriately, being involved in diverse activities, developing a sense of humor, and cultivating an optimistic attitude.

Teachers must recognize the impact of familial socialization on students and must attempt to relate equally to students from diverse living arrangements. By recognizing each student as an individual who demonstrates unique qualities and talents, teachers can do much to promote mental health. Words of praise and encouragement as well as appropriate guidance coupled with realistic, clear-cut expectations will help build a classroom atmosphere that enhances emotional well-being. Teachers must also listen and show their acceptance, support, and concern.

All people are exposed to stress. Stress is defined as the body's physical and/or psychological response to an unanticipated event. Stress may result from a pleasant event (eustress) or unpleasant event (distress). Prolonged distress can have a debilitating health effect. Anything that elicits a stress response is called a stressor. Regardless of the type of stress experienced, the body reacts with a three-stage response, general adaptation syndrome (GAS). The three stages are alarm, resistance, and exhaustion. All stages are the result of hormonal messages that the stress event triggers. People can relieve the effects of stress through exercise, progressive relaxation techniques, deep breathing, meditation, visualization, biofeedback, humor, music, and effective time management. Developing effective communication patterns is one of the best methods of protecting against negative stressful responses.

Students in grades 7 through 12 have many concerns in the areas of mental/emotional health. These can involve questions of right and wrong, appropriate actions, friendships, and dealing with negative feelings.

DISCUSSION QUESTIONS

1. Describe the link between mental and physical health.
2. Discuss the relationship between a positive self-image and emotional health.
3. Discuss the importance of expressing one's emotions in a positive way.
4. Describe several causes of distress.
5. How are defense mechanisms used to cope with distress?
6. Describe how effective communication can help reduce distress.
7. Discuss depression and suicide as they apply to adolescents.
8. How can good decision-making skills help one deal with distress?
9. Discuss the role of the family and the teacher in promoting mental health.
10. List the rules that can help an individual maintain emotional health.

■ ■ ■   *ACTIVITIES FOR TEACHING MENTAL HEALTH*
AND STRESS REDUCTION

The process of developing good mental health and finding strategies that can consistently reduce stress is lifelong. Throughout life we are constantly under the influences of situations, pressures, and people that can affect our emotional health and that serve as sources of stress. The activities in this section are suggestions for helping students identify feelings, situations, and behaviors that can influence their own emotional health.

The Shield

This activity is designed to help students identify feelings about themselves and their families. Once students become familiar with this technique, they can make up additional questions for it. You should emphasize having students react honestly to each statement.

1. What is something I like about my family?
2. If I could change one thing about my family, what would it be?
3. One way my family has influenced my life is _____ .
4. Three words that describe my family are _____ .
5. My mother/father makes me angry when _____ .
6. Other people see my family as _____ .

Ask students to share their shield with one other person. One student can begin by responding to number 1 and then the other student can respond to number 1. Continue this until all 6 areas have been covered.

Processing Questions

1. What did you learn about each other's family?
2. Did you have any thoughts or feelings that were the same? Different?
3. What comments do you have about your family in general?

Students can ask each other questions about their shield. No questions should be allowed until all 6 areas of the shield have been covered. Have students put the shield away and then the partners can introduce each other's family to the group.

Facts About Me

Ask students to complete the following statements. Stress to students the importance of honest responses.

1. Other people see me as _____ .
2. My greatest strength is _____ .
3. My greatest weakness is _____ .
4. As a child, I _____ .

5. The person who has influenced my life most is _____ .

6. Nothing is so frustrating as _____ .

7. Members of the opposite sex see me as _____ .

8. It is fun to _____ .

9. Loving someone is _____ .

10. Five years from now, I _____ .

11. I get angry at _____ .

12. I feel hurt when _____ .

13. When I'm alone, I _____ .

14. My greatest dream is to _____ .

15. Religion is _____ .

16. For me, suicide is _____ .

Place students into groups of 3 to 5 and have all group members read their answers. After each group member has provided an answer, ask the members to discuss their feelings concerning their responses or those of another group member. Follow this format until all questions have been answered.

Processing Questions

1. What did you learn about yourself?
2. Were you surprised by any of your responses?
3. How did you feel doing this?

My Personal Assessment

To help understand our emotional health, we must have insight into our own self-perceptions. This activity is designed to help students identify their perceptions of themselves.

Prepare a worksheet with the following questions. Emphasize the importance of honestly assessing perceptions. Ask students to check the statement that best describes themselves.

1. How do you get along with others?

   _____ Very well with friends if they know me well

   _____ Well liked by most people

   _____ Respected but not necessarily well liked

   _____ Very few friends

2. Your attitude toward other people could best be described as:

   _____ Cold and distant

   _____ Indifferent

   _____ Really like other people

   _____ Depends on the person

3. How would you describe your temperament?

_____ Easygoing, slow to anger

_____ Excitable

_____ Cool, calculating

4. What is your best personal characteristic?

_____ Loyalty, trustworthiness

_____ Intelligence

_____ Sense of humor

_____ Dependability

5. Do you consider yourself to be:

_____ Forgiving

_____ Vindictive

6. How do you react to criticism?

_____ Ignore it

_____ Resent it

_____ It hurts, but keep it to yourself

_____ Accept and attempt to learn from critical statements

7. Are you more:

_____ Dependable

_____ Undependable

8. What do you see yourself as being?

_____ Concerned with your own welfare first

_____ Concerned with other people

9. Which adjective best describes you?

_____ Warm

_____ Friendly

_____ Cold

_____ Indifferent

10. What do you see your attitude toward life as being?

_____ Open-minded

_____ Flexible

_____ Indifferent

_____ Conforming

Processing Questions

1. If others looked at your responses, do you think they would check the same characteristics for you that you did for yourself?

2. What are the characteristics you are most proud of?

3. Can you identify problem areas or characteristics that represent potential problems for your emotional health?

Tending My Emotional Health

Have students complete the following chart to help them determine their present opportunities for enhancing their emotional health. Ask them to check the location that offers the best opportunity for the stated behavior.

	Location		
Opportunity to:	Home	School	Peers
Give and receive love			
Increase self-discipline			
Gain worth and recognition			
Express yourself			
Be yourself			
Follow your value system			
Receive positive feedback			
Have fun			
Feel successful			
Say what you really think			

Processing Questions

1. Where is your best opportunity to enhance emotional health?
2. What are some ways the other locations might help develop your emotional health?
3. What other opportunities for enhancing emotional health can you identify in your life?

Friends Should Be

Provide students with a list of the following groupings. Ask them to rank within each group (1, 2, 3) the characteristics they consider most important to look for in a friend. Share the responses with the class.

A	B	C
_____ Smart	_____ Honest	_____ Loyal
_____ Popular	_____ Dependable	_____ Conscientious
_____ Funny	_____ Dedicated	_____ Trustworthy

D	E	F
_____ Open	_____ Quiet	_____ Healthy
_____ Discreet	_____ Bubbly	_____ Happy
_____ Closed	_____ Talkative	_____ Successful

Processing Questions

1. What characteristics seem to be most important to you?
2. What other characteristics would you add?
3. What turns you off as far as developing a friendship with another person?

What Do I Have?*

This assessment is based on the National Association for Mental Health's characteristics of mentally healthy people. In the column on the left you will find a characteristic listed. In the middle column, mark an "X" if you think you possess that characteristic. In the column on the far right, make a list of your behaviors that are indicative of that characteristic.

	Characteristic	Do you possess	Indicative behaviors
1.	Feel comfortable about self		
2.	Feel right about others		
3.	Able to meet the demands of life		

Processing Questions

1. What criteria did you use to decide whether you possessed each of these characteristics?
2. Would others agree with your assessment? Why or why not?
3. How did you decide what behaviors exemplified each of these characteristics?

The Stressors of Life**

The following stress scale represents an adaptation of Holmes and Rahe's Life Event Scale. It has been modified to apply to college-age adults and should be considered a rough indication of stress levels and health consequences for teaching purposes.

Have students determine their stress scores by adding up the number of points corresponding to the events they have experienced in the past 12 months.

---

*Taken from the Instructor's Manual to accompany *Understanding Your Health* (p. 19) by Wayne A. Payne, Dale B. Hahn, and Susan C. Lipnicky, 1989, St. Louis: Mosby Yearbook.

**Source: Reprinted with permission from The Social Readjustment Scale, *Journal of Psychosomatic Research*. Vol II, 1967, Oxford, England: Pergamon.

1. Death of a close family member _____ 100
2. Death of a close friend _____ 73
3. Divorce between parents _____ 65
4. Jail term _____ 63
5. Major personal injury or illness _____ 63
6. Marriage _____ 58
7. Firing from a job _____ 50
8. Failure of an important course _____ 47
9. Change in health of family member _____ 45
10. Pregnancy _____ 45
11. Sex problems _____ 44
12. Serious argument with close friend _____ 40
13. Change in financial status _____ 39
14. Change of major _____ 39
15. Trouble with parents _____ 39
16. New girl- or boyfriend _____ 37
17. Increase in work load at school _____ 37

18. Outstanding personal achievement _____ 36
19. First quarter/semester in college _____ 36
20. Change in living conditions _____ 31
21. Serious argument with instructor _____ 30
22. Lower grades than expected _____ 29
23. Change in sleeping habits _____ 29
24. Change in social activities _____ 29
25. Change in eating habits _____ 28
26. Chronic car trouble _____ 26
27. Change in the number of family get-togethers _____ 26
28. Too many missed classes _____ 25
29. Change of college _____ 24
30. Dropping of more than one class _____ 23
31. Minor traffic violations _____ 20

Total _____

Interpretation: If your score is 300 or higher, you are at high risk for developing a health problem. If your score is between 150 and 300, you have a 50-50 chance of experiencing a serious health change within 2 years. If your score is below 150, you have a 1-in-3 chance of a serious health change. Use of effective stress reduction techniques can reduce the chances of experiencing a serious health change.

How Hardy Are You?

Following are 12 items similar to those that appear on a hardiness questionnaire. Properly evaluating an individual's hardiness requires more than one quick test, but this simple exercise can be a good indication of one's own "hardiness." Have students write down how much they agree or disagree with the following statements, using this scale:

0 = Strongly disagree
1 = Mildly disagree
2 = Mildly agree
3 = Strongly agree

_____ A. Trying my best at work makes a difference.

_____ B. Trusting to fate is sometimes all I can do in a relationship.

_____ C. I often wake up eager to start on the day's projects.

_____ D. Thinking of myself as a free person leads to great frustration and difficulty.

_____ E. I would be willing to sacrifice financial security in my work if something really challenging came along.

_____ F. It bothers me when I have to deviate from the routine or schedule I have set for myself.

_____ G. An average citizen can have an impact on politics.

_____ H. Without the right breaks, it is hard to be successful in my field.

_____ I. I know why I am doing what I'm doing at work.

_____ J. Getting close to people puts me at risk of being obligated to them.

_____ K. Encountering new situations is an important priority in my life.

_____ L. I really don't mind when I have nothing to do.

Scoring: These questions measure control, commitment, and challenge. For half the questions, a high score (agreement) indicates hardiness; for the other half, a low score (disagreement) does. To obtain scores on control, commitment, and challenge, students should first write in the number of their answer—0, 1, 2, or 3—above the letter of each question on the score sheet. Then add and subtract as shown. (To get a score on control, for example, add the answers to questions A and G, add the answers to B and H, then subtract the second number from the first.)

Scores on commitment, control, and challenge added together produce a score for total hardiness. A total score of 10–18 = hardy personality; 0–9 = moderate hardiness; below 0 = low hardiness.

_____ + _____ = _____	_____ + _____ = _____	_____ + _____ = _____
(A) (G)	(C) (I)	(E) (K)
_____ + _____ = _____	_____ + _____ = _____	_____ + _____ = _____
(B) (H)	(D) (J)	(F) (L)
Control Score = _____	Commitment = _____	Challenge score = _____

_____ + _____ + _____ = _____

Control   Commitment   Challenge   Total
Hardiness
Score

Paths to hardiness: Three techniques are suggested to help become happier, healthier, and hardier:

- *Focusing.* Recognize signals from the body that something is wrong. Focusing increases the sense of control over plans and puts individuals psychologically in a better position to change.
- *Reconstructing stressful situations.* Think about a stress episode and then write down three ways the situation could have gone better and three ways it could

have gone worse. Doing this helps show that things could have been worse and, even more important, that better ways to cope are available.

■ *Compensating through self-improvement.* It is important to distinguish between what can be controlled and what cannot. A way to regain control is by taking on a new challenge or task to master.

Analyzing My Use of Time

Managing our time effectively and efficiently can significantly contribute to the feelings of control we have over our lives. A by-product of this sensation of control is reduced stress and tension as we are able to meet daily demands with less effort. Since the basis of change is recognizing that change is needed and then determining the areas that need change, a good place to begin with time management needs is by analyzing your current time management. Have students make several copies of this log and keep track of their time for a week. They should include all activities—from classes to meals to driving time to conversations with friends. At the end of the day and week, have them rate each hour as to how important the activities that occurred during that time were. Taking time to relax, talk to friends, and be alone are considered important to total well-being and should not be discounted.

	Daily Log		
Time	Activities	Where?	Essential, important, or trivial?
6–7 A.M.			
7–8			
8–9			
9–10			
10–11			
11–12			
12–1 P.M.			
1–2			
2–3			
3–4			
4–5			
5–6			
6–7			
7–8			
8–9			
9–10			
10–11			
11 P.M.–6 A.M.			

Analyzing Your Log

1. Which activities did you find to be the most productive for you? Which were the least?
2. Where were your most productive activities performed? Your unproductive activities?
3. What time of day did you find to be the most productive for you—morning, afternoon, or evening?

The analysis should be based on the full week's activities. You are looking for patterns of behavior that yield the best results for you. You may find that you work best at home, or in the dorm in the afternoons, or at the library in the evenings. Using this assessment, try to find the best patterns of achievement for you.

Assertive Communication: Getting What I Want

Meeting our needs has several aspects. One manner to accomplish this is to effectively express feelings, and we can practice this by learning to express likes and dislikes about someone or something. Girdano, Everly, and Dusek (1990) developed the following technique, the Assertiveness Ladder, to improve student assertiveness. Have students follow the instructions and steps outlined here:

The Assertiveness Ladder is a hierarchy of assertiveness exercises that you might attempt in your daily contacts with other people. The exercises are listed in order from least to most difficult. Start slowly at the bottom and progress up through the list. You might spend a week or two practicing each one before moving up to the next. If you begin to experience anxiety, drop back to the previous exercise for another week, then try to move up again through the list.

Exercise 1: Greeting Others. Many unassertive people are too shy to greet others or initiate conversations. This exercise consists of initiating at least two exchanges or conversations per day with individuals whom you would not consider close friends. It may be difficult at first, but continue trying. You may meet some very interesting people.

Exercise 2: Complimentary Statements. This exercise involves giving others compliments. This is a social behavior that may lead to greater social horizons. Many unassertive people neglect to give compliments by rationalizing "Oh, that's dumb," or "Why would they care what I think?" Giving compliments is polite and people probably do care what you think, so give it a try.

Exercise 3: The Use of "I" Statements. Many unassertive people are hesitant or afraid to use the word *I*. The reason is that the use of "I" shows ownership, and disagreement with an "I" statement by someone else is often seen by the unassertive person as a rejection of him or her personally. This is not usually the case, though. Don't be afraid to take a position. Let your preferences be known: If you don't, they will never be realized.

Exercise 4: "Why?" This exercise involves asking "why?" Many unassertive people feel that to ask why represents a challenge—it does not. "Why?" simply asks for additional information. In this exercise you should ask "why" at least twice a day from people you consider to be "above" you in status, position, or respect—your boss, for example. If you think the word "why" may be too threatening to that person, substitute, "What makes you think that?" or "How is that so?" or "Could you help me to understand that better?"

Exercise 5: Spontaneous Expression of Feelings. Unassertive people often repress feelings. This exercise consists of having you spontaneously react on a feeling level to someone else's statement or behavior. Repressed feelings are hazardous to your health and well-being, so express them a little at a time. Try to express your emotional reaction at least twice a day. You'll find it gets easier the more you practice. Remember, sometimes it is better to take the risk of hurting someone else's feelings than to keep your feelings bottled up. If that person is your friend, he or she will understand.

Exercise 6: Disagreement. This exercise involves disagreeing with someone when you feel that person is wrong. Many people take such disagreement personally, but that is a problem they must work out for themselves. If the other person is secure, he or she will know that disagreement can be a healthy and positive force for new ideas. Give it a try, but be sure not to be arbitrary—if you disagree with someone, make sure you really believe in what you are saying.

Exercise 7: Eye Contact. Maintaining eye contact is often one of the most difficult things for the unassertive person to do. You may find it awkward at first, but continue trying. The best way to attempt maintaining eye contact is to start with short intervals, 2 to 3 seconds in length. Eventually extend it to 4 to 5 seconds, then 9 to 10 seconds. It is important that you don't stare at people; this is too often interpreted as a challenge. Therefore, use this time interval technique. When you break eye contact it is important not to look down—maintain your basic eye level. Don't look down!

Processing Questions

1. How did you feel as you advanced up the assertiveness ladder?
2. What were the greatest obstacles to overcome at each step?
3. Did you feel better after you successfully completed each exercise?

Silent Steps

Divide students into groups of 5 to 7. Provide each group with a sealed envelope that contains a sheet of colored construction paper cut into 5 to 7 shuffled jigsaw pieces. Each group should receive a different colored puzzle with differently shaped pieces of equal difficulty. Instruct each group member to select a puzzle piece randomly from the envelope on your signal to start. The students must reconstruct the pieces nonverbally without telling each other where specific pieces should go or fit together. The first group to reconstruct the sheet of construction paper wins; members should raise their hands, not talk. Wait until all groups have solved their puzzles, then discuss students' feelings about this nonverbal game. Did they feel frustrated? Helpless? Confused? Confident?

■ ■ ■   *ACTIVITIES:* BULLETIN BOARDS

Communications Bulletin Board

Define the term *communication*. Have the students make a bulletin board display that shows the different ways people communicate with each other (e.g., telephone, writing letters).

Mental Health Resources

Compile a list of resources available to the community for mental health. Make a bulletin board comprised of information about and/or from agencies that deal with mental health and treatment.

■ ■ ■   *ACTIVITIES:* DISCUSSION AND REPORT STRATEGIES

Question Box

Supply a large, colorful question box and encourage students to submit questions that they want to discuss regarding personal fears, worries or dilemmas. Questions are anonymous. Set aside a particular time for about 30 minutes each week to discuss as many of these as possible.

Picture the Emotion

Photograph students in a variety of situations. Post the photographs on a bulletin board and ask students to comment on the emotions being expressed in the photographs, such as happiness, love, sorrow, fear, and anxiety. This will help students explore their emotions and the emotions of those around them.

Mental Health in Music

Have students compose songs that describe healthy living. They can bring in records that describe a human relationship. Discuss the feelings depicted in the music. Pay attention to the tone of the music as well as to the words of the song.

Freedoms/Responsibilities

On a sheet of paper students should list new freedoms they have acquired within the past year. Opposite each freedom they should list its accompanying responsibilities. Discuss the question, "What will happen if you do not accept the responsibility that accompanies the freedom?"

■ ■ ■   *ACTIVITIES:* LEARNING ENHANCEMENTS

Following are several titles of videotapes that would be appropriate for use in junior high, middle school or high school. This list represents a sample of videos available from several sources. The videos listed were found in one of the following sources:

Human Relations Media
175 Tompkins Avenue
Pleasantville, NY 10570-9973

Films for the Humanities & Sciences
P.O. Box 2053
Princeton, NJ 08543-2053

Unmasking Depression. Follows the lives of 4 people and describes their fears, emotional pain, and thoughts of suicide. Each person explains how he or she overcame depression in ways that can assist others. Grades 9–12; 28 minutes; video or 16mm.

Anorexia and Bulimia. Explains the effects of both disorders on body functioning. A nutritionist demonstrates the extremes to which people with these conditions will go. Grades 7–12; 19 minutes; video or 16mm.

Stress. Examines how stress can affect people of all ages and demonstrates a variety of methods for coping with the pressures of life. Grades 7–12; 26 minutes; video or 16mm.

Stress and Immune Function. Investigates the relationship between stress and illness. Examines the studies that link stress to cancer, respiratory function, herpes, and autoimmune disease. Grades 7–12; 26 minutes; video or 16mm.

Managing Stress, Anxiety and Frustration. Defines stress and its causes and effects and provides suggestions and techniques for dealing with it. The filmstrips include: (1) What Is Stress? (2) Stress and the Body; (3) Relaxation Techniques; (4) Life Management Skills. Grades 8–12; 15–18 minutes per filmstrip; filmstrip or video filmstrip.

Student Stress. Two-part series that assesses some of the reasons why stress symptoms among young people have increased in the past 15 years. Offers suggestions for dealing with a variety of stressful situations. Grades 7–12; 38 minutes; video.

REFERENCES

Chandler, C., & Kolander, C. (1988). Stop the negative, accentuate the positive. *Journal of School Health, 58,* 295–297.

DeSpelder, L., & Strickland, A. (1987). *The last dance* (2nd ed.). Mountain View, CA: Mayfield.

Girdano, D. A., Everly, G. S., & Dusek, D. E. (1990). *Controlling stress & tension: A holistic approach.* Englewood Cliffs, NJ: Prentice-Hall.

Goodwin, L., Goodwin, W., & Cantrill, J. (1988). The mental health needs of elementary school children. *Journal of School Health, 58,* 282–287.

Greenberg, J. S., & Dintiman, G. B. (1992). *Exploring health: Expanding the boundaries of wellness.* Englewood Cliffs, NJ: Prentice-Hall.

Grollman, E. A. (1988). *Suicide.* Boston: Beacon Press.

Hales, D. (1992). *An invitation to health*. Redwood City, CA: Benjamin/Cummings.

Hamrick, M., Anspaugh, D., & Ezell, G. (1986). *Health*. New York: Merrill/Macmillan.

Jones, J. (1985). *Promoting mental health of children and youth through the schools*. Presentation at the American School Health Association convention, Little Rock, AK.

Mayo Clinic. (1989). Depression. *Mayo Clinic Health Letter, 7,* 4.

Olsen, L., Redican, K., & Baffi, C. (1986). *Health Today* (2nd ed.). New York: Macmillan.

Selye, H. (1975). *Stress without distress*. New York: New American Library.

Trucano, L. (1984). *Students speak—A survey of health interests and concerns: Kindergarten through twelfth grade*. Seattle: Comprehensive Health Education Foundation.

CHAPTER 7

Substance Use and Abuse

Ultimately the most important weapons in the war on drugs are the least tangible ones—self-discipline, courage, support from the family, and faith in one's self. The answer is traditional values. If we want to stop our kids from putting drugs in their bodies, we must first ensure that they have good ideas in their heads and moral character in their hearts.   Former U.S. President George Bush

OBJECTIVES

After reading this chapter, you should be able to

- Define substance use and abuse
- Identify reasons for substance abuse
- Describe the various effects of different drugs on the body
- State the physiological, psychological, and sociological effects of commonly used substances
- Define designer drugs
- Give examples of the signs and symptoms of substance use and abuse
- Describe the most effective drug abuse education programs
- List recommendations for schools to reduce drug abuse problems among their students

SUBSTANCE OR DRUG ABUSE

For too long, an epidemic of illicit drug use has afflicted America's young people, robbing many of life itself and preventing many more from fulfilling their hopes and dreams. Drugs have torn apart families, corrupted the nation's values, and devastated countless communities. Drugs have affected all parts of our society, sparing no one—no social class, no region, no neighborhood, and no school.

Over the past decade, however, this epidemic of substance abuse has begun to recede. Today, fewer young people are abusing illegal drugs than at any time since 1979. Young people deserve much credit for turning away from drugs, and their hardening attitudes toward drugs have been documented in national attitudinal surveys. (National Commission on Drug-Free Schools, 1990).

Still, far too many young people are abusing alcohol and other drugs that pose serious health hazards to them. For example, alcohol-rated traffic accidents remain the leading cause of death among young people. For this reason, teachers need to continue to discourage substance abuse among young people.

For many people, the word **drug** is an emotionally charged term associated with such substances as heroin, cocaine, marijuana, and LSD. These substances are drugs, of course, but so are antibiotics, aspirin, the caffeine in a cup of coffee, and the alcohol in a glass of table wine. All of these substances share the ability to bring about change. Taken under a physician's direction, drugs can help alleviate certain medical problems. If a person uses tranquilizers that have been prescribed for someone else, however, that is misuse. If someone relies on tranquilizers as an emotional crutch, use turns into abuse. Likewise, many people enjoy a glass of wine with a meal, but drinking a glass of wine while under the influence of a drug such as an antihistamine or a sleeping pill is misuse. Drinking a quart of wine a day constitutes abuse. **Drug misuse** is the inappropriate use of medicines, whether intentional or not, and includes not following directions for proper medication, "lending" prescribed medicine to other people, and using old medicines for current problems. To some degree the difference between use and abuse is a value judgment. More objectively, **substance abuse** can be defined as the ingestion of any substance that produces deleterious effects, either physically, psychologically, or both. Not surprisingly, drug education is one of the most controversial aspects of health education. Many disagree over how to approach the subject. In fact, some parents would prefer ignoring the subject altogether.

In this chapter, we examine substances that are commonly abused or misused. Some of them have little or no therapeutic value. Over-the-counter drugs, such as cough medicines, can have beneficial effects when used carefully. Because many individuals wrongly consider these drugs to be essentially harmless, however, misuse and abuse are common. Prescription drugs, such as tranquilizers, are more closely controlled, but these substances are also widely abused. Finally, we look at illegal substances, such as heroin, hallucinogens, cocaine, and marijuana.

Reasons for Substance Abuse

Individuals misuse or abuse drugs for a variety of reasons. Young people are especially likely to do so for the following reasons:

Curiosity. We all have an intrinsic desire to experience the unknown, and this desire is especially pronounced during the ages of strong peer influence, when many of a youngster's friends are trying drugs.

Spiritual Search. The search for the meaning of life and one's reasons for existence is as old as time. People for generations have used mind-altering chemicals to try to answer these questions (Girdano & Dusek, 1988).

Low Self-Esteem. Many individuals have poor opinions of themselves. By using drugs, these individuals attempt to avoid coming to grips with their own feelings of inadequacy. Drugs thus serve as a coping mechanism.

Peer Pressure. Particularly during adolescence, individuals have a strong need to belong to "the group." If peers are abusing drugs, that puts strong pressure on all members of the group to do likewise.

Adult Modeling. Young people want to feel grown up, and they view taking drugs as a form of adult behavior to emulate. Smoking tobacco or marijuana, drinking alcohol, or taking pills may all result from adult modeling.

Mood Alteration. Some people take drugs simply to change their psychological state. The mellow feeling or the excitement produced causes this behavior.

HEALTH HIGHLIGHT
Drug Use Among Adolescents

The National Adolescent Student Health Survey found that drugs remain a severe problem among young people. According to the survey:

- About 1 out of every 10 adolescents smoked marijuana in the past month.
- Nearly 15% of eighth-grade students and 35% of tenth-grade students report having tried marijuana.
- 6% of eighth-grade students and 15% of tenth-grade students report having used marijuana during the past month.
- About 1 out of every 15 adolescents have tried cocaine.
- 5% of eighth-grade students and 9% of tenth-grade students report having tried cocaine.
- 2% of eighth-grade students and 3% of tenth-grade students report having used cocaine during the past month.
- About 1 out of every 5 adolescents have tried sniffing glue.
- 20% of eighth-grade students and 21% of tenth-grade students report having tried sniffing glue.
- 7% of eighth-grade students and 5% of tenth-grade students reported having sniffed glue in the past month.

Source: Adapted from *The National Adolescent Student Health Survey—A Report on the Health of America's Youth,* 1989, a cooperative project of the U. S. Department of Health and Human Services, Office of Disease Prevention and Health Promotion, Centers for Disease Control, and National Institute on Drug Abuse. Oakland, CA: Third Party Publishing Company.

Boredom. Many young people, especially teenagers, are at loose ends about their place in society. Childhood activities no longer interest them, but they are not yet able to engage in adult activities. As a result, they feel bored with life.

Alienation. Some individuals think they have little or no power to control their destiny. They may also feel unwanted and unloved. Often, such individuals have few friends and view themselves as misfits in society. Drugs provide an outlet for expressing these feelings of alienation. Alienation may also cause the person to rebel against parental and other adult authorities.

Youth at high risk for illegal substance and alcohol abuse include the economically disadvantaged; children of substance abusers; school dropouts; pregnant teens; victims of physical, sexual, and psychological abuse; runaways or homeless children; and youth who have committed a violent or delinquent act. High-risk youth are different from regular at-risk youth because they have multiple problems that are complex and interrelated (National Drug Policy Board, 1988).

The drug problem is very real in the United States and is receiving great attention. Although no one knows the exact number of drug fatalities, drug-related deaths in 1987 numbered about 37,000. Unlike in previous decades, today's substance user is more likely to use a variety of drugs than to be a single substance user. One bright spot shines through these statistics. A survey of high school seniors conducted for the National Institute on Drug Abuse by the Institute for Social Research at the University of Michigan reflected an attitude that substance use is harmful (National Drug Policy Board, 1988).

EFFECTS OF DRUGS ON THE BODY

Drugs are chemicals that alter normal body activities. First, a substance either mimics, facilitates, or antagonizes the body's normally occurring functions. Second, a substance can have one of four effects on a cell: it can increase activity, decrease activity, increase sensitivity, or disrupt the cell so that normal activity is sporadic. Third, the effect of a substance depends on the concentration of the drug at the site of action (Ray & Ksir, 1987). The effects of drugs result from their biochemical actions. This action depends on the substance reaching the desired site and on the body's chemistry. Other factors include the route of administration, distribution, dosage, user expectations, and frequency of use.

Route of Administration

Drugs can be taken orally in the form of pills, capsules, or liquids. They may be injected intravenously (directly into the bloodstream through a vein), intramuscularly (into a muscle), or subcutaneously (under the skin). Certain substances may be inhaled. Drugs can also be administered topically; that is, by external application of the substance to the skin or mucous membranes.

HEALTH HIGHLIGHT
Factors That Increase the Risk of Substance Abuse

1. Poor self-esteem.
2. Families in which one or more members (generally parents or older siblings) smoke, drink alcohol, or abuse other drugs.
3. Family disruption by:
   a. divorce
   b. death in the family
   c. poor parent/child relationship
   d. family rules and discipline that are *undefined, permissive,* or *harsh.*
4. Socializing mostly with friends who are substance-abusers, making it even more difficult to resist the "peer pressure."
5. Exposure to the media presentation of substance abuse as an important part of popularity, fun, and sex appeal.
6. Poor social skills.
7. Poor academic performance.

(These factors appear to increase the *probability* of drug use—they should not be considered factors *indicating* drug use.)

Source: *Substance Abuse Prevention Activities for Secondary Students* by P. Gerne and T. Gerne (1991), Englewood Cliffs, NJ: Prentice-Hall.

The amount of time required for a drug to take effect after use depends largely on the technique employed to administer it. The substance administration method yielding the strongest, fastest effect is intravenous (IV) injection. This procedure is considered the most dangerous because the risk of infection, vein collapse, or overdose is extremely high. Overdose is a significant problem with IV injection because chemicals enter the circulatory system rapidly and without intervening or protective factors. Smaller amounts of a drug are needed than for any other form of application.

Intramuscular injection works most rapidly in the deltoid muscle and least rapidly in the buttocks, because buttocks have a poorer blood supply. Subcutaneous injection can be extremely irritating to the tissue. Topical administration is usually short acting and may damage the skin or mucous membrane because the chemical being administered often is an irritant.

Even oral ingestion creates problems. This technique requires the drug to enter the bloodstream by passing through the stomach, which may destroy it or alter it into an inactive form. Then, the substance must be lipid (fat) soluble to cross cell membranes and target the problem. Lipid-soluble products tend to remain in the body and show cumulative effects. Water-soluble products are rapidly excreted, on the other hand. Lastly, substances absorbed in the digestive tract go to the liver before being absorbed into general circulation. (The liver also breaks down substances for excretion.) Ultimately, oral ingestion hinders control of the actual dosage absorbed by the body.

Distribution

The bloodstream carries drugs to various parts of the body. Some drugs, like aspirin, are absorbed and then excreted quickly. Other drugs accumulate and are excreted very slowly. It may take several days to build up the drug in the body to a level that will produce the desired therapeutic effect. Once built up, only maintenance doses are needed to maintain the drug's level. Certain heart medications are of this type.

Dosage

Dosage is the amount of a drug administered. The dosage determines the effect of the substance on the body, or the dose-response relationship. The larger the amount taken, the greater the probability of several different effects. The threshold dose is the minimum amount required to produce a therapeutic effect. The dose that obtains the maximum effect is called the maximum dose. The effective dose is the dose needed to produce a desired effect. A lethal dose is the amount that will produce death. The ratio between the effective dose and the lethal dose is the therapeutic index. This is obtained by dividing the amount of a lethal dose by the amount required for an effective dose. The higher the index, the lower the chance of a given dosage being lethal.

Another important concept concerning dosage is the potency, or the difference in effective doses among drugs that are used for the same purpose. For example, substance A may require twice the dosage to achieve the same effect as substance B. Therefore, substance B is a more potent drug. The time required for the substance to produce an effect after the body receives it is called the time-action response. As a general rule, the quicker the effect, the shorter its effectiveness.

The presence of more than one drug can produce what is called **synergism**, whereby the drugs' combined action is greater than the sum of the effects of any one of the drugs taken alone. For example, some drugs potentiate, or increase the effect of another drug. The effect of one substance may be enhanced because of specific enzymes, formation of more potent metabolites, or unknown reasons. It is frightening that pesticides, traces of hormones in meat and poultry, traces of metals in fish, nitrites, nitrates, and a wide range of chemicals used as food additives have been shown to interact with and potentiate some drugs. The classic example of synergism causing a dangerous potentiation is that a safe dose of alcohol mixed with a safe dose of a barbiturate can become lethal by depressing respiration. Conversely, a drug that acts as an antagonist blocks or interferes when used in combination with another drug, or it may inhibit a normal biological compound, such as a hormone.

Expectations of the User

The mood of the user and the setting in which the drug is taken may also affect the reaction to a drug. If the substance is expected to help a problem or produce a particular effect, then the probability of that effect is greater. The effect may occur even when the substance administered is only a placebo, or inert substance. The placebo effect is quite common. Friends, soft lights, and music may help create an environmental setting for particular drug effects.

Placebos are often effective against pain. This effect was not understood until the endorphins and enkephalins were discovered. Both are peptides (biochemical chains of two or more amino acids) produced by the body and have an action similar to morphine. Enkephalins were first isolated from the brain and endorphins from the pituitary gland. Research has shown that endorphins and enkephalins alleviate pain. Physicians are just beginning to realize the importance of the mind in controlling disease and pain, but it is clear that placebos can affect the release of biochemical substances already present in the body if the mind believes a desired effect can be achieved (Witters, Venturelli, & Hanson, 1992).

Frequency of Use

When used frequently, some drugs require larger dosages to maintain the effect. This is called **tolerance**. Tolerance takes several forms: disposition tolerance, cross-tolerance, pharmacodynamic tolerance, and reverse tolerance. **Disposition tolerance** refers to the rate at which the body disposes of a drug. Certain drugs tend to increase the rate of action of enzymes in the liver and, consequently, deactivation of the drug. Alcohol and barbiturates are examples of drugs that cause the liver to produce metabolic enzymes. These enzymes are not very discriminating; therefore, tolerance to one substance may lead to tolerance of other drugs that are pharmacologically similar. This effect is called **cross-tolerance**. Usually a heavy drinker will exhibit tolerance to barbiturates, tranquilizers, and anesthetics.

Evidence indicates that a considerable degree of central nervous system tolerance to certain drugs may develop independent of changes in the rate of absorption, metabolism, or excretion. Called **pharmacodynamic tolerance**, this occurs when the nerves or other target tissues adapt to the substance, decreasing the effect of the same concentration of a chemical. In the case of **reverse tolerance**, users will have the same response to a lower dose of a drug that they had with initial higher doses. Reverse tolerance is believed to be primarily a learning process and not a physiological response. However, it is possible for some drugs, such as marijuana, to be stored in the fat cells and released later as the fat cells are broken down (Ray & Ksir, 1987). Usually, tolerance to a substance that requires increasing amounts of a chemical to maintain normal body functioning will lead to a physical dependence.

Some drugs, such as aspirin, cause neither tolerance nor dependence. **Psychological dependence**, or **habituation**, occurs when taking a substance becomes a habit and fosters a feeling of satisfaction or psychic drive that requires repeated administration of the substance to produce an effect or avoid discomfort (Carroll, 1989, p. 89).

Addiction is a term with various meanings. It is sometimes used interchangeably with dependence, either physiological or psychological, yet at other times appears to be synonymous with substance abuse. The model of addiction-producing drugs is based on opiates, which require the development of tolerance, along with physical and psychological dependence. Opiates, alcohol, and barbiturates are examples that fit the traditional addiction model.

OVER-THE-COUNTER DRUGS

Drugs that can be purchased without a prescription and that are used for self-medication are called **over-the-counter (OTC)** drugs. There are thousands of OTC drugs. These include aspirin and other analgesics, cold remedies, antihistamines and allergy products, vitamins, laxatives, antacids, and mild sedatives. Prescription drugs, in comparison, can be obtained legally only through a physician's order. Prescription drugs typically are more potent than OTC drugs.

Most OTC drugs are somewhat effective in relieving symptoms of the mild illnesses and disorders for which they were developed, as long as they are used according to directions. Despite regulation by the Federal Trade Commission and other government agencies, however, advertising claims for many OTC products often mislead consumers into overestimating the effectiveness of these drugs. As a result, when the product fails to produce instant relief, some individuals may exceed the recommended dosage in hopes of boosting or speeding up aid. This sort of misuse can be dangerous.

Individuals should also recognize that using any medication, including aspirin, involves risk—even when the directions are carefully followed. First, allergic reaction is a possibility. In rare cases, such reactions can be fatal. Second, relief provided by an OTC drug may mask symptoms of another illness or underlying disorder. For this reason, people should self-medicate only when the problem is minor and obvious, as in the case of a mild cold.

Another risk of using OTC drugs is synergism. As explained earlier, if two or more drugs or medications are taken at the same time, one substance can increase or decrease the potency of another. This synergistic reaction can have harmful—even fatal—results.

As with any drugs, OTC drugs can have a stronger effect on children than on adults. Recently, for example, children's aspirin, formerly thought to be safe, has been identified as causing a severe reaction that can lead to death under certain conditions.

DEPRESSANTS

Drugs that slow down, inhibit, or depress the nervous system are classified as **depressants**. The most commonly used depressant drug is alcohol. Dozens of other depressants are available, most of them prescription drugs. Whether obtained legally or illegally, however, depressants are among the most commonly misused and abused drugs.

Depressants have four main effects on the body. As sedatives, they can produce relaxation. As tranquilizers, they can reduce anxiety and relax muscles. As hypnotics, they can promote sleep. As anesthetics, they can minimize sensation. Various depressant drugs differ in their potencies, but in sufficient amounts they can all produce these four effects.

The sedative-hypnotics include barbiturates and tranquilizers. Examples of barbiturates by trade name include Amytal, Nembutal, and Seconal. Commonly prescribed tranquilizers include Valium, Librium, and Miltown. Both of these types of drugs are usually taken orally, although some can be given intravenously as a general anesthetic.

Barbiturates

Barbiturates have historically caused one of the nation's biggest drug abuse problems. Users often take barbiturates, generally known as downers, as a way of escaping from the problems of daily living. Abusers of this type of drug "fog out" and feel removed from the cares of existence. The potency of such drugs increases when combined with alcohol, which often results in fatal overdoses that cause cardiorespiratory failure. More commonly, barbiturate abuse results in mental confusion, dizziness, and loss of memory.

Barbiturates are highly addictive. Physical as well as psychological dependency can quickly develop. Withdrawal from barbiturates can be life-threatening and should occur only under close medical supervision.

Tranquilizers

Tranquilizers are classified as major and minor. The major tranquilizers, such as Thorazine, are used to treat psychosis. Minor tranquilizers, such as Valium and Librium, are prescribed for stress and anxiety. They are also useful as muscle relaxants. Partly because they are so widely prescribed, however, such tranquilizers are often abused. Physical and psychological dependency can result. Symptoms of physical dependency include drowsiness and slurred speech. Psychological dependency may be characterized by increased irritability and irrational fear. As with barbiturates, withdrawal from tranquilizers can be highly traumatic.

Cross Tolerance and the Depressant Drugs

The body can develop a tolerance to depressant drugs quickly. Higher and higher doses of the drug must be taken to produce the desired relaxing effect. Tolerance to one kind of depressant drug also produces tolerance to other types of depressant substances that are not even being taken. This phenomenon is known as **cross tolerance**. The danger of cross tolerance may not be as obvious to drug abusers as it should be. Once the body has developed tolerance to one depressant drug, the individual may decide to switch to another depressant, hoping to achieve the same desired effect. However, because of cross tolerance, the outcome is not the one that was hoped for. A higher dose may then be resorted to. If the new drug is more potent, it may constitute a fatal overdose.

NARCOTICS

For the most part, **narcotic drugs** come from opium and its derivatives, although some are synthesized substances. Such drugs act on the central nervous system and gastrointestinal tract. While they are excellent painkillers, they can be highly addictive, both physically and psychologically. Opium is derived from the opium poppy, which also goes into morphine, codeine, and heroin.

Morphine is a potent painkiller used primarily to relieve severe pain such as that caused by acute sickle cell crisis and heart attack. Codeine is often used in conjunction with acetaminophen to relieve moderate pain. In addition, codeine is effective in suppressing the cough reflex. Heroin is not used for medical purposes.

Heroin is one of the most dangerous abused drugs. Much heroin is produced illegally in Asia and smuggled into the United States. The drug can be smoked, swallowed, injected under the skin, or injected directly into a vein. The latter method is used most often by heroin addicts because the drug reaches the bloodstream most quickly this way. The desired effect is a sudden rush of euphoria, followed by a dreamy state of complete relaxation. This period may last up to several hours, depending on a variety of factors including the strength of the dosage. "Street" heroin is always sold in an adulterated state, usually mixed with milk sugar, so that the actual percentage of heroin is small.

Although considered physiologically "clean," in the sense that it does not damage organs, heroin is extremely addictive, and a user soon may live for no other reason than to inject more heroin. Tolerance also quickly develops, leading to a need for higher and higher or more frequent doses of the drug. The result is too often a fatal overdose, which results in death because of cardiorespiratory failure.

Withdrawal from heroin is agonizing. It is characterized by chills, fever, diarrhea, and vomiting. However painful, heroin withdrawal is seldom life-threatening. Still, most heroin addicts, even when they would like to quit, find it almost impossible to do so because of the craving they have developed for the drug.

The dangers of heroin use are manifold. Aside from weight loss, lethargy, sexual dysfunction, and the constant problems of withdrawal that require regular doses of the drug, injection of heroin can lead to other health problems, including hepatitis and AIDS due to dirty needles and anemia due to disregard for proper nutrition. Toxic adulterants in heroin sold on the street can also kill.

After heroin was outlawed in 1914, heroin addiction declined steadily to a low point during World War II. Heroin addiction peaked in the early 1950s, but it dropped again to another low point in the early 1960s. The upsurge in marijuana and other hallucinogenic drug use was accompanied in the 1970s by another upsurge in heroin use, with an estimated 300,000 to 400,000 addicts by the mid-1970s. The number who had used heroin or other opiates in the past was estimated at 3 million. In 1975, the percentage of high school seniors who had ever used heroin was 2 percent, with 1 percent having used it the preceding year. By 1982, both of these figures had been halved. By 1982, daily use had virtually disappeared among high school seniors. The use of heroin and other opiates continued to decline or stabilize at a low level through the 1980s. A 1990 survey reported 48,000 current users of heroin in the over-25 age group. In 1990, 1% of the high school seniors surveyed reported having ever used heroin and 8% reported some experience with other opiates. In the population aged 12 to 17, the lifetime prevalence has remained less than 12 percent since 1979. (Akers, 1992, pp. 93–4).

STIMULANTS

Stimulants are drugs that stimulate, or speed up, the nervous system. Physiologically, the stimulant drugs increase heart rate, blood pressure, and amount of circulating blood sugar. They also constrict the blood vessels and dilate bronchial tubes and the pupils of the eyes. Some can produce a temporary euphoria.

Caffeine

The most common stimulant is caffeine, contained in coffee, tea, cola drinks, and even chocolate. Caffeine is a mild stimulant that is often abused. Nonetheless, it is a drug and should be recognized as one that can lead to health problems.

Caffeine is absorbed quickly into the bloodstream and reaches a peak blood level in about 30 to 60 minutes. It increases mental alertness and provides a greater feeling of energy. However, high doses of caffeine can overstimulate and cause nervousness and increased heart rate. Caffeine can also cause sleeplessness, excitement, and irritability. In some cases, high doses of caffeine can induce convulsions.

Coffee or cola drinking, let alone chocolate eating, is not drug abuse under most commonly accepted standards, but some individuals seek out caffeine for its own sake, in OTC products and in illegal substances to produce a caffeine "high." Because it is not considered a dangerous drug, the opportunities for caffeine abuse are often overlooked.

Amphetamines

Amphetamines represent a more serious stimulant drug abuse problem. These drugs have limited legitimate and useful medical applications, but their wide availability causes widespread abuse. Examples of commonly prescribed amphetamines include Benzedrine, Dexadrine, Methadrine, Ritalin, and Narodin. Because of the possibility of dependency, the uncertainty of side effects, and the questionable nature of some applications, use of amphetamines has come under closer scrutiny in the last few years. For example, although amphetamines do suppress hunger, most doctors no longer recommend them as "diet pills." Still, 20% of adolescent girls and 7% of the boys reported in 1989 that they had tried such pills to lose weight (U. S. Department of Health and Human Services, 1989). Treatment of hyperactive children with Ritalin, which curiously seems to act as the opposite of a stimulant among such individuals, has also been called into question.

Still, stimulant drugs remain easy to obtain, and this has resulted in continued drug abuse problems. The general street name for such drugs is "speed," because of the way they seem to speed up the nervous system. Amphetamine pills are also known as "uppers." Abusers of amphetamines pass into an extremely excited state and may feel omnipotent until the drug begins to wear off. A depressed period (called a *crash* by abusers) then follows, leading to a craving for more amphetamines.

As with many drugs, amphetamine craving often undermines a person's regard for good personal health practices. Because these drugs inhibit appetite, poor nutrition leading to weight loss often results. An amphetamine user soon becomes a physical and psychological wreck, often experiencing episodes of paranoia and psychosis. Once the stimulating effects diminish, chronic users frequently enter sometimes severe depressions (Payne, Hahn, & Dinger, 1991).

Whether amphetamines result in true physical dependency is open to debate, but strong psychological dependency is not. Long-term use of these drugs can damage the heart, liver, and kidneys. Speech problems and facial twitches may also be apparent. In high doses, amphetamines can cause hallucinations, delusions, and disorganized behavior. Withdrawal from amphetamines is not life-threatening, but the process does result in depression and anxiety. Professional treatment is often necessary.

Cocaine

Known on the street as "snow" or "coke," cocaine is an illegal drug that continues to rise in popularity. Currently, cocaine trafficking and consumption represent the most significant drug problem in the United States (U. S. Department of Education, 1987). More than 25 million Americans have tried cocaine, with 6 million using it at least once a month. The number of new users is rising at an estimated rate of 5,000 per day (U.S. Dept. of Justice, 1987). According to the recent National Adolescent School Health Survey (U.S. Dept. of Health and Human Services, 1989), more than one out of every 20 students reported having used cocaine in their lifetime, and 3% reported using cocaine during the past month. The good news from this survey is that the great majority of adolescents perceive a great risk from using cocaine powder (69%) or crack cocaine (74%) occasionally.

Cocaine is legal and useful for limited medical purposes. Because of its vasoconstrictive and anesthetic properties, cocaine is used as a local ingredient in Brompton's cocktail, a preparation for treating severe pain in individuals with a terminal illness.

Cocaine trafficking and consumption represent the most significant drug problem in the United States.

Cocaine produces a feeling of intense euphoria and boundless energy. As this fades, sometimes severe depression follows, along with the strong desire for another dose or "hit." Although cocaine does not cause physical dependence, psychological dependence is common and can be very potent. Withdrawal symptoms from cocaine are limited to mild depression and anxiety with limited use. Paranoid thoughts, hallucinations, and psychosis can occur with heavy, extended use.

Cocaine is most often found in the form of a white powder, which the user generally sniffs or "snorts" through the nostrils. The drug then enters the bloodstream through the nasal membranes. Cocaine concentration in the blood rapidly increases for about 20 minutes, peaks at 1 hour, then gradually declines for 3 or more hours after use (Witters, Venturelli, & Hanson, 1992).

Following intravenous administration, the total amount of cocaine enters the bloodstream in a few minutes. The peak occurs in 3 to 10 minutes. This "high" precedes a depression that may last 10 to 40 minutes (Witters et al., 1992). Oral use is not common in the United States, but the high is comparable to other forms of use.

A process used for purifying or refining cocaine is called **freebasing**. This method produces a more potent form of the drug and an accelerated, intense high. The drug is heated to a high temperature and mixed with other substances (some highly volatile, occasionally resulting in explosion). The remaining mixture is then smoked in a water pipe.

Recently, a new form of cocaine has become popular. "Crack" and "rock" get their names from the sound made by the crystals when heated and the rocklike appearance. Crack may be 90% pure, compared to 15% to 25% purity in regular cocaine. The drug is smoked in a glass water pipe, which allows rapid absorption into the blood. Crack reaches the brain in less than 10 seconds, with the high lasting from 5 to 7 minutes. Following this intense rush, crashing depression may occur and last two to three times longer than the high.

Many people perceive smoking to be less dangerous, but this route provides direct absorption via the lungs, into the blood, and to the brain in less than 10 seconds. The speed with which crack acts and the purity it displays make it very dangerous. Crack is widely available for about $5 a hit, dispelling the notion that cocaine is an upper-class drug.

Cocaine's action on the body most directly affects the cardiovascular system. The heart rate increases and small blood vessels constrict, resulting in increased blood pressure. This sudden increase in cardiac activity, coupled with vaso-constriction, leads to an elevated risk of cardiac ischemia resulting in heart attack or rhythm disturbances. These risks are not unique to IV use nor limited to massive doses. In addition, the absence of an underlying heart condition does not allow a person to avoid cardiac consequences (Isner & Clarke, 1989). Most crack-related deaths result from brain hemorrhage, blocking of the heart's electrical system, or lung failure associated with heart and vessel complications (Witters et al., 1992).

The number of individuals admitted to hospitals for cocaine-related emergencies rose from 5,200 in 1983 to more than 26,000 in 1987 (U.S. Department of Justice, 1987). These figures reflect an upsurge in smoking cocaine, as well as increased availability and use of crack. Other problems associated with cocaine include nasal septum deterioration from snorting cocaine, and, less often, convulsions.

INHALANTS

Substances that are inhaled to produce altered states are called **inhalants**. These substances are classified as volatile solvents and aerosols. Common chemicals inhaled are nail polish remover, lacquer thinners, glue, gasoline, and liquid correc-tion fluid. Inhalation is a rapid means of ingesting substances, equal to intravenous injection in the time it requires to reach the brain. Altered consciousness is possible within 1 to 2 minutes of inhaling a large concentration, 5 to 10 minutes with low doses. Inhalants can also be ingested through the mouth. This method is called *huffing,* and it is not as prevalent as inhaling.

Most volatile substances are classified as depressants, although some may have hallucinogenic characteristics. The user may experience the "high" or relaxation associated with alcohol. Cardiac arrhythmias and consciousness alteration can occur immediately. Long-term effects include liver and kidney damage, peripheral nerve damage, decreased blood cell formation, organic brain syndrome (i.e., impaired short-term memory, lethargy, loss of muscle coordination), and an increased rate of cancer (Witters et al., 1992).

The most common inhalant abusers are younger children, prison inmates, and individuals from low socioeconomic groups. Abusers are generally experimenters or transient users who move on to other drugs. Young and very poor individuals comprise the group of chronic abusers.

DESIGNER DRUGS

Designer drugs are substances produced synthetically by underground chemists and sold under the false assumption that they are some other drug. Chemists alter compounds to give the appearance of the original drug, and to some extent, the effects, but designer drugs contain only legal substances. They are often called look-alikes. The most familiar designer drugs are amphetamine look-alikes that contain caffeine, ephedrine, and phenylpropanolamine—the same ingredients as in many over-the-counter diet and cold compounds. Designer cocaine may be comprised of powdered sugar and a topical anesthetic such as benzocaine. The user experiences sinus numbing, but the cocaine rush is absent. Naive users may be fooled, but experienced coke users will quickly recognize the imposter.

In addition to differing in chemical makeup, some designer drugs are more dangerous than the drugs they imitate. They may contain very dangerous drugs that can be lethal in very small amounts. When the user injects the usual dose, death may result. Other effects such as brain damage and paralysis have occurred. Designer drugs were banned in the United States by a bill passed in 1986.

HALLUCINOGENS

Hallucinogens are substances—occurring naturally or produced synthetically—that distort the perception of reality. Such drugs cause sensory illusions that hinder ability to distinguish fact from fantasy. Perhaps the most widely known hallucinogen is LSD (lysergic acid diethylomide), which was first synthesized in 1938. Although still occasionally used in medical research, the drug has no everyday therapeutic applications. Even a tiny amount is enough to cause hallucinations, which manifest themselves in intensified colors, individualized sound perceptions, and bizarre visions, which may be pleasant or extremely frightening.

In mentally unstable individuals, LSD can produce psychotic reactions. Users also risk so-called flashbacks, in which they suddenly have hallucinations long after having last ingested the drug. LSD neither causes physical dependency nor seems to result in brain damage or birth defects, as once supposed. However, a "bad trip," or unpleasant experience while under the influence of the drug, can have long-lasting psychological effects.

Other hallucinogens are either products of peyote, a kind of cactus that grows in Mexico and the American Southwest, or are made synthetically. Most mimic the effects of LSD, but some are particularly dangerous because of their unpredictable side effects. One of the more common of these illegal drugs is PCP (phencyclidine hydrochloride), known as "angel dust." Originally synthesized as an animal tranquilizer, PCP is a relatively easy chemical to manufacture illegally. The drug is usually mixed with tobacco or marijuana and ingested by smoking. PCP produces perceptual distortions, feelings of depersonalization, and changes in body image. Apathy, sweating, and auditory hallucinations may also result. High doses produce a stupor and overdose coma that can last for several weeks, followed by weeks of a confused mental state. In some individuals PCP also has been reported to precipitate extremely violent behavior, including murder.

MARIJUANA

After alcohol and nicotine, marijuana is the third most popular recreational drug in the United States. One-quarter of U.S. high school students report having used marijuana in their lifetime, and 10% report using it during the past month. Only about half of these students believe a great risk is associated with smoking marijuana. Further, more than half of the students believe that it would be easy for them to get marijuana (U. S. Department of Health and Human Services, 1989).

Marijuana is a prepared mixture of the crushed leaves, flowers, small branches, stems, and seed of the hemp plant, *Cannabis sativa*. Hashish is a more potent resin derived from this plant.

Marijuana is a hard drug to classify. Depending on various factors, including the amount of drug taken, the type of drug, the setting, and the mood of the user, cannabis intoxication may resemble the effects of alcohol, a sedative, a stimulant, or a hallucinogen. Marijuana in low to moderate doses causes a sedative effect. However, at higher dose levels, marijuana produces effects quite similar to the mind-expanding psychedelics. Like the powerful psychedelics, there is little cross-tolerance between marijuana and LSD, for example. In average doses, it acts much like alcohol. In addition, it distorts time, increases heart rate, increases appetite and thirst, dilates blood vessels in the eyes, and may cause muscular weakness. Some individuals may act emotionally unstable or anxious or experience sensory distortions. The ability to think seems to decline because of effects on short-term memory. The ability to drive a car effectively is hindered because of impaired perception and motor coordination.

The health effects from long-term marijuana use are still under investigation. Several major problems can result from intense marijuana abuse. Current research indicates that chronic bronchitis, cancer, and emphysema can result from long-term marijuana smoking—in fact, the risk of these diseases is greater from marijuana than from tobacco, since marijuana smoke goes into the body unfiltered. Reports have also suggested that marijuana smoking adversely affects the body's ability to fight disease (Payne et al., 1991).

Marijuana affects the reproductive system in various ways. It affects the sympathetic nervous system, increasing vasodilation in the genitals, and thus delays ejaculation. Chronic marijuana use has been shown in some studies to reduce testosterone (male hormone) levels and lower sperm counts, but results are not consistent (Payne et al., 1991). High doses over a period of time can lessen sexual desire and cause impotence. This probably occurs because of the decreased testosterone, which is the result of THC affecting either the hypothalamus, the pituitary, or perhaps both glands. The number of sperm ejaculated decreases, the proportion of abnormal sperm increases, and the motility of sperm declines in marijuana users.

Studies of the effects of marijuana on adolescents in the 12- to 15-year-old range has raised many questions but provided few answers. Its effect on the reproductive system, as well as on psychological and sociological development, is unknown. However, even the advocates of more liberal marijuana laws agree that its use should be limited to those over a particular age.

Although marijuana tolerance can develop, the frequent user may actually require less to gain the effects of the drug over time. While physical dependence seems rare, a danger of psychological dependence does exist. For some time, marijuana has been under investigation for possible medical use. In fact, marijuana has been used for numerous medical purposes since the ancient Chinese first employed the cannabis plant as a therapy. Some patients not helped by conventional therapies may be treated successfully with marijuana. Cannabis also might be combined effectively and safely with other drugs to produce a treatment goal. According to Carroll (1989), marijuana has been used medically in the following ways:

Glaucoma. Marijuana has been found to reduce the vision-threatening intraocular pressure of glaucoma. Older patients experience undesirable physical and psychological side effects, however. Despite providing relief for some patients, marijuana neither prevents glaucoma nor improves vision.

Chemotherapy-Caused Nausea and Vomiting. Cancer chemotherapy can prolong survival in patients with certain cancers, but the accompanying nausea and vomiting may interfere with a person's ability or willingness to continue therapy. Marijuana has been proven effective in controlling nausea and vomiting. The U. S. government has established a program to make marijuana available through capsules (containing THC, the active ingredient in marijuana) and cigarettes through specified pharmacies to physicians who want to use the drug on their chemotherapy patients. Some cancer patients report anxiety. Also, marijuana does not help reduce nausea and vomiting for everyone.

Appetite Stimulant. Research now suggests that cancer patients who use marijuana in conjunction with chemotherapy find their appetite increases.

Antiasthmatic Effect. Long-term marijuana smoking constricts the airways. However, short-term smoking has actually produced a bronchodilation effect in patients with bronchial asthma; therefore, the drug is considered useful in the treatment of asthma.

Muscle Relaxant Action. Limited studies suggest that marijuana is effective in relieving the muscle spasms common in patients with multiple sclerosis.

Analgesic Action (Pain Relief). Some test subjects in research studies did attest to marijuana's pain-relieving effects; however, they also tended to experience "mental clouding" and other undesirable pharmacological effects. Marijuana, therefore, is not considered any more effective than currently available analgesics.

Treatment for Drug Abuse. Research has failed to find marijuana useful in treating alcoholism. No evidence proves that marijuana is more effective than currently available treatment for opiate withdrawal.

Should marijuana become an accepted drug? Marijuana is an unstable substance that has a poor shelf life. Research has found that it contains at least 400 chemicals, some of which may be harmful. Very few drugs in today's pharmacopoeia are crude drugs (the whole plant, rather than the essential active ingredients).

ANABOLIC STEROIDS

Anabolic steroids are hormone drugs. Anabolic steroids contain androgens and are used therapeutically for replacement of the hormone in males with malfunctioning testes. Sometimes steroids are administered for prolonged periods during puberty to stimulate proper male development.

Anabolic steroids cause a pronounced increase in muscle mass and body weight. This effect draws athletes (male and female) to these drugs. Body builders use these drugs to build muscle mass and improve their physiques. Athletes in other strength and endurance events (such as swimming) have used them for building muscle mass, too. Half of these athletes are using them illegally, while the other half obtain them through physicians.

Continued, frequent use of these drugs can cause damage to the body. Anabolic steroids can cause unwanted physical changes, such as breast enlargement and shrinking of the testes in men, and growth of facial hair and decreased breast size in women. Steroid use by teenagers can stunt growth by closing the spongy parts of bones that expand during growth. Headaches, anxiety, increased aggressiveness, insomnia, and possible paranoia are other side effects associated with steroids.

Physicians and educators have combined their efforts to prevent abuse of steroids among their clients and students. Also, various athletic contests have started testing for steroid abuse, and athletes who violate these rules face suspension from competition. The most celebrated case of a suspension due to steroid abuse involved Canadian sprinter Ben Johnson, who lost his gold medal at the 1988 Olympics when his drug test proved positive (Witters et al., 1992).

Table 7.1 summarizes information about the various drugs discussed thus far.

Table 7.1   Terms of Drug Abuse

Marijuana			
Type	**What called**	**What looks like**	**How used**
Marijuana	Pot Grass Weed Reefer Dope Mary Jane Sinsemilla Acapulco gold Thai sticks	Dried parsley mixed with stems that may include seeds	Eaten Smoked
Tetrahydro-cannabinol	THC	Soft gelatin capsules	Taken orally Smoked
Hashish	Hash	Brown or black cakes or balls	Eaten Smoked
Hashish oil	Hash oil	Concentrated syrupy liquid varying in color from clear to black	Smoked—mixed with tobacco
Inhalants			
Type	**What called**	**What looks like**	**How used**
Nitrous oxide	Laughing gas Whippets	Propellant for whipped cream in aerosol spray can Small 8-g metal cylinder sold with a balloon or pipe (buzz bomb)	Vapors inhaled
Amyl nitrite	Poppers Snappers	Clear or yellowish liquid in ampules	Vapors inhaled
Butyl nitrite	Rush Bolt Locker room Bullet Climax	Packaged in small bottles	Vapors inhaled
Chlorohydro-carbons	Aerosol sprays	Aerosol paint cans Containers of cleaning fluid	Vapors inhaled
Hydrocarbons	Solvents	Cans of aerosol propellants, gasoline, glue, paint thinner	Vapors inhaled

Table 7.1   *continued*

Depressants			
Type	What called	What looks like	How used
Barbiturates	Downers Barbs Blue devils Red devils Yellow jacket Yellows Nembutal Seconal Amytal Tuinals	Red, yellow, blue, or red and blue capsules	Taken orally Injected
Methaqualone	Quaaludes Ludes Sopors	Tablets	Taken orally
Tranquilizers	Valium Librium Equanil Miltown Serax Tranxene	Tablets Capsules	Taken orally

Stimulants			
Type	What called	What looks like	How used
Cocaine	Coke Snow Flake White Blow Nose Candy Big C Snowbirds Lady	White crystalline powder, often diluted with other ingredients	Inhaled through nasal passages Injected Smoked
Crack cocaine	Crack Freebase rocks Rock	Light brown or beige pellets or crystalline rocks that resemble coagulated soap; often packaged in small vials	Smoked

Table 7.1 *continued*

Stimulants			
Type	What called	What looks like	How used

Amphetamines	Speed
	Uppers
	Ups
	Black beauties
	Pep pills
	Copilots
	Bumblebees
	Hearts
	Benzedrine
	Dexedrine
	Footballs
	Biphetamine
		Capsules
		Pills
		Tablets
			Taken orally
			Injected
			Inhaled through
			  nasal
			  passages

Metham-
phetamines
	Crank
	Crystal meth
	Crystal
	Methedrine
	Speed
	Ice
		White powder
		Pills
		A rock that resembles a
		  block of paraffin
			Taken orally
			Injected
			Inhaled through
			  nasal
			  passages

Additional stimulants	Ritalin Cylert Preludin Didrex Prestate Voranil Tenuate Tepanil Pondimin Sandrex Plegine Ionamin	Pills Capsules Tablets	Taken orally Injected

Hallucinogens			
Type	What called	What looks like	How used

Phencyclidine	PCP
	Angel dust
	Loveboat
	Lovely
	Hog
	Killer weed
		Liquid
		Capsules
		White crystalline powder
		Pills
			Taken orally
			Injected
			Smoked—can be
			  sprayed on
			  cigarettes,
			  parsley, and
			  marijuana

Table 7.1 *continued*

Hallucinogens			
Type	What called	What looks like	How used
Lysergic acid diethylamide	LSD Acid Green or red Dragon White lightening Blue heaven Sugar cubes Microdot	Brightly colored tablets Impregnated blotter paper Thin squares of gelatin Clear liquid	Taken orally Licked off paper Gelatin and liquid can be put in the eyes
Mescaline and peyote	Mesc Buttons Cactus	Hard brown discs Tablets Capsules Tablets and capsules	Discs can be swallowed, chewed, or smoked Taken orally
Psilocybin	Magic mushrooms Mushrooms	Fried or dried mushrooms	Chewed and swallowed

Narcotics			
Type	What called	What looks like	How used
Heroin	Smack Horse Brown sugar Junk Mud Big H Black tar	Powder, white to dark brown Tarlike substance	Injected Inhaled through nasal passages Smoked
Methadone	Dolophine Methadose Amidone	Solution	Taken orally Injected
Codeine	Empirin compound with codeine Tylenol with codeine Codeine Codeine in cough medicines	Dark liquid varying in thickness Capsules Tablets	Taken orally Injected

Table 7.1 *continued*

Narcotics			
Type	What called	What looks like	How used
Morphine	Pectoral syrup Hypodermic tablets	White crystals Injectable solutions	Injected Taken orally Smoked
Meperidine	Pethidine Demerol Mepergan	White powder Solution Tablets	Taken orally Injected
Opium	Paregoric Dover's powder Parepectolin	Dark brown chunks Powder	Smoked Eaten
Other Narcotics	Percocet Percodan Tussionex Fentanyl Darvon Talwin Lomotil	Tablets Capsules Liquid	Taken orally Injected

Designer Drugs			
Type	What called	What looks like	How used

Analogs of
  fentanyl
  (narcotic)
	Synthetic
	  heroin
	China white
		White powder resembling
		  heroin
			Inhaled through
			  nasal
			  passages
			Injected

Analogs of
  amphetamines
  and metham-
  phetamines
  (Hallucinogens)
	MDMA
	  (Ecstasy,
	  XTC, Adam,
	  Essence)
	MDM
	STP
	PMA
	2,5-DMA
	TMA
	DOM
	DOB
		White powder
		Tablets
		Capsules
			Taken orally
			Inhaled through
			  nasal
			  passages

Analogs of
  phencyclidine
  (hallucinogens)
	PCPy
	PCE
	(PCP) TCP
		White powder	Taken orally
			Injected
			Smoked

Reprinted with permission of Merrill, an imprint of Macmillan Publishing Company, from *Teaching Today's Health,* Third Edition, by David J. Anspaugh and Gene Ezell. Copyright © 1990 by Merrill Publishing Company.

DRUG EDUCATION

Evaluation research on drug education programs designed to encourage prevention done over the last three decades indicates that these programs have not been effective. In fact, the findings state that these programs essentially had no effect on curbing drug use. Although studies of the more recently developed program are more optimistic, the findings still do not provide strong evidence of impact. The goal of these programs has been to influence three basic areas: knowledge, attitudes, and behavior. They have had some success in increasing knowledge and, to a lesser extent, changing attitudes toward drugs; however, increases in knowledge and changed attitudes do not mean much if the actual drug behavior does not change. In fact, programs that only increase knowledge tend to reduce anxiety and fear of drugs, and may actually increase the likelihood of drug use. For example, one approach in the past was to provide students with complete information about drugs, from the names of every street drug, to how the drugs are usually ingested, to detailed descriptions of the drugs' possible effects and the possible consequences of an overdose. Given the inquiring nature of children and adolescents, such an approach could well amount to a primer on how to take drugs, not how to avoid them.

The only effective approach to drug education is one in which students come to see that drug taking constitutes unnecessary self-abuse. Teachers must provide information about realistic alternatives. Too often, teachers try to ignore the real appeal of drugs such as marijuana or alcohol by encouraging students instead to take up a sport or go bike riding or learn to play a musical instrument. Nothing is wrong with such suggestions, but they fail to take into account the personal problems that are tempting students to try drugs.

The social-influence education programs show the most promise in reducing or delaying onset of drug use. Psychological approaches that stress social influences and skills are more effective than other approaches. Programs that are most effective in influencing both attitudes and behavior are "peer programs" that include refusal skills—with more direct emphasis on behavior—and/or social and life skills. Refusal skills can be taught through role-playing that helps students learn the responses they will need to refuse a drug in a real situation. This program demonstrates that practicing can make saying "no" much easier, and that being prepared for negative peer pressure in advance is better than being caught unprepared. When helping students develop refusal skills, the teacher should assist them by identifying situations in which persuasion to use drugs is likely to occur. Recognizing that students with high self-esteem are more likely to be successful in using refusal skills, the teacher should pay particular attention to enhancing students' self-esteem through a variety of learning strategies (Papenfuss, 1989). Several self-help groups also can help the substance abuser. Figure 7.1 lists some of these groups.

Something appears to be reducing drug abuse, whether that is better educational programs, media campaigns, or other programs. Almost all of the indicators of drug abuse decreased significantly in the 1980s. Magazine and television campaigns, school- or community-based prevention programs, or various treatment programs might have brought about the change. Also, the general reduction in drug use in

Figure 7.1   Self-help groups for substance abusers and their families

Parents of Adolescents

Tough Love
P.O. Box 1069
Doylestown, PA 18901
215/348-7090
Parent support groups for dealing with teenagers' unacceptable behavior. Help in starting groups, self-help manual, parent support network, newsletter.

Alcoholism

Alcoholics Anonymous
P.O. Box 459
Grand Central Station
New York, NY 10163
212/686-1100
Members share experiences, strengths, and hopes with each other so they may solve common problems and help each other recover from alcoholism. Bimonthly newsletter "Loners Internationalist" includes networking by mail.

Al-Anon Family Group
World Service Office
P.O. Box 862
Midtown Station
New York, NY 10018-0862
800/356-9996
Provides help for family members and friends of problem drinkers by offering comfort, hope, and friendship through shared experiences. "Lone Member Letterbox" newsletter. "Al-Anon Speaks Out" newsletter for professionals. Guidelines for developing new groups.

Alateen
World Service Office
P.O. Box 862
Midtown Station
New York, NY 10018-0862
800/356-9996
For younger family members who live in an alcoholic family situation to learn effective ways to cope with problems. Helps members achieve detachment from alcoholic family member. Newsletter, pen pal, "Loner's Service." Chapter development kit.

National Association for Children of Alcoholics
P.O. Box 421691
San Francisco, CA 94142
Support and information for children of alcoholics of all ages and those in a position to help them.

Drug Abuse

Narcotics Anonymous
P.O. Box 9999
Van Nuys, CA 91409
818/780-3951
Fellowship of recovering addicts meeting to "stay clean of all drugs."

Families Anonymous
P.O. Box 528
Van Nuys, CA 91408
818/989-7841
For relatives and friends concerned about the use of drugs and alcohol or related behavioral problems. Referrals to local groups. Guidelines for developing groups. Newsletter "12-Step Rag."

Nar-Anon Family Groups
P.O. Box 2562
Palos Verdes, CA 90274-0119
213/547-5800
Fellowship of relatives and friends of drug abusers. Follows the 12-step program adapted from Alcoholics Anonymous and Al-Anon. Helps members learn to achieve peace of mind and gain hope for the future.

National Federation of Parents for Drug-Free Youth
1423 N. Jefferson
Springfield, MO 65802
417/836-3709
National Red Ribbon Campaign
4600 Eisenhower Avenue
Alexandria, VA 22304
Information, networking, newsletter, and guidelines for parents forming groups to address drug abuse problems among adolescents.

American society may be the result of changes in social norms and an informal control system unrelated to conscious and deliberate prevention, treatment, or law enforcement efforts (Akers, 1992). The National Commission on Drug-Free Schools (1990), echoes this optimism as well. The commission's investigations showed that students in schools and colleges have taken leadership roles in peer programs to prevent alcohol and other drug abuse on their campuses; parents have organized party safe-home networks; schools in a variety of communities have developed programs for high-risk students who need help with drug abuse and other problems; and law enforcement officers and public housing residents have banished drug gangs from their neighborhoods.

As a teacher, you must become aware of the drugs that are commonly abused in your community so that you can act and react appropriately. Your knowledge of abused drugs should include street names of the substances, symptoms of their use, and possible consequences of abuse.

What should you do if you realize that your school has a drug problem? This question has no definitive answers, but you must begin with a solid informational base about just what drugs do and do not do. Then, any action taken will be based on fact. The U. S. Department of Education (1987) recommends that schools take the following actions to combat the drug abuse problem in schools:

1. Determine the extent and character of drug use and establish a means of monitoring that use regularly. This would mean conducting anonymous surveys of students and school personnel; identifying areas where drugs are being used and sold; meeting with parents to determine the nature and extent of drug use; informing the community of the results of the assessment of the drug problem.
2. Establish clear and specific rules regarding drug use that include strong corrective actions. School policies should specify what constitutes a drug offense by defining types of illegal substances and type of violations; by stating the consequences for

HEALTH HIGHLIGHT
Symptoms of Possible Substance Abuse

- Sudden or gradual changes in grades
- Absence from classes
- School suspensions
- Withdrawal from family and other social functions
- Breaking curfew or lying
- Playing one authority figure against another
- An increase in arguments with others
- A persistent and nagging cough
- Weight loss
- Difficulty sleeping
- Vagueness about new friends and what they do together
- Associating with an older crowd

Source: "Is Your Child Using Drugs?" by Harold T. Hunton, Nov. 1991, *Alternatives*. Rockville, MD: Institute for Human Resources.

violating the policies; by describing procedures for handling violations; by enlisting legal counsel to ensure that the policy is drafted in compliance with applicable laws; and by building community support for the policy.

3. Enforce established policies against drug use fairly and consistently. Also, implement security measures to eliminate drugs on school premises and at school functions. The enforcement practices should be reviewed regularly to ensure that penalties are uniformly and fairly applied. (pp. 19–23)

The National Commission on Drug-Free Schools (1990) adds to this list of recommendations in its objectives for attaining drug-free schools: Schools should:

1. Develop and evaluate all drug abuse education and prevention programs.
2. Develop standard operating procedures for selecting and using drug education programs, activities, and materials, concentrating on what research has shown to reduce drug use.
3. Establish firm, no-use policies with appropriate sanctions.
4. Work with local law enforcement officials to ensure that laws on drugs, including alcohol and tobacco, are enforced fairly and consistently throughout the community.
5. Reward students who participate in programs and activities that promote being alcohol and drug-free.
6. Identify students most at risk of drug use, and develop prevention programs for them.
7. Help develop a broad-based community task force to address the community's problems with alcohol, tobacco, and other drugs. (pp. xii–xiii)

A drug education program is not an easy undertaking. For every strategy proposed, critics have raised good and plausible arguments as to why that strategy is the worst one possible. Some people—including many parents—think the best approach is no approach at all; if adults don't mention drugs, they reason, then the problem doesn't really exist. This view seems out of touch with reality, and yet it is understandable considering how so many drug education programs have led to unfortunate results.

The use of scare tactics in any health education program, including drug abuse education programs, is counterproductive. Adolescents soon learn to recognize the difference between fact and possible fiction. Attempts to equate the dangers of marijuana with those of heroin, suggestions that any drug can kill or permanently impair an individual, and other dire warnings, no matter how true, are often disregarded as propaganda.

Teachers must never lie about the dangers of drugs nor play down the problems that may make drugs seem to be an appealing way to cope. Effective drug education walks a fine line, one that requires teachers' sensitivity to the environment in which students must live and function. Teachers must point out that, no matter what the circumstances, each individual has a choice about substance use or abuse. Drug education must be a part of a comprehensive mental health education program. Only when students realize that drugs are not the answer to a problem, but part of the problem, can instruction be considered successful.

■ ■ ■   *STUDENT CONCERNS:* SUBSTANCE ABUSE

As students move through grades 7 through 12 many issues of concern surface in the substance abuse area. The statements reflected under the various grades below were taken from *Students Speak—A Survey of Health Interests and Concerns: Kindergarten Through Twelfth Grade.* Typical student responses were as follows:

Grade 7

How do drugs affect your health?
What do you do if a friend asks you to take drugs?
Why do people change if they get hooked on certain drugs, like heroin?
How many kinds of drugs are there that aren't like aspirin?
I would like to know the history of drugs.
How do they prove what drugs do to you?
How do drugs affect an unborn baby and why?
What do you do when your best friend asks you to have some pot?
What are drugs made of and what are their effects?
Why do people use drugs?
Why is getting high so bad?
I would like to know more about drug addiction.
Teach more about hard drugs—and I mean the truth, because every kid by the ninth
    grade has been offered dope and stuff. Don't treat us like we don't know anything!
I want to know what to say to friends when they ask if you take drugs or drink.
Why do some people get a "high" feeling from drugs while others have no effect?
Why do kids turn to drugs when something is going wrong?

Grade 8

What are the effects of drugs such as marijuana and cocaine after you take them?
    Does it stay with you?
Why are drugs habit forming?
How addictive are drugs?
I think if people knew what kind of stuff they were getting into when they take
    drugs, they might be less inclined to do these things.
What do you do if your friend is on drugs?
I would like to know more about common drugs like caffeine and how they affect
    you and how not to get addicted.
How do aspirin and other kinds of drugs affect our body?
What effect do drugs have on the heart and brain?
How do drugs affect your mind?
How will smoking pot affect you over a long period of time?
Why do people who are under pressure use drugs?
How do you handle someone who is stoned or high?
How do drugs, both abused and not abused, affect your body while being taken?
    What about after-effects, long-range effects, and the effect they can have on
    your children?
How do you handle yourself under drugs? Can you take any safely?

Grade 9

Can drugs have any effect on heredity?

What part of the body does each kind of drug affect?

Why do people abuse drugs?

I think you should know when and how to take medicines and to include what is in each type of medicine.

What is involved in the rehabilitation of drug victims?

What are the regulations on drugs?

Why do some people force other people into drugs?

How do drugs affect the mind?

How come some drugs make people act one way and the same drug makes a different person act another way?

How do marijuana and speed affect the baby in the female and the sperm in the male?

How do drugs overcome a person's will and cause someone to get hooked?

What, if any, are the permanent effects of drugs on the body?

What drugs affect an unborn child?

What effect does too much aspirin have on the human brain?

What influences people to use drugs?

What kinds of nonprescription medicines would suit your body best?

Grade 10

How do you say no to unwanted drugs?

How can drugs affect your everyday capabilities?

How do drugs affect your life?

Why do people use drugs?

I would like to know more about the use of medicine. What can it do to your body?

What kinds of things are we running from when we use drugs?

SUMMARY

A drug is any substance that alters bodily functions. Drugs can be used or abused. Reasons for substance abuse include low self-esteem, peer pressure, adult modeling, mood alteration, boredom, curiosity, and alienation.

Drugs act on the body by stimulating or depressing cellular activity. Even when drugs are prescribed for medical purposes, substance abuse can result.

Over-the-counter drugs are usually safe when taken as directed, but ingestion of any drug, no matter how mild, can cause health hazards. Advertisements for OTC drugs often lead people to believe that they are safer and more effective than the compounds actually are. Particularly dangerous drugs include barbiturates and amphetamines, known commonly as "downers" and "uppers." Barbiturates are depressants, and amphetamines are stimulants. Both, if abused, can cause serious health problems or death.

One of the most dangerous stimulants in our society is cocaine. Crack (or rock) cocaine is cheap and readily available. Crack is smoked and the bloodstream absorbs it in less than 10 seconds. Most crack-related deaths result from brain hemorrhage, blocking of the heart's electrical system, lung failure, or associated heart and vessel complications.

Narcotics are in some ways much more dangerous than barbiturates. This class of drugs includes opium, morphine, and heroin. Heroin is extremely addictive. Use of such drugs can lead to psychological breakdowns and irrational acts. As with any street drug, the user can never be sure of just what a dose contains. Hallucinogens include such drugs as LSD and PCP. Although not physically addictive, such drugs also can cause psychological breakdowns and irrational acts.

Marijuana, for various reasons, is in a class by itself. Although not extremely dangerous, its use can lead to personal and social harm. The stronger derivatives of the cannabis plant, including hashish and hashish oil, are more potent and can lead to even greater harm. Ongoing research is determining the medicinal effects of marijuana.

Substance education is a difficult topic, with no easy clue to the correct course. Teachers must provide factual information, but they must avoid making substance education a primer on how to take drugs. Effective drug abuse education programs are needed to change not only knowledge and attitudes, but behavior as well. The U. S. Department of Education and the National Commission on Drug-Free Schools list several recommendations to help schools fight the war against drugs for their students and school personnel. Community mores and lifestyles must be considered so that information and advice given are realistic and practical. The best course is to build self-esteem in students so that they will not regard drugs as a viable alternative for coping with personal problems. A person with high self-esteem will not be as vulnerable to the pressure to abuse drugs.

DISCUSSION QUESTIONS

1. What is the definition of a drug? Give examples of substances that qualify as drugs under this definition.
2. List six common reasons for substance abuse, especially the reasons that apply to young people.
3. What factors contribute to the misuse and abuse of over-the-counter drugs?
4. Discuss the drug cocaine and its various forms.
5. Why is marijuana considered to be a harmful substance? How can it effectively be used medicinally?
6. What approach to substance education is the most effective and why?
7. What policies should schools employ to reduce the drug abuse problem on their campuses?

■ ■ ■ *ACTIVITIES FOR TEACHING SUBSTANCE USE AND ABUSE*

Check It Out! (Surveying Non-Prescription Drugs)*

Concept/Description. It is important to read and abide by the information given on over-the-counter (OTC) or non-prescription drugs to avoid possible injury or illness.

Objective. To make students aware of the information found on OTC drug labels and containers.

*From the book *How to Survive Teaching Health,* by Kenneth G. Tillman, Ph.D., and Patricia Rizzo Toner, M.Ed., © 1990, West Nyack, NY: Parker.

Materials

Clean, empty bottles or boxes from typical non-prescription (OTC) medications, such as pain relievers, cold remedies, nasal sprays, etc.
Non-prescription drug survey questions
Pens or pencils

Directions

1. Place the non-prescription containers at various locations around the room.
2. Write survey questions on the board, or distribute a survey sheet.
3. Ask students to answer the questions based on the information they gained by carefully reading the labels. NOTE: The questions will vary according to the type of containers you have.

A Day in the Life (Describing an Abuser)*

Concept/Description. Drug and alcohol abuse occurs in all age groups, professions, ethnic backgrounds, income levels, and in both sexes.

Objective. To have students describe their perception of a day in the life of an alcoholic or drug addict and to help them to see that alcohol and drugs affect all walks of life.

Materials

Paper
Pens and pencils

Directions

1. Have students write a few paragraphs about a typical day in the life of a drug or alcohol addict. Describe the person and how they looked, dressed, acted, etc.
2. Ask students to volunteer to read their descriptions.
3. From the papers, determine if students believe the average abuser to be a skidrow alcoholic or drug addict. Did anyone describe the user as a woman? Did anyone mention a professional, such as a business person, doctor, teacher, police officer, etc.?
4. Discuss how alcohol and drug addiction affects all ages, professions, ethnic backgrounds, income levels, and both sexes.

Variation. For extra credit, have students ask three adults to describe a drug addict or alcoholic and jot down their responses. Discuss how adults perceive the typical abuser. What could influence their perceptions? (Knowing a relative who has a drug or alcohol problem, previous courses on alcohol or drugs, etc.)

My Attitudes**

1. What do you think of when you hear the word "drunk?"
2. What do you think of when you hear the word "stoned" or "high?"

**"My Attitudes" and "Playing it Safe" (on p. 175) adapted from *Substance Abuse Prevention Activities for Secondary Students* by P. Gerne and T. Gerne, 1991, Englewood Cliffs, NJ: Prentice-Hall.

3. What do you think of when you hear the word "addict?"
4. What do you think of when you hear the word "alcoholic?"
5. What do you think of when you hear the word "junkie?"
6. How would you feel if your parents found you drinking a beer?
7. How would you feel if your parents found you smoking marijuana?
8. What would you do if someone in your family had a drinking problem?

Playing it Safe**

Complete the following stories on a separate sheet of paper.

1. Your friend has just gotten his driver's license. He wants to take you for a drive around the neighborhood. You jump at the chance! He stops off at a friend's house. Your driver decides to drink a few beers with his friend. After they finish a six-pack, he wants you to get back into the car so he can take you home. You don't drive. No one is at your house. You. . . .
2. Mrs. Potter is a single parent who has to work. She sends her 3-year-old son Chris to a day care center. You work as a teacher's aide after school. You notice that the neighbor who picks up Chris on her way home has the smell of liquor on her breath today, and she seems unsteady on her feet. You. . . .
3. Mary has had too much to drink. Her friend wants to help her to "sober up" before she drives home, so she gives her a cup of coffee. Mary gets her coat to leave for her car. You. . . .
4. Your older brother shouts out to your mother, who is working in the kitchen, "I'm taking the keys to the car. I need to pick up something at the store. I'll be right back." You notice he looks "high." You. . . .
5. You are being picked up for a date by someone you really like and want to impress. When he comes, he seems a little slow to respond to your questions and the whites of his eyes appear red. He is driving a new red convertible. He hands you a long-stemmed red rose. You. . . .

■ ■ ■   *ACTIVITIES:* LEARNING ENHANCEMENTS

The following films and videotapes offer additional instruction in substance abuse. Unless otherwise specified, these materials may be acquired by contacting:

Films for the Humanities and Sciences
  800/257-5126

The Addicted Brain. This documentary takes viewers on a tour of the world's most prolific manufacturer and user of drugs—the human brain. The biochemistry of the brain is responsible for joggers' highs, for the compulsion of some people to seek thrills, for certain kinds of obsessive-compulsive behavior, even for the drive to achieve power and dominance. This program explores the cutting edge of developments in the biochemistry of addiction and addictive behavior. 26 minutes, color.

The Power of Addiction. The program covers both chemical and behavioral addiction, describes the signs of compulsive behavior, and analyzes such possible causes of addictive behavior as neurotransmitter imbalance and genetic and environmental factors. It also examines the physiological and psychological mechanisms of cocaine addiction and recovery from it. 19 minutes, color.

Addiction Caused by Mixing Medicines. Nonaddictive prescription drugs can and often do lead to addiction, and one of the primary dangers of mixing prescription drugs—individually prescribed for specific purposes—is the addictive effect. In this program, an addictionologist and a clinical pharmacist explain how mixing medicines can lead to problems, which groupings of drugs are likely to cause problems, and how dangers can be minimized. 19 minutes, color.

Drug and Alcohol Rehabilitation. This program focuses on the treatments in use to overcome chemical dependency. The program also covers two controversial therapies currently in use: aversion therapy for alcoholism and methadone treatment for drug addiction. Viewers learn what the addict must do to avoid relapse. 19 minutes, color.

Drug Prevention. Who will run things if an entire generation of adults is permanently out to lunch? The problem of who will be the role models is addressed in this program. Joining Phil Donahue are Susan Newman of the Scott Newman Center and Sue B. Rusche of Families in Action. 28 minutes, color.

Teen Addiction. A profile of a high school student recovered from addiction to drugs and alcohol. He discusses the factors that led to his addiction. His parents talk about the effect their son's problems had on their family life and what compelled them to force their son into treatment. A specialist in adolescent medicine offers insight into how parents and siblings may act as enablers. 19 minutes, color.

Kids and Drugs. This program presents the stories of five teenagers and their battles with drug and alcohol abuse. It also provides insight from experts and explores parental denial, children's denial, warning signs, and the stress that addiction causes the family. 28 minutes, color.

Why People Take Drugs. This program covers some of the basics of drug use and abuse: the definition of drugs, factors that influence people's opinions about drugs, and the problem of drug abuse. Parodies of game shows, soap operas, and other popular TV formats deliver the message. 15 minutes, color.

Caffeine, Nicotine, and Prescription Drugs: The "Invisible" Drugs. Caffeine, nicotine, and prescription drugs affect us greatly and can be dangerous (and sometimes lethal). A takeoff on a shopping network covers the dangers of tobacco, and private investigators on a soap opera parody get closer to the truth about our problem character, a would-be teenage junkie. 15 minutes, color.

The Risks of Illegal Drug Use. The facts about illegal drugs, their inherent dangers, and the risks involved in their use are the focus of this program. "Pay the

Price" has students answer questions on drugs. And our soap opera heroine is in danger of following in her mother's footsteps toward alcoholism. 15 minutes, color.

Speak Up, Speak Out: Learning to Say NO to Drugs. This video gives teens specific techniques to resist peer pressure. A teen is asked to host a party where there will be drugs and alcohol. He has to learn to use his own best judgment in handling the situation. Includes a teacher's guide and catalog cards. 15 minutes. ETR Assoc., 800/321-4407.

Coping with Peer Pressure. Viewers learn to cope with peer pressure by looking ahead to the consequences of their actions and being honest with themselves. Private investigators help a girl whose low self-esteem nearly led her astray to find herself, and some soul-searching has beneficial results. 15 minutes, color.

Cocaine: The End of the Line. The program explains the origin of cocaine, how it works, and how cocaine use is dangerous; shows how cocaine kills and injures otherwise healthy young people; defines the typical coke user; explains why cocaine is so addictive and why addiction is so difficult to overcome; and provides a quiz on some of the myths about cocaine. 58 minutes, color.

Icy Death. Hosted by Colin Quinn, this video explores the dangers of this highly addictive and dangerous substance. What is ice? Where did it come from? Why is it so deadly, and how can we avoid it? This 26-minute video answers these questions and gives children and adults a real-life look at the frightening consequences of drug abuse. It comes with a leader's guide, fact sheets, and quiz. Health Edco, 800/299-3366 Ext. 295.

Marijuana Use and Its Effects. This program discusses the use of marijuana and its effects on the nervous, respiratory and reproductive systems. Updated visuals on all versions, and music under soundtrack on the slide and VHS versions highlights the presentation. Health Edco, 800/299-3366 Ext. 295.

Me, Myself, and Drugs. This video gives students in middle school an understanding of the cultural pressures and consequences of drug use. Students examine: messages we get to use drugs by adults, commercials, how drugs work within the body, and ways to deal with peer pressure. 35 minutes. ETR Assoc., 800/321-4407.

REFERENCES

Akers, Ronald L. (1992). *Drugs, alcohol, and society: Social structure, process, and policy.* Belmont, CA: Wadsworth.

Carroll, C. R. (1989). *Drugs in modern society* (2nd ed.). Dubuque, IA: Wm. C. Brown.

Girdano, D., & Dusek, D. (1988). *Drug education: Content and methods* (4th ed.). New York: Random House.

Hunton, H. T. (1991). Is your child using drugs? *Alternatives, 1.*

Gerne, P., & Gerne, T. (1991). *Substance abuse prevention activities for secondary students.* Englewood Cliffs, NJ: Prentice Hall.

National Commission on Drug-Free Schools (1990). *Toward a drug-free generation: A nation's responsibility.* Washington, DC: Author.

National Drug Policy Board. (1988). *Progress report 1987*. Washington, DC: U.S. Government Printing Office.

Papenfuss, R. L. (1989). *A teacher's guide for your choice . . . our chance*. Bloomington, IN: Agency for Instructional Technology.

Payne, W., Hahn, D., & Pinger, R. (1991). *Drugs: Issues for today*. St. Louis: Mosby.

Ray, O., & Ksir, Charles. (1987). *Drugs, society, and human behavior* (4th ed.). St. Louis: Mosby.

Trucano, L. (1984). *Students speak—A survey of health interests and concerns: Kindergarten through twelfth grade*. Seattle: Comprehensive Health Education Foundation.

U.S. Department of Education. (1987). *What works: Schools without drugs*. Washington, DC: U.S. Government Printing Office.

U.S. Department of Health and Human Services. (1989). *The national adolescent student health survey: A report on the health of America's youth*. Oakland, CA: Third Party Publishing.

U.S. Department of Justice (Office of Justice Programs). (1987). *Report on drug control: Implementation of the Anti-Drug Abuse Act of 1986*. Washington, DC: Author.

Witters, W., Venturelli, P., & Hanson, G. (1992). *Drugs and society* (3rd ed.). Boston: Jones & Bartlett.

CHAPTER 8

Alcohol and Tobacco

The abuse of alcohol [and tobacco] and the use of illegal drugs have ravaged families, and have infiltrated our streets, neighborhoods, and schoolyards. The American public has finally said, "We've had enough," and is joining forces against [alcohol and tobacco] use.
U.S. Center for Substance Abuse Prevention

OBJECTIVES
After reading this chapter, you should be able to

- Describe the alcohol and tobacco abuse problem among adolescents
- Detail why adolescents begin to use alcohol and tobacco
- Explain how adults can influence alcohol use among adolescents
- Describe how tobacco advertising influences adolescents to use tobacco products
- Describe the various effects of alcohol and tobacco on the body
- Explain the relationship between alcohol and accidents among adolescents
- Describe the four basic stages of alcohol addiction
- List recommendations for schools to reduce alcohol and tobacco abuse problems among their students

Alcohol and tobacco use by adolescents continues to be a problem, despite declining levels of use and increased awareness of the dangers of these substances. According to the American Medical Association (1990), 28% of eighth graders and 38% of tenth graders report occasions of heavy drinking. Further, alcohol use among young people appears to stimulate progression to other drug use. Alcohol and tobacco use among adolescents is correlated with other problems, including suicide, homicide, school dropout, delinquency, early sexual activity, sexually transmitted diseases, problem pregnancy, and motor vehicle crashes. Alcohol-related traffic crashes are the leading cause of death and spinal cord injury for young Americans. Nearly 7% of boys aged 12 through 17 had used some form of smokeless tobacco within the last month. Young people, especially teenage girls, are taking up smoking at younger ages. Initiation of smoking behavior now occurs almost entirely during adolescence. Young adults are unlikely to develop alcohol and tobacco problems if they do not start using these substances during childhood and adolescence.

Many teachers say that alcohol and tobacco use is at least a moderate problem in their schools, according to a report published by the National Center for Education Statistics (Appalachian Educational Laboratory, 1992). In a survey of 1,350 elementary and secondary school teachers nationwide, 54% of secondary teachers reported that alcohol and tobacco use is a concern. Many added that prevention programs and policies for reducing alcohol and tobacco use have little or no effect.

ALCOHOL

Ethyl alcohol is the active ingredient in beer, wine, and distilled beverages such as whiskey. Ethyl alcohol is not as toxic as are some other forms of the chemical, such as methyl alcohol, which is used as rubbing alcohol. In this discussion, we use the term **alcohol** to refer to ethyl alcohol.

Alcohol is a colorless, flammable liquid formed by the fermentation of fruits, juices, or cereal grains. Alcoholic beverages contain varying amounts of alcohol, depending on the type of beverage. Beer usually contains from 5% to 7% alcohol. Wines may vary from 11% to 20%. Distilled beverages have the highest alcohol content. This content is reflected in the *proof* of the beverage, a number that is twice the alcohol content. For example, 100 proof whiskey contains 50% alcohol, whereas 90 proof contains 45%.

Effects of Alcohol

Alcohol is a central nervous system depressant. In small doses, the substance has a mellowing or tranquilizing effect. The individual may feel relaxed and free from tension. As a result, behavior may become less inhibited, leading to the misconception held by some that alcohol is a stimulant. Actually, what appears to be stimulated, or at least animated, behavior results from the anesthetic, depressant effect that alcohol has on the cerebral cortex area of the brain.

The effects of alcohol upon the body correspond with the amount of alcohol in the system. The amount of alcohol can be measured. In large amounts, alcohol impairs brain activity, muscular control, coordination, memory, reaction time, and judgment. Heavy intake over a short period can dull the senses. Continued heavy drinking can result in coma and death. Table 8.1 summarizes the effects of alcohol by percentage in the bloodstream.

Long-term consumption of alcohol can damage the brain and liver. The brain may be damaged to the extent that memory, judgment, and learning deteriorate. Alcohol-caused damage may result in cirrhosis of the liver, a potentially fatal condition. Cirrhosis occurs rarely in nonalcoholic drinkers. Recent research has shown the harmful effects of even moderate amounts of alcohol consumed by

Table 8.1   Effects of Alcohol on the Body

Percentage in bloodstream	Effects
0.05	Careless behavior; some loss of self-control; some loss of judgment
0.10	Poor judgment; greater loss of self-control; serious loss of coordination
0.20	Very drunk; slurred speech; staggers when walking
0.40	Unconsciousness; passes out
0.70	Death occurs

Source: *Teaching Today's Health* (p. 370) by David Anspaugh and Gene Ezell, 1990, New York: Merrill/Macmillan.

pregnant women. The alcohol can have a deleterious effect on the developing fetus, resulting in a condition known as fetal alcohol syndrome. A child born with this condition may suffer permanent impairment. Characteristics of the condition include low birth weight, smaller head circumference, abnormal formation of the nose, small fingernails, smaller stature, poor joint movement, ear abnormalities, and mental retardation.

In moderation, alcohol does not seem to harm the body permanently; however, an adult who decides to partake of alcoholic beverages should exercise care. Alcohol should be consumed slowly, with adequate food in the stomach. Imbibers should also recognize that tolerance to alcohol builds up so that they require more of the substance to produce the pleasant, mellow effect. Drinking without recognizing the potential dangers of alcohol can lead to tragedy.

Who Drinks?

As mentioned earlier in this chapter, American Medical Association research (1990) shows that 28% of eighth graders and 38% of tenth graders report occasions of heavy drinking.

According to a survey by the Center for Substance Abuse Prevention (1989), most 1987 high school seniors (92%) had at least tried alcohol before graduation, and 66% reported having used alcohol at least once during the 30 days before being questioned. Boys and girls reported similar lifetime and annual rates of alcohol use, although daily alcohol use among senior boys was almost 2.5 times that of senior girls. Seniors not planning to attend college were twice as likely to drink daily as seniors with college plans. Seniors in the southern and western regions of the country were somewhat less likely to use alcohol than seniors in the northeastern and north central regions. High school dropouts had overall higher rates of alcohol and other drug use. (See Table 8.2.)

Two-thirds of all U.S. adults consume alcoholic beverages. Various surveys of college students indicate that more than 90% drink alcohol. Twelve percent of adults are currently classified as heavy drinkers (many of whom would be considered alcoholics).

Of those who drink, 70% consume only 20% of the alcohol sold. The other 30% of the drinking public consumes the other 80% of the alcohol sold. Just 10% of the drinkers consume roughly half of all the alcohol sold in the United States (Payne, Hahn, & Pinger, 1991, 143–144).

Altogether, approximately 75% of all men and 60% of all women are drinkers. Although women choose to drink less overall than men, the percentage of those who do drink is increasing, especially among women under 35. The primary age for drinking is between the ages of 21 and 34. Older people choose to drink the least. Over the age of 65, only 7% of men and 2% of women are heavy drinkers. At any age, men are two to five times more likely to be heavy drinkers than women.

Why Do People Begin Drinking?

As discussed in Chapter 7, young people begin abusing drugs, including alcohol and tobacco, for the following reasons:

Table 8.2 Trends in Alcohol Behaviors and Perceptions Among High School Seniors, United States, 1975 to 1987

	Percent Saying 'Great Risk' If . . .				Percent Saying 'Most or All' of Best Friends . . .	
	Try 1 or 2 alcoholic drinks	Take 1 or 2 drinks nearly every day	Take 4 or 5 drinks nearly every day	Take 5 or more drinks once, twice weekend	Drink alcohol	Get drunk at least once a week
1975	5.3	21.5	63.5	37.8	68.4	30.1
1976	4.8	21.2	61.0	37.0	64.7	26.6
1977	4.1	18.5	62.9	34.7	66.2	27.6
1978	3.4	19.6	63.1	34.5	68.9	30.2
1979	4.1	22.6	66.2	34.9	68.5	32.0
1980	3.8	20.3	65.7	35.9	68.9	30.1
1981	4.6	21.6	64.5	36.3	67.7	29.4
1982	3.5	21.6	65.5	36.0	69.7	29.9
1083	4.2	21.6	66.8	38.6	69.0	31.0
1984	4.6	23.0	68.4	41.7	66.6	29.6
1985	5.0	24.4	69.8	43.0	66.0	29.9
1986	4.6	25.1	66.5	39.1	68.0	31.8
1987	6.2	26.2	69.7	41.9	71.8	31.3

Source: *Drug-Free Communities: Turning Awareness Into Action* (p. 20) by Center for Substance Abuse Prevention, 1989, Washington, DC: U.S. Department of Health and Human Services.

Curiosity
Spiritual search
Low self-esteem
Peer pressure
Adult modeling
Mood alteration
Boredom
Alienation

Adolescence is a transition between childhood and adulthood, with confusing, uncomfortable changes occurring physically and emotionally. Early adolescence is a time of particular vulnerability, when children seem to try to loosen family constraints and are compelled to find their places within other social groups. Alcohol use is sometimes perceived as a vehicle to that place and to the comforts that group acceptance brings.

Adolescents are naturally curious—exploring new ideas, behaviors, and relationships. They feel the need to take risks, to exercise their judgment and their independence. In the process, some become users of alcohol and other drugs. Schools, families, and friends need to support them in channeling their curiosity away from using alcohol. Adults, who have a direct impact on the alcohol-using behavior of young people, are unaware of how their own behavior influences kids. Ways in which adults may unknowingly contribute to adolescent alcohol use include

- School officials who do not believe that a drug and alcohol problem exists in their schools
- Salespeople in convenience stores and bartenders who sell and serve without checking identification
- Judges who allow alcohol-impaired drivers off the hook, sometimes even for repeat offenses
- Parents who do not want to appear hypocritical because they too used drugs years ago (Center for Substance Abuse Prevention, 1989)

Consequences of Alcohol Use

Alcohol can interfere with an adolescent's motivation to do well in school, become involved in useful activities, or form healthy relationships—ones that do not revolve around alcohol and other drug use. As a result, alcohol compromises intellectual growth, social skills, and self-confidence. Study results (Office of Substance Abuse Prevention, 1989) show that most young people who consistently use alcohol lack social and peer resistance skills and have less than optimal bonds with their families, schools, and communities. They often want desperately to belong, even to the extent of doing things that go against their better judgment.

Because alcohol can reduce inhibitions, young people who use alcohol are more likely to become involved in risk-taking behavior. For instance, they may engage in sexual relations because their judgment is altered. Participation in behaviors such as intravenous drug use or unsafe sex will put a young person at risk for contracting AIDS.

Over the past 30 years, life expectancy has increased for every age group in the United States except young people (under 18) and young adults (18 to 25 years old). Three-fourths of all the deaths among this age group are attributed to injuries, suicides, and homicides, and a large proportion of these are related to risky lifestyles that include alcohol.

Drinking and Accidents

Alcohol remains the primary cause of automobile accidents among young drivers. Alcohol is involved in 50% or more of all fatal traffic accidents. Without question, drinking and driving don't mix. Nearly 8,000 teenagers are killed each year in accidents involving alcohol. It is estimated that another 40,000 teenagers are disfigured each year in accidents involving alcohol. Alcohol can magnify the accident risk for young, relatively inexperienced drivers. Also, young people are especially at risk from alcohol-related accidents because of their low tolerance to the substance.

Two of the many groups that are making people aware of the problem are Mothers Against Drunk Driving (MADD) and Students Against Drunk Driving (SADD). MADD also mobilizes the public to help individuals modify their drinking habits and protests the judicial system when someone with a history of driving drunk is allowed to continue driving. MADD has been successful in reducing the legal blood-alcohol content (BAC) in various states and has initiated several effective programs to limit drinking and driving. SADD started as a school health education program in Wayland High School near Boston. This organization helps students save their own lives and the lives of others, educates students on the problem of drinking and driving, develops peer counseling among students about alcohol use, and increases public awareness and prevention of alcohol abuse everywhere. An important feature of the SADD program is a teenager-parent contract whereby the teenager agrees to call the parent for advice and/or transportation at any time from any place if the teenager or his driver has had too much to drink. The parent in return agrees to transport the teenager in such a situation, and also agrees to seek sober transportation for himself in a similar situation (Schlaadt & Shannon, 1990).

Alcoholism and Alcohol-Related Problems

The area for greatest concern regarding alcohol may be the potential for alcoholism among young people. According to the National Council on Alcoholism, alcoholism is the number-one drug problem among the nation's youth. Forty percent of children have tasted alcohol by age 10. The average age for taking a first drink is just under 13. Nearly 30% of teenagers have experienced negative results from abuse of alcohol, ranging from auto accidents to arrests to detrimental effects on schoolwork and other results mentioned earlier in this chapter. Ironically, 42% of fourth-graders failed to recognize alcohol as a drug. Only 72% of children in the upper grades realize it is a drug, and, therefore, dangerous.

Definitions of the term alcoholism vary from source to source. The World Health Organization defines alcohol dependence as a psychic and/or physical state charac- terized by a compulsion to take alcohol to experience its psychic effects and sometimes to avoid its absence (Witters, Venturelli, & Hanson, 1990). Alcoholics use the substance in such a way that it disrupts their personal, social, and occupational behavior, either partially or totally. Anyone—rich or poor, young or old—is suscep- tible. As many as 10 million Americans have a serious drinking problem.

Alcoholism is considered a disease. Research has not completely explained the causes of alcoholism, but genetic predisposition is one possible cause of alcoholism. Research involving identical twins born to alcoholics, some of whom were adopted by other families at birth and raised without knowledge of their biological parents' problems, illustrates the presence of some inherited traits. Recent studies also suggest that genetically predisposed persons show less intense responses to low doses of alcohol than normal subjects. Therefore, they may be less able to estimate their level of intoxication when drinking. This could make it more difficult for them to know when to stop drinking. New technology is now enabling researchers to identify which genes predispose an individual to alcoholism (Payne et al., 1991).

Regardless of heredity's influence, social and psychological factors also influence the development of alcoholism. Because alcohol use is generally accepted in our society, many individuals feel free to indulge. Too often, however, use leads to misuse and alcoholism. The drug becomes a crutch for dealing with everyday problems until the individual can no longer get along without it.

Alcohol-related problems are all too familiar in our society. Aside from the thousands of traffic deaths and injuries that alcohol abuse causes each year, alcohol also contributes to the high divorce rate, job absenteeism, crimes of violence, suicide, and social disorder.

Figure 8.1 outlines the path of chemical dependency in adolescents.

Treatment of Alcoholism

Alcoholism, like many other diseases, can be treated successfully. Because physical withdrawal from alcohol can be fatal, attempts to terminate alcohol use in alcoholics should be done only under medical supervision. There are three phases to any program that seeks to help the individual withdraw from the drug. Identification, the first phase, involves helping the person understand he is dependent and needs help. The second phase is treatment. This involves helping the alcoholic work through personal problems, build greater self-esteem, learn more effective methods for coping with life, and stop destructive drinking. The third phase is aftercare. This involves helping the alcoholic stay sober. Alcoholics can never return to even social drinking, or they will fall back into their devastating former lifestyle.

Alcoholics and their families can receive help from many sources, including such nonprofit groups as Alcoholics Anonymous (AA). AA is a support group of fellow

Figure 8.1   Four basic stages of alcohol and other drug use

Stage 1

Too many youngsters and adults believe that the first use of alcohol and other drugs is safe. For youths, using drugs such as tobacco and alcohol is often, unfortunately, viewed as normal. However, because young bodies are particularly susceptible to alcohol and other drugs and their effects, there is no such thing as totally "safe" use of any mind-altering drug by a youngster. In stage one, however, there may be no outward behavioral changes caused by the use of drugs.

Stage 2

The second stage involves more frequent use of alcohol or other drugs as the person actively seeks the euphoric effects of a mind-altering drug. At this point, the user usually establishes a reliable source, and may add mid-week use of alcohol or other drugs to previous habits of weekend use at parties. Among adolescents, significant clues now include changes in friends, deterioration of school performance, and possibly a general lack of motivation.

Stage 3

In stage three, there is intense preoccupation with the desire to experience euphoric effects. Daily use of mind-altering drugs, depression, and thoughts of suicide are common. Family troubles increase and the adolescent may be having problems with the law.

Stage 4

In the fourth stage, increasing levels are needed just to feel OK. Physical signs such as coughing, frequent sore throats, weight loss, and fatigue—which may have begun to appear earlier—are now common. Blackouts and overdosing also are more common, family life is a disaster, and crime may be becoming a way of life to obtain money to buy drugs.

alcoholics designed so that members help each other remain sober. The key to AA is for members to admit that they have lost control over their drinking behavior. As part of the spiritual basis of this program, members turn their life over to a higher power for help in managing. Many commercial alcoholic treatment programs also are available. These can be expensive, but many health insurance companies now pay for such treatment.

Al-Anon, Alateen, and Alatot are groups specifically established to assist the families of alcoholics. Al-Anon is a group for relatives and friends of alcoholics. Alateen and Alatot are groups designed for children of alcoholics. These groups are designed to help friends and relatives understand the alcoholic and thereby better cope with the alcoholic's lifestyle. These groups also help the individuals learn from each other (Witters et al., 1992). These groups also help family members understand the roles they play as codependents; that is, the behavior by family members may enable the alcoholic to continue his lifestyle. For example, if a spouse calls her alcoholic husband's employer and tells the employer that her husband will not be at work because he is sick, this action enables the alcoholic to continue his behavior.

Objectives for Reducing Alcohol-Related Problems

Among the alcohol-related objectives of the *Healthy Youth 2000 Initiative* (American Medical Association, 1990) are the following:

1. Reduce deaths among people aged 15 through 24 caused by alcohol-related motor vehicle crashes to no more than 18 per 100,000. In general, there is a need to improve surveillance of injuries caused by motor vehicle crashes.
2. Increase by at least 1 year the average age of first use of alcohol by adolescents aged 12 through 17. This objective is particularly important because the use of drugs at preteen ages appears to predict both greater involvement with alcohol and other drugs and less likelihood of recovery.
3. Reduce the proportion of young people who have used alcohol in the past month. Use of alcohol has been shown to jeopardize physical, mental, and social development during the formative years, and to endanger the successful transition from school to the workplace.
4. Increase the proportion of high school seniors who perceive social disapproval associated with the heavy use of alcohol, and increase the proportion of high school seniors who associate risk of physical or psychological harm with the heavy use of alcohol. Recently, investigators reported that the 10-year decline in marijuana use by high school seniors could be directly attributed to the dramatic increase in the perceived risk of psychological and physical harm and the increased perception of social disapproval associated with regular use of marijuana. In a comparable fashion, these two prevention factors may also be instrumental in the future prevention of alcohol use, particularly by adolescents. This initiative further states that schools should provide effective educational programs on alcohol and other drugs, preferably as a part of a quality school health education. (pp. 9–12)

TOBACCO

Tobacco has been used for hundreds of years. It can be snuffed, chewed, placed between the gum and lips, or smoked.

The most popular method of tobacco use is smoking. Cigarettes became popular in the early 1900s. Before then, tobacco was usually chewed or smoked in a pipe. Cigarettes were provided free to soldiers in both World Wars I and II, a practice that helped many soldiers start or strengthen an addiction to tobacco. Although the dangers of tobacco smoking are now much better understood, an estimated 42% of adult men and 31% of adult women still smoke.

Tobacco use is of special concern to the U.S. Department of Health and Human Services. According to this agency, smoking is directly responsible for about 390,000 deaths each year in the United States; thus, we can fairly blame smoking for more than one of every six deaths in our country.

The prevalence of smoking among adolescents increased steadily from the 1950s until the beginning of the 1970s. By that time the majority of those in the 12- to 17-year-old group had experimented with cigarettes. About half as many girls as boys then were regular smokers. The prevalence of smoking among boys stabilized at that point, but it continued upward among girls; by the end of the decade, their rate of smoking equaled that of the boys. Prevalence among both teenage boys and girls has declined since 1977. At the beginning of the 1980s, less than half of 12- to 17-year-olds had ever smoked. About 15% were regular (at least once weekly) smokers, 10% were daily smokers, and 3% smoked a pack of cigarettes or more a day; and only one in a hundred was classified as a heavy smoker (Akers, 1992).

The really disheartening news, however, is that some one million teens start smoking each year, and many go on to become addicted for life. In fact, about 90% of adult smokers began their addiction as children or adolescents, and these young smokers will account for many health problems in the future. The younger people are when they start to smoke, the more likely they are to become long-term smokers and to develop smoking-related diseases. Preventing youngsters from taking up smoking is far more cost-effective than treating the addiction later in life and far less expensive than treating the resulting diseases (Sullivan, 1990).

The National Adolescent School Health Survey (U.S. Department of Health & Human Services, 1989) identified the following facts regarding the perceptions and use of tobacco among adolescents:

1. About 6 out of every 10 students reported having tried cigarettes sometime in their lives.
2. More than 8 out of every 10 students believe that it would be easy for them to get cigarettes.
3. About half of the students believe there is a great risk associated with smoking one or more packs of cigarettes a day.
4. Approximately three-quarters of the students believe that their close friends would disapprove of them smoking one or more packs of cigarettes a day.
5. More boys (12%) than girls (1%) reported having used chewing tobacco or snuff during the past month. (pp. 73–75)

Daily cigarette smoking often starts in the seventh through ninth grades. Very few people begin to smoke after high school. Because cigarettes are so addictive, three-quarters of those who are daily smokers in high school are still smoking years later (Center for Substance Abuse Prevention, 1989). Further, most new users of smokeless tobacco products are adolescent males.

HEALTH HIGHLIGHT
Tobacco Use Among Adolescents

The National Adolescent Student Health Survey found that drugs remain a severe problem among young people. According to the survey:

- One of every 5 adolescents smoked cigarettes during the past month.
- 51% of eighth-grade students and 63% of tenth-grade students report having tried cigarettes.
- 16% of eighth-grade students and 26% of tenth-grade students report having smoked a cigarette in the past month.
- 12% of boys and 1% of girls report having chewed tobacco or used snuff during the past month.
- More than one-fourth of adolescents report one occasion of heavy drinking during the past 2 weeks.
- 77% of eighth-grade students and 89% of tenth-grade students report having tried an alcoholic beverage.
- 34% of eighth-grade students and 53% of tenth-grade students report having had an alcoholic beverage during the past month.
- 26% of eighth-grade students and 38% of tenth-grade students report having had five or more drinks on one occasion during the past 2 weeks.
- About 1 out of every 10 adolescents smoked marijuana in the past month.
- Nearly 15% of eighth-grade students and 35% of tenth-grade students report having tried marijuana.
- 6% of eighth-grade students and 15% of tenth-grade students report having used marijuana during the past month.
- About 1 out of every 15 adolescents has tried cocaine.
- 5% of eighth-grade students and 9% of tenth-grade students report having tried cocaine.
- 2% of eighth-grade students and 3% of tenth-grade students report having used cocaine during the past month.
- About 1 out of every 5 adolescents have tried sniffing glue.
- 20% of eighth-grade students and 21% of tenth-grade students report having tried sniffing glue.
- 7% of the eighth-grade students and 5% of the tenth-grade students reported having sniffed glue in the past month.

Source: Adapted from *The National Adolescent Student Health Survey—A Report on the Health of America's Youth,* a cooperative project of the U.S. Department of Health and Human Services, Office of Disease Prevention and Health Promotion, Centers for Disease Control, and National Institute on Drug Abuse, 1990, Oakland, CA: Third Party Publishing Company.

Effects of Tobacco Smoking

According to the U.S. Surgeon General's Office, cigarette smoking is the primary avoidable cause of death in our society and the most important health issue of our time. Cancer is the second leading cause of death in this country, and smoking accounts for nearly one-third of all cancer deaths. Prevention of smoking in young people is a critical goal, particularly in view of the limited success that many smokers have in quitting (U.S. Department of Health and Human Services, 1989).

About 90 percent of adult smokers began their addiction as children or adolescents.

The primary drug in tobacco is **nicotine**. A typical filtered cigarette contains between 1 and 2 mg of nicotine; the smoker absorbs about 90% of this amount when inhaling. Smoking constricts the blood vessels, decreasing the skin temperature. Nicotine acts as a stimulant on the heart and nervous system, increasing the heartbeat and blood pressure. In addition, smoking decreases the blood's ability to carry oxygen because of the carbon monoxide in tobacco smoke, which is more easily picked up by hemoglobin.

Cigarette smoke also contains chemicals known collectively as **tars**. These substances have been identified as carcinogens, or cancer-causing agents. Smoking is a major cause of lung cancer and may contribute to other forms of malignancies as well.

Besides running an increased risk of developing cancer, smokers also have much higher rates of coronary heart disease. Emphysema, a breathing disorder that results from deterioration of lung tissue, is also associated with cigarette smoking, as are many other respiratory diseases.

The relationship between smoking during pregnancy and the effects upon a developing fetus has been established. An estimated one-third of U.S. women of childbearing age are smokers. It is estimated further that only 5% to 10% of these women quit smoking during pregnancy. Girdano and Dusek (1988) summarized some of the most important findings related to smoking and pregnancy:

- Cigarette smoking during pregnancy causes a reduction in infant birth weight.
- Cigarette smoking is related to significantly higher fetal and neonatal mortality.
- Cigarette smoking is associated with an increase in spontaneous abortions. (pp. 204–205)

Both male and female cigarette smokers experience more lost days of work, days of bed disability, and long limitation of activity due to chronic diseases than do people who never smoked. In studies, current and former smokers also report more hospitalization than nonsmokers in the year prior to being interviewed. Even though most studies show a reduction in the risk of mortality among former smokers, data on disability and illness often show continued high risk among former smokers. All measures of smoking disability are dose-related; that is, the more smoking there is, the greater the likelihood of developing a disability (Carroll, 1989).

Although cigarette smokers run the highest risk, use of tobacco in other forms can also lead to serious problems. For example, pipe smoking is related to cancer of the lip. Both pipe and cigar smokers run a higher risk of developing cancer of the mouth, larynx, and esophagus. Snuff dippers, or people who use smokeless tobacco, have a higher incidence of cancer of the gums than do nonusers.

Why People Smoke

Individuals begin smoking for some of the same reasons that they start drinking. Adult modeling and peer pressure are certainly factors. The appeal of cigarette advertising also plays a part. According to Schlaadt and Shannon (1990), once a person has developed a smoking habit, one or more of the following reasons may apply:

- *Stimulation.* Smokers claim that smoking helps wake them up, organize their intellectual activity, and enhance their energy level.
- *Relaxation or tranquility.* Smokers say that smoking helps promote and enhance pleasant feelings. Smokers also believe that smoking reduces negative feelings.
- *Stress reduction.* Smokers use cigarettes in times of stress or personal discomfort. Smoking is seen as a tranquilizer, again helping to reduce negative feelings.
- *Physiological and/or psychological dependence.* The smoker is dependent on cigarettes; there is a psychological and possibly physical dependence on cigarettes.
- *Habit.* Smoking is done simply out of habit, although the smoker gets very little pleasure from smoking. The person may have minimal awareness of the act of smoking, sometimes lighting one cigarette while another one is still burning. (pp. 130–131)

A very forceful motivation for smoking is advertising. Cigarette manufacturers spend more than $3.2 billion each year promoting cigarettes and the acceptance of smoking. Cigarette advertising reveals very few facts about cigarettes, but rather appeals to individual needs, a memory of good feeling, the universal need for companionship, and a desire for escape and adventure. Cigarette ads also are designed to reduce one's anxieties about growing old, being alone, or losing one's health or sex appeal.

According to the Centers for Disease Control (1990), cigarette advertising and promotion may increase cigarette consumption among children and adolescents by encouraging them to experiment with and initiate regular use of cigarettes. Tobacco companies' promotional activities are also designed to encourage trial and purchase of tobacco products among younger people. Free samples may encourage initiation of tobacco use among children and adolescents, especially when samples are distributed at youth-oriented events, such as concerts. Tobacco company sponsorship of sporting events allows cigarette brand names to be shown or mentioned on television (even though cigarette commercials are prohibited in the broadcast media), and such sponsorship is reported to increase cigarette brand recognition among children.

The impact of such advertising on young potential smokers is substantial (Girdano & Dusek, 1988). A recent poll indicated that Joe Camel (a character used in Camel cigarette ads) was the most recognizable media cartoon character among young children, tying with Mickey Mouse. In response to this poll, the former U.S. Surgeon General called for Camel to remove Joe Camel from its ads. A U.S. senator commenting on the camel campaign pointed out that any company that marketed a product that killed off its clientele (e.g., tobacco) must advertise strongly to attract new customers (e.g., young people).

Advertising of tobacco products to females has been successful. By the mid-1990s, the percentage of women who smoke is expected to exceed that of men who smoke. The explanation is not only that more females than males have taken up the habit in the past decade but also that fewer females have quit. Advertising tobacco products to females benefits from the fact that smoking artificially and temporarily holds down body weight, and societal pressure for girls and women to be slender is intense. Weight control is one of the most important reasons girls start smoking and one of the biggest barriers preventing them from quitting. Since adolescents are very concerned about body image and since adolescent girls are prone to low self-esteem, they are particularly vulnerable to tobacco advertising (Mintz, 1991). The effects of the resulting tobacco use among females have been devastating. Lung cancer has overtaken breast cancer as the number one cause of cancer death among women, and lung cancer death rates among women continue to increase at an unrelenting pace. Other smoking-related diseases, such as heart disease and emphysema, also are exacting a terrible toll on women. For example, women who smoke are more than three times as likely to have a heart attack as women who have never smoked (Sullivan, 1990).

The youth market represents a significant share of all tobacco expenditures. U.S. children under 18 spent $1.26 billion for a billion packs of cigarettes and 26 million containers of smokeless tobacco. The profit for manufacturers was $221 million (Mintz, 1991).

Second-Hand and Sidestream Smoke

Although an individual may choose not to smoke, being in an enclosed area where others smoke forces him to smoke involuntarily. Sidestream smoke is the smoke that comes from a burning cigarette. Second-hand smoke is exhaled from the smoker. This smoke has much higher concentrations of some irritating and hazardous substances than mainstream, or inhaled, smoke. Carbon monoxide is especially significant with second-hand smoke. Several people smoking in an enclosed area can exceed the Environmental Protection Agency's safe limit recommendation. Furthermore, most standard air-filtration systems do not remove carbon monoxide gas from the air. Only dilution with fresh air can lower carbon monoxide levels.

Nicotine from sidestream smoke generally settles out of the air, with only small amounts being absorbed from heavily polluted air. Other carcinogens are absorbed in small amounts, but their carcinogenic effect is not known.

Other substances from sidestream smoke probably are not hazardous, just irritating to nonsmokers. Individuals with cardiovascular or broncho-pulmonary diseases can suffer. In addition, children of parents who smoke are more likely to have bronchitis, pneumonia, and reactive airway diseases, especially during the first year of life and as adolescents.

Reducing the Hazards of Smoking

The best way to avoid the hazards of smoking is simply not to smoke. This means not beginning in the first place or giving up the habit if smoking has already begun. Individuals who smoke should also recognize the possible harmful effects of second-hand smoke on others. Inhaling smoke produced by a smoker can aggravate respiratory conditions and may even be the cause of such conditions in a nonsmoker.

Those who refuse to stop smoking can reduce the effects of smoking by choosing cigarettes with less tar and nicotine, by smoking fewer cigarettes, by taking fewer puffs and not inhaling so deeply, and by not smoking the cigarette all the way down to the end.

Smokeless Tobacco

Advertising claims have made smokeless tobacco seem to be a safe alternative to smoking tobacco. Evidently, this effort has been successful, because smokeless tobacco is the only type of tobacco product whose use has increased in recent years. Advertisements for this product feature athletes and run in adventure and sports magazines, thereby appealing to young people, and adolescents have gotten the message. Nearly 12 million try smokeless tobacco every year, and 6 million are regular users (Avis, 1990).

Smokeless tobacco comes in three forms: loose leaf, snuff, and plug. Chewing tobacco is sold as either loose leaf or a plug. Snuff is finely ground tobacco that is placed between the cheeks and gums. This method of use is called **dipping**. Sometimes the user places snuff on the back of the hand and sniffs it up the nose. Plugs are solidly formed, like a brick, and must be cut with a knife. Plugs of tobacco are then placed between the teeth and gums, causing the person to salivate.

The Surgeon General's report (U.S. Department of Health and Human Services, 1986) indicates the following health risks associated with the use of smokeless products:

- The risk of cancer of the cheek and gum may be 50 times higher for snuff users.
- Smokeless tobacco can lead to the development of leukoplakia (white patches) in the mouth, particularly where the tobacco products have been placed. These white patches represent a precancerous condition.
- Smokeless products contain many carcinogens (cancer-causing agents), including nitrosamines, hydrocarbons, and polonium.

Other problems associated with smokeless tobacco identified by McDermott and Marty (1986) and Brubaker and Loftin (1987) include:

- Excessive abrasions of tooth surfaces caused by abrasive grits in tobacco.
- Increased heart rate and blood pressure.
- Suppressed immunological responses, which reduce the ability to ward off disease.
- Increased number of dental caries.
- An association with gingival (gum) inflammation.
- An association with cancers of the pharynx, esophagus, urinary tract and pancreas.
- Darkening of the teeth, resulting in bad breadth.

Preventing and/or Reducing Tobacco Use

As stated earlier in this chapter, about 90% of adult smokers began their addiction as children or adolescents, and these young smokers account for many future health problems. The younger a person is when he starts to smoke, the more likely he is to become a long-term smoker and to develop smoking-related diseases. Preventing youngsters from taking up smoking is far more cost-effective than treating the addiction later in life, and far less expensive than treating the resulting diseases. As with so many other health issues, tobacco addiction should be attacked with prevention measures, including a vigorous effort to discourage children and youth from ever starting to use tobacco (Sullivan, 1990).

The *Healthy Youth 2000* initiative (American Medical Association, 1990) includes objectives related to reducing and preventing tobacco use among adolescents. Two of them are:

- Reduce the initiation of cigarette smoking by children and youths so that no more than 15 percent have become regular cigarette smokers by age 20 (currently 30 percent of youths become regular cigarette smokers by that age). Experimentation with smoking is occurring at younger and younger ages, and initiation now occurs almost entirely during adolescence.
- Reduce smokeless tobacco use by males aged 12 through 24 to a prevalence of no more than 4 percent (currently 6.6% of males aged 12 through 17 use smokeless tobacco). Most new users of smokeless tobacco products are adolescent males. Oral cancer has been shown to occur several times more frequently among smokeless tobacco users than among nonusers and may be 50 times as frequent among long-term snuff users. All smokeless tobacco products contain substantial amounts of nicotine. Their use can support nicotine dependence and may lead to cigarette use. (pp. 7–8)

As stated in the alcohol objectives in this chapter, the *Healthy Youth 2000* initiative states that a carefully planned, comprehensive school health education program can make a big difference in preventing the onset of smoking. Louis Sullivan (1990) launched another initiative to reduce and/or prevent tobacco use among adolescents: improving the enforcement of state laws against smoking by minors. As a result of a study by the U.S. Department of Health and Human Services (HHS), Sullivan reported that children in this country can easily buy cigarettes virtually anytime they want to in violation of the law. HHS also found that where state and local officials take their responsibilities seriously, however, and devise workable and effective enforcement tools, these laws can be successfully enforced. Sullivan proposed a model law that would include the following:

1. Create a licensing system (similar to that for alcohol) so a store could sell tobacco only if it avoids selling to minors.
2. Set a graduated schedule of penalties—monetary fines and license suspensions—for illegal sales.
3. Place primary responsibility for investigation and enforcement in a designated state agency, but allow local law enforcement and public health officials to investigate noncompliance.
4. Ban the use of vending machines to dispense cigarettes.

Preventing the use of tobacco products would do more to enhance the length and quality of life in the United States than any other possible step.

■ ■ ■   *STUDENT CONCERNS:* ALCOHOL AND TOBACCO

As students move through grades 7 through 12, they have many questions about alcohol and tobacco. The following statements from students in various grades are from *Students Speak* (Trucano, 1984).

Grades 7 and 8:

How does chewing tobacco affect a person?
How does alcohol affect your brain?
What do you do if a friend asks you to drink?
If alcohol and tobacco are so bad for you and cause so much death, why aren't they against the law like cocaine and marijuana?
How do you cope with an alcoholic?
How harmful are cigarettes?
How can a kid stop his parents from smoking?
If teenagers smoke in front of children, will it have an effect on them?
I would like to know about alcoholism.
How can we get adults to go to alcoholic counseling?
What do you do if your father or mother becomes an alcoholic?
Does tobacco give everyone some kind of problem?
I want to know how tobacco can do something to people.

Grade 9

What does smoking cigarettes do to the unborn baby?

What is worse, marijuana or cigarettes?

SUMMARY

Alcohol is one of the most commonly used and abused drugs. In small or moderate doses, this drug has a tranquilizing or mellowing effect. But alcohol can easily lead to psychological and physical dependency, sometimes resulting in alcoholism, a disease that can wreck lives. Adolescents begin using alcohol because of curiosity and peer pressure, and because they are modeling adult (usually their parents') behavior. Alcohol-related accidents are the leading cause of injuries and death to adolescents. Alcoholism can and does afflict adolescents. Alcoholics and their families can seek help from many sources, such as Alcoholics Anonymous.

Smoking tobacco is also a serious health problem. Smokers often become psychologically and physically dependent on tobacco. Adolescents begin smoking for the same reasons they begin using alcohol and other drugs. Tobacco companies' advertising and promotions have led many adolescents to start smoking and to use smokeless tobacco. Smoking is a difficult habit to break, but failure to do so can lead to a variety of serious diseases, including cancer and emphysema. The sidestream smoke from the end of a cigarette and the second-hand smoke exhaled by a smoker can cause similar problems to nonsmokers who live or work with smokers. Smokeless tobacco can lead to similar problems.

DISCUSSION QUESTIONS

1. Describe the effects of alcohol upon the body at various blood alcohol concentration levels.
2. Discuss the psychological and sociological effects of alcohol.
3. Explain the path to chemical dependency among adolescents.
4. Detail the relationship between drinking alcohol and having motor vehicle accidents.
5. Detail the impact of advertising upon adolescent tobacco use.
6. List six reasons why individuals may begin smoking tobacco.
7. Describe the effects of second-hand smoke on a nonsmoker.
8. Discuss the adverse effects of smokeless tobacco.

■ ■ ■ *ACTIVITIES FOR TEACHING ABOUT ALCOHOL AND TOBACCO*

Why Do Some People Smoke?*

Have students complete the following exercise:

Read the following statements carefully to understand some of the reasons why people smoke. Then, place the letter that appears in front of the sentence under one of the four headings below, which identifies the "pay-off" for the smoker.

*Source: *Substance Abuse Prevention Activities for Secondary Students* by P. Gerne and T. Gerne, 1991, Englewood Cliffs, NJ: Prentice-Hall.

A. I smoke cigarettes in order to keep myself from slowing down.
B. Handling a cigarette is part of the enjoyment of smoking it.
C. Smoking cigarettes is pleasant and relaxing.
D. I light up a cigarette when I feel angry about something.
E. When I run out of cigarettes, I find it almost unbearable until I can get more.
F. I smoke automatically without even being aware of it.
G. I smoke to stimulate myself, to perk myself up.
H. Part of the enjoyment of smoking a cigarette comes from the steps I take to light up.
I. I find cigarettes pleasurable.
J. When I feel uncomfortable or upset about something, I light up a cigarette.
K. When I am not smoking a cigarette, I am very much aware of the fact.
L. I light up a cigarette without realizing I still have one burning in the ashtray.
M. I smoke cigarettes to give me a lift.
N. When I smoke a cigarette, part of the enjoyment is watching the smoke as I exhale it.
O. I want a cigarette most when I am relaxed and comfortable.
P. When I feel blue or want to take my mind off cares and worries, I smoke.
Q. I get a real gnawing hunger for a cigarette when I haven't smoked for awhile.
R. I've found a cigarette in my mouth and didn't remember putting it there.

For Stimulation	To Reduce Tension	The Rituals	It's a Habit

List some healthy alternative behaviors for each category to help someone stop smoking.

Teenager Alcohol Questionnaire*

Ask students to complete this questionnaire:

1. Do you lose time from school due to drinking?	Yes	No
2. Do you drink because you are shy with other people?	Yes	No
3. Do you drink to build up your self-confidence?	Yes	No
4. Do you drink alone?	Yes	No
5. Is drinking affecting your reputation—and do you care?	Yes	No
6. Do you drink to escape from study or home worries?	Yes	No
7. Do you feel guilty after drinking?	Yes	No
8. Does it bother you if someone says you drink too much?	Yes	No
9. Do you have to take a drink when you go out on a date?	Yes	No
10. Do you make out generally better when you have a drink?	Yes	No
11. Do you get into financial troubles over buying liquor?	Yes	No
12. Do you feel a sense of power when you drink?	Yes	No
13. Have you lost friends since you started drinking?	Yes	No
14. Have you started hanging out with a crowd where the stuff is easy to get?	Yes	No
15. Do your friends drink less than you do?	Yes	No
16. Do you drink until the bottle is done?	Yes	No
17. Have you ever been to a hospital or been "busted" (arrested) for drunk driving?	Yes	No
18. Have you ever had a complete loss of memory from drinking?	Yes	No
19. Do you "turn off" to any studies or lectures about drinking?	Yes	No
20. Do you think you have a problem with liquor?	Yes	No

A "yes" to two or more of the above questions ought to be a warning that the respondent is on shaky ground. Alcoholism? Possibly. These are some of the early warning signs.

■ ■ ■ *ACTIVITIES:* DECISION STORIES*

Have students work on the following sample problems:

1. Mr. Brown and Mr. Smith live next door to each other. Each week, Mr. Brown mows his lawn. When he does, the grass shoots from his mower on to Mr. Smith's porch. Mr. Smith is getting tired of sweeping his porch after Mr. Brown mows. What could he say or do?
2. Sue just bought her favorite tape and has not even opened the package. Donna asks to borrow the tape for her party that afternoon. Donna has lost or broken Sue's tapes in the past, but they are good friends. What could Sue do or say?

*Source: *How To Survive Teaching Health* by K. Tillman and P. Toner, 1990, West Nyack, NY: Parker.

3. Dan asks Beth to meet him at the movies. When Beth gets there, Dan buys a ticket for himself only. Beth has $3.00, and the movie costs $4.50. What could Beth do or say?

4. Bill, who is 16, asks Jamie his brother, who is 21, to buy some alcohol for him and his friends. Bill promises he won't drive, but lately Bill has been getting into a lot of trouble. What could Jamie do or say?

5. Mr. and Mrs. Wilson have a cocktail party. Their 15-year-old daughter Jennifer asks for a glass of wine. What do you think her parents should do or say?

6. At a party, every person there is either doing coke or smoking pot. When Jean walks in with her friend Ashley, who is new in the neighborhood, another friend offers them some drugs. Jean accepts. Ashley is very uncomfortable and has no desire to use any drugs, but wants desperately to "fit in." What could Ashley do or say?

■ ■ ■   *ACTIVITIES:* LEARNING ENHANCEMENTS

The following films and videotapes can supplement lessons about alcohol and tobacco. Unless otherwise specified, these materials may be acquired from:

Films for the Humanities and Sciences
    800/257-5126.

Drug and Alcohol Rehabilitation. This program focuses on the treatments in use to overcome chemical dependency. The program also covers two controversial therapies currently in use: aversion therapy for alcoholism and methadone treatment for drug addiction. Viewers learn what the addict must do to avoid relapse. 19 minutes, color.

Fetal Alcohol Syndrome and Other Drug Use During Pregnancy. This program profiles an eight-year-old boy born with FAS, showing how alcohol enters the bloodstream of the fetus; it describes the common characteristics of children with FAS and the learning disabilities, mental handicaps, and behavioral problems that are common. The program also explores babies born to cocaine-addicted mothers, illustrating how cocaine affects the fetus and explaining that crack babies are at risk for low birth weight, impaired brain growth, and malformed kidneys and genitals. 19 minutes, color.

Alcohol's Effect on the Body. This program illustrates the wide-ranging negative effects of alcohol on the human body and on society. Dr. Ruth Liver delivers the facts on alcohol in the body; drugs and alcohol strain relationships on the soap opera parody, "The Young and the Breathless"; and a fitness instructor describes how alcohol can ruin your appearance. 15 minutes, color.

Caffeine, Nicotine, and Prescription Drugs: The "Invisible" Drugs. Caffeine, nicotine, and prescription drugs affect us greatly and can be dangerous (and sometimes lethal). A takeoff on a shopping network covers the dangers of tobacco, and private investigators on the pseudosoap opera get closer to the truth about the problem character, a would-be teenage junkie. 15 minutes, color.

Alcohol Addiction. Access and attitudes explain why people begin to drink; genetic predisposition may explain why some people cannot stop. At the Rutgers University Alcohol Research Lab, this program explores the nature of alcohol addiction. The conclusion is that addiction is a biochemical disease still best treated by behavioral means. 28 minutes, color.

Alcohol and the Family: Breaking the Chain. This program analyzes the signs of alcoholism and shows how a family member, coworker, or friend can help break the chain; discusses the impact of alcoholism on the children of alcoholics; and evaluates the options and prognosis for alcoholism treatment. 25 minutes, color.

Children of Alcoholics. Alcohol abuse means physical or psychological abuse of the family as well, which geometrically increases the number of victims, frequently leads to alcoholism in other family members, and invariably leaves deep scars. In this specially adapted Phil Donahue Program, Suzanne Somers tells of growing up in an alcoholic family; she is joined by members of her family, all of whom have struggled with and overcome alcoholism. 28 minutes, color.

Adult Children of Alcoholics: A Family Secret. In this program, famous adult children of alcoholics speak out about childhood nightmares and adult behavior that continues to reflect the problem of a parent's alcoholism: some chose alcoholic partners, others developed drug, gambling, or other addictions. All speak of the difficulties of coping with the damage inflicted by an alcohol-centered childhood. 52 minutes, color.

Smoking and Lung Cancer. Smokers are 10 times more likely to develop lung cancer than nonsmokers; the more they smoke, the higher the risk. Early detection, before cancerous cells metastasize, is critical to successful treatment and survival. This program profiles a man who had lung cancer and gave up smoking. 19 minutes, color.

Kick the Habit. This program focuses on the effects of cigarette smoking on the body and on the battle against smoking. It shows the efforts being made to educate people to the hazards of smoking, explains the conditioning process by which people become hooked on cigarettes, and presents evidence of the dangers of secondary smoke. 19 minutes, color.

If You Love Someone Who Smokes. This program shows how a tough New York City cop responded when told that he had terminal lung cancer. With failing breath and growing determination, Ken McFeely joined media guru Tony Schwartz to make some of the most successful public service messages ever aired to warn people about the hazards of smoking. If you love someone who smokes, make sure he or she sees this program. 52 minutes, color.

Smoking: Following the Crowd. Why, in the face of all that we know about the negative effects of smoking today, do young people still take up this dangerous, addictive habit? This 15-minute video answers this question as well as many others about smoking. With up-to-date information and fast-moving graphics, the video shows the foolishness of following the crowd, especially when it comes to smoking. Health Edco, 800/299-3366, ext. 295.

Smoking ... Hazardous to Your Health. This video details the exact effects of smoking on the body, heart, and lungs, and the diseases triggered by smoking. 29 minutes. Health Edco, 800/299-3366, ext. 295.

Smoking—Kicking the Habit. From hypnosis seminars to aversion-therapy clinics, this video takes a look at some of the many programs designed to help people stop smoking. It warns about dubious, high-cost programs, and gives special emphasis to preventing teens from starting smoking. 29 minutes. Health Edco, 800/299-3366, ext. 295.

Smoking and Health. Vivid photography in this program details lung cancer, emphysema, bronchitis, heart attacks, bladder cancer, strokes, burns, and other consequences of smoking. Health Edco, 800/299-3366, ext. 295.

Showdown on Tobacco Road. This award-winning program for junior high through adult viewers looks at smokers' versus nonsmokers' rights in America, presenting provocative views from all sides of the issue. Conversations with experts and people who participated in the story's important events are combined with Hollywood film footage to give an overview of smoking in our culture from the 1880s to the present. 57 minutes. ETR Assoc. 800/321-4407.

Fire without Smoke. This informative filmstrip on video provides facts on the history of smokeless tobacco and its increasing use today. The program, developed by the Public Health School at Loma Linda University, helps teenagers understand the severe health problems associated with smokeless tobacco use and explores the reasons why some young people may still be tempted to try it. 16 minutes. ETR Assoc. 800/321-4407.

Dirty Business. This video attacks the tobacco industry for the subtleties in its advertising. It exposes tactics that the industry uses to lure new and young smokers to tobacco products. 24 minutes. ETR Assoc. 800/321-4407.

The Chews Blues. This video discusses the results of chewing tobacco, from bad breath to mouth and throat disease. It is designed to provide information for students to make their own decision regarding the use of tobacco products. 23 minutes. ETR Assoc. 800/321-4407.

The Tobacco Action Curriculum. This program includes a 15-minute video along with worksheets and activities designed to introduce the student to the hazards of smoking and chewing tobacco. Anson-Schloat Live Action Videos, Spring 1993, 175 Tomkins Ave., Pleasantville, NY 10570-9973 or 800/833-2004.

REFERENCES

Akers, Ronald L. (1992). *Drugs, alcohol, and society: Social structure, process, and policy.* Belmont, CA: Wadsworth.

American Medical Association. (1990). *Healthy youth 2000.* Chicago: Author.

Appalachian Educational Laboratory (1992). *R&D Notes, 6,* Charleston, WV: Author.

Avis, Harry. (1990). *Drugs & life.* Dubuque, IA: Wm. C. Brown.

Carroll, Charles R. (1989). *Drugs in modern society* (2nd ed.). Dubuque, IA: Wm. C. Brown.

Center for Substance Abuse Prevention. (1990). *What you can do about drug use in America.* Washington, DC: U.S. Department of Health and Human Services.

Center for Substance Abuse Prevention. (1989). *Drug-free communities: Turning awareness into action.* Washington, DC: U.S. Department of Health and Human Services.

Centers for Disease Control. (1990). Current trends: Cigarette advertising—United States, 1988. *Morbidity and Mortality Weekly Report, 39,* 261–265.

Gerne, P., & Gerne, T. (1991). *Substance abuse prevention activities for secondary students.* Englewood Cliffs, NJ: Prentice-Hall.

Girdano, D., & Dusek, D. (1988). *Drug education: Content and methods* (4th ed.). New York: Random House.

Mintz, M. (1991, May 6). The nicotine pushers: Marketing tobacco to children, *The Nation,* 577, 591.

Payne, W., Hahn, D., & Pinger, R. (1991). *Drugs: Issues for today.* St. Louis: Mosby.

Schlaadt, R., & Shannon, P. (1990). *Drugs* (3rd ed.). Englewood Cliffs, NJ: Prentice-Hall.

Sullivan, L. W. (1990, May 24). Statement before the Committee on Finance, U.S. Senate, Washington, DC.

Trucano, L. (1984). Students speak—*A survey of health interests and concerns: Kindergarten through twelfth grade.* Seattle: Comprehensive Health Education Foundation.

U.S. Department of Health and Human Services. (1989). *The national adolescent student health survey—A report on the health of America's youth.* A cooperative project of the U.S. Department of Health and Human Services, Office of Disease Prevention and Health Promotion, Centers for Disease Control, and National Institute on Drug Abuse. Oakland, CA: Third Party.

U.S. Department of Health and Human Services, Public Health Service. (1986). *The health consequences of using smokeless tobacco: A report of the advisory committee to the Surgeon General.* Bethesda, MD: Author.

Witters, W., Venturelli, P., & Hanson, G. (1992). *Drugs and society* (3rd ed.). Boston: Jones and Bartlett.

CHAPTER 9

Human Sexuality and Family-Life Education

Sex is a serious topic. The well-being of individuals, couples, families and even an entire society can depend on matters that are fundamentally sexual. K. Hass and A. Hass, *Understanding Sexuality*

OBJECTIVES

After reading this chapter, you should be able to

- Identify the goals of a family-life education program
- Discuss the social aspects of sexuality and family living
- List criteria for mate selection
- Discuss marriage, parenthood, and divorce
- Trace the psychological development of sexuality
- Describe the anatomy and physiology of the male and female reproductive systems
- Discuss the various types of contraception
- Explain the problems of family abuse and violence

PROGRAM GOALS

Family-life and sex education are among the most controversial areas facing teachers. Many people view discussion of this subject as an attempt to teach sexual technique and corrupt the morals of today's youth. If that were true, family-life education would involve little more than teaching the act of coitus. Family-life education does deal with sexuality, but that is not the same thing as sex. **Sexuality** involves one's total being and identity. An effective family-life program helps develop an individual's sexuality. This includes appreciation for oneself and the opposite sex, ability to develop fulfilling personal and family relationships, acceptance of sexual roles (mother, father, sister, brother, friend, wife, husband), recognition of reproduction-related bodily functions, understanding of the part emotions play in sexual behavior, maturing of attitudes toward the function of sex in life, appreciation of the responsibility of being a member of a family, and overall, development of a healthy attitude toward life.

The primary responsibility for teaching facts, attitudes, and values about family life remains with parents. Frequently, however, the education students receive at home about family life does not match their level of questioning, need, and interest. School is not the only source of information outside the home—churches and other organizations can also contribute significantly. The school, however, is an increasingly important source of education in this field. Before any family-life curriculum can be taught, parental approval must be obtained (see Chapter 2). Most communities will support such a program if the school administration and community really understand what is to be taught. Approval is a most important first step that cannot be ignored.

Students must learn an appreciation for self early in life and build on that continually to feel comfortable with their sexuality through the preadolescent, adolescent, and adult years. As all aspects of health education should emphasize, students must recognize that they will eventually need to accept the responsibility of their sexuality.

If society is not willing to promote comprehensive family-life education, then that component of a young person's total being will be shortchanged. Personal and social problems such as unwanted pregnancies, sexually transmitted diseases, sexual nonresponsiveness, and divorce will continue to plague society. A worthwhile educational effort in sex and family life must include social, psychological, moral, and biological components. This chapter examines these areas of concern.

SOCIAL ASPECTS OF SEXUALITY AND FAMILY LIVING

Various cultural, historical, legal, religious, and other institutional factors influence families and sexual roles within families. It is important to remember that families take many forms. With this in mind, some typical characteristics of the family will be examined.

Types of Families

The family fulfills a most important role in providing stability for the individual and society. The term **family** describes two or more persons living together who are related by blood, marriage, or adoption (Eshleman, 1991). A **nuclear family** might be composed of a husband and wife, a brother and sister, one parent and a child or children, or both parents and one or more children. An **extended family** consists of a number of nuclear family groupings, often with no blood ties. Extended family members can include uncles, aunts, grandparents, or cousins.

Because most people marry, they will be part of at least two nuclear families, one they are born to and one they join after selecting a marriage partner. The nuclear family to which we are born is the first and most basic provider of socialization. The extended family also influences our socialization.

The Changing Nature of the U.S. Family

U.S. youngsters in past generations generally grew up in one city or town, married someone from the surrounding area, and settled nearby. Members of the extended family probably also lived in the area.

In today's society the nuclear family may be intact, but the extended family probably is not. For example, parents and grandparents may live in widely separate locations. As a result, grandparents may visit only on holidays or other special occasions. Thus, the interaction among these family members is not as frequent as in the past. The mobility of today's society and frequent job changes or transfers have served to separate the nuclear family from the extended family.

The advent of two-career households has brought about several changes. Families tend to have fewer children, and parents often leave the children's care to day-care centers or other individuals who are not family members. Consequently, a child may come in contact with caretakers who influence the child's social/ psychological and value system development.

Divorce may also change children's perspectives and the roles and responsibilities they must handle. Currently, one out of every five children lives with one parent, 90% with the mother. It has been estimated that by the end of this century, 50% of all children under the age of 18 will have spent some time living with only a female parent (U.S. Bureau of the Census, 1988). Hass and Hass (1993) have suggested that divorce leads to a significant increase in sexual problems, juvenile delinquency, and emotional and psychological maladjustment.

Technology has influenced the family. Easy access to transportation has enabled families to move throughout the country easily. Sometimes this has led to family members engaging in activities as individuals rather than as a unit. Television and other media have presented a variety of social values to students. In the past, the value system an individual initially accepted was a combination of beliefs fostered by the church, family, and school. Now, young people can witness a whole spectrum of values in a relatively short period of time by viewing, listening, or reading.

What an individual becomes socially, morally, and psychologically depends on all of the factors just described. Understanding the world is perhaps more difficult than ever before because of these societal changes and a barrage of mixed signals. It is no wonder, then, that many young people are confused about their roles in and the expectations of society.

While the family is changing, people will always need to be bonded to others through closeness, sharing, and love. Changes in child-rearing and household responsibilities have required family members to make adjustments, but a complete upheaval in the basic family structure has not occurred and seems unlikely.

MATE SELECTION

Although we can choose from various lifestyles, more than 90% of the U.S. population marries at least once. About four out of five who divorce marry again. Courtship, then engagement, usually precede marriage. The length of each phase, including the marriage, depends on the couple. Too often the partners do not take advantage of the courtship and engagement to learn useful information about each other. Unfortunately, we drift from a romantic movie script to the day-to-day reality of marriage. Many people do not know what their partner expects of the marriage; others never realize that marrige is not one long romantic adventure. As wonderful and exciting as initial mate selection can be, both partners should try to keep in mind the realistic aspects of marriage.

Love and Intimacy

From the socialization process we learn that we are supposed to form relationships and "fall in love." Attempting to define **love** is a most difficult task. Love has been defined as "that condition in which happiness of another person is essential to your own" (Heinlein, 1961, p. 345). This highly romantic definition of love surfaces in popular songs, the scenario of Romeo and Juliet, and the explanation for Edward VIII's leaving the throne to marry Mrs. Simpson. Certainly, the element of caring must be present. Without caring, what is thought to be love may be only strong desire. We may pretend to be in love in order to have sex or gain wealth and status. The problem is determining what love really is. Erich Fromm (1956) wrote that caring and respect for another are central to love, and that people can achieve a meaningful type of love only if they are secure in their own identity. Fromm goes on to define mature love as "union under the condition of preserving one's integrity, one's individuality" (p. 17). Fromm suggests that a lover must feel this way: "I want the loved person to grow and unfold for his own sake and in his own ways, and not for the purpose of serving me" (p. 24).

The English language has only one word, love, to describe a wide variety of feelings and relationships. The ancient Greeks used a variety of terms to describe more precisely the different kinds of love. *Eros* referred to passionate or erotic love. *Storge* meant affection such as the feelings parents have for their children. *Philia* indicated the type of love in friendships, and *agape* referred to a kind of love associated with the traditional Christian view of being undemanding, patient, kind, and always supportive.

Our society divides love into three types: romantic, rational, and mature. **Romantic love** is an intense emotional experience that can totally captivate our existence. **Rational love**, which is based on accepting the partner's imperfections as well as affections, is more likely to lead to fulfilling, long-lasting relationships. **Mature love** is characterized by communication and separateness of the partners. It involves respect, admiration, and the desire to help each other. Lovers who exhibit maturity in their relationship are best friends who are committed to each other and their relationship.

To help explain the concept of love, Coutts (1973) has described five levels of love. The first, called *sentimentality,* centers on one's own feeling, needs, fears, and insecurities. If people remain at this level, they become insensitive and exploitative in their relationship. The second level is *awareness.* Sharing and caring develop mutually between the partners, and an intimacy emerges based on facts, not impressions. The third level is *involvement,* in which the partners see what is needed and work very hard at offering support. The fourth level is *dedication,* in which the partners are willing to sacrifice some of their needs, safety, and comfort. The fifth level of loving is *commitment.* This is the most powerful of all love relationships. It encompasses intellect, emotions, body, lasting awareness, and involvement. As difficult as love is to define and identify, Peele & Brodsky (1976) developed several questions to help distinguish between healthy and problematic love.

1. Do both lovers have a secure belief in their own value?
2. Are the lovers improved by the relationship?
3. Do the lovers maintain serious interests outside the relationship, including other meaningful personal relationships?
4. Is the relationship integrated into, rather than being set off from, the totality of the lovers' lives?

5. Are the lovers beyond being possessive or jealous of each other's growth and expansion of interest?
6. Are the lovers also friends? Would they seek each other out if they should cease to be primary partners? (pp. 83–84)

As love develops, so does intimacy. Like love, intimacy needs time to develop and goes through several stages. Calderone (1972) identifies those stages as:

1. *Choice:* Two people meet; they like each other and begin to become closer.
2. *Mutual:* Their desire for closeness is mutually shared.
3. *Reciprocity:* They give to each other and grow by confiding in each other. There is an equal sharing of confidences.
4. *Trust:* Their deepest feelings and thoughts are accepted.
5. *Delight:* They have unconditional acceptance of one another and delight in the relationship.

To be intimate means to be vulnerable. It means a risk of rejection or suffocation of oneself. However, compatible partners replace those risks with trust and satisfaction. Essentially, individuals must remain responsible for themselves yet help each other with their goals, problems, and desires. Enjoying, sharing, and caring should be the outcomes of living with someone with whom love and intimacy are shared.

Why People Marry

There is no single reason why people marry. People marry for both personal and societal reasons. Some marry because they do not want to be alone. They want someone to share confidences with, and they want to give and receive affection. A happy marriage can offer intimacy, sharing, support, and stimulation for personal growth.

Some people marry for economic reasons. For example, they may wish to pool their incomes, or the husband may provide financial security to the wife and children, while the wife runs the home and cares for the children. Most people marry because they enjoy a person and can depend on that person in times of need. Theoretically, marriage provides someone to share both joy and sorrow.

Dating and Courtship

Most people engage in some form of dating. The development of an extensive dating system seems to be a modern U.S. innovation. Dating as courtship is influenced by parents, the church, and other institutions that have a vested interest in continuing a traditional form of society. Dating helps us develop skills for selecting our mates. The beneficial features of dating are in aiding the processes of socialization, personality development, and learning to get along with the opposite sex.

Choosing a Partner

Typically, the characteristics that people look for in a marriage partner include dependable character, emotional stability, pleasing disposition, mutual attraction, good health, desire for home and family, and refinement (Kephart, 1991). We tend to marry someone from more or less the same background as ourselves. We may be attracted to certain types of people, but we seldom consider how various factors affect the chances of a successful marriage. Love and personal background are some of the factors that are involved in selecting a marriage partner.

Love

As difficult as it is to define, most people marry because of their feelings of love for their partner. A desire for sharing experiences and sexual intimacy, as well as a deep concern for the partner, are the ingredients of love. As important as this factor is, two people can maintain love only if they develop communication, understanding, and a desire to enhance each other's happiness. The nature of love tends to change during a marriage; emotions often enhance it over the years. Certainly, love should not be confused with sexual attraction. Although sexual desire may confirm a feeling of love for one's partner, a couple's good sexual relationship does not ensure love.

Background

We all bring unique histories to our relationships. Several factors seem to be important considerations in the selection of a potential mate. Included are age, race, health, education, intelligence, religion, economic status, family background, and previous marital status.

Age. Research indicates that the younger the age of the couple, the less chance the marriage has of surviving. Between 50% and 67% of marriages in which the individuals are below age 20 end in divorce. The average age of marriage in the United States is now 24 for men and 21 for women. For men, marriage before age 22 decreases the probability of marital success. In 4 out of 10 marriages, the man is 3 to 9 years older than the woman. Certainly, age differences are not uncommon, but the motives for marrying someone extremely older or younger should be examined. For example, does the older person represent a parental figure or offer immediate economic security?

Race. In many communities, interracial marriages are not well accepted and may present difficult barriers, even though the percentage of such marriages has been increasing steadily. Besides the societal problems an interracial couple faces, problems concerning customs, values, and attitudes often crop up. While these factors are present in any marriage, they may be even more pronounced in an interracial marriage and should be discussed when such a marriage is contemplated.

Health. Factors such as genetics may be important if one or both partners have conditions that they could pass on to offspring. Conditions such as alcoholism or mental health problems are indications of possible problems for a marriage. An important component of success in marriage is the mental and physical health of the partners. Warning signs of serious problems in either area should not be ignored.

Education. Although marriages can succeed when the partners have different educational levels, it is important for each person to assess his feelings when a wide disparity in educational levels is present. A pronounced difference in this area could lead one partner to having feelings of inferiority. However, any differences can be overcome if love, interests, and expectations are similar.

Intelligence. Like education, differences in intelligence should not hinder a relationship if the partners have the freedom to be themselves. The positive aspects should be emphasized. A point of warning is that wide variations in intelligence can lead to the couple drifting apart because educational, social, and intellectual interests may become different as the partners develop their individuality.

Religion. One of the most difficult aspects to overcome is the difference in religious affiliation and devotion of the partners. Although interfaith marriages are quite common, few couples take the time to discuss religious beliefs regarding raising children, sexual behavior, and finances. For some, religion has little meaning, whereas for others, it has the potential to unify—or serve as a powerful wedge in—the relationship. The couple, their parents, and clergy should discuss this area thoroughly so that the partners clearly understand the issues and obligations surrounding their religious views.

Economic Status. Adequate income can be essential to a successful marriage, because this factor represents a major area of potential contention. A couple should examine their values and determine whether their available income allows for the lifestyle they desire or whether marriage would be better delayed. Job potential should be assessed to determine whether the desired lifestyle requires both partners to work full time.

Insel and Roth (1988) list several additional factors that should be considered.

- *Tolerance for differences:* Tolerance brings us a long way toward coping with differences of background, viewpoint, interest, and energy level. Is there the freedom to be yourself and retain your own identity in this relationship?
- *Values and taste:* What are the values and tastes of the couple in terms of religion, politics, music, art, recreation, and types of people? Do these coincide in most areas?
- *Self-esteem:* Do you and your partner like yourselves? The more at ease you are with yourself, the more nourishing it is possible to be as a partner.
- *Authority:* Who makes the final decisions? Authority works best when shared and is probably best when divided according to time and talent.
- *Energy level:* How do your energy levels compare with each other's? Does one of you want to be constantly on the go or constantly at home?
- *Communication skills:* Can the unpleasant things that arise be talked about? Can the two of you communicate positive feelings of praise, support, and empathy? Can you listen to one another? Can both partners express his/her feelings and thoughts without fear of the other person's response? (p. 115)

Marriage

Most people view marriage as the cornerstone of family organization. Reiss (1980) defines **marriage** as "a socially accepted union of individuals in husband and wife roles, with the key function of legitimation of parenthood" (p. 50). Eshleman (1981) identifies six areas that have been found to be societally sanctioned for marriages, regardless of social or economic background. They are

1. A heterosexual union, including at least one male and one female.
2. The legitimating or granting of approval to the sexual relationship and the bearing of children without any loss of standing in the community or society.
3. A public affair rather than a private, personal matter.
4. A highly institutionalized and patterned mating arrangement.
5. An assuming of mutual and reciprocal rights and obligations between the spouses.
6. A binding relationship that assumes some permanence. (p. 82)

Marriage serves many functions for individuals, including establishment of a family, companionship, economic strength, emotional security, a sexual outlet, and children. The greater the success in meeting these needs, the greater the likelihood the marriage will remain intact. Because each year more than 2 million marriages take place in the United States, it seems safe to say that marriages exist to fulfill basic needs associated with the husband–wife relationship. To meet these individual needs, each partner must be committed to the marriage, develop effective communication, and accept the responsibility to nurture and enhance the marriage.

Parenthood

When children enter a family, the married couple must assume new roles. The wife must become a mother and the husband, a father. The exclusive attention of the partners toward each other as well as the time demands and interests of the couple must change. Parenthood is a most difficult task, yet couples are expected to fulfill this role automatically with little or no formal training. Parenthood is a lifetime commitment. Individuals can quit their jobs or divorce their mates, but they have no honorable way to withdraw from the role of father or mother. Many groups now offer parenthood education programs that promote parenting skills. These courses attempt to teach ways to facilitate communication between parents and children, improve methods of discipline, and develop appropriate behavior for parents and children.

Advantages and Disadvantages of Parenthood

The obvious advantage of parenthood is the opportunity to love and nurture another human being. The psychological pleasure from being part of a loving family and helping direct its development can bring a couple closer together and provide them the long-term benefit of pride in having done so. Besides the extreme economic cost of having and raising children, parenthood usually requires a career adjustment for at least one of the partners. Further, children reduce the couple's emotional sharing time. Instead, the parents spend time in guiding and showing affection to the children. Parents thus will need to change or eliminate some personal activities in order to have time for the children.

Single Parenthood

Parenthood is difficult when two partners share the nurturing and love that each child requires. It can become even more difficult if only one parent is present. Some individuals cope quite successfully with single parenthood, whereas others struggle with the many roles and situations they face in raising their children.

A single parent may encounter various problems. The demands of working and maintaining a home may be so overwhelming that children's emotional needs may not be met adequately, for example. The single parent may also have trouble properly supervising the child. Arranging for the child's care and supervision is difficult and may take a large share of the budget, especially in households headed by women. Finally, the single parent may have unfulfilled emotional and sexual needs. Unmet emotional needs can develop because of the lack of time to seek or spend in a relationship. Because most single parents wish to hide their sexual involvement, finding a time and place for it can present problems. Nevertheless, being a single parent is not the end of the world. It is important that single parents have sufficient financial, material, and emotional support to meet their own and their children's demands.

Divorce

The most frequent method for dissolving a marriage is through divorce. In 1980, one person had divorced and not remarried for every 10 who were in an intact marriage. Two-fifths of first and second marriages end in divorce. Although the rate of separation can only be estimated for unmarried people who live together, the rate is considered to be greater than 50%.

Divorce is usually viewed as a failure of the family system as well as a great personal crisis. Often, however, it is also a way to end the physical abuse or emotional tension of a marriage. Personal factors most often given as reasons for divorce include financial problems, physical abuse, mental abuse, drinking, in-law problems, lack of love, adultery, and sexual incompatibility. Most societies allow divorce today. During the last 15 years, divorce rates have risen throughout the world. Kephart (1991) lists six social factors that have contributed to the increased divorce rates.

1. *Changing family functions.* Outside sources may now fulfill functions that were once considered primary family responsibilities. These may include medical, religious, and recreational aspects of family life.
2. *Casual marriages.* Hasty and youthful marriages complicated by pregnancy are often unstable.
3. *Jobs for women.* With greater job opportunities available to a large number of women, a great barrier to divorce for many women has been removed.
4. *Decline in moral and religious sanctions.* Although not openly stated by all churches, most have taken a more liberal attitude toward divorce. Also, society does not attach the severe stigma to divorce that it once did.
5. *The philosophy of happiness.* If happiness does not materialize to the degree anticipated, divorce or separation is accepted as a way of dealing with the feeling.
6. *More liberal divorce laws.* The liberalization of divorce laws, including no-fault divorces, has made it easier to terminate a marriage. (p. 470)

The emotional impact of a divorce is extreme. Anyone who has experienced a divorce usually describes it as a painful, devastating experience. Problems with

Divorce is a traumatic experience for all family members involved.

finances, personal adjustment, and children create an extremely stressful situation. Children whose parents are divorcing may develop deep feelings of guilt, fear, and anger. Many times children believe they must take sides in the conflict, which only serves to enhance their guilt feelings. The emotional conflict between the parents may prevent them from recognizing the children's worries about their own welfare and future. It is important to remember that despite the family fighting, the children will continue to love both parents. Sensitive parents and understanding teachers are especially important for children during and after a divorce. Many children require counseling, but this must usually come from a private source, not the school system.

PSYCHOLOGICAL ASPECTS OF SEXUALITY AND FAMILY LIVING

People have a wide variety of options for displaying their psychological and physiological traits. Also, today's society allows greater flexibility in sex roles. This section deals with the psychological aspects of human sexuality and family life that help determine how people feel and react as individuals.

Gender Development

From birth, social expectations largely guide **gender development**. Parents consciously and unconsciously manipulate their children's gender development from infancy based on the sole criterion of sex. From dress and toys to behavior, the child learns to accept the parameters of being either a girl or a boy. By age 2, children know what sex they are and understand some of their society's expectations for that sex.

By the time children have reached school age, task orientation and emotional responses are based almost solely on what they have learned about gender. Children's activities reflect traditional social images of adult roles. Boys focus on achievement and sports, whereas girls are pointed toward personal beauty or other "feminine" interests. This is not to say that girls do not participate in sports or aggressive activities, but these activities are not stressed for girls to the extent they are for boys.

Throughout the school years, students observe traditional concepts of adult roles. For example, most elementary teachers are female, whereas most administrators are male. Boys typically are encouraged to achieve, compete, and develop occupational goals. Girls typically are encouraged to comply, depend on others, and sacrifice their occupation and position to males.

Gender identification is an important determinant of expectations and conduct. Society places a great deal of emphasis on socializing and maintaining gender differences. In some cases this process may be beneficial—in others, detrimental—to the potential of both boys and girls.

Sex Roles

Since the 1960s, more people have recognized that both males and females have a right to expand their individual potential and not be confined within traditional roles and stereotypes. Children learn traditional **sex roles** in the same ways as gender identity. Sex roles should reflect the individuality of people, not their gender. Such an emphasis can eliminate factors that inhibit the complete development of the individual. Sharing household duties, child rearing, and economic responsibilities can contribute to the personal development of both partners. Males need not always be aggressive, nor females always passive.

Overcoming traditional sex roles is not easy because they are established early in life and constantly reinforced throughout the years. Self-evaluation and a sense of adequacy are linked to sex role behavior as defined by parents and peers in childhood. Some say that sex roles are a natural part of growing and learning; however, tradition should not be used to psychologically lock people into sex roles that inhibit their growth as individuals.

Developing Sexuality

All aspects of human sexuality develop over a long period, from early childhood through the adult years. The groundwork for sexual values begins to develop in infancy, as children learn trust, initiative, and love. As they grow older, children try to achieve self-confidence in their interactions with parents, adults, and peers. Development of self-confidence is crucial to development of the child's sexuality. If children grow up feeling at ease with themselves, they are more likely to appreciate themselves and members of the opposite sex.

Anything that affects a child's developing identity will eventually affect her sexuality as well. A child who learns to be defensive, unforgiving, or mistrusting in daily life will carry over these attitudes into the sexual component of her personality. Consequently, children must learn to give and receive love and have a positive self-image if they are to be at ease with their sexuality later in life.

BIOLOGICAL COMPONENTS OF SEX EDUCATION

All teachers need a basic knowledge of the human reproductive system and genetics.

Genetics

The human body is made up of trillions of cells that provide for various specialized functions. Each cell contains a nucleus. This nucleus contains **genes** that provide the hereditary information in smaller rod-shaped bodies called **chromosomes**. Twenty-two pairs of autosomal chromosomes account for individual facial features, hair color, height, body build, and myriad other characteristics. Gender is determined by the twenty-third, or sex-determining, chromosomal pair. One member of the pair is called an X chromosome. The other can be either an X or Y chromosome. If two Xs pair, a female develops. An XY pairing produces a male offspring.

Mitosis is ordinary cell division. This process results in two new cells that each contain the full complement of 46 chromosomes. **Meiosis** is the cell division that forms the sperm and ovum. These cells are called **gametes** and contain only 23 chromosomes. When a male gamete (sperm) unites with a female gamete (ovum), the 23 pairs unite to determine gender. The ovum always contains the X chromosome, whereas the sperm can have either an X or Y chromosome. If a sperm with a Y chromosome fertilizes the egg, the baby will be a male, or XY.

The Male Reproductive System

The male reproductive system, shown in Figure 9.1, is not cyclical and thus not as hormonally or endocrinologically complex as that of the female. The major male sexual endocrine glands are the two testes, or **testicles**, which are contained and protected in a saclike structure called the **scrotum**. At puberty, the testes begin producing mature **sperm**, the male reproductive cells. Attached to the top of each testis is the **epididymis**. This structure consists of tightly coiled tubes through which the sperm pass to the **vas deferens**. The two vas deferens serve as storage areas for the mature sperm and are the means by which sperm move to the urethra. The two vas deferens eventually form into one structure called the **ejaculatory duct**. This tube connects with the **urethra**. The urethra is a tube that runs the length of the **penis**. The penis is the male organ for sexual intercourse and consists of spongy material

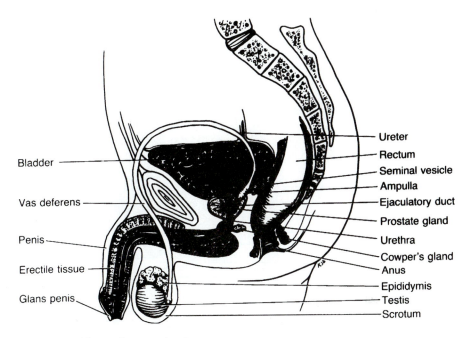

Bladder

Vas deferens

Penis

Erectile tissue

Glans penis

Ureter
Rectum
Seminal vesicle
Ampulla
Ejaculatory duct
Prostate gland
Urethra
Cowper's gland
Anus
Epididymis
Testis
Scrotum

Figure 9.1   The male reproductive system

called erectile tissue. The head of the penis is called the **glans penis**. This area contains many nerve endings and is very sensitive to sexual stimulation.

The **seminal vesicles**, the **prostate gland**, and the two **Cowper's glands** manufacture substances important to the sperm and ejaculation. The seminal vesicles produce a simple sugar, fructose, that adds volume to the ejaculatory fluid, called semen, and activates the movement of the sperm. The prostate gland provides a highly alkaline milky fluid that helps to neutralize the high acidity of the vagina and facilitates the movement of sperm through that organ. The pea-sized Cowper's glands also produce an alkaline fluid that lubricates and neutralizes the acidity of the urethra. The Cowper's glands secrete this substance prior to ejaculation. The combined fluid produced by the seminal vesicles, prostate, and Cowper's glands, along with the sperm it contains, is **semen**.

It should be noted that the testes manufacture mature sperm on a consistent basis from puberty through old age. Upon release of the interstitial cell-stimulating hormone (ICSH) into the bloodstream from the anterior lobe of the pituitary, the testes also secrete **testosterone**. Although it plays many diverse roles, testosterone triggers the male adolescent growth spurt, which accompanies the development of secondary sex characteristics.

The Female Reproductive System

The female reproductive system, shown in Figure 9.2, is comprised of the **external genitalia** and the internal organs consisting of the **vagina, uterus, fallopian tubes,** and **ovaries**. The external genitalia are the **labia majora** (the outer lips) and the **labia**

Fallopian tube
Ovary
Bladder
Mons veneris
Urethra
Clitoris
Labium minus
Labium majus

Uterus
Rectum
Vagina
Anus

Figure 9.2   The female reproductive system

minora (inner lips). The **clitoris** is a small structure at the top of the labia majora that facilitates sexual stimulation. The vagina is an elastic canal extending from just behind the cervix to the opening of the external genitalia. It serves as the organ for sexual intercourse and as the birth canal. The uterus is a pear-shaped organ that serves as a cavity where the fetus develops. The uterus has three layers, called the **perimetrium** (outer layer), the **myometrium** (muscular layer), and **endometrium** (inner layer). It is the endometrium that is sloughed off during menstruation. Two armlike projections called the fallopian tubes branch from the uterus. These tubes are 3 to 5 inches long and have fembria (small fingerlike projections) at the far ends next to the ovaries. Through these tubes the eggs, or **ova**, pass. If fertilization takes place, it occurs in the upper third of one of the fallopian tubes. Two ovaries produce ova and secrete hormones that cause the development of the female secondary sex characteristics such as the rounding of the female figure, breast development, voice change, and pubic hair appearance.

Each ovary contains 200,000 to 400,000 saclike structures called **follicles** that store immature egg cells. At the onset of puberty, due to the release of the follicle-stimulating hormone (FSH) into the bloodstream from the anterior lobe of the pituitary, several follicles are activated in the ovary each month. Only one will evolve into a mature ovum. Simultaneously, the follicle is secreting **estrogen**, which signals the womb, or uterus, to prepare for a potential pregnancy by filling its lining with blood and nutrients for the embryo. As the maturing follicle and its ovum move to the surface of the ovary, with the follicle continuing to secrete estrogen, the luteinizing hormone (LH) is released into the bloodstream from the anterior lobe of the pituitary. The LH production causes the follicle to rupture and release the mature ovum into the fallopian tubes. This process, **ovulation**, usually occurs midway into the monthly reproductive cycle of 28 days (see Figure 9.3).

During ovulation, estrogen is at its highest level and causes cessation of additional secretions of FSH. At the same time, LH continues to be secreted and produces closure of the ruptured follicle. The empty follicle, now called the **corpus luteum**, and the mature ovum begin to produce another hormone in addition to estrogen called **progesterone**. Progesterone further prepares the uterus for implantation of a fertilized egg and continues to maintain the uterus during pregnancy. Simultaneously, the levels of estrogen begin to decrease.

From the moment conception occurs, the woman's body begins to change. Through pregnancy a weight gain of 17 to 24 pounds is normal and considered desirable because this helps ensure adequate development of the fetus. The average fetus weighs approximately 7 pounds at birth. Figure 9.4 follows the development of the fetus through each trimester.

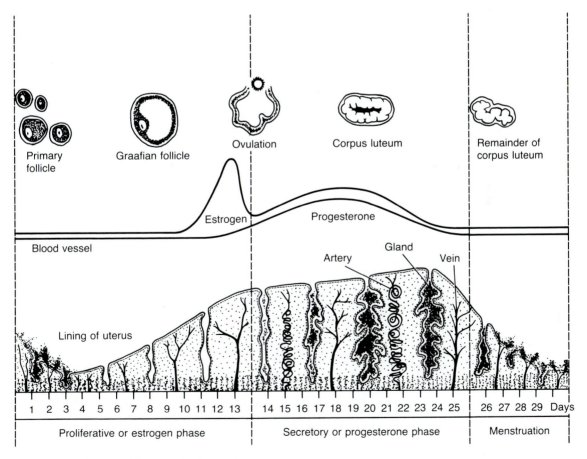

Figure 9.3 The monthly reproductive cycle

Figure 9.4   The development of the fetus

First trimester development

A small mass of cells is implanted in the uterus.

Development into a fetus begins.

Major organ systems are present and recognizable.

During the fourth to eighth weeks, the eyes, ears, arms, hands, fingers, legs, feet, and toes develop.

By the seventh week, the liver, lungs, pancreas, kidneys, and intestines have formed.

By the end of the first trimester, the fetus weighs two-thirds of an ounce and is about 4 inches in length.

From this time on, development consists of enlargement and differentiation of the existing structures.

Second trimester development

By the end of the fourteenth week, movement can be detected.

By the eighteenth week, a fetal heartbeat can be detected.

By the twentieth week, the fetus will open its eyes.

Around the twenty-fourth week, the fetus is sensitive to light and can hear sounds. It will also have periods of sleep and wakefulness.

Third trimester development

Fat deposits form under the skin.

During the seventh month, the fetus turns in the uterus to a head-down position.

By the end of the eighth month, the fetus weighs an average of 5 lb. 4 oz.

At birth, the infant weighs approximately 7.5 lb and is 20 in. long.

If the mature ovum is not fertilized within 24 to 48 hours after ovulation, it disintegrates, thus diminishing the amount of estrogen and progesterone in the bloodstream. Around the twenty-fourth day of the cycle, the corpus luteum also stops secreting progesterone and estrogen. As a result, several days later the uterus expels its blood-rich lining through the vagina. This process is referred to as **menstruation**. Following menstruation, the reproductive cycle begins again in preparation for possible fertilization and pregnancy. Menstruation begins with puberty. The onset of menstruation is called **menarche**.

CONCEPTION AND PREGNANCY

Conception occurs when a single sperm fertilizes an egg to produce a zygote. To facilitate conception, the sperm undergo biochemical changes that enable them to penetrate the egg. This process is referred to as **capacitation** (Denney & Quadagno, 1992). Conception usually occurs in the upper third of the fallopian tube and must take place in the first or second day following ovulation. When a sperm enters an egg, the membrane thickens to prevent further penetration by sperm.

Indications of Pregnancy

The first indication that a woman may be pregnant is often a missed menstrual period. The woman may develop morning sickness, or nausea. The term **morning sickness** is not altogether appropriate, because nausea can occur at any time of the day. The breasts may increase in size, and the nipples may enlarge and darken. The woman may also need to urinate more frequently. One of the most common methods for determining pregnancy is a laboratory test based on the presence in the urine of a hormone called human chorionic gonadotrophin. This hormone, which becomes detectable about 9 days after the missed menstrual period, is produced by the developing placenta (uterine lining). Home pregnancy tests available over the counter test for this hormone; the tests are about 98% effective. Although they can be used the first day after a missed period, the accuracy increases after 9 days when more chorionic gonadotrophin is present. A physician should confirm whether the woman is actually pregnant.

Pregnancy lasts an average of 266 days from the time the egg is fertilized or 280 days from the first day of the last menstrual period if menses are based on a 28-day cycle. Very few women actually have a 28-day cycle, which makes it difficult to pinpoint when conception occurred. Nine calendar months, the common gestation period, is midway between 266 and 280 days.

The Embryonic Period

Immediately after conception, the zygote begins to divide to form other cells. It travels down the fallopian tube and within 10 days attaches to the uterine wall. From the time it attaches to the wall until the eighth week, it is called an **embryo**. The embryo divides into three layers of cells which produce the various body organs and systems. The innermost layer, the **endoderm**, becomes the digestive and respiratory systems; the next layer, the **mesoderm**, forms the skeletal, muscular, circulatory, and reproductive systems; and the **ectoderm**, or outermost layer, becomes the nervous system and skin. The head develops first, the lower body, last. After 8 weeks, the embryo is called the **fetus**.

HEALTH HIGHLIGHT
Calculating the Due Date*

To find out when the baby is due, use the following formula:

1. Add 1 week to the first day of the last menstrual period.
   Example: January 1, 1993 + 7 days = January 8, 1993.
2. Subtract 90 days.
   Example: January 8 – 90 days = October 8, 1992.
3. Add one year.
   Example: October 8, 1992 + 1 year = October 8, 1993.

*60% of births occur within 5 days of a date calculated in this manner.

The amnion is a thin protective membrane filled with a fluid called **amniotic fluid**. This fluid serves as insulation and protection for the embryo against shocks and blows to the mother's abdomen. The fluid also allows for changes in position as growth and movement occur. The **umbilical cord** connects the **placenta** and the embryo.

The placenta is the organ through which the embryo receives nutrients, vitamins, antibodies, and other substances such as drugs, alcohol, and diseases. The fetus also emits waste products, such as nitrogen compounds and carbon dioxide, which are carried through the umbilical cord, diffused through the placenta and eliminated in the mother's urine and through her lungs. This is accomplished even though the fetus's and mother's blood do not mix. The placenta is expelled shortly following the birth of the child and is referred to as the **afterbirth**.

Multiple Births

Several factors contribute to multiple births. Heredity, age of the mother, and fertility drugs are thought to be significant factors (McCary, 1984). Multiple births occur more often in some families than in others. Women in their thirties are more likely to have multiple births than are women in their twenties.

Identical twins develop from a single fertilized ovum that divides to form two individuals. Such twins are always the same sex and look very much alike. **Fraternal twins** develop from two different ova. Although the ova are fertilized at about the same time, fraternal twins may not be of the same sex and may look no more alike than any other siblings born to the same parents.

Triplets usually involve two fertilized ova, one of which separates and then develops into twins. **Quadruplets** usually involve two fertilized ova that then divide and develop into two pairs of identical twins.

CHILDBIRTH

The process of birth occurs in three stages, referred to as **labor** (see Figure 9.5). This process begins when the amniotic sac that has protected the fetus ruptures and the amniotic fluid flows from the vagina. Labor pains occur at regular intervals, usually 15 to 20 minutes apart, with the cervix dilating to 3 to 4 inches to permit the emergence of the fetus through the vagina. This first stage of labor may last 12 to 16 hours (or even longer) for the first birth, but usually is shorter in subsequent births.

The second stage begins when the cervix has fully dilated and the baby's head enters the vagina. It ends with the birth of the baby. Contractions are quite severe and last from a minute to a minute and a half, with a 2- to 3-minute interval between contractions. The contractions move the baby down the birth canal. Just before the head of the child appears, it rotates to the side to pass the pelvic bone. The neck and shoulders emerge, and the rest of the body follows rather quickly.

The third and final stage lasts only a few minutes and consists of the delivery of the placenta. The placenta separates from the wall of the uterus and is expelled as afterbirth. It is examined to determine that all of the organ has been delivered. Occasionally, complications do arise during labor. For example, some conditions

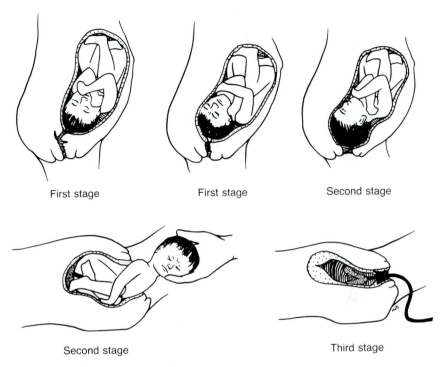

First stage   First stage   Second stage

Second stage   Third stage

Figure 9.5   The three stages of birth

may require a **cesarean section**. Under this procedure, an incision is made through the abdominal wall. Another incision is made in the uterus and the baby is removed. Cesarean sections are usually done because of a contracted pelvis, in which the baby is unable to pass into the vagina. Other reasons are that the baby is in a breech (buttock or leg first) position; the placenta has prematurely separated from the uterus, causing a loss of oxygen; a vaginal infection is present; or the mother is incapacitated because of injury or trauma. To help identify potential complications, a fetal monitor may be used during the birth process.

Methods of Delivery

Several methods are commonly used to help reduce the pain associated with labor. A general anesthetic is sometimes used to induce a light sleep in which the mother is partly awake. The problem with any type of general anesthesia, however, is that it also enters the baby's bloodstream and can cause sluggish respiration in the infant. A complaint against local anesthetics is that they are often used unnecessarily, therefore increasing the potential for harm to the woman and the infant. Anesthetics may also dull the experience and excitement of birth. Another procedure used to ease delivery is a surgical incision in the vagina called an **episiotomy**. This is done to prevent undue stretching or tearing of the vagina.

Today, many couples want the father to be present and the mother to be totally aware during childbirth. A method known as **prepared childbirth** is an outgrowth of this desire. Introduced to the United States by the French physician Fernand Lamaze, it is known as the **Lamaze technique**. This technique requires pretraining sessions to learn relaxation and controlled breathing. This type of childbirth is not an endurance test, because a mild painkiller may be given, but the use of a general anesthetic is avoided unless the mother so chooses during labor. The husband is taught how to help his wife relax through birth. A major advantage of the Lamaze method is that both the man and the woman learn what happens to the woman's body during birth and what to expect during delivery. Prepared childbirth may be done either at the hospital or in a special childbirth center where a midwife usually assists in the labor process.

Frederick Leboyer, another French physician, developed a procedure that attempts to provide a nonviolent birth for the baby. This approach advocates placing the baby in warm water immediately after birth and surrounding the baby with dim lighting and very little noise. Leboyer believed this type of environment makes birth gentler for the baby. He also advocated not cutting the umbilical cord immediately and allowing breathing to begin gradually (Leboyer, 1966).

In addition to alternative methods of birth, some women are choosing to have their children in birth centers or in their own homes. The **alternative birth center**, which may be associated with a hospital, typically emphasizes the needs and desires of the mother. The birthing room may consist of a double bed and be decorated more like a bedroom than a hospital room. This provides a homelike situation but with any necessary medical equipment readily available. Many hospitals now allow the newborn to remain in the mother's room for most of the day. At night the child is taken to a central nursery. This allows the mother an opportunity to become accustomed to the child and learn proper techniques for caring for the infant. Other women prefer to have their babies in their homes. However, it may be difficult to find a physician who is willing to deliver in a home. Some states do allow midwives to deliver babies in the home setting; the major drawback of this option is the lack of emergency medical equipment. Advantages are that it costs less, places control in the parents' hands, and allows the woman to avoid procedures she finds unnecessary or objectionable.

Breast-Feeding

At one time, few women in the United States breast-fed their babies. However, a group called the La Leche League has been instrumental in educating American women about the advantages of breast-feeding.

Breast-feeding seems to be an important means of bonding between the mother and child by ensuring close contact and by providing a sense of security for the baby. Additional advantages are that the mother's milk is easier on the baby's digestive system; has more iron, vitamins, and minerals; contains more antibodies that provide immunity against allergy and disease; is always the right temperature; and is free from bacteria. In addition, sexual interest returns more rapidly for breast-feeding women than for non-breast-feeding women (Denney and Quadagno). The American Academy of Pediatrics strongly recommends breast-feeding.

Any woman who does not enjoy breast-feeding should discontinue it, because it can detract from the mother-child relationship. Other possible disadvantages of breast-feeding are that any substances the mother ingests (such as alcohol, nicotine, cocaine, or prescription drugs) can have a negative effect on the baby; some women find that their breasts drip milk, which can become a nuisance for them; the baby may not drink enough milk, leaving the breasts swollen and tender; the nipples may become sore; it may be difficult for the mother to know if the baby is consuming enough; and the father may feel he is not part of the process because he cannot feed the baby, whereas the mother may feel "tied down" doing all the feeding. Finally, some women feel that breast-feeding prevents them from resuming their regular activities or returning to work.

Preventing Conception

For many people the problem is not how to conceive, but how to prevent conception. **Contraception**, or the prevention of pregnancy, can take many forms. It can involve preventing ovulation, fertilization, or implantation. Some of the common methods employed are coitus interruptus, rhythm, fertility awareness, condoms, vaginal spermicides, diaphragms, cervical caps, hormonal contraceptives (the "pill"), intrauterine devices (IUDs), vaginal sponges, and sterilization. Two of the newest methods that are extremely effective include injectable progesterone and implants (Norplant). Sterilization should be considered a permanent procedure for prevention of pregnancy. Table 9.1 summarizes the advantages and disadvantages of various types of contraceptive devices.

Abortion

Abortion is the removal of an embryo, or fetus, from the uterus. If the body rejects the embryo, however, it is called *spontaneous abortion* or **miscarriage**. Most miscarriages occur in the second or third month of pregnancy. Some of the causes of miscarriage include diseases such as syphilis, genital herpes, and diabetes; poor uterine environment; a defective fetus; or malformations of the female reproductive organs.

Probably no health issue has caused more controversy than that of artificially induced abortions. Many consider it an act of murder. Others believe, just as strongly, that abortion is a matter of choice for the individuals involved. In 1973 the U.S. Supreme Court ruled that every woman is entitled to an abortion, if she so desires. Two landmark decisions—*Roe v. Wade* and *Doe v. Bolton*—provided that an abortion could be performed during the first trimester if a woman and her physician so chose. In 1976 the Supreme Court ruled that the right to choose or reject an abortion was the sole right of the pregnant woman.

The abortion issue is far from settled, however. Many states have circumvented the 1973 ruling by establishing laws that make abortions more difficult to obtain. Congress has placed restrictions on government-paid abortions by prohibiting Medicaid funds from being used to pay for the procedure, except when the mother's life is in danger. The issues surrounding abortion are now being more hotly debated

Table 9.1   Advantages and Disadvantages of Various Contraceptive Methods

Method	Advantages	Disadvantages
Contraceptive pill	Highly effective; no loss of spontaneity.	Contraindicated for women with blood clots, history of stroke, impaired liver function, cancer of the breast or reproductive organs, migraine headaches, hypertension, diabetes. Side effects may include nausea, weight gain, headaches, spotting, yeast infections, discharge, gallbladder disease, hypertension.
Mini-pill	Highly effective; no loss of spontaneity; fewer side effects than regular pill.	Irregular menses, amenorrhea.
IUD	Effective: no loss of spontaneity.	Possible infections or sterility.
Cervical cap	Less messy than diaphragm; similar in terms of effectiveness.	Must be inserted 5 hours prior to intercourse and left in place 6–8 hours after intercourse.
Diaphragm	No serious side effects. When used with nonoxynol 9 offers some protection against STDs.	Must be used with spermicide, can be inserted up to 2 hours prior to intercourse and must be left in place 6–8 hours.
Condom (male and female)	Easy to use; good protection against STDs.	Loss of sensation; possible breakage; loss of spontaneity.
Contraceptive sponge	Easy to use; some protection against STDs (contains nonoxynol 9)	Must be inserted 24 hours before intercourse and left in place 6 hours after.
Vaginal spermicides (foams, jellies, etc.)	Easy to use; some STD protection.	Messy; loss of spontaneity; not very effective when used alone.
Norplant/progesterone implants	Almost 100% effective for 12–18 months; no loss of spontaneity.	Irregular cycles; expensive.
Vaginal rings	No loss of spontaneity; lasts 1–6 months.	Fairly expensive; no protection against STDs.
Tubal ligation	Permanent and effective.	Permanent; some risk.
Vasectomy	Permanent and effective.	Permanent.
Coitus interruptus	None.	Poor effectiveness; no STD protection
Basal body (rhythm)	Accepted by religious groups; inexpensive.	Prolonged periods of abstinence; time consuming; difficult to do.
Cervical mucus	See above.	See above.

Source: *Contraceptive Technology,* 15th ed., by R. A. Hatcher, 1990, New York: Irvington.

than at any previous time. Both prochoice and antiabortion groups continue to spread their messages. The outcome is yet undetermined and will probably not be settled in the next few years.

Methods Used for Abortion

Following are the procedures used for aborting a pregnancy:

Vacuum Curettage. This is the most widely used technique for performing abortion. The procedure is done under local anesthesia. The cervix is dilated, a tube inserted into the uterus, and the contents of the uterus are aspirated.

Dilation and Curettage (D & C). A common procedure used in many gynecological procedures, dilation and curettage is occasionally used in abortions. The woman must be under general anesthesia. D & C is more painful than vacuum curettage because it causes more blood loss and requires greater dilation.

Prostaglandins. These agents are powerful biochemicals that are either injected directly into the amniotic sac or are placed in the vagina as suppositories. These agents cause the uterus to expel the fetus. They are used for second trimester abortions.

Alternatives to Abortion

A number of options are available besides abortion in the case of unwanted pregnancy. The woman may choose to keep the child or place the infant up for adoption. If the mother is a teenager, and unwed, parenting will be very difficult. Many times she must rely on her parents or other relatives to aid in caring for the child. Unfortunately, too often the maturity necessary to be a good parent is lacking. The mother faces the difficulty of furnishing a secure, supportive place for the child to grow and develop, providing adequate nutrition, and developing sufficient economic resources. The options open to a single, young parent may be severely lacking socially, educationally, and economically. Even if marriage occurs, the chances of a teenage marriage surviving are much less than if marriage occurs later in life.

Adoption is a difficult decision, but many couples are willing to provide the love, closeness, and resources a child may need. In fairness to both the child and the natural mother, the best choice for both is often adoption. Being an adoptive parent is virtually no different from being a natural parent. The same love, rewards, and frustrations are experienced by both parents and children.

PROBLEMS OF ABUSE AND VIOLENCE

Spouse Abuse

Spouse abuse occurs in all social and economic classes. The wife is usually the subject of the abuse, but in some cases the wife physically abuses the husband. Only a small percentage of abuse cases are ever reported.

The typical wife abuser seems to be a man who is angry, resentful, and suspicious, yet extremely dependent on his wife's support and nurturing. To the outside world, he may appear to be self-assured and independent. Unfortunately, he harbors deep feelings of insecurity and is unable to vent his anger on what he views as a threatening world. Abusive husbands see themselves as outclassed and unable to achieve the ideal image of life that they developed during their upbringing.

Perhaps the most mystifying question is why women remain in such a deplorable situation. Many women consider themselves to blame for the abuse and think they actually deserve what happens. Others have a very real fear of having to deal with the spouse if they should call the police: what happens after the police leave or the husband is released from jail? Finally, many women are reluctant to leave because they have nowhere to go and no obvious way to support themselves or their children.

Evidence suggests that if a husband and wife seek professional help together, often they can eliminate violence in the home. Unfortunately, abusive husbands rarely are willing to seek therapy as a solution. If a husband refuses to seek outside help, a wife should not remain in the household and expose herself to additional abuse.

Child Abuse

Child abuse is a particularly difficult problem to combat because the abuse usually occurs in the home and because many people are reluctant to intervene and report what they consider a family matter. The National Center on Child Abuse and Neglect estimates that one million children suffer abuse by their parents each year. Of these children, as many as 100,000 to 200,000 are physically abused; 60,000 to 100,000 are sexually abused; the remainder are neglected. Each year, more than 2,000 children die because of abuse or neglect. An estimated 200,000 to 500,000 sexual assaults occur each year in the United States to females between infancy and 13 years of age. Other researchers have estimated that 27% of females and 16% of males are sexually molested before they reach their sixteenth birthday (Calderone & Johnson, 1989). Still other studies indicate that one in four women and one in seven men are abused during their lifetime.

Aside from the obvious physical consequences, abusive treatment can seriously handicap a child's psychological development. Many abused children are emotional cripples their entire lives. A child who is abused loses the chance to be a child. Unable to understand why they are being punished, these children come to believe that they deserve such treatment because they are "bad." They see the world as cold and hostile and have little faith in themselves or in their ability to succeed in life. They learn that using force is an acceptable way to deal with others and, most tragically, they often become child abusers themselves.

Many parents become abusive because of their own history of abuse, failure to understand their children's needs, or as a response to unmanaged stress. They typically do not have the self-confidence, ingenuity, and ability to cope with crises within the family. For them, any crisis presents a greater danger than for someone with better coping skills. Even a minor occurrence may cause loss of self-control and an abusive attack on the innocent child. In many instances, abusive adults reverse roles with their children, requiring the child to love and care for them without providing the emotional support the child needs. With sexual abuse, the abuser may actually convince himself that he is doing a child a favor by showing the child the "facts of life" in a more loving way than an outsider would use (Office of the Attorney General, 1985). Abusers can be rehabilitated if the matter is brought to the attention of the proper authorities. Successful therapy seems directly related to the perpetrator's willingness to change.

Every state has laws that compel teachers to report suspected abuse. Not every bruise should be considered abuse, but if teachers observe a pattern of injury, they should report this concern. Proper authorities may be the state department of family and child services or a local health agency.

Incest

Sexual intercourse between two persons who are too closely related by blood or affinity to be legally married is considered **incest**. When the act occurs against the will of a party involved, it is coercive. Most incest goes unreported; thus, it is difficult to know its exact rate of occurrence. Father-daughter incest was once thought to be the most common, but some researchers now believe that brother-sister incest is (Renshaw, 1983). The exact cause of incest is unknown, but fathers who force such

---

HEALTH HIGHLIGHT
Indicators of Sexual Abuse

Psychological Signs

1. Fear of being alone with a specific person.
2. Sleep disturbances such as nightmares, fear of going to bed, and fear of sleeping alone.
3. Irritability or short temper.
4. Clinging to parent or parents.
5. Unexplained fears.
6. Changes in behavior and schoolwork or in relating to friends or siblings.
7. Behaving like a younger child (regression).
8. Sexual sophistication or knowledge greater than age group.
9. Fear of going home or running away from home.

Physical Signs (Caused by Sexual Acts)

1. Difficulty in walking or sitting.
2. Pain or itching in genital areas.
3. Torn, stained or bloody underwear.
4. Bruises or bleeding in external genitals, vagina, or anal areas.
5. Sexually transmitted diseases.
6. Pregnancy.

Source: *Human Sexuality* by N. W. Denney and D. Quadagno, 1992, St. Louis: Mosby.

behavior on their daughters tend to be domineering in the home situation, possibly to compensate for their lack of social skills outside the home.

Virtually every society has taboos against incest. Besides the obvious social problems, inbreeding can cause serious genetic consequences. A study done in Japan compared marriages between cousins with those between nonrelated persons. Children of the blood-related partners had significantly poorer school performance, physical skills, and certain measures of health than did the offspring of the nonrelated marriage partners. In addition, incest may cause conflict within the family, guilt, and resentment that may last a lifetime for the individuals involved. Finally, incest is not bound by a family's educational or economic level. The evidence indicates that families from all walks of life can be affected.

Rape

Rape is the act of forcing someone to have sexual intercourse against her will. It is a crime of violence and often is not sexual in nature or motivation. Forcible rape is distinguished from statutory rape, which is intercourse with a partner below the age of consent, regardless of whether force is involved. In her book *Against Our Will* (1986), Susan Brownmiller asserted that rape is essentially an act of aggression, control, and degradation aimed at proving male superiority. The typical rapist is a 20- to 24-year-old man from a low-income, culturally deprived background. The rapist is typically of low to normal intelligence. The family backgrounds of rapists are typically unstable, and the rapist often expresses feelings of inadequacy and low self-esteem. A history of teenage offenses is common.

In an attempt to deal with the various personalities that commit rape, a classification system has been developed (Cohen, Garofalo, Boucher, & Seghorn, 1977). The four types are (1) the aggressive-aim rapist, (2) the sexual-aim rapist, (3) the sex-aggression-fusion rapist, and (4) the impulse rapist. The aggressive-aim rapist is motivated by a desire to hurt his victim. The emotional state during the rape is one of anger. The attacker's victim is typically a stranger. Hurting the victim, not sex, is the intent. For the sexual-aim rapist, the motivation is clearly sexual. He uses a minimal amount of violence and aggression and is highly sexually aroused. The act is usually committed outdoors, and the victim can escape easily if she resists this type of attacker. The sex-aggression-fusion rapist seems to be sexually excited by violence. Rapist-murderers are an extreme version of this type. Needless to say, the sex-agression-fusion rapist is the most dangerous; fortunately, he is also the rarest. The impulse rapist has neither a sexual nor an aggressive motive; he commits rape on impulse. He sees an opportunity and seizes it and is not bound by normal societal restraints against rape. The motivation is that the rape is satisfying to him.

Group or gang rapes occur most often when group members seek esteem by challenging their peers to join in an assault. Responsibility for the assault shifts from the individual to the group. The attacks are usually planned in advance, with the attackers generally between the ages of 15 and 19.

Many myths are associated with rape. Among these myths are the patently absurd notions that women secretly want to be raped, some women deserve to be raped, rape keeps women in line, nice women do not get raped, and rape is provoked by the woman. Nothing in the research substantiates these claims even partially. They may ease the rapist's guilt feelings, but the fact remains that he has committed a heinous act of aggression and violence against an innocent victim.

An area of great concern is "date" or "acquaintance" rape. Anytime one person forces another to have sex, it is rape. It does not matter if the people know each other, if they are dating, or even if they have engaged in sex in the past. Rape is a violation of will. Several studies have reported that almost 15% of college women have been raped, with 84% to 89% of these women having known the rapist. Only 2% of these rapes were ever reported (Koss, Gidycsz, & Wisniewski, 1988). In a study of women at Kent State University, it was found that one out of eight women had been raped on a date. More than 90% of these women did not report the rape. These women frequently feel guilty and responsible for what has happened. Often, women feel pressured into sex because they lack the ability to insist on abstaining.

Men need to learn that "no" means exactly that! The miscommunication associated with many dating situations is a major contributor to date rape. What the woman considers appropriate dress, for example, may seem provocative or sexual to the man. An invitation to her apartment to watch TV may be just that to the female, but the male may see a signal or invitation for sexual intercourse. Myths, misinformation, and misconstrued intent are often real issues. Both males and females need to realize that sexual intercourse should occur only by mutual consent, and that when one person says "no," that should stop further advances. Presence in a compromising situation (e.g., attending a party where alcohol and other drugs are being abused) and failure to clearly communicate perceptions and intent can contribute to circumstances that can result in acquaintance rape. Regardless of circumstances, however, having sex with any woman who protests is rape and the person should be prosecuted.

A victim of rape may react in one of two ways. The expressive reaction may include hysteria, crying, guilt, and fear. This type of reaction may first appear as a very controlled reaction, followed later by a severe emotional reaction. The second type is referred to as the silent reaction. In this case, the victim may tell no one of the attack because she feels responsible for the rape or believes she could have prevented it. Unfortunately, this reaction may also be motivated by the fact that many men reject their wives or girlfriends after a rape. Regardless of the type of reaction, victims of rape suffer from a wide variety of conditions, including rectal bleeding and pain, irritation of the genitals, headache, nervousness, sleeplessness, fear, nausea, a sense of humiliation, and a desire for revenge.

Counseling is extremely important in helping the victim work through her feelings. Many cities have rape crisis centers designed to help victims with physical and emotional problems. Many centers also help victims with the police and court procedures.

Self-defense instruction is important for women in avoiding rape. Women need proper training before trying self-defense, because improper technique can cause even greater physical harm to the victim. Others suggest that we need to change the way we socialize males and females. The stereotype of weak and passive females versus aggressive males seems to be one root cause of rape. In societies in which males are taught to be nurturing rather than aggressive, rape is virtually unknown (Mead, 1935).

IMPLICATIONS FOR FAMILY-LIFE EDUCATION

Few subjects in society evoke more discussion and controversy than family-life and sex education in our schools. It is amazing that one of the most significant aspects of our being is such a taboo topic. Humans are sexual from the moment they are born until well into old age. The adage that we are sexual beings from womb to tomb is certainly true. While humans have learned a great deal about sexuality that can be incorporated in the educational process, we often repress and hide information about sex and avoid discussing sexuality with our children. Many people believe it is better to ignore problem pregnancies, the increasing rate of STDs, and the many sexual misconceptions of the nation's youth.

Some groups oppose family-life/sex education because they think the less adolescents know about sex, the less likely they are to engage in it. Research, however, has indicated that informing young people about sexual manners has actually decreased premature and irresponsible sexual behavior.

Parents greatly influence their children's views concerning sexuality. Parents provide the young child with a basic orientation by the verbal and nonverbal messages they send concerning nudity, masturbation, sexual values, and so on. If parents believe that sex is shocking, dirty, or disgusting, or that one sex should be submissive, those beliefs are transmitted to the child. These types of messages are likely to interfere with enjoyable, healthy sexuality in the adult years. It is important to note that information children and adolescents get about sex and sexuality from parents is more likely to be accurate and positive than what they learn from peers. Adolescents are more likely to view sex as "dirty" or something to be "ashamed of" if they learn about it from peers. Research indicates that adolescents who report good communication with parents are more likely to use contraception than those adolescents who report poor communication. In addition, adolescents whose parents educate them about sex are more likely to behave in ways consistent with their knowledge. This is important, since a number of studies have indicated that increased knowledge in sexual matters results in changes in sexual behavior (Fan & Shaffer, 1990).

Because many parents feel inadequate or unable to deal with sexual topics and issues, schools have been asked to fill the void. Indications are that well over 90% of parents favor family-life/sex education programs in junior and senior high schools. Topics typically taught are sexual physiology, STDs, pregnancy, and childbirth. Topics such as relationships, communications, dating, and contraception may also be covered. Subjects least likely to be discussed are masturbation, abortion, and homosexuality (Sonenstein & Pittman, 1984).

Because there is some resistance to family-life programs, any program's success depends on involving the community in the planning process. People are more comfortable if they have opportunities to give input and to view the actual content, materials, and activities associated with the curriculum. Successful family-life programs were found to have a high degree of parental involvement, administrative efforts at teacher training, a cooperative relationship between the school and a family planning agency, and strong support from the school board (Scales, 1984).

Despite the school's involvement, the family should teach each child values. The school can provide knowledge, decision-making training, and opportunities for examining sexuality issues in a nonthreatening environment. At best, family-life programs in the school can strive to help students recognize and have insight into their own values.

CONCEPTS TO BE TAUGHT IN FAMILY-LIFE/SEX EDUCATION

Bruess and Greenberg (1981) suggest teaching the following topics and concepts in grades 7 through 12:

Lower Secondary Grades

1. Overview of biological material
2. More detail on birth control
   a. How various methods work
   b. Research in contraception
3. More on intimate sexual behavior
   a. How far to go
   b. Why individuals feel the way they do
   c. Why people behave sexually the way they do
4. Dating and interpersonal relationships
   a. What to expect from a date (both the person and the experience)
   b. Why people date; why some do not date
5. Variations in sexual behavior
   a. Homosexuality
   b. Voyeurism
   c. Transvestism
   d. Exhibitionism

Upper Secondary Grades

1. Birth control research and details
   a. Population dynamics
   b. Abortion
2. Dating decisions
   a. Dating standards and regulations
   b. Premarital sexual behavior
   c. Communications
3. Contemporary marriage patterns
   a. Companionship and patriarchal structures
   b. Communes and group marriages
   c. Three-way marriages
   d. Living together
   e. Contract marriages
4. Sexual myths
5. Moral decisions
6. Control of sex drives
7. Parenthood
   a. Childbirth
   b. Child rearing
   c. Sex education of children
8. Masculinity and femininity

9. Research in sexuality
    a. Human sexual response
    b. Sexual dysfunction
    c. Sterility
    d. Pornography
10. Sexuality and legality
    a. Personal behavior
    b. Treatment and information
    c. Sex education
11. Historical and social factors affecting sexuality
    a. Selected historical accounts related to sexuality
    b. Cultural aspects of sexuality
12. Sexuality and advertising

■ ■ ■   *STUDENT CONCERNS:* HUMAN SEXUALITY

From *Students Speak* (Trucano, 1984), typical concerns of students were as follows:

Grades 7 and 8

How do boys feel when they find out their girlfriend is pregnant?
Why are girls always to blame for pregnancy?
How can you prevent hurt from divorce?
Why do some families fight a lot?
How can you prevent child abuse?
How do pregnant teenagers cope with their problems?
What makes a strong, loving family?
What are ways of solving family problems?
Why do we have sexual urges?
I would like to learn a lot more about sex, more than we do learn, not just about
    reproduction but about feelings between boys and girls.

Grades 9 and 10

How can the guy be made to take more responsibility in a teenage pregnancy?
How does sex affect you after it's over?
When you get a check-up and discuss birth control with your doctor what occurs
    in this medical check-up?
How can you tell if you are going to marry the right person?
How can you say "no" to a partner?
How do you keep your values when you are in a car with a girl?
How do you know when you are mature enough for sexual activity?
Do contraceptives really work; are they harmful?
What makes people have sexual feelings towards the opposite sex?
How do you know the difference between caring for a person and being actually
    in love?

Grades 11 and 12

Why does society somewhat set a time period when sexual activity is O.K., such
    as when a girl is over 21?

What risks are taken using birth control?

What makes you want to have sex?

Do most teenage marriages fail?

What causes people to abuse their children?

How does a child deal with being abused?

When is the right time to have sex?

How does teenage pregnancy affect future lifestyle?

What are the different choices of birthing processes and what is involved in each?

In choosing a mate, how can you tell if you have anything in common?

How can I be sure about marriage so it won't end in divorce?

What changes may arise in a person or persons after getting married?

What makes people get upset over things that don't have to do with them?

How can you value your own ideas so you won't be influenced so much by peers to do something you really would not have done by your own standards?

SUMMARY

No area in health education is more controversial than that of sex and family-life education. Sex and family-life education aims to develop an appreciation of self and others and to aid students in becoming responsible members of society. This process must start early in life and be reinforced each year for children to develop a healthy appreciation of their own sexuality.

Family-life education consists of many components, including the biological aspects of families, dating, mate selection, marriage, and parenthood. These components are all part of each person's sexuality. Each fulfills basic needs of the individual or society and serves to maintain an institutionalized social pattern. The American family is in transition and is a subject of greater stress. However, the family as the basic unit of society continues to thrive.

Family-life education in the schools is a highly controversial area. While many people support the role of the school in educating students about sexuality issues, others vehemently oppose it. Schools can only provide the knowledge base and assist students in decision making and communication skills. The family must provide the value base for each student's decisions.

DISCUSSION QUESTIONS

1. Why do some people oppose family-life education?
2. What qualifications should a teacher have for teaching sex and family-life education?
3. What are secondary sex characteristics?
4. Discuss the female/male reproductive cycle.
5. Discuss the development that occurs during each trimester of pregnancy.
6. What are the important functions the family serves?
7. What are the shortcomings of inflexible sex roles?
8. Differentiate and explain the different types of family abuse.
9. What are the implications for family-life education in today's schools?
10. What arguments could be presented for a family-life education program?

■ ■ ■   *ACTIVITIES FOR TEACHING ABOUT FAMILY LIFE EDUCATION*

■ ■ ■   *ACTIVITIES:* GAMES

A Riddle

Have students read the following story and answer the questions.

A father and his son were involved in a car accident in which the father was killed and the son was seriously injured. The father was pronounced dead at the scene of the accident. The son was taken by ambulance to a local hospital and was immediately wheeled into an operating room. A surgeon was called. Upon seeing the patient, the attending surgeon exclaimed, "Oh, my God, it's my son!" Can you explain this?

Note: The father was killed in the accident and the attending physician is not the boy's stepfather.

Answer: The surgeon was the boy's mother.

Processing Questions

1. Are some jobs thought of as masculine? Feminine?
2. Why do you think some jobs have been assigned to women? To men?
3. Did you stereotype the doctor? Why?
4. What are some role models you have?
5. Who are some of the models you look to for sexual identity?

Ideas

Ask students to write about (or just think about) some of their ideas about sex. The teacher may give a few examples: sexual intercourse, love, reproduction, marriage, sex organs, penis, vagina, man, woman, kissing, masculinity and femininity, jokes, movies, *Playboy, Playgirl,* and so on.

Divide the students into groups of 2 or 3 and have each group define sex and sexuality. Explain that their ideas are only tentative and will probably change as they learn more information. Also, explain that some may be uncomfortable discussing sex and sexuality because of its personal meaning and individual values. Most people did not talk about sex openly until the mid-1900s. Our society today seems to discuss sex more frequently and openly as a normal part of human life.

In a large group, provide an opportunity for students to exchange some of their ideas about sex and sexuality. The teacher (on newsprint or chalkboard) may want to record many of the ideas for later discussion.

Processing Questions

1. What does the word "sex" generally refer to? What about "sexuality"?
2. Do sex values change and develop as one becomes older?

Married and Unmarried Folks—Happiness Inventory

Explain to students that this activity is designed to help them discover some attitudes people have about married and single people. It will also help them discover which group may have a better chance for happiness in our culture.

Divide students into groups of 6 to 8. Pass out Happiness Inventories. For each item in the inventory, have students check the group that they believe is the happiest, healthiest, and so forth. Provide each small group with a tally sheet.

Draw a large tally sheet on newsprint or a chalkboard. Have one person from each group report the classification that received the most checks for each category.

Discuss with the entire group the attitudes toward marriage indicated by the results of the Happiness Inventory.

	Happiness Inventory			
	Unmarried		Married	
	Men	Women	Men	Women
Healthier				
Wealthier				
More travel opportunities				
More social life				
More attractive				
More power				
More freedom				
More optimistic				
Live longer				
More emotionally stable				
Better jobs				
Considered more dependable				
Better drivers				

Processing Questions

1. Why do you think married/unmarried people are happier?
2. What are some positive and negative ways that we describe single men and women?
3. What attitudes in society today make it easier for single women to be happier than they might have been in the past?

Meeting Mr. Male/Ms. Female

Break students into groups of 2 to 4. On the drawing provided, see if they can place the correct terms in the appropriate space provided. Give them 15 minutes to complete the activity.

Terms

Penis	Urethra	Clitoris	Labia minora
Scrotum	Bladder	Fallopian tubes	Cervix
Testes	Epididymis	Uterus	Ovary
Vas deferens	Seminal vesicle	Prostate gland	Labia majora
Semineferous tubules	Glans penis	Vagina	

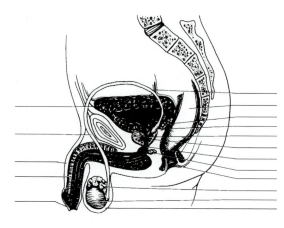 

Processing Questions

1. How many terms did your group correctly identify?
2. Can you tell the various functions of the reproductive system?
3. How did you feel naming the various parts of the human anatomy with members of the opposite sex? Why?

Pick a Date

Provide a set of questions to the person (boy or girl) who is to "pick a date." Assign three people of the opposite sex to be interviewed by this person as prospective dates. The person choosing a date asks each of the three people two questions. After hearing the answers, she must choose the person that she believes best answers the questions. The interviewer then tells the group why she picked that person.

The class may disagree with the interviewer's choice. Encourage such controversy. Have the class discuss the choice after each set.

Since the questions have no set answers, the "dates" being interviewed can say whatever comes into their heads. Interviewers may wish to choose questions that parents might ask if *they* could choose their child's date.

Processing Questions

1. How do you decide: Where to go on a date; when to come home; whether the date will be single, double, or in a group?
2. When should a person begin dating?

Questions for girls to use in interviewing boys:

1. What do you like best about dating?
2. If someone tried to flirt with me while I was out with you, what would you do?
3. How do you feel about going steady?
4. If I liked you a lot, but my parents didn't, how would you go about changing their minds? Would you try to change their minds?
5. What would you do if I called you and asked you out for a second date?
6. What do you like or dislike about blind dates?

7. What do you like to do best on a date?
8. How do you react to a girl who always seems to choose the most expensive items on the menu, suggests that you go to expensive concerts, and so on?
9. What types of gifts do you choose for a girl you are dating a lot?
10. What do you do when you are getting a girl home long past her curfew?

Questions for boys to use in interviewing girls:

1. What do you like or dislike about double-dating?
2. Where do you most like to go on dates?
3. What is your reaction when a guy tries to kiss you on the first date?
4. If you found that you were very bored after we had been together a few hours, what would you do?
5. Suppose you really like me. How would you let me know?
6. If another guy tried to flirt with you while you were out with me, what would you do?
7. What would you do if I started flirting with someone else while we were out together?
8. If it appeared that I was not going to get you home on time, what would you do?
9. If I did something on the date that you did not approve of, such as drinking too much or using drugs, what would you do?
10. If we really liked each other, but your parents did not like me, what would you do?

Questions a parent might like to ask a son's date:

1. What do you like most about my son?
2. How do you feel when the boy says that he has a curfew?
3. How does your family feel about my son?
4. What would you do if you became really bored on a date with my son?
5. How would you act if he tried to go "further" than you wanted to?
6. If I invited you to come to our house for dinner, what are some things you would do while you were here? What are some things you would not do?
7. Where do you want to go on your first date with my son?
8. What would you do if my son drank too much on a date with you?
9. How do you feel about going steady?
10. What type of behavior would make you decide after one date that you would not go out with my son again?

Questions a parent might like to ask a daughter's date:

1. How important do you think it is to have her home on time? What reason do you think should be considered for not getting her home on time?
2. What would you do if you realized the two of you were not able to meet her curfew deadline?
3. How would you behave if she flirted with someone else while she was out with you?
4. If we invited you for dinner, what are some things you would do or not do in our home?
5. What do you consider good reasons for breaking a date with any girl?
6. What would you do if you felt that we did not like you?

7. If you really liked our daughter, but we asked you not to see her anymore, what would you do?
8. Where are you going on this first date, and how will you get there?
9. If her curfew is earlier than yours, what will you do?
10. What characteristics do you look for in a date?

Prove Yourself

Tell this story to the class and have students discuss it: Bill was 13 years old and had just moved into the neighborhood. After a few days, he met the other boys his age in the neighborhood and started doing things with them. The group decided that Bill had to prove himself to the group by lifting something worth $10 from one of the large discount stores.

Processing Questions

1. What should Bill do?
2. How do you think he felt?
3. What kinds of pressures were on Bill?
4. What would you do?

The Road to Independence

Divide participants into three groups. Direct each group to list the major steps toward independence for a designated age group: birth to 6, 6 to 12, and 12 to 18. Remind the group that small accomplishments such as crawling, feeding oneself, tying one's shoes, and so on are steps to independence.

After completing the lists, have participants create a road to independence by writing the various steps on pieces of paper cut in the shape of footprints and attaching them to a long piece of butcher paper. The different age categories should be designated on the road. An alternative road could be created with pictures depicting the various milestones such as a baby feeding himself, teens having fun with the caption "first boy-girl party" or a picture of a first date.

Processing Questions

1. What milestones have you had in your life so far?
2. What milestones do you expect in the future?
3. What are some of the alternatives that might occur?

Sex Information Sources

Distribute the following possible sources for obtaining sex information. Ask students to rank items (1 to 12) to indicate the best sources. There are no right or wrong answers.

_____ minister

_____ counselor

_____ physician

_____ teacher

_____ parents   father _____ mother _____

_____ friends

_____ magazine

_____ books

_____ relative

_____ pornographic materials

_____ movies and television

_____ other sources _____

Group students in pairs and have them discuss and compare their sources of sex information for approximately 3 to 5 minutes. In a large group, encourage the groups to share their sex information sources and explain their choices. The teacher could list their comments on newsprint or the chalkboard.

Processing Questions

1. Why are some parents (adults) not comfortable talking about sex with their children? Do you think their parents talked to them about sex?
2. How do you think we learn most sex information?
3. Is trust important in discussing sex with others? Why or why not?

What's Important?

Each student will make two lists: One list should contain the five most important qualities he or she looks for in a male, the other should contain the five most important qualities he or she looks for in a female. Compile four lists: what males look for in males; what males look for in females; what females look for in males; and what females look for in other females.

Processing Questions

1. How do the two sexes differ in their views of what's important in the opposite sex?
2. What seems to be important in relationships of the same sex?
3. Do males and females have the same standards for evaluating males? For evaluating females?
4. How do you account for differences in the lists?

Who, What

Ask students to indicate how they perceive individual and group attitudes concerning sex roles and traits. Have them circle the choice that most closely indicates their views:

W=women   M=men   ND=no difference.

1. Less judgmental of other people?   W   M   ND
2. Is more concerned with what others   W   M   ND
   think?
3. More sexual activity?   W   M   ND
4. A better driver?   W   M   ND
5. More emotional?   W   M   ND
6. More sexually aggressive?   W   M   ND

7. More talkative?	W	M	ND
8. Better at manual labor?	W	M	ND
9. More scheming?	W	M	ND
10. Better organized?	W	M	ND
11. More concerned with sex?	W	M	ND
12. More thoughtful of others?	W	M	ND
13. A better parent?	W	M	ND
14. More concerned about work?	W	M	ND
15. More money-wise?	W	M	ND
16. Carry purses?	W	M	ND
17. Kiss father?	W	M	ND
18. More likely to express emotions?	W	M	ND
19. Score higher on tests of verbal ability?	W	M	ND
20. Score higher in mathematics?	W	M	ND
21. Less likely to risk failure?	W	M	ND
22. More active physically?	W	M	ND

Processing Questions

1. Did your list indicate more males or females?
2. For those traits that you thought were different, what do you feel accounted for the differences?

Why, Mommy?

Have the class break into groups of 3. Provide a list of discipline dilemmas. Instruct each trio to choose a reporter. Assign three dilemmas for the triad to discuss. Allow time for discussion, then have reports on the decisions of each triad. Instruct the participants not only to make a decision about how a child should be disciplined but also to be prepared to answer the questions children usually ask, such as "Why are you making me do this?" and "Why are you being so mean?" The seriousness of child abuse should be discussed, along with the types of punishment that constitute abuse.

Suggested Discipline Dilemmas

If you were the parent, what would you do if:

1. Your 5-year-old son hit a female playmate because she snatched his toy?
2. Your 3-year-old would not eat his spinach?
3. Your 2-year-old had a temper tantrum in the doctor's office?
4. Your 4-year-old wet the bed repeatedly?
5. Your second-grader begged you to be allowed to stay up beyond her bedtime for a TV special and she had school the next day?
6. Your 5-year-old woke up from a nightmare and wanted to sleep with you?
7. Your fourth-grade child wanted to watch horror movies on the late show Saturday?
8. Your grade school child confessed that he had lied to you about doing his homework?
9. Your preschool child has been undressing and playing doctor?

10. Your elementary school child has been using "dirty" words?
11. Your 13-year-old wants to go out on single dates?
12. Your 15-year-old girl wants to go out with a man of 25?
13. Your 16-year-old girl went to a birth control clinic without your knowledge?
14. Your 15-year-old son asks you about sexually transmitted diseases?
15. You discover a dent in the car after your son has been driving?
16. You come home from work to find your daughter and her boyfriend upstairs in her room?
17. Your 17-year-old daughter gets in an hour after the time you both had agreed that she would be home?
18. Your 17-year-old son gets home an hour after the time you both had agreed that he should be home?
19. Your teenage daughter seems to be spending all her time in her room and rarely goes out with friends.
20. Your 14-year-old refuses to go to church anymore?
21. Your 17-year-old continually plays his stereo louder than you can take?
22. Your 16-year-old wants to buy a motorbike?
23. Your son was caught with marijuana in his locker?
24. Your daughter wants to date a young man who has had several car wrecks?
25. Your 13-year-old son has a number of friends much older than he is?
26. Your 12-year-old gripes about anything you ask her to do around the house?
27. Your 10-year-old son never picks up anything of his own?
28. Your 12-year-old son always seems a little dirty?

Processing Questions

1. What are some of the behaviors that require more serious discipline?
2. What are some acceptable forms of discipline?
3. Is discipline always necessary?

"Sex As" Questionnaire

Sex can be used behaviorally for many reasons. When used broadly, the term *sex* can refer to flirting, wearing provocative clothing, or using perfume as a seductive device. After having students complete the following questionnaire, have small groups form to discuss how sex can be used in each of the ways listed.

> Directions: Try to identify with this list of "Sex As" and pick those phrases that most represent your feelings. Try to identify with at least 3. Place a "+" before the ones you choose.

_____ Sex as purely playful activity.

_____ Sex as a way to have babies.

_____ Sex as fun.

_____ Sex as an expression of hostility.

_____ Sex as punishment.

_____ Sex as a mechanical duty.

_____ Sex as an outlet from physiological or psychological tension.

_____ Sex as a protection against alienation.

_____ Sex as a way of overcoming isolation or loneliness.

_____ Sex as a way to communicate deep involvement in another's welfare.

_____ Sex as a form of "togetherness."

_____ Sex as a reward.

_____ Sex as revenge.

_____ Sex as an act of rebellion.

_____ Sex as an experiment.

_____ Sex as an adventure.

_____ Sex as a deceit.

_____ Sex as a form of self-enhancement.

_____ Sex as proof.

Sex Role Dislikes/Likes*

This activity is a discussion of what males dislike about females and what females dislike about males. Begin by dividing the class into groups by gender—one all male and the other all female. Each group brainstorms about what they dislike about the opposite sex. After about 10 to 15 minutes, have each group select a representative to read the list that their group developed. Both groups can then discuss stereotypes of sex roles. This can be followed up by the same groups discussing what they like about the opposite sex (this should help eliminate any ill feelings associated with the first phase of this activity).

■ ■ ■   *ACTIVITIES:* BULLETIN BOARDS

Hey, Sexy! (Sex in Advertising)

A mere glance at a newspaper or magazine reveals many advertisements with sexual images, from the "manly" man to the "womanly" woman, suggesting how use of certain products will automatically result in sex/romance/conquest.

Sex is a popular strategy for selling products. For this bulletin board, use a variety of illustrations showing how frequently and often how subtly sex is used in advertising. Students can then comment on the advertisements and how they perceive the sex in the ads, if at all.

Sexy Collage*

All the sexual overtones in advertising affect our behavior, although we frequently don't recognize it. By having students make their own collages illustrating what

*Source: *Health education learner-centered instructional strategies* by J. S. Greenberg, 1989, Dubuque, IA: Wm. C. Brown.

they perceive sex to be, they may come to realize just how much these overtones are influencing them both consciously and unconsciously. These collages can be posted for classroom viewing for comparison and recognition of differences between the sexes and among individuals. These similarities and differences can be discussed orally or the following questions can be written out for personal introspection.

Processing Questions

1. To which advertisement appealing to sexual needs are you most likely to respond?
2. What could this advertisement influence you to do?
3. How was this advertisement presented to you (television, newspaper, magazine)? Would you have reacted differently if it was presented in another media?
4. What would you tell younger males and females to help them not be influenced by advertisement as much as you are?

■ ■ ■   *ACTIVITIES:* LEARNING ENHANCEMENTS

The following titles are appropriate for use in sex and family-life programs.

Let's Talk About Responsibility. This two-part program guides students toward clarifying their personal beliefs and aids in establishing a standard of responsibility. 28 minutes. Sunburst Communications, 800/431-1934.

Coming Together. Program covers the physiological events behind reproduction. 28 minutes. Sunburst Communications, 800/431-1934.

Understanding Human Reproduction. Provides students with a thorough understanding of the basics of human reproduction. 39 minutes. Sunburst Communications, 800/431-1934.

Choosing to Wait: Sex & Teenagers. Examines the reasons why people choose to remain virgins until marriage. 28 minutes. Sunburst Communications, 800/431-1934.

Birth Control for Teens. Examines the statistics on pregnancies among unwed teens. Also examines ways to teach teens how to avoid pregnancy without advocating premarital sex. 28 minutes. Films for the Humanities and Sciences, 800/257-5126.

My Parents Are Getting a Divorce. Looks at divorce in today's society and examines the reasons for these high rates. Helps identify the problems teenagers face when parents divorce. 28 minutes. Sunburst Communications, 800/431-1934.

Daddy Doesn't Live Here Anymore. Uses case histories to illustrate the problems of living in a one-parent household. Discusses how to foster cooperation, understanding, and love. 72 minutes. Sunburst Communications, 800/431-1934.

Human Sexuality and the Life Cycle. Topics such as secondary sex characteristics, teenage pregnancy, marriage, gradual decline of sex drive, concerns of handicapped persons, and prolonged vitality of many aging adults. 58 minutes. Sunburst Communications, 800/431-1934.

REFERENCES

Bossard, J. (1932). Residential propinquity as a factor in marriage selection. *American Journal of Sociology,* 219–224.

Brownmiller, S. (1986). *Against our will.* New York: Simon & Schuster.

Bruess, C. E., & Greenberg, J. S. (1981). *Sex education—theory & practice.* Belmont, CA: Wadsworth. ,

Calderone, M. (1972). Love, sex, intimacy and aging as a life style. In *Sex, love, intimacy—Whose life styles?* New York: SIECUS.

Calderone, M. S., & Johnson, E. W. (1989). *The family book about sexuality.* New York: Harper & Row.

Coutts, R. (1973). *Love and intimacy: A psychological approach.* San Ramon, CA: Consensus.

Denney, N. W., & Quadagno, D. (1992). *Human sexuality.* St. Louis: Mosby.

Eshleman, J. (1991). *The family: An introduction* (7th ed.). Boston: Allyn & Bacon.

Fan, D. P., & Shaffer, C. L. (1990). Use of open-ended essays and computer content analysis to survey college students' knowledge of AIDS. *Journal of American College Health, 38,* 221–243.

Fromm, E. (1956). *The art of loving.* New York: Harper & Row.

Greenberg, J. S. (1989). *Health education learner-centered instructional strategies.* Dubuque, IA: Wm. C. Brown.

Hass, K., & Hass, A. (1993). *Understanding sexuality.* (3rd ed.). St. Louis: Mosby.

Hatcher, R. A. (1990). *Contraceptive technology* (15th ed.). New York: Irvington.

Heinlein, R. (1961). *Stranger in a strange land.* New York: Putnam.

Insel, M., & Roth, W. T. (1991). *Core concepts in health.* Mountain View, CA: Mayfield.

Kephart, W. (1991). *The family, society and the individual.* Boston: Houghton Mifflin.

Koss, M., Gidycsz, C., & Wisniewski, N. (1988). The scope of rape: incidence and prevalence in a national sample of higher education students. *Journal of Clinical Psychology, 55,* 162–170.

Leboyer, F. (1975). *Birth without violence.* New York: Knopf.

McCary, J. (1984). *Human sexuality.* New York: Van Nostrand.

Mead, M. (1935). *Sex and temperament in three primitive societies.* New York: Morrow.

Office of the Attorney General. (1985). *Child abuse prevention handbook.* Sacramento, CA: Author.

Peele, S., & Brodsky, A. (1976). *Love and addiction.* New York: New American Library.

Reiss, I. (1988). *Family systems in America* (4th ed.). New York: Holt, Rinehart & Winston.

Renshaw, D. (1983). *Incest: Understanding and treatment.* Boston: Little, Brown.

Scales, P. (1984). *The front line of sexuality education.* Santa Cruz, CA: Network.

Sonenstein, F. L., & Pittman, K. J. (1984). The availability of sex education in large city school districts. *Family Planning Perspective, 16,* 19–24.

Trucano, L. (1984). *Students speak—A survey of health interests & concerns: Kindergarten through twelfth grade.* Seattle: Comprehensive Health Education Foundation.

U.S. Bureau of the Census. (1988). *Marital status and living arrangements: Current population reports,* Washington, DC: U.S. Government Printing Office.

CHAPTER 10

Nutrition

Of the many things you can do to enhance your well-being, none is more important than maintaining proper nutrition. The mind and body cannot function optimally without the proper supply of nutrients and energy obtained from food.   G. Edlin and E. Golanty, *Health and Wellness: A Holistic Approach,* 4th ed.

OBJECTIVES

After reading this chapter, you should be able to

- Discuss the factors that determine food choices
- Describe cultural differences in eating patterns and preparation of foods
- Discuss the USDA's food pyramid
- List the basic functions of the different categories of food
- Discuss the purpose of vitamins and minerals in the body
- List healthy ways to snack
- Describe the effect of hunger and malnutrition on a student's physical and intellectual development
- Describe the characteristics of an anorexic and/or bulimic victim
- List several hints to help a student reduce or add weight
- Determine the nutrient value of a food by reading the food label

KNOWLEDGE AND NUTRITION

Human beings must eat to survive. The well-nourished student is more apt to reach her full potential physically, mentally, and intellectually.

Americans today know more about nutrition than at any other time in history, yet this knowledge has not translated into proper nutritional behavior for everyone. For years, the majority of us paid little attention to nutrition, other than to eat three meals a day and perhaps take a vitamin supplement. This dietary regimen might have prevented major nutritional deficiencies, but medical evidence now links this same diet to a variety of chronic diseases (Yarian, 1991).

Americans live in a very food-affluent society, yet many Americans—not just the poor—are malnourished. An unwillingness to alter lifestyle to meet sound nutritional standards and concessions to convenience are often at the heart of this condition. In our fast-paced society, people opt to skip meals, especially breakfast, or to eat a poorly balanced meal at a fast-food restaurant. Many parents and teachers fail to set good examples with their own nutritional habits.

Nutrition education has been included as a priority by the U.S. Department of Health and Human Services in the Year 2000 Health Objectives for the Nation (*Healthy People 2000,* 1990). Nutrition education is essential to improving our health status. Studies indicate that sound school nutrition programs can produce positive outcomes (Crockett, Mullis, & Perry, 1988).

Helping students develop sound nutritional habits should be one of teachers' major goals in elementary health instruction. To accomplish this, teachers must do more than simply provide information. They must counter the impact of television commercials and other sources. They also must help students recognize that although the food they eat strongly depends on their culture and lifestyle, they can learn to control these influences. Teachers must also dispel misconceptions associated with food and nutrition, help students become informed consumers, and develop in them an appreciation of nutrition.

FOOD HABITS AND CUSTOMS

Every culture has its own food habits and customs. Approaches to nutrition in part reflect the food resources available. In addition, U.S. food habits and customs reflect the multicultural nature of our society. At one time, cooking and food preferences differed significantly by region. Seafood was a major part of the diet on the East Coast; wild game provided much of the meat eaten in the rural South; Mexican and Native American cultures influenced the cuisine of the Southwest. Today, these regional differences have faded, largely as a result of refrigeration and modern transportation. Getting fresh fish is now almost as easy in Kansas as it is in Massachusetts. Cultural intermixing has also diminished regional differences and expanded the range of dishes commonly eaten. Pasta, for instance, is no longer eaten only by Americans of Italian extraction. Chinese, French, German, Mexican, and Middle Eastern dishes have also become popular.

Economic, Personal, and Lifestyle Factors

As an affluent, multiethnic nation, we have a greater variety of foods and dishes to choose from than almost any other people on earth. This does not mean, however, that Americans can afford to eat anything they like. Inflation has influenced the eating habits of all Americans, especially those of the poor. People living near or below poverty level often must subsist on cheap starchy foods, which are filling, if not particularly nutritious.

Although economics influence the diet most of us cannot blame lack of money for poor nutritional habits. Instead, we must look for the reasons in personal preferences and lifestyles. Personal preference for a food often has little or nothing to do with the nourishment that food will provide. For example, parents typically pass food preferences on to their children. We develop prejudices against foods because of bad experiences; when a food causes an allergic response or gastrointestinal upset, for example. The most popular foods among one's subculture and peer group also influence food choices. Finally, we might choose a food because of the way it looks, smells, and tastes.

The national lifestyle also influences our nutritional habits. When the United States was mostly a rural, agrarian society, breakfast was a major meal. The main meal of the day was served at noon. These two meals provided the necessary energy for performing farm labor and chores. Evening dinner was typically a lighter meal. Today, the reverse is true. Most Americans eat a light breakfast, and some skip breakfast entirely. Lunch is also a light meal, often eaten in haste. The largest meal of the day is in the evening, because more time is available to prepare and eat such a meal. Unfortunately, this meal usually precedes general physical inactivity, then sleep, behavior that can hinder digestion. Many people also rush through their meals, which reduces the nourishment received from the foods. It overloads the stomach, which is not able to break it down adequately for the small intestines.

Teachers cannot do much to change our hectic national lifestyle. They can, however, emphasize the importance of beginning the day with a good breakfast that will provide energy needed for classes and studying. In recent years, several studies have documented the benefits of breakfast consumption. Considerable research indicates that skipping breakfast impairs academic performance. Consuming breakfast, on the other hand, has been associated with improved overall nutritional status. Breakfast skippers have been found to have significantly higher cholesterol levels than breakfast consumers despite lower daily fat and cholesterol intake (Resnicow, 1991).

Teachers can also emphasize the value of a balanced, nutritional lunch and a reasonable evening meal. This is not to suggest that teachers should criticize the eating patterns of any student's family, and certainly not any religious or ethical dietary restrictions a family might have, but they can be a source of information about sound nutritional practices and encourage students to consider changes in their diet that could improve their nutrition. Teachers can also stimulate students' curiosity about trying new dishes that could add needed variety to their diets.

Teachers also should emphasize that snacking on junk food, such as candy, may spoil a student's appetite for a regular meal as well as contribute to tooth decay. Though teenagers can benefit from snacking, they often fall into the habit of constantly eating the same foods. Snacks sometimes even substitute for, rather than supplement, teens' regular meals, and these snacks may not provide the variety of nutrients these youngsters need. Thus, while snacking is regarded as a potential asset to the teenager's diet, it can become a liability if it results in more calories than needed. Obesity often starts during the teenage years, and poor snacking habits can contribute to obesity (Weinstock, 1991).

Food is one of the delights of every civilization. Preparation of some dishes in many cultures is an art. Eating a fine meal is an aesthetic experience, not just fulfillment of nutritional requirements, but even the simplest dish can provide great pleasure. Teachers can use this positive approach in presenting nutritional concepts. Too often nutrition is taught as a grim and dry subject, divorced from the human perspective. No wonder students often emerge from health education with scorn for nutritional principles; they associate nutrition with the imagined somber atmosphere of a health food store!

NUTRIENTS

Humans require about 40 essential nutrients in the proper amounts and proportions to remain healthy (Edlin and Golanty, 1992). Food's most basic function is to provide these nutrients to the body. **Nutrients** are the substances in food needed to support life functions. One vital function of nutrients is providing energy that the body needs. This energy, produced as a by-product of food consumption, is measured in calories. A calorie is defined as the amount of heat energy required to raise the temperature of 1 kg of water 1°C. All foods have specific caloric values, and a given amount of food will produce a certain number of calories when broken down by the body.

The number of calories needed by the body daily depends on two factors: (1) the individual's basal metabolism and (2) the amount of energy expended in daily activities. Basal metabolism is the minimum amount of heat that the body produces when at rest. This heat, among other things, is necessary to maintain a normal body temperature. The amount of energy an individual expends varies, depending on her activities. Thus, someone who engages in heavy physical labor each day needs more calories than someone who works in an office. Young students need fewer calories per day than active adults, because their smaller bodies burn less energy.

Although caloric requirements differ with age, basal metabolism, and daily activities, the Food and Agricultural Organization of the United Nations recommends a daily minimum intake for adults of 2,650 calories. However, more than half the people in the world exist on fewer than 2,200 calories per day (Jones, Shainberg, & Byer, 1986). During periods of rapid growth, students need more calories. For example, a 10-year-old boy requires an average daily intake of about 2,300 calories, with this amount rising to 2,900 calories by age 13. A 10-year-old girl requires an average daily intake of 2,200 calories, and 2,400 calories at age 13. Three categories of nutrients provide caloric energy: carbohydrates, fats, and proteins. Together, they make up most of the elements in the foods we eat.

Carbohydrates

Foods rich in carbohydrates form about half of the typical U.S. diet. **Carbohydrates** are either simple sugars, derived from such foods as table sugar and honey, or more complex compounds, derived from such foods as cereals and potatoes.

Carbohydrates are found in foods as monosaccharides, disaccharides, and polysaccharides. The monosaccharides are glucose (found in honey and fruits), galactose (human breast milk, fruits, and honey), and fructose (fruits and honey). The disaccharides are sucrose, a combination of glucose and fructose (found in bananas, green peas and sweet potatoes), lactose, a combination of glucose and galactose (found in milk), and maltose, a disaccharide composed of two glucose units (used in candy flavoring and brewing beer). Many adults, especially Asians and African Americans, suffer from lactose intolerance. In other words, undigested lactose is not absorbed and remains in the gastrointestinal tract, resulting in bloating, a large amount of gas, and abdominal cramping. This malady can be treated through a high-protein, high-carbohydrate, low-to-moderate-fat, high-calorie diet. The polysaccharides contain many glucose molecules and include (1) glycogen, which is synthesized in the liver and muscles and serves as a reserve source of blood glucose; (2) cellulose, found in many vegetables; and (3) starch, found in plant seeds, cereal grains, and some vegetables.

The body breaks carbohydrates down into glucose, and this metabolism produces energy. Each gram of carbohydrates yields 4 calories. If carbohydrates are not abundant in the diet, protein and fat must be metabolized to produce needed energy.

Carbohydrates must be constantly replenished in the blood, either by eating or by breaking down glycogen stored in the liver and muscles.

Carbohydrates are important to the diet; approximately 58% of total caloric intake should come from this category. Foods rich in carbohydrates include rice, spaghetti, noodles, bread, breakfast cereals, and potatoes. Many vegetables, fruits, and fruit juices also contain some carbohydrates. Although candy and cookies are sources of carbohydrates, they contain a large amount of refined sugar, which contributes to tooth decay and increases caloric content without providing additional nutrients.

Proteins

Protein means "to come first." **Proteins** are essential nutrients: No organism can live and almost no biological process can take place without protein.

A protein molecule is composed of smaller structures called **amino acids.** *Essential* amino acids must be provided by the diet, while *nonessential* amino acids are synthesized by the body. Amino acids are building blocks necessary for several body functions, including making its own protein. Proteins are present in every cell, in enzymes, and in body secretions. Proteins provide calories but also serve other important, complex functions. They are important components of DNA and RNA molecules, which determine individuals' genetic makeup. Proteins also help build new cells and tissues in growing bodies, maintain tissues that are already built, and play a role in manufacturing blood, enzymes, hormones, and human milk. Proteins also convert into antibodies to combat infection.

Proteins provide 4 calories per gram. Protein should comprise about 12% of a student's total caloric intake. Most students require approximately 60 grams of protein daily. Meat, poultry, legumes, milk, and other dairy products are all good sources of this essential nutrient.

Protein is of particular concern to strict vegetarians, who avoid eating any animal products. Because animal-based foods are the only source of complete proteins (i.e., proteins containing all the essential amino acids), people who consume only plant-based foods need to eat a variety of foods to ensure adequate protein in their diet. For example, nuts and seeds contain one combination of amino acids, grains contain a different combination, and legumes (dried peas and beans) contain another combination. Vegetarians need to eat foods from at least two of these groups throughout the day, although not necessarily at the same time.

Fats

Fats, or lipids, are the most concentrated source of calories we ingest. Fats provide 9 calories per gram, as compared with 4 grams for proteins and carbohydrates.

There are two types of fatty acids: saturated and unsaturated. Dietary sources of saturated fatty acids include animal fat, butter, tropical oils, chicken eggs, and whole milk. Unsaturated fats are found in certain vegetable oils, such as corn, olive, soybean, peanut, and safflower. The more saturated a fat is, the harder it is at room temperature. Polyunsaturated fats, found in vegetable and fish oils, may reduce serum cholesterol levels (Lankford & Jacobs-Steward, 1986).

Fats are an important part of our diets, a fact that is sometimes overlooked because of the association of fats with cardiovascular and other health problems. Fats serve several vital functions, however. The energy they provide spares protein for tissue synthesis. Fats also serve as carriers of the fat-soluble vitamins A, D, E, and K. As food, they provide satiety, because the rate at which the stomach empties is related to the fat content. The higher the fat content, the slower the food empties from the stomach. Fats also make food taste better.

Fats are an important part of all cells, membrane structures, and tissues. Additionally, fats provide protection in the adipose tissue just under the skin. This layer of adipose tissue also helps maintain a constant body temperature despite changes in the environmental temperature. Similarly, fats provide a layer of protective shock-absorbing tissue between the kidneys, reproductive organs, and other organs. They also provide padding for the cheeks, palms of the hands, and balls of the feet.

Fats should comprise no more than 25% to 30% of total caloric intake. These fats should be equally divided among polyunsaturated, saturated, and monounsurated fats. (Monounsaturated fats are fatty acids that lack two hydrogen atoms and have one double bond between carbons—that is, oleic acid. These are found abundantly in the triglycerides in olive oil, which are contributing factors in atherosclerosis.) Major food sources of fat include butter, cream, lard, and salad dressings. Olives, nuts, and avocados also have a significant fat content.

Blood Cholesterol

An issue closely related to ingestion of fats, obesity, and health risks is blood **cholesterol** levels. Cholesterol is a vital part of the body, but too much of it can result in health risks. Cholesterol is a waxy, fatlike substance found mainly in the liver, kidneys, and brain. Cholesterol has two sources—diet and liver production. The main way to control the cholesterol our bodies produce is through medication under medical supervision. We can control the amount of cholesterol we ingest through our diets.

Most of the cholesterol is transported through the body as lipoproteins. There are different forms of lipoprotein, and they are classified by their density. The most important forms of lipoprotein are **low-density lipoprotein cholesterol** (LDL) and **high-density lipoprotein cholesterol** (HDL). Many blood tests will provide only a total blood cholesterol reading, but a more important factor is the ratio of HDL to total cholesterol. The smaller the ratio, the lower the cardiovascular risk.

Even though some foods are labeled truthfully as containing no cholesterol, these foods might be high in saturated fats (e.g., coconut or palm oil), which will cause the body to produce more blood cholesterol. Although the body produces cholesterol regardless of the foods ingested, a healthy diet can improve the blood cholesterol level. Generally, foods of animal origin, particularly eggs and organ meats, should be reduced, whereas fruits, vegetables, and whole grains should be increased. These foods will increase the amount of fiber in the diet, which will aid in digestion, increase intestinal motility, and may lower cholesterol. People on high-fiber diets have been shown to excrete more cholesterol and fat than those on low-fiber diets. One reason is that the high-fiber diet shortens food's transit time through the digestive tract, and so allows less time for cholesterol to be absorbed. When cholesterol from the diet is thus reduced, the body must turn to its own supply to make necessary body compounds. Diets high in fiber are typically low in fat and cholesterol anyway—another advantage of emphasizing fiber (Turner, Sizer, Whitney, & Wilks, 1992). High-fiber diets may also help prevent constipation and may reduce the risk of obesity, hypoglycemia, heart disease, cancer, and diabetes (University of California, 1992).

Recent findings suggest that fish oils rich in unsaturated fats called Omega-3 fatty acids actually change the chemistry of the blood to lower cardiovascular risk. Specifically, these fatty acids may lower blood triglycerides, highly saturated fats that contribute to blockage in the arteries. The oil in some seafood depresses LDL and raises HDL. Seafood high in Omega-3 fatty acids includes anchovies, herring, mackerel, salmon, sardines, and tuna (Allsen, Harrison, & Vance, 1989).

Other Nutrients

In addition to the three major nutrients, water, minerals, and vitamins are vital to human nourishment.

Water

Discussions of nutrition often overlook water, but it is second only to oxygen in importance to body functioning. A person can survive longer without food than without water.

Water is an essential component of body structure. It also acts as a solvent for minerals and other physiologically important compounds. In the body, it transports nutrients to and waste products from the cells. Water also helps regulate body temperature. Water comes from fluids and solids in the diet and from metabolism of energy nutrients within the tissues. The amount of activity and the climate are important factors influencing the amount of water a person needs. Because students usually participate in more physical activities, they perspire more and therefore need more water than many adults. Water is also lost through exhaled air. The recommended daily intake is the equivalent of six to eight glasses of water, although solid foods and other beverages provide much of this.

Minerals

The body needs organic compounds—carbohydrates, fats, and proteins—for proper nutrition. It also needs inorganic materials, such as minerals. The body contains these inorganic elements in small amounts, but they play a vital role in nutrition. The major minerals needed by the body are calcium, phosphorus, potassium, sulfur, sodium, chlorine, and magnesium. Food sources for these major minerals include

Calcium: milk, cheese, sardines, salmon, green vegetables
Phosphorus: milk, cheese, lean meat
Potassium: oranges, bananas, dried fruits
Iron: green vegetables, organ meats
Sulfur: eggs, poultry, fish
Sodium: table salt, beef, eggs, cheese
Chlorine: table salt, meat
Magnesium: green vegetables, whole grains

Other mineral elements, known as trace elements and required in lesser amounts, are zinc, selenium, magnesium, copper, iodine, fluorine, chromium, molybdenum, and cobalt.

Minerals function in the body in several ways. After the organic compounds have been oxidized, minerals remain to form actual body parts. For example, calcium, magnesium, and phosphorus are components of the bones and teeth. Minerals also act as regulators and are necessary to certain body functions. For example, minerals contribute to the water and electrolyte balance of the body and are important in the transmission of nerve impulses. Minerals contribute to the osmotic pressure of body fluids and to the maintenance of neutrality—the acid-base balance of the blood and body tissues. Finally, they regulate the heartbeat.

Elevated amounts of some minerals may cause health problems. For example, elevated levels of sodium are associated with high blood pressure and cardiovascular disease. Restricting intake of salt, according to the American Heart Association, is safe, feasible, and probably useful in preventing hypertension in many people. Sodium can be restricted through the diet by curtailing use of table salt, using sodium-free salt substitutes, drinking low-salt milk, and eliminating high-sodium prepared foods (Yarian, 1991).

A lack of essential minerals can cause malnutrition. For example, iron-deficiency anemia is a major health problem in the United States and Canada and even more so in the rest of the world. Students deprived of iron show a lack of motivation and less ability to work and play (Turner et al., 1992). This deficiency occurs most frequently in infants, adolescent males, and females during child-bearing years.

Vitamins

No group of nutrients has captured the interest of the public more than vitamins. Vitamins first came to the public's attention when researchers discovered that scurvy could be cured by eating fresh fruits containing vitamin C. These and other vitamin-related discoveries through the years have demonstrated the importance of vitamins in maintaining good health.

Today, vitamin-enriched foods and vitamin supplements are popular. Unfortunately, many people equate vitamins with good nutrition; some mistakenly believe vitamins contain all the nutrients essential to life. Charlatans have exploited these beliefs by promoting the unproven use of megavitamins to cure diseases (Allsen et al., 1989). In fact, large doses of some vitamins can be dangerous.

Vitamins are organic compounds that every part of the body requires to maintain health and prevent disease. The diet must supply them, because the body cannot synthesize them in the required amounts. Vitamins foster growth, promote the ability to produce healthy offspring, maintain health, aid in the normal function of the appetite and digestive tract, and help the body's resistance to bacterial infections. Vitamins are classified as either fat-soluble or water-soluble.

Fat-Soluble Vitamins. **Fat-soluble vitamins** dissolve in fat and are found in the fatty parts of food and body tissues. They are stored in the body until needed, so it is not necessary to consume them every day. The fat-soluble vitamins transported by lipids through the body are A, D, E, and K.

Vitamin A is important in promoting growth and health of body tissues as well as enhancing the function of the immune system. This vitamin also enhances vision by helping the retina function properly, permitting us to distinguish between light and shade and to see various colors distinctly. Dermatologists use a form of vitamin A to treat acne and other skin disorders. Overdoes of vitamin A may result in yellowish, dry, scaly skin and dry, irritated eyes. It can also affect the brain development of a fetus and cause spontaneous abortions.

Vitamin D is needed to prevent and cure rickets, a deficiency disease in which bones fail to harden. Vitamin E triggers certain essential enzyme reactions, and it prevents vitamins A and C from being metabolized too quickly. Vitamin K is essential for the synthesis of prothrombin, a substance needed for normal blood coagulation.

Water-Soluble Vitamins. **Water-soluble vitamins** dissolve in water and are associated with the watery parts of food and body tissues. The body cannot store these vitamins. Since excess amounts are usually excreted in the urine, these vitamins must be provided in the diet on a regular basis. The water-soluble vitamins include the B vitamins and vitamin C.

The B vitamins are essential to daily nutrition. Known as the B-complex group, they help body systems combat stress and maintain energy reserves. The B-complex group includes vitamin B_1 (thiamine), vitamin B_2 (riboflavin), vitamin B_3 (niacin), vitamin B_5 (pantothenic acid), vitamin B_6 (pyridoxine), vitamin B_{12} (cobalamin), folic acid, and biotin.

Thiamin is necessary for carbohydrate metabolism. It aids in the release of energy from food. Riboflavin helps body cells use oxygen, promotes tissue repair, and helps the nervous system function properly. Niacin is essential to growth; without it, thiamine and riboflavin could not function properly in the body. Pantothenic acid helps increase vitality and influences glandular functions. Pyridoxine is necessary for healthy teeth and gums and helps maintain normal body cholesterol. It also aids in production of antibodies. Cobalamin works in conjunction with folic acid and iron to build normal blood cells and prevent pernicious anemia. Folic acid aids in the proper growth and reproduction of blood cells and contributes to healthy skin. Biotin is necessary for proper metabolism of fats, carbohydrates, and protein. Biotin also helps produce antibodies.

Vitamin C, or ascorbic acid, is vital in preventing scurvy, in forming and maintaining collagen (the cementing material that holds cells together), in metabolizing some amino acids, and in functioning of the adrenal glands.

Vitamins sometimes serve as catalysts for important body functions. Although required only in small amounts, they are vital to good nutrition. Unlike minerals, however, they do not become part of the body (as calcium does in the teeth and bones). Overdosing on vitamins can cause serious side effects: loss of coordination, nausea, rashes, diarrhea, and fatigue. Excess amounts of the fat-soluble vitamins, stored in the body, can reach toxic levels. Even water-soluble vitamins, when taken to extreme, can be dangerous. The key is moderation and a well-balanced diet featuring a range of healthy, vitamin-rich foods.

HEALTH HIGHLIGHT
Vitamin Facts

Vitamin	U.S. RDA*	Best Sources	Functions
A (carotene)	5000 IU/day	Yellow or orange fruits & vegetables, green leafy vegetables, fortified oatmeal, liver, dairy products	Formation and maintenance of skin, hair and mucous membranes; helps us see in dim light; bone and tooth growth.
B₁ (thiamine)	1.5 mg/day	Fortified cereals and oatmeals, meats, rice and pasta, whole grains, liver	Helps body release energy from carbohydrates during metabolism; growth and muscle tone.
B₂ (riboflavin)	1.7 mg/day	Whole grains, green leafy vegetables, organ meats, milk and eggs	Helps body release energy from protein, fat and carbohydrates during metabolism.
B₆ (pyridoxine)	2 mg/day	Fish, poultry, lean meats, bananas, prunes, dried beans, whole grains, avocados	Helps build body tissue and aids in metabolism of protein.
B₁₂ (cobalamin)	6 mcg/day	Meats, milk products, seafood	Aids cell development, functioning of the nervous system and the metabolism of protein and fat.
Biotin	0.3 mg/day	Cereal/grain products, yeast, legumes, liver	Involved in metabolism of protein, fats and carbohydrates.
Folate (folacin, folic acid)	0.4 mg/day	Green leafy vegetables, organ meats, dried peas, beans and lentils	Aids in genetic material development and involved in red blood cell production.
Niacin	20 mg/day	Meat, poultry, fish, enriched cereals, peanuts, potatoes, dairy products, eggs	Involved in carbohydrate, protein and fat metabolism.
Pantothenic Acid	10 mg/day	Lean meats, whole grains, legumes, vegetables, fruits	Helps in the release of energy from fats and carbohydrates.
C (ascorbic acid)	60 mg/day	Citrus fruits, berries, and vegetables—especially peppers	Essential for structure of bones, cartilage, muscle and blood vessels. Also helps maintain capillaries and gums and aids in absorption of iron.
D	400 IU/day	Fortified milk, sunlight, fish, eggs, butter, fortified margarine	Aids in bone and tooth formation; helps maintain heart action and nervous system.
E	30 IU/day	Fortified & multi-grain cereals, nuts, wheat germ, vegetable oils, green leafy vegetables	Protects blood cells, body tissue and essential fatty acids from harmful destruction in the body.
K	**	Green leafy vegetables, fruit, dairy and grain products	Essential for blood clotting functions.

* For adults and children over 4. IU = international units. mg = milligrams. mcg = micrograms.

** There is no U.S. RDA for vitamin K; however the Recommended Dietary Allowance is 1 mcg/kg of bodyweight.

† Many of the symptoms outlined under this heading can also be attributed to problems other than vitamin deficiency. If you have these symptoms and they persist, consult your doctor.

HEALTH HIGHLIGHT
Vitamin Facts *continued*

Deficiency Symptoms†	Toxic?	Processing Tips	Did You Know?
Night blindness, dry and scaly skin, frequent fatigue	Yes, in high doses, but beta-carotene is nontoxic.	Serve fruits & vegetables raw and keep covered and refrigerated. Steam veggies; broil, bake or braise meats.	Lowfat and skim milks are often fortified with Vitamin A which is removed with the fat.
Heart irregularity, fatigue, nerve disorders, mental confusion	No, high doses are excreted by the kidneys.	Don't rinse rice or pasta before and after cooking. Cook in minimal water.	Pasta and breads made of refined flours have B_1 added since it is lost in the milling process.
Cracks in corners of mouth, skin rash, anemia	No toxic affects reported.	Store foods in containers that light cannot enter; cook vegetables in minimal water; roast or broil meats.	Most ready-to-eat cereals are fortified with 25% of the U.S. RDA for B_2.
Convulsions, dermatitis, muscular weakness, skin cracks, anemia	Long-term megadoses may cause nerve damage in hands and feet.	Serve fruits raw or cook for shortest time in little water; roast or broil meats.	Since B_6 aids in use of protein in the body, the need for B_6 increases with protein intake.
Anemia, nervousness, fatigue, and, in some cases, neuritis and brain degeneration	No toxic effects reported.	Roast or broil meat and fish.	Vegetarians who don't eat any animal products may need a supplement.
Nausea, vomiting, depression, hair loss, dry, scaly skin	No toxic effects reported.	Storage, processing & cooking do not appear to affect this vitamin.	Biotin deficiency is extremely rare in the U.S.
Gastrointestinal disorders, anemia, cracks on lips	Some evidence of toxicity in large doses.	Store vegetables in refrigerator and steam, boil or simmer in minimal water.	Deficiencies can occur in premature infants and pregnant women.
Skin disorders, diarrhea, indigestion, general fatigue	Nicotinic acid form should be taken only under doctor's care.	Roast or broil beef, veal, lamb and poultry. Cook potatoes in minimal water.	Niacin is formed in the body by converting an amino acid found in proteins.
Fatigue, vomiting, stomach stress, infections, muscle cramps	No toxic effects reported.	Eat fruits and vegetables raw.	It is believed some pantothenic acid is produced in the G.I. tract.
Swollen or bleeding gums, slow wound healing, fatigue/depression, poor digestion	Intakes of one gram or more can cause nausea, cramps and diarrhea.	Do not store or soak fruits and vegetables in water. Refrigerate juices & store only 2–3 days.	Smokers may benefit from an increased intake of vitamin C.
In children: rickets and other bone deformities. In adults: calcium loss from bones.	High intakes may cause diarrhea & weight loss.	Storage, processing & cooking do not appear to affect this vitamin.	Sunlight starts vitamin D production in the skin.
Muscular wasting, nerve damage, anemia, reproductive failure	Relatively nontoxic.	Store in air-tight containers away from light.	Most fortified cereals have 40% of the RDA.
Bleeding disorders in newborn infants and those on blood-thinning medications	Not toxic as found in food.	Store in containers away from light.	Vitamin K is also formed by bacteria in the colon.

Source: Nestle Information Service, *Nestle Worldview, 3,* Winter 1992.

Information for this chart was obtained from the Food and Drug Administration, the American Institute for Cancer Research and the United States Department of Agriculture/Human Nutrition Information Service.

Food sources for some vitamins include

A: liver, whole milk, butter, dark green leafy vegetables
C: citrus fruits, broccoli, tomatoes, potatoes
D: eggs, liver, fortified milk
E: margarine, salad dressing
K: egg yolk, liver, milk, cabbage
Thiamin (B_1): pork, beef, liver, eggs, fish, whole grains, legumes
Riboflavin (B_2): milk, green vegetables, cereals
Pyridoxine (B_6): pork, milk, eggs, legumes
B_{12}: seafood, meats, eggs, milk
Niacin: milk, eggs, fish, poultry
Folacin: spinach, asparagus, broccoli, kidney beans
Biotin: milk, liver, mushrooms, legumes

NUTRITIONAL NEEDS

About 50 different nutrients are needed to maintain health. Because no food contains all the nutrients, we need to ingest a variety of foods to satisfy nutritional needs. One way to ensure this variety and a balanced diet is to daily choose the types of foods identified in the Food Guide Pyramid (Figure 10.1) from the U.S. Department of Agriculture. The pyramid emphasizes foods from five food groups shown in the three lower sections. None of the food groups is more or less important than the others—to be healthy, one should eat the suggested number of servings from all of the groups. The USDA food pyramid was created as a guide to a well-balanced diet (Boyle & Zyla, 1992).

Characteristics of the Types of Food

Fruits are usually good sources of vitamin C, vitamin A, and fiber. Citrus fruits are especially good sources of vitamin C. Two to four servings daily (at least one of which provides vitamin C), each about equal in size to an orange, are recommended.

Vegetables usually provide vitamin A, vitamin C, and fiber. Vegetables are low in calories if served without added fat. Dark green, leafy vegetables like spinach, kale, collard greens, mustard greens, and broccoli are high in vitamin A, vitamin C, and calcium. Orange vegetables like carrots, sweet potatoes, and squash are also high in vitamin A. Three to five servings daily (at least one of which provides vitamin A), each about equal in size to a small potato, are recommended.

Bread, cereal, and pasta are high in iron, protein, and some B vitamins. Although the actual amount of protein is small in each serving, eating many grain foods each day can provide some of the daily requirement for protein. Whole-grain products contain more fiber, vitamins, and minerals than refined products. Six to eleven servings daily, each about equal to the size of a slice of bread, are recommended.

Dried beans and peas supply protein and iron. This category also includes nuts, lentils, peanut butter, and tofu. These foods are usually low in cost and can be

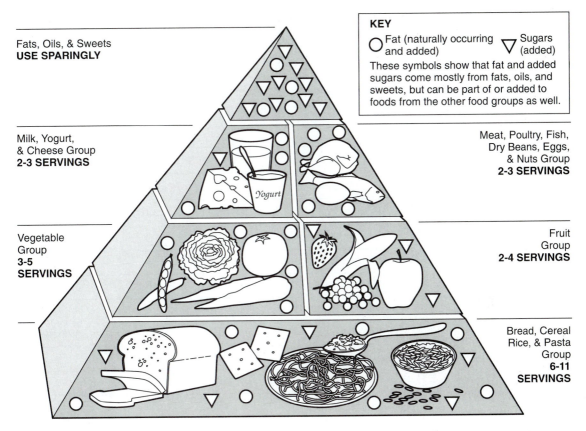

Fats, Oils, & Sweets
USE SPARINGLY

KEY
○ Fat (naturally occurring and added)   ▽ Sugars (added)
These symbols show that fat and added sugars come mostly from fats, oils, and sweets, but can be part of or added to foods from the other food groups as well.

Milk, Yogurt, & Cheese Group
2-3 SERVINGS

Meat, Poultry, Fish, Dry Beans, Eggs, & Nuts Group
2-3 SERVINGS

Vegetable Group
3-5 SERVINGS

Fruit Group
2-4 SERVINGS

Bread, Cereal Rice, & Pasta Group
6-11 SERVINGS

Figure 10.1   USDA food guide pyramid

Source: United States Department of Agriculture, 1992.

prepared a variety of ways. Nuts and peanut butter are high in fat and therefore high in calories. A combined total of two to three servings per day from this group and/or the meat, poultry, fish, and eggs group is recommended.

Meat, poultry, fish, and eggs are high in protein and iron. Lean meats, poultry without skin, and most fish are lower-calorie choices. A serving in this group is 3 oz. A combined total of two to three servings per day from this group and/or the dried beans and peas group is recommended.

Milk and cheese provide calcium and protein. Low-fat milk and cheese made from low-fat milk are lower-calorie choices. These products have the same amount of vitamins and minerals but a lower percentage of fat. Two to three servings daily are recommended for this food group.

Another food group includes sweets and fats. These are added to other foods, thus increasing the number of calories. These foods supply few nutrients for the calories they contain and are usually expensive. Beverages such as alcohol and soft drinks are included in this group. The USDA made no recommendation for foods in this group; they should be used sparingly.

Recommended Daily Allowances

Another guide to proper nutrition is the Recommended Daily Allowances (RDAs). This is a basic dietary guide for the population as a whole. The National Research Council (NRC) updated the RDAs in 1989 (see Table 10.1). The recommendations reflect the specific climate and general energy needs of the U.S. population. The NRC obtained statistics from large groups of people living in the United States to

Table 10.1 Changes in the RDAs, 1980 to 1989

Source: Reprinted with permission from *Recommended Dietary Allowances:* 10th ed. copyright 1989 by National Academy of Sciences. Courtesy of the National Academy Press, Washington, DC.

Nutrient	1980[1]		1989[2]	
	M	W	M	W
Protein (g)	56	44	63	50
Vitamin A (mcg)	1,000	800	no change	
Vitamin D (mcg)	5	5	no change	
Vitamin E (mg)	10	8	no change	
Vitamin K (mcg)	—	—	80	65
Vitamin C (mg)	60	60	no change	
Thiamin (mg)	1.4	1.0	1.5	1.1
Riboflavin (mg)	1.6	1.2	1.7	1.3
Niacin (mg)	18	13	19	15
Vitamin B_6 (mg)	2.2	2.0	2.0	1.6
Folate (mcg)	400	400	200	180
Vitamin B_{12} (mcg)	3.0	3.0	2.0	2.0
Calcium (mg)	800	800	no change	
Phosphorus (mg)	800	800	no change	
Magnesium (mg)	350	300	350	280
Iron (mg)	10	18	10	15
Zinc (mg)	15	15	15	12
Iodine (mcg)	150	150	no change	
Selenium (mcg)	—	—	70	55
M = Men				W = Women

[1]Figures are for ages 23-50; a man 5 feet 10 inches tall weighing 154 pounds; a woman 5 feet 4 inches tall weighing 120 pounds.

[2]Figures are for ages 25-50; a man 5 feet 10 inches tall weighing 174 pounds; a woman 5 feet 4 inches tall weighing 138 pounds.

establish the criteria for the recommended allowances. These allowances, while only estimates of the nutritional needs of Americans, are useful for dietary planning to ensure proper amounts of various nutrients.

FOOD-RELATED PROBLEMS

Problems concerning food have been a part of human life from the earliest times. In earlier ages, crop failures have led to famine and war. Even today, starvation kills hundreds of thousands in very poor nations each year. Although the United States also has some problems with hunger, few students actually face starvation. Unfortunately, many Americans are undernourished or malnourished. Overweight and obesity are also common.

Undernutrition

Typically, an undernourished person is also underweight, but this is by no means absolutely true. Undernutrition implies that the individual is not getting enough nutrients. This can occur even if the person is consuming more than enough calories. Thus, weight is not necessarily an indication of nutritional status. In the United States, undernutrition is most likely to occur in infants, children, and adolescents, whose nutritional requirements for tissue growth and development are high. Undernutrition may inhibit growth, delay maturation, limit physical activity, and interfere with learning (Montoye, Christian, Nagle, & Levin, 1988). Undernutrition has many causes; poverty and lack of nutrition understanding are two major factors. Many Americans are undernourished simply because they cling to nutritionally deficient eating habits. Dietary practices dictated by cultural taboos, religious beliefs, and cultural patterns also sometimes lead to nutritional deficiencies. Occasionally,

HEALTH HIGHLIGHT
RDAs Versus "Daily Values"

The U.S. Food and Drug Administration (FDA) has proposed a major revision of the listing of nutrition information on labels. This proposal would change from RDA listing to "Daily Values" for the purpose of calculating the amount of nutrients that are in the food package. The FDA has elected to establish in its Daily Values age-adjusted *average* levels for vitamins, minerals and protein recommended for various age/sex groups in the RDA, instead of the highest recommended values. Averaging for these nutrients was considered necessary by the FDA because it would be contrary to public health goals to base values for fat, for example, on the highest recommended intake. The new averaging approach for all nutrients would give consumers a more current, unified "measuring stick" to compare the content of all labeled nutrients among different foods. These Daily Values would include not only protein and several of the vitamins and minerals previously listed under the U.S. RDAs, but for the first time, fat, cholesterol, fiber, sodium and other food components would be included. To this date, these proposals have not yet been adopted.

Source: *FDA Backgrounder*, 12 February 1992, pp. 1–2.

the cause is physiological. A poorly functioning body might fail to use nutrients supplied to it. For example, a disease such as hyperthyroidism can affect growth regardless of the quality of diet. In addition, people with certain allergies or conditions have difficulty absorbing nutrients.

Psychological factors can also lead to undernutrition. Hurried meals in haphazard settings may be deleterious because of the type and amount of food as well as how the food is eaten. The noise and confusion that often accompany rushed meals can compromise digestion.

Anorexia and Bulimia

An improper concept of one's nutritional state can cause health problems such as anorexia nervosa. **Anorexia nervosa** means nervous lack of appetite. This is a syndrome characterized by loss of appetite, aversion to food, and weight loss. A psychological disorder more than a simple eating disorder, it means that a drive for thinness and a fear of fatness result in life-threatening emaciation and a host of other problems.

The major characteristics of anorexia are outlined in Figure 10.2. Its central features are difficult to specify because the disorder emerges over time as a complex mixture of a relentless drive for thinness, the effects of starvation, and commonly associated psychological disturbances (e.g., low self-worth and mistrust of others).

Significant weight loss is one of the cardinal features of anorexia. The anorexic person approaches weight loss with a fervor, convinced that her body is too large. Lost weight is viewed as an accomplishment. The value that our culture places on thinness contributes to these attitudes held by anorexics. This drive for thinness accompanies an extreme fear of becoming fat. This unreasonable fear of weight gain may be expressed by the person weighing herself several times each day and becoming very anxious with any weight increase. Anorexics also have a distorted body image—they are unable to recognize their appearance as abnormal. They will insist that their emaciated figure is just right or even too fat (Levine, 1987).

Anorexics are typically compulsive, perfectionist, and highly competitive. The anorexic person sometimes suffers from a poor self-image due to a feeling of incompetence, so she becomes consumed with losing weight to demonstrate to herself and others that she is in total control. If a friend, parent, or teacher admonishes the anorexic person for looking too thin, she may take this as a compliment, for it means others are aware of her disciplined approach to weight loss. Psychological counseling and family therapy are needed to correct some anorexic cases.

The long-term effects of anorexia include psychological problems such as obsessions, compulsions, paranoia, social withdrawal, and depression. Sufferers may become irritable, hostile, indecisive, depressed, defiant, and resistant to change. Arguments with parents and other authorities over eating habits become power struggles for control. Anorexia nervosa can involve overexercising, self-induced vomiting, and the use of laxatives and diuretics. Starvation can interrupt normal brain-body functions such as sleep, proper blood pressure, muscle strength, immunity to disease, and sexual drive. Vomiting upsets the potassium-sodium balance

Figure 10.2 Central features and other information related to anorexia nervosa

Source: *How Schools Can Help Combat Student Eating Disorders: Anorexia Nervosa and Bulimia* (p. 38) by M. Levine, 1987, Washington, DC: National Education Association.

Central Features

1. An iron determination to become thinner and thinner
2. An extreme fear of becoming fat
3. Significant weight loss
4. A distorted body image
5. Difficulty in accurately interpreting hunger and other internal sensations (for example, anger)
6. Refusal to maintain a healthy body weight
7. Abnormal reproductive functioning

Effects of Starvation*

1. Obsession with food and food preparation
2. Unusual eating and drinking habits
3. Emotional disturbances
4. Social withdrawal
5. Binge-eating

Commonly Associated Characteristics

1. Hyperactivity
2. Perfectionism coupled with a profound sense of ineffectiveness
3. Binge-eating
4. Purging via self-induced vomiting, laxatives, and/or diuretics

*Although there are significant individual differences in the ways in which people respond to weight restoration, many of the effects of starvation persist for at least several weeks after nutritional rehabilitation has been in effect.

---

necessary for proper functioning of nerves and muscles (including the heart), causes enamel erosion and tooth degeneration, and creates lesions in the esophagus.

The anorexic person may start losing weight to become more popular, yet as the illness progresses, the anorexic becomes increasingly alienated from other people. Obsession, fear, and starvation cause the anorexic to become lonely (Levine, 1987).

Anorexia victims can lose more than 25% of their total body weight. Anorexia nervosa affects girls more than boys, but the incidence among males is increasing. Girls and boys are equally affected by anorexia athletica, in which the young person reduces fatness for optimal athletic performance (Burckes-Miller & Black, 1988).

With a related disorder, **bulimia**, a person eats large quantities of food during short periods and attempts to control her weight through self-induced vomiting or laxatives. Bulimia among females is thought to result from a lack of self-esteem and a desire to become an "ideal" woman (Edlin & Golanty, 1992). Like anorexia, this condition can have serious health consequences, and medical help and counseling are essential.

The symptoms of undernutrition include lusterless hair, poor teeth, pale skin, dermatitis, inflamed eyes, sore tongue, fissures at the corners of the lips, muscular

Anorexia nervosa is a psychological disorder more than a simple eating disorder involving a preoccupation with thinness.

weakness, apathy, increased susceptibility to infections, shortness of breath, extreme nervousness, irritability, and sometimes weight loss (Lamb, 1990).

A simple solution to undernutrition is to eat more of the proper nutrients, assuming these foods are available. If lack of knowledge is the only cause of the problem, then suggestions for proper food selection might remedy the situation. A balanced diet that includes a variety of foods, sufficient complex carbohydrates, and minimal fat, sodium, and cholesterol can be extremely beneficial to an undernourished student (Hamrick, Anspaugh, & Ezell, 1986).

Hunger and Learning

Hunger is a physiological and psychological state that occurs when food needs are not satisfied. Research has shown that hunger has an effect on learning behavior. Hunger increases nervousness and irritability and reduces interest in learning situations. Students who are hungry will have less interest in what is being taught and will be unable to concentrate.

Hunger and malnutrition lead to weakness and illness. A variety of avitaminoses (vitamin-deficiency disorders) can result from malnutrition. Hunger can also influence a student's development and brain function. Furthermore, malnourished students are more susceptible to infections, which can impair growth even more.

Nutrition and Cancer

The type of foods we eat seem to have some relationship to the possibility of certain cancers. For example, some carcinogens (cancer-causing agents) may be introduced to the body through foods, either by accident or in an additive. Also, a diet deficient in some nutrients may increase one's chances of some cancers. The lack of fiber in one's diet may be a factor in intestinal, bowel, or colon cancer. Further, a diet that includes an excess of some nutrients might predispose one to cancer. An excess of animal protein and/or excess vitamin and mineral supplements, for instance, may alter the absorptive system so that it allows carcinogens to adversely affect the body. Also, high-fat diets are correlated with breast and colon cancer.

Any discussion of diet and cancer should contain some precautions to the reader. First, be wary of a *single* study claiming results connecting a food or diet with cancer. One study reporting something needs to be validated with other studies under other conditions. Also, remember that when a type of food is connected with a cancer, that diet may also be deficient in another nutrient; that is, what is *not* consumed may be more important than what *is*.

In general, the following practices are recommended to reduce the chances of contracting some form of cancer through a diet:

- Eat a variety of foods.
- Do not rely too heavily on one type of nutrient.
- Increase your intake of fresh fruits, cereals, and vegetables.
- Reduce your intake of animal proteins (meat) and fat.

Nutrition and Athletic Performance

An important relationship exists between the foods one eats and the way the body performs. In particular, the foods one includes in a diet can enhance or hinder athletic performance. For example, certain types of athletes need a more readily available source of energy, and thereby need to consume more carbohydrate and fat calories. Both high-intensity, short-duration activities (such as sprinting) and endurance-type activities require a sufficient amount of glucose in the muscles. The best source for this is carbohydrates. In addition, athletes need to include Vitamin B foods in their diet when an activity expends many calories. Usually, athletes do *not* require extra protein. Proteins are not a good source of energy for the muscles, and the typical diet includes enough protein to support muscle growth. If, however, the athlete is exercising in extremely high temperatures and/or is losing significant fluids through perspiration, protein needs are greater.

The Role of the Teacher

Teachers should provide accurate information concerning nutrition and should teach students how to make wise decisions to help prevent undernourishment. They need to emphasize the importance of eating a good breakfast and lunch, and they should encourage students to socialize when they are eating. Teachers can help students appreciate the taste, smell, color, and texture of food and thereby increase their interest in it. In addition, teachers have an excellent chance to be exemplary role models by eating the right foods in the right way while at school.

Overweight and Obesity

Recent research indicates that obesity increased 54% for children ages 6 to 11 and 39% for ages 12 to 17 between 1963 to 1965 and 1976 to 1980. Very little of this increase can be linked to heredity. Rather, lifestyle seems to play the primary role in the development of obesity. The longer students remain obese, the greater the probability they will be obese adults (Price, Desmond, & Rupert, 1990).

The health risks of obesity, such as degenerative diseases and shorter life span, may not be of immediate concern to secondary school students, but maintaining a correct weight is important for many other reasons.

Obesity can be considered a physical handicap at any age because it affects physical activity. Also, overweight students face many emotional problems. In a society that emphasizes thinness, overweight students may be isolated and shunned, ridiculed, stared at, and rejected. As a result, overweight students may lose their sense of self-worth and withdraw from others. To complicate matters, many overweight students find satisfaction in nothing else except eating, which causes them to gain even more weight, further alienating them from peers.

Being overweight becomes a health problem when weight is 15% to 20% above normal. Of course, body build and an individual's lean-to-fat ratio also must be considered. Different people gain weight in different places in the body. Those who typically gain weight in the lower portions of the body (usually females) do not face as many health risks as those who gain weight in the upper body (usually males). A person might have a stocky build and weigh more than the desirable level for her height and age, but the percentage of body fat might be within the normal range. More often than not, however, obesity is self-evident.

Obesity is a problem that reflects the individual's physical, social, and emotional environment. Usually, the condition results from a lack of exercise, overeating, improper food habits, or emotional problems. The increased popularity of video games and other sedentary activities, for example, has contributed to the decline in exercise by students. Some people simply enjoy food too much. Others overeat to reduce anxiety, using food as a tranquilizer. Still others eat because of anger or boredom. Family habits sometimes contribute to obesity: The family may not exercise, may overeat, and may rely on snacking.

Weight Control

Weight reduction demands self-discipline and commitment. Overweight people must accept personal responsibility for their condition. If an emotional problem is the cause, that problem must be treated first to ensure long-lasting success at weight control, because the overweight condition is only a symptom of a deeper problem. Before any reducing plan is begun, a physician should be consulted.

Obese persons must consume fewer calories than they expend daily, but this is easier said than done. Dieters should use a diet that is similar to the one to which they are accustomed so they do not feel as restricted and tempted to quit dieting. Besides restricting caloric intake, they need to incorporate exercise into the overall plan to lose and maintain the loss.

Other techniques that have helped people lose weight are to:

- Arrange to eat in one place only
- Remove all unnecessary fat when cooking and eating meat
- Avoid gravies, using herbs and spices for seasoning instead
- Start meals with filling, low-calorie dishes like soup or celery sticks
- Eat fresh fruit instead of processed (canned fruit, juice, etc.)
- Eat regular meals—a missed meal may make you even more hungry during the day
- Use raw vegetables for snacks
- Eat baked, broiled, or boiled foods without adding fat
- Use a salad-sized plate rather than a dinner plate so the portions look larger
- Cut food into small bites and eat slowly
- Brush teeth after each meal; sometimes the aftertaste of food can stimulate the appetite
- Exercise moderately and regularly
- Develop hobbies; sometimes people substitute food for friends and outside activities

People should not lose weight too rapidly. Rapid weight loss might result in exhaustion, kidney problems, dehydration, reduced cardiovascular output, decreased strength, decreased growth, and decreased endurance.

In determining whether they are overweight, people should consult ideal weight statistics, not reports of average weights. Some weight tables will provide data on "average" weight; but, as noted earlier, the average person in the United States is overweight. Ideal-weight tables should be used as the standard for evaluating weight.

In addition, weight alone should not be the issue. Body fat (or lean-fat ratio) is even more critical. A student who is large framed might appear overweight, yet her body fat might be very acceptable. Conversely, a student with small bones might weight in within an acceptable range but actually have high body fat. Also, a person who combines a dieting program with an exercise program might be losing fat and gaining muscle. Since muscles weigh more than fat, the result might not be lost pounds but rather lost fat—a healthy condition. However, since most dieters are concerned only with how much they weigh, they might be disappointed that they are not losing weight. Again, a dieter should focus on the lean-fat ratio, not weight alone.

Therapy and Counseling

Attempts at weight reduction generally succeed more when they involve a "buddy system" or peer support group. Teachers can help by getting together several students who have a similar goal of weight reduction and having them eat together and share their concerns and problems. Teachers can also educate obese and overweight students about proper nutrition and encourage physical activity. To promote the obese student's emotional health, teachers need to offer security and acceptance without pitying or overprotecting the student. Offering support will produce much better results than constant harassment or criticism. Trying to reduce the student's anxiety while helping build self-esteem and independence are also important.

OTHER FOOD-RELATED ISSUES

Food Quackery

Some obese people may understand the need to diet but may want to do so as painlessly as possible. These people are vulnerable to fad diets advertised to help a person lose weight quickly. Some of these fad diets are expensive, useless, restricted in variety, and sometimes even detrimental to health. Most fad diets are directed at adults, rather than students, but students are impressionable. These diets must be put into proper perspective. In reality, most people who are overweight do not need to read a book about how to lose weight. Simply eating less of everything will usually cause them to reduce, if they follow the diet conscientiously.

Food quackery goes beyond diet books and weight-loss clinics that employ dubious methods. Many nutritional experts consider the whole "natural and health foods" segment of the industry quackery. Both of these areas prey on fears and uncertainties about foods and nutritional requirements. No accepted legal definition exists for "natural foods," and retailers continue to sell granola, dried fruits, and so on at inflated prices, all the while hinting that these products are healthier. "Health foods" such as bee pollen and algae extracts fall into the same category. Such foods are not harmful to health, but their "health" benefits are debatable. Advocates of natural, health, and "organic" foods claim that additives or pesticide residues in regular foods can cause disease or even lower the nutritional value of the food, but many of these claims are exaggerated. By and large, the Food and Drug Administration and other supervisory agencies do a good job of preventing potentially harmful or unsafe foods from reaching the market. Teachers can help students become informed consumers of food products and develop a good knowledge of nutritional principles. But nutrition should not become an obsession, as it is with many food faddists. Students should also be taught to recognize the difference between nutrition and food panaceas.

Food Myths

In spite of the level of education and communication in our country, nutritional myths and misconceptions still prevail. People cling to many false beliefs about food without regard to research findings or nutrition experts' advice. The sad thing about these fallacies is that they end up causing many people to become malnourished. Some of the more common food-related myths are the following (Jones et al., 1986):

Myth: All diseases are due to a faulty diet.
Reality: Some diseases are the result of a genetic predisposition or other environmental cause.

Myth: Everyone needs vitamin supplements.

Reality: A person who is healthy and eats a good variety of foods does not need vitamin supplements.

Myth: Megavitamins have a therapeutic effect on several physical conditions.

Reality: Continued use of megavitamins can be wasteful (because the body will rid itself of the excess) and sometimes can be harmful (if the body is unable to eliminate the excess amounts).

The most effective means of destroying these myths is through nutrition education. Teachers need to develop lessons designed to enlighten their students about these food misconceptions.

Food Labeling

A tremendous amount of nutritional information is available today, but many Americans are still misinformed and confused about the foods they buy and eat. The U.S. Food and Drug Administration (FDA) has attempted to ameliorate this problem by establishing regulations for advertising and labeling of food products (Hamrick, Anspaugh, & Ezell, 1986). These regulations have resulted in improved labeling designed to list all nutrients in the product and to make the information on food labels more meaningful to consumers. For example, nutrients are listed on the label in order by weight. Typically, the label will provide nutritional information based on one serving of the food product rather than on the entire can or package.

HEALTH HIGHLIGHT
Healthy Fast Foods?

Sample healthy menus			
	Calories	Fat (g)	% Calories from fat
McDonald's			
McLean Deluxe, side salad (no dressing), 1% low-fat milk	460	13	25
Muffin, fat-free, apple bran	180	0	0
Burger King			
Broiler Chicken Sandwich, side salad (no dressing), orange juice	374	8	19
Frozen yogurt, vanilla	120	3	23
Hardee's			
Real Lean Deluxe Burger, side salad with reduced-calorie Italian dressing, orange juice	530	21	36
Cool Twist Cone, vanilla/chocolate	190	6	28

Source: Excerpted from "Hazardous Salads, Healthy Burgers," June 1992, *University of California at Berkeley Wellness Letter,* © Health Letter Associates, 1992.

Manufacturers must use nutritional labeling when they add any nutrient to packaged food or when they make some nutritional claim for their products. Labeling is also meant to stop unsupported generalizations and fraudulent statements. Nutritional labeling of food products is being sought for nearly all foods. This would be difficult for foods like fresh fruits, but labeling of all food products would benefit the consumer.

The FDA and the U.S. Department of Agriculture (USDA) have launched a major effort to improve the format and content of food labels. In November of 1992, the FDA proposed regulations covering topics such as nutrition information, serving sizes, descriptive words, and health messages. These changes are designed to clear up confusion in some labels and to help the consumer make healthy choices. These changes would force manufacturers to list certified color additives, label fruit and vegetable juices, require grocery stores to display nutrition information on the 20 most popular raw fruits, vegetables, and types of fish, require these changes for virtually all packaged foods; define serving sizes; and define descriptors such as "light," "lean," and "low-fat" (Foulke, 1992, p. 9).

NUTRITIONAL EDUCATION

In emphasizing sound nutrition to students, teachers need to provide interesting and personalized learning opportunities. Students should learn to make their own responsible food choices. Of course, the home and school must work together to make the student's nutrition education a success.

The School Lunch Program

Many times school lunches are criticized for being bland and lacking in nutrition. A 1987 study of school foods found that their fat and sodium content significantly exceeded the recommended amounts (*Mayo Clinic,* 1988). The goals of school lunches are to:

1. Provide one third of the student's RDA
2. Serve a minimum of five items with minimum portions
3. Use resources provided by the government
4. Appeal to students. If the school offers vending machines with less-healthy choices, however, the student may choose those instead of the school lunch
5. Break even financially—a major problem, because most school systems operate on a limited budget

Even under these constraints, many school lunches provide varied, nutritious meals. A well-planned school lunch program also provides excellent nutrition learning opportunities. The federal school lunch program was established to provide nutritionally sound meals at low cost to students. These lunches help teach students good food choices. They each consist of a half-pint of whole milk; 2 oz of lean meat, poultry, fish, or cheese; a three-fourths-cup serving of two or more vegetables or fruits or both; one slice of whole-grain or enriched bread or its equivalent; and one teaspoon of butter or fortified margarine. Some schools now offer alternative lunches of salads and/or sandwiches.

For students who bring their lunches from home, teachers can provide several examples of nutritious sack lunches (e.g., a sandwich including some type of lean meat and lettuce on whole-wheat bread, banana, raisins, and milk).

In the cafeteria, teachers can help students learn table manners, sitting posture, and appropriate social behavior. The planning, preparation, and serving of meals by the cafeteria staff can also provide excellent learning opportunities for students.

■ ■ ■   *STUDENT CONCERNS:* NUTRITION

As students move through grades 7 to 12, they raise many issues of concern regarding nutrition. The following statements reflecting the various grades were taken from *Students Speak* (Trucano, 1984):

Grade 7

What is a good diet that a teenager could go on if he or she is overweight?
What is a good food to snack on?
Why are certain foods not nutritious?
How do you know what foods are good or bad?
I'd like to learn how dangerous food additives are.
How can you stay at the weight you want to be?
How can some people eat a lot of food, not necessarily good food, not exercise and still be thin?
How do you lose or gain weight and be safe about it?
Does the food you eat affect being physically fit and looking good?
I would like to know more about food and what kinds are healthy or good for you and which are not good for you.
How does the body transform leftover calories that are not burned into stored fat?
What would happen if you didn't eat?
What sorts of food do you eat to keep healthy?
What natural foods give the longest energy?

Grade 8

How do you get thin easily?
I think this section is very important because most people our age don't really know about what they eat and how to be more physically fit.
I think this would be quite important; there are more and more people who suffer from weight problems. I think if people knew more about this and learned when they are younger they might not have this problem now.
What foods keep the body going best all day?
How can you be a vegetarian and still be healthy and full of energy?

How do you diet without starving; does dieting change your personality?
I would like to know what foods contain.
How do you diet correctly and successfully?
How does the food you eat really affect how good you look?

Grade 9

I would like to know the significance of health foods and various vitamins.
I would like to take a class that would help me with my personal nutrition.
How can a vitamin help cut down on stress?
What foods are fattening and which are not?
Are diet pills helpful or bad for you?
What kinds of food should you eat if you want to stay fit?
Does diet food really help people who are overweight?
How do you get motivated to control weight?
What is the best way to diet?
What is bad about wrong foods?
Why do some eat a lot and not gain weight while others eat the same amount and gain a lot of weight?
How does weight affect body functions?
What are good foods?
What effect can junk foods have on one's complexion, mental attitude, and physical growth?
How can a teenager lose weight and still keep healthy?

Grade 10

What happens to people physically and psychologically when they have an unbalanced diet?
How can you keep weight down?
How can you gain weight when you are under stress of alcoholic parents and do not have much attention?
What vitamins are in different foods?
How can junk food affect your body over a period of time?
Teach us all the definitions of all of the preservatives and additives in food that we eat.
What will being overweight do to you in the long run and what is the influence of being in pretty good physical shape all your life even if you just sit at your office desk for 8 hours a day?
Tell me more about how to lose weight and stay healthy all of my life.
Talk more about bad diets that are coming out these days.
How does one maintain proper weight?
What happens when you don't get all the nutrients you are supposed to?
How do you go on a diet by eating the right foods and staying healthy and losing weight all at the same time without feeling weak?
What kind of foods are good for good complexion and healthy hair?
Why do our bodies require so much variety in foods?

Grade 11

What does it take to lose weight?

What is a quick way to lose pounds, in days, and still stay healthy, and keep the weight off?

Does food really affect the way you perform athletically and emotionally?

What type of diet is recommended to be the best and safest?

I think we should discuss the possible disadvantages of vitamins, such as people who take too many and jeopardize their health.

Do diet pills work as well as they say?

Grade 12

I would like to learn the effects of sugar, carbohydrates, and other commonly over-eaten foods and how they affect the body.

What is good nutrition for healthy people?

What are the effects of different fad diets?

I would like more information on the nutritional value of fiber foods such as grains and oatmeal products.

Appropriate weight-loss methods would benefit those who really don't know how to lose weight.

SUMMARY

Although food is basic to human existence, food choices often have little to do with good nutrition. Socioeconomic factors, personal preferences and habits, cultural customs, and religious and ethical beliefs all determine what food we select.

The eating habits of U.S. students are often poor. This is due primarily to the habits of their parents, hurried lifestyles, and lack of nutrition education. Healthy snacks can help supplement an otherwise poor diet. The development of positive lifetime eating habits in students is a critical issue.

Food's basic function is to provide nutrients to the body. All foods have specific caloric values. The USDA's food pyramid and the revised recommended daily allowance tables can be used to plan a healthy diet.

Food problems abound among students. Hunger and malnutrition affect a student's growth and learning. Lack of activity is leading to more overweight students. Pressure from peers to be thin or to look good encourages anorexia and bulimia. These conditions are physical and emotional handicaps. Therapy and counseling are needed to correct these problems.

Food quackery preys on the fears and misconceptions people have about foods. Students should be taught to distinguish between truth and misleading statements. Food labels are provided on most foods to help determine the nutritional value of a food.

Students should learn how to make responsible choices about food. Teachers and parents must work together for nutrition education to be successful.

DISCUSSION QUESTIONS

1. Describe why U.S. diets are typically insufficient even though we live in an affluent country.
2. What factors determine one's selection of foods?
3. Discuss the importance of complex carbohydrates in the diet.

4. Discuss some healthy ways to snack to enhance your diet.
5. List the food sources for proteins.
6. Differentiate between saturated and unsaturated fats.
7. Describe the importance of water to the body structure.
8. What beneficial roles do minerals play in body function?
9. Discuss the role of vitamins in helping the body use minerals.
10. Describe the use of the USDA's food pyramid in selecting proper foods.
11. Discuss the typical characteristics of an anorexic person.
12. Describe obesity as an emotional and physical handicap.
13. How can food labels be helpful to consumers?
14. Discuss the importance of the school lunch program.

■ ■ ■   *ACTIVITIES FOR TEACHING NUTRITION*

The following activities for students include puzzles, value-oriented strategies, experiments and demonstrations, discussion-oriented strategies, and learning enhancements (filmstrip and videotape information).

■ ■ ■   *ACTIVITIES:* NUTRITION PUZZLES

Nutrition Scramble*

Have students complete the following exercise.

Name: _____   Date: _____

Nutrition

Directions: Unscramble the letters below to form fifteen terms associated with nutrition.

1. **TTNRIUENS**   _ _ _ _ _ O _ _ _
2. **EWRTA**   O _ _ _ _
3. **ACBRHODYARETS** _ O _ _ _ _ _ O _ _ _ _ _
4. **NEOIPRT**   _ _ _ O _ _ _
5. **SAFT**   _ O _ _
6. **IIAVMNTS**   _ _ O _ _ _ _ _
7. **SMNEIRLA**   _ _ _ _ _ O O _
8. **LGSCUEO**   _ _ _ O _ _ _
9. **EMTA**   _ O _ _
10. **RSGNIA**   _ _ _ _ O _
11. **EEEASBVGTL**   _ _ _ _ _ _ O O _ _
12. **RFTIU**   _ _ _ O _
13. **EBRFI**   _ _ _ O _
14. **GMEUESL**   O _ _ _ _ O _
15. **YRDIA DPORCUST** O O _ _ _   _ _ _ _ _ _ _ _

Rearrange the circled letters to form advice a person should follow in order to maintain a healthy lifestyle.

_ _ _   _   _ _ _ _   _ _ _ _ _ _ _ _ _ _   _ _ _ _

*Source: *Health Education Puzzles and Puzzlers* by Karen Geswein Zipprich. Copyright 1989, J. Weston Walch, Publisher. Further reproduction is prohibited.

Nutrition Hidden-Word Puzzle*

Instruct students to find the words hidden in this puzzle.

Name: _____   Date: _____

Nutrition

Directions: Find the words in the puzzle and circle them. The words are spelled horizontally, vertically, diagonally, forward, or backward.

```
N  S  U  G  A  R  Z  I  N  S  O  C  U  L  O  N  I  T  E  R  V
U  N  I  M  A  I  H  T  E  B  I  A  F  I  B  O  O  T  N  G  E
T  A  E  Z  N  E  N  V  G  Y  O  R  V  I  T  A  L  P  I  I  G
R  C  N  C  M  U  I  D  O  S  L  B  E  E  L  A  I  N  D  O  E
I  L  Z  N  O  T  A  M  I  C  H  O  L  E  S  T  E  R  O  L  T
E  O  A  M  I  N  O  A  C  I  D  H  V  I  T  A  U  O  I  M  A
N  I  Z  D  O  O  R  P  C  Z  O  Y  R  Y  G  N  E  Z  F  O  B
T  Z  D  L  U  E  O  R  H  Y  K  D  I  G  E  S  T  I  O  N  L
B  A  O  H  T  O  P  E  E  M  L  R  F  L  S  O  S  G  L  O  E
E  S  H  A  L  S  D  B  E  E  I  A  L  G  A  H  T  H  A  R  S
A  C  W  N  N  I  O  I  S  O  T  T  G  O  S  Y  H  O  C  P  T
B  O  O  A  I  M  R  F  E  S  K  E  P  L  A  R  E  N  I  M  E
O  R  E  O  S  O  T  T  V  T  I  N  I  M  I  N  E  N  N  U  I
I  B  E  G  L  I  O  N  I  E  T  O  R  P  O  K  N  I  Z  G  Y
T  I  U  A  U  N  I  A  C  I  N  S  N  A  C  K  L  Z  S  O  R
N  C  C  R  D  F  O  L  I  L  A  F  T  P  O  U  Y  I  E  M  T
I  A  F  O  S  L  E  B  A  L  T  A  O  U  R  T  A  E  M  A  L
O  C  Y  G  R  E  N  E  N  Z  Y  M  E  S  N  E  V  I  U  T  U
B  I  O  T  I  N  R  U  L  S  N  I  M  A  T  I  V  N  G  I  O
L  D  A  E  B  E  M  U  M  U  I  S  E  N  G  A  M  I  E  V  P
U  R  E  O  C  H  L  C  I  S  T  G  U  M  M  U  I  C  L  A  C
```

Words to find:

Additives	Cheese	Folacin	Mineral	Snack
Amino acid	Cholesterol	Fruit	Niacin	Sodium
Ascorbic acid	Diet	Iodine	Nutrient	Sugar
Beans	Digestion	Iron	Nuts	Thiamin
Biotin	Eggs	Labels	Oils	Vegetables
Bread	Energy	Legumes	Poultry	Vitamins
Calcium	Enzymes	Liver	Protein	Water
Calorie	Fats	Magnesium	Retinol	Zinc
Carbohydrate	Fiber	Meat	Salt	
Cereal	Fish	Milk		

*Source: *Health Education Puzzles and Puzzlers* by Karen Geswein Zipprich. Copyright 1989, J. Weston Walch, Publisher. Further reproduction is prohibited.

Digestive System Identification*

Ask students to fill the blanks in for the following diagram.

Name: _____   Date: _____

The Digestive System

Directions: Match each label below with the correct number corresponding to the illustration. Write the letter of the label in the blank provided.

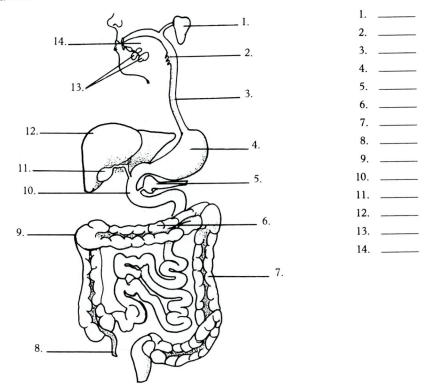

1. _____
2. _____
3. _____
4. _____
5. _____
6. _____
7. _____
8. _____
9. _____
10. _____
11. _____
12. _____
13. _____
14. _____

A. Transverse colon

B. Tongue

C. Esophagus

D. Gall bladder

E. Liver

F. Salivary glands

G. Small intestine

H. Pharynx

I. Large intestine

J. Stomach

K. Pancreas

L. Appendix

M. Descending colon

N. Salivary gland

*Source: *Health Education Puzzles and Puzzlers* by Karen Geswein Zipprich. Copyright 1989, J. Weston Walch, Publisher. Further reproduction is prohibited.

ACTIVITIES: VALUES-ORIENTED STRATEGIES

Looking at Myself*

Instruct the students to use the following scale and place the number next to each body part or other characteristic listed that describes their feelings about that part of themselves.

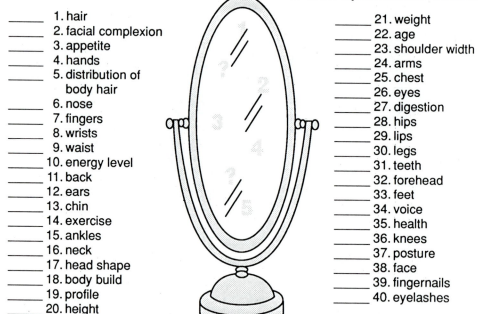

Looking at Myself

Directions: Using the scale below, place the number next to each body part or other characteristic listed that describes your feeling about that part of yourself.

Scale:

1. I have strong feelings and wish I could change this.
2. I don't like this, but I can put up with this.
3. I have no particular feelings about this.
4. I am satisfied with this.
5. I consider myself fortunate with this.

_____ 1. hair
_____ 2. facial complexion
_____ 3. appetite
_____ 4. hands
_____ 5. distribution of body hair
_____ 6. nose
_____ 7. fingers
_____ 8. wrists
_____ 9. waist
_____ 10. energy level
_____ 11. back
_____ 12. ears
_____ 13. chin
_____ 14. exercise
_____ 15. ankles
_____ 16. neck
_____ 17. head shape
_____ 18. body build
_____ 19. profile
_____ 20. height

_____ 21. weight
_____ 22. age
_____ 23. shoulder width
_____ 24. arms
_____ 25. chest
_____ 26. eyes
_____ 27. digestion
_____ 28. hips
_____ 29. lips
_____ 30. legs
_____ 31. teeth
_____ 32. forehead
_____ 33. feet
_____ 34. voice
_____ 35. health
_____ 36. knees
_____ 37. posture
_____ 38. face
_____ 39. fingernails
_____ 40. eyelashes

Scoring: Add up all the point values you assigned to the characteristics and divide the sum by 40. Your score should fall between 1 and 5.

A score closer to 5 indicates you are very comfortable with your body image. A score closer to 1 indicates that you are very uncomfortable. You may need to think about changing your attitude to improve your self-esteem about your body image. You may also want to consider healthful ways to change your appearance.

*Source: *Entering Adulthood: Looking at Body Image and Eating Disorders* by Susan Fiarranto, 1991, Santa Cruz, CA: Network. Reprinted with permission of ETR Associates/Network Publications.

280

Media Messages*

Instruct the students to answer the following questions about any advertisement. Then have them complete the Scoring and Interpretation section, following Steps I through IV.

Media Messages

Directions: Answer the following questions about an advertisement. Then complete the *Scoring and Interpretation* section, following *Steps I-IV.*

What is the name of the advertised product? _____

What kind of product is it? Circle or fill in the blank space below.
Diet (weight control)   Alcoholic beverage (beer, wine, liquor)
Clothing   Other _____
Tobacco product

Rate the advertisement on each of the following factors, using this scale:
SA = Strongly Agree   D = Disagree
A = Agree   SD = Strongly Disagree
U = Undecided   NA = Not Applicable

Circle *one* choice for each statement.

Generally, the advertisement:		Score
1. Suggests that use of the product will produce a positive body image.	SA A U D SD NA	_____
2. Shows a socially negative body image.	SA A U D SD NA	_____
3. Suggests the product is a solution for boredom.	SA A U D SD NA	_____
4. Associates the use of the product with fun or pleasure.	SA A U D SD NA	_____
5. Associates the use of the product with being attractive.	SA A U D SD NA	_____
6. Encourages the use of the product as a method of problem-solving.	SA A U D SD NA	_____
7. Suggests that everyone is using the product.	SA A U D SD NA	_____
8. Suggests that people who use the product are mature.	SA A U D SD NA	_____
9. Shows the model using the product.	SA A U D SD NA	_____
10. Suggests that the product will improve performance (intellectual, physical, spiritual, etc.).	SA A U D SD NA	_____
	Total:	_____

---

*Source: *Entering Adulthood: Looking at Body Image and Eating Disorders* by Susan Fiarranto, 1991, Santa Cruz, CA: Network. Reprinted with permission of *ETR* Associates/Network Publications.

Scoring and Interpretation of Results

Step I. Use the following scale to score your responses.

    [SA] Strongly Agree   = 5 points
    [A] Agree   = 4 points
    [U] Undecided   = 3 points
    [D] Disagree   = 2 points
    [SD] Strongly Disagree = 1 point
    [NA] Not Applicable   = 0 points

Step II. Add your points for each statement:

Total Points: _____ Points

Step III. After you have added up the total points, place an X on the point of the following line that best represents your total points.

Total Points

10	20	30	40	50

Little Impact on Body Image   **High Impact on Body Image**

Step IV. Write your comments regarding your analysis or evaluation of the body image in the advertisement. (e.g., What decisions did you reach about the body image?)

_____

_____

_____

_____

_____

_____

_____

The Perfect Body*

Instruct students to describe their idea of a "perfect" body. If the student is a male, have him write about a perfect male body. If the student is a female, have her write about a perfect female body.

What's Perfect?

Directions: Write a short paragraph about your idea of a "perfect" body. If you are a male, write about a perfect male body. If you are a female, write about a perfect female body. Keep your ideas to yourself. Complete Part II after your class discussion.

Part I
A perfect body is...

Part II
Some of the things that influence this view of perfect are...

---

*Source: *Entering Adulthood: Looking at Body Image and Eating Disorders* by Susan Fiarranto, 1991, Santa Cruz, CA: Network. Reprinted with permission of *ETR* Associates/Network Publications.

Privacy Circles*

Instruct the students to complete this exercise by indicating who they would talk to in the following hypothetical situations.

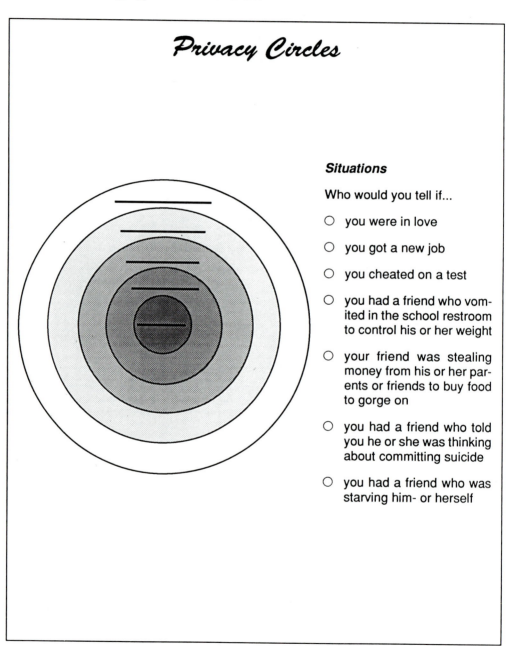

Privacy Circles

Situations

Who would you tell if...

○ you were in love

○ you got a new job

○ you cheated on a test

○ you had a friend who vomited in the school restroom to control his or her weight

○ your friend was stealing money from his or her parents or friends to buy food to gorge on

○ you had a friend who told you he or she was thinking about committing suicide

○ you had a friend who was starving him- or herself

Source: *Entering Adulthood: Looking at Body Image and Eating Disorders* by Susan Fiarranto, 1991, Santa Cruz, CA: Network. Reprinted with permission of ETR Associates/Network Publications.

■ ■ ■   *ACTIVITIES:* EXPERIMENTS AND DEMONSTRATIONS

Exercise and Obesity*

Concept

Body weight is overwhelmingly dependent upon the balance between caloric intake and caloric expenditures.

Students

Designed for tenth-grade students of average academic ability.

Technique

Laboratory experiment.

The directions that follow describe a procedure for using laboratory rats to demonstrate the effects of exercise on obesity. Although it requires a significant amount of equipment and supplies, the various steps are relatively simple and require no special skills. If problems are encountered in obtaining the necessary materials through normal channels, they may often be borrowed from the school's science department. Actually, in many schools there may be advantages in conducting this learning activity as a joint project in conjunction with the science program. The directions here are for an experiment of relatively modest proportions. There are many obvious ways of embellishing this program should conditions permit.

1. Sometime prior to the start of a unit of study on exercise or weight control, obtain the following materials:
   - eight mature white rats with ages ranging between thirty and sixty days
   - eight small animal cages complete with water bottles and feeding trays
   - twenty-five lbs of cedar shavings
   - twenty-five lbs of rat pellets
   - one clean garbage can approximately two feet in diameter
   - one pair of leather gloves
   - one small scale, preferably of the triple-beam balance type and sensitive to the nearest gram.

2. Set up the cages and the garbage can in a suitable location. The back of the classroom is preferable if space and supervision are available. Put one rat in each cage and make food and water continuously available. These animals will bite occasionally so leather gloves should be used when handling them.

3. Record the weight of all food added to each cage. At the end of each week, weigh the food remaining in the dish of each cage and subtract it from the total of all the food added to determine the amount of food each animal consumed

---

*Source: *Creative Teaching in Health* (3rd Ed.) by Donald A. Read and Walter H. Greene, 1989, Prospect Heights, IL: Waveland.

each week. Also weigh and record their body weight once per week on the same day and hour.

4. After approximately two weeks, or until such time as stable baseline readings are obtained for body weight and food consumption, randomly assign four rats to an "exercise" group and four to a control group. Fill the garbage can one-half full of water of moderate temperature. Using the leather gloves, place the exercise rats in the water once each morning and allow them to swim for thirty to sixty minutes. Repeat this activity with the same animals in the afternoon so that they have two exercise sessions per day Monday through Friday. Have one student available during these sessions to serve as "lifeguard"; he or she should remove and cut short the sessions of any rats that become exhausted and sink to the bottom. This is particularly important during the first week while the animals are adapting to the training program.

5. Continue this regimen for three or four weeks, and maintain the continuous monitoring of body weight and food consumption. At the end of this time compare the totals for the two groups. A typical pattern of results will show a small to moderate weight loss among the exercise rats together with slightly higher food consumption.

The manner in which this experiment is worked into the regular class activities will normally vary according to local conditions. If the animals can be housed in the health education classroom, for example, then students of all or most of the sections that meet there throughout the day can be involved in their care and in carrying out the experiment. For example, the exercise session could be rotated among the morning and afternoon class sections on a regular basis. One caution, however: try to avoid variations in the conditions for the weighing of the food and the animals. If the animals must be housed elsewhere, then it may be best to have a small group of students undertake full responsibility for the project for extra credit or for the completion of a major assignment. They could then provide an elaborate report to their section and, where possible, to all the other tenth-grade sections.

The use of four animals in each group is about minimal for predictable results. The use of fewer rats may still provide a worthwhile learning experience; however, there will be a great possibility that individual differences may distort the findings. Other pitfalls include the onset of puberty if immature rates are used or pregnancy if cross-sexed animals are housed in the same cage.

■ ■ ■   *ACTIVITIES:* DISCUSSION-ORIENTED STRATEGIES

Eating Disorders*

Have students read each of the following statements. Have them circle the letter *T* if the statement is completely true, and circle the letter *F* if the statement is partly or completely false. The key, with correct answers circled, follows.

*Source: *Entering Adulthood: Looking at Body Image and Eating Disorders* by Susan Fiarranto, 1991, Santa Cruz, CA: Network. Reprinted with permission of ETR Associates/Network Publications.

Check Your Knowledge

Directions: Read each of the following statements. Circle the letter **T** if the statement is completely true; circle the letter **F** if the statement is partly or completely false.

T   F   1. Teens may develop unusual eating behaviors as a way to become independent and rebel against authority, such as parents and teachers.

T   F   2. Eating a lot of food in a short time is called bingeing.

T   F   3. Insisting that your body is fat, even when you're very thin, is a symptom of anorexia nervosa.

T   F   4. Being teased by friends about being fat or needing to diet can trigger an eating disorder.

T   F   5. Thinking about food all the time is a symptom of eating disorders.

T   F   6. Feeling depressed often is a symptom of eating disorders.

T   F   7. Losing too much weight due to starvation is a symptom of anorexia nervosa.

T   F   8. Most weight-loss diets provide normal ways to eat for a lifetime.

T   F   9. Forcing yourself to vomit is one of the common behaviors of anorexia nervosa.

T   F   10. Only females are affected by bulimia.

T   F   11. Diet pills are a good way to help people lose weight and keep it off.

T   F   12. People can become addicted to diet pills.

T   F   13. People with eating disorders have low self-esteem.

T   F   14. Most people with anorexia nervosa deny that their eating behavior is a serious problem.

T   F   15. People with eating disorders believe that a thin body will bring them happiness and success.

Check Your Knowledge

Key

Directions: Read each of the following statements. Circle the letter **T** if the statement is completely true; circle the letter **F** if the statement is partly or completely false.

(T) F 1. Teens may develop unusual eating behaviors as a way to become independent and rebel against authority, such as parents and teachers.

(T) F 2. Eating a lot of food in a short time is called bingeing.

(T) F 3. Insisting that your body is fat, even when you're very thin, is a symptom of anorexia nervosa.

(T) F 4. Being teased by friends about being fat or needing to diet can trigger an eating disorder.

(T) F 5. Thinking about food all the time is a symptom of eating disorders.

(T) F 6. Feeling depressed often is a symptom of eating disorders.

(T) F 7. Losing too much weight due to starvation is a symptom of anorexia nervosa.

T (F) 8. Most weight-loss diets provide normal ways to eat for a lifetime.

T (F) 9. Forcing yourself to vomit is one of the common behaviors of anorexia nervosa.

T (F) 10. Only females are affected by bulimia.

T (F) 11. Diet pills are a good way to help people lose weight and keep it off.

(T) F 12. People can become addicted to diet pills.

(T) F 13. People with eating disorders have low self-esteem.

(T) F 14. Most people with anorexia nervosa deny that their eating behavior is a serious problem.

(T) F 15. People with eating disorders believe that a thin body will bring them happiness and success.

more satisfying life
800/232-0366.

Nutrition Test. Sho
and reading food la
nutritional value po
food versus taking
Council, 800/232-0

Eating Behavior. F
reasons for overeati
and Food Nutrition

Eating Light—Eati
weight problems, t
nutritionally adequa
leader's guide comp
Nutrition Council, 8

Exercise for Life. F
program explains th
not exercising. 16 n

Fat or Fit Test. Des
loss. Explains why
many suggestions fo
Council, 800/232-0

Introduction to the
tians, will find this
individual counseli
works, this progra
emphasizing variety
use the Food Excha
Food Nutrition Cou

Healthy Mother, He
learn the importanc
sickness, money sa
discussed. 18 minut

Eating Disorders a
risk, physiologic ef
loss, factors precipi
an eating disorder.
athletes. Great for n
Food Nutrition Cou

Peak Performance
Maine's Summer Sp
classes, and for use

REFERE

Allsen, P. E
ness fo
ed.). Du
Boyle, M., &
ed.). Ne
Burckes-Mi
ders: A
19, 22–
Crockett, S.
trition ed
School F
Edlin, G., &
A holisti
Bartlett.
Foulke, J. (1
posals to
9–13.
Hamrick, M.
Health. N
Jones, K., S
sions VI.
Lamb, L. (19
date. *The*
Lankford, T.
tions of
York: Wil
Levine, M. (1
eating di
Washingto
Mayo Clinic
Clinic N

Eating Habits*

Instruct students to think about their eating patterns and habits. What, how much, when, where, and why do they eat? For each of the following questions, have the students check the answer that best describes their eating patterns.

Your Eating Habits

Directions: Think about your eating patterns and habits. What, how much, when, where and why do you eat? For each of the following questions, check the answer that best describes your eating patterns.

What do I usually eat?

☐ A varied and balanced diet that includes only moderate amounts of fat, sugar and salt

☐ Deep-fat fried and breaded foods

☐ Extras, such as salad dressings, potato toppings, spreads, sauces and gravies

☐ Sweets and rich desserts such as candies, cakes, pies

☐ Snack foods high in fat and sodium, such as chips

How much do I usually eat?

☐ A single small serving

☐ A large serving

☐ Two servings or more

When do I usually eat?

☐ At mealtimes only

☐ While preparing meals or clearing the table

☐ After school

☐ While watching television or participating in other activities

☐ At school breaks

☐ Anytime

Where do I usually eat?

☐ At the kitchen table or dining room table

☐ At restaurants or fast-food places

☐ In front of the television or while reading

☐ Where I am preparing the food

☐ Wherever I happen to be when I'm hungry

Why do I usually eat?

☐ It's time to eat.

☐ I'm starved.

☐ Foods look tempting.

☐ Everyone else is eating.

☐ Food will get thrown away if I don't eat it.

(Adapted from U.S. Department of Agriculture, Human Nutrition Information Service. 1986. Nutrition and your health: Dietary guidelines for Americans. *Home and garden bulletin* No. 232-2.)

*Source: *Entering Adulthood: Looking at Body Image and Eating Disorders* by Susan Fiarranto, 1991, Santa Cruz, CA: Network Reprinted with permission of *ETR* Associates/Network Publications.

Cost Analysis

Investigate comm
cost, services off
diet clinics comp
consideration fo

Comparison of

Make a study of
qualifications, le
shots, hypnosis,

Comparison of

Visit the local d
available or visit
dieting.

Evaluation of [

Compile magazin
devices. Evaluate
objective facts, ps
do something for

Analysis of "Fa

Write to adolesc
Figuring length
pound of weight

Survey of Fam

Make a survey of
aids, products an
for consumer ed
and *A Diet for Li*

■ ■ ■   *ACTIVITIES:* L

How to Live Lon
properly and ex
outlines ways to
emotional change

*Source for these six
Loya, 1983, Reston, V

CHAPTER 11

Concepts for Teaching Communicable Disease

The human species coexists with a large number of microorganisms. In most instances, we and our microbiologic associates live in harmony. Of the wide spectrum of organisms found in nature, only a relatively small proportion cause disease in humans. Leonard V. Crowley, *Introduction to Human Disease*

OBJECTIVES

After reading this chapter, you should be able to

- Identify the various pathogens
- Describe the typical stages through which a disease progresses
- Describe how the body is protected from disease
- Discuss the major communicable diseases
- Discuss the major sexually transmitted diseases

Many conditions influence the quality of life. Over the past centuries, the types of diseases which have killed and debilitated mankind have changed. At one time, infectious diseases were the big killers of humans. Today, chronic diseases are the leading causes of death. Some people say that infectious disease—in the form of the AIDS epidemic—will again become our biggest enemy.

COMMUNICABLE DISEASES

At various times throughout history, such communicable diseases as the plague, smallpox, syphilis, and polio have been common throughout the world. Occasionally, a disease such as Legionnaires' disease will cause a short-term epidemic. Currently, the AIDS epidemic threatens the welfare of our citizens. In addition, minor ailments such as the common cold and influenza are constant problems.

The Pathogens

Microorganisms (or **microbes**) are invisible, living agents that are found throughout the environment. Most of the time, these microbes do no harm and may even promote certain body functions. Some microbes can harm humans, however. This type of microbe is known as a **pathogen**. When a pathogen invades the body, it is called an **infection**. When an infection is transmitted between humans or from animals to humans, it is known as a **communicable disease**.

Pathogens take one of six general forms. In order of size, from smallest to largest, pathogens are classified as viruses, bacteria, rickettsias, fungi, protozoa, and helminths (more commonly referred to as parasitic worms) (see Figure 11.1).

Figure 11.1   The six major pathogens known to cause diseases in humans

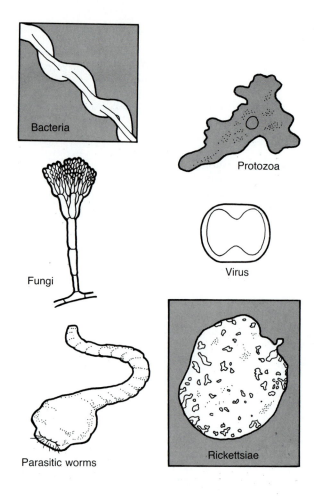

Viruses

Viruses are the smallest pathogens. There are 150 viruses known to cause disease. They can be viewed only with an electron microscope. Because viruses must rely on a living host to survive, they are known as **obligate intracellular parasites**. Viruses consist of a protein structure that contains DNA and RNA. Once the viruses attach themselves to a host cell, they begin reproducing new viruses. Eventually, the host cell bursts, releasing the viruses to start the process again.

Drugs for treating viral infections are limited. Some medications can block viruses' reproductive cycle. The body also produces **interferon**, a protein substance that helps the cells reject the invading viruses. Interferon does not destroy the viruses, however.

Some of the more common viral diseases are the common cold, influenza, hepatitis, mumps, measles, chicken pox, herpes, infectious mononucleosis, and AIDS.

Bacteria

Bacteria are small, single-celled microorganisms. More than 1,500 species of bacteria are known, but only about 100 of those are pathogenic to humans. Bacteria occur in three shapes: spherical (coccus), spiral (spirella), and rod-shaped (bacillus). Pathogenic bacteria cause harm through the release of **toxins** (poisons). They need not invade the cell to do damage. The toxins kill and dissolve the cells near the site of the infection. The damaged cells nourish the bacteria. The infection can spread deeper into the tissue or pass to other parts of the body through the bloodstream. Some pathogenic bacteria can cause damage by growing in such large numbers as to interfere with normal organ functioning. They do this without producing a toxin.

Some of the diseases caused by bacteria include tuberculosis, strep throat, tetanus, dental caries (cavities), gonorrhea, Legionnaires' disease, syphilis, and several types of food poisoning.

Rickettsias

Rickettsias resemble both viruses and bacteria. Rickettsias range in size between that of the viruses and bacteria. They can produce toxins that destroy tissue. Insect **vectors** (carriers) transmit rickettsia diseases to humans. The most common carriers of rickettsias are fleas, lice, mites, and ticks. Rocky Mountain spotted fever, typhus, and Q fever are common rickettsia diseases.

Fungi

Fungi are plant-like organisms that include molds and yeasts. Fungi can vary in size from microscopic single cells to multicellular. Fungi contain no chlorophyll and must live off a host. Most fungi do no harm to humans, but several do cause diseases such as ringworm, jock itch, and candidiasis (a yeast infection). Several types of fungi are quite useful to humans. Mushrooms, which are one form of fungi, are included in a variety of dishes.

Protozoa

Protozoa are single-celled microscopic animals. These pathogens are associated with diseases such as malaria, African sleeping sickness, and amoebic dysentery. The most common protozoal disease in this country is trichomoniasis, a sexually transmitted disease. Many of the protozoal diseases remain in the body and alternate between active and inactive states.

Helminths

Helminths, or **parasitic worms**, range in size from the relatively small pinworm to a length of several feet for some tapeworms. Parasitic worms are divided into roundworms (pinworms and hookworms) and flatworms (tapeworms and flukes). The roundworms cause a variety of mild infections. The flatworms have the potential to be deadly in large numbers. Usually, parasitic worm infections enter the body through contaminated food and drink. Beef, pork, and intestinal roundworms cause problems in humans.

Figure 11.4   Types of immunity

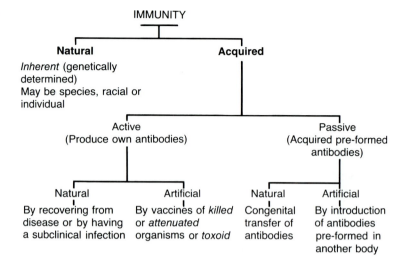

IMMUNITY

Natural
Inherent (genetically determined)
May be species, racial or individual

Acquired

Active
(Produce own antibodies)

Passive
(Acquired pre-formed antibodies)

Natural
By recovering from disease or by having a subclinical infection

Artificial
By vaccines of *killed* or *attenuated* organisms or *toxoid*

Natural
Congenital transfer of antibodies

Artificial
By introduction of antibodies pre-formed in another body

The Immune System

If the defenses listed in Figure 11.3 do not prevent development of a disease, the host body turns to another powerful line of defense. **Immunity** is the state of being protected from infectious diseases. When a pathogen invades the host, the immune system swings into action to destroy the infectious agent. Anything that invades the body and causes the immune system to react is called an **antigen** (foreign body). The body develops **antibodies** that destroy or lessen the effects of the invading antigen. Each type of antibody is specific for each type of antigen. For example, antibodies for measles have no effect on the common cold antigen.

Lymphocytes are the type of white blood cells most responsible for this reaction to occur. Two forms of lymphocytes are T-lymphocytes and B-lymphocytes. T-lymphocytes circulate through lymphatic tissue and the bloodstream, neutralizing antigens. T-helpers or T-suppressor cells either increase or release the response of other lymphocytes. B-lymphocytes produce antibodies. When stimulated by an antigen, these cells produce antibodies that destroy the antigens.

Immunity can be developed through having a disease (natural immunity) or through artificial immunity. Artificial immunity is acquired by vaccination with dead or attenuated (weakened) organisms or toxins (poisons). Injecting antibodies for a particular antigen will provide short-term protection against a disease, as Figure 11.4 illustrates.

SELECTED INFECTIOUS DISEASES

Diseases usually found in schools include the common cold, influenza, strep throat, and the childhood diseases of chicken pox, mumps, and rubella (German measles). To a lesser extent, diseases such as infectious mononucleosis, hepatitis, and AIDS are now affecting the classroom. In the school situation, respiratory diseases constitute the greatest problem (see Figure 11.5). Students face more days of

Figure 11.5   Respiratory diseases

Chicken Pox	Poliomyelitis
Diphtheria	Rheumatic Fever
German Measles (Rubella)	Scarlet Fever
Influenza	Smallpox (Variola)
Measles (Rubeola)	Streptococcal Throat Infection
Meningococcus Meningitis	Tuberculosis
Mumps (Parotitis)	Whopping Cough (Pertussis)

restricted activity and school absenteeism because of respiratory conditions than any other disease.

The Common Cold

The cold is the most common of all the infectious diseases found in the school setting. A cold alone is not considered serious, but secondary infections resulting from improper care can be a problem.

At least 50 different viruses can cause the common cold. Symptoms usually develop within 24 hours after exposure and include teary eyes, obstructed breathing, and a runny nose. When a fever is present, it indicates a secondary infection. Once a cold develops, it will run its course in 7 to 14 days.

Colds have no cure; consequently, antibiotics are of no benefit. Once developed, bed rest, good nutrition, and plenty of fluids are the best medicines. Over-the-counter drugs may mask symptoms, but they will not cure a cold. A cold is most contagious during the first 24 hours.

Streptococcal Throat Infection

Strep throat is commonly found in the school setting. The causative agent is the streptococci bacteria. The infection is passed primarily through sneezing, coughing, or the use of soiled objects, such as handkerchiefs, that reach the mouth. Incubation time for strep throat is three to five days. Symptoms may include sore throat, fever, nausea, and vomiting. In some cases, individuals may develop a rash on the neck and chest area. Treatment is through the use of antibiotics. Students should be excluded from school until the fever and sore throat are gone for 24 to 48 hours.

Influenza

Influenza, or flu, is a commonly experienced virus. Three strains of the virus have been isolated, with a multitude of mutations within each strain. Strain A is the most pathogenic, followed by strains B and C. A person may develop short-term immunity to one strain, but that immunity does not transfer to a different variety. Fortunately, the flu is not extremely hazardous to normally healthy people. Death does result more frequently in adults over 65, children under 5, and people experiencing chronic diseases.

Influenza symptoms include aches and pains, nausea, diarrhea, fever, and coldlike ailments. The best treatment for flu is to get ample bed rest, ingest plenty of fluids, eat nutritious foods, and take medicine, if prescribed. While obvious symptoms last only a few days, a feeling of weakness may persist for some time, so extra rest may be needed. It is important to take extra care following the flu, so that complications do not develop. Since influenza is caused by a virus, Reye's syndrome can develop as a secondary disease. The syndrome is almost always confined to people under the age of 18. It is characterized by brain and liver damage. Evidence suggests it is often related to taking aspirin for a viral infection (Thomas, 1984).

Infectious Mononucleosis

Infectious mononucleosis is thought to be initiated by the Epstein-Barr virus and is transmitted through saliva, hence its more common name, the "kissing disease." In reality, mononucleosis does not seem to be highly contagious. Initial symptoms may include moderate fever, discomfort, lack of appetite, fatigue, headache, and sore throat. Lymph nodes usually enlarge as does the spleen about one-third of the time. Occasionally, mild liver damage may occur leading to jaundice for a few days. Diagnosis is made using a blood test. A positive test indicates extremely high levels of white blood cells, as well as mononuclear cells. Treatment consists of possibly prolonged bed rest, sound nutrition, and medicine for secondary problems as indicated. For 2 to 3 months after recovery, the individual may feel depressed, lack energy, and feel sleepy during the day. Symptoms may linger for up to a year after infection.

Hepatitis

Hepatitis is a disease that has long created a public health hazard, occasionally reaching epidemic proportions in specific populations and parts of the country. Hepatitis causes inflammation of the liver. Characteristic symptoms are fever, diarrhea, nausea, loss of appetite, skin rashes, tenderness in the upper right abdomen, dark yellow urine, and possibly jaundice.

Four types of hepatitis have been isolated. Hepatitis A, or infectious hepatitis, is often the result of poor sanitary conditions. A major problem with Hepatitis A is that it is a major sexually transmissible disease. Hepatitis B, or serum hepatitis, is transmitted primarily by sharing contaminated needles among addicts. Hepatitis B is more serious than hepatitis A, with higher potential for liver damage. Non-A, non-B hepatitis, also called hepatitis C, resembles both A and B but is classified as neither. Hepatitis occurring after a blood transfusion is usually this type. Hepatitis D, or delta hepatitis, is the newest and most potent variation. Hepatitis D can only be contracted by a person suffering from hepatitis B. It is most often spread among intravenous drug users (Crowley, 1988).

Treatments for any form of hepatitis are limited, and relapses may occur. Bed rest and inactivity may be necessary for months. Passive immunization with antibodies directed against viral hepatitis A and B are available. A new drug called interferon alfa is now available for patients with chronic hepatitis B. However, a four-month course of treatment resulted in a 40% remission (Sheldon, 1992).

SEXUALLY TRANSMITTED DISEASES (STDs)

AIDS (HIV Infection)

Human Immunodeficiency Virus (HIV) is responsible for the development of Acquired Immunodeficiency Syndrome (AIDS). Until the infected person actually develops full-blown AIDS, he is referred to as being HIV positive. A person infected with the HIV virus will sometimes experience symptoms that resemble the flu or mononucleosis. These symptoms will usually occur within 2 weeks of exposure. The symptoms subside and the person generally feels well. The breakdown of the immune system and the development of opportunistic diseases require several years; consequently, additional symptoms may not be noticed for years. The following signs and symptoms may indicate a serious situation if they persist for more than 2 weeks:

- Fatigue or tiredness
- Night sweats, chills, or fever
- Unexplained loss of more than 15 pounds
- Swelling in lymph nodes of the neck, armpits, or groin
- Persistent sore throat or white patches in mouth/throat
- Persistent cough
- Bleeding from any part of the body for any unknown reason
- Chronic diarrhea
- Pink, brown, or purplish spots on the skin

The HIV virus causes the body's immune system to break down. The body's normal defense system becomes unable to fight off invasive agents, enabling opportunistic diseases to develop. These diseases are not usually seen in healthy individuals but frequently occur in people who have poorly operating immune systems. Common opportunistic diseases seen in AIDS include Kaposi's sarcoma, Hodgkin's disease, thrush, cytomegalovirus, *Toxoplasma gondii, Pneumocystis carinii,* and tuberculosis. As with all pathogens, antibodies are produced when HIV invades the bloodstream, but, for some yet unknown reason, the antibodies have no effect on the virus. The HIV virus is detectable because of the presence of these antibodies in the blood.

Normally, the incubation period for severe AIDS is 5 to 10 years, although it can be more or less time. The average incubation period between infection and the development of severe AIDS is 8 to 10 years. Although it may take a number of years for full-blown AIDS to develop, once the HIV is present it can be transmitted from the infected person to others. There is no way to predict which of those infected with HIV will develop AIDS symptoms. A milder form of HIV that does not meet the definition of full-blown AIDS is symptomatic HIV infection. This condition can be very serious and is characterized by swollen lymph nodes, persistent fevers, chronic fatigue, weight loss, and candidiasis of the mouth, or thrush. Individuals with symptomatic HIV infection can get better, stay the same, or develop full-blown AIDS.

The majority of people who develop AIDS live 2 to 5 years. Some AIDS victims have survived 9 or 10 years, but no one has recovered. AZT and other drugs seem to inhibit development of AIDS, but death is inevitable. Half of all victims with AIDS have already died.

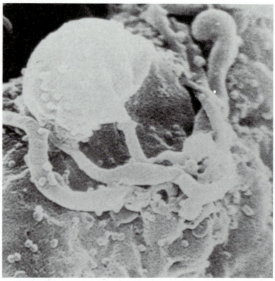

Population of white blood cells infected with HIV

HIV virus budding from the surface membrane of a T-4 lymphocyte (white blood cell)

The breakdown of the immune system resulting from AIDS makes the victim extremely susceptible to a number of serious diseases, including Kaposi's sarcoma (a cancer that causes lesions, usually purplish and blotchy) and *Pneumocystis carinii* pneumonia (PCP). This type of pneumonia is seen in people with suppressed immune functioning. Pneumonia is the most common disease seen. Also found frequently in AIDS victims is toxoplasmosis, which causes fatigue, lymph-node infections, liver and lung infections and inflammation of the brain (encephalitis). *Dementia candida,* a fungal infection of the mouth and throat, is common. Another virus, cytomegalovirus, frequently causes infections of the brain, eyes, and lungs. Hodgkin's disease, a cancer of the lymph nodes, is frequently found in the AIDS victim. Tuberculosis is also a significant problem, not only for the AIDS victim but also for those around the infected person, since the disease is very contagious.

Primary transmission is through sexual contact. Anytime people exchange body fluids through sexual contact, exposure to HIV is possible. Secondary transmission occurs among intravenous drug users. While blood transfusions were once risky, recent screening techniques have reduced the chances of contracting the HIV virus this way to approximately 1 in 1 million. Although AIDS has affected homosexuals disproportionately, in recent years heterosexual transmission of AIDS has become more common. The World Health Organization predicts that by the year 2000, heterosexual transmission will be the primary means of infection (Mann, 1989). In fact, the potential AIDS epidemic from heterosexual transmission of HIV is staggering. An estimated 1 million Americans are already infected with HIV, and each of their sex partners is at risk. Considering that the incubation period can be as long as 10 years and that the HIV-infected person may be unaware of the disease, transmission will grow geometrically. Another estimate indicates that up to 70% of all

HIV infections will result from heterosexual intercourse by the year 2000 (Jackson, 1992, p. 40).

Unfortunately, HIV has no cure. Emphasis must be placed on prevention, particularly practicing safer sex. Although they are not foolproof, the following rules can help prevent infection:

1. Use a condom for all sexual activity.
2. Reduce or limit the number of sexual partners. Ask potential partners about health, past sexual history, and knowledge of safe sex practices.
3. Avoid the use of intravenous drugs or the sharing of needles, including steroids. Avoid sharing of toothbrushes or razors that may be soiled with blood.
4. Mutually monogamous relationships lower the risk of HIV infection significantly, assuming that neither partner has been exposed to HIV.
5. Abstinence from sex, assuming no previous exposure to HIV, is the surest way to protect against infection.

HIV infection is not contracted through contact with food, eating utensils, clothing, furniture, swimming pools, or insects. Shaking hands, coughing, sneezing, or even living with an HIV positive person will not transmit the disease. HIV has been found in tears, saliva, and urine, but transmission through contact with these substances has not been directly implicated (Peterman, 1986).

Without a cure, treating HIV infection is predicated on delaying the onset of AIDS. The drug that seems to be most useful is AZT, or Zidovudine. AZT slows down the replication of HIV and seems to help the immune system respond to the infection. Maximizing the drug's effectiveness requires early identification and treatment. Some side effects, such as severe anemia and bone marrow damage, may become so serious that treatment must be discontinued.

Several drugs are in clinical trials to determine their effectiveness. One drug, called DDC, has potential but has caused nerve damage in patients. Another drug, DDI, has been found to be less effective than AZT but also seems to be less toxic. One treatment that may hold promise is using several drugs in combination or alternating treatment between two or more drugs. Certainly any hope for a cure is years if not decades away, but better treatment procedures may surface in the next few years.

Gonorrhea

Some medical historians believe gonorrhea has been a problem since biblical times. This STD is caused by a bacterial organism called *Neisseria gonorrhoeae*. The incubation period is usually 3 to 5 days, but can be as long as 10 days. Between 1 and 2 million people report new cases of gonorrhea each year. Gonorrhea represents a health threat to sexually active women and men and to children born to infected mothers. The disease can be contracted through oral, anal, and vaginal sexual contact.

The symptoms in men include initial pain when urinating accompanied by a thick yellow-green discharge from the penis. In some men the lymph nodes in the groin area may become swollen. The majority of men will exhibit symptoms but a small percentage may exhibit minor or no symptoms whatsoever.

In women the disease is asymptomatic in 80% of the cases. Even if a discharge is present, many women mistake it for normal mucus discharge associated with the menstrual cycle. If the infection has been present for a long time, a woman may experience abdominal pain, discomfort, or cramping. Fever and vaginal bleeding may be present. All these symptoms may indicate the presence of pelvic inflammatory disease (PID) (discussed later in this chapter).

New strains of the gonorrhea bacteria have appeared that make treatment difficult, since they are penicillin-resistant. The test for determining if gonorrhea is present consists of a smear test or culture of the discharge. Accurate identification of the type of gonorrhea strain is imperative for proper treatment. Broad-spectrum antibiotics combined with some form of penicillin are the preferred approach to treatment. For those allergic to penicillin, tetracycline can be used.

Untreated gonorrhea can cause sterility, heart and circulatory problems, and arthritis.

Chlamydia

Because chlamydia has symptoms similar to gonorrhea, the two diseases are often mistaken for each other. Chlamydia is now estimated to be the number one sexually transmitted disease in the United States, with 3 to 4 million new cases reported each year.

Chlamydia causes sterility in both men and women. In men it can result in painful swelling in the epididymis. Infection of the ovaries and fallopian tubes results in PID infection and sterility in females. Chlamydia can cause eye infections, pneumonia, and ear infections in newborns, who contract the disease during the birth process. Tetracycline is the treatment of choice, since penicillin is ineffective against the disease. Chlamydia bacteria are also responsible for another STD, lymphogranuloma venereum.

Pelvic Inflammatory Disease

An extremely serious complication of gonorrhea and chlamydia can be pelvic inflammatory disease. This condition is a severe infection of the pelvic and abdominal region. It is characterized by severe pain in the lower abdominal areas, fever, menstrual irregularities, recurring infections, ectopic pregnancy, and the need for hysterectomy. Psychologically, severe depression seems to accompany the condition.

Syphilis

Syphilis is caused by a bacterial pathogen, a spirochete known as *Treponema pallidum*. The disease is transmitted by oral-genital, genital, or anal-genital contact. It also can be contracted by kissing or touching an infected area. Syphilis usually proceeds through four distinct stages: stages are primary, secondary, latent, and late syphilis.

Primary syphilis is characterized by the development of the chancre (pronounced shanker). This sore is found at the site where the spirochete has entered the body. In males, the site is usually the penis. In females, the chancre most often appears on the vaginal wall or on the cervix. If contracted through oral sex, the chancre will appear in the mouth or throat. The sore is about the size of a dime, painless, and highly contagious. Obviously, because of the location, detection in the female is difficult. Multiple chancres are possible if the spirochete has entered the body at several places. If nothing is done, the chancre will disappear in 3 to 6 weeks.

Secondary syphilis will develop anywhere from one month to a year after the chancre associated with primary syphilis disappears. Symptoms of this stage include a skin rash, white patches in the mouth and throat, hair loss, low-grade fever, headache, swollen glands, or sores around the mouth. These sores contain millions of spirochetes and are highly contagious. Symptoms may last for months or disappear within weeks. Without treatment, the disease simply goes into hiding.

During the third stage or latent syphilis, no signs or symptoms appear. The spirochetes are beginning to invade the body's organs and the infected person may periodically exhibit some of the symptoms of secondary syphilis. After a period of 2 to 4 years, the disease is rarely transmitted to others. A pregnant woman, however, can transmit the disease to the fetus after the first trimester. This is referred to as congenital syphilis. Congenital syphilis can lead to blindness, deafness, birth defects, disfigurement, or death in a child. Left untreated in adults, the disease will continue to invade the body's organs and leads to the development of the fourth stage. While syphilis can be cured during the latent stage, any damage done cannot be corrected.

The fourth stage is called late syphilis. After years of infection, several conditions may develop. They include heart damage, such as a ruptured aorta or valve damage, or central nervous system damage resulting in blindness, deafness, paralysis, or insanity.

The diagnostic technique used to determine if syphilis is present is a blood test called UDRL. Early diagnosis and treatment can lead to a complete cure. Penicillin is the drug of choice.

Genital Herpes

More than 20 million people in the United States are thought to have genital herpes, and another half-million new cases appear each year. The virus that is responsible for this condition is herpes simplex, type II. The incubation period is between 2 and 20 days after exposure. Symptoms include the development of one or more extremely painful blisterlike sores around or on the genitals. The blisters eventually rupture and form wet, open sores. After several days, the sores will crust, dry, and finally disappear. The virus is still in the body, but will travel to the base of the nerve endings that supply the infected areas and remains dormant until a stimulus reactivates it. A stimulus can be any of a variety of conditions, including exposure to sunlight, poor nutrition, increased stress, or a repressed immune system.

Genital herpes is dangerous for a pregnant woman and her fetus, since the disease can be transmitted to the child during the birth process. To eliminate this danger, a cesarean delivery may be utilized. In addition, women with herpes are at greater risk for cervical cancer. For men, other than reactivation of the disease, the dangers seem to be somewhat less.

308   CHAPTER ELEVEN

Herpes has no cure at this time. The use of condoms may prevent their transmission. The drug acyclovir (trade name: Zovirax) lessens the length of time the blisters are present and reduces the severity of the symptoms. A prescription drug, acyclovir is available in capsules or ointment. Capsule form seems most effective, since the ointment appears to work only in the initial infection. Either capsules or the ointment helps to relieve symptoms but does not kill the virus.

Genital Warts

Genital warts are caused by the human papilloma virus (HPV). The incubation period is from 1 to 6 months. The warts appear on the glans penis, vulva, vaginal wall, and cervix. Genital warts are common in the rectal area of homosexual males. It is estimated that 10 million people are infected with HPV.

Genital warts usually appear as soft, moist, pink or red swellings. Several may be found in the same location. They are described as resembling a cauliflower in appearance. Genital warts tend to recur in people who have been treated. Of particular concern is that HPV has been linked to cervical cancer and cancer of the penis.

The warts may be frozen, cauterized, or treated topically with podophyllum. This drug removes the wart but does not kill the virus. All sexual partners should be evaluated, since the infection seems to be readily transmittable (Nuovo, 1990).

Chancroids

A chancroid is a localized, highly contagious STD caused by the bacterium *Haemophilus ducreyi*. The incubation period is 3 to 7 days. The disease is characterized by painful papules that quickly break down into ulcers with ragged edges. The lymph nodes in the groin area may become enlarged and rupture, causing severe tissue damage.

Since the bacterium does not exist in temperate climates, the disease is rare in the United States. Cases usually occur when someone has visited a tropical region and had contact with prostitutes. Treatment consists of the antibiotic sulfonamide.

Candidiasis (Yeast Infection)

A type of yeast called *Candida albicans* is the causative agent of this condition. The body normally keeps this yeast in check, but under certain conditions such as pregnancy, poor nutrition, antibiotic therapy, or use of the contraceptive pill, candidiasis may develop. Common sites include the vulva, vagina, penis, and mouth. Symptoms include a burning sensation, itching, and a whitish discharge. Normally the infection is not spread sexually, but if one partner has the condition it is advisable to use condoms. Several over-the-counter medications are available to effectively treat the condition. The infection is rare in men. When a yeast infection occurs in children, it is called thrush and usually effects the mouth.

Urinary Tract Infections

Urinary tract infections (UTIs) are referred to by the area of infection. The infection is called urethritis if the urethra is involved, cystitis if the bladder is involved, and pyelonephritis if the kidneys are infected. Women are much more prone to develop UTIs than men because their urethra is only $1\frac{1}{2}$ inches and consequently more susceptible to bacterial infections. Bacteria thus have a shorter distance to travel to infect the bladder and kidneys. Symptoms include frequent and/or painful, burning urination, chills, fever, fatigue, and blood in the urine.

UTIs seem to be caused by pregnancy, sexual intercourse and use of the diaphragm, bike riding, bubble baths, douches, urinary stones, enlarged prostate, vaginitis, and stress (Renner, 1990). Antibiotics are prescribed for UTIs.

Pubic Lice

Pubic lice or crab lice are sexually transmitted about 90% of the time (Jackson, 1992). The *Phthirus pubis* is called a crab louse because it resembles a small crab. Contact with toilet seats, towels, and bedding may also transmit the lice. The louse is found in the pubic hair and is about the size of a pinhead. It may be as long as a month after contact before the infestation becomes severe enough to be noticed. Females may need to lay eggs several times, and these may need to mature before the symptoms appear. The pubic louse feeds on blood and the bite is very itchy; consequently, an overwhelming desire to scratch the area will be the first sign. It is possible to spot the lice or nits (eggs laid by female lice) earlier, but usually the itching has already begun.

Prescription shampoo is available (Kwell or Lindane). The treatment includes using the shampoo and combing the pubic area with a special comb. The process must be repeated a week later to kill any nits not eliminated with the first application. Over-the-counter products also are available for treatment. The same protocol for these products is followed as for prescriptions. Bedding and clothing should be washed in hot water and sexual contact avoided until treatment is completed.

Trichomoniasis

Trichomonas vaginalis, a protozoa, is the pathogen that causes this infection. Both men and women transmit the disease, but women are most often infected. In females the infection causes a foamy, yellow-green vaginal discharge accompanied by a most unpleasant odor. Other symptoms include burning, itching, and painful urination. All symptoms are most likely to occur during or shortly after menstruation. Males are generally asymptomatic.

Treatment consists of oral metronidazole. All sex partners should be treated, since the disease can "ping-pong" back and forth. Sexual intercourse should be avoided until the condition is cured.

■ ■ ■   *STUDENT CONCERNS:* COMMUNICABLE DISEASE

Issues of concern in the communicable disease area for grades 7 through 12 center around sexually transmitted diseases and their prevention. Students also seem to have a general interest in how the body fights disease. Students in the lower grades appear to have a general lack of understanding as to what diseases are transmitted sexually. This information was taken from *Students Speak* (Trucano, 1984). Typically, concerns of the students are as follows:

Grades 7 through 8

Can you ever get rid of VD (STDs)?
Can you get VD if you don't have sex at all?
What kind of disease can sex cause?
What causes disease?
Can you catch a disease if you have already had a shot for it?
What diseases are really serious and which ones aren't?
How are stress, worries, and fear related to diseases you get?
What most commonly makes you sick?

Grades 9 through 10

Why is immunization so important?
Tell us about diseases that can't be cured.
Why do we only get VD (STDs) when we have sexual intercourse?
How does our immune system work?

Grades 11 through 12

Which immunizations are important to your body?
Do immunization shots ever wear out?
How can you tell when you have VD (STDs)?
How do you prevent and control STDs?
What are the effects of STDs on the unborn?

SUMMARY

Many diseases have affected humans throughout the course of history. Today, the big killers are cardiovascular disease and cancer. AIDS is the newest infectious disease to threaten human welfare.

Infectious diseases are caused by pathogens. When the infection is transmitted among humans or from animals to humans, it is known as a communicable disease. The six types of pathogens include viruses, bacteria, rickettsias, fungi, protozoa, and helminths (parasitic worms). The viruses are the smallest of the pathogens. About 150 cause disease in humans. The viruses are obligate, intracellular parasites—they require a living host to survive. The bacteria occur in three shapes (spherical, spiral, and rod-shaped). They cause damage by releasing toxins (poisons) or interfering with cell functioning. Most rickettsia diseases are transmitted by vectors (carriers). Rickettsias resemble both viruses and bacteria. Most fungi cause no harm to mankind. Conditions such as ringworm and candidiasis are the result of fungi. Protozoa are single-celled microscopic animals. Many of the protozoal diseases can alternate between active and inactive states. Parasitic worms range in size from relatively small to several feet in length. Parasitic worms are divided into roundworms and flatworms.

When a pathogen invades a human host, the reaction to the invasion proceeds through several stages, called the incubation, prodromal, clinical, convalescence, and recovery stages. The immune system is one way the body has to protect itself. Other body defenses include the skin, body secretions, mucus membranes, enzymes, and compounds in blood, interferron, and other natural substances.

Many diseases can affect the student, including the common cold, influenza, infectious mononucleosis, and hepatitis. The sexually transmitted disease that is of greatest concern is acquired immunodeficiency syndrome (AIDS or HIV). The virus attacks the immune system but may not manifest itself for several years. Some HIV-positive individuals may develop ARC (AIDS-related complex), a milder form of HIV infection that does not meet the definition of full-blown AIDS. The majority of people who develop AIDS live 2 to 5 years. Primary transmission is through sexual contact. No cure exists at this time, but the drug AZT seems to help the immune system respond to HIV. While the disease has afflicted a disproportionate number of homosexuals, researchers predict that the number of heterosexual cases will increase significantly over the next decade. Prevention depends on education and safer sex practices.

Other significant STDs include gonorrhea, chlamydia, syphilis, genital herpes, genital warts, and chancroids. Other diseases that are transmitted sexually but can also be contracted through other means are candidiasis, urinary tract infections, trichomoniasis, and pubic crabs.

DISCUSSION QUESTIONS

1. List and describe the pathogens.
2. Discuss immunity and the various protective mechanisms the body has to protect itself against disease.
3. Trace the typical stages of a communicable disease.
4. Describe the antigen/antibody response.
5. Select any communicable disease and discuss its signs and symptoms.
6. Describe how HIV affects an individual with the virus.
7. List the ways an individual can practice safer sex.
8. Discuss the dangers associated with viral STDs.
9. List the dangers of bacterial STDs.
10. What are some diseases that can be contracted through both sexual and nonsexual means?

■ ■ ■ *ACTIVITIES FOR TEACHING COMMUNICABLE DISEASES*

Name That Disease

This activity is designed to encourage group involvement when teaching in the area of communicable diseases. After introducing the types of pathogens, how diseases are transmitted and how to protect against each disease, have the students brainstorm as many communicable diseases as they can. The teacher may add to this list or may choose to add some uncommon diseases that can serve as special challenges to students.

Have students list one disease each on a set of index cards. Distribute cards to the students and ask them to obtain the following: cause of the disease, how it is transmitted, signs and symptoms, serious results, length, and treatment.

When all diseases have been investigated, place the index cards in a large box. Divide the class into groups and ask each group to identify the diseases according to various clues as provided (e.g., symptoms of a particular disease). Each group may have an opportunity to review the index cards prior to beginning the game. The team that can guess the correct disease with the fewest clues will eventually achieve the most points. Guessing the disease from only one clue is worth 10 points; 2 clues equal 8 points; 3 clues are worth 6 points; and 4 clues are worth 4 points.

Disease Detective

This activity is designed to help students identify all the potential places where diseases may be spread. After studying how communicable diseases spread, ask students to survey locations such as their home, the cafeteria, restrooms, and their own personal habits that could transmit diseases. Index cards may be used to list the location, behavior, incident, or situation. Bring the index cards back to class and discuss them. Divide the class into groups and have them list ways diseases are transmitted and the methods of prevention. As a final activity, have students design a bulletin board entitled "Protection Against Disease." The board should reflect information learned in the disease investigation.

Discussion Questions

1. Did you find some surprises about how diseases may be transmitted?
2. How many of you have personal habits that could lead to disease transmission? Can you name some?
3. What steps can be taken to eliminate some of the risks identified in the survey?

Watching Johnnie Grow

This activity requires some special materials. Needed are petri dishes, cotton swabs, and an incubation oven. If the oven is unavailable, keeping the dish near a warm heater will do. The science teacher can supply the medium for the sample, or raw potatoes can be used. Ask students to take a sample from their mouths, ears, hands, and so on with the cotton swabs. Place each sample on a separate petri dish and label its origin. Place the samples in a warm area and observe them over the next few days. Leave one petri dish uncontaminated for purposes of having a control sample.

Processing Questions

1. Where did you find the bacteria growing?
2. What protects us from invasions of these bacteria?
3. How can we enhance the possibility that these will not infect us?

What's My Feeling?

Following are some unfinished sentences that allow students to express their thoughts. The teacher can add sentences if she chooses:

Pathogens are _____ .

People with AIDS are _____ .

I believe communicable diseases are _____ .

Immunization should _____ .

Children who are not inoculated _____ .

Hepatitis is a disease that _____ .

STDs should be _____ .

The most dangerous pathogens are _____ .

Disease transmissions could be _____ .

Flu vaccines _____ .

Sneezing is _____ .

Washing hands is _____ .

Processing Questions

1. Were any of your answers unusual? Why?
2. Did any of your answers surprise you?
3. What is the most important statement you made? Why?

The Patient*

Divide the class into several groups and provide the following scenario. Ask the students to first make their decisions on an individual basis and then on a group basis.

> You are a highly trained group called County Medical Helpers. Each of you has been specifically trained to administer first aid, recognize communicable disease, and set up appointments for the doctor. Your primary responsibilities are to visit the residents of your county and identify those people who are in need of medical assistance.
>
> The people in your rural community are poor and uneducated.
>
> There is only one traveling doctor who visits once a week. He makes the final diagnosis and treatment. The day before his regular visit you are informed that the doctor will have only enough time to see 5 patients. You are to bring them to the church basement, which is used for the doctor's office. Your group has identified 10 people who need medical assistance. Your job is to select the 5 who will see the doctor.

1. Mary, age 79, severe cold, chronic cough, possible pneumonia.
2. John, age 15, suspected tuberculosis.
3. Bobby, age 9, sudden fever, weakness, coughing, aching pain in the back and extremities, possible influenza.
4. Susan, age 19, home from college, symptoms indicate polio or mononucleosis.
5. Sam, age 24, syphilis.
6. Linda, age 43, infectious hepatitis.
7. Mary, age 5, trachoma.
8. Virginia, age 7, smallpox.
9. Charles, age 54, AIDS-related complex.
10. Butch, age 29, polio.

Processing Questions

1. Did all group members agree on the 5 patients who were to see the doctor?
2. What considerations were given to your choices?
3. Which 5 did your group select and why?
4. What are the consequences, if any, for those patients not selected?
5. What might have been done to prevent these 10 people from acquiring their diseases?

*Source: *Health Games People Play* (pp. 125–126) by R. Engs, E. Barnes, and M. Wanty, 1975, Dubuque, IA: Kendal/Hunt.

Getting to Know Mr. Pathogen

The names of various diseases are listed in this table. Leaving all but the "Disease" column blank, ask students to fill in the chart and discuss it when all students have completed it.

Disease	Causative Agent	How Contracted	Signs and Symptoms	Prevention
Cold	Virus	Direct or Indirect	Runny nose, sore throat, cough, and headache	Avoid contact
Influenza	Virus	Direct or Indirect	Fever, aching, coughing, tired	Avoid contact
Hepatitis A	Virus	Direct: food and water	Nausea, fever, pain in abdomen, yellow skin/eyes	Avoid contact
Hepatitis B	Virus	Blood transfusion, dirty hypodermic needles, sexual	Same as above	Screen blood donors; don't use unsterilized needles; practice safe sex
Mononucleosis	Virus	Direct contact	Swollen lymph glands, sore throat	Avoid contact
Poliomyelitis	Virus	Direct and Indirect	Swollen lymph glands, stiff joints	Immunization
Rabies	Virus	Bites from infected animals—dog, cat, skunk, bat	Low-grade fever, restlessness, hyperactivity, disorientation, perhaps serious intense thirst, eye and facial muscles paralyzed	Immunization of pets
Strep throat	Bacteria	Throat discharge	Fever, sore throat	Avoid contact
Syphilis	Bacteria	Sexual contact	Chancre at site of entry	Know sex partner, practice safer sex
Gonorrhea	Bacteria	Sexual contact	Discharge, painful urination; no symptoms in females	See above
Herpes	Virus	Sexual contact	Painful sores and blisters in genital area	See above
Chlamydia	Bacteria	Sexual contact	Discharge or maybe no symptoms	See above
Genital warts	Virus	Sexual contact	Small cauliflower-like bumps	See above
AIDS	Virus	Sexual contact	Loss of weight, fever, swollen glands, fatigue, extremely ill with opportunistic diseases	See above

Processing Questions

1. Which diseases can be cured?
2. How are these diseases treated?
3. Are some symptoms different in males than in females for any of these diseases?
4. Why have STDs been increasing in the last few years?

Staging a Disease

This activity is designed to help students understand what happens when a disease invades the body. Assign one disease for the entire class. Students should list every occurrence at the various stages of the disease. Start with the incubation stage, then the prodromal, illness, and recovery stage. Describe all the mechanisms the body employs to help the individual recover. Students should identify the immune system response that is occurring throughout the illness.

Processing Questions

1. What are some ways the disease can spread?
2. What are some of the body's defenses against disease?
3. How could this disease have been prevented?
4. What are some ways the body might have been attempting to prevent the disease before the person became ill?

Minidocumentary on Communicable Diseases

This activity is conducted like the television shows "60 Minutes" or "20/20." The class can be divided into groups with each group assigned a particular disease. Each group then is taped doing a "show" focusing on that disease. Once completed, the video can be used for review or shown at parent-teacher association functions.

How the Minidocumentary Works

Groups will answer several questions about their diseases. The students will decide the characters needed to enact and name each. As an example, say a group chooses gonorrhea. The group's assignment would be to research and prepare the following questions on an index card:

Dr. _____ , a leading STD investigator from _____ University is here to introduce leading experts to answer some important questions concerning gonorrhea.

1. What are the signs and symptoms?
2. Track the course of the disease from contact to conclusion.
3. Are the symptoms different for males and females?
4. How is the disease treated?
5. What is the test for the disease?
6. What are some special facts concerning the disease?

The rest is left up to the students; they must find the correct answers. Two students from the group must be chosen to fill the spots of commentator and interviewer. The commentator's job is to introduce the group's segment and make some concluding statements. The interviewer is responsible for interviewing the specialists (students with the most enthusiasm and originality seem best suited for these roles).

Videotaping should take place on a small set that allows focusing on all the "stars" at the same time. Interviewers should dress in appropriate attire (e.g., lab coats, stethoscopes, etc.). Students may be evaluated on the amount of research done and their ability to answer the questions correctly. With a little enthusiasm, originality, and humor, even a seemingly dull subject can become an exciting and refreshing educational tool that can be used for learning as well as showcasing health education.

■ ■ ■   *ACTIVITIES:* BULLETIN BOARDS

Disease Prevention

Develop a board titled "Disease Prevention and Control." Illustrate the methods by which diseases are transmitted and provide examples of how to control and prevent their spread.

Practicing Safer Sex

Using an owl to illustrate "Be a Wise Owl—Practice Safer Sex," list the ways people can help protect themselves against sexually transmitted diseases.

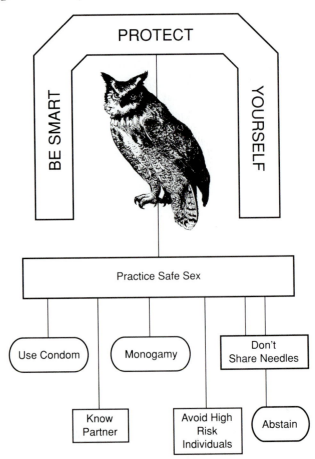

Invasion of the Pathogens

Illustrated here is a possible design for a bulletin board that emphasizes how the body's defenses work to protect against disease.

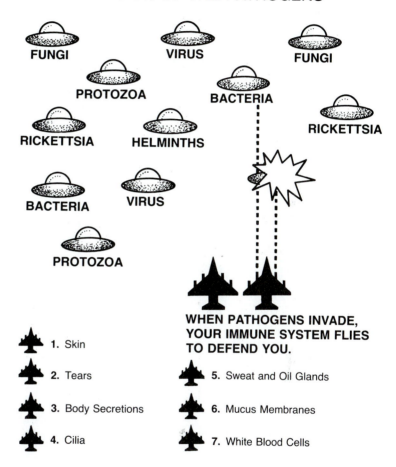

INVASION OF THE PATHOGENS

FUNGI

VIRUS

FUNGI

PROTOZOA

BACTERIA

RICKETTSIA

HELMINTHS

RICKETTSIA

BACTERIA

VIRUS

PROTOZOA

WHEN PATHOGENS INVADE, YOUR IMMUNE SYSTEM FLIES TO DEFEND YOU.

1. Skin
2. Tears
3. Body Secretions
4. Cilia
5. Sweat and Oil Glands
6. Mucus Membranes
7. White Blood Cells

■ ■ ■ *ACTIVITIES:* PUZZLES, WORD SEARCHES, AND WORD SCRAMBLES

Activities such as puzzles, word searches, and scrambles are well-suited to enhancing and reinforcing learning. Several computer programs can generate these activities. Many school systems have purchased such programs. They also may be found at computer stores. Examples of these follow.

Word Scramble

Have students unscramble the following words (the key is on the right).

gahtposne	(pathogens)	snxito	(toxins)
brmeisco	(microbes)	trovesc	(vectors)

survies   (viruses)   tacinoibun   (incubation)
carebiat   (bacteria)   dalmropor   (prodromal)
stekracisit   (rickettsias)   yercover   (recovery)
niguf   (fungi)   ityummin   (immunity)
orazotpo   (protozoa)   gatinen   (antibodies)
nslehtmhi   (helminths)

Word Search

The following is an example of a word search. Have students find the words listed in the right column. Words may appear horizontally, vertically, or diagonally.

```
N E S Q Z S R E L L E G O J D D J L I T O
I M O M P G O T P I M M U N I T Y O E V N
T U B E R C U L O S I S T L P C W U A L C
E P G A O I N F L U E N Z A T Z Q B H E M
T F R S T I U X I T M Q M B H F W R S L E
A Z C L O I Q D O D N Y Y I E O O B G I V
N U Q E Z S R M M U M P S P R E Q I L D B
U D O S O Z Z A Y O F U N G I B Z B H R F
S G B Y A N V Y E I N C U B A T I O N S O
E F J L D G B J L U C O G V H J U W E Y X
G W J O V R A O I R A L N C S D E H I T G
H H I F M U C C T F C E O U I S J C R N H
F U K C H S T J I W G N R H C Z D J Q N J
U N C A N K E S S O P I Y P E L G C U V N
M H B F H Y R I H T V L G T K W E H C Y N
R Y P I C L I T K F X Y F R I K O O I G M
J T W W R P A T G S H E P A T I T I S I S
V X M V R P D H K L T F N M T X L M I I O
W S O Y A B Q C P M Z N C Y L B K Z N I S
```

MONONUCLEOSIS
INCUBATION
DIPTHERIA
PROTOZOA
TETANUS
VIRUS
POLIOMYELITIS
HEPATITIS
IMMUNITY
BACTERIA
MUMPS
TUBERCULOSIS
INFLUENZA
PATHOGEN
MEASLES
FUNGI

■ ■ ■   *ACTIVITIES:* DISCUSSION AND REPORT STRATEGIES

Think About It

Form several groups in the class to discuss the following questions:

1. Should health-care workers be tested for HIV? What should be done if they are determined to be HIV-positive?
2. Do patients have the right to know if their dentists, physicians, or nurses are HIV-positive? Why or why not?
3. Does a physician have the right to refuse to treat an HIV-positive patient?

After the groups have had an opportunity to discuss the questions, ask a spokesperson from each group to report on the important points from that group's discussion.

The Right to Sue

Ask students to write a paragraph concerning their feelings about the right to sue someone who gave them an STD. Instruct the students to not place their names on their paper. After completing the papers, put them on the bulletin board and ask students to read them. Discuss important points made in the various papers.

■ ■ ■   *ACTIVITIES:* LEARNING ENHANCEMENTS

The following films and tapes are appropriate for teaching communicable diseases.

Lyme Disease. This video-filmstrip presents current information on preventing, recognizing, and treating Lyme Disease. 15 minutes. Films for the Humanities and Sciences, 800/257-5126.

AIDS: Our Worst Fears. This filmstrip-cassette explains what is known and not known about HIV/AIDS, who is at greatest risk, and what precautions should be taken to protect against infection. 15 minutes. Sunburst Communications, 800/431-1934.

STDs. This is a two-part video. Part I presents the signs, symptoms, prevention, and cures for most of the major STDs. Part II discusses the moral and ethical dilemmas faced by teens with STDs. 36 minutes. Sunburst Communications, 800/431-1934.

Bacteria and Viruses. This video explores the differences between bacteria and viruses and how immunization protects against diseases. Programs show how bacteria multiply and the body response to invasion by pathogens. 20 minutes. Films for the Humanities and Sciences, 800/257-5126.

The Common Cold. This video covers the current state of knowledge about cold viruses and how they can be prevented from entering the body. 28 minutes. Films for the Humanities and Sciences, 800/257-5126.

The Human Immune System: The Fighting Edge. Information is presented on how the immune system works. Describes the stories of a body born without an immune system, a man with B-cell Lymphoma, a long-living survivor of AIDS, and a woman who had a severe allergic reaction. 52 minutes. Films for the Humanities and Sciences, 800/257-5126.

Vaccines & Prevention Medicine. Examines the technology that has led to development of new vaccines. Investigates controversies surrounding vaccine production, side effects, and liability concerns. 26 minutes. Films for the Humanities and Sciences, 800/257-5126.

REFERENCES

Crowley, L. V. (1988). *Introduction to human disease* (2nd ed.). Boston: Jones and Bartlett.

Engs, R., Barnes, E., & Wanty, M. (1975). *Health games people play.* Dubuque, IA: Kendal/Hart.

Hamrick, M. H., Anspaugh, D. J., & Ezell, G. (1986). *Health.* New York: Merrill/Macmillan.

Jackson, J. K. (1992). *AIDS, STDs and other communicable diseases.* Guilford, CT: Dushkin.

Mann, J. (1989). *Global AIDS into the 1990s.* Paper presented at the World Health Organization's Fifth International Conference on AIDS, Montreal, Canada.

Nuovo, C. J. (1990). Human papilloma virus types and recurrent cervical warts. *Journal of the American Medical Association, 263,* 1223–1226.

Peterman, T. A. (1986). Sexual transmission of human immunodeficiency virus infection in the United States. *Journal of the American Medical Association, 256,* 2222–2226.

Renner, J. (1990, May). Urinary infections common to women. *Healthline,* 5.

Sheldon, H. (1992). *Boyd's introduction to the study of disease* (11th ed.). Philadelphia: Lea & Febiger.

Thomas, C. L. (Ed.) (1984). *Taber's cyclopedic medical dictionary.* Philadelphia: F. A. Davis Co.

Trucano, L. (1984). Students Speak—*A survey of health interests and concerns: Kindergarten through twelfth grade.* Seattle: Comprehensive Health Education Foundation.

CHAPTER 12

Concepts for Teaching Chronic and Noninfectious Diseases

The Nation has within its power the ability to save many lives lost prematurely and needlessly. Healthy People 2000

OBJECTIVES

After reading this chapter, you should be able to

- Describe the anatomy and physiology of the heart and circulatory system
- Discuss the types of cardiovascular disease
- Identify the risk factors associated with cardiovascular disease
- State the major types of cancer
- Describe the possible causes of cancer
- Discuss some of the trends in diagnosis and treatment of cancer
- Discuss various other chronic and noninfectious conditions
- Plan strategies for teaching about chronic disease

CHRONIC AND NONINFECTIOUS DISEASE

A number of chronic and noninfectious diseases commonly afflict humans. Diseases of this type are not "caught," but rather are developed over time, often are progressive in effect, and may be due to genetic predisposition. Under normal circumstances, these conditions do not usually lead to death, but they are uncomfortable and, in more severe cases, can cause suffering. Although medicine is used in treatment, development of a lifestyle geared toward wellness may decrease both the incidence and the effects of these diseases.

THE CARDIOVASCULAR SYSTEM

Chronic diseases affecting the cardiovascular system are now among the leading causes of death. The cardiovascular system is complex and is subject to a range of diseases.

Anatomy and Physiology

The heart is composed of specialized muscle tissue called **cardiac muscle**. This muscle is extremely thick and strong and has amazing endurance capacity. Although the heart is only the size of a fist and weighs a mere 8 to 10 oz, it contracts an average of 70 to 80 times a minute, 100,000 times a day, nearly a billion times in an average life of 70 years, pumping 30 to 40 million gal. of blood.

Located transversely in the chest, the heart is encased in a fiber sac called the **pericardium**. The lining inside the heart is the **endocardium**. The actual cardiac muscle tissue is referred to as the **myocardium**. The heart functions as a double pump, separated by a thick wall, called the septum. When blood is in a deoxygenated state—that is, when it has circulated through the body and delivered oxygen while accumulating carbon dioxide and waste products—it enters the heart in the right, upper chamber, known as the **atrium**, by means of two large veins known as the superior and inferior vena cava. Blood moves from the right atrium to the right ventricle through the tricuspid valve. From the right ventricle, the blood passes through the pulmonary valve into the **pulmonary artery**. The right half of the heart is known as the pulmonary pump because it pumps only deoxygenated blood to the lungs. In the lungs, carbon dioxide is exchanged for oxygen. While under normal circumstances deoxygenated blood carries approximately 14 ml of oxygen per hundred ml of blood, oxygenated blood carries 20 ml of oxygen per 100 ml of blood.

From the lungs, oxygenated blood travels through the pulmonary veins back to the left atrium. The pulmonary vein is the only vein that carries oxygenated blood. From the left atrium, blood is pumped through the mitral valve to the left ventricle. It passes from the ventricle through the aortic valve into the aorta and to the rest of the body via the systemic aorta. Because the left half of the heart must pump blood to the entire body, it is usually somewhat larger and stronger than the right half (see Figure 12.1).

Upon leaving the heart, blood travels throughout the body as part of the circulatory system. Blood containing oxygen and nutrients travels away from the heart, first in arteries, then arterioles, then capillaries. Oxygen, carbon dioxide, nutrients, and waste products are exchanged through the very thin walls of the capillaries. Even the heart receives its nourishment in this manner. The waste products and carbon dioxide that are picked up by the blood are then returned to the heart in its deoxygenated state through venules (small veins), then veins, before reentering the vena cava to the right atrium (see Figure 12.2).

Figure 12.1   Diagram of the heart

Source: *Teaching Today's Health* (3rd ed.) by David Anspaugh and Gene Ezell, 1990, New York: Merrill/Macmillan.

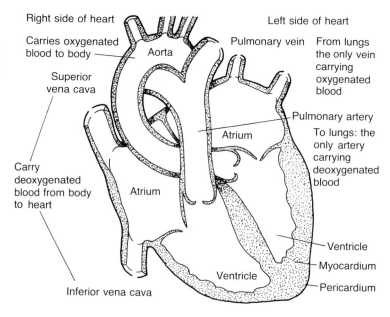

Right side of heart

Carries oxygenated blood to body

Aorta

Superior vena cava

Carry deoxygenated blood from body to heart

Atrium

Atrium

Ventricle

Inferior vena cava

Ventricle

Left side of heart

Pulmonary vein — From lungs the only vein carrying oxygenated blood

Pulmonary artery

To lungs: the only artery carrying deoxygenated blood

Ventricle

Myocardium

Pericardium

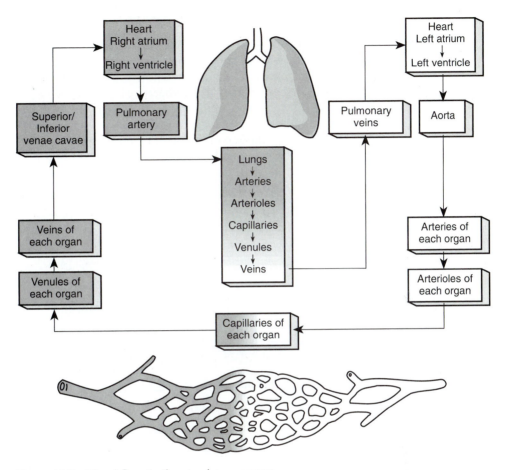

Figure 12.2   Blood flow in the circulatory system

The heart has its own system for controlling its rhythmic pace. This mechanism begins with a group of specialized cells called the sinoatrial (SA) node or pacemaker. The sinoatrial node emits electrical impulses that travel toward the atrioventricular (AV) node, where a momentary pause occurs before the electrical impulses are distributed through the *bundle of HIS or AV bundle*. The bundle of HIS is a band of fibers in the myocardium through which the cardiac impulse is transmitted from the AV node to the ventricles. It begins at the AV node, follows the septum and divides left and right. Its ends are called the Purkinje fibers. Normally the heart beat begins with the SA node. The SA node causes both of the atria to contract (Anderson & Anderson, 1990). As the electrical charge spreads to the AV nodes through the bundle of HIS and Purkinje fibers, the ventricles contract. This conduction of electrical charge occurs slightly later in the ventricles and accounts for the characteristic "lub-dub" sound heard through a stethoscope (Thibodeau & Anthony, 1988).

Types of Cardiovascular Disease

The most common cardiovascular diseases originate not in the heart, but in the arteries. **Arteriosclerosis** is the generic term for a collection of diseases characterized by hardening of the arteries. The most common form of arteriosclerosis is known as **atherosclerosis**. Atherosclerosis is a degenerative disease that begins early in life, perhaps as early as 2 years of age. Atherosclerosis is the result of a buildup of plaque, fat, and other materials that aggregate at sites of damaged cells inside arterial walls. The earliest formations are composed of fatty streaks in the inner lining of the arteries. As atherosclerosis progresses, the arteries harden and thicken. With this hardening, the arteries begin to lose their ability to dilate and constrict, which they must do to meet all of the body's requirements for oxygen in the various parts (see Figure 12.3).

Figure 12.3   Progressive narrowing of a coronary artery

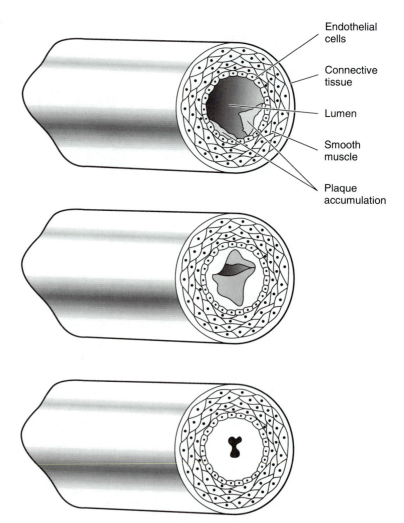

Endothelial cells

Connective tissue

Lumen

Smooth muscle

Plaque accumulation

Over time, more and more plaque accumulates, gradually narrowing the flow of blood through the arteries. This narrowing can result in **ischemia**, diminished blood flow. Also, as channels narrow, the chances for developing a **thrombus**, or stationary blood clot, increase. If the channels become sufficiently narrow, a free-floating clot, or **embolus**, can become stuck and block blood flow, resulting in a heart attack, or **myocardial infarction**. A myocardial infarction may be severe enough to result in death or may be sufficiently mild so that heart function can return to normal. In either event, a certain amount of heart tissue dies, and heart tissue does not regenerate. In time, scar tissue can form; if it is located in strategic areas, full recovery from a heart attack may not be possible. If atherosclerosis affects arteries going to the brain (the carotid and cerebral arteries), a **stroke** (shortage of blood to the brain) may result.

Coronary heart disease (disease of the coronary vessels, rather than of the heart itself) is the leading cause of death in the United States today. Coronary atherosclerosis is the leading form of coronary heart disease. Current research has indicated that some heart attacks may be caused by spasms (cramping) in the coronary arteries. The origin of these spasms is unknown at this time, although some researchers believe a relationship between stress, tension, and heart spasms is possible. Other experts attribute spasms to an overabundance of calcium in cells that are being deprived of oxygen or to the release of chemical substances at diseased sites, which causes the artery to close down. When these spasms occur in cases where sufficient atherosclerosis is present, the chances of having a heart attack increase. An **aneurysm**, a ballooning in an artery or vein due to weakened or damaged arterial walls, is another source of coronary heart disease. An aneurysm in the brain arteries causes hemorrhaging, which results in a stroke (Crowley, 1988).

Other forms of heart disease include congenital heart defects that originate during the development of the fetus. These difficulties usually involve the septum or valves of the heart not functioning properly. With congestive heart failure, the heart has lost strength and cannot pump all the blood out of the chambers, compromising circulation. The number-one reason for congestive heart failure is uncontrolled high blood pressure or **hypertension**, although it may also be due to a previous heart attack, atherosclerosis, or birth defect. Hypertension usually has no symptoms and may affect people of all ages, including children. Men are more susceptible than women to high blood pressure and African Americans are more susceptible than other people (American Heart Association, 1992).

The common childhood illness of strep throat is the source of an infection that can cause rheumatic heart disease. Undiagnosed strep can result in rheumatic fever. In a portion of these cases, rheumatic heart disease results, damaging one or more of the heart's valves. Commonly known as a heart murmur, the valves in the heart either cannot fully open (stenosis), or do not close properly (insufficiency) (Berkow, 1987).

Angina pectoris is defined as chest pains. Angina is neither a heart attack nor a disease. It is a frequent symptom of coronary heart disease, however. An angina attack usually lasts less than 5 minutes, often after extraordinary exercise or stress. A primary symptom is a squeezing sensation in the chest, as if a weight had been placed there. Some experience pain somewhere else in the upper body—frequently the left arm—or feelings similar to indigestion or heartburn. Angina usually subsides with rest and medication. The positive aspect of angina is that it is an early sign of progressive heart disease. For one third of all victims, a heart attack is the first symptom. Recognized and properly treated, angina can lead to prevention of more serious heart disease or even a heart attack.

Risk Factors Associated with Cardiovascular Disease

Some factors associated with increased risk of developing cardiovascular disease cannot be changed. *Heredity* is the primary unchangeable risk factor. In families with high incidence of heart attack, especially heart attacks before age 60, the risk is greater for any individual in that family to develop cardiovascular disease. *Age* and *sex* also influence risk. As one ages, chances of suffering from cardiovascular disease increase. For example, women under 35 seldom have problems, and 75% of all heart attacks occur after age 65. Last, *race* is an uncontrollable risk factor. African Americans have close to a 45% greater chance of developing hypertension than whites. This statistic may reflect the environment rather than genetics, however.

Several factors associated with increased risk *can* be altered, at least partially. The easiest risk factor to control is *smoking*. The noxious products found in cigarettes— tars, carbon monoxide, and nicotine—adversely affect the body. These products increase heart rate, raise blood pressure, stimulate the production of unneeded

Smokers are at great risk for developing cardiovascular disease.

adrenalin, shorten the coagulation time of the blood, reduce the blood's ability to carry oxygen, increase arterial spasms, and elevate cholesterol levels. The smoke destroys the alveoli in the lungs and paralyzes the cilia, which are the first line of defense against dirt and chemicals in the air. Cigarette smoking contributes more to heart disease than it does to lung cancer. Although nicotine is not labeled a drug, the withdrawal effect from it is real. This is a major problem when trying to quit.

Elevated levels of specific types of **cholesterol** are clearly associated with increased risk. Some cholesterol is needed for bodily functions. Ten percent of the weight of the brain is cholesterol, for example. Cholesterol is so important to normal functioning that the body produces endogenous cholesterol for its own use. It is important to differentiate between the different types of cholesterol because each performs differently. Very low density lipoprotein cholesterol (VLDL) and low-density lipoprotein cholesterol (LDL) are considered "bad" cholesterol. They circulate throughout the body, depositing fat and cholesterol in all parts, including the muscles and arteries. If the walls of the arteries have roughened, this cholesterol can be added to the plaque already present, thereby contributing to heart disease. High-density lipoprotein cholesterol (HDL), on the other hand, is involved in reverse transport. HDL "picks up" fat from the cells and lining of the arteries and delivers it to the liver, where it is degraded and eliminated or used to form other tissue. People with high levels of HDL have an independent factor that seems to *lower* the risk for heart disease. Although it is important to reduce total cholesterol levels, specifically LDL and VLDL cholesterol, increases in HDL independent of the others are good for *preventing* heart disease. Table 12.1 contains the recommendations for levels of total cholesterol, LDL cholesterol, and the ratio of total cholesterol to HDL cholesterol.

The major component of VLDL is triglycerides. Triglycerides make up 95% of human fat. High levels of triglycerides are, by themselves, a minor risk factor contributing to cardiovascular disease.

Hypertension, or persistently high blood pressure, is the third alterable risk factor for cardiovascular disease. It is also the leading cause of stroke. Blood pressure is the pressure blood exerts on arterial walls as it circulates. When blood pressure reaches a certain level, medical and/or lifestyle measures are needed to lower it. Because hypertension tends to run in families, family history is one of the main indicators. Weight loss, salt restriction, stress management, potassium and/or calcium supplements, a low-fat diet, and exercise are all possible recommendations, depending on individual cases.

Inactivity, or hypokinesis, is another primary risk factor for developing cardiovascular disease. Hypokinesis is defined as very little movement. Too much rest leads to significant reduction in organ size, bone demineralization, and loss of lean body mass. Physical activity, on the other hand, decreases the chance of heart attack; heart attacks tend to be less severe and occur later in life and the recovery level is higher.

Although no one knows for certain whether the tendency to be *obese* is more genetic or environmental, it is known that among people who suffer from cardiovascular disease, obesity and high total cholesterol are the most frequent risk factors. The national norms for weight are no more than 20% over desirable weight

Table 12.1 Recommended Cholesterol Levels

Risk of total cholesterol	
Cholesterol (mg/dl)	Risk
<200*	Desirable level
200–239	Borderline
≥240†	High level

Risk of LDL cholesterol	
LDL cholesterol (mg/dl)	Risk
<130	Desirable level
130–159	Borderline—high risk
>160	High risk

Ratio of total cholesterol to HDL cholesterol		
Risk	Male	Female
Very low ($\frac{1}{2}$ average)	Under 3.4	Under 3.3
Low risk	4.0	3.8
Average risk	5.0	4.5
Moderate risk (2 × average)	9.5	7.0
High risk (3 × average)	Over 23	Over 11

Source: American Heart Association.
* < less than
† ≥ equal to or greater than

(desirable being based on the Metropolitan Life Insurance tables). However, obesity is *not* equivalent to being overweight. Obesity is based on a ratio of lean to fat tissue. The threshold for obesity among males is 22% to 23% or higher of fat compared to total body weight. Among females, 30% to 32% or higher fat is considered obese.

Diabetes (see the discussion later in this chapter) increases the risk of cardiovascular disease because a lack of insulin results in a breakdown of the arteries, higher cholesterol levels, and a higher incidence of arteriosclerosis.

CANCER

The term **cancer** refers not to one disease, but rather to a large group of diseases. Cancer is characterized by uncontrolled growth and spread of abnormal cells or **neoplasms**. These neoplasms often form a mass of tissue called a tumor. Tumors can be **malignant** (cancerous) or **benign**. Benign tumors usually cause no harm; however, if they are located in an area where they obstruct or crowd out normal tissues or organs, benign tumors can be life-threatening. For example, a benign tumor in the brain could restrict the flow of blood. Benign tumors are enclosed in a fibrous capsule that prevents their spreading to other areas of the body. Malignant tumors are not so constrained. To determine if a tumor is malignant or benign, a **biopsy** (microscopic examination of tissue) must be done.

Types of Cancer

There are four major categories of tumors. They are **carcinoma, sarcoma, lymphoma**, and **leukemia**. Carcinoma is the most common form of cancer. Cancers of the skin, breast, uterus, prostate, lung, stomach, colon, and rectum are examples of carcinoma. Sarcomas are cancers of the connective tissue. Muscle, bone, and cartilage cancers are examples of sarcomas. These cancers occur less often than carcinoma, but usually spread more quickly. Lymphomas are cancers that affect the lymph nodes. Leukemia is cancer of the blood-forming cells, causing an overproduction of immature white blood cells. Data on the incidence and deaths by site and sex from cancer appear in Table 12.2.

How Cancer Spreads

Malignant tumors are not contained in a fibrous capsule. Consequently, the malignant cells can spread from one part of the body to another. This process of spreading is known as **metastasis**. Cancers metastasize by invading adjacent tissues or dislodging and moving through the blood and lymphatic vessels to other parts of the body. Early diagnosis is vital for any type of cancer, because once the cancer metastasizes, treatment becomes much more difficult. As the malignant cells spread, they begin to disrupt the chemical functioning of the normal cells in the area they invade, affecting the RNA and DNA. When this disruption occurs, mutant cells that differ in form, quality, and function develop.

Causes of Cancer

Even though we understand *how* malignant cells spread, we do not understand *why* this process occurs. Researchers have suggested that the DNA alters cells to allow the growth of cancer cells. These **oncogenes** (cancer-causing genes) are present in chromosomes, and scientists theorize that stress, viruses, radiation, or some other **carcinogenic** (cancer-causing) agent activates these oncogenes. Whether these genes are present through genetics or develop because of exposure to some carcinogen is not known. The answer to this question could lead to a better understanding of cancer and provide the basis for more effective treatment.

A range of other factors may cause cancer.

Genetic Factors

Most cancers are not genetically linked. Whether people tend to inherit a cancer-prone immune system remains a controversial notion. Because of the complexity of environmental and lifestyle factors, isolating a single cause is difficult. Certain cancers, such as breast, stomach, colon, prostate, lung, and uterus, appear to run in families. Again, whether this is genetic or environmental remains a question.

Table 12.2   Cancer Incidence and Deaths by Site and Sex, 1992 Estimates

Cancer Incidence by Site and Sex*		Cancer Deaths by Site and Sex	
Male	Female	Male	Female
Prostate 132,000	Breast 180,000	Lung 93,000	Lung 53,000
Lung 102,000	Colon and Rectum 77,000	Prostate 34,000	Breast 46,000
Colon and Rectum 79,000	Lung 66,000	Colon and Rectum 28,900	Colon and Rectum 29,400
Bladder 38,500	Uterus 45,500	Pancreas 12,000	Pancreas 13,000
Lymphoma 27,200	Lymphoma 21,200	Lymphoma 10,900	Ovary 13,000
Oral 20,600	Ovary 21,000	Leukemia 9,000	Uterus 10,000
Melanoma of the Skin 17,000	Melanoma of the Skin 15,000	Stomach 8,000	Lymphoma 10,000
Kidney 16,200	Pancreas 14,400	Esophagus 7,500	Leukemia 8,300
Leukemia 16,000	Bladder 13,100	Liver 6,600	Liver 5,700
Stomach 15,000	Leukemia 12,200	Brain 6,500	Brain 5,300
Pancreas 13,900	Kidney 10,300	Kidney 6,400	Stomach 5,300
Larynx 10,000	Oral 9,700	Bladder 6,300	Multiple Myeloma 4,500
All Sites 565,000	All Sites 565,000	All Sites 275,000	All Sites 245,000

*Excluding non-melanoma skin cancer and carcinoma in situ.
Source: American Cancer Society.

Viral Causes

Although evidence is still under investigation, it indicates that viruses enhance the probability of cancer developing. There is evidence that the herpes viruses may contribute to the development of some forms of leukemia, Burckitt's lymphoma, Hodgkin's disease, cervical cancer, and some forms of leukemia (Donatelle, Davis, & Hoover, 1991).

Diet

A number of foods have been linked to cancer. Although useful as preservatives, many of the food chemical additives and preservatives have been associated with cancer. For example, the cyclamate saccharin and the nitrosamines have been linked to cancer. It has been estimated that 40% to 50% of cancers are caused by environmental chemicals such as pesticides, herbicides, preservatives, and other chemicals. The Food and Drug Administration (FDA) has developed a list of more

HEALTH HIGHLIGHT
Cancer Terms to Know

Some terms commonly used in the language of cancer:

- **Antibody:** a substance made by specialized cells in the body that defends the body from infections due to viruses, bacteria, and other foreign substances
- **Benign:** a noncancerous growth
- **Biopsy:** removal and microscopic examination of tissue from a living body for diagnosis
- **Cancer:** a general term for more than 100 diseases involving abnormal, uncontrolled growth of cells
- **Grading:** a method physicians use to identify the severity of cancer
- **Malignant:** a growth of cancerous cells
- **Metastasis:** the spread of cancer from one part of the body to another; cells in the new site are like those in the original growth
- **Remission:** a lessening or stopping of symptoms of a disease when the disease is under control
- **Staging:** a numerical method indicating the extent to which the cancer has spread; helps determine best form of treatment and prognosis
- **Tumor:** a palpable mass; may be malignant or benign

than 14,000 chemicals suspected of causing cancer. Instead of concerning itself with the ill effects of all these chemicals, the American Cancer Society has developed the following nutritional guidelines for preventing cancer.

1. Eat a variety of foods. No one food provides all the nutrients. Include foods such as fruits and vegetables, whole grain cereals, lean meats, fish, poultry without skin, beans, and low-fat dairy products.
2. Maintain desirable weight. Obesity increases the risks for colon, breast, gallbladder, and uterine cancer.
3. Avoid too much fat, saturated fat, and cholesterol. A low-fat diet may reduce the risks for cancers of the breast, prostate, colon, and rectum. A low-fat diet also will help control weight and reduce the risk of heart disease.
4. Eat foods with adequate starch and fiber. Starch and fiber can be increased by eating more fruit, vegetables, potatoes, and whole grain breads and cereals. A high-fiber diet helps reduce the risk of colon and rectal cancer.
5. Include foods high in vitamins A and C. Foods such as carrots, spinach, oranges, strawberries, and green peppers are high in vitamin C. Vitamin A can be found in dark green and deep yellow fresh vegetables. These foods may help reduce the risk for cancers of the larynx, esophagus, and lungs.
6. Include cruciferous vegetables. Foods such as cabbage, broccoli, brussel sprouts, and cauliflower may help prevent cancer. These are high in fiber.
7. Reduce consumption of salt-cured, smoked, and nitrate-cured foods. Consuming these foods in large amounts is associated with higher incidence of cancers of the esophagus and stomach.
8. If you drink alcohol, do so in moderation. Heavy drinking is associated with cancer of the mouth, throat, esophagus, and liver.

Psychological Factors

Research has demonstrated a link between the mental state and health. Negative emotional states contribute to disease. People who have no social support and are lonely or depressed have been shown to be more susceptible to cancer than their mentally healthy counterparts. Depression seems to suppress the activity of the body's immune system, thus reducing resistance to disease. While psychological factors play a part in the development of cancer, they are not as significant as other risk factors.

Radiation and Chemical Causes

One of the most dangerous sources of cancer is exposure to the sun. In 1990, more than 600,000 people were diagnosed with either melanoma, basal-cell, or squamous-cell carcinomas. This represents an increase of more than 200,000 cases from 1980. The increase has been associated with increased exposure to the sun and the depletion of the ozone layer. People must understand that less sun is better and no sun is best when attempting to prevent skin cancer. Cigarette smoking is strongly associated with lung, bladder, and mouth cancers. Radiation from diagnostic X-rays and radioactive substances is potentially a cause of bone marrow, skin, and thyroid cancers. Asbestos has long been associated with lung cancer. Coal dust is linked to lung, bladder, and scrotum cancers. Synthetic estrogens are related to vaginal, cervical, and uterine cancers. The list goes on. Many of the chemicals with which people have daily contact are carcinogenic.

Warning Signals of Cancer

The American Cancer Society recommends watching for the following warning signs. The chances of survival are significantly better with early detection and diagnosis. None of the risk factors are sure indicators of cancer, but they should be investigated by a physician. The warning signs are as follows:

- Change in bowel or bladder habits
- A sore that does not heal
- Unusual bleeding or discharge
- Thickening or lump in the breasts or elsewhere
- Indigestion or difficulty in swallowing
- Obvious change in a wart or mole
- Nagging cough or hoarseness

Trends in Diagnosis, Treatment, and Research

The American Cancer Society says that anyone surviving cancer 5 years after diagnosis is considered to be cured. The emphasis continues to be on the importance of early detection and treatment. Often treatment will combine several therapies. The following list indicates the direction of current methods in treatment and research (American Cancer Society, 1990; *Mayo Clinic Health Letter,* 1992):

1. A genetic fusing of cancer cells with normal cells can produce disease-fighting "monoclonal antibodies," specific antibodies tailored to seek out chosen targets on cancer cells. Their potential in the diagnosis and treatment of cancer is under study.

2. New understanding of the causes of pain in cancer patients has increased the options for control. Regular use of oral pain medicines, infusions, or injections of analgesics (procedures to interrupt pain pathways) are among the effective approaches available.

3. Studies with agents like synthetic retinoids (cousins of vitamin A), and other substances are being undertaken to see if recurrences of certain cancers can be prevented. Another step is to see if these agents can reduce cancer in high-risk groups. For example, studies of dietary intervention will examine the effect of low-fat diets in women at high risk of developing breast cancer.

4. New approaches to drug therapy use combination chemotherapy and chemo-therapy with surgery or radiation. New classes of agents are being tested for their effectiveness in treating patients resistant to drug therapies now in use.

5. Many patients with primary bone cancer now are treated successfully by removing and replacing a section of bone rather than by amputating the leg or arm. Drugs and radiation therapy are being used effectively in bone cancer surgery, resulting in dramatic improvement in survival.

6. New high technology diagnostic imaging techniques have replaced exploratory surgery for some cancer patients. Magnetic resonance imaging (MRI) is one example of such technology under study. It uses a huge electromagnet to detect tumors by sensing the vibrations of the different atoms in the body. Computer-ized tomography (CT scanning) uses X-rays to examine the brain and other parts of the body. Cross-section pictures are constructed which show a tumor's shape and location more accurately than is possible with conventional X-ray tech-niques. For patients undergoing radiation therapy, CT scanning may enable the therapist to pinpoint the tumor more precisely to provide more accurate radiation dosage while sparing normal tissue.

7. Immunotherapy holds the hope of enhancing the body's own disease-fighting systems to control cancer. Interferon, interleukin-2, and other biologic response modifiers are under study. Recently, interferon was made available as the treatment for hairy cell leukemia, a rare blood cancer of older Americans. Interleukin-2 is under very active research in the treatment of kidney cancer and melanoma. Also under investigation are colony-stimulating factors that encour-age production of white blood cells. This enables the patient to tolerate higher doses of medication while decreasing the chance of infection.

8. Many cancers are caused by a two-stage process through exposure to substances known as initiators and promoters. Research scientists are exploring ways of interrupting these processes to prevent the development of cancer.

9. The transfusion of blood components is becoming increasingly available and effective as a support in cancer therapy. Platelets are used to prevent hemor-rhaging, and red blood cells, to combat anemia. Infections, a common compli-cation in cancer patients, can now be better anticipated, and with new drugs and antibodies, better controlled and treated.

10. New technologies have made it possible to use bone marrow transplantation as an important treatment option in selected patients with aplastic anemia and leukemia. Bone marrow transplantation for other cancers is under study. The administration of larger doses of anticancer drugs or radiation therapy may be

tolerated by some patients if their bone marrow is stored and later transplanted to restore marrow function (autologous bone marrow transplants).

11. Hyperthermia is a way to increase the heat or temperature of the entire body or a part of the body. It is known that heat can kill cancer cells. A cell temperature of 45° C kills cancer cells. A temperature of 42°–43° C makes the cell more susceptible to damage by ionizing radiation (X-rays). Studies are under way to learn if hyperthermia can increase the effect of radiation or chemotherapy. The value of hyperthermia has yet to be established and this technique, although appearing to be useful, is the cornerstone of many types of cancer quackery.

12. With medical progress producing longer survival periods for many cancer patients, clinical concerns are expanding to include not only patients' physical well-being, but also their psychosocial needs. The patient's and family's reactions to the disease, sexual concerns, employment and insurance needs, and ways to provide psychosocial support have emerged as important areas of research and clinical care.

13. Improvements in cancer treatment have made possible more conservative management of some early cancers. In early cancer of the larynx, many patients have been able to retain their larynx and their voice; in colo-rectal cancer, fewer permanent colostomies are needed; and the surgery required in many cases of breast cancer is often more limited.

14. Prostatic ultrasound, a rectal probe using ultrasonic waves producing an image of the prostate, is currently being investigated as a potential means to increase the early detection of occult, or not clinically suspected, prostate cancer.

15. Neoadjuvant chemotherapy has been successful against certain types of cancers. This involves giving chemotherapy to shrink the cancer and then removing it surgically. Part of this research is with tumor necrosis factors or proteins that destroy tumor cells. The body produces small amounts of this protein naturally and researchers are now looking for ways to make larger amounts.

RESPIRATORY DISORDERS

The term *allergy* can be used synonymously with the term *hypersensitivity*. Both terms refer to an exaggerated response to an antibody-forming substance (antigen). Many people with the most common allergic disorders have an inherited tendency to develop this hypersensitivity. Although those who suffer from allergies may think that the vast majority of people experience hypersensitivity, each specific reaction is theoretically harmless to 80% of the population.

One of the most common forms of allergic reaction is hay fever. Typical symptoms include itchy sensations in the nose and roof of the mouth; watery, itchy eyes; and sneezing. Hay fever that occurs in the spring is associated with grass pollens, the summer version is related to grass and weed pollens, and fall hay fever is related to weed pollens. Nonseasonal hay fever may result from breathing irritating substances. The annoying symptoms associated with hay fever can be decreased or alleviated by using oral antihistamines or another drug, limiting contact with the source of irritation, or administering injections to desensitize the subject to the isolated cause(s).

Asthma occurs most frequently in children and young adults. Although many children do outgrow the symptoms, people of all ages suffer from the disorder. Extrinsic asthma is allergy-related and may occur with other allergic problems. Intrinsic asthma, on the other hand, seems to be stimulated by factors such as infections, emotional or physical fatigue, irritants in the air, and emotional situations. During an asthmatic attack, the large and small airways narrow due to spasms in the bronchial tubes or swelling in the mucous membrane. Attacks are characterized by wheezing, coughing, difficult breathing, and shortness of breath. The frequency and duration of asthmatic symptoms vary greatly but can be potentially dangerous. Drugs can often provide relief.

Deep inside the lungs are tiny air sacs, called alveoli. Oxygen diffuses into the bloodstream and is carried throughout the body through the membranes of these sacs. The alveoli are also the site where carbon dioxide is diffused from the blood for eventual elimination from the body. With **emphysema**, the membranes of the sacs lose their elasticity. This loss of elasticity results in gradual lessening of the alveoli's ability to accomplish the necessary exchange of gases. Breathing becomes more and more difficult. The best treatment is avoiding pollution in the atmosphere, especially cigarette smoke. Other devices to aid in breathing difficulties may also be used.

Chronic bronchitis is a type of bronchitis associated with the effects of smoking or air pollutants. Symptoms of chronic bronchitis are a continuous cough that is present for at least 3 months of 2 consecutive years and excretion of large amounts of sputum due to increased mucus secretions in the trachea and bronchial tubes. Chronic bronchitis is often called "smoker's cough," and if it continues unhindered, both the number and size of the mucus-secreting glands increase. This can cause vulnerability to other respiratory diseases or permanent blockage of the airways. If the affected person smokes, smoking should be stopped. If possible, removal to a less polluted environment is recommended.

OTHER NONINFECTIOUS DISORDERS

Diabetes mellitus is a complex disorder of carbohydrate, fat, and protein metabolism. It results primarily from a relative or complete lack of insulin secretions by the beta cells of the pancreas or from defects of the insulin receptors. This lack of insulin or lack of receptor sites in target cells results in excessive amounts of sugar in the blood and urine. **Hyperglycemia** (high blood sugar) is the hallmark symptom of diabetes. Obesity is a contributing factor to lack of receptor sites in older people. Insufficient amounts of insulin are available to metabolize sugar, the primary source of fuel. When fat is metabolized without sugar, a residue called a **ketone body** develops, increasing acid in the bloodstream. Sufficient amounts of ketone bodies produce a diabetic coma and can cause death. Genetically determined diabetes may be caused by inadequate secretion of insulin. The condition may also result from a deficiency of beta cells brought on by other causes such as infection, pregnancy, drugs, or obesity. Diabetic patients have increased incidence of atherosclerosis, which is often earlier and more severe. Characteristically, the earliest symptom of diabetes is excessive urination.

There are two main types of diabetes: insulin-dependent and non-insulin-dependent. Insulin-dependent diabetes usually appears in people under the age of 35, most commonly between the ages of 10 and 16. This type is the most severe form and usually develops rapidly. The insulin-producing cells in the pancreas are destroyed as a result of an immune response after a viral infection. Insulin production ceases almost immediately; without injections of insulin, coma and death can occur.

Non-insulin dependent diabetes is usually of gradual onset and occurs mainly in people over 40. In some cases a combination of dietary measures, weight reduction, and exercise keeps the condition under control without the injection of insulin.

Extra care with hygiene is part of treatment. Diabetics are very prone to infection, so it is important for them to maintain sterile conditions for shaving and to treat cuts and abrasions carefully. The feet and legs are particularly susceptible to infection. Insulin is given by injection, although some experimentation with an insulin pump is also under way.

Colitis is the most frequently diagnosed gastrointestinal disease. It consists of an inflammatory condition of the large intestine. Sometimes it occurs sporadically in the form of irritable bowel syndrome; it can also progress to more serious chronic conditions. Irritable bowel syndrome is characterized by bouts of pain and diarrhea or constipation. Emotional stress is often associated with colitis. Ulcerative colitis increases the tendency toward colon cancer.

Diverticulosis is caused by the development of small sacs in the colon, which may be due to lack of dietary bulk. Feces accumulate in these sacs, which can eventually lead to ulceration and bleeding. Although the condition frequently is asymptomatic, rectal bleeding or pain in the left abdominal area may indicate a need for a medical checkup. Fatal hemorrhage may result if undiagnosed (Thomas, 1984).

Peptic ulcers are ulcerations of the mucous membrane and are usually located in the lower end of the esophagus, stomach, and duodenum. Pain, described as uniform and "gnawing," is the main symptom. Peptic ulcers seem to be the result of an imbalance in acid secretion and production of protective mucous factors. Usually, stress is seen as a precipitating factor. Treatment includes a combination of diet and medication. Prognosis is guardedly favorable, but recurrences are common (Thomas, 1984).

DISEASES OF THE BONES AND JOINTS

The most frequent causes of lost work days may well be arthritis and rheumatic diseases. Difficult to diagnose, **arthritis** is characterized by inflammation of joints, usually accompanied by changes in structure. The specific cause of arthritis is not known, but the cause may be related to an antigen-antibody reaction. The most prevalent age for onset is between 30 and 40. The beginnings of the disease may be sudden or progressive, and deformity of the joints is often observable. Exercise and/or physical therapy is encouraged to maintain range of motion in the affected joints. Arthritis has no cure, and treatment is nonspecific. If the pain is intense, bed rest may be required for a short time. Salicylates (aspirin) are commonly used to ease pain. Antiinflammatory drugs and certain types of steroids also may be used. Long-term use of steroids is not recommended due to undesirable side effects, however. In severe cases, surgery is a possibility.

Osteoarthritis is the most prevalent form of arthritis. It is also the type most easily controlled. In osteoarthritis, the cartilage at certain joints breaks down. Because nearly 90% of all people over 60 years of age show signs of osteoarthritis, the degeneration of the joints is largely attributed to the aging process. When the cartilage that covers the bones in certain joints becomes rough and pitted, it restricts movement and causes pain. The pain can be minor, or it can prevent the simplest of movements and even make getting a good night's sleep impossible. Osteoarthritis can neither be cured nor stopped once it has started, but extreme disability is rare.

Rheumatoid arthritis may be the most well known form of arthritis. It is described as a chronic destructive, sometimes deforming, collagen disease that has an autoimmune component. Rheumatoid arthritis tends to occur in the joints that are most "active" by attacking the synovial membrane that is responsible for lubricating the joints. Rheumatoid arthritis can be extremely destructive to the ends of the joints. Some characteristics are morning stiffness, pain or tenderness on motion in at least one joint, swelling in at least one joint, symmetric swelling of the same joint on both sides of the body, and/or subcutaneous nodules. Ten percent of all people who suffer from rheumatoid arthritis will eventually be disabled, despite all treatment.

Juvenile rheumatoid arthritis is a rare form of arthritis that affects children and lasts more than three months. Juvenile arthritis occurs more often in girls than in boys. It most commonly starts between the ages of two and four or around puberty. The three main types that occur are Still's disease, polyarticular juvenile arthritis, and Pauciarticular juvenile arthritis. Still's disease usually begins with an illness characterized by fever, rash, enlarged lymph nodes, abdominal pain, and weight loss. The symptoms last several weeks with joint pain, swelling, and stiffness appearing several months later. Polyarticular juvenile arthritis begins with pain, swelling, and stiffness in a number of joints. Pauciarticular juvenile arthritis involves four or fewer joints (American Medical Association, 1989, p. 871).

In any of the three types of juvenile arthritis, damage incurred to the epiphyseal plates can impair skeletal development. In most children the arthritis disappears after several years, although some are left with permanent stiffness and joint deformity.

Low back pain afflicts 8 out of 10 Americans. It is the major cause of disability in people aged 20 to 45 years of age. Back injury is the single most expensive medical cost in industry today. Although low back pain is only a passing problem for some people, for many, it is the beginning of a lifetime of discomfort. Preventing pain can be very simple. It begins with overall fitness. A body that is strong and fit is not as susceptible to injury as one that is overweight and out of shape. Strong abdominal and back muscles are especially important. Practicing good posture techniques is also essential. Learning to lift properly, with the legs and not the back, may make the difference between pain and comfort. Also, not managing stress well and suffering from psychological problems can enhance the chances of developing low back pain.

If back pain is a problem, a person can take steps to alleviate it. The use of heat, massage, and whirlpools can relax muscles. Rest is very important for complete recovery. Pain relievers are also effective but should be taken only on the advice of a physician.

■ ■ ■   *STUDENT CONCERNS:* CHRONIC AND NONINFECTIOUS DISEASES

Several areas are of particular concern to students in grades 7 through 12. Following are some typical questions about topics of concern from *Students Speak* (Trucano, 1984).

Grades 7 through 8

How do people get cancer?

What is cancer and why do some people get it and others don't?

What diseases does smoking give you other than cancer?

Why do some people get diseases in certain families but not other members of that family?

What causes diseases?

What can happen to your heart if you are not physically fit?

How do diseases come about, like multiple sclerosis, polio, and mental illness?

How do you cope with diseases and handicaps?

What diseases are really serious and which ones aren't?

How are stress, worries, and fears related to diseases you get?

How do you find out if we have a disease that got passed down by the family?

Grades 9 through 10

What causes cancer and related things?

What causes leukemia?

What things cause epilepsy in children?

What are some warnings of cancer, heart attack, and strokes?

How does your diet affect the diseases you get?

In a mild case of diabetes where can one get sugar-free goods and how can one deal emotionally with it?

If a disease is wiped out, like smallpox, and you stop immunization, can that disease come back?

What helps prevent diseases in the body?

Grades 11 through 12

I would like to learn more about cancer. A lot of people in my family have died from cancer and I would like to understand it better.

What types of diseases are passed through heredity?

What makes people get upset over things that don't have to do with them?

How can you value your own ideas so you won't be influenced so much by peers to do something you really would not have done by your own standards?

We should know about different types and treatments for diseases like diabetes and cancer.

Emphasize what our bodies take in to know what kind of diseases may develop later.

SUMMARY

Many diseases have affected humans throughout history. Today, the greatest killers are cardiovascular disease and cancer. The cardiovascular system is responsible for carrying the blood throughout the body. Besides the heart, it includes a complex array of arteries, arterioles, capillaries, venules, and veins.

Arteriosclerosis is the generic term for a collection of diseases that affect the cardiovascular system. These diseases are characterized by hardening of the arteries. The most common form, atherosclerosis, results from a buildup of plaque in the arteries. Over time, the arteries sufficiently narrow or become congested. When this situation occurs in the arteries of the heart, it causes a heart attack, or myocardial infarction. If atherosclerosis occurs in the neck or brain, the result is a stroke. Other conditions of the heart and cardiovascular system include congenital heart defects, congestive heart failure, angina pectoris, hypertension, and rheumatic heart disease. The risk factors for cardiovascular disease include heredity, gender, age, race, cigarette smoking, high cholesterol, hypertension, inactivity, obesity, and diabetes.

Cancer is really a term to describe a number of conditions characterized by uncontrolled growth and spread of abnormal cells, or neoplasms. These neoplasms form tumors and can be benign (noncancerous) or malignant (cancerous). A microscopic examination (biopsy) must be done to determine if the tumor is malignant or benign. Types of cancer include the carcinomas, sarcomas, lymphomas, and leukemia. The process of the cancer cells spreading from one part of the body to another is known as metastasis. Cancers have many causes, including oncogenic, viral, dietary, psychological, environmental, and chemical factors. Careful attention should be paid to the risk factors, because early detection and diagnosis are important.

Many noninfectious diseases affect humans and cause discomfort and suffering. They include respiratory disorders, digestive disorders, and diseases of the bones and joints.

DISCUSSION QUESTIONS

1. Trace the blood through the heart and circulatory system.
2. Describe the major cardiovascular diseases.
3. Discuss the major risk factors associated with cardiovascular disease.
4. Discuss the various types of cancer.
5. Describe how cancer spreads from one body location to another.
6. List the things a person can do to protect herself against cancer.
7. Describe the two types of diabetes and how they can be controlled.
8. Select two respiratory conditions and describe them.
9. Discuss the difference between osteoarthritis and rheumatoid arthritis.
10. Describe ways to prevent injury to the back.

■ ■ ■

ACTIVITIES FOR TEACHING ABOUT CHRONIC AND NONINFECTIOUS DISEASES

■ ■ ■

ACTIVITIES: GAMES

Risko*

MEN

Find the column for your age group. Everyone starts with a score of 10 points. Work down the page *adding* points to your score or *subtracting* points from your score.

		54 OR YOUNGER	55 OR OLDER

1. WEIGHT

Locate your weight category in the table below. If you are in . . .

		54 OR YOUNGER	55 OR OLDER
		STARTING SCORE **10**	STARTING SCORE **10**
	weight category A	SUBTRACT 2	SUBTRACT 2
	weight category B	SUBTRACT 1	ADD 0
	weight category C	ADD 1	ADD 1
	weight category D	ADD 2	ADD 3

2. SYSTOLIC BLOOD PRESSURE

Use the "first" or "higher" number from your most recent blood pressure measurement. If you do not know your blood pressure, estimate it by using the letter for your weight category. If your blood pressure is . . .

			EQUALS	EQUALS
A	119 or less	SUBTRACT 1	SUBTRACT 5
B	between 120 and 139	ADD 0	SUBTRACT 2
C	between 140 and 159	ADD 0	ADD 1
D	160 or greater	ADD 1	ADD 4

3. BLOOD CHOLESTEROL LEVEL

Use the number from your most recent blood cholesterol test. If you do not know your blood cholesterol, estimate it by using the letter for your weight category. If your blood cholesterol is . . .

			EQUALS	EQUALS
A	199 or less	SUBTRACT 2	SUBTRACT 1
B	between 200 and 224	SUBTRACT 1	SUBTRACT 1
C	between 225 and 249	ADD 0	ADD 0
D	250 or higher	ADD 1	ADD 0

4. CIGARETTE SMOKING

If you . . .

(If you smoke a pipe, but not cigarettes, use the same score adjustment as those cigarette smokers who smoke less than a pack a day.)

			EQUALS	EQUALS
	do not smoke	SUBTRACT 1	SUBTRACT 2
	smoke less than a pack a day	ADD 0	SUBTRACT 1
	smoke a pack a day	ADD 1	ADD 0
	smoke more than a pack a day	ADD 2	ADD 3
		FINAL SCORE EQUALS	FINAL SCORE EQUALS

WEIGHT TABLE FOR MEN

Look for your height (without shoes) in the far left column and then read across to find the category into which your weight (in indoor clothing) would fall.

YOUR HEIGHT FT IN	WEIGHT CATEGORY (lbs.) A	B	C	D
5 1	up to 123	124-148	149-173	174 plus
5 2	up to 126	127-152	153-178	179 plus
5 3	up to 129	130-156	157-182	183 plus
5 4	up to 132	133-160	161-186	187 plus
5 5	up to 135	136-163	164-190	191 plus
5 6	up to 139	140-168	169-196	197 plus
5 7	up to 144	145-174	175-203	204 plus
5 8	up to 148	149-179	180-209	210 plus
5 9	up to 152	153-184	185-214	215 plus
5 10	up to 157	158-190	191-221	222 plus
5 11	up to 161	162-194	195-227	228 plus
6 0	up to 165	166-199	200-232	233 plus
6 1	up to 170	171-205	206-239	240 plus
6 2	up to 175	176-211	212-246	247 plus
6 3	up to 180	181-217	218-253	254 plus
6 4	up to 185	186-223	224-260	261 plus
6 5	up to 190	191-229	230-267	268 plus
6 6	up to 195	196-235	236-274	275 plus
ESTIMATE OF SYSTOLIC BLOOD PRESSURE	or less	120 to 139	140 to 159	160 or more
ESTIMATE OF BLOOD CHOLESTEROL	199 or less	200 to 224	225 to 249	250 or more

Because both blood pressure and blood cholesterol are related to weight, an estimate of these risk factors for each weight category is printed at the bottom of the table.

© 1985 American Heart Association

WOMEN

Find the column for your age group. Everyone starts with a score of 10 points. Work down the page *adding* points to your score or *subtracting* points from your score.

		54 OR YOUNGER	55 OR OLDER
1. WEIGHT			
Locate your weight category in the table below. If you are in . . .		STARTING SCORE **10**	STARTING SCORE **10**
	weight category A	SUBTRACT 2	SUBTRACT 2
	weight category B	SUBTRACT 1	SUBTRACT 1
	weight category C	ADD 1	ADD 1
	weight category D	ADD 2	ADD 1
2. SYSTOLIC BLOOD PRESSURE		EQUALS	EQUALS
Use the "first" or "higher" number from your most recent blood pressure measurement. If you do not know your blood pressure, estimate it by using the letter for your weight category. If your blood pressure is . . .	A 119 or less	SUBTRACT 2	SUBTRACT 3
	B between 120 and 139	SUBTRACT 1	ADD 0
	C between 140 and 159	ADD 0	ADD 3
	D 160 or greater	ADD 1	ADD 6
3. BLOOD CHOLESTEROL LEVEL		EQUALS	EQUALS
Use the number from your most recent blood cholesterol test. If you do not know your blood cholesterol, estimate it by using the letter for your weight category. If your blood cholesterol is . . .	A 199 or less	SUBTRACT 1	SUBTRACT 3
	B between 200 and 224	ADD 0	SUBTRACT 1
	C between 225 and 249	ADD 0	ADD 1
	D 250 or higher	ADD 1	ADD 3
4. CIGARETTE SMOKING		EQUALS	EQUALS
If you . . .	do not smoke	SUBTRACT 1	SUBTRACT 2
	smoke less than a pack a day	ADD 0	SUBTRACT 1
	smoke a pack a day	ADD 1	ADD 1
	smoke more than a pack a day	ADD 2	ADD 4
		FINAL SCORE EQUALS	FINAL SCORE EQUALS

	YOUR HEIGHT FT IN	WEIGHT CATEGORY (lbs.)			
		A	B	C	D
WEIGHT TABLE FOR WOMEN	4 8	up to 101	102-122	123-143	144 plus
	4 9	up to 103	104-125	126-146	147 plus
Look for your height (without shoes) in the far left column and then read across to find the category into which your weight (in indoor clothing) would fall.	4 10	up to 106	107-128	129-150	151 plus
	4 11	up to 109	110-132	133-154	155 plus
	5 0	up to 112	113-136	137-158	159 plus
	5 1	up to 115	116-139	140-162	163 plus
	5 2	up to 119	120-144	145-168	169 plus
	5 3	up to 122	123-148	149-172	173 plus
	5 4	up to 127	128-154	155-179	180 plus
	5 5	up to 131	132-158	159-185	186 plus
	5 6	up to 135	136-163	164-190	191 plus
	5 7	up to 139	140-168	169-196	197 plus
	5 8	up to 143	144-173	174-202	203 plus
	5 9	up to 147	148-178	179-207	208 plus
	5 10	up to 151	152-182	183-213	214 plus
	5 11	up to 155	156-187	188-218	219 plus
	6 0	up to 159	160-191	192-224	225 plus
	6 1	up to 163	164-196	197-229	230 plus
ESTIMATE OF SYSTOLIC BLOOD PRESSURE		119 or less	120 to 139	140 to 159	160 or more
ESTIMATE OF BLOOD CHOLESTEROL		199 or less	200 to 224	225 to 249	250 or more

Because both blood pressure and blood cholesterol are related to weight, an estimate of these risk factors for each weight category is printed at the bottom of the table.

WHAT YOUR SCORE MEANS

0-4	You have one of the lowest risks of heart disease for your age and sex.
5-9	You have a low to moderate risk of heart disease for your age and sex but there is some room for improvement.
10-14	You have a moderate to high risk of heart disease for your age and sex, with considerable room for improvement on some factors.
15-19	You have a high risk of developing heart disease for your age and sex with a great deal of room for improvement on all factors.
20 & over	You have a very high risk of developing heart disease for your age and sex and should take immediate action on all risk factors.

WARNING

* If you have diabetes, gout or a family history of heart disease, your actual risk will be greater than indicated by this appraisal.
* If you do not know your current blood pressure or blood cholesterol level, you should visit your physician or health center to have them measured. Then figure your score again for a more accurate determination of your risk.
* If you are overweight, have high blood pressure or high blood cholesterol, or smoke cigarettes, your long-term risk of heart disease is increased even if your risk in the next several years is low.

HOW TO REDUCE YOUR RISK

* Try to quit smoking permanently. There are many programs available.
* Have your blood pressure checked regularly, preferably every twelve months after age 40. If your blood pressure is high, see your physician. Remember blood pressure medicine is only effective if taken regularly.
* Consider your daily exercise (or lack of it). A half hour of brisk walking, swimming or other enjoyable activity should not be difficult to fit into your day.
* Give some serious thought to your diet. If you are overweight, or eat a lot of foods high in saturated fat or cholesterol (whole milk, cheese, eggs, butter, fatty foods, fried foods) then changes should be made in your diet. Look for the *American Heart Association Cookbook* at your local bookstore.
* Visit or write your local Heart Association for further information and copies of free pamphlets on many related subjects including:
  • Reducing your risk of heart attack.
  • Controlling high blood pressure.
  • Eating to keep your heart healthy.
  • How to stop smoking.
  • Exercising for good health.

SOME WORDS OF CAUTION

* If you have diabetes, gout, or a family history of heart disease, your real risk of developing heart disease will be greater than indicated by your RISKO score. If your score is high and you have one or more of these additional problems, you should give particular attention to reducing your risk.
* If you are a woman under 45 years or a man under 35 years of age, your RISKO score represents an upper limit on your real risk of developing heart disease. In this case, your real risk is probably lower than indicated by your score.
* Using your weight category to estimate your systolic blood pressure or your blood cholesterol level makes your RISKO score less accurate.
• Your score will tend to overestimate your risk if your actual values on these two important factors are average for someone of your height and weight.
• Your score will underestimate your risk if your actual blood pressure or cholesterol level is above average for someone of your height or weight.

*Source: American Heart Association.

UNDERSTANDING HEART DISEASE

In the United States it is estimated that close to 550,000 people die each year from coronary heart disease. Coronary artery disease is the most common type of heart disease and the leading cause of death in the United States and many other countries.

Coronary heart disease is the result of coronary atherosclerosis. Coronary atherosclerosis is the name of the process by which an accumulation of fatty deposits leads to a thickening and narrowing of the inner walls of the arteries that carry oxygenated blood and nutrients to the heart muscle. The effect is similar to that of a water pipe clogged by deposits.

The resulting restriction of the blood supply to the heart muscle can cause injury to the muscle as well as angina (chest pain). If the restriction of the blood supply is severe or if it continues over a period of time, the heart muscle cells fed by the restricted artery suffer irreversible injury and die. This is known as a myocardial infarction or heart attack.

Scientists have identified a number of factors which are linked with an increased likelihood or risk of developing coronary heart disease. Some of these risk factors, like aging, being male, or having a family history of heart disease, are unavoidable. However, many other significant risk factors, including all of the factors used to determine your RISKO score, can be changed to reduce the likelihood of developing heart disease.

APPRAISING YOUR RISK

* The RISKO heart hazard appraisal is an indicator of risk for adults who do not currently show evidence of heart disease. However, if you already have heart disease, it is very important that you work with your doctor in reducing your risk
* The original concept of RISKO was developed by the Michigan Heart Association.
* It has been further developed by the American Heart Association with the assistance of Drs. John and Sonja McKinlay in Boston. It is based on the Framingham, Stanford, and Chicago heart disease studies. The format of RISKO was tested and refined by Dr. Robert M. Chamberlain and Dr. Armin Weinberg of the National Heart Center at the Baylor College of Medicine in Houston.

* RISKO scores are based upon four of the most important modifiable factors which contribute to the development of heart disease. These factors include your weight, blood pressure, blood cholesterol level, and use of tobacco.
* The RISKO score you obtain measures your risk of developing heart disease in the next several years, provided that you currently show no evidence of such disease.
* The RISKO heart hazard appraisal is not a substitute for a thorough physical examination and assessment by your physician. Rather, it will help you learn more about your risk of developing heart disease and will indicate ways in which you can reduce this risk.

How Does It Get Where It Is Going?

This activity is designed to help students understand how the blood is circulated throughout the body. If desired, the student can be given a handout and colored pencils to trace the flow through the heart and circulatory system. Deoxygenated blood should be drawn in blue and oxygenated blood in red.

Directions for Activity: Trace the flow of the blood throughout the cardiovascular system using the blue pencil for deoxygenated blood and the red pencil for oxygenated. Label the valves in the heart muscle.

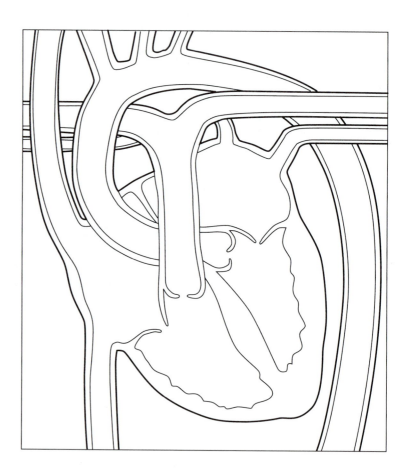

Knowing the Signals

This activity is designed to acquaint students with warning signs of cancer and to associate those potential dangers to the possible sites and how to prevent or protect against the various cancer sites.

Directions: Listed here are the warning signs for cancer. In the adjacent columns, fill in the sites for cancer most often associated with the warning sign. In the last

	Warning Sign	Common Site of Development	Prevention/Protection
1. **C**	hange in bowel or bladder habits.		
2. **A**	sore that doesn't heal.		
3. **U**	nusual bleeding or discharge.		
4. **T**	hickening or lump in breast or elsewhere.		
5. **I**	ndigestion or difficulty in swallowing.		
6. **O**	bvious change in wart or mole.		
7. **N**	agging cough or hoarseness.		

column, write suggestions about how to protect against or prevent each type of cancer.

Processing Questions

1. What type of check-ups should most concern people under 30?
2. What is the most common site of cancer?
3. What seem to be the most important factors in prevention?

Exercise for Cardiovascular Health

Exercise is an important aspect of preventing or delaying cardiovascular disease. To help students understand the concept of calories used in exercise and the intensity necessary to achieve cardiovascular fitness, the following activity is suggested: Expending two thousand calories per week at 60% to 80% of the maximum heart rate seems to be the upper threshold for cardiovascular fitness.

Directions: Secure a chart that provides caloric factors for various activities. Select an activity that you enjoy and find the calories expended in that activity per pound per minute (calories/min/lb). Then, for each pound you weigh, multiply that weight times calories/min/lb. This will give the approximate number of calories you will use per minute in this activity. Multiply this number by the number of minutes you would ordinarily engage in this activity. This will provide you with the amount of calories expended in one exercise session. Target heart rate is figured next.

CALORIC EXPENDITURE: (*example*)
Body weight in pounds: <u>150 pound</u> male.
Activity: <u>Soccer</u>
Calories used = <u>150 lbs × .097</u> = 14.55 calories/min.
<u>14.55 × 40 minutes</u> = 582 calories/40 min of exercise.

Target Heart Rate (THR)

To achieve cardiovascular fitness, exercise intensity should be between 60% and 80% of maximum heart rate for a person with no previous history of cardiovascular disease. Target heart rate (THR) can be determined in the following manner:

Estimated Target Heart Rate = 220 − your age × 60%–80%.

Example:

220 − 18 = 202 estimated maximal heart rate (EHR_{max}).

$$202\ EHR_{max} \qquad\qquad 202\ EHR_{max}$$
$$\underline{\times\ .60} \qquad\qquad\qquad \underline{\times\ .80}$$

121.2 = lower limit THR   161.6 = upper limit THR

Divide both numbers (upper and lower limits) by 6 to determine the heart rate for a 10-sec count:

121.2 ÷ 6 = 20.2   161.6 ÷ 6 = 26.9 or 27

The range for which cardiovascular conditioning can be achieved is between 20 and 27 beats per 10-sec count for an 18-year-old person.

Processing Questions

1. If soccer is your choice of activity, how many days per week of this activity would it take in the preceding example to expend 2,000 calories? How many days a week would it take with the activity or activities you would choose?
2. What does the range of 20–30 beats per second mean?
3. What do the terms *frequency, intensity,* and *duration* mean in relationship to exercise?
4. Can you plan an exercise program that incorporates the necessary factors for achieving cardiovascular fitness?

The Asthma Quiz

This quiz provides an opportunity for the teacher to provide a great deal of information to the student. Within this framework the important facts concerning asthma can be presented. One approach is to have the students correct the false statements so that they are all true. In addition, the students can add important statements/facts concerning each question.

Directions: If you think the answer is false, circle false. If you believe the statement is true, circle true. Your teacher will discuss the correct answers.

Asthma Pop Quiz

1. Asthma is a rare disease among children and adults in the United States. · TRUE OR FALSE?
2. Asthma is caused by psychological problems · · · TRUE OR FALSE?
3. Asthma attacks are caused by blocked sinuses. · · TRUE OR FALSE?
4. Many things can provoke an asthma attack. · · · · TRUE OR FALSE?
5. Overprotective or negligent parenting can cause a child to get asthma. · TRUE OR FALSE?
6. Asthma attacks are uncomfortable and inconvenient, but not dangerous. · TRUE OR FALSE?
7. Asthma attacks appear suddenly, without warning. · TRUE OR FALSE?
8. There is no cure for asthma, but it can be controlled through care & treatment. · · · · · · · · · · · · · · · · · · · TRUE OR FALSE?
9. There are different types of medicine for treating asthma. · TRUE OR FALSE?
10. There is no clear way to know how well the lungs are functioning. · TRUE OR FALSE?
11. Smoke can make an asthma attack more severe. · TRUE OR FALSE?
12. People with asthma should avoid exertion and exercise as much as possible. · · · · · · · · · · · · · TRUE OR FALSE?
13. My doctor is in total control of my asthma management program. · TRUE OR FALSE?

The Family Tree*

This activity (p. 350) is taken from the American Heart Association's Schoolsite Program. It is designed to help make the student aware of heredity in the development of heart disease. Ask students to take the information home and discuss or have the parents help fill out the questionnaire. When they are returned, discuss the information and ask students to write a summary of their family histories.

Processing Questions:

1. Were there any surprises in your family history?
2. What would be the most important factor for you to attempt to change?
3. Did your mother's family or your father's family have more risk factors for cardiovascular disease?

Facts of Life*

This activity (p. 351) helps students focus on the major risk factors for cardiovascular disease. With modification, this is an excellent way to identify cancer risks and other chronic conditions.

   Directions: Answer each question by filling in the blanks with either a word or statement.

---

*Source: *Heart Decisions* by the American Heart Association, 1989, Dallas: Author.

SAMPLE FAMILY HISTORY

This is the family history of John who is 13 years old. John has one sister, Marie, who is 20. Neither John nor his sister like to play sports or do any kind of vigorous exercise. Marie is a little overweight.

John's mom, Susan, is 42 years old. She too is overweight and neither enjoys nor finds time to exercise. John's dad, George, is 43 years old and smokes a pack of cigarettes a day. He plays handball three times a week. At his last checkup, the doctor told him that he had a high level of blood cholesterol.

Susan has two sisters, Alice, who is 35 and Kathy, who is 46. Both sisters have high blood pressure and do not like to exercise. Alice is overweight. Susan's mother is 70, has no real health problems, but does not exercise. Susan's dad died at age 55 from a stroke. He had high blood pressure and diabetes during the last ten years of his life. He was also overweight and did not like to exercise.

George has 2 brothers, Sam, who died of a heart attack at age 50; Howard, who is 55; and one sister, Louise, who is 62. Sam had high blood cholesterol, smoked, and was overweight. He did not exercise. Howard smokes and doesn't like to exercise. No one has been in contact with Louise for several years. George's dad and mom separated several years back, and they haven't had any contact with his dad. His mother is 82 and in very good health for her age. She still goes walking every day.

Name →

INSTRUCTIONS

Draw in the males and females in your family tree. In each box write the number for each risk factor existing in that individual.
1. High Blood Cholesterol
2. High Blood Pressure
3. Cigarette Smoker
4. Overweight
5. Limited Exercise
6. Stroke
7. Diabetes
8. Heart Attack
9. Don't Know

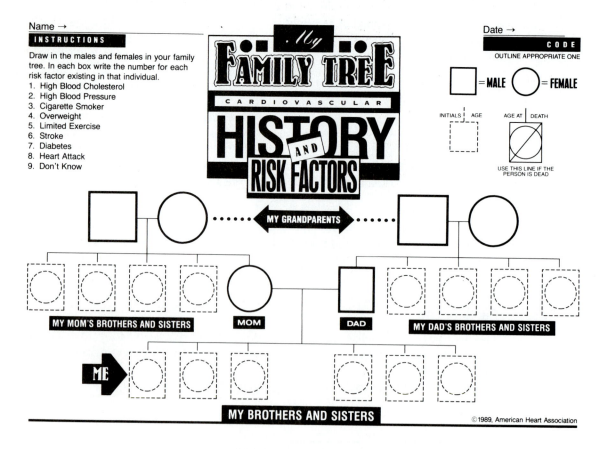

Date →

CODE
OUTLINE APPROPRIATE ONE

☐ = MALE   ◯ = FEMALE

INITIALS | AGE   AGE AT | DEATH

USE THIS LINE IF THE PERSON IS DEAD

My FAMILY TREE

CARDIOVASCULAR

HISTORY AND RISK FACTORS

MY GRANDPARENTS

MY MOM'S BROTHERS AND SISTERS   MOM   DAD   MY DAD'S BROTHERS AND SISTERS

ME   MY BROTHERS AND SISTERS

©1989, American Heart Association

NAME _____   DATE _____

THE REAL FACTS OF LIFE

1. What is the name for diseases of the heart and blood vessels?

_____   _____

2. List five cardiovascular diseases.   a. _____

    b. _____   c. _____

    d. _____   e. _____

3. What term describes characteristics and behaviors that lead to an increased chance or risk of developing cardiovascular disease?

_____

4. A _____ risk factor is one that medical research has proven definitely increases a person's chance of developing cardiovascular disease.

5. A _____ risk factor is one that medical research has proven appears to increase a person's chance of developing cardiovascular disease.

6. List seven *major* risk factors and then indicate if the factor is controllable or noncontrollable.

    1) _____

    2) _____

    3) _____

    4) _____

    5) _____

    6) _____

    7) _____

7. List three *contributing* risk factors and then indicate if the factor is controllable or noncontrollable.

    1) _____

    2) _____

    3) _____

©1989, American Heart Association

Wellness*

Draw a Wellness Chart on the chalkboard:

Wellness Chart

| Death | Critical | Medium | Low | Low | Medium | Optimum |

Illness   **Wellness**

Discuss "wellness" with the class. Point out that sick people have different levels of sickness. For example, they might be just a little bit sick and have a sore throat, or more sick and have to go to a hospital for appendicitis, or even sicker and have a heart attack. In the same way "well" people have different levels of "wellness." For example, they might not be sick, but they might not be very well either, having difficulty walking a few miles to the shopping center. Or they may be more well and able to ride a bicycle five miles. Or even more well and able to compete in a marathon.

Explain that we all have some control over whether we are ill or well, and, more than that, we have some control over our levels of illness and our levels of wellness. We can choose to live in certain ways, and our level of wellness will be low, or we can live in other ways and make our level of wellness higher. If a person eats good food, exercises, rests enough, and doesn't smoke, she can have a very high level of wellness. However, if that person eats the wrong kinds of foods, never exercises, gets too little rest, and smokes cigarettes, her level of wellness will not be as high. Smokers might not be sick, but they are not very well either. Point out that these kinds of decisions have something to do with how long we live, how well we can do the things we like to do, whether people like to be around us, and even whether we have to be in a hospital or not.

Tell the students that you are now going to describe three individuals. You'd like the class to evaluate each for their level of wellness:

1. *Teen X* exercises daily, handles personal and social pressures well, and does not smoke cigarettes.
2. *Teen Y* exercises occasionally, is sometimes overwhelmed by school pressures, and smokes a few cigarettes at parties and other social gatherings.
3. *Teen Z* hates to exercise, handles pressures by "pigging out" on junk food and smoking even more.

Processing Questions

1. What factors keep you from achieving high-level wellness?
2. What factors have been identified in class that keep other members of your classroom from achieving high-level wellness?

---

*Activity taken from *Breathing Easy—Smoking and Health* Teaching Guide for Junior High School Teachers, 1984, Pittsburgh: American Lung Association.

3. What are the long-range effects of negative behavior?
4. What are the short-term effects of negative behavior?

Decisions, Decisions

As students grow and mature, decision-making skills become increasingly important. The choices made in relation to chronic diseases and conditions can have either a positive or a negative impact. Discuss the importance of decision-making skills and developing a systematic approach to deciding what is appropriate. Present a tough decision such as whether to smoke cigarettes. Present the following model and allow students to use it to solve the decision under consideration.

Decision-Making Model

1. What are my options?
2. What are the positive and negative consequences of each choice?
3. Is this a choice that I can put off?
4. If I cannot delay making this decision, have I made a similar choice in the past? If so, was it a good choice and can I make the same one now?
5. Whom can I talk to for advice about this decision?

Once these questions are answered:

6. What is my decision? How can I best act on this decision?

Processing Questions

1. Did using the model make the decision easier? Why? Why not?
2. What factors were important in deciding what to do?
3. Were there any factors that were surprising in making this decision?

Important Pursuits

Games have great value in helping students gather information, review content material, and prepare for tests. Using games the student is familiar with helps the learning process, since the focus can be on the material rather than on how to play the game. Questions can be developed by the teacher or the students, and any of the diseases studied can be included. This game is adaptable for all grade levels. Health games can be created for Monopoly, Jeopardy, Bingo or any other games with which the students are acquainted.

Directions: Following are the steps necessary to prepare to play the health game "Important Pursuits." With the materials provided, develop the game and be prepared to have fun.

1. On sheets of 15 × 15 cardboard, draw the game board shown in the example.
2. Select six main topics (see A through L).
3. Divide the board into segments with the correct number of spaces for the categories.
4. Assign each topic area a separate color. Using index cards of that color, write questions on one side and the answers on the other. Color coding will help keep the questions separate.

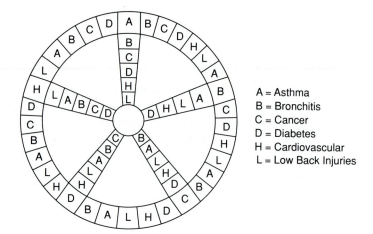

A = Asthma
B = Bronchitis
C = Cancer
D = Diabetes
H = Cardiovascular
L = Low Back Injuries

5. Once the game is ready to play, select two or more teams. Provide each of the teams with a token to move through the board. Use dice to determine the amount of spaces moved with each turn.
6. All teams must begin at the hub and end at the hub. To win, a team must be the first to arrive at the hub (exactly) and correctly answer a question of choice posed by the other team.

Processing Questions

1. What new facts did you learn from playing this game?
2. What are some additional questions that might be added to the game?
3. What are two important facts learned during the game?

How Your Heart Works*

The following crossword puzzle (p. 355) is designed to help students understand the heart. Have them fill in the answers and then point out the answers using a heart model or diagram.

■ ■ ■   *ACTIVITIES:* DISCUSSIONS AND REPORTS

Debate Abate

Have students debate whether smoking should be banned from all public buildings and offices. One group will propose banning smoking, while the other group will oppose that stance.

Letters to the Editor

Have students compose letters to the editor warning of the lifestyle factors that can lead to either cardiovascular disease or cancer. The student may wish to approach

*Source: *Heart Decisions* by the American Heart Association, 1989, Dallas: Author.

Name   Date

how your HEART WORKS

CROSSWORD PUZZLE

ACROSS

2. The valve between the left atrium and the left ventricle
3. The heart is classified as a ____
6. Blood vessel which carries blood to the heart
8. The heart is a little larger than your ____
10. ____ regulate the flow of blood through the heart
12. One function of the heart is to ____ blood to the lungs
14. The tough, muscular wall of the heart
16. Upper chamber of the heart
17. From the right side of the heart blood goes to the ____

18. Lining of the heart
19. Waste gas: carbon ____

DOWN

1. The valve between the left ventricle and the aorta

4. The valve between the right ventricle and the pulmonary artery
5. The heart pumps blood to each body ____
6. Lower chamber of the heart
7. Fiber-like bag surrounding the heart
9. Wall which divides heart cavity down the middle
11. The valve between the right atrium and the right ventricle
13. The artery/vein connecting lungs and heart
15. ____ is pumped through the body to nourish all of the tissues
16. Great trunk artery which receives blood from the left ventricle

©1989, American Heart Association

the situation from the perspective of what our society should do to help reduce or alleviate risks.

What's the Combination?

For further research, students can investigate how the tars in tobacco smoke are linked to cancer or how carbon monoxide affects the development of heart disease.

Predict-A-Problem

Provide an index card with a situation that has potential to develop a chronic condition (e.g., low back pain, arthritis, cancer, etc.). Have students read the situation aloud and then ask them to describe possible immediate and long-range effects. Ask them to provide solutions as to how the situation might be corrected.

Observe a Stress Test

Find out if a hospital or fitness center in your area does exercise tolerance testing and/or thallium treadmill testing for clinical purposes. Ask if they will allow the class an opportunity to observe one or two tests. Students should write reports on their observations regarding the procedure and its results.

■ ■ ■   *ACTIVITIES:* BULLETIN BOARDS

Diabetes

Construct a bulletin board on diabetes with the following elements:

Diabetes and you
Diabetes is: a lack of insulin.
Without insulin, your body cannot get the energy it needs.
Risk groups
Control methods

Heart Disease

"How to Have a Healthy Heart" can be the subject of a bulletin board. Include the following:

Risk Factors	Prevention
1. Age	1. Exercise
2. Male Sex	2. Stress Management
3. Family History	3. Decrease Fat Intake
4. Smoking	4. Don't Smoke
5. High Blood Pressure	5. Eat More Fruit
6. Hyperlipidemia	6. Eat More Vegetables
7. Obesity	7. Lose Weight

■ ■ ■   *ACTIVITIES:* LEARNING ENHANCEMENTS

Several videotapes are appropriate for use in the junior high, middle school, or high school setting. This list represents a selection of videos available from several different sources.

All of the following materials can be obtained by contacting the Films for the Humanities and Sciences, 800/257–5126.

Cancer: Progress in Treatment. This video examines the latest range of surgical, radiological, and chemotherapeutic treatments available. Also looks at a variety of explanations for the rising cancer death rate. 19 minutes.

Diet: The Cancer Connection. Nutritionists and medical specialists look at the controversy surrounding diet and the risk of developing cancer. 26 minutes.

Preventing Cancer. Deals with the area of known and suspected carcinogens as well as ways to prevent cancer and cancer recurrence based on the National Cancer Institute guidelines. 19 minutes.

How to Beat Cancer. This video discusses the causes of cancer and the search for new therapies. Reasons why people are surviving cancer, including advances in early detection techniques and treatments. 58 minutes.

Immune System Disorders. Examines how the immune system determines what is normal, reports on the current state of immune disorder research, and discusses the possible future for treatment of immunological disorders. 28 minutes.

Heart Disease. Describes the sometimes subtle symptoms and warnings of heart disease and what to do. Also explains the risk factors and preventive measures. 19 minutes.

Reversing Heart Disease. Only lifestyle changes can reverse heart disease and offset the effects of family history. Video shows the benefits of exercise, diet, and stress reduction in lowering risk and improving total health. 19 minutes.

Bacteria and Viruses. Shows how bacteria multiply and differentiates between those that are beneficial and those that are harmful. Also explains the differences between bacteria and viruses and how the immune system provides antibodies against future attacks. 20 minutes.

REFERENCES

American Cancer Society. (1992). *Cancer facts and figures*. New York: Author.

American Heart Association. (1992). *Heart facts, 1992*. Dallas: Author.

American Medical Association. (1989). *Home medical encyclopedia*. New York: Random House.

Anderson, K. N., and Anderson, L. E. (1990). *Mosby's pocket dictionary of medicine, nursing, and allied health*. St Louis: C.V. Mosby.

Berkow, R. (Ed.) (1987). *The Merck manual of diagnosis and therapy* (15th ed.). Rahway, NJ: Merck.

Crowley, L. V. (1988). *Introduction to human disease* (2nd ed.). Boston: Jones & Bartlett.

Donatelle, R. J., Davis, L. G., & Hoover, C. F. (1991). *Access to Health*, Englewood Cliffs, NJ: Prentice-Hall.

Greeley, A. (1991). No safe tan. *FDA Consumer, 25,* 16–21.

Hamrick, M. H., Anspaugh, D. J., & Ezell, G. (1986). *Health*. New York: Merrill/Macmillan.

Mayo Clinic. (1992, March). Curable cancers. *Mayo Clinic Health Letter, 10,* 3.

National Cancer Institute fact book. (1987). Bethesda, MD: Office of Cancer Communications.

Report of the second task force on blood pressure control in children, 1987. *Pediatrics, 79,* 1–25.

Thibodeau, G. A., and Anthony, C. A. (1988). *Structure and function of the body.* St. Louis: Times Mirror/Mosby.

Thomas, C. L. (Ed.) (1984). *Tabor's cyclopedic medical dictionary.* Philadelphia: F. A. Davis.

Trucano, L. (1984). *Students speak—A survey of health interests and concerns: Kindergarten through twelfth grade.* Seattle: Comprehensive Health Education Foundation.

U.S. Public Health Service. (1980). *Health in the United States in 1980.* Washington, DC: U.S. Government Printing Office.

CHAPTER 13

Consumer Health

Today a pharmacist can be a consumer's best friend when it comes to figuring out medication mysteries such as drug side effects, interactions and how to take prescriptions so that they'll do the most good. D. Blumenthal, "Pharmacists help solve medication mysteries," in *FDA Consumer*

OBJECTIVES

After reading this chapter, you should be able to

- Analyze the role of advertising in consumer purchases
- List various advertising approaches
- Discuss how quackery affects health care
- State criteria for selecting a health care professional
- State criteria for selecting a health care facility
- List the rights of the consumer
- Discuss private and governmental agencies that help protect the consumer

A NATION OF CONSUMERS

We are all consumers. A consumer is anyone who selects and uses products to fulfill personal needs and desires. Consumer products range from the clothes we wear to the foods we eat to the over-the-counter drugs we buy for self-medication. Consumer services include those provided by physicians, dentists, and other medical professionals. In this chapter, we examine the area of **consumer health**—the selection and use of health-related products and services. At first glance, this may seem to be only a small percentage of consumer goods and services, but in fact it describes many things. For example, buying a car may not seem to be a health-related matter, but it is: One car might be safer to operate than another. Also, spending too much on such a major purchase may require a person to cut corners on more direct health-related spending.

This chapter cannot cover all aspects of consumer health, only those that most influence health. In addition to products and services, we look at consumer psychology and how various forces attempt to manipulate consumer attitudes and behavior. In addition, we discuss consumer rights, consumer-oriented legislation and government agencies, and the role of the teacher in consumer health education.

ADVERTISING AND CONSUMER BEHAVIOR

Everyone has needs and desires to consume goods and services. From childhood, we are barraged with advertising that attempts to blur the line between needs and desires. A need becomes a desire, and a desire is perceived as a need. Our economic system is built on supply and demand, and marketers do all that they can to increase that demand.

This manipulation of consumer psychology and behavior begins in early childhood, often through Saturday morning television commercials aimed specifically at young children. Typical products promoted are toys, candy, and breakfast cereals. As students grow older, the messages and products change, but the message is still one of persuasion. Although, by law, advertising of any kind may not be false or misleading, advertisers use sophisticated methods to stimulate desire and create a belief about need.

Businesses spend more than $60 billion a year on advertising; health-care companies spend more money on advertising than any other industry. Approximately 5% to 35% of the gross sales of drugs and health aids is spent on advertising (Cornacchia & Barrett, 1985). A great deal of psychological research goes into advertising to ensure that it reaches and manipulates the target group—children, teenagers, homemakers, young adults, or older adults. The entire point of these efforts is to get consumers to buy a particular product or engage in a specific activity. Advertising's main function is to persuade, not inform.

Consumers choose from among dozens of different brands of products. In many ways, U.S. consumers are fortunate to have so great a choice. Competition for the consumer dollar also stimulates development of better, more efficient products and services. Consider the level of quality that would be available if only one brand of each type of product or service were offered. Having so much choice, however, makes it more difficult to make correct, informed decisions about purchases. Many of the products on the market are virtually indistinguishable from one another in quality and effectiveness. Price may be the only difference, and even that may not be much of a factor. For example, all brands of aspirin are essentially the same in quality and effectiveness, regardless of advertising claims to the contrary.

Because the primary purpose of advertising is to persuade, most advertising contains little informational content. Even what seems to be informational is carefully selected to make the product being advertised appear uniquely better in some way. Certainly, no one would expect a company to state, "Our product is no different from our competitors' products, but please buy ours anyway."

Advertising Approaches

Advertising is a sophisticated kind of manipulation. Advertising experts understand that, despite the lack of information about the actual merits of a product, advertising can convince consumers to seek out one particular brand from among dozens of very similar products on the market. The reason for this is that advertising appeals less to logic than to emotion. By making a particular product sound more appealing, *for any reason,* an advertiser can increase the product's market share. This can be done in a variety of ways, almost all of them noninformational in nature. Following are typical approaches used to create appeal.

Cost

Two advertising approaches are related to the cost of the product. If the item is priced lower than the competition, the advertising will emphasize its *value*. If the product costs more than comparable items, however, *quality* will be stressed over price.

HEALTH HIGHLIGHT
Recognizing Fraudulent Advertising

Bogus remedies are big business in the United States. In fact, $4 to $5 billion a year is spent on cancer remedies of no proven value, $2 billion on worthless cures for arthritis, and $10 billion on diet products and gimmicks. Government controls have not eliminated advertising of quack remedies, partially because the legislation still has loopholes. Each consumer should assume the responsibility to recognize fraudulent advertising by the following signs:

1. It uses words like "miracle," "cure," or "breakthrough."
2. It does not identify the ingredients.
3. It claims to have support from experts who are not named or fully identified.
4. It offers the substance only through the mail or door-to-door.
5. It makes claims of effectiveness for a variety of conditions.
6. It declares the product is all "natural."
7. It emphasizes opposition or disapproval by the medical profession.
8. It includes testimonials from people who were "cured."

Source: Excerpted from the *Harvard Medical School Health Letter,* October 1984.

Repetition

Consider the number of times you have seen a television commercial only to see it repeated 5 minutes later. A mistake by the broadcaster? A waste of money by the advertiser? Not at all. Advertising experts understand the impact of repetition, even if such repetition may annoy or puzzle the consumer. They know that constant repetition of the same message has an impact on the consumer. Even when the consumer attempts to ignore or block out the commercial, as is usually the case, the message gets through to some degree. A catch phrase, a jingle, or a visual image is remembered. When the consumer goes to make a choice in a store, that memory can be the deciding factor. More often than not, consumers will choose a product they have heard about over one they have not heard about, even when the message essentially provides no useful information.

Testimonials and Authority Figures

Some commercials or advertisements attempt to persuade consumers by offering testimonials from celebrities. Most informed adults (and many children) realize that the person offering the testimonial is being paid well and may not even use the product regularly. These advertisements have the appeal of reflected glory, however; by using a product, you will share something with a famous movie star or athlete. Testimonials by "plain folk," often supposedly done on "hidden camera," attempt to persuade consumers that people just like themselves have found the product effective. Note that while the camera may be "hidden," these commercials never claim that the person offering the testimonial does not know that he or she is making a commercial. Such individuals, who may or may not be professional actors, are paid for their services.

Comedy Appeal

Some advertisers use comedy to promote purchases of their product. Because nothing is funny about most health problems, this approach is of limited use, but it has been applied to analgesic and antacid products quite successfully.

Bandwagon Appeal

This widely used approach attempts to convince the consumer that "everyone" uses the product. Typical phrases employed are "the nation's leading," "used by millions," "preferred by most for more than 20 years," and so on. These ads imply that if the product is so widely used, it must be good and effective. Left unsaid is that advertising alone may have created the widespread use of the product, regardless of effectiveness or need.

Scientific Appeal

This is the "hospital tested" or "doctors recommend . . ." approach. Testing a product in a hospital means nothing. The product may have been tested and found neither better nor worse than similar products. That many doctors recommend the ingredients in a product does not mean they endorse a particular product containing those ingredients. The scientific appeal may also involve an actor recommending the product on a scientific-looking set with laboratory equipment or medical books in the background. The actor may also be wearing a white laboratory coat to heighten the effect.

Snob Appeal and Superiority

Snob appeal can either be one of the most blatant or the most subtle of approaches. Testimonials based on snob appeal attempt to get the consumer to identify with the famous person endorsing the product. Snob appeal can also be fostered by insinuating that the consumer being addressed is much smarter than most people and that the facts presented in the commercial or advertisement will be the sole deciding factor in that person's decision to buy or not buy the product. "People who know, use . . ." is the basic message used to manipulate the consumer with this ploy.

Fear Approach

The fear method of manipulation is a favorite with insurance companies. "One out of every 10 Americans will spend some time in a hospital this year. Will you be one of them?" The statistics used may be technically accurate but still misleading. In any case, the consumer must ask—but often does not—if this insurance company will provide the best coverage for the dollars spent.

Other Common Advertising Approaches

Many advertisers combine the preceding approaches with visual and/or emotional imagery. Whether it is a magazine ad or television commercial, the visual aspects are just as important as the written or spoken message. If the visual message of the commercial is pleasant, the reader or viewer will more likely associate positive thoughts with the product. Packages and advertisements can be powerful stimuli. Students should be made aware of this.

Advertisers also use subliminal messages, which are thought to appeal to the emotions or subconscious mind. An ad for an alcoholic beverage had "sex" written in several places on the picture of a drink, pictures of food are displayed for an instant during films, and verbal suggestions to do or buy something are hidden in tapes of music in certain situations (Corry, 1983).

What consumers must learn to recognize is that almost any commercial or advertisement contains some puffery, regardless of the approach used to convey the message. Advertising tries to manipulate us into feeling better about using one product over another, but often the health benefit of Brand X is the same as that of Brand Y. People must develop an understanding of how advertising seeks to influence them, so that, when serious health problems arise, they will not be deceived by advertising claims and will not fail to seek out proper treatment. Consumers must recognize the limited effectiveness of all over-the-counter drugs and self-medication.

OTHER INFLUENCES ON PRODUCT AND SERVICE CHOICES

Consumer decisions result not only from advertising but also from an individual's education level, family beliefs, religion, socioeconomic status, community, and personal goals. A host of other factors may be involved, including one's physical and emotional needs, motives, and personality (Corry, 1983). Individuals may model their buying patterns and selections on those of family members, friends, or peers. The more status or importance of the person being modeled, the greater the influence that person has.

With all these influences, it might seem that a person can hardly be blamed for sometimes making poor choices about consumer health products and services. But this denies self-responsibility. We can't blame everything on advertising or outside influences; people often make harmful health decisions independently of either. They may use advertising claims to support these decisions, for example, by trying to use over-the-counter products to cure ill health when they know that they should be seeking more effective medical treatment. These people are only too willing to create a false sense of security or relief by accepting advertising claims uncritically or by enlarging on such claims themselves to find easy answers where no such answers exist. In the final analysis, consumers can make informed choices if they desire to do so. By accepting responsibility, consumers can then seek out information on products and services, analyze them on their own merits, and make informed decisions.

CONSUMER MYTHS AND MISCONCEPTIONS

Some consumer health myths might be classified as folk beliefs. Although not based on any scientific facts, many of these myths are widely believed. Here are some common consumer health myths (Cornacchia & Barrett, 1985):

1. Extra doses of vitamins give more pep and energy.
2. Arthritis and cancer are partly caused by a lack of vitamins and minerals.

3. Substantial weight loss can occur through perspiring.
4. A daily bowel movement is necessary for good health.
5. Most things that advertisements say about health and medicines are true.
6. Wearing brass or copper jewelry can help arthritic and rheumatic conditions. (p. 5)

In some instances, belief in certain of these myths can lead to unwise consumer health decisions. For example, belief in the need to take supplementary vitamins can cause a person to spend money unnecessarily on all sorts of vitamin and tonic products, when, in fact, most people get all the vitamins their bodies need from a normal, balanced diet. Similarly, a belief that "organic" or "natural" foods are somehow better than regular produce available in stores can lead to wasteful spending on overpriced specialty products. Some consumer health myths are believed because the person is desperate for relief. Sufferers of arthritis, which is an incurable condition at present, may wear a copper bracelet, believing the myth about the curative properties of copper. They may also spend money on mud baths or other worthless forms of supposed therapy. Since some of these treatments do provide relaxation, leading to a feeling of temporary relief, they are not entirely without value. Consumers who place their faith in them, however, are deluding themselves if they think they have long-term benefits.

Consumer misconceptions also lead to wasteful spending and, occasionally, actual harm to health. Perhaps the most common misconception is that manufacturers sell only necessary products; therefore, if a product is on the market, it must be fulfilling a need. In fact, many products are marketed to create a need that does not actually exist. A few years ago, for example, some manufacturers began marketing feminine deodorant sprays. With regular bathing and other sanitary measures, such a product is not needed, but millions of dollars' worth have been sold. Many mouthwashes, tonics, and other nostrums also provide few health benefits; however, constant advertising reinforces the notion that they are necessary.

Shipley and Plonski (1980) note that even better educated people are often ignorant about consumer health information and have many misconceptions. For example, when surveyed, only 49% of college students responded correctly to a series of questions on health care. Of this same group, 42% believed that popular magazines always checked health articles for scientific accuracy before publishing them. The greatest number of misconceptions concerned health insurance, terminology, legislation, and nutrition.

Clearly, consumers must become better informed to make wise health decisions. They must recognize the negative impact that myths and misconceptions can have on personal health. They must also become more aware of how advertising seeks to manipulate consumer behavior and must learn to reject appeals to the irrational in favor of factual information.

Obtaining facts about health products and services is not always easy. By law, advertisers must tell the truth about their products, prove the claims they make, be specific about any guarantee or warranty, and avoid making misleading statements. Additionally, the advertising code subscribed to by most business advertisers puts forth similar guidelines. Most products are still made to sound more effective than they really are, however. Ultimately, the consumer is responsible for seeing through this puffery and making wise decisions accordingly.

QUACKERY

There are many models of medical treatment. Some of them are valid and time-tested; some are new and not universally accepted. People who practice some models of medicine, however, do not seek scientific validation and, in fact, avoid scientific inquiry. The first category of medical models includes conventional medicine practiced by physicians who are licensed and certified in their field. The second category includes such approaches to health care as biofeedback and holistic health, which may be of value in treating certain health conditions. The third category is **quackery**, the use of worthless approaches that often promise miracle results.

Quacks usually try very hard to appear scientific. Their offices may closely resemble conventional physicians' offices, even down to the framed degrees (often from diploma mills) on the walls. They may dress as physicians—in white laboratory coats or with stethoscopes around their necks—employ scientific-looking gadgets, and use scientific-sounding mumbo jumbo to explain their supposed treatments. But it is all a sham, and a quack will always find an excuse for not subjecting it to independent scientific scrutiny. Although some quacks may sincerely believe in the efficacy of their treatments, most are simply out to victimize the consumer to make money.

Quackery flourishes in the United States for a variety of reasons. The primary reason is ignorance. Many people do not know the difference between legitimate and illegitimate medical practitioners. They accept anyone who claims to be a doctor or a healer at face value. Quackery also thrives because quacks often promise cures or relief that legitimate medical practitioners cannot offer. Those suffering from incurable diseases may find the false hope that quacks hold out irresistible. Because nothing else can help them, they turn to quacks in desperation. People also sometimes consult quacks to avoid the high cost of legitimate medical attention; the quack promises a quick, inexpensive cure. In other instances, people turn to quacks because they wish to avoid surgery or other complicated legitimate medical treatment. Some people may not realize the difference between scientifically proven methodologies and legitimately trained professionals versus those who are trained in treatments outside this body of knowledge. Still, of course, many people actually believe quacks' claims (Payne & Hahn, 1989).

Quackery can involve deception in several areas, including medicine, drugs, healing devices, and diets. Hamrick, Anspaugh, and Ezell (1986) identified some of the warning signs of quacks:

- Offers of a guaranteed, quick cure for an illness with a "miracle" drug or treatment
- Uses of fear strategies to convince the patient of his need for the cure
- Claims of victimization by other physicians or the American Medical Association
- Underrating traditional medical practice
- No use of surgery
- Use of devices, gadgets, and secret formulas to convince patients that their illness is cured (p. 69)

In some instances, quacks do seem to provide relief or cures. In these cases, the patient may be a hypochondriac with no actual physical problem. If the person believes that help is being provided, the "problem" disappears. When an actual problem does exist, the body's natural healing powers may be responsible for a cure, but a quack gets the credit. Finally, temporary relief or remission may be mistaken for a cure.

Quackery treatments, medications, and devices shortchange not only consumers' wallets, but possibly also their health. Quackery delays proper treatment and increases the possibility of a more serious outcome. Using good sense and seeking information from physicians or a reputable health agency is a good start to obtaining proper care (Greenberg & Dintiman, 1992). Some nonprofit agencies that may be able to help provide reliable information and referrals include Consumers Union, American Cancer Society, Arthritis Foundation, American Heart Association, American Lung Association, American Medical Association, American Dental Association, and Better Business Bureaus. Federal agencies that can provide information (and also attempt to protect the consumer) include the Food and Drug Administration, Federal Trade Commission, Consumer Product Safety Commission, and the U.S. Postal Service.

HEALTH CARE IN THE UNITED STATES

The U.S. health care delivery system is in critical condition. Rising medical care costs are one of the top concerns of government, which is paying an increasing portion of its budget for health care. The reasons for increasing health care costs include current reimbursement practices, the increasing cost of new technologies, the ballooning cost of treating diseases such as AIDS, the growing number of elderly, and the inflation of pharmaceutical prices. Another factor in high health care costs, particularly in hospitals, is the need to absorb the costs of care for the poor and uninsured.

The poor and elderly are suffering most from the current health care delivery system. Government programs such as Medicare and Medicaid help, but many individuals find their portion of these bills financially overwhelming. In fact, most people over 65 are paying more of their income for health care now than they did before Medicare went into effect in 1966 (Hamilton, 1982). The U.S. Department of Health and Human Services (DHHS) is attempting to reduce costs under the Medicare plan by setting fees for hospital treatments according to diagnostic related groups, or DRGs. DHHS sets a fee for a specific procedure, and if the hospital charge exceeds the set amount, the hospital must absorb the difference (Olsen, Redican, & Baffi, 1986).

National Health Insurance

The problem of providing adequate health care to all Americans has been recognized for many years. Congress has made several attempts to establish a national health insurance plan. In theory, under such a plan the federal government would finance the cost of medical coverage for families below the poverty level, while other families would have deductions from their income to support the system. Various plans have been introduced to provide equal access to health care for all citizens. Advocates of national health care insurance say such a system would promote cost control by requiring health care institutions to provide care within their annual budgets and put doctors on salary. In general, physicians oppose this approach. They and other opponents protest that national health insurance would impose too much government control and intervention in health care. Another criticism is that this system of health care would foster an impersonal, assembly-line approach to providing treatment because doctors on salary would no longer be competing for business and thus would have less incentive to provide high-quality, personalized care. A final criticism is that national health insurance would simply cost too much, with most of the burden falling on middle-income families.

Health Maintenance Organizations

As the debate about national health insurance continues, the private sector has made other attempts to provide better, more economical health care. One promising approach is the health maintenance organization (HMO). These private health care centers provide prepaid group programs that offer a full range of medical services. Good HMOs emphasize preventive medicine. They try to keep their patients well rather than treating them after they have developed serious, expensive health problems. HMOs assume that it is cheaper to keep people well than to treat them after they become ill. This type of care has its advantages and disadvantages, as do all forms of medical care. Some advantages commonly cited for HMOs include lower cost, a centralized location for many services, fewer laboratory tests, less paperwork, and an emphasis on prevention. Some disadvantages include possible long waits for service, limited choice of primary physician, an emphasis on cost-effectiveness over patient needs, inconvenient location, limited coverage when traveling and difficulty in maintaining coverage after a job change (Cornacchia & Barrett, 1991).

Medical Insurance

As fees for medical and health care services continue to climb, having medical insurance is more important than ever. Today, group plans cover many workers at their place of employment. Typically, such plans pay 80% of medical costs, with the individual responsible for the remaining 20%. Premiums for this coverage are paid for by employer contributions and employee pay deductions. Group insurance plans typically have a deductible that the insured is responsible for paying before the insurer (third party) covers costs. Most of these plans provide good coverage, but one problem is that coverage ceases if the employee leaves the company.

A variation of the third-party reimbursement method as described in the previous paragraph includes the use of preferred providers (PPOs). PPOs are intended to minimize insurance claim filing and costs. The employer contracts with an insurance company and specific health care providers. The employee agrees to use only the health care professionals and institutions under contract. The employer and employee pay lower insurance premiums, the insurance companies save on paperwork and claim filing, and physicians increase their patient load.

Another attempt to hold down health care costs is through a managed care plan. This consists of several procedures used by insurance companies to provide quality care, yet hold the line on cost. Managed care usually involves the following features (Isaacs, 1990):

- Preadmission review—nonemergency situations must be approved before hospital admission
- Mandatory second opinion for elective surgery
- Preadmission testing—as many tests as possible are done on an outpatient basis
- Concurrent review—cases are reviewed to determine if treatment can be provided at home
- Discharge planning—reviews types of support and equipment needed for home after discharge
- Case management—determines appropriate setting for continued treatment

Many individuals pay for their own medical insurance. Self-employed people have no other choice. Taking out personal and family medical insurance, while it can be expensive, has certain advantages. The type and amount of coverage can be tailored to individual needs. However, the more extensive the coverage, the more expensive the premiums. Nonetheless, every individual should try to have some sort of medical insurance.

WHEN TO SEEK HEALTH CARE

Sometimes deciding when to seek medical attention can be difficult. Some individuals tend to wait too long before seeking health care, while others may unnecessarily seek help. For many, their ability to tolerate discomfort determines whether they seek help. Health care decisions are largely personal and based on the perceived severity of the symptoms. Being in tune with one's body and understanding the signs and symptoms of illness can help with the decision to seek or wait to get medical attention.

A number of symptoms indicate a need for medical attention. Blood in urine, stool, vomit, or sputum should be investigated. Pain in the abdomen, especially when accompanied by nausea, may indicate a wide range of conditions, from appendicitis to pelvic inflammatory disease, all of which need a physician's attention. A stiff neck accompanied by fever may indicate meningitis. Obviously, any disabling injury requires prompt medical assistance (Anspaugh, Hamrick, & Rosato, 1991).

Presence of fever is another area of concern when deciding to seek medical care. A fever is an indication that the immune system is fighting an infection. Left untreated, however, a fever may damage various body organs and structures. Self-treatment in the form of aspirin, acetaminophen, or ibuprofen will usually lower the temperature. If the condition does not improve in 24 to 36 hours or a low-grade temperature persists over a long period, a physician should be consulted.

SELECTING A HEALTH CARE PROFESSIONAL

Nearly everyone should have a primary care physician. If a medical emergency arises, a person can seek help immediately from a trusted health care professional who knows the patient's history. Having a personal physician or other health care professional helps a person maintain good health through regular checkups or consultations with the provider about health concerns. A health care professional should be selected carefully. Hamrick, Anspaugh, and Ezell (1986) offered some suggestions for making this selection:

1. Choose your physician while you are in good health. If you wait until a medical crisis arises, you will have to rely on whomever you can find. Having a physician you trust and feel comfortable with before a crisis will lessen anxiety.

2. To locate physicians who are accepting new patients, telephone the local county medical society. The number can be found in the Yellow Pages. If you are not sure what kind of physician you need, such as a specialist or a general practitioner, the medical society can also offer some initial advice. Generally, you will be given the names of two or three physicians you can call. A local hospital can also be a good source of information about physicians who are accepting new patients.

3. Select a board-certified family practitioner for a family physician, a pediatrician for children and a gynecologist for females (see the Health Highlight on health care specialists for other types of providers).

4. Check the credentials of physicians you are considering. Don't be afraid to ask questions about how the person is keeping current in the field.

5. Get details about office hours, emergency care, whether house calls will be made, and so forth. Also try to determine how long a patient usually has to wait before seeing the doctor.

6. Determine the fee schedule for checkups and different types of treatment. Doctors often base their fees on recommended prices recorded in a fee schedule book produced by the American Medical Association. The fees are recommended ranges, not fixed prices, and a physician may charge on the high or low end. Keep in mind that the most expensive physician is not necessarily the best.

7. Choose a physician who is able to communicate with you in terms you can understand. You have a right to know what is going on during any treatment, and the doctor has an obligation to keep you informed. Regardless of their medical skills, however, some physicians are better communicators than others.

8. Choose a physician you feel comfortable with. The doctor's age, sex, and personal manner may all be factors that make you more comfortable or less comfortable. Set up an appointment to talk with the professional to see whether he or she is willing to communicate openly and honestly.

9. Choose a physician you can have confidence in. Even if the person is highly qualified and well thought of in the profession, you may be put off by some personal quality.

10. Don't be afraid to change physicians if you are not satisfied with the way you are being treated. Find a doctor with whom you feel comfortable. (pp. 39, 40, & 53)

CHOOSING A HEALTH CARE FACILITY

Most people are not eager to choose a health facility such as an emergency room or hospital. Unfortunately, most people will need the services of these facilities at times throughout their lives. Consequently, a health care facility should be chosen long before it is needed.

HEALTH HIGHLIGHT
Health Care Specialists

Name of specialist	Field of specialty
Medical Specialists	
Allergist	Allergic conditions
Anesthesiologist	Administration of anesthesia (for example, surgery)
Cardiologist	Coronary artery disease; heart disease
Dermatologist	Skin conditions
Endocrinologist	Diseases of the endocrine system
Epidemiologist	Investigates the cause and source of disease outbreaks
Family practice physician	General care physician
Gastroenterologist	Stomach, intestines, digestive system
Geriatrician	Diseases and conditions of the aged
Gynecologist	Female reproductive system
Hematologist	Study of blood
Immunologist	Diseases of the immune system
Internist	Treatment of diseases in adults
Neonatologist	Newborn infants
Nephrologist	Kidney disease
Neurologist	Nervous system
Neurosurgeon	Surgery of the brain and nervous system
Obstetrician	Pregnancy, labor, childbirth
Oncologist	Cancer, tumors
Ophthalmologist	Eyes
Orthopedist	Skeletal system
Otolaryngologist	Head, neck, ears, nose, throat
Otologist	Ears
Pathologist	Study of tissues and the essential nature of disease
Pediatrician	Childhood diseases and conditions
Plastic surgeon	Use of material to rebuild tissues
Primary care physician	General health and medical care
Proctologist	Disorders of the rectum and anus
Psychiatrist	Mental illnesses
Radiologist	Use of X-rays
Rheumatologist	Diseases of connective tissues, joints, muscles, tendons, etc.
Rhinologist	Nose
Surgeon	Treats diseases by surgery
Urologist	Urinary tract of males and females and reproductive organs of males
Dental Specialists	
Dentist	General care of teeth and oral cavity
Endodontist	Diseases of tooth below gum line (performs root canal therapy)
Orthodontist	Teeth alignment, malocclusion
Pedodontist	Dental care of children
Periodontist	Diseases of supporting structures
Prosthodontist	Construction of artificial appliances for the mouth
Other Specialists	
Chiropractor	Emphasizes the use of manipulation and adjustment of body structures to treat disease
Naturopathic physician	Emphasizes lifestyle and dietary therapies in the prevention and treatment of diseases
Optometrist	Examines and tests eyes for visual defects
Osteopath	Emphasis on structural integrity of the body; uses manipulation along with medical therapies
Podiatrist	Care and treatment of the foot
Psychologist	Study of human behavior

Emergency rooms should be used only in an absolute emergency. Most ERs are understaffed, overcrowded, and very busy. Long waits are likely for less serious problems. Tests are more difficult to arrange and the cost for ER care is higher than those of a visit to a physician's office.

When you have time to select a hospital, it is wise to discuss with your physician the available options. Many times, physicians have admitting privileges at more than one hospital. You should find out as much as possible about the hospital. Some possible questions to consider include:

- Why does your physician use this hospital?
- What is the patient-to-nurse ratio?
- What are the room rates?
- What are the costs of laboratory services, X rays, and so on?
- How frequently does the hospital perform the procedure you require?
- Have there been or are there now any malpractice suits against the hospital?
- Can you tour the hospital?

Choosing a hospital is serious business. Don't be afraid to ask questions; your life may depend on it.

HEALTH RELATED PRODUCTS

Americans spend billions of dollars each year on health care products ranging from over-the-counter (OTC) drugs to cosmetics. Many of these products are used to help relieve symptoms, aid in curing illnesses, and provide aesthetic effects. Unfortunately, many products are not needed, don't provide the advertised effect, and may have the potential to cause detrimental health consequences.

Over-the-Counter (OTC) Drugs

More than half a million OTC health care products are available. These vary widely from mouthwashes to pain relievers. In fact, some of the most beneficial OTC drugs can also create problems. For example, pain relievers such as aspirin and ibuprofen (a nonsteroid anti-inflammatory drug) can damage the lining of the stomach, which can lead to ulcers, among other problems. Large dosages have been associated with kidney damage. Another pain reliever, acetaminophen, also relieves pain and reduces fever. This is the drug of choice for relieving pain in children. Heavy doses, however, can cause bleeding and liver damage. All these pain relievers should be taken with a full glass of water to help avoid irritating the lining of the stomach.

Two other frequently used (and potentially hazardous) OTC products are nasal sprays and laxatives. Nasal sprays relieve congestion by shrinking the blood vessels in the nose. If used for too long, more spray often is required to maintain effectiveness and the vessels actually begin to swell, worsening the congestion. This is called the **rebound effect**. Prolonged use also can result in bleeding and partial or complete loss of smell. Another product that holds potential for misuse is laxatives.

Some contraceptive products, such as condoms, are sold over-the-counter whereas others, such as birth control pills, require a prescription from a physician.

Many people, especially the elderly, consider a daily bowel movement necessary. Chronic laxative use destroys much of the flora in the intestinal tract, worsening constipation. Bulk laxatives are better, but exercise and a high fiber diet are much safer alternatives for promoting regular defecation.

Cosmetic Products

Many health care related products are intended for external use. Although some of these have little effect, massive advertising campaigns and misconceptions about their effectiveness have made them popular. These products are intended for skin, hair, and mouth care.

Skin Products. Some products are designed to prevent or cure acne, rejuvenate skin, prevent body odor, or protect against excessive sunlight. Acne products, combined with washing the face using a mild soap, may help control the condition. Over-the-counter skin rejuvenators have never been proven effective at actually changing skin properties. A moisturizer can help with the dry skin associated with aging, but it does not actually change the skin. Retin-A, a prescription drug, does seem to help delay skin deterioration and restore a more youthful appearance for those individuals who can use it. Retin-A irritates the skin and may result in peeling, blotching, or other undesirable side effects. Deodorants and antiperspirants can help control body odor, but no product can prevent sweating in extremely hot weather or during exercise (in fact, this is not desirable, since sweating is the body's primary means of cooling itself). Regular washing is essential to remove the bacteria that cause odor.

Hair Products. Hair products run the gamut from removing hair to restoring, cleaning, and coloring it. Several products are designed to remove hair. Obviously, shaving can be used under almost all circumstances, and is safe except for the risk of cuts. Tweezers can be used to pluck unwanted hair, but they present some danger of infection if the skin is unclean. Chemicals can be used to soften and remove hair at the root; wax can be warmed and used to tear hair from the roots as the wax hardens on the skin; and a fine pumice stone can be used to prevent hair from growing above the skin. While these products are usually safe, if sometimes painful, skin reactions, irritations, and infections are always possible. A dermatologist should be consulted if any symptoms appear.

Most hair restoring products do not work. One drug, minoxidil (Rogaine), does seem to grow limited amounts of hair in some people. A prescription drug, minoxidil has never been shown to totally restore hair (Folkenberg, 1989). Hair transplants can replace hair loss, but they are extremely expensive, painful, and may take a year or more to complete. Before considering transplant surgery, a person should seek multiple medical opinions.

Products used to clean the hair are generally safe. A wide variety is available; personal preference usually determines the choice of a particular product. People occasionally have allergic reactions to hair products. Most people consider dandruff a hair problem, but it is actually a scalp problem. The scalp tends to slough off dead skin cells, or dandruff. If hair is washed daily, dandruff is not usually a problem, so a special hair product is not needed to help fight dandruff—any shampoo will remove the flakes. People with a severe problem may wish to use an antidandruff shampoo, however. Antidandruff shampoos, considered a drug by the FDA, can help control dandruff but cannot cure it. Dandruff may represent a social or psychological problem but usually poses no medical or health threat unless it is a symptom of psoriasis, seborrhea, or dermatitis, which require a physician's attention.

Hair coloring products should be used with caution, since many of these products can cause skin irritation or harm the eyes when in direct contact. These products have cosmetic use only. The user should test the product on a small area of the hair prior to covering all the hair with the product.

Mouth Products. Mouth products include toothpaste, mouthwashes, and gargles. Many toothpaste products, when combined with dental flossing, serve to protect against tooth decay. Living in an area with fluoridated water also helps in preventing dental caries. A toothpaste with fluoride should be used. Toothpastes with whiteners contain abrasives that damage the teeth.

Mouthwashes and gargles do little to eliminate unpleasant odors or treat sore throats. Bad breath may be the result of postnasal drip, gum disease, poor oral hygiene, and consumption of substances such as onions, tobacco, alcohol or garlic. Bad breath also may be a symptom of other conditions such as infections, tumors, or diabetes (Cornacchia & Barrett, 1993). Mouthwash can only mask these odors. Excessive use of these products can actually dry the mucous membranes, further irritating a sore throat.

CONSUMER RIGHTS AND PROTECTION

One of the basic premises of this book is that individuals should be responsible for their own health behavior. This is certainly true for consumer health. With so much competition for every dollar we spend, and with so much available to buy, consumers need to guard against wasteful spending on products and services of dubious value. For the most part, consumers do not protect themselves properly by informing themselves. Fortunately, government agencies and private organizations have stepped in to establish consumer rights and offer some protection. On March 15, 1962, in his Special Message on Protecting the Consumer Interest, President John Kennedy stated that additional legislative and administrative actions were needed to assist consumers in exercising their rights. Kennedy outlined these rights (Cornacchia & Barrett, 1985):

- *Right to safety:* to be protected against the marketing of goods that are hazardous to health or life
- *Right to be informed:* to be protected against fraudulent, deceitful, or misleading information or advertising
- *Right to choose:* to be assured that consumer interests will receive full and sympathetic consideration in the formulation of government policy on consumer matters

In 1970 and 1971, Mary Gardiner Jones of the Federal Trade Commission and consumer activist Ralph Nader further extended the definitions of consumer rights to include these:

- The right to expect quality of design, workmanship, and ingredients in products and services
- The right to be charged fair prices
- The right to receive courteous and respectful treatment from firms
- The right to expect consumer products and services whose use by the consuming public is consistent with the values of a humane society
- The right to redress of legitimate grievances related to purchased products and services

These consumer rights, of course, are meaningless unless they are backed up with the power of legislation. Over the years, hundreds of federal, state, and local laws have been passed to ensure the rights of consumers and to protect consumers from fraudulent or harmful products and services.

Consumer Protection Agencies

Many federal agencies work to protect the consumer. One of the most active of these agencies is the Food and Drug Administration (FDA). The FDA's responsibilities include periodic inspection of foods, drugs, devices, and cosmetics. The agency demands proof of the safety and effectiveness of any new drug before it is marketed and has the power to recall possibly unsafe drugs or other substances from the market. The FDA also enforces the law against illegal sales of prescription drugs, investigates therapeutic devices for safety and truthfulness of labeling claims, and checks imported foods, drugs, devices, and cosmetics to ensure that they comply with U.S. laws.

Another government agency, the Federal Trade Commission (FTC), is responsible for eliminating unfair or deceptive practices in commerce that curtail competition. In other words, this agency protects the free enterprise system from a company creating a monopoly on a product or service, or using fraudulent trade techniques. The FTC has the authority to stop the dissemination of advertising for foods, drugs, devices, or cosmetics when such action is in the best interest of consumers. Also, if a label on a product is misleading, the FTC can order that product withdrawn from store shelves.

The Consumer Product Safety Commission (CPSC), established by the federal government in 1973, protects the public against unreasonable risks of injury from products. This commission oversees the enforcement of the Flammable Fabrics Act, the Federal Hazardous Substances Act, and the Poison Prevention Packaging Act, among many others. Under these acts, the CPSC is responsible for regulating the manufacture for sale of all highly flammable wearing apparel and fabrics. This is especially helpful for the consumer, because the majority of fabrics used in today's clothing will burn quite easily.

In January 1964, President Lyndon Johnson established the President's Committee on Consumer Interests. This committee was replaced by the Office of Consumer Affairs in 1971. The main purpose of this office is to act as a consumer voice in the presidential administration. This organization also coordinates all governmental activities in the field of consumerism; investigates consumer problems; handles consumer complaints; facilitates communication on consumer affairs among the government, business, and the consumer; and helps disseminate useful information to the consumer.

Various department-level organizations within the federal government also aid the consumer. The Department of Commerce encourages industries to avoid packaging proliferation that can lead to consumer confusion in shopping. This department can request mandatory packaging standards. The organization also provides statistics on population, gross domestic product, corporate profits, personal income, retail sales, balance of payments, manufacturing, and housing, all of which helps the government and consumers understand the present status of the nation's economy. The Department of Labor provides the consumer price index (CPI), the measure of changes in the nation's economy and currency. This agency also surveys employment trends and studies prices of various commodities. The U.S. Department of Agriculture (USDA) inspects meat and food animals prior to slaughter to prevent any diseased meat from reaching the stores. The USDA establishes grades of meat to help the consumer identify the different quality levels. The U.S. Postal Service investigates any incidence of mail fraud and regulates attempts to sell worthless or harmful merchandise or medicines through the mail.

Private Agencies

Many private agencies also assist the consumer by providing accurate, unbiased information about products or by attempting to eliminate fraud and deception by businesses. For example, Consumers Union publishes *Consumer Reports,* a magazine that provides impartial information about products. This publication lists the best buys and the most reliable products for a number of categories. *Consumer Reports* also helps the consumer by critically explaining advertising for many products.

Better Business Bureaus are private, nonprofit, business-supported groups that assist the consumer in mediating misunderstandings between customers and businesses. These groups provide information about a company, help resolve complaints against companies, foster ethical advertising and selling practices, alert consumers to bad business practices, and provide the media with information on consumer subjects. Better Business Bureaus have no legal powers, but they can arbitrate between consumers and businesses. When a bureau discovers illegal practices and a business refuses to cooperate, the bureau turns the matter over to the appropriate law enforcement agency. These bureaus are one of the more important sources of help for consumers who need assistance, especially concerning health products and devices (Cornacchia & Barrett, 1985).

Many cities have chambers of commerce supported by local businesses. These organizations often publish a business-consumer relations code of ethics. Their work is quite similar to a Better Business Bureau in that they act as liaisons between the consumer and business. They also protect the consumer by attempting to eliminate fraudulent business practices.

Even with all of these government and private agencies working to protect the consumer, the individual is ultimately responsible for being informed about products and services.

CONSUMER HEALTH EDUCATION

Consumer health education teaches consumers how to make wise decisions about buying and using products and services, especially in health-related areas (Corry & Galli, 1985). Students need to learn about consumer rights and responsibilities. The rights were outlined earlier in this chapter; the responsibilities include obtaining accurate information about products and services, being skeptical of advertising claims, recognizing the differences between needs and desires, and making wise consumer choices.

The most important component of consumer health is prevention. By learning about and striving for proper nutrition, exercise, and rest, students can avoid the need for many consumer health products such as vitamin supplements, tonics, and diet products. Understanding the dangers of substance abuse will help avert the need for potentially hazardous drugs, whether prescription or over-the-counter products.

The importance of critical thinking cannot be overemphasized in teaching consumer health education. Students should recognize that a product's being advertised on television or in a newspaper does not render it worthwhile or useful. They should learn to see how advertising can foster demand. In addition, they should learn not to accept advertising claims or promises without thinking. Help your students recognize that many of the claims in advertising are meaningless. For example, a product may be touted as "new" or "improved." Is "new" necessarily better? "Improved" in what way? If a product is advertised as being "25% more effective," students should ask, "More effective than what?" Often the question has no answer.

Consumer education is designed not to teach students *what* to buy, but rather *how* to buy. Students should be encouraged to get the facts, comparison shop, consider the consequences of all purchases, and budget their money. By learning the importance of wise consumer behavior, students can incorporate the concepts you teach into their own value system. Finally, students should understand their rights as consumers and what recourse they have if they are victimized in the marketplace. All consumers have legal rights. Exercising these rights can help put an end to shoddy and deceitful health care practices and services as well as worthless health care products.

■ ■ ■ *STUDENT CONCERNS:* CONSUMER HEALTH

Some of the issues of concern in consumer health are listed for grades 7 through 12. The information was taken from *Students Speak* (Trucano, 1984). Typical concerns of the students are as follows:

Grades 7 through 8

If you are on medication prescribed by your doctor should you take medicines over-the-counter?
I would like to know more about medicines.
When do you go for a health checkup?
What do doctors do?
Why do you get checkups?
What can't there be lady doctors for girls and men doctors for boys because some people get embarrassed?
How do you know if you have a good doctor?
Are there any medicines that you shouldn't take together and are there any liquids that you shouldn't take with them?
Why do we have so many drugs such as aspirin?
How do you read directions on labels of medicine?

Grades 9 through 10

We need to know how to get medical care.
How do you go about picking a good doctor that you can trust?
How careful should we be when purchasing health products?
Why are the costs of medical treatment so high?
Why are people not informed of health regulations so they know what to expect from a hospital; why don't they know about prices before checkups?
What can you and can't you refuse at a hospital?
Are all the tests the doctors do necessary?
How can you know if a doctor is a quack or not?

Grades 11 through 12

How come it costs so much to be ill?
What are the rights of patients?

Who sets health regulations?
What kind of health care is best?

SUMMARY

A consumer is anyone who selects and uses goods and services. Consumer health education concerns products that directly or indirectly affect health. Consumer decisions about products and services can influence overall health.

Consumers learn about available products primarily through advertising. Although laws and regulations govern the content of advertisements, the primary goal of advertising is not to inform, but to persuade. Advertising seeks to manipulate consumer psychology and behavior by confusing wants with needs and by fostering desires. Thus, an advertisement for a product may mislead without being legally deceitful. Most marketers of health care products try to give the impression that these products are more effective than they actually are. Even when consumers understand this on a rational level, they may still be persuaded to buy a product because of an emotional appeal or because of steady repetition of the advertisement.

Quackery is widespread in the United States, despite legal measures designed to prevent it. Many consumers who turn to quacks for relief are either desperate or gullible. Money spent on quacks is money wasted. More important, resorting to a quack can delay or prevent a person from seeking proper medical attention.

The high cost of health care delivery is a problem today. While various plans for national insurance schemes have been suggested, they have run into opposition from many different interest groups. An alternative, health maintenance organizations, can provide some of the benefits of national health insurance, but only limited numbers of people are members of such groups. Private and company medical insurance plans, including preferred provider plans, are important safeguards against the financial burdens of serious illness.

A physician and health care facility should be selected with care. Consumers should seek out quality professionals whom they can trust to deliver good care at fair prices.

Many government and private agencies have been established to protect the consumer. These agencies evaluate the quality and effectiveness of health-related products and also police business practices. Each consumer, however, bears the responsibility for learning enough to make wise consumer decisions. Helping students become informed consumers is part of the teacher's job in teaching consumer health education.

DISCUSSION QUESTIONS

 1. How does advertising manipulate consumer psychology and behavior?
 2. Discuss the most typical advertising approaches.
 3. Describe the influences, other than advertising, that affect consumer behavior.
 4. List and discuss some common health-related consumer myths.
 5. Discuss the teacher's role in combating consumer misconceptions.
 6. Discuss the role of the Better Business Bureau in protecting consumers' rights.
 7. What are some considerations that should be made when selecting a physician?
 8. Describe how one might go about selecting a health care facility.
 9. Describe the potential of DRGs on health care costs.
10. Discuss alternative forms of health care.
11. What are some of the agencies that help protect the health consumer?

■ ■ ■   *ACTIVITIES FOR TEACHING CONSUMER HEALTH*

Why Do I Buy?

Have students think about a product that they occasionally buy (it need not be a health-related item). List the following reasons why people might buy a product. Have each student determine which three of these reasons most likely influence the purchase of the product they are thinking about. Students may provide other reasons if they wish to do so.

1. Advertising has convinced me that this is the best product of its kind.
2. My friends all use this product so I use it, too.
3. This is the cheapest product of its kind.
4. This is the only product of its kind available for me to buy.
5. I like the packaging.
6. My family has told me that this is a good product.
7. I think this product has the highest quality.
8. I have tried other brands and I like this one better.
9. I don't really know why I buy this particular product, but I do.
10. I like other people to know that I use this brand of product.

Processing Questions

1. What are the reasons for purchasing this product?
2. Do the reasons for selecting the product relate to your value system?

Assessing Attitudes

Duplicate statements such as those shown here and have students assess their own attitudes about each one. The purpose of this activity is to increase students' awareness of why they make certain consumer choices.

	Agree	Disagree	Not Sure
1. Most television commercials give accurate information about the product advertised.	____	____	____
2. If my friends have a certain product, I usually want to buy that product, too.	____	____	____
3. I only buy products that I need.	____	____	____
4. Advertisers must tell the truth.	____	____	____
5. Only products and services that are useful are sold.	____	____	____
6. I sometimes buy things that I don't need.	____	____	____
7. There is not much point to saving money.	____	____	____
8. Sometimes I buy things without knowing very much about how good they are.	____	____	____
9. Health care products are always safe to use.	____	____	____
10. The products I buy for myself can affect my health.	____	____	____

Processing Questions

1. With how many of the questions did you agree, disagree, or were not sure? What does this tell you about your feelings?
2. What suggestions do you have for being a better consumer after doing this activity?

Budget Diary

Have each student keep a notebook diary of all purchases made for a week or longer. Every purchase made should be recorded in the diary along with the reasons for that purchase. Money spent on food, snacks, toys, video games, school supplies, transportation, books and magazines, pet supplies, hobbies, and health care products should all be recorded. Explain to the class that the amount of money each student spends is less relevant than how the money is spent. After the diaries have been completed for the assigned time period, have students analyze their purchases.

Processing Questions

1. What items did you buy that brought you a great amount of pleasure?
2. What items disappointed you?
3. Do you think that you spent any money unwisely? Why?
4. Does this diary suggest ways that you could budget your spending money better? How?
5. What does this diary tell you about your consumer habits? Does the way you spend your money follow certain patterns?

The Home Medicine Cabinet

Assign students the task of investigating their own medicine cabinets. A list can be made of all medicines, their cost, their purpose and the effectiveness as perceived by the user. Have them list and then discard medicines that have expired. Students can compare their lists in class to learn about the average number and kinds of medicines in medicine cabinets and the total amount of medicine that needs discarding.

Processing Questions

1. Were you surprised by the number of products you found?
2. What were the health products found most often?
3. What does this tell you about your family's and your own use of OTC products?

Know Thy Medicine

To give students an opportunity to familiarize themselves with information provided on over-the-counter drugs, have students bring in and then mount OTC drug labels on notecards. These cards can then be used for a variety of activities such as classifying the cards by kinds of medicine (why they are being taken) or by instructions for how often they should be taken—once, twice, three times a day, or more.

Processing Questions

1. What were three concepts learned from this activity?
2. For what purpose were the health products identified used? Do you think they really work?
3. What are the dangers associated with the products?

Scrambled-up Health

Through the media, people are constantly bombarded with ads about goods and services that purport to improve health or appearance. The following items have some scrambled words that name some items that should be considered with discretion. Have students unscramble the words and write them in the blanks.

Beware of

1. Religious faith _____ . (rsleahe)
2. Advertisements where the only "evidence" is _____ of other people. (nistmstoeie)
3. So-called doctors whose only degrees are from unaccredited or nonexistent _____ . (tnisotsituin)
4. Products that miraculously cause weight _____ , such as "body wrapping." (odcruetin)
5. High-potency _____ that make extravagant claims about their effect. (ansivitm)
6. Very expensive cures or remedies that may not be harmful by themselves, but are totally _____ . (viftecefine)
7. Overuse of medicines that may be _____-forming. (bahti)
8. Medicines that may alleviate symptoms temporarily, but prevent a possibly sick person from seeking the _____ help that is needed. (oinspfolresa)
9. Using medicine that has been _____ for someone else whose symptoms are similar. This is especially dangerous because the problems causing the sickness and how two people react may be entirely different. (rsiepcbdre)

Answers: 1. healers; 2. testimonies; 3. institutions; 4. reduction; 5. vitamins; 6. ineffective; 7. habit-forming; 8. professional; 9. prescribed.

Processing Questions

1. As you unscrambled the words, what specific examples came to mind?
2. Are these guidelines that could be used to protect yourself or that you should be aware of?
3. What is the most important thing you learned from this activity?

Slogans—Do They Sell?

Listed next are several slogans used to sell products. Can you identify the products? Do the slogans influence your purchasing in any way? Using these as examples, identify some health-related slogans by having students bring their own to class for others to identify. Put each slogan on a notecard with the answer on the back.

1. Can't beat the feeling	A. Burger King
2. This is the new generation of _____	B. Pontiac
3. Good time, great taste	C. Chevrolet
4. We build excitement	D. Diet Coke
5. Just for the fun of it	E. Kodak
6. The heartbeat of America	F. Dr. Pepper
7. We do it like you'd do it	G. Oldsmobile
8. _____ really satisfies you	H. Coca-Cola Classic
9. For the times of your life	I. McDonald's
10. Just what the doctor ordered	J. Snickers

Answers: 1. Coca-Cola Classic; 2. Oldsmobile; 3. McDonald's; 4. Pontiac; 5. Diet Coke; 6. Chevrolet; 7. Burger King; 8. Snickers; 9. Kodak; 10. Dr. Pepper.

Processing Questions

1. Do slogans sell products? How?
2. What message is portrayed in each of the slogans listed above?
3. Does the wording really state anything about the worthiness of the product? What kinds of information do we really need in order to make a wise decision?

Do Only Ducks Quack?

Develop a class discussion around the topic of quacks and quackery. Possible questions include:

1. What is quackery?
2. Why does quackery continue to flourish?
3. Who are the people most likely to believe what quacks say?
4. How can consumers be protected from quackery?
5. What should you do if you think a legitimate physician is in error?
6. Why would people give testimonials about products that have no proven value?
7. What are some health concerns for which getting people to buy products would be easy?

After the discussion, divide students into groups. Each group is to develop and build its own fraudulent medical device, product, or service to present to the class.

Students need to formulate advertisements to stimulate interest in their phony product. You may want to videotape groups so the phony claims can be discussed. Projects can also be displayed in the classroom after completion.

Processing Questions

1. Did the claims made by the various groups seem realistic?
2. Would some people believe these claims? Why?
3. What are three concepts we can learn from this project?

Health Promotion Agencies

The following list describes agencies involved in health promotion programs. Have students write the letter of the agency next to the description of its functions. (Not all letters will be used.)

_____ 1. Enforces laws for labeling and safety of cosmetics, medicines, and food.

_____ 2. Responsible for inspecting and grading meat and poultry.

_____ 3. Prevents false advertising from being sent through the mail.

_____ 4. Has offices all over the country to handle consumer complaints and keep track of businesses engaged in fraudulent practices.

_____ 5. Involved in the examination and testing of electrical devices to ensure safety in operation.

_____ 6. In charge of coordinating federal efforts in the field of health care.

_____ 7. Promotes cancer research and educational programs dealing with all aspects of cancer.

_____ 8. Under the guidance of the United Nations, oversees programs dealing with disease, nutrition, and sanitation in all member countries.

_____ 9. Establishes regulations for the manufacture and sale of biological products, researches health problems and provides information to the public, and assists local and state health departments.

_____ 10. Within a specific political division, maintains clinics, laboratories, and staffs of nurses and other personnel to aid in prevention and control of diseases.

Answers: 1. i; 2. k; 3. c; 4. a; 5. e; 6. h; 7. g; 8. j; 9. h; 10. l.

a. Better Business Bureau
b. Department of Health and Human Services
c. U.S. Postal Service
d. National Association for the Prevention of Blindness
e. Underwriters Laboratory
f. American Heart Association
g. American Cancer Society
h. U.S. Public Health Service

   i. Food and Drug Administration
   j. World Health Organization
  k. U.S. Department of Agriculture
   l. State and local health departments
 m. American Red Cross

Processing Questions

1. What other types of health protection functions do the identified agencies perform?
2. How many are government agencies?
3. Do the nongovernmental agencies have any real power to protect the public? What kind?

Advertising: Don't Buy It Hook, Line, and Sinker

Distribute the following items and have students circle the appropriate letter that best completes the statement or answers the question.

1. When a product's package says "free coupon inside," the advertising appeal being used is:
   a. Costs/rewards
   b. Scientific appeal
   c. Snob appeal
   d. Testimonial/authority figure
2. People who purchase and use goods and services are called:
   a. Advertisers
   b. Consumers
   c. Researchers
   d. Shopkeepers
3. Advertising is designed to do all of the following except:
   a. Entertain
   b. Inform
   c. Persuade
   d. All of the above
4. The most serious health-related consequence of not understanding advertising techniques is:
   a. Dependence on a stimulant drug
   b. Failure to seek out proper treatment
   c. Feelings of total frustration
   d. Loss of one's self-respect
5. In evaluating an advertisement that features an endorsement by a famous person, the *most* important question should be:
   a. How is this person qualified to judge the product?
   b. How much money is this person being paid?
   c. Does this person really like the product?
   d. Does this person use the product regularly?

Answers: 1. a; 2. b; 3. b; 4. b; 5. a.

Processing Questions

1. What is the most important thing we learned from this activity?
2. What are some other techniques advertisers use to convince people to purchase a product?
3. Is there anything harmful in using gimmicks to persuade people to purchase a product?

Is There a Difference?

Many products are indistinguishable once removed from their packaging. To demonstrate this, bring in some different brands of cola, toothpaste, and mouthwash. Provide small amounts of three or four different brands and have the students make taste comparisons. Let them try to guess which cup contains a particular brand.

Processing Questions

1. Is it possible to distinguish among the different products?
2. Was the product selected the one you would personally choose?
3. What influenced your opinion about a particular product?

Which Is Better?

Ask students to recommend a particular health-related product such as a shampoo or soap. Then have students trade the products they now use with someone using another brand of shampoo or soap. Let each volunteer use the alternate product for a week or two, then report the results. Did the alternate shampoo or soap do the same job, or did the students note differences? Were any differences a matter of individual preference? Could certain products be more or less effective for different individuals? Be sure to note that differences or a lack of difference in OTC products may not hold true for prescription medications.

Processing Questions

1. Was the product used as effective as your normal product?
2. Were some products more effective for others than for you? Why?
3. Why do you think people select different products?

Consumer Health Tick-Tack-Toe

This game can be played either by two players or by the whole class divided into two groups. Have each side or player come up with a health-related question for one of the tick-tack-toe squares. The opposing side or player elects to try to answer a question for a particular square. The opposing side or player, however, should not know what the question is for that square. If an incorrect answer is given, no mark on the tick-tack-toe board is to be made for that square. Each side plays in turn until there is a winner.

Processing Questions

1. What did you discover as you played the game?
2. If you could select one piece of information to know from the game, what would it be?
3. How can you use the information gained from the game?

■ ■ ■   *ACTIVITIES:* BULLETIN BOARD

Which Would You Buy?

Prepare, or have your students help you prepare, a bulletin board display of different brands of a particular health-related product, such as a shampoo, soap, analgesic, or food. Make a collage of pictures from magazines of the different products under the heading "Which Would You Buy?" Then have students discuss the merits of and differences among the various products.

Needs and Wants

Ask students to prepare bulletin board displays of various products that they consider either needs or wants. Point out that buying wanted products is not necessarily negative—unless it prevents someone from being able to afford necessities. Discuss this point with the class and elicit different views about needs and wants.

Don't Be Taken In

Ask students to find advertisements that they believe are deceptive or misleading. Have each student display an example and explain to the class what he or she thinks is deceptive about the advertisement.

■ ■ ■   *ACTIVITIES:* OTHER STRATEGIES FOR LEARNING

Dr. I. M. Quack

Have each student invent a quack product or service and try to convince the class that this product or service is actually of value. Encourage imaginative creations. For example, one student might try to convince the class that magnetic energy can cure arthritis. Another might claim to have invented a product that will cure the common cold. The class should listen to each presentation without interruption, then afterwards point out its fallacies.

Finding a Doctor

After discussing the procedures that can be used for locating a qualified physician, have students role-play the techniques. For instance, let one student play the part of a representative from the county medical society who can recommend physicians who are accepting new patients. Another student can simulate a telephone call to ask for the names of such physicians. Or, one student can play the part of a doctor while the other plays the part of a prospective client. The latter should ask questions about availability of services, fees, qualifications of the doctor, and so forth.

Where Can I Go For Help?

Have students research legitimate health care services available in the community and write reports on their findings. Community health resources include private physicians, dentists, therapists, hospitals, clinics, health maintenance organizations, telephone referral services, and so on.

Panel Presentation on Consumer Agencies

Divide the class into small groups, and have each research an assigned consumer protection agency, such as the Food and Drug Administration, the Federal Trade Commission, Better Business Bureaus, and so forth. Each group should present a short panel presentation. Be sure that all members of every group participate in the presentations.

What's the Pitch?

Have students watch and analyze a television commercial of their choice and then prepare a written report explaining what advertising technique is employed in the commercial, such as snob appeal, fear, humor, testimonials, or the scientific approach. Students should note the actual amount of useful information contained in the commercial and decide to what extent the commercial concerns irrational considerations.

Scrambled Words

Have students unscramble each of these words that relate to consumerism.

1. mocmlaceri (commercial)
2. qyuracek (quackery)
3. singiadevrt (advertising)
4. elagl githrs (legal rights)
5. aeetngura (guarantee)

Agencies That Help Consumers

Divide the class into groups and have each research a particular government or private agency that works to help the consumer. Each group should prepare a bulletin board display that illustrates and explains the functions of one particular agency.

Not All Doctors Are the Same

Divide the class into small groups, and have each research the work of a particular medical specialty. Include general practitioners, gynecologists, pediatricians, dermatologists, psychiatrists, and so on. Let each group prepare a bulletin board display explaining the services offered by each kind of specialist.

Listen Carefully

Tape some representative radio or television commercials. Then play them back for the class. First, play the commercial in its entirety, asking students to listen or watch for any misleading presentation. Then play the commercial again, this time stopping the tape to discuss statements made, such as "Newly improved," or "America's number one choice." Note that many statements and claims that seem to say something are actually meaningless. Singing commercials are among the least informative. An old adage on Madison Avenue says: "If you don't have anything to say, sing it."

Comparison Shopping

Have students develop a list of five or six health care products such as toothpaste, deodorant, soap, eyedrops, dental floss, and antiseptic cream. Let each student comparison shop for these items and report on which stores in the community sell each brand of product for the best price. This can be done either by visiting stores or by checking prices in newspaper advertisements. You may wish to have the students comparison shop for specific brands that they normally use, or you may suggest that the students look for the cheapest and most expensive brand of each type of product. Compare the results in a class discussion.

■ ■ ■   *ACTIVITIES:* LEARNING ENHANCEMENTS

The following video titles can help in teaching consumer health:

America's Healthcare Dilemma: Who Pays? This video discusses the changes necessary to provide a health care system for the uninsured or underinsured. Examines what the standards for basic care should be and who will pay for them. 26 minutes. Films for the Humanities and Sciences, 800/257-5126.

Health Maintenance Organizations. Describes how an HMO differs from traditional health care and what the advantages of this system are. 19 minutes. Films for the Humanities and Sciences, 800/257-5126.

How to Choose a Doctor. The program explains how to choose and evaluate medical professionals and discusses how to use a referral service. 19 minutes. Human Relations Media, 800/431-1934.

How to Talk to Your Doctor. Follows several people through the medical system from the emergency room to a regular clinic visit to the intensive care unit. Provides tips for communicating patient needs. 26 minutes. Human Relations Media, 800/431-1934.

REFERENCES

Anspaugh, D. J., Hamrick, M., & Rosato, F. D. (1991). *Concepts and applications of wellness.* St. Louis: Times Mirror/Mosby.

Blumenthal, D. (1991, Jan.—Feb.). Pharmacists help solve medication mysteries. *FDA Consumer, 25,* 1.

Cornacchia, H., & Barrett, S. (1993). *Consumer health: A guide to intelligent decisions.* St. Louis: Times Mirror/Mosby.

Corry, J. (1983). *Consumer health: Facts, skills and decisions.* Belmont, CA: Wadsworth.

Corry, J., & Galli, N. (1985). The role of the school in consumer health education. *Journal of School Health, 55,* 4.

Folkenberg, J. (1989). Hair apparent? For some, a new solution to baldness. *FDA Consumer, 22,* 10.

Greenberg, J. S., & Dintiman, G. B. (1992). *Exploring health—Expanding the boundaries of wellness.* Englewood Cliffs, NJ: Prentice-Hall.

Hamilton, P. (1982). *Health care consumerism.* St. Louis: Mosby.

Hamrick, M., Anspaugh, D., & Ezell, G. (1986). *Health.* New York: Merrill/Macmillan.

Isaac, F. (1990). *Health insurance today.* Chicago: Blue Cross-Blue Shield.

Olsen, L., Redican, K., & Baffi, C. (1986). *Health today* (2nd ed.). New York: Macmillan.

Payne, W. A. and Hahn, D. B. (1989). *Understanding your health* (2nd ed.). St. Louis: Times Mirror/ Mosby.

Shipley, R., & Plonski, C. (1980). *Consumer health: Protecting your health and money.* New York: Harper & Row.

Trucano, L. (1984). *Students speak—A survey of health interests and concerns: Kindergarten through twelfth grade.* Seattle: Comprehensive Health Education Foundation.

CHAPTER 14

Concepts for Teaching Environmental Health

The quality of the environment on Earth has deteriorated to the point that the continued existence of life is threatened. In order to reverse present destructive trends caused by people-related activities and styles of life, an environmental literacy and an environmental ethic must become a basic objective of education at all levels—within school systems, the community and the home. Barbara Robinson, *Environmental Education*

OBJECTIVES

After reading this chapter, you should be able to

- Discuss the responsibility of every human being in caring for the environment
- Describe the study of ecology
- Describe an example of an ecosystem
- Relate the connection between overpopulation and environmental pollution
- Explain the impact of various chemicals upon air pollution
- Detail the conditions that lead to water pollution
- Suggest solutions to remedy the different types of environmental pollution
- Discuss recycling as a solution to solid waste control
- Give examples of legislation designed to control environmental pollution

HUMAN IMPACT UPON THE ENVIRONMENT

Maintaining personal health is largely an individual responsibility. Yet we do not live in a vacuum; we are all subject to the influences of our environment. Thus, a person may attempt to exercise the most positive of personal health behavior and still be subjected to health hazards in the form of contaminated drinking water, polluted air, and urban stress factors, such as noise and overcrowded living conditions. Clearly, our environment has an impact on health.

Human beings are the dominant species on earth because of our power to control, manipulate, and alter our surroundings. To a large extent, we have learned to use the natural resources of the planet for our own benefit. In doing so, however, we have also created a host of environmental problems. For a long time, many of these problems went unrecognized, but with the growth of technology and industry they became increasingly obvious. Even then, many people preferred to ignore what was happening to our environment, accepting it as "the price of progress."

Today, more people are becoming aware of the negative impact human activity has had upon the environment. Many of the negative changes that have occurred were not necessary, and awareness has helped us avoid making the environment worse. We can no longer plead ignorance about how our activities affect our world. We also are increasingly recognizing our responsibility toward protecting the environment and preserving our natural resources for future generations.

Ecology is the study of interactions in the environment. This study follows three basic natural laws:

1. Every system within nature is connected to every other system.
2. Once created, matter is never destroyed but is recycled in one way or another.
3. Natural resources are finite and nature's capacity to absorb the by-products of human technology is limited.

These three laws, separately and together, have powerful implications for the health of all people and the state of the environment. At first, these principles may seem beyond the individual's control, but this is not so. Each of us has a responsibility both to understand the laws of ecology and to realize that what we do as individuals affects the action of these laws. This is the most important single concept in the teaching of environmental health education.

Students must become aware that they are part of the planet's overall ecosystem and, as intelligent members of that ecosystem, they have both rights and responsibilities concerning the environment. This is a vital concept that must be stressed. Environmental health involves three main areas: ecosystems and ecology, pollution of the ecosphere, and preservation of the ecosphere. Each of these areas will be discussed in this chapter.

ECOSYSTEMS AND ECOLOGY

Each living thing, whether plant or animal, is part of an immediate **ecosystem** or habitat in which the living and nonliving components interact and interrelate. For example, all the organisms in a particular field or pond form an ecosystem. By interacting in a balanced fashion with all other parts of the ecosystem, a given species within that ecosystem can generally continue to thrive while perpetuating its population. This interrelationship and interdependence with other animals and plants in the environment produces a web of common sharing of most natural resources, including air, water, territorial space, sunlight, and soil minerals. An example of an ecosystem is shown in Figure 14.1. Nonliving natural resources are usually referred to as the **physical environment** comprising the given ecosystem, while living organisms are referred to as the **biotic environment** of the ecosystem.

Both environmental components of an ecosystem influence each other. When the physical environment is altered significantly, the biotic environment also changes significantly, and vice versa. As a result, ecosystems follow an interwoven natural organization of cycles between groups within the system to balance and stabilize the community. Yet, balance and stability themselves are dynamic processes, changing to adapt to the alterations in these cycles, which are changed by the varying interactions among the residents of the neighborhood and their use of natural resources. Since ecosystems are inherently unstable, therefore, they require an input of energy to maintain equilibrium or homeostasis. This input of energy produces a closed, self-sustaining cycle that fosters chains of interconnections. For example, decomposition within the system nurtures new life, one species feeds off another, and so forth. By nature's rules, all resources are recycled and continually reused in some form, since energy is always constant.

In addition, ecosystems are in continuous interaction with one another and are joined by the actions of the various physical and biotic environments to form a total worldwide ecosystem called the **ecosphere** or **biosphere**.

Figure 14.1 Ecosystem of a marsh

Source: *Environmental Education* by B. Robinson and E. Wolfson, 1982, New York: Teachers College Press.

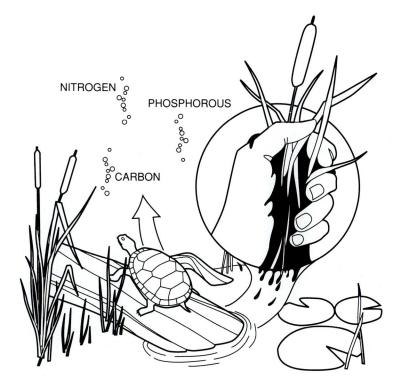

Humans, unlike any other species, can extensively manipulate both the physical and biotic environments of ecosystems, indirectly affecting the ecosphere as a whole. While many of these alterations in and of themselves are not inherently damaging, their cumulative impact has taken its toll on the ecosphere, sometimes overwhelming natural recycling mechanisms. Ecologists have pleaded for us to develop a greater understanding of the scientific principles that govern ecosystems to increase our awareness about our impact on the ecosphere. That way, more of our decisions about how we interact with the environment will be based on knowledge and logic rather than ignorance or greed. Ecologists have also warned of the grave danger facing our entire planet from depletion or pollution of its rich natural resources, which are finite and must be preserved for future generations.

POLLUTION OF THE ECOSPHERE

Pollution is the contamination of the environment resulting from an overabundance of substances that render the physical surroundings unfit, unsafe, or unsanitary for use or habitation by the residents of the ecosystem. While pollutants may initially appear to affect directly only a limited or select population within the ecosystem, such as birds and marine life, these substances eventually have an impact on all members of the ecosystem because of the interdependence and interaction between organisms. Human activity is the major cause of environmental pollution, but humans often experience the results of contamination much later than other

HEALTH HIGHLIGHT

Healthy People 2000 Objectives Related to Environmental Health

1. Reduce asthma morbidity, as measured by a reduction in asthma hospitalizations to no more than 160 per 100,000.
2. Reduce outbreaks of waterborne disease from infectious agents and chemical poisoning to no more than 11 per year.
3. Reduce the prevalence of blood lead levels . . . among children aged 6 months through 5 years to no more than 500,000 and zero respectively.
4. Reduce human exposure to criteria air pollutants, as measured by an increase to at least 85 percent in the proportion of people who live in counties that have not exceeded any EPA standard for air quality in the previous 12 months.
5. Increase to at least 40 percent the proportion of homes in which homeowners/occupants have tested for radon concentrations and that have either been found to pose minimal risk or have been modified to reduce risk to health.
6. Reduce human exposure to toxic agents by confining total pounds of toxic agents released into the air, water, and soil each year.
7. Reduce human exposure to solid waste-related water, air, and soil contamination, as measured by a reduction in average pounds of municipal solid waste produced per person each day to no more than 3.6 pounds.
8. Increase to at least 85 percent the proportion of people who receive a supply of drinking water that meets the safe drinking water standards established by the EPA.
9. Reduce potential risks to human health from surface water, as measured by a decrease to no more than 15 percent in the proportion of assessed rivers, lakes, and estuaries that do not support beneficial uses, such as fishing and swimming.
10. Perform testing for lead-based paint in at least 50 percent of homes built before 1950.
11. Expand to at least 35 the number of states in which at least 75 percent of local jurisdictions have adopted construction standards and techniques that minimize elevated indoor radon levels in those new building areas determined to have elevated radon levels.
12. Increase to at least 30 the number of states requiring that prospective buyers be informed of the presence of lead-based paint and radon concentrations in all buildings offered for sale.
13. Eliminate significant health risks from the National Priority List hazardous waste sites, as measured by performance of clean-up at these sites sufficient to eliminate immediate and significant health threats as specified in health assessments completed at all sites.
14. Establish programs for recyclable materials and household hazardous waste in at least 75 percent of counties.
15. Establish and monitor in at least 35 states plans to define and track sentinel environmental diseases.

Source: *Healthy People 2000,* U.S. Department of Health and Human Services, 1990, Washington, DC: U.S. Government Printing Office.

members of the ecosphere. As a result, although pollution of the environment has been occurring for centuries, we have only relatively recently become aware that polluting constitutes self-destructive behavior. The most crucial areas of concern include problems caused by overpopulation, air pollution, water pollution, hazardous chemical pollution, solid waste pollution, radiation pollution, and noise pollution.

Overpopulation

Many environmental health problems arise not so much from misuse of technology as from the sheer numbers of people on the planet. Earth simply does not have enough natural resources to support an unlimited human population.

In 1950, about 2.5 billion people occupied the earth; by 1990, the world population had reached 5.3 billion people. The population is expected to exceed 6 billion by 2000—an increase of over 17% in only a decade—and by the year 2050, that figure should reach between 10 and 10.5 billion. China currently has 1.1 billion, India has 833 million, the Commonwealth of Independent States (formerly USSR) has 289 million and the population of the United States is 250 million people (Payne & Hahn, 1992).

World shortages of food have already been occurring, largely because the population appears to be increasing twice as fast as the food supply. Even with advances in agricultural techniques and a more equitable balancing of food distribution and consumption, the earth's resources are going to be strained or depleted within the next century unless dramatic changes in lifestyles occur (Edlin & Golanty, 1992).

The consequences of uncontrolled world population growth go beyond the issue of food. In addition to hunger, it could cause joblessness, environmental devastation, and uncontrolled urban growth. In the last decade or two, many countries have attempted to deal with the problem of overpopulation by means of governmental incentives to limit births. Ethical and moral controversy surrounds the issue, which is understandably a very delicate and highly personal one to most individuals. Regardless of the ethical or moral considerations, however, overpopulation is a serious environmental problem that must be addressed—not only by governmental and private agencies but by the schools as well. Information about family planning and parenthood should be provided to junior high and high school students, and elementary school health programs should provide a foundation about families and population. Children need to understand that our planet will soon be unable to support the growing human population if reproduction rates continue at the present rate. While the solutions are not easy and decisions must ultimately be made by each individual, a world perspective should be provided as well. When one realizes that the world's population is increasing at the rate of 255,000 people per day or 90 million per year, it becomes easier to conceptualize overpopulation as a legitimate environmental health problem (Smith & Smith, 1990).

Air Pollution

Human beings, all 5.3 billion of us, need air more desperately than any other material for survival. People can endure drought, famine, and drastic temperature changes, but oxygen deprivation will result in death after only a few minutes. Yet most of us think very little about the air we breathe, what it contains, or how as a finite supply it is replenished and kept clean. Almost no oxygen was present in the atmosphere at the earth's creation, but an abundance of carbon dioxide was available for sustaining plant life. Over an evolutionary period, green plants began producing oxygen as a waste product of photosynthesis; today, the atmosphere is composed of approximately 80% nitrogen and 20% oxygen. While plants have been responsible for producing the oxygen humans and other animals need for life, humans have been largely responsible for polluting the atmosphere with a variety of harmful gases and other substances. The result is air pollution, an increasing environmental health problem in the United States and many other nations.

Exposure to high concentrations of air pollutants can cause a variety of health problems, ranging from sneezing and coughing to labored breathing and death. Individuals who are most sensitive to air pollution are usually older adults and people who have chronic respiratory or cardiovascular conditions. The chief air pollutants include carbon monoxide and nitrogen oxides, sulfur oxides, hydrocarbons, and particulate matter.

Carbon Monoxide and Nitrogen Oxides

Carbon monoxide, which accounts for almost half of the total emission of air pollutants, is a colorless, odorless, toxic gas whose chief source is the automobile. Because of hemoglobin's greater affinity for carbon monoxide than for oxygen, the blood is deprived of oxygen. An environment in which heavy traffic is present provides significant levels of carbon monoxide, and diminished physical and mental functioning can result from long-term exposure. Adverse effects include impaired breathing, hearing, vision and thought (Kane, 1987).

Nitrogen oxides, which account for about 6 percent of air pollutants, are chemically very similar to carbon monoxide. Poisonous nitrogen oxides, such as nitrogen dioxide and nitric acid, produce comparable physiological disturbances in the circulatory system. Nitrogen oxide combines with water vapor in the air to form nitric acid, a brown gas capable of corroding metal and destroying vegetation. As with carbon dioxide, the major source of nitric acid is the automobile.

HEALTH HIGHLIGHT
Global Warming: The Greenhouse Effect

Though it is still being debated, scientists predict that rising levels of carbon dioxide and other gases in the atmosphere are creating a greenhouse effect—trapping heat, affecting the earth's atmosphere, and causing a global warming trend. The atmospheric level of carbon dioxide, the primary greenhouse gas, has risen 25% since the 1850s. Most of the increase is due to the combustion of wood and fossil fuels, including coal, natural gas, and gasoline (mainly auto exhaust).

The EPA has estimated that the earth's overall temperature will rise as much as 8 degrees over the next 50–60 years if this trend continues. The result would be:

- melting of ice at the north and south poles
- rising sea levels
- coastal flooding
- permanent damage to some coastal areas
- expanded desert areas
- impeded growth of crops and livestock in some areas, and
- diminished world food supplies.

Source: *Life & Health: Targeting Wellness.* 1992, by M. Levy, M. Dignan, & J. Shirreffs, New York: McGraw-Hill.

Emissions from automobiles and other internal combustion engines is a major source of air pollution. This source produces most of the manufactured carbon monoxide. For example, 40% of the pollutants in the smog (smoke and fog combined) in cities like Los Angeles comes from automobile exhausts (Levy, Dignan, & Shirreffs, 1992).

Sulfur Oxides

Next to carbon monoxide, sulfur oxides are the most abundant air pollutant. These are poisonous gases that come from factories and power plants burning coal or oil containing sulfur. These gases form sulfur dioxide, a poison that irritates the eyes, nose, and throat, damages the lungs, kills plants, rusts metals, and reduces visibility (Edlin & Golanty, 1992).

Hydrocarbons

Although no specific ailments or irritations can be directly linked to the release of **hydrocarbons** (compounds comprised of hydrogen and carbon, these substances constitute an important component of smog. They account for 10% to 15% of all air pollution emissions.

Particulate Matter

Particulate matter refers to any nongaseous pollutant found in the air, whether liquid or solid. These pollutants include such substances as ash, soot, asbestos, and lead. Particulate matter is estimated to comprise approximately 8% of air emissions. Prolonged exposure to these pollutants can cause deterioration of the respiratory tract surfaces, particularly the cilia.

Lead

Sources of airborne lead are primarily smelters and automobile exhausts. (Unleaded gasoline has eased the problem of automobile exhaust pollution somewhat.) Health hazards from high concentrations of lead include irritability, anemia, convulsions, severe intestinal cramps, loss of consciousness, and kidney and brain damage. Lead enters the body primarily through the respiratory tract and sometimes through the stomach walls. Signs of lead poisoning are behavioral problems, anemia, decreased mental functioning, vomiting, and cramps.

Asbestos

In the past, asbestos was widely used in construction and manufacturing; because of that, most exposures occur in occupational settings. Asbestos can cause serious respiratory problems, such as emphysema, and has been implicated in lung cancer.

Toxic substances, the final major source of air pollution, are generally the products of technology and have not been studied extensively. These substances include natural elements such as arsenic and mercury and synthetic products such as polyvinyl chlorides, asbestos, and pesticides. Some are highly toxic, causing cancer and death.

Conditions Resulting from Air Pollution

Air pollution causes serious damage to human well-being, property, and plant and animal life. In addition, air pollution can lead to serious environmental problems, including acid rain and temperature inversions.

Pollution Damage. In terms of human welfare, air pollution exacerbates such respiratory conditions as coughs, colds, asthma, pneumonia, and bronchitis, as well as cancer and even heart disease. Pollution can also severely harm animals and plant life. When crop dusters spray pesticides, only about a quarter lands on the crop, less than 1% may hit the target insects, and the rest drifts miles away. The insecticides kill birds, frogs, and predatory insects. Falcons and eagles have become extinct in some local areas as a result of pesticide spraying. Herbicides sprayed on forest lands have caused miscarriages, cancer, and birth defects and wiped out local wildlife as well as pets and livestock. Vegetation may change color or fail to pollinate. Animals grazing on affected land can be contaminated.

Finally, air pollution damages our houses, apartments, and public buildings. Buildings become darkened and discolored as a result of air pollution. Contaminants damage public works of art and monuments. Unfortunately, today's high technology produces new pollutants faster than the scientific community is able to study their effects. These by-products may pose as-yet-undiscovered serious health problems.

Acid Rain. The primary cause of acid rain is the burning of fossil fuels in electric generating plants. The burning converts the sulfur in fuel to sulfur oxides. If rain, snow, dew, or mist are present, sulfuric and nitric acids form. Most of the sulfur pollution originates east of the Mississippi River. Much of the pollution that originates in the United States is deposited in Canada. Throughout the eastern parts of Canada and the United States, acid rain changes soil acid levels, ruins the eggs of amphibians and fish, and makes lakes and streams more acidic. As the water becomes more acidic, life begins to disappear from the water, thus disrupting the ecosystem and eventually affecting all of our lives.

Temperature Inversions. When a warm air mass moves over cooler air near the ground, a temperature inversion results. The cooler air cannot be dissipated. Temperature inversions decrease visibility and allow pollutants to build up, making the air unsafe for breathing. The trapped pollutants are subjected to sunlight, causing them to produce other pollutants, such as ozone. The temperature inversion eventually disperses, but illness and even death have resulted from this condition.

Water Pollution

Like air, water is essential to life. Despite its importance, we dump everything from animal fertilizer and detergents to industrial wastes and sewage into our precious water supply. In addition, when pollutants are channeled into nonflowing bodies of water, such as lakes, eutrophication—accelerated growth of algae—occurs. As algae growth skyrockets on a diet of inorganic pollutants, especially nitrogen and phosphorous, a blanket of slime covers the water. The algae die, resulting in bacterial decomposition that consumes the oxygen present. This oxygen deficit kills off fish and other lake inhabitants, many of which are valuable as food resources.

When pollutants are dumped into nonflowing bodies of water, algae form, robbing the water's inhabitants of their essential oxygen and killing them.

Eventually, the body of water becomes contaminated beyond use. Even flowing bodies of water, such as streams and rivers, that undergo natural purification can be badly polluted if sufficient amounts of wastes are dumped.

Water pollution has numerous sources. The main ones are industrial wastes, animal fertilizers, human sewage, and thermal pollution.

Industrial Wastes

Chemical by-products from the manufacture of paper, steel, oil, pesticides, and the life account for more than half of the water pollution in this country. Despite water pollution laws, an abundance of diverse industrial wastes continues to be disposed of in lakes, streams, and rivers throughout the country. Many, like lead and mercury, are known to be toxic to humans. An important concern about any industrial waste product is the length of time the environment takes to break it down and the amount that humans and other organisms can tolerate.

Animal Fertilizers

Agriculture is one of the major sources of water pollution. Many animal fertilizers are particularly rich in nitrogen, thus adding to the problem of eutrophication and oxygen depletion of bodies of water. Also, use of fertilizer often results in diminishing returns: The more fertilizer used, the less it helps (Levy, Dignan, & Shirreffs, 1992).

Human Sewage

Although contamination of water from human waste is much less serious than it once was, it still can occur in varying degrees if a community's sewage treatment system is antiquated or not regularly inspected. Sewage should undergo two treatment stages, primary and secondary. During the primary stage, water, which has been allowed to settle in a holding tank, is ridded of large objects through a filtration process that passes the liquid over a series of screens. During the secondary treatment stage, smaller particles of organic material and microbes are removed through additional filtration techniques, dispersement over beds of stone, and chemical purification. The final step usually involves the addition of chlorine to disinfect the water of any remaining bacteria and make it safe for recycling.

Thermal Pollution

Numerous industries, including those involved in generating nuclear power, use water as a coolant for their equipment. Water absorbs heat from the equipment and is channeled back to its source, where it increases the source water temperature. While this process seems harmless enough, the warmer water is, the less oxygen it will absorb, and the less oxygen absorbed, the slower organic matter in the lake or river decomposes. Since power-generating plants heat particularly large volumes of water, the parent waterway is certainly at risk. In addition, the high temperatures drastically affect much of the aquatic life.

Effects of Water Pollution

Polluted water can transmit many pathogens. For example, typhoid fever, dysentery, cholera, and parasitic worms are just a few of the diseases that can be transmitted through polluted water. Viruses from human waste carried in contaminated water can cause hepatitis. Bacteria found in polluted water can cause intestinal disorders. Other materials found in polluted water, such as asbestos fibers, can cause cancer.

Polluted water can be particularly harmful to fish, birds, and animals. For example, herbicides, phosphates, fertilizers, sewage, and industrial wastes kill numerous fish and birds. These products also promote the growth of algae, which changes the ecological balance. In addition, they produce odors and foul-tasting drinking water. Fish also may be affected by rising water temperature, which retards their reproduction, destroys their food supplies, or kills them.

The oil slicks of recent years and their devastation of wildlife have been widely publicized. Oil coats the gills of fish, killing them. It covers feathers of birds, preventing them from flying. Oil-covered beaches are also expensive to clean, and the public loses recreational areas.

Hazardous Chemical Pollution

The hazardous chemicals that pollute our environment are numerous and varied. They include not only the toxins deposited in our air and waterways, but also the pesticides sprayed on crops, the chemicals transported along our railways and highways for use in industry, and those contained in commonly used household products.

Pesticides

With the 1962 publication of Rachel Carson's *Silent Spring,* people grew more conscious of the hazards of pesticides, toxic chemicals used to kill insects and other pests that destroy crops. In past decades, the harm caused by the widespread use of chlorinated hydrocarbons like aldrin, dieldrin, and DDT as pesticides was not fully recognized. These chemicals are particularly dangerous not only because they are toxic, but also because they accumulate in human tissue, since they are fat-soluble. Traces of DDT, probably the most widely disseminated pesticide in the world, are said to exist in all Americans. DDT was banned from use in the United States (Edlin & Golanty, 1992).

Chlorinated hydrocarbons decompose very slowly and remain toxic to a wide variety of animal life for long periods. Organophosphorous pesticides like diazinon, parathion, and malathion exhibit similar properties and are even more poisonous than the chlorinated hydrocarbons.

Although worldwide food production must be increased to meet the demands of a growing population, extensive use of pesticides can cause great harm to environmental health in the process. Questions still must be answered concerning the implication of long-term exposure to moderate or even minimal levels of pesticides. Evidence shows that these chemicals can damage the human reproductive and nervous systems, for example. It is obvious, therefore, that the use of pesticides must be limited and controlled to protect all inhabitants of our ecosphere.

Industrial Chemicals

One of the newest, most dangerous environmental threats is the transportation of industrial chemicals from state to state and from country to country. While transportation itself is not inherently dangerous, leakage or spills of chemical substances most certainly is. In fact, hardly a week goes by without news of such an accident that causes disability or death. Accidents involving the transportation of oil and other petroleum products (e.g., the Exxon Valdez in Alaska) have also resulted in major oil spills that have damaged some of our nation's most beautiful beaches and killed or endangered countless birds and marine life.

In response to this increasingly dangerous threat, many state governments and the federal government have formed special subcommittees to study the problem of transporting industrial chemicals. Movement of radioactive material across states for industrial and burial purposes has caused particular concern. More controls and safeguards need to be implemented in transporting hazardous chemicals of any kind, whether by truck, ship, or train.

Household Products

Before the recent ban on spray cans containing fluorocarbon propellants and detergents containing phosphates, numerous household products contaminated the environment by releasing these agents into the air and water, respectively. Fluorocarbons destroy the protective ozone layer of the atmosphere that shields us from the sun's damaging ultraviolet rays, while phosphates serve as excellent nutrients for bacteria, protozoa, and algae, promoting eutrophication of lakes, streams, and rivers. These examples serve as an excellent illustration of the dangers involved in releasing seemingly harmless compounds into our surroundings from heavily used household products like cleansers, polishes, waxes, and sprays of all kinds without first studying their environmental impact before marketing them.

Solid Waste Pollution

Until recently, the public virtually ignored the problems related to the disposal of solid wastes. Each year in the United States, we junk about 7 million autos, 75 billion cans, bottles, and jars; and 200 million tons of trash and garbage. The U.S. Public Health Service has categorized over 90% of the thousands of authorized hazardous waste disposal sites as posing "unacceptable" health risks. Hazardous wastes consist of materials that are flammable, corrosive, toxic, or chemically reactive. About 35 million tons of such wastes are produced each year in the United States (Edlin & Golanty, 1992).

Today, we use more and more "convenience" products that are easily disposed of and replaced—everything from disposable diapers, dishes, and food containers to plastic wraps, sanitary products, and paper napkins. The price of this convenience has been the growing problem of solid waste disposal. The unsightly junkyards, dumps, and scattered litter that dot our land are more than just eyesores. They are a public health hazard as well.

Many solid waste materials are not biodegradable and remain in the environment for long periods because they do not decay or cannot be burned easily. The piles of refuse serve as excellent breeding grounds for microorganisms, rats, insects, and other disease carriers. In addition, agricultural waste products from orchards, feedlots, and farms add significantly to the total solid waste that must be disposed of each year. How, then, do we rid ourselves of all this refuse? Methods primarily used today include dumps, sanitary landfills, recycling, and incineration.

HEALTH HIGHLIGHT
The Shrinking Ozone Layer

The ozone layer is a part of the upper atmosphere where ozone traps the most dangerous ultraviolet radiations. Ozone is created by the energy of sunlight acting upon ordinary oxygen. Chlorofluorocarbons (CFCs)—gases used in fire extinguishers, refrigerators, and air conditioning units—rise into the atmosphere and damage this protective layer. Formerly, there were high levels of CFCs in aerosol cans, but strict regulations control CFC levels in these products now. Also, more consumers are changing to nonaerosol sprays which contain little or no CFCs.

The results of a shrinking ozone layer include increases in skin cancer, particularly malignant melanoma. Most countries have agreed to cooperate to reduce this problem and to produce alternatives to the chemicals causing the ozone layer to shrink; however, some scientists believe that the replacements are more powerful greenhouse gases that also may contribute to global warming.

Source: *An Invitation to Health* (5th ed.), by D. Hales, 1992, Redwood City, CA: Benjamin/Cummings.

Dumps

Most solid waste in this country is deposited in open, minimally managed dumps. Some garbage is burned to condense the material. Besides being extremely unsightly, open dumping grounds can pose a serious threat to a community's health if the insect or rodent population gets out of control. Dumps are popular, however, because they are inexpensive in the short term.

Sanitary Landfills

Unlike the open disposal in a dump, sanitary landfills require covering the solid waste with soil each day after it has been compacted. Once covered with dirt, the landfill is bulldozed, smoothing out and compressing the area. A properly operated sanitary landfill requires predetermined design and engineering of the site as well as continued daily maintenance from a crew of sanitation workers. However, the benefits of a well-functioning landfill can be numerous. Because refuse is covered daily, it considerably lowers the risk of a contaminated water supply or of disease due to the breeding of flies, mosquitoes, rats, and the life. Since burning is not necessary, the technique does not contribute to air pollution. In addition, after the location has been completely filled in, it can serve some other valuable purpose, such as a site for housing, recreation, or industry.

Sanitary landfills do pose some problems, however. Land itself is growing scarcer and more expensive, not all types of terrain are suitable to serve as landfills, and the surrounding water table must be low enough. In addition, residents often oppose the establishment of a sanitary landfill nearby for fear that it will lower property values.

Recycling

Many products can be recycled, or reused in another mode, including paper, glass, metal, and many plastic products. This method of solid waste control gained some popularity during the environmentally conscious era of the late 1960s and early 1970s. Today, many communities require households to recycle some materials. Other communities provide recycling centers to which residents can bring recyclable materials. Some communities merely ask residents to place recyclable materials out for pickup in front of their homes. These projects have decreased the amount of unrecycled solid waste significantly.

Incineration

Like dumping, incineration is a very old method of waste disposal that adds to environmental pollution because of the release of particulate matter into the atmosphere during burning. Of particular danger is the release of hydrogen chloride from burning plastic materials, which are mainly composed of polyvinyl chloride. Upon contact with moisture in the air, hydrogen chloride forms hydrochloric acid, an especially corrosive agent that causes respiratory irritation.

On the other hand, the energy and heat produced as a by-product of incineration can be used in homes and industry. Many locations throughout Europe have successfully incinerated solid wastes for this purpose; some locations in the United States are also trying it. Many incinerators in this country would need to be redesigned and rebuilt to accomplish this on a broad level. As it stands, incineration is already one of the costliest waste disposal methods. Nevertheless, incineration as a generator of energy deserves more investigation.

Radiation Pollution

Individuals are exposed to radiation daily from both natural sources, such as sunlight, and artificial sources. The artificial sources of radiation are of most concern. Radio-active materials release energy in the form of a stream of particles generally referred to as radiation. Alpha and beta radioactive particles do not easily penetrate the human body, but gamma particles do. Gamma rays are much like X rays. If an individual is exposed to a high enough dosage of gamma radiation, a number of adverse effects result, ranging from nausea, hair loss, and diarrhea to cell mutation, anemia, and death.

Individuals in the United States come into contact with radiation mainly through medical testing and X rays. Although X rays are generally safe, many instances of unnecessary exposure have been reported. Intervals of several months should elapse between X rays if multiple X rays are necessary. Pregnant women, particularly during the first trimester, should avoid X rays entirely if possible, because radiation can cause cell damage and mutation in the developing fetus.

Exposure to low-level radiation for a prolonged period is also of great concern for individuals whose work surroundings or home environment may be near a radioactive source. Radiation adversely affects the digestive system and the tissues that form the blood. Significant doses of radiation can cause infertility, miscarriages, and birth defects (Kane, 1987). As a result, opponents to the use of nuclear power as an energy source are becoming more vocal. They fear both the potential for a nuclear accident and the dangers of mishandling the disposal of nuclear wastes. On the other hand, supporters of nuclear power believe that through implementation of the Nuclear Regulatory Commission's guidelines, nuclear power can be a safe, viable, and much needed energy source for the future.

Noise Pollution

With more and more U.S. people living in metropolitan areas, the problem of noise as a pollutant is also growing. Noise pollution is a problem for almost every urban dweller and a particular cause of concern among people living near airports, employees working in manufacturing or industry, and commuters who must endure hours of noise each week traveling in cars, trains, buses, and subways. Also, listening to loud music, especially through earphones, is a noise pollutant that is a potential cause of hearing loss.

Noise levels are calculated in decibels (db), with 1 db representing the minimum level of hearing for humans. A sound that is 10 times as loud would be 10 db, another 100 times as loud would be 20 db, one 1000 times as loud would be 30 db, and so forth. Some typical noise levels include whispering (30 db), normal conversation or sewing machine (60 db), busy traffic (70 db), truck noise (90 db), airplane overhead or chainsaw (100 db), rock concert in front of speakers (120), shotgun blast (140 db), or a rocket pad during launch (180 db).

Temporary hearing impairment may result from even limited exposure to a loud noise source 80 to 85 db and above, while permanent hearing loss can result from lengthy or chronic exposure to loud noise. High-frequency hearing in particular seems to be affected. Sounds below 70 db appear relatively safe to the human ear, regardless of exposure duration (Payne & Hahn, 1992).

Apart from hearing impairment, noise can cause many detrimental side effects of its stressful nature. Headaches, sleeping difficulty, increase in anxiety, and elevated blood pressure are just a few. As a result, noise pollution should be abated.

PRESERVATION OF THE ECOSPHERE

Conservation and protection of our natural resources must stem from both individual and public action. Both are needed to stabilize and eventually reverse the deleterious cycle of contamination plaguing the ecosphere. Legislation and implementation of healthier environmental practices have been instituted. Enacting additional measures could serve to improve the quality of living for us and for future generations.

Population Control

The problems resulting from overpopulation are well recognized in such countries as China and India, where the governments have established incentives to limit child bearing. Prior to the availability of the condom and the diaphragm in the nineteenth century, birth control methods were generally unsafe and did not enjoy widespread use. The introduction to the general public of the birth control pill and the intrauterine device (IUD) in the 1960s, however, along with improved female and male sterilization techniques introduced in the 1970s, birth control has gained acceptance throughout the world. In addition, information about contraceptive methods is now disseminated to preteens, teenagers, young adults, and older adults alike. Although some individuals and groups believe instruction about birth control is ill-advised in a school setting, many school systems nevertheless have incorporated such instruction into the curriculum. The establishment of various kinds of family planning services throughout the United States and in many other nations has also aided in increasing contraceptive education.

In the United States, population growth has stabilized. The average age for marriage has increased and many young couples delay parenthood to advance educationally or professionally. In Third World countries, where population control is more of a problem, efforts are needed to provide the same kind of education and services offered in the more technologically advanced nations. It must be recognized, however, that decisions about pregnancy are deeply personal, cultural, religious, and social in nature and should be based on free choice.

Air Pollution Control

Congress established the Environmental Protection Agency (EPA) in 1970 as the federal environmental watchdog agency. Under the provisions of the Clean Air Act of

1970, the EPA set national ambient air quality standards for **criteria pollutants**, the most common air pollutants. Examples of criteria pollutants are ozone, particulate matter, carbon monoxide, sulfur dioxide, lead, and nitrogen dioxide. The EPA also determines the potential health hazards for **hazardous pollutants**, those known to cause death or serious illness. Examples of hazardous pollutants are asbestos, beryllium, mercury, vinyl chloride, arsenic, benzene, and coke oven emissions (Smith & Smith, 1990).

Air quality standards were initially issued in 1971 by the EPA and were amended in 1987. Many geographic regions have made progress in reducing air pollutants, but much work remains.

Water Quality Control

Although federal controls regarding water pollution have not been as extensive as those for air pollution, the Federal Water Pollution Control Act was enacted in 1973 as a means of developing a national system that would require any institution, industry, or company that discharges substances into waterways to meet EPA standards. In addition, congress passed the Safe Drinking Water Act in 1974, which covers 40,000 community water supply systems and another 200,000 private systems. This act requires these systems to meet federal drinking water safety standards and is considered a difficult law to enforce (Edlin & Golanty, 1992).

Hazardous Chemical Control

With governmental regulation of DDT in 1973, national attention focused on the dangers of pesticides in general. As a result, more sensible approaches to crop spraying have evolved. Nonetheless, the widespread use of pesticides still poses a danger to environmental health.

Solid Waste Control

In the 1970s, Congress created the Superfund for the purpose of cleaning up old dump sites filled with solid and hazardous wastes. Under this law, the EPA can clean up a dump site, and then recover the costs from those responsible through lawsuits. In addition, in 1988 the EPA set forth a plan that called for Americans to recycle 25% of their household trash by 1992. Voluntary recycling efforts aid these mandatory efforts. (Levy, Dignan, & Shirreffs, 1992).

The United States, like many other nations, is still struggling with the problem of solid waste. Until citizens recognize that many solid waste disposal programs are ineffective or unacceptable, the situation is unlikely to change. More public awareness and action are needed to draw attention to the problem of solid waste disposal. In addition, individual efforts to decrease the daily use of disposable products that are not easily biodegradable as well as efforts aimed at recycling can assist greatly.

Radiation Exposure Control

Guidelines exist for allowable ranges of radiation exposure from medical testing, X rays, and consumer products emitting small amounts of radiation, such as television sets. However, the long-term effects upon health of even low or "safe" levels of radiation are still poorly understood. *Any* radiation may in fact be deleterious to health. As individuals, we must become more educated and aware of both the benefits and dangers of using radiation and nuclear power.

Noise Pollution Control

Acceptable noise levels for school, home, and work environments have not been determined. Each individual, therefore, must exercise personal judgment in deciding how much noise exposure is not only tolerable but safe. Employees in industry are, of course, issued protective ear devices, but the general public is not guaranteed the same protection on noisy highways or in neighborhoods near loud noise sources. Greater awareness of the harmful effects of noise, both physical and psychological, may lead to public action and legislation in the years ahead.

■ ■ ■   *STUDENT CONCERNS:* ENVIRONMENTAL HEALTH

Students in grades 7 through 12 have many issues of concern about environmental health. The statements reflected under the various grades are from *Students Speak* (Trucano, 1984):

HEALTH HIGHLIGHT
What You Can Do

Because environmental health is such a major problem involving so many people, you may feel that an individual effort may be futile; however, such is not the case. First, you can become informed and become involved on a local as well as a national and/or international level.

Further, the following specific daily actions will contribute to a healthier environment:

1. Reduce air pollution by using your auto less frequently—carpool, walk, or ride a bike when you can;
2. Recycle paper, aluminum, glass, and plastics;
3. Do not pour solvents, cleaners, or other toxic chemicals down the drain;
4. Purchase products in biodegradable containers when available;
5. Put grass clippings, leaves and vegetable waste into a compost heap. If you don't have a lawn, contribute these materials to someone who does;
6. Use low-phosphate dish and laundry detergent;
7. Limit the use of pesticides, and when you use them, use organic fertilizers and insecticides;
8. Insulate your home with fiberglass or cellulose insulation instead of rigid urethane foams containing CFCs; and,
9. Minimize the use of gasoline-powered lawn mowers (use electric), charcoal lighter fluid (use newspaper), and chemical paint thinners (use water-soluble latex paint).

Source: *Personal Health Choices* by S. Smith and C. Smith, 1990, Boston: Jones and Bartlett.

Grade 8

> How do you cope with disasters or natural catastrophes that you might be involved with?

Grade 9

> How do you control panic during an accident or disaster?
> What causes cancer and related things?
> Are the health regulations strong enough to protect society?
> Are the new medical machines safer or more dangerous than the out-of-date machines?
> What are the effects of radiation on the body?

Grade 10

> I think a knowledge of what to do in a disaster and how to prevent infant accidents is important.
> How can accidents be prevented?

Grade 11

> I would like to learn more about cancer. A lot of people in my family have died from cancer and I would like to understand it better.

SUMMARY

Individual efforts undertaken to maintain and promote personal health, no matter how responsible and diligent, cannot ensure high level wellness unless the environment in which one lives is free of dangerous levels of pollutants and therefore conducive to quality living—not just mere survival. To maintain the natural resources upon which all living things depend, we must understand how we interact with and influence our ecosystem, our immediate habitat.

Many human inventions have cause havoc in the natural ecological chains or webs within ecosystems. Because ecosystems, like the residents within them, are interdependent and thus form one worldwide ecosphere, the deleterious impact of human growth and technology affects the entire planet. In sheer numbers alone, our species is stretching the capacity of land, water, and food supplies to accommodate us. In addition, particularly in the highly industrial nations, human lifestyles have resulted in an abundance of pollution problems that the natural cycles within the ecosphere cannot accommodate. Our automobiles release dangerous pollutants into the air. Industry adds still other toxins. Runoff from agriculture and industrial dumping contaminate our water. In addition, hardly a week goes by without some incident involving the accidental leakage or spilling of highly lethal substances being transported.

These environmental health problems, coupled with those of solid waste disposal, radiation exposure, and noise pollution, have resulted in ecological crises never before witnessed. Continued research and education, which will spark responsible action on the part of both governments and individuals, can help preserve the ecosphere. It is our job as educators to provide instructional and consciousness-raising experiences to the children we teach so that their children and grandchildren will enjoy continued health and well-being in a sound environment.

DISCUSSION QUESTIONS

1. Define and differentiate between the terms *environment* and *ecology.*
2. Identify three basic laws of ecology and tell how each affects the state of the environment.
3. What is the ecosphere and how do human beings interact with elements of it?
4. What impact does overpopulation have upon the state of the environment and what problems directly or indirectly stem from overpopulation?
5. What are the major sources of air pollution? Describe the harmful effects of specific air pollutants upon human health.
6. Why are pesticides a particularly dangerous form of pollution?
7. What steps can be taken to more effectively manage and control solid waste?
8. What threats to environmental health does the transportation of hazardous substances pose?
9. What is noise pollution? How does it affect environmental health?
10. How can each individual help to preserve the ecosphere? Give specific suggestions.

■ ■ ■ *ACTIVITIES FOR TEACHING ENVIRONMENTAL HEALTH*

■ ■ ■ *ACTIVITIES:* PUZZLES AND GAMES

Health or Hazard? A Post-China Syndrome Game*

How important is it to teach about ionizing radiation or noise protection or industrial safety? For most students, these three topics seem remote and removed from the classroom. However, the movie, *The China Syndrome,* made the Three Mile Island incident and the hazards of radiation hauntingly realistic. Students and teachers in the Harrisonburg area were undoubtedly affected and students elsewhere certainly felt curiosity and a need to know more facts. What better place to bring together the topics of radiation and health hazards of the working environment than in an environmental health course or in a unit on environmental health? And how better to make learning more fun than with a game?

Fun and success with such a game, called "Health or Hazard?", are attributed to proper orientation and to student involvement and discovery. Orientation to the game consists of a cognitive introduction to the basic forms of radiation (e.g., ionizing—alpha, beta, gamma rays, and non-ionizing—microwaves) and how to use time, distance, and shielding for protection. A cognitive introduction to health hazards of the working environment should cover the detrimental effects on humans of noise, dust, gases, and toxic liquids. Protection measures would include environmental manipulation, medical surveillance, management decisions, and personal protection. Students should be taught to adapt such principles to specific hazards (that is where much of the learning occurs).

*Source: *Health Education Teaching Ideas* (pp. 104) by R. Loya, Reston, VA: American Alliance for Health, Physical Education, Recreation, and Dance.

Following cognitive input, the teacher should divide the class into three equal-sized and intellectually-matched groups. One group will be student referees with responsibility for awarding points and making decisions regarding disagreements between sides. Their preparation will consist of correctly matching hazards with proper health protection methods.

The two other groups will be competing teams. Each team should prepare itself independently. Based on the cognitive information given in class, each team should prepare an array of "offensive" hazards and an arsenal of "defensive" health protection measures. Each hazard and each health protection measure should be written on a separate index card large enough so that it can be read across a classroom.

The spirit of competition between the two sides fosters a spirit of cooperation on each side. Team members naturally help each other in learning the associations between hazards and the proper health protection.

Competition begins after about fifteen minutes of preparation. Each side alternately chooses a player from the opposite team to "challenge." Each challenge is considered a "round." Each team alternately assumes an offensive and defensive position.

During the round the offensive player chooses a hazard with which to "attack" the defensive player. The hazard is hidden from view until the offensive and defensive players face each other in the front of the classroom. The defensive player brings his arsenal of methods. On a signal from the judge, the offensive player flashes his hazard. The defensive player has fifteen seconds to respond by showing the card with the correct health protection measure against that hazard. If the correct health protection measure is not on one of the defensive player's cards, the defensive player has the same fifteen-second time limit to write the proper health protection on a separate index card. No coaching from teammates is allowed.

A score results when either side wins a "round." Decisions regarding which side wins will be made by the student judge for that particular round. The student judge must decide whether the defensive player's response is correct and made within the fifteen-second limit. (The time should be kept by another judge.) If the defensive player displays the correct response within the time limit, the defensive side scores a point. If not, the offensive side wins a point. The first team to win a predetermined number of points wins.

For greater variety and excitement, more than one hazard can be introduced at one time, forcing the defensive players to respond more quickly. This game can be played at the pace of the students. It is fun, exciting, and a harmless way to learn health protection measures against radiation and hazards of the working environment.

Health and Safety Education from the Trash Can*

As educators, we constantly dream of ways to obtain effective visual aids to help us develop concepts; however, the difficulty of getting school monies appropriated for

---

*Source: *Health Education Teaching Ideas* (pp. 106–107) by R. Loya, Reston, VA: American Alliance for Health, Physical Education, Recreation, and Dance.

visual aids to enhance classroom presentations too often confronts us. I am going to share a secret of how to cope with, even *enjoy,* two problems of our everyday existence—teaching on a shoestring budget and taking out the trash! The trash can offers unlimited potential for collecting an abundance of effective teaching aids. My recent practice of accumulating discarded items provides a wealth of invaluable materials for the classroom that we can use effectively to develop important health and safety concepts.

In my collection is a necktie which is ripped and tattered. It makes me think back to early spring, several years ago. I was itching to get my boat in the water so, on returning home from church, I announced that anyone who wanted to go to the lake should be ready to leave in five minutes. My wife objected saying that I had promised to build some kitchen shelves for her and that I was not leaving the house until the job was done. Needless to say, I was in no mood to build kitchen shelves! Rushing like a madman, I started to cut a board with the circular saw and the next thing I knew, my tie was tangled in the saw blade which was rapidly approaching my throat! Looking at the mutilated tie and thinking about the close call, I suddenly realized what a perfect visual aid this would make in teaching about hazard potential of various items of clothing. I saved the tie and it became the first of many items in my "trash can collection."

A plastic cup brings to mind a personal example of how an accidental poisoning might occur. I wanted to make a smoking machine out of a liquid detergent bottle so I went into our kitchen, grabbed the soap bottle, and poured its contents into a plastic cup, placed the plastic cup on the window sill and began making the smoking machine.

About a week later, Tom was making lemonade for the twins and found only one clean glass in the cupboard. Looking around, he spied the plastic cup on the window sill and filled it with lemonade for Robby. Robby took a big drink and started to cough and choke tearfully. His mother came running in and said, "What's the matter? Is your lemonade too sour?" She took the glass from him and sampled it herself to see what was wrong, and she's been blowing bubbles ever since! This is an excellent example of how poisonings occur in the home! We are fortunate that the glass didn't contain drain cleaner, automatic dishwasher detergent, or other toxic substances which would have caused extensive tissue damage. By this example, we can learn quite a lesson about proper storage.

Other trash that can be used to teach about poisons is abundant. A paint can with a "lead-free" label is an appropriate visual aid when teaching about lead poisoning. A rusty, swollen or dented food can might be the focus of questions designed to stimulate an awareness of food poisoning.

Once your trash collection becomes well known, others will bring you items and stories to add.

"I'd like to donate this to your trash collection," said one of my students as he handed me an old extension cord. The cord was peeling and cracked and dried out with wires exposed. He had used this under the carpet for several years. Instead of just telling students not to run extension cords under rugs, this cord can show how friction will break down the insulation. When students were asked to suggest ways that the cord might have become so abused, they told of pets which had chewed through extension cords and about times when heavy duty appliances were used on light duty extension cords causing the cord to deteriorate. One of the values of utilizing items from the trash can is that they act as discussion stimulators providing students with opportunities to share personal experiences.

One such experience involved a handmade sweater which our twins decided to use as a replacement for their lampshade when redecorating their room. The light bulb encrusted with charred wool and the tiny sweater with a hole the size of a grapefruit tell the rest of the story. Luckily, it was a wool sweater! Had it been made with synthetic yarn, it could have caused a fire instead of smoldering as it did. With the seater and light bulb or other wearing apparel the concept of flammability in clothing could be explored.

The topic of home fires is rich with bizarre stories. This past summer, I heard a lot of commotion in the kitchen, so I came running in from the back yard and saw flames shooting out from behind the refrigerator. The coils on the back of the refrigerator had come into contact with the plug; over a period of time, vibrations had caused the coils to cut through the insulation. The melted plug is a good reminder that we should regularly check our electrical appliances.

In my trash collection I have a dish towel that touched the lower heating element in the oven. A section of it burned away when it was being used as a pot holder and the unsuspecting cook had a fire.

As a child, you probably enjoyed playing with tape measures. Jeff was no exception. While watching TV, he was reeling out a tape measure and watching it spring back. As he reeled it out, the end dropped between a chair and the far wall; Jeff flew out of his chair, eyes like saucers and hair standing on end. The metal tape had come into contact with the prong of a lamp plug which was not all the way into the receptacle. The other end hit the aluminum frame around the sliding glass patio door. At the contact points, the tape melted and charred. Jeff's tape clearly illustrates how seemingly harmless activities can be dangerous if the right conditions exist.

The average person can do little to prevent the unexpected; however, a safety conscious individual can take measures to guard against common hazards. When purchasing electrical appliances how careful are you to look for the Underwriters Laboratory (U.L.) label? When I found a battery charger at an unbelievably low price I looked on the display card and found the U.L. label. It wasn't until sometime later that I realized the U.L. approval applied only to the cord and plug—not the battery charger. How often we have been led into a false sense of security by not reading the fine print!

Items like the extension cord, sweater, refrigerator plug, tape measure, and U.L. labels are discarded daily. Alert your friends and students to save these types of items for you. It has been our experience that students are much more willing to listen, share, and remember examples of home hazards than they are to memorize lecture notes of do's and don'ts.

Hundreds of suffocations occur in homes each year. Students become directly involved when I introduce the subject of suffocation by placing a plastic bag over my head. I demonstrate when plastic bags are and are not dangerous. A plastic bag, tied in knots, will illustrate the proper method for its disposal.

My mother-in-law receives shirts from the cleaners in plastic bags which she uses for jobs around the house. When the twins were three, they discovered those bags in Grandmother's kitchen. They were just the right size to get over their heads. I happened to walk in just as Robyn pulled one down over her eyes and nose. Had she been more successful, she would have been in great danger of suffocation. A larger plastic bag in my collection was on a crib mattress at a hotel which could have tragic consequences if tired parents don't take time to check for such hazards.

Many other household helpers can be hazards. We all know that power tools should be handled with great respect, but often there is a tendency to abuse or be careless with "everyday" tools. You probably have a screwdriver with a blade that chipped because the tool was used as a chisel, a crowbar, or something else for which it wasn't designed. When there is finally an opportunity to tighten a screw, there's not enough blade. As you apply pressure, trying to turn the screw, there is danger of personal injury as pressure causes the broken blade to slip from the screw head.

Another example is my 98¢ bargain hammer which was designed for light use such as driving tacks or small nails. When the kids decided to build a fort in the back yard, they used my hammer to drive spikes. Half the spikes went in crooked so they tried to pull them out. All of a sudden the claw broke, and there was a flying missile that might have put out an eye. These would-be-architects also damaged my hammer so that the head would no longer fit. To avoid upsetting me, they left it on the workbench just as they had found it, saying "Wrong." A week later, as I was working on a project the hammer head flew off and sailed through the garage window onto the hood of my car. Are you saving your plastic bags, broken screwdrivers and hammers as aids in developing concepts relating to hand tools and home safety?

Annually, hundreds of youngsters are fatally injured as a result of home firearm accidents. Many of these accidents occur because youngsters don't understand the danger of firearms. It is not uncommon for children to consider .22 caliber guns as toys because of the small size of the cartridge. In an attempt to make students appreciate the destructive capabilities of a small bore gun, I showed them a soft drink can which was shot with a .22 hollow point. This mutilated metal creates a lasting impression when used to illustrate the damage a .22 caliber bullet could inflict on a human body. Gunshot wounds can also be explored with X rays obtained from a radiologist. My X ray of a skull that had been penetrated by a BB clearly illustrates the importance of safe gun handling.

These items are examples of numerous objects that can be recycled from the trash to the classroom. As educators know, the more we can do to allow students to identify with our subject matter the more we can enhance the learning process. By using common items of junk as a focal point for discussing real life situations, teachers can help students develop important concepts concerning their own health and safety. Tight school budgets and rising inflation might be just the motivating factors to encourage rummaging through the trash for classroom stimulators.

Ecology Games*

Ecology is currently a "hot" topic in health education courses in colleges and high schools. The topic is relevant, the subject matter is current, abundant resource material is available, the mass media are active on the topic, public and private agencies are concerned, and the students are involved in changing attitudes and legal approaches toward ecological matters. Still, the competent health education teacher, with all of this support, seeks fresh ideas in teaching ecology. Your department editor has experimented with a learning approach in ecology which is current, innovative, educationally sound, economical, appropriate to several school levels and allows for student creativity. This method is the game simulation technique, which allows students to create their own ecology games with ecology problems and solutions presented in the games.

The rationale for using this instructional technique is, to some extent, based on the games theory which was developed in the 1960s at Johns Hopkins University and other institutions. The games simulation theory, which has been used extensively in social studies, political science, and consumer education, uses reproduced materials, documents, historical events, and historical persons in a game setting with the rules and regulations for the game based on the possibilities found within that game. Rules and regulations are based on the many combinations which have or could occur in the interplay of people, places, and events. Learning opportunities for the student are many, varied, and allied in theme. Creative situations are different for each student and each group. In brief, the game simulation method produces an excellent learning situation. Granted, this approach is rather a simple one, but it can be modified for use on the college and high school levels and, perhaps, the junior high school level merely by making local classroom adaptations.

It is noted that several commercial games are marketed in the area of ecology. *SMOG, Litterbug,* and *Cleanup* are good examples of these. *Pollution,* a commercial product using game simulation, is suitable for use with junior high school students through adults. The learning experiences described here are different from the commercial games in several respects. Some of these differences are as follows:

1. The students provide the input and knowledge necessary to develop their own game.
2. The game conditions are current.
3. The game situation can be scaled to local problems.
4. The creative aspect is present.
5. Small-group work is educational and fun.
6. Decisions must be made by the players that are relevant to their needs.

---

*Source: *Health Education Teaching Ideas* (pp. 108–109) by R. Loya, Reston, VA: American Alliance for Health, Physical Education, Recreation, and Dance.

Materials Needed

Six or eight pieces of cardboard, scissors, felt tip pens or crayons, glue, and scrap paper are sufficient.

Class Organization

Group leaders are appointed, and six to eight students are grouped in the areas of population, water, air, noise, and others as class size warrants. An extensive bibliography is handed out several classes prior to this experience. Students are oriented as to the purpose of the class: to develop a game related to their area of interest. This game must contain rules and regulations, include choices and chances, and involve a decision-making process. Some of the rules may be preplanned, or they may be developed on the spot. The model of monopoly may be used where dice are rolled or number cards may be developed as a means for the students to travel around the board, encounter the different situations, and experience learning opportunities. Chance cards are placed at appropriate areas, and students have to decide on a course of action. (For example: A student draws a card and has the choice of additional waste controls in the company in which he owns stock, or he has an increased dividend of two dollars. What will he/she take?) Who wins the game and how winners are declared are parts of the game which the group must establish in their rules and regulations.

Starter Ideas

In case your students need kick off ideas, here is an approach one class used.

NOISE POLLUTION: A player starts out with normal hearing. He moves and lands on a square of rock music (3 decibels hearing loss), construction (−5 decibels), or sonic boom (+ nervousness to your physical condition). Chance cards might be safety legislation, adding carpets and drapes in house, etc.

Desired Outcomes

The following teaching points are among those that should be made forcefully and vividly while ecology games are being used.

1. The "random chance approach" to ecology matters, as expressed by the dice or cards, is insufficient in real life. Cooperative planning must take place if we are to win the ecology game of life.
2. There is a total involvement needed of legal methods, legislative processes, citizenship practices and concepts, industrial concerns, religious beliefs and practices, and genuine concern about people and our environment.
3. An understanding of the interrelationships of ecology systems and subsystems is a prerequisite to effective action.
4. Careful selection in the means of correcting the different ecology problems, so as not to produce additional problems of ecology, is important.
5. There should be a greater concern for and knowledge about ecology with its problems and promises.

The kind of game simulation and game development outlined briefly here has worked for this teacher on the college level. The students like it, and its use creates an effective learning situation. Other health teachers on different levels in other locales might well use this approach to help their students learn more about ecology.

Environmental Health Scramble*

Instruct students to complete the following exercise.

Name: _____   Date: _____

Environment and Health

Directions: Unscramble the letters below to form fifteen terms associated with environment and health.

1. **LPLTUNIOO**   _ O _ _ _ _ _ _

2. **CIXOT AETWS**   _ _ _ _ O _ _ _ _

3. **DAIITRONA**   _ O _ _ _ _ _ _

4. **ESSARLOO**   _ O _ _ _ _ _ _

5. **HMCCELISA**   O _ _ _ _ _ _ _

6. **TXHUSAE**   _ _ _ O _ _ _

7. **WAGEES**   _ _ _ _ _ O

8. **LLPTOOUIN**
   DDSAATNR XDINE   _ _ _ _ _ _ _ O

   _ _ _ _ O _ O _   _ _ O _ _

9. **BCRONA OOXDIEMN**   _ _ _ O _ _   _ _ O _ _ _ _ _

10. **UFOLORRACONSB**   O _ _ O _ _ _ _ _ _ _ _ _

11. **GSMO**   _ O _ _

12. **IEONS**   _ _ _ _ O

13. **ERPSRITAYOR**
    LAMINEST   O _ _ _ _ _ _ _ _ _ _

    _ _ _ O _ _ _ _

14. **HHTLAE AZADHR**   _ _ O _ _ _   _ _ _ _ _ _

15. **LDSIO SWTEA**   _ _ _ O _   _ _ _ _ _ O

Rearrange the circled letters to form the first step to be taken in order to contribute to public and environmental health.

_ _ _ _ _   _ _ _ _ _   _ _ _   _ _ _ _ _ _ _

*Source: *Health Education Puzzles and Puzzlers* (p. 22) by K. G. Zipperich, 1989, Portland, ME: J. Weston Walch.

■ ■ ■ *ACTIVITIES:* EXPERIMENTS AND DEMONSTRATIONS

Plants Respond to Environmental Changes*

Plants and animals face threats in their environments and must respond effectively in order to survive. Man can learn from his observation of plant adaptations to their "natural" environment, even though he makes fewer adaptations, preferring instead to devise ways to make his life more comfortable.

A plant's response to stimuli, such as sun and water, indicates life, and this life is maintained by achieving some kind of fitness to the environment with all its variables.

The natural habitat for reindeer moss is a rock surface in the Arctic; it has developed a fitness for this kind of environment over eons of time. Severe climatic change would demand that the reindeer moss adapt to the change and become "fit" for a new kind of existence, or die.

Cacti are symbolic of desert areas, a fit environment for the unusual plant, simply because the cacti can store water in the large stems during sparse rainy periods. The stored water is gradually absorbed during droughts. Cacti also have shallow root systems to quickly take up moisture from the surface soil. Man, caught on a desert, can make his own adaptation to the unusual dryness by breaking a cactus stem and drinking stored water.

Strong, constant winds along the West Coast or severely cold mountain tops destroy certain kinds of trees, yet other trees develop a fitness to these conditions and survive. Not only do the trees survive, they develop visible patterns of change and adaptation.

Suggested Activities

1. Show the effect of desiccation on a variety of small growing plants for two weeks. Do the plants revive and grow when water is given again on a regular basis? Make other environmental changes on additional plants; observe and record results.

2. Discuss your experiences with plants growing in unusual places you may have visited: (1) the desert, immediately following the spring rains; (2) near the tree line on high mountains, both "new" rocky mountains and "aged" green mountains; (3) the far North, in late spring or early summer; (4) swamplands.

3. Report any changes which have occurred to large shrubs and trees still growing in the immediate vicinity of an industrial building, oil refinery, or limestone crushing plant which was erected within the last two years. Why do you think these changes occurred? How long will the plants probably survive?

---

*Source: *Health Education Guide* (pp. 216–217) by M. Barrett, 1974, Philadelphia: Lea & Febiger.

■ ■ ■   *ACTIVITIES:* DISCUSSION AND REPORT STRATEGIES

Guidelines for a Recycling Project*

Health educators and their students may become involved in local environmental action by helping to establish a community newspaper recycling program. One such program has been successfully operated since July 1971 by the Greeley (Colorado) Committee on Environment. The committee, appointed by the city council in 1969, originally consisted of about a dozen members—businessmen, housewives, teachers, and faculty members. Other members have been added, including a staff member of the local newspaper—a recent journalism graduate, keenly interested in the committee's work, whose added publicity efforts have greatly helped the success of the project.

The committee decided to undertake a newspaper recycling project after learning that 50% or more of the volume of municipal solid waste is made up of paper and paper products, and that about half of that volume consists of newspapers and magazines. They contacted a paper salvage company in Denver, which assured the committee that they would purchase the paper they collected.

A subcommittee was appointed to find a building to serve as a central collection center. In a long, unfruitful search they found building owners reluctant to permit storage of newspapers because of the potential fire hazard, or desiring to secure a long-term tenant. They investigated the possibility of securing a railroad car on a convenient siding, but learned that a car couldn't be spared. A local trucking firm, learning of the project, offered to spot a semi-trailer in a local shopping center parking lot on collection day, then haul the trailer to the paper salvage company in Denver. Permission was gotten to use the parking lot area—far enough away from the main parking lot traffic pattern, yet permitting smooth in-and-out traffic flow along both sides of the trailer. Arrangements were made with the local police department for traffic control and with the city street department for portable barricades to channel traffic flow along both sides of the trailer.

The second Saturday of the month was selected and publicized as collection day. The Committee on Environment loaded the trailer that first Saturday, while a subcommittee sought volunteer groups to furnish labor for loading in subsequent months. The first day's collection yielded 27 tons. Seeing what the collection could amount to, the committee decided to share the monetary return from the sale of paper with the groups which offered to help—one-third to the committee, one-third to the morning volunteer group, and one-third to the afternoon group. The news media carried the story of the committee's plans for continuing the paper collection on the second Saturday of each month. Volunteer groups, wanting to earn money for their projects, were soon put on a waiting list as groups were assigned collection days several months in advance.

A telephone answering service agreed to receive calls from aged persons and others unable to bring their papers to the collection center. Trucks and station

*Source: *Health Education Teaching Ideas* (pp. 110–111) by R. Loya, 1983, Reston, VA: American Alliance for Health, Education, Recreation, and Dance.

wagons, furnished by members of the groups working at the collection center, collected papers from callers. Most people who wanted pick-up service made their calls ahead of the 10 A.M. deadline on collection day. There was little cause for concern over abuse of the service.

The Committee on Environment hopes that Greeley will soon combine its trash collection with recycling on a city-wide basis. However, though the technology is available for such an undertaking, the market for recycled materials needs to be expanded. Even paper collection alone is not yet feasible on a city-wide basis; the paper salvage company says it would be unable to handle all of Greeley's paper along with all the other paper delivered to its docks.

Greeley's Committee on Environment can boast of a great deal of first-hand experience with what has become a widely accepted but not always practiced dictum: Man must live with his environment, not despoil it. People will cooperate, if properly informed and motivated with sound, well-planned projects.

Here are some suggestions for those who want to start their own recycling project.

A market for the materials to be recycled is a must. The company accepting secondary materials must be notified in advance of the start of your project.

Have adequate transportation available. Greeley's first Saturday collection filled a 40-foot van type semi-trailer. Every Saturday since, two trailers have been needed; in March 1972 a third truck was partially filled.

Advise city officials and the police department of your project.

Publicize each collection day, taking into account the different deadlines of daily and weekly newspapers and radio and television stations. Announce and adhere to opening and closing hours; remind people not to leave materials at any other time. Include phone numbers of key committee members and answering service, if any. Give clear instructions on how materials are to be tied, bundled, or boxed.

Liability insurance is a must.

Have adequate workers on hand—a minimum of 10 or 12—during all collection hours. At times even that may not be enough, though at other times it may be too many. Workers may need gloves for handling paper bundles. Lifting bundles by the heavy cord soon wears blisters on tender hands.

Someone should be responsible for receiving the checks by mail from the company purchasing the papers or other materials. A home address or Post Office box may be used. The same person should be authorized to write checks to the volunteer groups who furnish labor for your project, and should keep records of names and mailing addresses.

Federal Concern for Conservation of Human Resources*

Throughout the Federal government, agencies charged with such matters as public health, consumer protection, transportation, city planning, agriculture, and natural resources are thinking in terms of environmental impact. They are striving to

---

*Source: *Health Education Guide* (p. 230) by M. Barrett, 1974, Philadelphia: Lea & Febiger.

reconcile their actions with some elusive principle of ecological wisdom. State and local governments have established programs to cope with various aspects of the environment which threaten the quality of American life. Universities and other private organizations have turned their attention toward helping man develop a more sensible use of his environment. Industry is showing increasing awareness of its responsibilities in environmental management.

All of these concerned groups are now recognizing that their areas of concern are part of a larger, more complex problem which will not yield to piecemeal solutions—the problem of maintaining an environment conducive to human health and well-being in a world undergoing profound and accelerating change.

A primary goal of the Department of Health, Education, and Welfare (HEW) [now Health and Human Services] is to assure that the health and welfare of man will become, and remain, the chief focus of all actions affecting the environment.

The department and its consultants developed what may be called "A Strategy for a Livable Environment." This is a strategy to improve the status of man within his eco-system and to achieve the highest quality environment man is capable of achieving. The strategy includes a statement of tasks which should receive high priority if we are to establish a hospitable environment in which man can survive and also flourish.

The deteriorating quality of air is an immediate problem and should receive first priority. Excessive noise is an emerging problem and frequently becomes a portion of the task of urban improvement. Other portions of urban improvement are levels of tolerance for crowding, congestion, odor, general stress, and accident threats at home, in recreation, and in traffic. Consumer protection is a large task concerning flammable clothing and toys, appliances, cosmetics, foods, drugs, household chemicals, and poison control.

There can be no illusions about the difficulty of the many tasks ahead. The Department of HEW [HHS] cannot manage the environment. No single agency of the federal government, or of private enterprise, can do so. But the department can provide leadership to a national effort to protect the health and well-being of man, now and in the years to come. Participating in the national effort must be state and local governments, industry, research and development teams, national health agencies, professional organizations, and the universities.

Since the ultimate responsibility for improved maintenance and control of the environment rests with the individual citizen, there must be the reality of involvement of community citizens and of all segments of our society.

Suggested Activities

1. Discuss the organization and functions of these departments in the executive branch of the federal government: (1) Health and Human Services; (2) Housing and Urban Development; (3) Interior; (4) Agriculture; (5) Transportation. Do these departments have local offices in your community? If so, learn how they cooperate with other agencies to help solve the environmental problems of your community.
2. Assign committees to draft legislation designed to improve the quality of the environment. Have each proposed act reviewed by the class acting as a "committee of the whole." Send best regarded legislation to a state legislator or member of Congress.

Solid Wastes Accumulate and Despoil*

It has been estimated that 6 million cars go out of use every year and each urban resident throws away about 2,000 lbs. of rubbish and garbage each year. One report says that currently we are accumulating the fantastic sum of 360 million tons of solid wastes per year in the United States and spending at least $5 billion to collect and dispose of it. By 1980 these figures are expected to be three times greater.

The costs of collecting and disposing of our solid wastes are exceeded only by the costs for schools and roads. Few cities have approved, sanitary, and nuisance-free disposal methods. Open dumps are completely unsatisfactory, city incinerators contribute heavily to air pollution, and landfills have been used for longer terms than practicable and have deteriorated and polluted ground water supplies.

In addition to the obvious solid wastes picked up from residences, and automobiles and trucks, there are pathological wastes, explosives, building materials from construction and demolition, and slag from steel mills and mining operations.

Radioactive wastes may be gaseous, liquid, or solid. Some of these wastes are dispersed into the atmosphere or into streams where they continue to be radioactive for the life of the isotope. Many liquid wastes are concentrated and pumped into concrete-encased steel-lined tanks which are buried beneath the soil. Solid wastes are buried daily as they accumulate in nuclear research installations. The material is placed in containers which are then buried in shallow earth trenches beneath three feet of soil. Each isotope has its own rate of decay. No matter what the disposal, radiation from these wastes continues and may affect man later when the wastes are uncovered or the containers break open or rot away.

The Atomic Energy Commission (AEC) [now Nuclear Regulatory Commission (NRC)] is working with 900 radioisotopes of 100 elements. Many of these isotopes perform useful tasks for us, and may solve some of our environmental problems when we learn to use them successfully. Weigh these benefits against the risks of damaged cells for present generations, and damaged genes which affect succeeding generations!

Charles H. Fox, author of an AEC booklet, *Radioactive Wastes*, has this to say: "Mankind needs the tremendous energy represented by nuclear fuels, but their use will create vast quantities of radioactive wastes. Disposal of these must never be allowed to harm man, his environment, or his natural resources."

Suggested Activities

1. Report on the effectiveness of innovations in garbage and municipal wastes disposal, such as shipping from large cities to abandoned mines or piping material out to sea beyond the continental shelf.
2. Determine what laws or ordinances govern the handling of solid wastes in your community. Propose new ordinances or techniques for disposing of these wastes in a more effective manner.
3. If you live near a nuclear power plant, arrange a class visit to study the safety controls which prevent the contamination of air, water, and soil resources by

---

*Source: *Health Education Guide* (p. 221) by M. Barrett, 1974, Philadelphia: Lea & Febiger.

waste products from the plant. How are employees protected from radiation hazards while disposing of wastes?

■ ■ ■   *ACTIVITIES:* DRAMATIZATIONS

Nuclear Power Debate*

The nation is entering its second decade of crisis over energy resources and energy consumption. Gasoline has more than doubled in price in the past two years. The rising price of home heating oil threatens the health and welfare of poor people who are unable to pay their bills. Congress is considering a proposal to relax environmental standards for strip mining and air pollution emissions from coal-burning power plants. Rampant inflation, partly caused by skyrocketing energy costs, threatens public health as government slashes social programs to balance the budget.

Concurrently, the long term commitment of the nation to the nuclear pathway to energy independence is being reconsidered. The major accident at Three Mile Island, together with the less publicized but nonetheless serious incidents at Browns Ferry, Chalk River, Rocky Flats, and Idaho Falls, have thrown a pallor over the once rosy future of nuclear power. At this writing only one state in the country (Tennessee) is now willing to accept radioactive wastes for storage and disposal. Among the general public, concerns about radiation, the potential for sabotage and the contribution of nuclear power technology to nuclear arms development, have grown dramatically in recent years. Among those who define themselves as environmentalists, opposition to nuclear fission power is virtually unanimous.

But there are two sides to each of these questions. Proponents point to the impressive safety record of nuclear plants. They argue that without nuclear power, electricity would be much more expensive than it is now and the air would be more polluted from coal-fired power plants. They contend that there are benefits and risks to every energy alternative and nuclear benefits far outweigh the risks.

In a course I teach on health and the environment I attempted to broach the problem of presenting the conflicting information which clouds the nuclear question, by organizing a debate in which the students assumed the roles of various interested persons as described below. The purpose of the exercise was to provide the students with the opportunity to try on various viewpoints regarding nuclear power in a simulated real life situation. First I provided the students with readings from a range of perspectives; then I presented the pros and cons of each of the relevant issues in as unbiased a manner as possible. A general discussion ensued. Emphasis throughout was placed on determining the credibility of the information and on the subsequent identification by students of the issues, facts and feelings salient to their attitudes and values toward nuclear power. I found a plethora of biased materials written for the lay public from the local electric company and from

---

*Source: *Health Education Teaching Ideas* (p. 105) by R. Loya, 1983, Reston, VA: American Alliance for Health, Physical Education, Recreation, and Dance.

one of the local anti-nuclear groups active in my community. I augmented this with academically credible sources. (A list of references is available on written request).

The procedures for the debate that I have found to be most valuable are as follows:

1. During the class session prior to the scheduled debate, present or discuss the issues with reference to the articles which the students should already have read. Next, break the students into groups as per the directions below.
2. At the beginning of the second class, just before the debate, give each group 10–15 minutes to compare notes and ideas, and select one person to serve on the panel.
3. Solicit a volunteer or assign someone to be moderator. Charge this person with the responsibility for limiting the time for each presentation and facilitating the democratic opportunity for everyone who wants to speak at least once.
4. Ask those not on the panel to assume the roles of concerned citizens who have the right, and who will be given the opportunity, to ask questions or make statements.
5. Plan 30–40 minutes for the debate including questions and comments from concerned citizens not on the panel.
6. After the debate, open up the class to general discussion and give people the opportunity through discussion and voting to identify the issues, concerns and feelings most important to them, and to clarify and affirm their personal values with respect to nuclear power.

Directions to Role Players

You are a participant in a discussion among local residents and interested persons concerning the proposal by the electric company's directors to build a nuclear power plant in your neighborhood. Each of you may select one of the following roles but there must be at least one person for every role. For the purpose of the exercise attempt to assume the arguments of the role assigned as you perceive they would be. Each person on the panel will have a maximum of five minutes for an initial statement after which there will be time for rebuttal and open discussion.

Participants

Sal/Sally Slick is the electric company's spokesperson. She/he is an outstanding proponent of nuclear power whose special talent is putting the levels of risk posed by nuclear power into perspective with other risks from automobiles, coal mining, natural disasters, cigarette smoking, etc.

Bert/Bertha Booster is the Chamber of Commerce public relations person. Although this character may be either for or against nuclear power, she/he is indefatigable in boostering local business.

Conrad/Connie Concerned is a local resident who is the parent of two children who go to school in the vicinity of the proposed power plant.

Alan/Alice Academic is the local university scientist who is concerned with the balanced presentation of the facts. She/he will often bring out the other side of the argument so that everybody will be apprised of all the facts. She/he likes to put things in the perspective of risks and benefits.

Ed/Edna Ecology is a local environmental activist who is deeply concerned about the ecology of the river on which the plant is proposed to be built as well as a number of other environmental problems.

Be conscientious about limiting the time for each panel member to present and rebut. The purpose of the exercise is to get a range of viewpoints out in the open, not to resolve the issues or to judge the presenters. The 10–15 minutes in groups before the debate assures that each panelist will have a few good points to make, and is itself a good exercise in information sharing. However, you may want to provide the moderator with a few leading questions just to get the discussion going should it come to a standstill. Usually, the reverse occurs—it is hard to limit the debate. The role playing seems to provide many students with a comfortable vehicle for interaction, and the instructor with a method for examining a controversial health concern.

The External Environment Benefits Man*

There are many factors in the external environment which benefit man's internal environment. The absolute essentials for life are air, water, sunlight, and food. To these we must add shelter from the elements, protection from our enemies, and mental and emotional stimuli.

A list of desirable factors in the environment would include sunlight, clean air, pure water and food, fuels and other useful resources, good climate, transportation, family and friends, music or voice and other pleasant sounds, and the stimuli received from beauty, truth, and love.

Suggested Activities

Suggest ways in which life at school and at home can be made more healthful and more pleasant by changing a variety of physical, biologic, and socio-economic factors in the environment.

The External Environment Threatens Man*

Man is constantly threatened by factors in the environment which have an adverse effect on the mind and body. The body repairs minor internal damage and proceeds along the continuum from conception to death with little noticeable effect other than the normal aging process. When the threats become too great, man is forced to make a greater adaptation to this change in his environment so that he may maintain his health and happiness. His body must attempt to repair tissue damage, alleviate mental distress, and restore the internal environment to normal. When stresses exceed the body's limited capacity to adapt, physical and mental damage can result.

These are some of the factors in the external environment which threaten man and call for adaptive responses:

solar and other radiations
polluted air and water

---

*Source: *Health Education Guide* (p. 216) by M. Barrett, 1974, Philadelphia: Lea & Febiger.

harmful microorganisms
contaminated or inadequate foods
industrial and household chemicals
solid and liquid wastes
adverse weather and storms
tools and machinery
distribution and abundance of people
emotional and mental stresses
drugs
pesticides
garbage
rodents and insects
excessive noise
motor vehicles
poverty
crime
congestion of space
weapons and warfare

Suggested Activities

Explain the feelings you may have when trapped between floors in a crowded elevator. Compare these feelings with those you may experience at a class picnic in the park.

■ ■ ■   *ACTIVITIES:* ROLE PLAYS

Vehicles, Tools, and Machinery Are Environmental Hazards*

In industry, new processes and massive, highspeed, automated machines have created possibilities for accidental injury that go far beyond the worker's capability for self-protection. It is impossible for the worker to take sole responsibility for his own health and safety in a complex world of physical and chemical hazards which are little understood, even by the experts, and which are often beyond his control.

Every one of the 87 million people who go to work each day in the United States needs to be made aware of the hazards he confronts in the workplace and should be educated to exercise caution. Industry, labor, and governments must create a working environment in which such a person, exercising reasonable care, can be assured that sudden death or the slow process of industrial disease will not be the wages of his work.

Large corporations have a captive audience and find it not too difficult to develop a safety awareness among employees who work in a stable environment. However,

*Source: *Health Education Guide* (pp. 226–227) by M. Barrett, 1974, Philadelphia: Lea & Febiger.

agricultural workers usually work alone in a disorganized and variable environment. The accident rate among farm workers is the third highest of any major occupation; and the death rate from these accidents is a higher percentage than normal. Tractors, corn pickers, and similar power equipment are extremely hazardous to operate in rough terrain.

Job-related illnesses and injuries are, by definition, preventable. Is it possible to expect that traffic-related accidents and injuries which occur on the highways are preventable? Statistics from reliable sources indicate that almost 50% of all accidental deaths in the U.S. are due to motor vehicle injuries. Accidents are the leading cause of death for young persons up to age 36, and the fourth leading cause for persons over age 36, exceeded only by heart disease, cancer, and vascular lesions.

Travel for personal reasons or for the transportation of goods and services represents an increasingly significant environmental exposure which may affect man's health and well-being. In addition to increased exposure to accidents, man faces increased exposure to air pollution, congestion on the highways and in the airways, emotional stress, and many less visible threats.

The emotional condition and the behavior traits of an individual are factors in the potential for an accident with vehicles, tools, and machinery. The use of alcohol, marijuana, or any one of a wide variety of pharmaceutical preparations will be added factors in the accident syndrome. Some of the emotions and traits which are conducive to accidents are: aggressiveness, anger, discontent, excitement, inability to judge speed and distance, indecision, personal conflict, and boredom from the monotony and routine quality of the task at hand.

Suggested Activities

1. Role-play situations which demonstrate some paradoxes in safety and safe practices. Examples: (a) Immunizations have conquered many childhood diseases. Accidents, including the ingestion of poisonous materials now kill more children than all these diseases combined. (b) Man has annual physical examination, stops smoking and overeating, exercises regularly. Yet, he ignores car seat belts, climbs insecure ladder, and drives with excessive speed habitually. (c) Business man buys accidental death insurance at airlines counter before each flight; but precedes this with several drinks at cocktail party and fast drive to airport.
2. Study the traffic patterns of major streets in your community and access routes to schools and large businesses. Diagram an improved traffic flow which can be achieved through the use of one-way streets, directional traffic signals, or other devices to decrease potential traffic hazards.
3. Chart the accidents in your school this year due to vehicles, tools, or machinery. Write a paragraph suggesting measures that may be taken to prevent a recurrence of like accidents.
4. Determine what accident-prevention training courses are available in your community. Are they effective in helping citizens respond effectively to mechanical hazards?

20th Century Life Creates a Variety of Respiratory Diseases*

Occupational respiratory diseases, in terms of severity, represent one of the most important occupational health problems in America. Adequate controls would pay big dividends, both in reduction of human suffering and in dollars and cents savings to the workers affected, to industry, and to the taxpayer.

Three and a half million American workers are exposed to asbestos in their jobs. They face a dual threat; not only are they subject to the lung-scarring pneumoconiosis of their trade, asbestosis, but they are endangered by lung cancer associated with the inhalation of asbestos fibers. Recent studies of asbestos insulators showed that, of every 5 deaths in this group, one was caused by lung cancer—7 times the expected rate. Half of the men who had worked in the trade had x-ray evidence of asbestosis. One in every 10 deaths was caused by mesothelioma, a cancer of the lung pleura, so rare that it strikes only 1 in 10,000 in the general working population.

"Black lung," or coal miner's pneumoconiosis, is a disease caused by the inhalation of soft coal dust. It is a progressive, crippling lung disease, often complicated by emphysema in the later stages. The death rate from respiratory disease in soft coal mines is 5 times that of the general working population. Black lung, at a conservative estimate, affects more than 100,000 soft coal miners in the United States. Efforts are being made to control the respirable dust in the mines by the continuous enforcement of an air quality standard. President Nixon signed the Coal Mine Health and Safety Act in late December 1969.

There are other industries whose workers run an extremely high risk of respiratory disease. Of the 6,000 men who have been uranium miners, an estimated 600 to 1,100 will die of lung cancer within the next 20 years because of radiation exposure on the job.

Over 3,000 cases of silicosis are reported yearly in this country from exposure to free silica, the major ingredient of all rocks, soils, sands, and clay.

For years it was thought that byssinosis, the lung disease caused by inhaling cotton dust, was not a problem for American textile workers. Even though British workers using American cotton came down with this crippling lung disease, we relied on a limited x-ray survey done years ago which did not reveal a byssinosis problem. Now, our scientists are discovering that America's 230,000 cotton textile workers are also threatened by this respiratory disease.

Talc, diatomite, carborundum, sugar cane fiber, even dust from moldy silage, all produce their own form of lung damage wherever dust control and worker protection are inadequate.

Little has been done in the United States to prevent occupational respiratory disease. Too many productive people have become disabled, and died prematurely, because too little attention is given to controlling the dust, fumes, and vapors to which they are exposed. In West Virginia, it took a walk-out of 40,000 miners to bring about passage of a comprehensive state workmen's compensation law. It took a mine disaster killing 78 men to mobilize public and congressional opinion behind the passage of a national mine health and safety act.

---

*Source: *Health Education Guide* (p. 227) by M. Barrett, 1974, Philadelphia: Lea & Febiger.

The chronic inhalation of any foreign material—cigarette smoke, polluted air, coal dust, or asbestos fibers, and many others—can harm the lungs and cause disease. And since, for the most part, occupational respiratory diseases are entirely preventable, man has a responsibility to take action to prevent them.

Suggested Activities

1. Report on the action taken by the British Parliament to control pollution caused by the burning of soft coal and to control air quality in the soft coal mines.
2. Prepare a map of the United States that indicates the location of soft coal and hard coal mines. Indicate which states are writing legislation to implement the Federal Coal Mine Health and Safety Act signed by President Nixon in December 1969.

■ ■ ■ *STRATEGIES:* BULLETIN BOARDS

Adapting to Weather*

Make a diagram for the bulletin board which shows the changes in environment surrounding the Hoover Dam and its reservoir, or the Aswan Dam in Egypt, or of a similar construction project in your state.

■ ■ ■ *ACTIVITIES:* LEARNING ENHANCEMENTS

New Radiation: Types and Effects. This program considers three aspects of radiation: what ionizing radiation is, the harm it can cause, and the risks connected with it compared with the risks encountered in everyday living. 22 minutes. Films for the Humanities and Sciences, 800/257-5126.

New Radiation: Origins and Controls. This program considers the average doses of ionizing radiation to which people are subjected in the ordinary course of modern events, from both natural and artificial sources, the steps being taken to limit exposure, and those that should be taken to ensure public safety. 27 minutes. Films for the Humanities and Sciences, 800/257-5126.

Environmental Illness: Bad Chemistry. Perfumes, aerosols, plastic on television sets—for some people, these everyday chemicals may create health problems ranging from headaches to loss of consciousness. This program examines the medical and political dimensions of environmental illness (EI), the controversial and mysterious condition whose victims cannot tolerate common chemicals of modern life. Doctors specializing in EI believe the condition may result from damage to the immune system, but other physicians do not recognize EI as a medical condition and see those who treat it as "cult practitioners." The dispute has given rise to wide-ranging political action and heated infighting in the medical profession. EI sufferers are caught in the middle. 60 minutes. Films for the Humanities and Sciences, 800/257-5126.

*Source: *Health Education Guide* (p. 218) by M. Barrett, 1974, Philadelphia: Lea & Febiger.

Noise Pollution. Noise can cause high blood pressure, fetal damage, loss of brain cells, and hearing damage. Almost every type of occupation poses potential dangers from excessive noise, not to mention noise on the way to and from work and during recreational activities. This program looks at the latest research on the impact of noise on health, as well as efforts to minimize noise. 26 minutes. Films for the Humanities and Sciences, 800/257-5126.

Paul Ehrlich's Energy Watch. Biologist Ehrlich examines the problem of burning fossil fuels and the resulting damage to the earth's ecosystems and atmosphere. He also looks at plans to reverse the problem. 18 minutes. Anson-Schloat, 800/833-2004.

Paul Ehrlich's Earth Watch. Biologist Ehrlich takes students on a tour of planet Earth to study three problems: the exploding population bomb, the extinction of tens of thousands of species, and global warming. He also offers solutions that could save our environment. 18 minutes. Anson-Schloat, 800/833-2004.

The Greenhouse Effect. This video examines the effects that humans have on the global thermostat. The causes and effects of global warming are explored as well as the use of computer modeling to predict the earth's changing climate. 17 minutes. Anson-Schloat, 800/833-2004.

REFERENCES

Barrett, M. (1974). *Health education guide.* Philadelphia: Lea & Febiger.

Edlin, G., & Golanty, E. (1992). *Health and wellness: a holistic approach* (4th ed.). Boston: Jones and Bartlett.

Hales, D. (1992). *An invitation to health* (5th ed.). Redwood City, CA: Benjamin/Cummings.

Kane, W. (1987). *Understanding health* (2nd ed.). New York: Random House.

Levy, M., Dignan, M., & Shirreffs, J. (1992). *Life & health: Targeting wellness.* New York: McGraw-Hill.

Loya, R. (Ed.) (1983). *Health education teaching ideas.* Reston, VA: Association for the Advancement of Health Education.

Payne, W., & Hahn, D. (1992). *Understanding your health* (3rd ed.). St. Louis: Mosby.

Robinson, B., & Wolfson, E. (1982). *Environmental education.* New York: Teachers College Press.

Smith, S., & Smith, C. (1990). *Personal health choices.* Boston: Jones and Bartlett.

Tillman, K. G., & Toner, P. (1990). *How to survive teaching health: Games, activities, and worksheets for grades 4–12.* West Nyack, NY: Parker.

Trucano, L. (1984). *Students speak—A survey of health interests and concerns: kindergarten through twelfth grade.* Seattle: Comprehensive Health Education Foundation.

U.S. Department of Health and Human Services. (1990). *Healthy people 2000.* Washington DC: U.S. Government Printing Office.

Vivian, V. E. (1973). *Sourcebook for environmental education.* St. Louis: Mosby.

Zipprich, K. (1989). *Health education puzzles and puzzlers.* Portland, ME: J. Weston Walch.

Aging, Dying, and Death

Although death and taxes are said to be inevitable, living to be old is not.   A. Ferrini and
R. Ferrini, *Health in the Later Years,* 2nd ed.

OBJECTIVES

After reading this chapter, you should be able to

- Discuss aging as a normal part of the life cycle
- Describe how ageism affects the elderly in our society
- Describe the current demographic aspects of the American elderly
- Explain the factors that can help delay or retard the physiological changes that occur in aging
- List the reasons why elderly persons have problems with nutrition
- Describe Alzheimer's disease
- Enumerate suggestions for intergenerational contact programs for school-aged students and the elderly
- Discuss the factors that will lead to better quality lives for the elderly in the future
- Discuss the fears of a dying person
- Describe the relationship between personal beliefs and facing dying and death
- List ways in which family members cope with and help in times of a relative's death
- Describe healthy ways to grieve
- Discuss the purposes of funerals, hospice care, and living wills
- Describe effective methods of teaching about death

THE NORMALCY OF AGING

Aging is a normal developmental process, not a pathological phenomenon, as it is often viewed. When we speak of aging, we must avoid the misconception that the process affects only those over 65; each of us is aging every day. We generally consider the changes taking place in the body as "development" until postadolescence, and "aging" after that. Most people in our society view growth as positive and aging as negative; in fact, both are part of one process. The process of aging is a continuous experience that begins at birth and ends at death.

Exactly how we age is not clear. Many theories have been advanced, but some aspects of the aging process remain a mystery. We *have* managed to control the process, though: Advances in medical technology, improved health care delivery, reduced infant mortality, and control of diseases have resulted in more people living longer. The first part of this chapter examines the ramifications of this fact and consider how our society views aging.

THE SIGNIFICANCE OF AGING EDUCATION

Aging is a relatively new health education topic. Because the number and proportion of elderly people in the United States are expanding rapidly, education about aging and the aged is becoming increasingly important (Ferrini & Ferrini, 1989). Elders are having a tremendous impact on our society through their talents, wisdom, and psychological support for younger age groups.

People face many changes and challenges as they age, and the elderly face problems that affect all of us. Major challenges include income, fitness, acute illness, nutrition, housing, sexuality, mandatory retirement, and the changing character of U.S. society.

Our society places a great deal of emphasis on youth and productivity; often, we consider the elderly person's role less significant. Also, for financial (sharing housing costs) and social reasons (desiring to live with or near peers and living nearer service-oriented agencies), some elderly people have opted to move into housing and communities for the aged. This further segregates them from the remainder of society and makes them less visible.

Students today are more likely to lose significant contact with the older generations than in the past. Some students see older persons daily (e.g., grandparents), but the interaction is often not as meaningful as in the past (Bee, 1987). This lack of meaningful contact with the elderly, coupled with misleading stories they read and hear, often leads to fears and misconceptions. As a result, students need to learn about the elderly and aging early in their lives. They need to see that they themselves will one day be old. They also need to understand that the elderly were once young.

If schools fail to include aging education, myths and stereotypes about aging will continue to abound. The goal of health education is to teach all aspects of growth and development through the life cycle, including the latter stages. Studying aging will make secondary school students more aware of issues facing their parents and grandparents today. It will also prepare them for their own aging. Effective aging education can lead to more satisfactory relationships with the elderly by promoting understanding and empathy among others. A major objective of aging education is to promote and enhance the quality of life in all the years that a person lives.

DEMOGRAPHIC ASPECTS OF THE ELDERLY

At 75 years of age, life expectancy is 9 years for white men, 11.7 years for white women, 8.7 years for black men, and 11.1 years for black women in the United States. In addition to differences in life expectancy related to age, gender, and culture, geographic differences exist: The average life span is longest in Hawaii, Minnesota, and Iowa, and shortest in Washington DC, Louisiana, and several other southern states. These data seem to reflect racial and socioeconomic differences that affect health and opportunity.

White persons over 65 years old make up 12.9% of the white population, and 8.2% of the black population is over 65 years. Aged men make up 10% of the population; aged women, 14%. The ratio of aged men to women continues to decline. Overall, 12.3% of the total population is over 65 (Ebersole & Hess, 1990).

The number and proportion of people over 65 have grown faster during most of this century than any other segment of the population. In 1985, the United States had 28.5 million people age 65 and older. At the beginning of the century, less than 1 in 25 was 65 or over. Today, 1 person in 9 (or 12%) falls into this category. The number of people 55 and over in our population is expected to double by the year 2050.

A popular myth is that most elderly live in nursing homes or other homes for the aged. In fact, only 5% of older people in this country live in such institutions. The majority, 67%, live in a family setting. Because more women outlive their spouses, older women are less likely to live with a spouse than older men (Ferrini & Ferrini, 1989). Half of the elderly are concentrated in a very few states: California, Illinois, New York, Ohio, Pennsylvania, Texas, and Florida. Florida has the highest percentage of elderly in a state population—over 17% (Burdman, 1986).

Many social statistics regarding the elderly are depressing. For example, 14% of older people live below the poverty level. This is due to a variety of reasons, including mandatory retirement; low income levels during the working years, leading to lower retirement incomes; poor financial planning for retirement; and lack of opportunity to work, either for social or physical reasons. Just over 10% of elderly males and less than 5% of elderly females participate in the labor force (MacNeil & Teague, 1987). Again, some have been forced to retire, many are women who have never been in the labor force, and some are physically incapable of working. Less than one half of today's elderly have completed a high school education, and only 9% have graduated from college (Ferrini & Ferrini, 1993).

FACTORS RELATED TO AGING

Aging is a complex function, influenced by physiological, psychological, and sociological factors. Some of these factors are as follows.

Gender. Women have a longer life expectancy than men. This is due primarily to the fact that men are more susceptible to disease at every stage of life, especially chronic diseases. Also, men are more prone to stress than women.

Race. White have a higher life expectancy than nonwhites. This difference can be partly attributed to the fact that some nonwhites, especially African American males, are more prone to hypertension than whites. Also, the general differences in education, economic levels, living conditions, nutrition, and health care between whites and nonwhites are factors.

Personality. Individuals who are very nervous will probably not live as long as those who are more relaxed. Also, some personality types may be more prone to taking risks or may pursue a more physically taxing lifestyle.

Genetics. The genetic code in our bodies provides a blueprint that may dictate how long we will live. Genetic diseases also affect the number and quality of our years.

Employment and Income. The more money an individual has, the better diet and lifestyle the person usually enjoys. Also, people with higher incomes generally have less financial stress.

Education. The more education an individual has, the better job the person might get. Better educated individuals are also more likely to be aware of the importance of a good diet, proper exercise, and the dangers of tobacco and alcohol misuse. College graduates have a greater life expectancy than nongraduates.

Social Attitudes. Many of the elderly in our country today feel "old" because they behave the way the younger generation expects them to. Our society often treats the aged as sickly and unproductive. If people accept these social expectations of behavior, it will influence their lifestyles as they age.

Cultural Factors Related to Aging

Certain ethnic and cultural factors affect the ways that some people age and cope with the aging process. For example, Hispanics in our society face additional problems with poor housing, language barriers, and a lack of medical care and education. Younger Hispanics are changing the traditional ways that their families live—moving away from the extended family and breaking with the traditions of their culture. Personal privacy and pride often prevent Hispanics from taking the financial or medical aid offered by the government.

Native Americans are among the poorest people in the United States. Unemployment, malnutrition, and lack of resources complicate the aging process for the American Indian. Family support has long been a staple of this culture. Without resources, however, a family is unable to offer the traditional kinship support. Medical care is a special concern of Native Americans, especially since government-sponsored medical care is inadequate to meet their needs—one major reason for the low life expectancy in this ethnic group.

Asian Americans face a unique social challenge in their later years. Pre-World War II immigration laws in this country prohibited spouses and children from accompanying Chinese men immigrating to this country. As a result, elderly Chinese-American males far outnumber elderly Chinese-American females in this country. Thus, only 27% of elderly Chinese Americans live with a spouse, compared with 43% of the total older population. Obviously, these laws have disrupted their traditional patterns of kinship and community responsibility. Japanese Americans did not face such immigration barriers, but more than half of their elderly live alone, most of them widows. In addition, an inordinate number of Asian Americans face poverty and language barriers—both of which further challenge their elderly (Butler & Lewis, 1982).

THE AGING PROCESS

Before discussing the specific changes associated with the aging process, it should be emphasized that different people undergo these changes at different times. Most of them are gradual, and adjustments can often be made to offset them. Further, proper exercise and other preventive health measures can retard many of the changes.

Biological Aspects of Aging

The following physical changes occur to the body with the passage of time (Spence, 1989):

- Slight loss of height
- Gradual reduction of muscle mass
- Loss of elasticity in the lungs, which causes more effort in breathing
- Loss of calcium from the bone (possible osteoporosis)
- Cellular dehydration
- Epidermis becomes thinner
- Gradual reduction in strength and endurance

Another biological phenomenon associated with aging is **organic brain syndrome** (OBS), also known as **senility** or **senile dementia**. OBS is a general term to describe a progressive disease that results in abnormal intellectual function. OBS may also affect one's personality and behavior. A series of small strokes, nutritional deficiencies, or atherosclerosis may cause OBS.

The most common and the most perplexing form of OBS is *Alzheimer's disease* (or presenile dementia), which is characterized by a progressive, irreversible decline in mental functioning that interferes with daily living (Ferrini & Ferrini, 1993). Alzheimer's disease is not a normal process of aging, but is typically associated with older persons. It can occur as early as 45 years of age. The person afflicted with Alzheimer's becomes confused, suffers memory loss, suffers physical and mental decline, and is unable to recognize even close family members. Little is known yet about the cause, prevention, and treatment of Alzheimer's. Researchers have suggested a possible genetic link, because relatives of people who have developed symptoms before age 65 are more likely to contract Alzheimer's; however, many Alzheimer's victims have had no family history of the disease. Researchers have recently discovered a chromosomal link that may prove to be the cause of Alzheimer's. If this proves to be a cause rather than merely a symptom, it may be possible in the near future to develop a drug that will treat some of the symptoms of the disease (Spence, 1989).

Psychological Aspects of Aging

The psychological changes that accompany the aging process affect some elderly more than others. Many of these are the result of negative attitudes and behavior toward the elderly by the younger generation. Better treatment of and more positive attitudes toward the elderly would help improve detrimental attitudes and behaviors among elderly people. In helping individuals cope with the changes that occur, it must be recognized that the elderly face many losses, including peers, jobs, spouses, and physical senses. These problems of adjustment overwhelm some elderly people, whereas others are able to face the challenges and find satisfaction.

Sociological Aspects of Aging

Sociological aspects of aging include

- A loss of the child-rearing function (the empty-nest syndrome)
- Loss of one's spouse
- Mandatory retirement (or if voluntary, still a change in role)
- Problems with transportation
- Lack of community involvement
- Lack of knowledge about community resources
- Inadequate medical services
- Financial problems
- A need for leisure activities and use of time
- Loneliness
- Loss of role identification
- Victimization through crime or abuse

Again, it should be noted that many sociological aspects of aging result from discrimination and inappropriate treatment by younger people. Proper education and attitudinal changes in the general population could alleviate many of these detrimental changes among many elderly individuals. To see the validity of this premise, one need only compare the role of the elderly in the United States with that of the elderly in countries like Japan. In Japan, individuals enjoy higher social status and prestige as they grow older, almost the opposite of what happens in our country.

MAJOR CHALLENGES FACING THE ELDERLY

Chief among the challenges facing the American elderly is the lack of financial resources. As mentioned earlier, many elderly live below the poverty line. Inflation and low interest rates have eroded the savings many elderly acquired during their working years. Social Security retirement benefits are not sufficient to meet all of their needs.

Housing continues to be a major issue for the elderly. Nearly two-thirds of the elderly in our country own their own home. Even if the house is paid for, the owners must still cover taxes and insurance costs. Also, if the home is older, it has higher maintenance costs. Some elderly people have to make a decision between drastic improvements in their current home and moving, and many are limited financially as to where they can move. Some government housing is available based on current income—the less the income, the less the monthly payment. Some elderly share housing to reduce monthly costs. Many elderly have few housing options, however. Other housing alternatives are apartments for the aged, sponsored by private, public, and nonprofit church-related groups. Boarding homes and nursing homes that provide both intermediate and skilled care for the aged dependent (those dependent on others for care) also are available.

Maintaining good health is a major challenge of growing old. Individuals' health affects every aspect of life, including their relationships with a spouse, family, and community; income-producing ability; and leisure pursuits. The health problems that beset the elderly usually reflect the aging process, in addition to those related to environmental causes, trauma, and heredity. Chronic ailments, such as heart disease, are the most common health problems for the elderly.

Escalating medical and health-related expenditures are a major concern for the older population. Of economic necessity, health care for many elderly people is crisis-oriented. Because they cannot afford to visit a physician every time they are ill, many do not seek help until they feel it is absolutely necessary. Additionally, in many areas the elderly needlessly spend money on health remedies or do not maximize the health benefits they receive for their money. Federal programs such as Medicare and Medicaid have helped in some ways, but even these programs do not pay enough of the health care bills of some elderly because of the ever-increasing costs of health care delivery.

Medicare is a health insurance program for those age 65 and over that is designed to help pay for hospital and other medical costs. The hospital insurance helps pay for hospital care and certain follow-up care after the person leaves the hospital. The medical insurance primarily pays for a physician's services and outpatient hospital services. Medicare pays about half of the medical expenses incurred, and the patient must pay the remaining amount. Medicare has incorporated a prospective payment system based on diagnostic related groups and has frozen reimbursement levels for physicians accepting Medicare assignment. These reforms have saved money at the federal level, but they have cost hospitals, physicians, and the elderly more money. Further, the reforms have adversely affected the quality of health care for elderly persons (Brodsky & Ezell, 1985).

Some of the elderly's health problems reflect improper nutrition. Nutrition is as important for the elderly as it is for other age groups. Because of limited finances, loneliness, various disease states, and a reduction in the senses of smell and taste, many elderly skip meals or do not otherwise eat well. Sometimes, emotional problems, such as depression, keep elderly persons from eating. Because an elderly person's basal metabolism is reduced, caloric need is also reduced. For this reason, proper nutrition requires better planning. Less food is required, but the quality has to remain high. Programs such as Meals on Wheels, which delivers meals to home-bound elderly, and the federal government's Food Stamp Program and Nutrition Program for the Elderly (Title VII of the Older Americans Act of 1965, which is updated every 3 years) help defray the cost and improve the nutrition of poor elderly people.

Drug use by older adults may cause greater problems than it does for younger persons because of slower metabolic rates and more illnesses. Older persons commonly take many different drugs. Some recommendations to help prevent drug problems among the elderly include making sure when the medication is to be taken, keeping an up-to-date record of the drugs taken, keeping the physician informed of all medications taken, and discarding old medicines (Teague, 1987).

Medical quackery also affects the elderly. Arthritis sufferers—most of them older individuals—spend $300 million yearly on quack remedies. Other types of crime against the elderly range from muggings and theft to financial exploitation and physical abuse by members of their own family. Transportation is a major challenge for some elderly people, partly because many of them do not drive. Others drive, but have not adjusted to today's complicated traffic patterns. Also, those who drive with failing eyesight and hearing are more likely to be involved in accidents. The cost of automobile maintenance and gasoline prohibits some older persons from operating a car. Nondrivers must seek other means of transportation. Taxis can be expensive, and public transportation, although cheaper, is much less convenient; it requires more walking and takes more time. Often it is not designed with the elderly in mind. For these reasons, many elderly are restricted to their homes and apartments except for health care, groceries, and other necessities.

AGEISM

Ageism is a term used to describe discrimination against elderly people. The elderly are characterized in terms of the least capable, least healthy, and least alert. Our society promotes ageism by exalting youth and vigor and emphasizing efficiency, speed, and mobility. We are critical of those considered unproductive. This attitude causes much discrimination and fosters many false beliefs about the elderly (Ebersole & Hess, 1990).

Intergenerational misunderstandings are reduced when the old and young work, play, study, and socialize together. When the young and old see each other frequently and interact in meaningful ways, they generally express a high regard for each other (Ebersole & Hess, 1990). Younger people are quick to emphasize the problems that occur with aging and the aged. Although people do face special problems and challenges as they grow older, the problems are less severe than many young people believe. For example, it is a myth that most elderly are incapacitated. In fact, most older people are able to work and live independently. Only 5% of the elderly are institutionalized, and elderly individuals average fewer than 15 days a year in bed because of ill health. Here are some other misconceptions about the elderly (Ferrini & Ferrini, 1993):

1. "After age 65, life goes steadily downhill."
2. "Old people are all alike."
3. "Old people are lonely and ignored by their families."
4. "Old people are senile."
5. "Old people have the good life."
6. "Most old people are sickly."
7. "Old people no longer have any sexual interest or ability."

Intergenerational Contact

Intergenerational contact programs can be one of the most effective ways for secondary teachers to implement an aging-education program. Such an experiential approach to intergenerational contact has been implemented in programs through-out the country. Notable examples include the Foster Grandparent Program and the Retired Seniors Volunteer Program. Volunteers and paid-aide programs, tutoring projects, free lunches, and guest speaker days have helped involve the elderly with

---

HEALTH HIGHLIGHT
Empty Nest Syndrome: The Misperception

Many believe that, when the last child leaves home, the parent(s) feel sadness, worthlessness, and emptiness. This is a common misconception, according to the Institute for Human Resources. This stigma began in psychiatry, which believes that a woman's depression during menopause was associated with the empty nest syndrome—also a misperception. In fact, both parents are finding these years a time to take up new hobbies, get more involved in the community, or rekindle relationships.

Many parents have 30 or more good years left to invest in life after the last child leaves home. Some specialists suggest that parents should develop their pursuits while the nest is still full. That way their nest will never be "empty" after the kids have all gone.

Source: *Alternatives* (1992, 2nd quarter), Rockville, MD: Institute for Human Resources.

---

the schools. Giving students such opportunities to understand aging and the aged will help dispel many false beliefs. Better attitudes toward aging may also help students realize their full potential throughout their lives as they themselves age. By studying aging, students will be better able to understand and interact with their parents and grandparents.

AGING IN THE FUTURE

As a result of the increasing numbers of elderly people and greater realization of the complex issues that surround aging, many organizations, public and private, are offering expanded services to the elderly. These services include homemaking services, chore services, health services, personal counseling, mobility and transportation assistance, financial and income tax counseling, and visiting services. Portable meals for the homebound, lunch programs at senior citizens centers, employment services, and information and referral services that tell the elderly about the services available to them in their communities are also becoming more widely available. The elderly in the year 2000 will be better organized and more of a political and economic force in society. They should be able to do much to improve the quality of life for the aged (Ferrini & Ferrini, 1989). They will be better educated as a group than the elderly of today. Many will have been activists in organizations and movements in their younger years, concerned with such matters as environmental issues and women's rights. They will probably continue to be activists, helping to improve the quality of life for all older individuals. The elderly of the future will most likely have higher incomes, better retirement plans, better living standards, better housing, and better health care programs. The next generation of elderly Americans will be larger in number, comprise a higher percentage of the total population, and be more evenly distributed throughout the nation. Finally, more government and private organizations will probably be created to meet the needs of the elderly. The organizations' programs and services will most likely temper the negative attitudes of younger people toward the elderly.

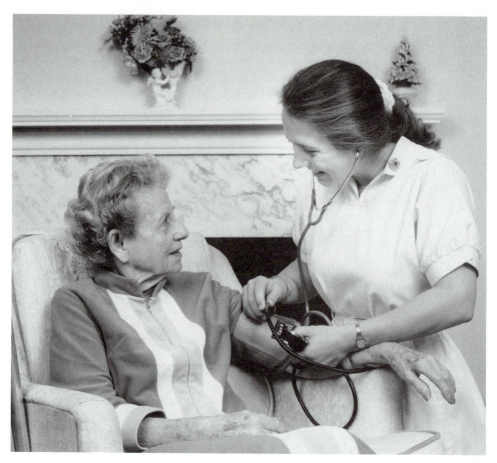

The elderly of the future will most likely have higher incomes, better retirement plans, better living standards, and better health care programs.

Young people need to consider several things when planning for later life. For example, better educated people will be better able to cope with the challenges of later life; therefore, younger adults should place an emphasis on continuing their education. Hobbies are also important to develop at an early age. Young adults should become active in organizations and/or movements in which they have concerns or interests, such as environmental issues, women's rights, and charitable organizations. This activity contributes to one's self-concept by providing a purpose in life, and it can add to the quality of life in later years. Finally, young adults should carefully consider financial planning for later years. A young adult may have trouble contemplating financial needs that are 30 to 40 years away, especially in a society that promotes instant gratification. Financial concerns usually top the list of problems for elderly people in our society, and this trend is likely to continue; therefore, young adults must develop a sound financial plan to ensure quality health care, housing, and living standards for themselves in later life.

CONSIDERING DEATH

Death is a vital part of the life cycle for every creature on earth. Death is part of the natural order that includes birth, growth, and aging. Death is very democratic; it respects no person. Death is a certainty; it will come to every person. These seem like elementary statements, but many people in contemporary society believe that life and death are mutually exclusive phenomena.

Contemplating death can be trying. The various aspects of dying and death are extremely complex and confusing because we do not comprehend so much about death. We have unanswered questions regarding death such as "If we are born to die, then why do we live?" "If death is natural, why do so many people regard it as bad?" None of the numerous attempts to answer these and similar questions have satisfied everyone. The "unknowns" have caused much confusion and surrounded death with an aura of mystery, but they have also been the source of many interesting attitudes and philosophies on the subject.

Death is as much a part of human existence—of human growth and development—as birth. Death limits our time in this world, and life culminates in death. Recognizing that death is a natural end to life can have a profound influence on our lives. Our lifestyles can depend on our attitudes toward death. Although much information on death and dying is available, many misconceptions and problems also still exist. For example, many physicians and clergy members have had little training in caring for the emotional needs of dying persons and their families. Physicians are trained to cure, but some lack the ability to be caring and comforting. Often, they avoid the crucial issues, thereby complicating the dying process. Even today, such courses are conspicuously absent at many of the seminaries and medical schools in our country (Oaks & Ezell, 1992).

Another problem with death and dying concerns children. Parents often "protect" their children from the trauma of death-related events, thinking they are doing the best thing. This treatment tends to promote fears and misconceptions, however. For example, students tend to regard death as happening only to the elderly because parents tell them not to worry about death until they are older.

In the remainder of this chapter, we examine these and other death-related issues. We also look at attitudes toward death, the needs of dying persons and their families, the grief experience, funerals and related rituals, and death education for students.

COMMON ATTITUDES TOWARD DEATH AND DYING

Many Americans' attitudes toward death are contradictory. Death both intimidates and fascinates us. We enjoy living, but we take risks by driving dangerously and taking part in high-adventure sports. We want safety and happiness, but we behave in self-destructive ways; for instance, by abusing drugs. We consider the subject of death a social taboo, but insist on reading and talking about it. We say we need nuclear weapons, but at the same time we are concerned about spiritual rebirth.

Our typical response to death is denial. This results from our resistance to imagining death, and is predicated upon our fears about the consequences of death, including dependency, loss of control, isolation, loneliness, pain, physical disfigurement, loss of dignity, and fear of the unknown (Kearl, 1989). We deny death by not planning for it (e.g., not making out a will), and by participating in high-risk activities as if we are impervious to dying.

Many people display an outright hatred of death. They hate death because they think people die too young or because they are afraid of what comes after death. The hate and fear might not result so much from the "unknown" factor as from the hopelessness regarding what lies beyond death.

Others believe that death should be considered a taboo topic for discussion. These people avoid open, honest discussions of dying and death (Kalish, 1985). Death is also a taboo topic because of the mystery and danger associated with it. This latter attitude reflects society's emphasis on youth and secularism.

Past experiences with death, early parental messages, cultural influences, life experiences, religious beliefs, level of education, and maturity all influence attitudes toward death. We form our attitudes from childhood experiences and carry those attitudes into adulthood. Findings from research indicate that negative attitudes toward death tend to be higher among females, African Americans, younger people, and those who do not characterize themselves as religious (DeSpelder & Strickland, 1992).

It is interesting that many people today who would rather not discuss death in an open and frank manner actually talk about death every day. For example, we hear "You'll be the death of me yet" or "My shoes are killing me" or "That loud noise scared me to death!" In other cases, death is the subject of jokes and humor. People who talk about death in these ways demonstrate an aversion to death as a topic of conversation as well as a fascination with death. They may be subconsciously trying to show themselves and others that death really doesn't bother them, even though serious contemplation of the subject makes them extremely uncomfortable.

We also treat death in a very special way. We set aside special places for death—funeral homes, cemeteries, hospices, and hospitals. We set aside special times for remembering deaths—Memorial Day; the Day of the Dead in Mexico; and Good Friday, a day for remembering the death of Jesus. In addition, the deaths of other celebrated and martyred persons have been remembered with special days. We have special symbols for death, such as the black armbands that athletes wear when a teammate has died, or a flag flown at half-mast in memory of someone who has died.

Several factors have contributed to our very narrow and stereotyped attitudes toward death and dying. We are so far removed from death that we fail to contemplate its nature. We blindly believe in modern medicine to the point that we subconsciously feel we may never die. Many never come to realize that death is a fact of life that all people must cope with and reason out for themselves. Most Americans say they want to die quickly or in their sleep. This response reflects a negative attitude and lack of preparation for a painful or slow death in which one is conscious of what is happening.

Many acceptable ways of causing death further confuse our attitudes. We normally detest the taking of another person's life, as in homicide, yet we train soldiers to do just that in war. In fact, we make heroes of soldiers who tempt death and kill the enemy. Every state in the nation has seen serious debate regarding capital punishment. Is it right to kill people because they have committed heinous crimes, such as murder? Does capital punishment deter these crimes? Another controversial issue involving death is abortion. Right to life groups say that abortion is murder, akin to genocide. Yet abortion is legal within certain guidelines, for example, if it is performed in the first trimester of pregnancy in some states.

Most of us have very negative attitudes toward death, primarily because we are uncomfortable with our own mortality. Many people associate death only with loss, pain, suffering, frustrated desires, and unachieved goals. We see death as a separation from persons we love, from places or objects we treasure, and from a part of our own self-identity, and we fail to see anything positive in death. Otherwise mature individuals often find themselves unable to cope with the thought of death. These individuals generally choose to try to ignore death, to pretend on a subconscious level that they are immortal. They adopt this attitude primarily out of a fear of death. Other peoples' deaths also remind us of our own vulnerability, causing us to feel totally helpless, as if nothing we can say or do will change a thing.

Many people try to avoid even mentioning death. When they do talk about it, they usually do so in the form of a joke. When the subject of their own death or the death of someone close comes up, they seem dismayed and uncomfortable until someone changes the subject, much to everyone's relief. When people refer to death, they often use euphemisms that do not imply the finality, totality, and complete separation from life that death represents. These euphemisms include "expired," "passed away," "departed," "gone to his rest," and "gone to her great reward." Such phrases make it easier to talk and think about death, because they soothe the harshness of its reality. Such euphemisms are an extension of the denial attitude that many of us take toward death. This denial carries over to other aspects of death as well. For example, many families have a deceased person's body embalmed so the body will "look alive" and "seem real" in the casket.

These attitudes toward death can have a profound influence on people's lives. If death is nothing but fear, and if fear prevents people from thinking and acting, they then become less than human. Also, if the fear of death does limit an individual's view of the future, this negative attitude can hinder the person's ability to plan ahead, to anticipate both hazards and opportunities in life.

Positive Approaches to Death

Death should not be considered taboo. It should be seen as a natural part of our existence. The more absolute death becomes, the more meaningful our life can become. Death is as much a part of human existence and the life cycle as birth. It is not an enemy to be conquered, but an integral part of life that gives meaning to human existence. Death sets a limit on our time in this life, urging us to do something meaningful with that time as long as it is ours to use. Dying is the final chance to grow, to become more truly who you are. Those who truly are reconciled to their own mortal existence are the ones who get the most out of life. Such a positive approach to death frees one to focus on the daily tasks of living life more fully.

A normal, healthy fear of death is considered essential to the preservation of life, because this fear leads us to take certain precautions. We should not allow this fear to affect our emotional health in a negative way, however. We must find ways to cope effectively with death and dying, and intellectualizing it is not enough. The quality of our life depends on our ability to acknowledge reality and to deal appropriately with death and dying. The first step in overcoming a fear of death is to face it openly and resolve any unrealistic fears by looking into the causes of those fears. Frank, open discussion about death can help a person to diminish fear, anxiety, aggression, and other conflicts associated with death and to develop a positive attitude.

Other media that have been used to help people confront death are religion, art, music, poetry, and love. For example, those who characterize themselves as religious tend to report less death anxiety than those who do not (DeSpelder & Strickland, 1992). Most religions believe that only the physical self dies and that one's spirit (or soul) survives.

People who have shared in the death of someone who understood death's meaning tend to develop a more positive attitude toward dying and death. Those who have a healthy attitude toward death and who consider it truly one phase of existence have profited from this frame of mind. Positive attitudes toward dying can enhance the meaning and richness of life for many, even for terminally ill persons. The awareness of one's mortality sometimes brings on a feeling of ecstasy from being freed from social constraints, for example (Kearl, 1989).

Personal Beliefs

Personal beliefs are helpful in coping with the reality of death and dying, whether these beliefs are called ethics, thoughts, meditations, or religion. People rely on personal beliefs to find comfort in the face of death. Some use religious beliefs as an escape, as if to gain personal exemption from the reality of death. While belonging to any religious group does not guarantee that one will face death any more positively, research does appear to show that maintaining a strong religious belief system diminishes the fear of death (Wass, Berardo, & Neimeyer, 1988).

NEEDS OF A DYING PERSON

Most Americans, when asked how they would want to die, say they wish to die in a sudden, unexpected way, or in their sleep. In other words, they want to die without knowing what is happening. In reality, though, most Americans will die of chronic illnesses. Those in this situation tend to feel powerless over their own destiny. They begin to realize their own mortality and sense a loss of independence.

Fear is the most typical psychological response that a dying person experiences. Dying persons often fear humiliation, a sense of failure, a loss of self-worth, and anxiety about the future. Other common reactions include fears of the unknown (i.e., not knowing what will happen after death), extinction, being disfigured, pain, indignity, insanity, and abandonment by friends and relatives (Wass, Berardo, & Neimeyer, 1988).

In a sense, dying people have no model to follow. They feel like strangers to the healthy living because no one understands what they are going through. Most dying people want to talk about death and their own illness, but unfortunately, they cannot always find anyone willing to discuss these matters.

Adjusting to Dying

Elizabeth Kubler-Ross (1975), a pioneer in the study of dying and death, devised a five-stage model describing the process many dying persons go through in coming to terms with their own death. Understanding these stages of adjustment to impending death is critical in understanding the needs of the dying person. Relatives of the dying person also go through these stages of adjustment, as we discuss later in the chapter.

In the first stage, called denial and isolation (sometimes referred to as shock), the patient, upon learning of the diagnosis of a terminal condition, reacts with disbelief. This is not surprising, because most people go through their whole lives pretending that they are not going to die. The diagnosis, however, brings the reality of one's death to a conscious level and does so with a tremendous impact. Some individuals, sadly, remain stuck in this stage until they draw their dying breath.

During the second stage, anger, the reality of impending death is beginning to seep into consciousness. People at this stage get angry at the doctors for not having a cure; at the nurses for not providing enough attention; at relatives for isolating, abandoning, or otherwise not meeting their needs; and at God for the injustice of impending death.

In the third stage, bargaining, the patient begins accepting the idea of death but tries to bargain for more time before actually having to face death. If a holiday or a special occasion, like a wedding, is coming up soon, the person asks God for more time. The person makes a promise, but then rarely keeps that promise, because when the first occasion comes and goes, the person often strikes another bargain with God.

The fourth stage of adjustment is depression. The patient is saddened by the fact that death is approaching and then starts the preparatory grief process for the losses death will bring. This time of adjustment can be very confusing and frustrating for relatives or helping staff because the dying person wants nothing to do with anyone. The individual is taking care of unfinished emotional business and is preparing for the arrival of death.

The depression stage can lead to the final stage of adjustment, acceptance, or resolution. People at this stage have come to terms with or resolved the meaning of death for their own lives. People who achieve this stage of emotional adjustment usually can die peacefully.

It should also be noted that the interpretation of Kubler-Ross' stages of adjustment has changed since they were originally presented. Each person is unique in death as in life, and everyone responds differently. Some may progress naturally through these stages, whereas others might reach one of the latter stages of adjustment, then regress. Further, all dying persons will not reach a stage of acceptance or resolution before they die.

NEAR-DEATH EXPERIENCES

The near-death experiences that have been recorded have remarkable similarities, leading many to believe that they are not merely dreams, as previously thought. Some physicians report not only that their resuscitated patients have similar experiences but also that the events occur in much the same sequence. Generally, people who have had such experiences describe a sensation of being out of their bodies, traveling through some tunnel or tubular conveyance, and entering into another world before they return to their bodies. Some of these people experience an "enlightenment," as if their knowledge has been broadened considerably. Others see cities of light, like heaven, or other light imagery. Many report a feeling of being "exposed"; in other words, they were not able to hide behind an emotional "mask," and their every thought and deed was portrayed openly (Kalish, 1985; DeSpelder & Strickland, 1992).

Many persons who experience near-death experiences as hospital patients undergoing surgery can recall procedures used on them and remember what each person in the room said. One patient, a nurse in a coma, recalled the exact procedures used with total recall. These patients also reported an instant replay of their own lives. Some patients have multiple experiences during a prolonged illness—some of these experiences are bad (usually the first ones), while others are very good. The patients themselves interpret whether the experience is good or bad. Sometimes the unpleasant experiences are so frightening that the conscious mind cannot cope with them, and the patient suppresses them into the subconscious.

Richard Kalish (1985) describes the common stages and events of near-death experiences:

1. Hearing others say that they are dead.
2. Experiencing a feeling of peace and quiet, especially during the early stages of their experiences.
3. Hearing a noise, which in many cases is a loud, sometimes unpleasant ringing, often concurrent with the feeling of being pulled rapidly through a dark cave, trough, tunnel, or the like.
4. Finding oneself "out of body," looking on one's own physical body from outside it, like a spectator. During this stage, many feel confused; others feel desperation, fear, "a release," or loneliness.
5. Meeting with others—friends and relatives who have already died, or a spiritual being.
6. Seeing "the light," the element of the experience that has the greatest effect on the individual. This light is usually dim, then growing brighter, with a magnetic attraction. Some believe the light to be Christ or an angel. This "being" either directs a certain thought to or speaks to the person.

7. Reviewing one's life, which consists of rapidly appearing memories, usually in chronological order complete with visual imagery, occurring with a startling intensity.

8. Approaching the "border" or "limit," which may be described as a body of water, a gray mist, a door, a fence, or a line, that separates the person having the experience from those in a more "permanent" existence.

9. Coming back, during which stage the person experiences a desperate desire to get back in the body. Deeper into the experience this desire diminishes and the return is resisted. Those who encounter the "being of light" especially report feeling secure and comfortable and in a blissful state. Some were drawn rapidly back through a dark tunnel and slipped back into their body as if into a pair of trousers. (p. 74)

THE FAMILY'S REACTION TO DEATH

Impending death affects family members of the dying person in various ways. Sometimes the family prohibits talk of death because members feel this may hasten death. Some family members think that a discussion of death would make the others more uncomfortable, and that any discussion may seem to reflect an inordinate interest in the dying person's estate. The loss of a key family member, like the head of a household, can threaten certain social and psychological arrangements. This can lead to enormous stresses and cause tension among all remaining members.

Besides grief, emotional reactions to the death of a family member may range from guilt and anger to fear, anxiety, and money worries. Sometimes the anger is directed toward the deceased person: "He died and left me with all these debts" or "She deserted us during a crucial time of our lives." Death is also a reminder of the survivors' own vulnerability, which evokes fear in itself. If the dying person lives in the home before death, tension and resentment can develop. When family members must sacrifice their own friends and activities to provide care, feelings of hostility and anger toward the dying person can develop. Anger then turns to guilt, which has been described as anger turned inward. Some family members tend to feel inadequate in such an overwhelming situation. They tend to want to protect themselves and the dying relative by not speaking to the person. This is wrong because it leads to emotional abandonment, worsening the situation for the dying person. That person needs compassion, not isolation.

The family can help the most, when circumstances permit, by maintaining an emotional and social environment consistent with the person's past life. This means keeping the person at home or in a hospice rather than in a hospital or nursing home. The family should include the dying relative as a participant in every discussion, especially those that involve decisions about that person's care and welfare. Relatives should do all they can to show their love and concern without doing it in ways that make the person feel guilty for being a burden to them. Family members should not allow their inability to face death to hinder the dying person's adjustment. When the person is ready to accept the reality of dying, the family should share that acceptance. An absence of support at this crucial time may result in the person dying without dignity.

THE GRIEF EXPERIENCE

Grief is usually described as sorrow, mental distress, emotional agitation, sadness, suffering, and related feelings caused by a death. **Bereavement** refers to a state of experiencing grief. **Mourning** is comprised of culturally defined acts that are usually performed when death occurs.

The closer the relationship of the bereaved to the deceased, the stronger the emotional response. Among emotions and patterns of behavior are sadness, anger, fear, anxiety, guilt, loneliness, tension, loss of appetite, weight loss, loss of interest in favorite things, decreased socialization, and disrupted sleep. These responses are usually greater when death is unexpected.

Grief, bereavement, and mourning are generally much less formal in the United States than in some other cultures. Today, people generally have greater freedom to determine for themselves what kind of grieving, bereaving, and mourning is appropriate (DeSpelder & Strickland, 1992).

Studies of mourning show that counseling sessions allowing survivors to talk about the deceased and work through their death-related problems are therapeutic (Leviton, 1985). Another form of therapy involves going to work, going to school, or participating in organizational activities. Americans seem in need of much more elaboration of death ceremonies than many other cultures. While the rituals are less formal, the need for these ceremonies remains. This helps explain why many in our society place a strong emphasis on the rituals of funerals and burials.

Funerals and Related Rituals

The **funeral** is an organized, group-centered response to death. It involves rituals and ceremonies surrounding the body of the deceased. The traditional funeral also addresses the needs of the mourners. Some religions include a eulogy of the deceased, and some include an open casket that survivors view as part of the ceremony.

An alternative to the traditional funeral is a **memorial service**. Memorial services are sometimes held in conjunction with a cremation (with the urn present or absent) or when the body is not present for some reason (e.g., if it has been donated to a medical school immediately upon death or the family prefers not to have the body present). This service is held in a church, chapel, home, or whatever place the family considers appropriate. The service is not a eulogy but rather a chance to show thankfulness for having known the person. It also gives an opportunity for families to express and share their grief. Generally, individuals who hold a memorial service are using this time to celebrate the life of the deceased while on earth rather than to mourn. Memorial services are most common among families with strong religious convictions and a belief in life after death, but they are becoming more common even among the nonreligious.

A primary purpose of the funeral is to dispose of the body. It also satisfies survivors' emotional needs, like grief and mourning. The visitation part of the funeral ceremony is important for friends to show their respect for the deceased and support for the survivors. Also, viewing the body, which is part of some funeral home visits, is important to some for realization (seeing and thus believing that the person is dead) and recall (providing an acceptable image for recalling the deceased). For these reasons, the funeral home visitation can be therapeutic for friends as well as family.

Cemeteries once were considered very sacred places where relatives could go in quiet and peace to show their respect for the dead. Now, however, many cemeteries are crowded, congested, and impersonal. The relatives of the deceased might also live many miles from the burial site. For these reasons, cemetery visits are less common than in the past. Survivors are less likely to use this ritual to work out grief and mourning among the survivors.

ISSUES SURROUNDING DEATH

Some death-related topics have become the focal point of controversy in recent years. These issues include the definition of death, the right to die, organ transplants and donations, wills, and suicide.

Definitions of Death

For thousands of years, the concept of the time of death was clearly defined as the cessation of bodily functions. Now, however, advanced medical technology can sustain life beyond the point at which death formerly would have occurred. The problem of defining it is much more complex—not just knowing when a person is dead, but being able to determine the exact moment of death. This is important in the case of potential organ transplants, when every second is critical.

Some say that a person is **brain dead** when the entire brain ceases to function even if respiration and circulation can be maintained artificially. Others argue that a person is dead when the outer surface of the cerebrum ceases functioning. (Such an individual may still breathe spontaneously via control of the brain stem, but thinking and reasoning ability have ceased.)

Definitions of death center around *brain, heart,* or *physiological* death when various organs cease to function, and *clinical* death when the person has a total lack of response to any external or internal stimuli, has no spontaneous respiration, has fixed and dilated pupils, shows a lack of brain-stem reflexes, and produces a flat EKG (no heartbeat). The definition of death has significance for more than organ transplants. It also indicates when life-support systems should be used.

Organ Donations and Transplants

Some people donate their organs or entire body for scientific and medical uses. This issue involves biological, medical, and legal ethics. For those who wish to donate an organ, the Uniform Anatomical Gift Act of 1978 sets guidelines underlying the donor laws of each state. Some individuals donate their entire bodies to medical schools for dissection. Other donated parts include eyes (for corneal transplants), ear bones (to temporal bone banks for use in research into ear diseases), kidneys (for kidney

HEALTH HIGHLIGHT

Questions Asked Most Often About Organ Donors

Currently only organ donations of kidneys, liver, heart, and the pancreas are accepted for donation. This acceptance is based on the definition of death discussed earlier in this chapter. The donor must die in a hospital, since surgery must be performed within hours for any organs to be used. The heart, for example, is suitable for transplantation for only 4 to 5 hours, as is the liver. For this reason, surgeries usually begin simultaneously for the donor and the recipient. Kidneys are suitable for transplantation for 36 to 48 hours.

To help encourage donors, several agencies have developed brochures that seek to answer the typical questions asked about organ donation. An article in *Health* also sought to provide answers for prospective donors (Byron, 1982). Some of the most asked questions and their answers follow.

1. Who will be the recipient?
   Answer: Who will receive the transplant is not always certain, nor is such information as the donor's name or hometown usually disclosed. (Recent involvement of the news media, however, has affected this greatly.) General information such as "the kidney of a 13-year-old who died in an auto accident was used," may be provided. Body parts from a person who is over 55 are not accepted for donation.
2. Will the donor suffer?
   Answer: The donor is legally dead and feels no pain. Because a surgical team removes the organ within two hours; consequently, surgery does not interfere with funeral arrangements.
3. Is there an age requirement for donors?
   Answer: Anyone 18 years or older and of sound mind may donate by signing a donor card. Anyone under 18 may become a donor if either parent or the legal guardian gives permission.
4. Should organ donation be mentioned in a will?
   Answer: This is not necessary; only the donor card is needed. Also, the will is usually read after burial. Family members and the physician should be informed about the desired donation in advance to help ensure cooperation.
5. Can an individual change his or her mind about donation?
   Answer: Simply tear up the card—nothing else is necessary.
6. When will the donation be used?
   Answer: The organs must be removed and transplanted within hours after death. The attending physician is responsible for determining death, but he or she cannot participate in either removing or transplanting the organ.
7. Will an estate be paid or have to pay for organ donation?
   Answer: No.
8. Besides organs, are other parts of the body useful?
   Answer: Such things as bones, cartilage, and other nonvital tissues such as eardrums and bones of the middle ear can also be used with very little rejection. Success rates have been reported as high as 70%.
9. What is the future of transplant surgery?
   Answer: Although much transplant surgery is still classified as experimental, the future is encouraging. Medical knowledge and technology are constantly improving. Today two-thirds of liver transplant patients live beyond the first year. Even when a transplant patient lives only a few months, most families consider the operation worthwhile, since it probably improved the patient's quality of life.
10. How does one become a donor?
    Answer: By signing a donor card, one may bequeath specific organs or parts. Donating the body for anatomical study is more complicated, and the body must be intact.
11. Where do I get a donor card?
    Answer: Most state driver's licenses have a space for donating organs. A uniform donor's card may be requested from several agencies, such as the National Kidney Foundation or a local eye bank.

transplants), pituitary glands (for use in producing growth hormone for those who lack this vital substance), and hearts (for heart transplants).

Few religions in our country restrict organ donations to help another patient regain health. Further, an organ donation need not interrupt or modify the planned funeral service for the donor in any way. A donor needs to carry a signed and witnessed donor card at all times. These donor cards are available from many agencies in the community, such as the local kidney dialysis clinic or the department of motor vehicles.

The Right to Die and Euthanasia

Euthanasia, also known as mercy killing, goes back to ancient times. Many Greek philosophers advocated euthanasia. Greeks and Romans alike agreed that people are the masters of their own bodies and have the right to decide their own fate. During the first century, on the Greek island of Cos, the elderly and the ill would gather at a banquet once a year and drink a poisonous chemical to promote death.

As early as 1906 in the United States, a bill was introduced in the Ohio state legislature to provide for voluntary euthanasia. In 1931, Dr. Milland, the newly elected president of the Society of Medical Officers of Health in Great Britain, gave a speech advocating the legalization of voluntary euthanasia for adults who were mentally competent and suffering from a fatal disease.

The Euthanasia Society of America was started by the Rev. Charles Francis Potter in 1938. This group included professionals who believed that the terminally ill had a right to die with dignity. This group became the Euthanasia Education Council in 1972; today it is known as the Euthanasia Society for the Right to Die. The mission of this group is to help introduce euthanasia-related legislation, such as that concerning the living will, which will be discussed later in this chapter (Wass, Berardo, & Neimeyer, 1988).

Euthanasia is not just a medical problem; it also involves legal, ethical, social, personal, and financial considerations. For this reason, the debate over euthanasia involves many professionals and paraprofessionals, as well as patients and their families. Arguments concern the dignity of the patients, the quality of their lives, their mental state, and sometimes their "usefulness to society." For example, a patient in a vegetative state is considered dead by some but not by others, and this case presents substantial ethical and logistical problems. Some say that to intervene in any way is to "play God," while others maintain that not allowing a patient to die violates the rights of the patient. Such procedures as using a life-support machine are sometimes seen as heroic acts, but others think they only prolong the patient's suffering. Therefore, the line between heroic procedures (or unnecessary care) and giving up (or neglecting the patient) is difficult to draw. This distinction would be simple it we could just ask patients which treatment they wanted, but this is not possible in a majority of cases, such as if a patient is in a coma.

Today, we are being forced to rethink our ideas and choices about life, dying, and death. The issue of euthanasia is an excellent example of this. In recent years, the emphasis in the euthanasia debate has shifted away from allowing people to die a natural, painless death and more toward allowing death to occur by withholding heroic medical treatment. Typically, patients for whom euthanasia is considered are terminally ill or have serious, life-threatening birth defects. Often, a decision to practice euthanasia means hastening the inevitable—letting the person die now rather than later—rather than a choice between life and death. Some argue that any trend toward euthanasia may be rooted in our fear of facing death. Using euthanasia to hasten death helps us avoid coping with the consequences of actually dying. Many times, medical staffs or families make the decision to prolong or end life, further complicating the issue.

The term *euthanasia* has come to imply a contract for terminating a person's life so he or she can avoid unnecessary suffering at the end of a fatal illness. Direct (or active) euthanasia is defined as a deliberate action to shorten life. It involves a procedure like injecting air or a chemical substance into the bloodstream. This is termed mercy killing and is still considered murder in our country, although some feel it should be permissible. In indirect, or passive, euthanasia, death is not induced; it is accomplished through the omission of an act or acts rather than commission of a life-taking act. For example, doctors might halt treatments that would prolong the life of a patient, or they might withhold treatment altogether. Several national polls and surveys show that the majority of Americans support passive euthanasia (Humphry & Wickett, 1987).

Rapid advances in medical technology have given the medical profession the ability to sustain or prolong life through extraordinary methods, so that those who might have died quickly now have a chance of survival with life-sustaining artificial support mechanisms. An adult in this country is considered to have the right to determine whether this type of medical technology should be employed. The person has the right to expressly prohibit life-saving surgery or other medical treatments. In other words, the right to die with dignity is inherent for every individual, as much so as the right to live. Some individuals fear the indignity and humiliation of merely existing as a vegetable, with others making decisions for them and caring for their every need. These people would rather die a "good death" than exist in this manner. The proponents of euthanasia state that saving a life is not always the same as saving people, as some do not wish to go on living or be revived. They argue that people should not be forced to extend their lives. This philosophy emphasizes the *quality* of life rather than just the literal existence of life.

Some states have passed laws to ensure their citizens the right to die. This type of legislation provides death with dignity to those who sign a legal document known as a living will, as shown in Figure 15.1. Signers of a living will anticipate a time when they cannot make or communicate decisions about their conditions and treatment but wish to reject artificial means of prolonging life. They ask, in most cases, for such treatment to be withheld. Those states that have not passed similar legislation are currently considering such a bill.

Wills

The **last will and testament** is a legal instrument declaring a person's intentions concerning the disposition of property, the guardianship of students, or the

Figure 15.1   Form for Last Will and Testament

LAST WILL AND TESTAMENT OF _____

A Resident of _____ County, in the state of _____ ,
being of sound and disposing mind and memory, and being ____ years of age (must be
18 in most states), do hereby make, declare, and publish this my Last Will and Testament,
hereby expressly revoking any and all other wills, including any and all codicils thereto, by
me at any time heretofore made.

I.

I direct that my just debts, together with my funeral expenses, be paid as soon as
practicable after my death.

II.

Subject to the foregoing, I will and bequeath to (In this paragraph dispose of all personal
property, such as household goods, government bonds, jewelry, and other personal
property, wherever situated, located, or to be found.)

III.

I will and devise to the following parties: (In this paragraph dispose of all real property, real
estate, etc., describing each parcel sufficiently so as to eliminate all doubt as to its
identity.)

IV.

(If the testator wants to leave property to one person for use during his or her lifetime and
at the death of such person leave the property to someone else, this may be
accomplished as follows:) I do hereby leave (<u>describing property</u>) to (<u>describing the
beneficiary</u>) for his/her life, and at his/her death I do hereby leave remainder of such
property to (<u>describing the beneficiary</u>).

V.

(Any property of the testator not disposed of by the will shall pass in a manner prescribed
by law, which may be contrary to the intention of the testator. It is therefore important that
the testator dispose of *all* of his or her property, including property the testator may
acquire after the time of the execution of the will and property that the testator may not be
aware he or she has an interest in. This may be accomplished by adding a clause like the
following:) I do hereby give, devise, and bequeath all the rest, residue, and remainder of
my property whether real, personal, mixed, or otherwise and wheresoever situated
to _____ [or to _____ ,
_____ and _____ in equal
shares].

VI.

I hereby nominate, constitute, and appoint _____ my (<u>sister,
brother, etc.</u>), Executor (or Executrix, if female) of this my Last Will and Testament, and to
the extent permitted I hereby excuse him or her from giving any bond, filing any inventory,

Figure 15.1 *Continued*

and making any report or settlement with any court as such Executor/Executrix. (It is a good idea to name an alternate in case the person named should predecease the testator. This may be accomplished as follows:) In the event that (the <u>named executor</u>) should predecease me, I do hereby appoint _____ Executor/Executrix of this my Last Will and Testament, and to the extent permitted by law I hereby expressly excuse him or her from giving any bond, filing any inventory, and making any report or settlement with any court as such Executor/Executrix.

IN WITNESS WHEREOF, I, _____ , the Testator (or Testatrix) do hereby publish and declare this to be my Last Will and Testament and have requested

_____ , _____ , and

_____ to become subscribing witnesses thereto, and have

hereunto set my hand this _____ day of _____ , 19 _____ .

(signature)

_____

Testator (or Testatrix)

Signed by the said <u>(Testator/Testatrix)</u> as for his/her Last Will and Testament, in the presence of us, the undersigned do who at his/her request and in his/her sight and presence and in the presence and sight of each other have hereunto signed our names as subscribing witnesses this day _____ of _____ , 19 _____ .

_____

_____

_____

(In most states, if the beneficiary named predeceases the tesator/testatrix, the "heirs" of the beneficiary will take title to the property bequeathed or devised. If the testator/testatrix does not want this result, but wants that property to pass to someone other than the "heirs" of the beneficiary if the beneficiary predeceases him or her, he or she may accomplish this result by adding the following sentence after a bequest or devise:) "In the event that (the <u>named beneficiary)</u> should predecease me, I do hereby bequeath/devise such property to _____ .

Source: *Dying and Death* by Judy Oaks & Gene Ezell, 1993, Scottsdale, AZ: Gorsuch, Scarisbrick.

administration of the estate after a person's death. A will is a legal document in which people outline how they want property and possessions to be distributed after their death. By constructing such a document, people can dictate how their property will be distributed, the cost and time of settling the estate can be reduced, an executor can be named, family quarrels can be avoided, a guardian can be appointed, and a testamentary trust can be created. For most people, ensuring the desired distribution of their property and possessions is sufficient reason for writing a will. A person can also enact a living trust, which entrusts an estate to another person while the owner of the estate is still alive. A living trust keeps the estate private instead of public, even when the owner of the estate dies. A living trust can avoid probate, legal fees, and some taxation when the owner of the estate dies.

Perhaps because ours is a society that denies death, most people delay writing a will. Others do not make out wills for reasons that border on superstition—i.e., "if I make out a will, I am admitting that I am going to die; therefore, I will die." In other words, the less we think about wills and dying, the less likely we are to die (Kalish, 1985). It is not surprising that most Americans, even many with sizable estates, do not have a will, because writing a will reminds people of their own mortality.

What Happens When No Will Is Left

A will is needed to ensure that personal property gets distributed as the deceased person desires, to avoid the consequences of estate and inheritance taxes, and to have some control over one's estate after death. For individuals who die without wills, property passes according to state law. In other words, the state will decide which relatives get which part of the estate, even if the deceased person may have wished otherwise.

Hospice

A **hospice** is a program, type of care, or facility that cares for the terminally ill and their families. Hospice care can be given in the patient's home, in a separate wing of a hospital, or in a separate facility. Generally, the goal of hospice care is to enhance the quality of a dying person's life during the last days and to allow the person to live as comfortably and inexpensively as possible.

Suicide

Suicide among school-aged students has increased dramatically in the last generation; the rate of increase in about the last 25 years is 132%. Suicide is the third leading cause of death among adolescents (Wass, Berardo, & Neimeyer, 1988). More guilt is associated with suicide than with any other type of death. Parents and other relatives blame themselves for the death. Some feel that a suicide reflects badly on the parents and family, but this is not always the case. Certain religions consider suicide morally wrong and teach that one who commits suicide cannot enter heaven.

No single answer explains why people wish to end their lives. The reasons are many and complex, but usually center around current and previous stresses, psychiatric and medical histories, alcoholism, frustration, hostility, revenge, hopelessness, failure, loneliness, aggression, and depression. Family problems, identity problems, and drugs can also contribute to feelings of anonymity and isolation leading to suicide (DeSpelder & Strickland, 1992).

People who commit suicide often provide clues such as changes in mood or behavior, excessive use of drugs or alcohol and/or decreased sleeping and eating habits.

Any suicidal threat, however subtle, must be taken seriously. Most individuals who commit suicide provide significant clues to their contemplated action. These include obvious changes in mood or behavior, excessive use of drugs, changes in habits, preoccupation with personal health, decreased academic performance, and insomnia.

Four steps are commonly recommended for helping someone who seems in danger of suicide. First, one should talk to the person who threatens suicide and determine how deeply troubled the individual really is. Second, one should not challenge the individual to act on the threat. Such a challenge may force the person to act to prove the validity of the threat. Third, someone can help the person postpone the decision and offer other options to consider. Fourth, one can be knowledgeable about resources that can provide aid. The person might have exhausted all personally known avenues of assistance and might need professional help.

Suicide prevention is a community responsibility, and everyone can play an important part in its resolution. However, many people have various misconceptions regarding suicide. Some of these misconceptions (and the truths) are shown in Figure 15.2.

Figure 15.2 Common myths about suicide

American society harbors many misconceptions concerning suicide. To help clear up some of the myths, the following list has been developed:

- *Myth:* People who talk about suicide won't commit suicide.
  Fact: Statistics indicate that eight out of ten individuals who commit suicide give definite warnings of their intentions.
- *Myth:* Suicidal people are fully intent on dying.
  Fact: Most suicidal people are ambivalent about living or dying. They are often willing to gamble with death in order to get the attention or help they desire.
- *Myth:* Once an individual attempts suicide, he is suicidal forever.
  Fact: People are usually suicidal for only a short period of time.
- *Myth:* Improvement following a suicide attempt means that the crisis is over.
  Fact: Most suicides that follow attempts occur within three months from the beginning of "improvement," or the initial lessening of the threat of suicide. The appearance of improvement may mean that the individual now has the energy to put his suicidal thoughts into action.
- *Myth:* Suicide occurs most often among the poor.
  Fact: Suicide is neither a rich person's curse nor a poor person's. It is represented proportionately throughout all strata of society.
- *Myth:* Suicide is inherited and runs in families.
  Fact: Suicide is an individual pattern and does not run in families.
- *Myth:* Suicidal people are mentally ill, and the act is psychotic.
  Fact: Although suicidal persons are extremely unhappy and depressed, they are not necessarily mentally ill.
- *Myth:* Asking whether a person is considering suicide will lead him to make an attempt.
  Fact: Asking a person directly will often minimize the suicidal feeling and act as a deterrent to the act.

Source: *Health* (p. 191) by M. Hamrick, D. Anspaugh, & G. Ezell, 1986, New York: Merrill/Macmillan.

STUDENTS AND DEATH

Students in our society no longer experience many aspects of the life cycle. Most do not live with grandparents or on farms, so they do not observe aging and death in their immediate environment. Education about death thus is necessary for the proper development of secondary school students. Death should be viewed as a natural topic for inclusion in education because students eventually experience the death of a loved one, a pet, or a classmate. Future secondary teachers should prepare themselves to teach about death, because it is an important part of students' mental health (Molnar-Stickles, 1985).

Students respond to their own imminent deaths within the framework of the stages just described. A dying student needs to be assured that death is not a punishment for something the student did or said.

Death Education

Positive attitudes toward death can help prepare succeeding generations to face death more realistically. We can help students accept the reality of death by preparing them properly for funerals and by allowing them to mourn, cry, recover from the loss of a pet or a relative, and express grief as part of a healing process. We should talk to students about death in whatever terms they can understand. This discussion can take either a religious or a factual point of view, depending on the parents' and the student's preferences.

We should explain the cause of death to eliminate any fear or guilt the student might develop as a result of experiencing a death. It is unwise to deceive the student by using euphemisms or half-truths. Another way to teach students about death is to allow—not force—a student to attend a funeral. A recommended method is to take them first to the funeral of a neighbor or distant relative. Because the parents would not be as physically or emotionally involved in such a situation, they could devote time and energy to the student. The funeral can be a teaming experience. Prepare the student before the funeral, ask him or her to watch for certain things during the funeral, and encourage questions afterward. Attending a funeral will help give the student a more complete understanding of death and make it more likely that the student will develop a healthy attitude about death.

Finally, students should be encouraged to talk openly about their fears and feelings. This will help eliminate any misgivings the students have and help the parents to respond more appropriately to the emotions expressed. Of course, this assumes that the parents know *how* to respond and that they will share their own emotions with the student.

Fortunately, people today are more willing to discuss death and dying. The many books available on the subject, the courses being taught in schools and universities, the increased number of bereavement societies and hospice groups, and the increasing number of documentaries, specials, and films in the media are evidence of this. The new openness about death is refreshing; it challenges the previous treatment of death as a taboo topic for conversation, research, and writing. Communication about death can improve the quality of our lives and help us grow as individuals. Even as a friend or parent, if we fumble through a discussion on death, it is very helpful.

Death is a universal part of living even though our society considers it a taboo topic. Students are interested in knowing more about the subject of death, but they are generally shielded from such exposure. Many parents are reluctant to talk with their children about death because they wish to protect them (and themselves) from the pain of loss. Students are often prohibited from some hospital wards, health care institutions, and other places where people are dying. As a result, they tend to learn about death through the media, which can be confusing and misleading.

Sooner or later, students must confront death to understand the needs of the dying, to have some preparation for the experience, and to deal with their own feelings. Death is a legitimate subject for students to study. It is an important topic worthy of open, informed, and sensitive discussion. Death education can increase students' understanding about death and dying, and, even though it might be painful for them and for the teacher, having such understanding can be essential for sound mental health.

In death education, teachers should come to terms with their own feelings about death and not just learn the material. They need to be aware of students' willingness to express their feelings on this sensitive topic and be ready to let them discuss the subject openly and frankly. Teachers should never tell students they need to wait until they are older to talk about death. Many times, adults use this ploy as an excuse to avoid their own insecurities about death. Teachers also need to answer any question at the students' level of understanding. The teacher's and students' feelings and emotions related to death should also be expressed—even encouraged—in the classroom. Teachers can use experiences in the classroom, such as the death of a flower, a pet, or a classmate, to teach students about death feelings and rituals.

■ ■ ■　*STUDENT CONCERNS:* AGING, DYING, AND DEATH

As students move through grades 7 through 12, many issues of concern surface regarding aging, dying, and death. The statements reflected here were taken from *Students Speak* (Trucano, 1984). Typical (verbatim) student responses were as follows:

Grade 7

What should you do if you are considering suicide?

I would like to know more about suicide and how cope with yourself when you are under stress.

How do you get out of a state of depression?

What do you do to prevent suicide or change somebody's mind about hurting himself or herself?

Are the reasons for suicide different with different people?

How can we keep our bodies up?

Why do some people go through changes in their body so easily and others take it so hard?

Grade 8

Now kids would rather go into suicide than stick around so I think this subject should be more fully studied.

At our age we have problems and need to release anger and confusion.

Dope and booze are popular and suicide is really climbing, too. I think we need all the info we can get on these things.

Why do people grow and change at different rates and why are some people smarter or more athletic than others?

What are the chances of someone getting, for example, a heart attack, if their grandpa did not but your father had one?

Do your ancestors affect how the child looks?

Will the heart, back, and eye problems that your parents have affect you now, near future, later life, your children? Can these problems be prevented now? How?

Grade 9

Are the people who commit suicide mentally ill or under a lot of stress?

What does the mental state of a person have to do with the wide number of suicides, homicides, and alcoholism?

How do you learn to like yourself so suicide and stress can be prevented?

What are the new studies about "preventing" aging?

Why do you shrink when you get older?

How do people become aged?

How can you slow down aging?

Grade 10

What can you do to help a friend when they think they are going to commit suicide?

Knowing more about suicidal signals.

Why do people age and not stay young?

Explain more on what happens when you get old such as senile and stages at which we see older people now, and we'll go through some day also.

What do you have to do to stay healthy all your life?

Grade 11

I think you should give out information about what to do or where to go if abused or thinking of suicide.

What should you do if you know of someone who has been sexually abused or contemplating suicide?

Grade 12

How does a child's behavior play a part in his or her aging?

SUMMARY

Aging is a normal part of the life cycle, not a pathological condition. We are all aging every day. The number of elderly has risen sharply in the past two decades, and this trend is likely to continue. In addition, life expectancies for all Americans are increasing.

The aging process remains poorly understood for the most part. Many factors, both intrinsic and extrinsic, also affect the aging process for each individual. Many biological, psychological, and sociological changes occur as a person ages. Some of these changes present unavoidable problems for the elderly, but other changes can be successfully accommodated.

Elderly people face many challenges in life, but these challenges affect all members of society. Finances, retirement, housing, health, nutrition, crime, and transportation are among these issues. Some of the problems the elderly face are the result of discrimination and misconceptions. Stereotypes about the elderly largely result from lack of knowledge and insufficient contact with the elderly. Intergenerational contact programs in schools can be one of the most effective ways to help students understand aging and the elderly, helping to dispel some of the many myths about aging. The elderly of the future will generally enjoy a better standard of living.

Death is the natural end to life, yet many in our society try to deny its existence. Death is mysterious because we do not know what is beyond death. Many people fear death and refuse to discuss the topic openly and frankly. Everyone, however, has personal beliefs about death. Some of these beliefs can help us face death because they help demystify it, but facing death is still a traumatic experience for the dying person and the survivors alike. The dying person has many emotional needs that relatives and medical professionals cannot satisfy. This may leave the dying person very lonely and feeling abandoned. A dying person also undergoes various stages of adjustment to impending death; by understanding these stages, we can better help the dying person.

Many controversies and issues surround death, including the definition of death, the person's right to die, organ donation and transplants, wills, and suicide. Most students in our society do not experience death close to home anymore. Students also go through definite stages in their understanding of death and are interested in knowing more about the subject of death. Thus, the study of death is a legitimate, worthwhile topic in secondary schools.

DISCUSSION QUESTIONS

1. Discuss the significance of aging education and death education in the school curriculum.
2. Describe the benefits of intergenerational contact.
3. Discuss the current demographics of elderly people in the United States.
4. Predict the typical lifestyle of elderly Americans in the year 2000.
5. Why do most people fear death?
6. How can the family help in the adjustment of a dying person?
7. Differentiate among grief, bereavement, and mourning.
8. Why is more guilt associated with suicide than with other types of deaths?

■ ■ ■   *ACTIVITIES FOR TEACHING ABOUT AGING, DYING, AND DEATH*

■ ■ ■   *ACTIVITIES:* VALUE-BASED ACTIVITIES ABOUT AGING

Rank Ordering*

Give students a list of categories and have them write down the age they think represents each group.

_____ Prime of life

_____ Middle age

_____ Retirement age

_____ Old age

Discuss with students why they picked the ages they did for each category. Some questions to ask: As we age, does our concept of what is middle age change? Is there a difference between men and women? With the average life span increasing, should the age of retirement be raised? Are there goals or activities that you have set for yourself to be reached before middle age, retirement, etc.?

*Source: *Health Education Guide* by M. Barrett, 1974, Philadelphia: Lea & Febiger.

■ ■ ■   *ACTIVITIES:* VALUE-BASED ACTIVITIES FOR DEATH AND DYING

A Teaching Strategy on Tragedy*

"Mary's life seemed to be at a perfect point! She was 16 years old, pretty, intelligent, enthusiastic, a varsity cheerleader, and had just been elected homecoming queen for her high school. She had a happy home life, with two brothers, four sisters, two parents, and a dog named Brownie. Mary loved life and had everything to live for. On a clear night in March, she was driving home from work, just getting ready to make the left hand turn off of Highway 617 into her driveway—when from nowhere a semi-truck started to pass her on the left. Mary died on March 23, 1976."

A similar tragedy may happen at any time in your community or school system. The question is, how do we prepare our students to handle the death of a friend or loved one properly? Is there ever a proper way to handle this situation?" Death 40 to 50 years ago was accepted as a natural culmination of life. However, today Americans try to cover it up and pretend that when death does occur they will be able to accept it. This idea has not proven to be valid in recent years. There appears to be an inescapable need to furnish our youth with a more comprehensive view of what death really means, how they can cope with a death when it occurs, and why it is important for them to carry on and live a more fulfilled life.

A death education unit taught in a health class needs to be implemented for the benefit of each student. If death is accepted as a natural part of life, an inevitable event in all existence, then we will be able to stress the importance of living life to the utmost for *today!* The main objective, it seems evident, is for the death unit to emphasize the need to develop in each individual a crisp zest for every undertaking, day-to-day, that one can. Life is rich in varied opportunities and the mission is to find and perceive each and every advantage that arises. We teach death in order to better live and understand the total process of life!

A Tragedy Strategy

Once the need for a unit on death education has been established, the next problem a teacher faces is just exactly how to introduce the unit into the classroom. One teaching strategy, which proved to be very functional in past health instruction and upon which this article is based, used a questionnaire entitled "You and Death," by Edwin Shneidman.[1] It contains approximately 72 questions which were condensed to 40 for class purposes. In essence, it entails answering the questions in an attempt to identify and clarify students' feelings and conceptions on death. The questionnaire proved to be a thought provoking and discussion stimulating technique to introduce the death unit.

[1]Edwin Shneidman, Center for Advanced Study in the Behavioral Sciences, in consultation with Edwin Parker and G. R. Funkhouser of Stanford University, "You and Death," *Psychology Today,* Communications Research Machines, Inc.; Del Mar, CA, August 1970, pp. 67–72.
*Source: M. Barrett: *Health Education Guide: A Design for Teaching* (2nd ed.). Philadelphia: Lea & Febiger, 1974. Reprinted with permission.

For a more complete and interesting discussion of the questionnaire, the students were instructed to mark a star by the most thought provoking questions; an "S" by those which most surprised them; a "T" beside the questions about which they would really like to talk with someone; and an "MI" in front of those questions they would like more information on as they went through the test. These marks pinpointed the areas of most interest for the ensuing discussion. They also symbolized to the students where their ideals and values needed to be researched and clarified further.

Four of the 40 questions that were clarified at some length in the classroom are discussed here. They exemplify the type of discussion that was carried on as a result of the questionnaire.

The first question seemed to influence the way in which the students answered the rest of the questionnaire: to what extent do you believe in a life after death? a. strongly believe in it; b. tend to believe in it; c. uncertain; d. tend to doubt it; e. convinced it does not exist.

Some students were confused about their feelings on the subject and therefore seemed to have a great deal of trouble completing the test. However, others answering the question either completely affirmatively or completely negatively had little trouble with the test. By discussing the question in greater detail it appeared that most of the students felt more at peace with their own feelings towards the subject and felt more open about their convictions because they found out that they were not the only ones who had trouble with the subject.

A second question prompting interest tried to clarify situations in which one would give up one's own life: For whom or what might you be willing to sacrifice your life? a. a loved one; b. an idea or moral principle; c. in combat or a grave emergency where a life could be saved; d. not for any reason.

Most of the students had a great deal of difficulty imagining sacrificing their lives for anyone or anything. Most of the members enjoyed their present lives. However, they all agreed that they would probably change their minds if they were confronted with a real life situation involving one of these choices.

Another thought provoking question had to do with the actual date of one's death: If it were possible, would you want to know the exact date on which you are going to die?

The catalyst of this discussion was supplied by one student's statement that "if I were told that I was going to live to be at least 40 years old, I would live life to its fullest and try to experience all that life affords and not wait for old age to do the things I've always dreamed of doing." Others responded that they would definitely not like to know when they were to die because it was a fearful subject for them and they would rather not think about it. Still another response was shared with the class by a student stating that it really doesn't matter to him whether or not he knew because his religious faith was so strong and he was so satisfied with his present life that anytime death came he would be ready.

Conclusions made from this question helped students to answer and discuss a fourth question: What effect has this questionnaire had on you? a. it has made me somewhat anxious or upset; b. it has made me think about my death; c. it has reminded me how fragile and precious life is; d. no effect at all; e. other effects (specify).

Most of the students responded to the question by either marking "b" or "e." The questionnaire did make them think about their own death but it also made them deliberate about their feelings on suicide. It also brought suppressed feelings out into the open and helped them to be more content with their ideas on death and dying.

As we discussed the whole topic of death once more in the summary, they felt also that they could have responded "c" as well. The discussion of death did remind them of the pricelessness of a fulfilled life and forced them to reevaluate their personal lives at the present time.

Strategy Evaluation

As a final evaluation of this experience, the students filled out a sheet of open-ended statements. These evaluations proved even more valuable than the discussion. It helped students to be more understanding of each other's personal feelings and views on death and the pricelessness of a fulfilled life.

The students were given no directions on the proper way to complete the statements and thus were forced to answer them with their own unique perceptions of the total experience. In sharing some of their answers it is my hope that each reader will see how successful the strategy proved to be for each participant. Some of the answers from the students follow.

I learned that . . .
- life, though often taken for granted is temporary, and protection of same, even promotion of same is of number one priority.
- "death education" can be an interesting topic if taught with the objective of living life better for now.
- I am able to stand firmly convicted to the belief in life after death—not fearing death as we know it here on earth.
- I am satisfied with my life and death concept.

I want to . . .
- find out more information about the stages of life when one's attitudes toward death change.
- live what life is afforded me to its fullest, but regretfully must adjust to constraints (some of which may be unnecessarily self-imposed).
- live my life to the fullest and when death comes, I hope to accept it gracefully and it accept me the same way.
- live daily with the attitude that today is my only opportunity to tell others why I don't fear death.

I hope that I . . .
- can live life productively, yet joyously—and never stray from the sense of perspective that enables me to "always smell the flowers . . ."
- can develop sharper opinions on some of the questions I was unsure of.
- if I discover I am scheduled to die soon, I can lead exciting final days and not spend my last days pouting and cursing my destiny.
- live to be a ripe old age!!

I was surprised to see that . . .
- some people didn't want to give their lives for others.
- when confronted with the possibility that even I might consider suicide, I really could not think of the way in which I would take my life.
- I don't have very many strong convictions about my attitude toward death.
- some refuse to seek the full life.

I was glad to see that . . .
- my religious faith is strong enough to answer most of these questions with ease.
- I was consistent in my thoughts on death.
- I did have to think as a result of this questionnaire about my feelings on death.
- others believe in God and put their trust in His promise for eternal life.
- Many treasure *living*—not as solely based on survival ethics, but on a *fulfilling* basis . . . "I want all from life that is good and beautiful."

I want to remember that . . .
- today may be my last—I need to keep a smile on my face and a rainbow in my heart!
- no matter what else I learn through my educational career I am sure to remember *today!*
- whatever I do with my life—the only important thing is to die with Jesus controlling my heart.
- death is not the end!
- life has order, peace, love and total appreciation of nature."

Death education can be a mind-expanding unit if taught with the objective of getting the students to learn to accept and understand death and to think of it as an inevitable end to life, as we know it here on earth. When they can accept this phenomenon, they can develop a more meaningful opinion about the necessity to *live* life to the utmost and to instill in themselves a zeal for a more fulfilled life.

It is vitally important that one learns that one does not have to wait for tragedy before confronting the fundamental and ineluctable questions related to death and dying with which one may be confronted. The requirement here is for one to be willing to participate and learn to understand and accept death as a natural part of all life.

The Survival Group*

These are survivors of a South Pacific cruise ship which sank 700 miles from known land. They have no supplies other than their clothes and what may be contained in their pockets. The seas and weather conditions preclude rescue for several days. The lifeboat cannot sustain them all for more than a few hours. Chances of survival are 40 percent with two persons eliminated; 80 percent with three eliminated. Rank order the individuals according to suitability for removal from the boat.

Source: *Activities for Health Decisions* by D. J. Anspaugh & M. H. Hamrick, 1983, Winston-Salem, NC: Hunter.

No one may volunteer to go over the side. Sharks would be attracted to the boat if someone were to get into the water to reduce weight in the boat, but still hold on to the side. This act would jeopardize everyone.

Individually rank the survivors and then in small groups come to a consensus as to how the group should be ranked.

Below, record your rankings of the eight persons. A ranking of *1* means most eligible for removal in your opinion.

Members of the survival group

1. *Male;* 59 years old; general practitioner, M.D.; widower; father of two adult children; vacationing; has had two severe heart attacks in the last five years; caucasian; U.S. citizen; alone on the trip.
2. *Female;* 31 years old; part-time secretary; married; mother of three—ages nine, seven, and four; visiting husband at overseas duty site; good health; U.S. citizen, black; children at home; alone on trip.
3. *Male;* sailor from downed ship; single; good health; Italian citizen; caucasian; no family or relatives; 24 years old; speaks no English.
4. Female; 28 years old; survival expert with paramedical training; married; no children; good health; U.S. citizen; caucasian; husband on ship.
5. *Male;* 30 years old; married; no children; survival expert and marine biologist; good health; U.S. citizen; wife on ship.
6. Male; 46 years old; protestant minister; married; father of one adult child; on missionary service in South Pacific; good health; Canadian citizen; caucasian; alone on trip.
7. *Male;* nine years old; brother to one other child in family; son of businessman and housewife; good health; U.S. citizen; caucasian; with family on trip.
8. Female; 59 years old; world-famous sculptress; single; fair health—asthma occasionally; mongol; Chinese citizen; alone on trip.

Person #1 _____   Person #5 _____
          2 _____   6 _____
          3 _____   7 _____
          4 _____   8 _____

Discussion Questions

1. How did you judge the people for ranking?
2. Were there differences between how the males ranked and how the females ranked? Why? Why not?
3. What changed (if any) your individual opinion from the final group opinion?

Understanding Death and Dying*

To understand life we must have insight into death and dying. To help with developing our understanding about death and dying, complete the following sentences. These will be discussed in small groups.

*Source: *Activities for Health Decisions* by D. J. Anspaugh & M. H. Hamrick, 1983, Winston-Salem, NC: Hunter.

Death is _____

I would like to die at (age) _____

I would like to die at (place) _____

When I die, I would like at my side _____

The greatest fear I have of dying _____

When I die, I'll be proud that during my life I _____

When I die, I'll be glad I didn't _____

If given one year to live, I would _____

When I die, I would like others to remember _____

Death and Dying—Opinionnaire*

Please circle the response which most accurately reflects your feeling. A-Agree, or mostly agree; D-Disagree, or mostly disagree. If you can't decide, circle the question mark (?), but try to circle as few ?'s as possible.

A	D	?	1. Too much money is spent on funerals.
A	D	?	2. Flowers are a beautiful way to pay tribute to a lost friend or loved one.
A	D	?	3. If I were dying from a serious illness, I hope the doctor doesn't tell me.
A	D	?	4. When I die, I hope it happens fast.
A	D	?	5. When a person is in a coma and will never recover, there is no reason to try to keep him alive on machines.
A	D	?	6. Death is a mystery that few people will ever understand.
A	D	?	7. It is best not to talk about death around young children.
A	D	?	8. Young children should be taken to funerals.
A	D	?	9. Most people are not fully appreciated until after they die.
A	D	?	10. Being dead is more honorable than being an invalid and a financial burden on the family.
A	D	?	11. Some funerals that I've attended were handled so badly that I've said, "I hope mine doesn't turn out like that."
A	D	?	12. Burying bodies in cemeteries is a waste of good productive land.
A	D	?	13. There is too much death in movies and TV.

*Source: *Activities for Health Decisions* by D. J. Anspaugh & M. H. Hamrick, 1983, Winston-Salem, NC: Hunter. Adapted from opinionnaire developed by David Wardlaw, Memphis-Shelby County Health Department, Memphis, TN.

A   D   ?   14. I would be willing to give my life for another if I owed them enough.

A   D   ?   15. My own death would probably scare me more than anything else I know.

A   D   ?   16. Expensive funerals usually mean that the family is trying to make up for the unfair way they had treated the person who died.

A   D   ?   17. If a dying person is in a lot of pain, I think that it is more humane to let the person die than to try to keep him alive as long as possible.

A   D   ?   18. It is natural for a person to dream about death.

A   D   ?   19. People should plan their own funerals.

A   D   ?   20. Most people have thought at least once about committing suicide.

A   D   ?   21. If doctors could predict when a seriously handicapped baby would be born, I think that they should be allowed to abort the pregnancy.

A   D   ?   22. It is difficult to know what to say when talking to someone who has just experienced a death.

A   D   ?   23. A strong religious belief really helps a person accept death better.

A   D   ?   24. Most funeral homes take advantage of the grieving family by selling them a funeral they often can't afford.

A   D   ?   25. It is quite common for a doctor to make a mistake in deciding the cause of death of one of his patients.

A   D   ?   26. I doubt that I would have the courage to work on a real human body if I were in an anatomy class.

A   D   ?   27. I would like to donate my body to science when I die.

A   D   ?   28. No matter how many improvements medical science makes, they will never be able to make man immortal.

A   D   ?   29. The right to die or live should be decided by the family rather than a doctor.

A   D   ?   30. Man should exhaust all possibilities in prolonging life including heart transplants, cryonics, etc.

Death and Dying Case Studies*

Have students read the following case studies and answer the questions.

Death and Dying—Case Study 1

On February 9, 1982, a child was born to Mr. and Mrs. Robert Houle at the Maine Medical Center. The child was horribly deformed. His entire left side was malformed;

---

*Source: *Activities for Health Decisions* by D. J. Anspaugh & M. H. Hamrick, 1983, Winston-Salem, NC: Hunter. Case studies developed by David Wardlaw, Memphis-Shelby County Health Department, Memphis, TN.

he had no left eye, was practically without a left ear, had a deformed left hand; some of his vertebrae were not fused. Also he could not be fed by mouth because of a fistula in his esophagus. Air leaked into his stomach instead of going to the lungs, and fluid from the stomach pushed up into the lungs. Further internal deformities were suspected.

As the days passed, the condition of the child deteriorated. Pneumonia set in. His reflexes became impaired and because of poor circulation, severe brain damage was suspected. The fistula, the immediate threat to his survival, could be corrected with relative ease by surgery. But in view of the associated complications and deformities, the parents refused their consent to surgery on the baby. Several doctors in the medical center felt differently, and took the case to court. The superior court judge ordered the surgery to be performed. He ruled: "At the moment of live birth a human being is entitled to the fullest protection of the law. The most basic right enjoyed by every human being is the right to life itself."

Questions

1. Do you think the operation should have been performed?
2. Should the parents have the right to make the "life or death" decision in this case?
3. Would your feelings be different if the child had only external deformities?
4. Who should decide questions such as these? What guidelines should be followed by those making such decisions?

Death and Dying—Case Study 2

On February 11, 1983, an 81-year-old grandfather removed his false teeth and announced to his family that he wouldn't need them anymore. Three weeks later, to the day, he died. His decision to die came after three years of living with hardening of the arteries or what is called "senility." His condition involved standing naked in front of the picture window, "talking" with a giant red rabbit that lived in the refrigerator, and being unable to control his bowels. His bizarre dressing habits, combined with his increasingly erratic behavior, meant the end of friendships that had remained intact for decades. Most people had known him as a proper man and a respected pillar of the community. His best friend said, "When you know what he was before, you just can't take him being like this."

Within a few days his condition deteriorated quickly as he refused to eat and drank very little. He spent most of his days in his room. When asked to come out for dinner he would say, "No I am just going to lie here until it happens." Three weeks after removing his teeth he died.

Questions

1. Is death ever better than life?
2. Should the family have intervened by placing the grandfather in a hospital or nursing home where proper nourishment could have been "forced" on him.
3. Was the grandfather's decision "tragic" or "heroic"?

Death and Dying—Case Study 3

On September 10, 1982, police found Samuel Moore, 29, in a spreading pool of blood in an Oakland, California, slum apartment, a .22-caliber bullet in his brain.

They arrested his friend, car polisher Andrew D. Lyons, 34. Moore didn't regain consciousness in the hospital, but a machine kept his heart beating.

Forty miles away at Stanford Medical Center, a 52-year-old retired construction engineer was in need of a new transplanted heart. A request was made to transplant Samuel Moore's heart. There were two days of argument: Was Moore dead? The county coroner was worried that cutting off Moore's power supply might mean that his death would not be considered murder. The coroner and district attorney finally consented to taking Moore's heart.

The charge against Lyons was changed from assault with a deadly weapon to murder. His lawyer argued that he was not guilty since the transplant had caused death and not the bullet wound. (The legal definition of death in California was cessation of heart beat and respiration.) The doctors argued that when the brain is dead the person is dead and that death occurred when the bullet entered the brain.

Questions

1. If you had been a member of the jury would you have found Lyons guilty or innocent?
2. Do you approve of the doctors removing the heart while it was still functioning with the help of machines?
3. In disputed cases such as this, who should have the responsibility of deciding whether a person is dead or not?

Death and Dying—Case Study 4

A major medical center was treating a man with terminal lymphosarcoma, a disease that involves continued bleeding from the mouth, nose and rectum. All the medical staff could do was to stop blood transfusing him and he would die shortly. He was leaving a young widow and two children who had adjusted to his expected death since for many weeks he had been foggy and unresponsive to them. He was still human to the extent that he had an almost limitless capacity to suffer. He seemed to plead with every reactive facial grimace for the doctors to let him die. He could not understand anything except for his own misery.

The medical center doctors, as do most doctors today, felt that they, in good conscience, should apply every effort to save or prolong his life even in the face of overwhelming odds. He was kept alive for 2½ months. Fifty units of blood at $35 per unit and 75 days of around-the-clock intensive care nursing at $130 per day, in addition to thousands of dollars worth of laboratory tests were used during that period.

Questions

1. Should the medical staff hasten his death by refusing to give needed transfusions?
2. If it is proper for a person to be allowed to die in a situation such as this, who should decide? The individual? the family? the doctor? the courts?

My Funeral

Planning their own funerals can help students face a number of issues related to death and consider the reality of death. Ask students to complete the following questionnaire and be prepared to discuss their responses.

My Last Illness and Death

Yes	No	
_____	_____	I ask that my family be allowed to stay close to me in my last moments.
_____	_____	At the time when I need their presence most I do not want, as is often the case in hospitals, the people who mean most to me to be sent out of the room.
_____	_____	Even after my death I want them to be allowed to remain with my body, if they desire.
_____	_____	Other desires:_____

Preparation of My Body

Yes	No	
_____	_____	I want my relatives or close friends, and not strangers, to wash and care for it as an act of mercy.
_____	_____	I do not want my body embalmed.
_____	_____	I do not want it to be made up to look as if I were still alive, healthy, youthful, or asleep.
_____	_____	I do not want my body put on display after it has been put in my coffin.
_____	_____	I wish to leave my body for scientific study or dissection by medical students.
_____	_____	I am willing to have an autopsy performed.
_____	_____	I am willing to donate any of my organs if they can be used in helping other people to recover health.
_____	_____	I want the remains of my body returned after dissection by the medical school, and buried as otherwise provided for herewith.
_____	_____	If necessary, I am willing for my estate to bear the costs of transportation to and from the medical school.
_____	_____	I am willing to let the medical school dispose of my remains as they deem proper.
_____	_____	I wish to have a funeral regardless of whether my body can be present.
_____	_____	I do not want a suit or dress to be bought for my dead body.
_____	_____	I do not want an elaborate coffin with plush or satin lining, or equipped with a mattress or inner spring.
_____	_____	I want a simple, unlined box of natural wood, which will disintegrate along with the body it contains.
_____	_____	I have prepared my own coffin, and wish to be buried in it.

Yes	No	
_____	_____	During the time between my death and my funeral I would like my body to remain at home, not in a funeral parlor.
_____	_____	I do not want a wake.
_____	_____	I would like my body to be brought to the church in the evening before my funeral.

My Funeral

I would like the following pieces of music to be played:

_____

_____

_____

I do not want the following pieces of music to be played:

_____

_____

_____

Yes	No	
_____	_____	I do not want electronic music played at any proceedings during the wake or funeral.
_____	_____	I do not want a display of flowers.
_____	_____	I do not want a car assigned to hold flowers.
_____	_____	If friends send flowers, I would like them to be delivered directly to hospitals, homes for the elderly, schools, churches or convents.
_____	_____	I hope that beautiful flowers will not be left to wither or rot on my grave, but that they will be distributed at once to cheer those who have come to my burial.
_____	_____	I ask, instead of flowers, that friends contribute to _____.
_____	_____	I do not wish to hire professional pall bearers; if possible, I desire to have my coffin carried by my friends.
_____	_____	I do not want a hearse. I prefer to be borne on a plain truck or station wagon. Other wishes: _____ _____

My Burial

Yes	No	
_____	_____	I wish that my body be buried as soon as possible after my death, and not delayed for the arrival of distant friends or relatives.
_____	_____	I would like to be buried in _____ cemetery.

Yes	No	
_____	_____	I have made arrangements for my grave, and own a plot in _____ cemetery, where I would like to be buried.
_____	_____	Should I die away from home, I direct that I be buried in the nearest _____ cemetery.
_____	_____	I would like my coffin to be lowered into the grave by hand, on ropes or straps, and not by mechanical devices.
_____	_____	If my family wishes to remain to fill my grave with earth, I direct that they be allowed to do so.
_____	_____	I want to be buried in the earth, not in a vault.
_____	_____	If the law requires a cement grave lining, I wish this to be filled with earth before it is closed, to facilitate the decay of my body.
_____	_____	I also want my coffin filled with earth.

Other desires: _____

_____

My Memorial

Yes	No	
_____	_____	I desire a simple gravestone to remind my friends of me.
_____	_____	I wish my name to be carved on my family's stone in _____ cemetery, even though my body is not buried there.
_____	_____	I would like a small memorial with my name to be put up in _____ church, to remind people of me.
_____	_____	I do not want any tomb stone or marker at my grave.

Other desires: _____

_____

Other Dispositions

Yes	No	
_____	_____	As the ocean is the source of all life, I would like my body to be returned to it, and be buried at sea. Thus, I do not need a coffin.
_____	_____	My body may be buried at sea in the box that was used to carry it on board ship.
_____	_____	I would like to be cremated.
_____	_____	I would like my ashes to be scattered.
_____	_____	I would like my ashes to be buried in the church yard.

Other Considerations/Directions Not Covered

_____
_____
_____
_____
_____
_____
_____

Signed: _____

Date: _____

Witnesses: _____

_____

■ ■ ■   ACTIVITIES: DYING AND DEATH ROLE PLAYS

PREVENTING SUICIDE* (*This list may be used with Suicide Myths*)

I. Myths about suicide
   A. The person who talks about suicide won't commit suicide.
   B. Suicide happens without warning.
   C. If you are concerned that a person is considering suicide and ask about it, you may be planting the idea in his mind.
   D. Suicide and attempted suicide are the same class of behavior.
   E. Suicide is a crazy or insane act performed only by the mentally ill.
   F. Suicide is inherited.
   G. The person who attempts suicide is fully intent on dying.
   H. Once a person is suicidal, he is suicidal forever.
II. Observable changes in behavior
   A. Sudden and unexplainable neglect of work or responsibilities
   B. Decrease in the ability to communicate
   C. Changes in daily living patterns
   D. Changes in social behavior
III. Observable changes in the person's emotional life
   A. Low self-esteem or self-deprecation
   B. Depression
   C. Hallucinations and delusions
   D. Withdrawal from life or agitated about the inability to eat or sleep
IV. Other characteristics of a person's life
   A. A family life marked by long-standing conflict, accompanied by rootlessness or transience
   B. The death or loss of parent or significant other
   C. A history of long-standing problems with recent escalation of certain problems

Source: Adapted from handout, *A Plan for Preventing Student Suicide,* by Donald E. Berg, Community Mental Health Center, Bellingham, WA.

D. Be alert for extreme mood swings. A person who is severely depressed one day, elated the next, and depressed again the day after may be struggling with the desire to live and the even stronger desire to die.

E. Be concerned when people start giving away the things they love. They may be telling you that they no longer have any reason to live.

F. Be alert for a crisis that may precipitate a suicide attempt. When suicidal individuals feel overwhelmed by external events—the loss of a job, the death of a parent, a pile of unpaid bills—they may feel that there is no way to cope with life as it is.

G. Listen for a suicide "plan." Suicidal people often talk about their death wish long before they try to kill themselves.

H. Take every suicide attempt seriously—no matter how ineffective it is. People who threaten to take their lives are crying for help. They want someone to save them from their intolerable situation.

I. Be aware that people who quickly bounce back from a suicide attempt and act as if nothing happened may try to kill themselves again within a short time unless they receive help.

Suicide Myths*

Goals

1. To examine and dispute commonly held beliefs about suicide.
2. To conduct open dialogue about personal and social attitudes toward suicidal behavior.

Materials

A series of cards or papers with one of the following myths stated on each (plus a summary list for viewing or distribution):

1. Suicidal people always give cues in advance of making a life-threatening gesture, such as withdrawing socially, giving away personal items, or abusing alcohol.
2. People who kill themselves rarely do so in the initial attempt.
3. Only when the depression in a suicidal person seems to lift can others feel the crisis has passed.
4. Suicidal people are so almost chronically, seeming constantly on the verge of another gesture to end their lives.
5. Most suicidal gestures are not serious but are merely help-seeking cries for rescue.
6. Suicidal tendencies are inherited.
7. Getting a suicidal person to talk about his or her despair is an excellent way to prevent him or her from acting self-destructively.
8. The root cause of a person's suicide can be found if the crises that result from his or her life circumstances are scrutinized.

---

*Reprinted with the permission of Lexington Books, an imprint of Macmillan, Inc., from *Thanatopics: Activities and Exercises for Confronting Death* by J. Eugene Knott, Mary C. Ribar, Betty M. Duson and Marc R. King. Copyright © 1989 by Lexington Books.

9. Suicide is a sign of insanity.
10. Suicide is a cowardly act.

Participants should sit in a circle, with the leader deciding how many myths, and therefore how many persons, per grouping.

Time

50 minutes.

Procedures

1. Introduce the exercise by saying, "We are going to have a short lesson in small groups that deals with a number of widely held beliefs about suicide in this society today. Some of them may be mythical rather than true statements."
2. Distribute cards or sheets with a statement printed on each (prepared in advance), one to each member of the group. Participants read the myths quietly to themselves and await the next instruction. If they are unsure of the meaning of the statement they received, they should privately seek clarification from the leader.
3. In turn, each member will:
   a. Read the statement aloud.
   b. Indicate whether he or she believes it is valid.
   c. Solicit agreement by a show of hands in the group.
   d. Ask any or all minority opinions to tell why they disagree with others.
   e. State why she or he chose the position.
   f. Invite open group dialogue about the statement (5 minutes).
      After calling time at 5 minutes, the leader restates the myth and gives a brief commentary on why the statement is invalid currently. He or she can also elaborate on the consequences, history, and possible methods for countering the myth, asking volunteers for their input in summary and for any specific (to the myth) questions.
4. The process is repeated for the rest of each group's membership until all have shared their myths. Obviously, any disclosure of the fact that all the statements are invalid will detract from the experience, so that should not be divulged in conducting the activity. Five minutes per group member is sufficient for the round.
5. After the round has been completed, each group should select a spokesperson and proceed to debrief the activity. Allow 15–20 minutes more for debriefing, and then solicit short summary statements from each spokesperson for another 10 minutes. Finish by distributing or displaying the collection of myths used.

Variations

The full set of myths can also be given as a sort of true-false listing. Then have participants debate their reasons for holding different positions along the same lines of discussion as above. Following debriefing, provide a key to the myths and make a brief lecture out of that set of explanations. Polling the total group at the conclusion of each statement if read aloud at the end, and possibly tallying the agreement for the total group, are variants to dealing with the information that can add significant demonstrations of social or group positions.

Debriefing

1. What basic motive(s) might underlie the support given to certain beliefs about suicidal behavior?
2. Were there any apparent sex, age, or other patterns of differences in beliefs held by your subgroup (or the whole membership, if polled)?
3. What particular myth(s) received the most support as valid? Which the least? What surprises emerged for you? Why?
4. Was there any felt or apparent wavering on any statement as a result of group pressure?
5. How might the knowledge gained here about myths about suicide affect your behaviors and attitudes?

■ ■ ■   *ACTIVITIES:* AGING GAMES
Games People Should Play*

Understanding what it is like to be old or chronically ill is an important concept for us all. Try these simulations and see what *your* attitude is toward each situation.

Arthritis/Stiff Joints

Materials needed:

Two elastic bandages (3–4 inches wide)
One pair of gloves

What to do:
To simulate stiff knees, wrap an elastic bandage around each knee and try walking around the room; then climb some steps.

Place the same elastic bandages around your elbow and try to put on a coat or eat/drink something.

To feel what it's like to have arthritis of the hands and wrist, put on the gloves and try to button your shirt or blouse.

Complete the following:
While doing this activity I realized _____

_____

To be like this all the time would _____

_____

*Source: Appeared in *Activities for Health Decisions* by D. J. Anspaugh & M. H. Hamrick, 1983, Winston-Salem, NC: Hunter. Adapted from Schnert, Keith W., M.D., "Put Yourself in Their Place," *Family Health,* Vol. 8, No. 4, April, 1976, pp. 38–41.

Stroke/Paralysis

Materials needed:

Pencil and paper, ping pong ball(s)

What to do:

If you are right-handed, take a pencil in your left hand (vice versa for the left-handed) and try to write your name. Would the bank accept your check or would you get an *A* in penmanship?

Place a ping pong ball in your mouth and call a friend on the phone. Did they recognize your voice?

Complete the following:

While doing this activity I realized _____

_____

To be like this all the time would _____

_____

Hearing Loss

Materials needed:

Cotton balls, earmuffs (stereo headphones)

What to do:

Place a cotton ball in each exterior ear canal, then put on the earmuffs. Attempt to talk to someone in another room. How many times did you have to ask that something be repeated?

Turn the television volume down to its lowest level, sit at the opposite end of the room and attempt to listen. Was it hard work? _____

Complete the following:

While doing this activity I realized _____

_____

To be like this all the time would _____

_____

Visual Problems

Materials needed:

Swim goggles or old glasses, wrinkled cellophane

What to do:

Put the cellophane over the glasses or goggles. Attempt to read the newspaper for a few minutes.

Complete the following:

While doing this activity I realized _____

_____

To be like this all the time would _____

_____

Loss of Smell

Materials needed:

Tissue paper

What to do:

Gently push one piece into each nostril. Then, grab an apple or your favorite snack and eat it. Not very tasty, is it?

Complete the following:

While doing this activity I realized _____

_____

To be like this all the time would _____

_____

Loss of Touch

Materials needed:

Rubber cement, needle and thread

What to do:

Cover the fingers with rubber cement and let it dry. Try to thread a needle.

Complete the following:

While doing this activity I realized _____

_____

To be like this all the time would _____

_____

■ ■ ■ ## *ACTIVITIES:* DYING AND DEATH
DISCUSSION AND REPORT STRATEGIES
Life and Death*

Although the various disease agents and accident situations that threaten to cause death tend to be overemphasized in many health education programs, the actual reality of death itself is generally ignored or avoided both in the classroom and in society at large. Reasons for this omission range from the rather frivolous reluctance to bother young people with such an unpleasant subject to very strong beliefs that this sensitive topic should be left to the church and the home. However, health educators, particularly those who are heavily involved in mental health work, have come to realize that the individual's knowledge of the eventual death of oneself and one's loved ones has a real presence, not only when death is imminent or has occurred, but for most of one's life extending from the first moment one is able to understand one's mortal status. There are many prominent examples of persons who

Source: Donald A. Read and Walter H. Green, *Creative Teaching in Health,* (3rd. ed.), pp. 200–3, 366–67 (copyright© 1980), reissued 1989 by Waveland Press, Inc., Prospect Heights, IL. Reprinted with permission from the publisher.

have been forced to take a hard look at death, either because of their own close escape or the actual death of someone very close to them, who have found that the experience had a positive effect on their day-to-day capacity to live with zest and maturity. Although it is both impractical and inadvisable to duplicate the intensity of these real experiences in the classroom, many of the same positive benefits can result from learning experiences designed to help students "come to terms" with this important health topic.

Concept

The nature of one's personal acceptance and adjustment to the inevitability of death has important effects on the strength and effectiveness of one's personality.

Students

Developed for twelfth grade, co-ed classes with average to above-average academic ability; also recommended for similar groups in grades 10 and 11.

Technique

Student Interview Project

Although death is an important area of study, both the realities of modern medical progress and the aforementioned universal habit of avoidance have combined to make the topic remote and abstract to most high school students. Moreover, the beneficial changes in student behavior that would hopefully result from a study of this sensitive topic generally take the form of altered feeling tone, increased peace of mind, and so forth, rather than the overt change sought in the study of nutrition, disease control, and other more traditional health topics. Consequently the real teaching challenge here is to provide reality and impact to an essentially abstract concept. Somehow the various issues, understandings, and subconcepts related to the study of death must be translated into terms and situations with which students can readily identify.

One way this task may be accomplished is through the use of good films or videotapes that realistically present death-related content. These materials may be very effectively worked into any well-planned presentation if they are available; however, at this writing such materials are generally scarce. Another, more practical approach in most teaching situations is to use a small group of students as the medium through which the needed material is conveyed to the class. This calls for the soliciting of three or four student volunteers from among those with better-than-average personal qualities (sensitivity, group acceptance, intelligence) who will then investigate the topic in a meaningful way and report it to the class. This general scheme can take many forms, depending on the particular conditions involved; however, the following description of specific steps may provide a useful basis for planning a teaching sequence in this area:

1. Arrange to meet with the student investigators for a minimum of five to ten minutes either at the back of the classroom during class time or at some mutually convenient time outside of class. During this meeting first acquaint the investigators with the basic benefits that can result from the study of death such as the ability to

- provide effective support and comfort for aggrieved friends and family members who have recently lost loved ones through death.
- provide effective support and comfort to friends and family members who are facing imminent death by terminal illness.
- adjust effectively to the loss of one's own loved ones through death.
- adjust effectively to a situation involving one's own imminent death.
- experience greater happiness and zest for life by coming to terms with the reality of eventual death.

Ask each investigator to use these basic points or objectives as the basis for interviewing a minimum of three persons on their feelings and opinions concerning death, including at least one young person (their own age), one mature adult (parents' age or older), and one person whose work routinely involves contact with dying or aggrieved persons. This last category might include such persons as ministers, priests, or rabbis; nurses on cancer wards, attendants at nursing homes, or other appropriate medical personnel; and morticians and funeral directors. Also advise each investigator to read one or more good articles on the topic before their interview and suggest any specific references you know to be worthwhile. Ask them to meet once on their own before the interviews to coordinate their efforts and once again following the interviews to plan a fifteen- to twenty-minute report to the class. Encourage the investigators to incorporate instructive aids in the form of tape recordings, pamphlets, and so forth, into their presentation but allow them to use a simple symposium format if they wish.

2. During the class meeting immediately preceding the report of the student investigators, generally introduce the class to the topic and the possible benefits of studying it. This may be accomplished by first showing a short film or reading them a synopsis of a good article or news item that relates to some aspect of adjustment to death. After they have had an opportunity to discuss the film or article for three or four minutes, present the following question by use of the chalkboard, overhead projector, or other means:

   What does death mean to you?
   a. The end; the final process of life.
   b. The beginning of a life after death; a transition; a new beginning.
   c. A joining of the spirit with a new cosmic consciousness.
   d. A kind of endless sleep; rest and peace.
   e. Termination of this life but with survival of the spirit.
   f. Don't know.
   g. Other.

   Ask each student to select one of the *a* to *f* selections if it seems reasonably close to what he or she believes and the other item if this is not the case. Following this, have each student write a paragraph in which his or her answer is more fully explained; allow them five to ten minutes for this task. Next tally the choices by a show of hands for each of the *a* through *g* selections, but make it clear that any student may choose not to reveal his choice. Once the tally is completed allow willing students to read their paragraphs to the class beginning with those who chose the most common category and then moving to a consideration of the less popular choices. Allow general discussion of the points raised by each presentation. If the class seems ready in terms of understanding and interest, cut short the individual analysis of paragraphs five minutes before the end of the class period and lead them into a discussion of the following question: "What effect can your beliefs about death have on your ability to live happily and effectively?"

3. Begin the following (second) class meeting with the reports of the student investigators. Unless the reporting team has devised a unique format, the general directions for the symposium should apply to their presentation. Once the basic reports have been completed the class should be ready to explore interesting subtopics in some depth. Many of the questions that might be profitably discussed relate directly to the basic objectives presented in item 1 such as:

- Through what stages must grief-stricken persons generally pass?
- How can one help the aggrieved person respond constructively to his grief? What words or actions should be avoided?
- What kinds of people combine zest for life with an acceptance of death? Do they have common occupations, religious beliefs, life experiences, and so forth, or are they diverse?

Other questions may be suggested by the categories of persons interviewed such as

- How do medical and hospital personnel generally seem to adjust to contact with dying persons?
- Are there apparent differences in how the younger versus older person feels about death?
- How do you think you would respond to news that you will die within six months?

These questions could be pursued in conventional class discussions or where conditions permit, in terms of time available and class readiness; these same questions could be explored by use of role-playing situations that they suggest.

Death Collage*

Goals

1. To have participants identify pictures and words they associate with death and life and to examine why they associate such symbols with one or the other.
2. To examine the interrelationships and/or distinctions made between life and death.

Materials

Work space, many magazines, scissors, glue, construction paper, large envelopes.

Time

Two 40-minute sessions or 1½ hours.

---

*Reprinted with the permission of Lexington Books, an imprint of Macmillan, Inc., from *Thanatopics: Activities and Exercises for Confronting Death* by J. Eugene Knott, Mary C. Ribar, Betty M. Duson and Marc R. King. Copyright © 1989 by Lexington Books.

Procedures

Session 1

Explain to the participants that they will be making individual collages about life and death. Allow them 30–40 minutes to go through magazines and cut out as many pictures and words having to do with life and death as possible and put them in their large envelope. Participants will take envelopes with them at the end of the session. Between sessions, if this is done in two sessions, participants are encouraged to look over the pictures and words and add to them. Instruct them not to discard any items at this time.

Session 2

At the beginning of this session have participants find a work space where they can arrange items and glue them on paper to make a collage. Discards may be made at this time. No further instructions should be given. Allow 15–20 minutes for this activity. At the end of this time, assemble all participants with their collages. Have each participant explain his or her collage and answer questions.

Debriefing

1. What kinds of items did you choose to represent life? death? Were they similar or different?
2. When you looked at them between sessions, did you have any difficulty identifying which ones were death and which ones were life?
3. Did you add any words or pictures between sessions?
4. Which group of items was easier to assemble? Why?
5. Were you more aware of possible inclusions between sessions than you were before you began this exercise?
6. When you began to construct your collage, did you mix or separate life and death items?
7. Are they part of one another or separate and distinct?
8. Did you communicate with anyone about this project—either in the group or outside the group?
9. Did anyone help you or did you help anyone else? Why or why not? Who?
10. Did you have any difficulty with any part of this activity?
11. Did the choosing of pictures and words, the putting them together, and the explaining of your collage give you any perspective or insight into your own attitudes toward life and/or death?
12. Did you discard any items? If so, what items, and why? If not, why not?

The Living Will*

Read the Living Will and then divide into small groups to discuss the following questions.

---

*Source: *Activities for Health Decisions* by D. J. Anspaugh & M. H. Hamrick, 1983, Winston-Salem, NC: Hunter. Courtesy of Concern for Dying Council, New York, N.Y.

To My Family, My Physician, My Lawyer and All Others Whom It May Concern

Death is as much a reality as birth, growth, maturity and old age—it is the one certainty of life. If the time comes when I can no longer take part in decisions for my own future, let this statement stand as an expression of my wishes and directions, while I am still of sound mind.

If at such a time the situation should arise in which there is no reasonable expectation of my recovery from extreme physical or mental disability, I direct that I be allowed to die and not be kept alive by medications, artificial means or "heroic measures." I do, however, ask that medication be mercifully administered to me to alleviate suffering even though this may shorten my remaining life.

This statement is made after careful consideration and is in accordance with my strong convictions and beliefs. I want the wishes and directions here expressed carried out to the extent permitted by law. Insofar as they are not legally enforceable, I hope that those to whom this Will is addressed will regard themselves as morally bound by these provisions.

Signed _____

Date _____

Witness _____

Witness _____

Copies of this request have been given to _____

_____

_____

Questions for Discussion

1. Should an individual have the right to determine how he is to die?
2. Who should determine when to "pull the plug"?
3. Does a person have a right to die if he chooses? By euthanasia? In the hospice?
4. Is the expense worthwhile for maintaining life when all seems hopeless?

Leading Causes of Death in the U.S.*

The purpose of this activity is to compare the changes in causes of mortality in the U.S. between 1900 and 1990. In the left column are listed the ten leading causes of death in 1900 in rank order. In the right column try to list in rank order the ten leading causes of death in 1990. See if you can identify the five causes of death that remain from the 1900 list. Add the remaining leading causes of death.

---

*Source: *Activities for Health Decisions* by D. J. Anspaugh & M. H. Hamrick, 1983, Winston-Salem, NC: Hunter.

	1900		1990
1.	Influenza and pneumonia	1.	_____
2.	Tuberculosis	2.	_____
3.	Gastroenteritis	3.	_____
4.	Heart disease	4.	_____
5.	Strokes	5.	_____
6.	Nephritis	6.	_____
7.	Accidents	7.	_____
8.	Cancer	8.	_____
9.	Diseases of early infancy	9.	_____
10.	Diptheria	10.	_____

Childhood Recollections*

Goals

1. To increase awareness of how personal attitudes about death and dying develop.
2. To identify how one's present attitudes and feelings toward death and dying relate to early experience.
3. To discover the extent to which one's feelings about death and dying are shared by others.

When people discuss and explore together their personal experiences and feelings about death, they often discover that their attitudes about death and dying are shared by others. In order to explore fully one's feelings about death, a structure for exploration is often necessary.

Insofar as childhood memories are reflections of the past, exploring and discussing such memories about death and dying can be less threatening than directly discussing one's current feelings. Through the process of exploration, participants are often able to generate memories and feelings they thought they had forgotten. These early experiences can then be reviewed to determine how they might be currently influencing one's attitudes about death.

Materials

Poster paper or chalkboard on which to write discussion questions.

Time

Minimum of 1 hour.

---

*Reprinted with the permission of Lexington Books, an imprint of Macmillan, Inc., from *Thanatopics: Activities and Exercises for Confronting Death* by J. Eugene Knott, Mary C. Ribar, Betty M. Duson and Marc R. King. Copyright © 1989 by Lexington Books.

Procedures

1. Instruct participants to form small groups of three to five members and find a comfortable location in the room.
2. Introduce the exercise:

> This activity is designed to assist us in remembering and talking about our childhood memories and experiences of death and dying. One of the purposes is to increase our awareness of how we felt about death as a child. This awareness may then help us understand our present feelings and assist us in clarifying what attitudes we might wish to change.
>
> You may find that you can't remember many experiences. You may also discover that someone else's memories remind you of a variety of experiences you had forgotten about.
>
> You may also find that there are some experiences you prefer not to discuss with your group. That is perfectly OK. Talk about only what you wish to talk about.

3. Introduce the first topic of discussion. Because some groups might require more time to discuss certain topics, allow flexibility by writing topic headings on the chalkboard and encouraging each group to move through the topics at a pace comfortable to each. Ask them to review in their mind's eye and share as they are willing and comfortable:

> What were some of your earliest experiences with death when you were a child? Was it a death of a person? a pet? What feelings do you recall about these experiences? Who did you talk to about your feelings? (pause)
>
> How did members of your family deal with their feelings about death and dying? What particular memories do you have about how your family expressed their feelings? (pause)
>
> What did you learn about death from your peers and close friends? (pause)
>
> What are your memories of times when you were responsible for killing some living things? What feelings did you have about these experiences? What feelings do you now have about these experiences? (pause)
>
> What are your early memories of times when you thought you were going to die or be killed? What feelings did you have about these events? Who did you turn to for help?

Debriefing

The following questions can be discussed among the entire group as a way of achieving closure for the activity:

1. What have you learned about your attitudes toward death through this exercise? How do you feel about this experience?

2. What other questions might we have discussed about our childhood memories of death?
3. What might be done to assist children in exploring their attitudes and feelings about death?

Journal*

Goals

1. To provide an opportunity for ongoing personal reflection and writing.
2. To identify patterns, puzzles, questions, answers, ideas, feelings, and resources.
3. To record and perhaps share growth, change, self-knowledge, new learning, and old learnings newly discovered.
4. To provide the facilitator with a regular, informal, nonthreatening means of communication and feedback from and with individuals in an ongoing group.

Materials

A notebook, diary, or other book with blank pages for each person.

Time

At least 30 minutes between sessions. Could be short daily entries or one or more longer entries weekly.

Procedures

Participants record reflections about each session between sessions. These journals should have no format requirements and should allow participants to write freely about the group experience, as well as any feelings, insights, observations, questions, answers, new learnings, new insights into old learnings, and any other related topic.

Journals should be read regularly by the facilitator with any needed follow-up noted. It is often helpful for the facilitator to write answers, comments, and reflections to each writer. The journals should remain a confidential and individual form of communication between participant and facilitator.

Variations

Journal entries can be shared with other group members at the beginning of each session on a voluntary basis *or* group members can form dyads and share journals with one another at some point in each session.

Audio cassettes can offer a quick, vocal form of exchange, including commentary with corresponding peers or group leaders; however, it can also be a more cumbersome way to document a longitudinal set of entries of great number or length. Obviously, this format requires audiotapes and recorders.

---

*Reprinted with the permission of Lexington Books, an imprint of Macmillan, Inc., from *Thanatopics: Activities and Exercises for Confronting Death* by J. Eugene Knott, Mary C. Ribar, Betty M. Duson and Marc R. King. Copyright © 1989 by Lexington Books.

Debriefing

This can take place regularly through reading, writing, and comments. At the end of the group sessions, the following questions would be a useful form of debriefing:

1. Was the journal helpful?
2. Was it easy or difficult? How?
3. What would you change or do differently?
4. Were comments helpful, or would you prefer no comments?
5. What types of entries did you make most often?
6. Did you share anything in your journal with others in the group? outside the group? If so, what prompted this sharing? What was the response? Would you share it again?
7. Will you continue to keep a journal? Why or why not?

■ ■ ■   *ACTIVITIES:* LEARNING ENHANCEMENTS

Aging

Exercise Can Beat Arthritis. This video is a specially designed system of nine gentle exercise routines that are easy to follow. The exercises help reduce arthritis pain, increase range of motion, strengthen muscles and joints, increasing energy, and reduce fatigue. 40 minutes. Health Edco, 800/299-3366, ext. 295.

Senior Flex. A safe and enjoyable approach to senior exercise, this video allows everyone to progress at his own pace. 46 minutes. Health Edco, 800/299-3366, ext. 295.

The Aging Process. This program explains the effects of aging on the mind and body, explores the damage and cell clock theories about why cells wear out, and examines the habits that affect both longevity and the quality of life. The program points out that it is never to late to mend one's ways. 19 minutes. Films for the Humanities and Sciences, 800/257-5126.

Studies in Aging. This program reports on current research to determine the effects of aging. It features a 74-year-old father and his 38-year-old son, as well as the community of Roseto, PA, subject of a landmark study in aging begun in 1964. 19 minutes. Films for the Humanities and Sciences, 800/257-5126.

Ageless America. The focuses of this program: caring for the elderly, why women live longer than men, the prospect of aging for a new generation of the middle-aged with fewer children and many more single women, the "sandwich generation" of adults with responsibility for aging parents and young children, and the process and problems of aging itself. 52 minutes, color. Films for the Humanities and Sciences, 800/257-5126.

Factors in Healthy Aging. A half-century-long study that examined the mental health of Harvard graduates over their lifetimes is used to illuminate the predictors of healthy aging. The impacts of diet, smoking, drinking, family history, and personality are discussed. New research is highlighted that offers the possibility of altering our genetic structure to enable us to live longer and in better health. 28 minutes, color. Films for the Humanities and Sciences, 800/257-5126.

Caring for the Elderly. An overview of the various methods of care available for the aging, from day-care centers and group housing to respite care and nursing homes. This program profiles a middle-aged couple and talks to social workers, senior citizen advocates, and nursing home administrators to clarify the issues and options. 19 minutes, color. Films for the Humanities and Sciences, 800/257-5126.

The Wit and Wisdom of Aging. Norman Cousins, himself a survivor of death sentences passed by his doctors, worked with "terminal" cancer patients who refused to die as scheduled. The will to survive and to be healed are potent medicines; in many cases, the incurable have been cured. 26 minutes, color. Films for the Humanities and Sciences, 800/257-5126.

How to Live Past 100. Is there a secret to living past the age of 100? This program examines the lives of some centenarians to seek clues to longevity and to determine the reasons for the increasing number of centenarians. The program also looks at the most common health hazards for the elderly, the relationship between social and physical activity and longevity, and whether intelligence declines in old age. 19 minutes, color. Films for the Humanities and Sciences, 800/257-5126.

Slowing the Clock. We can't stop the aging process, but this program shows how we can at least slow down its effects. The focus is on the current research centering on the role that the thymus gland and so-called "free radicals" play in aging. 26 minutes, color. Films for the Humanities and Sciences, 800/257-5126.

Death and Dying

Why Suicide? Find out why some teens find life unbearable. All four teens in this program have attempted suicide. From PBS. 30 minutes. Health Edco, 800/299-3366, ext. 395.

Suicide: The Teenager's Perspective. This program deals with peer groups, one promising solution to the increasing number of teen suicides. Teenagers are accustomed to going to their friends with their problems; in this case, the friends have been trained to recognize the signs of impending suicide. In his program, Jim Wells, a nationally recognized expert on suicide, says that even as teens are taking their own lives, they do not really want to die. The purpose of this program is to provide some help before an attempt is made. 26 minutes, color. Films for the Humanities and Sciences, 800/257-5126.

Teenage Suicide. This documentary explores some of the reasons teens commit suicide and the recent increase in suicides and describes some of the behavior patterns to which family and friends should be alert. A young man who attempted suicide describes his calls for help and how he hoped they would be heeded. 19 minutes, color. Films for the Humanities and Sciences, 800/257-5126.

Gifted Adolescents and Suicide. Intelligent and accomplished beyond their years but emotionally immature, isolated, and vulnerable—these are the adolescents who are at high risk. This specially adapted Phil Donahue program features two couples who lost intellectually superior 17-year-olds to suicide, a gifted adolescent who attempted suicide, and specialists in adolescent psychology. The program points out how parents and teachers need to recognize the pressure of expectations on superachievers. 26 minutes, color. Films for the Humanities and Sciences, 800/257-5126.

The Right to Die. The medical, ethical, and legal dilemmas of dying patients and their physicians and nurses are discussed in this video. 26 minutes. Films for the Humanities and Sciences, 800/257-5126.

The Biology of Death. Films for the Humanities and Sciences, 800/257-5126.

Teen Suicide. This Phil Donahue show brings family members and friends of suicide victims and teens who have attempted suicide together with a psychotherapist. This program seeks to find ways to stem the tide of increasing suicide rates among teens, to help others recognize the signals and warning cries of potential suicides, and to show what kind of help is available. Films for the Humanities and Sciences, 800/257-5126.

Children Die, Too. Dr. Sandra Fox of Boston's Good Grief Program discusses how people can help each other after the death of a child. A pediatric oncology nurse explains how a cancer treatment team can help families through a child's terminal diagnosis and treatment. The program also discusses how children express grief. 26 minutes. Films for the Humanities and Sciences, 800/257-5126.

Saying Good-Bye. Almost no one will escape the pain of surviving a loved one. This program talks to people who have gone through this difficult time to find out how they dealt with their grief: a support group for widows, a woman whose parents died within a year of each other, and a woman whose husband died of cancer. Also interviewed are a hospital chaplain and the director of a hospice. 26 minutes, color. Films for the Humanities and Sciences, 800/257-5126.

Coping with Loss. This program uses the Challenger tragedy as the starting point to show the reactions of schoolchildren and the opinions of educators and therapists about helping children deal with loss. It also profiles the family of a person who is dying, showing the psychological importance of grieving. 19 minutes, color. Films for the Humanities and Sciences, 800/257-5126.

The Forgotten Mourner. When there is a death in the family, friends flock to comfort spouses and parents of the bereaved, while siblings and grandparents are overlooked. Mourners who have been overlooked are joined in this specially adapted Phil Donahue program by a clinical psychologist in discussing how mourners can best be comforted. 28 minutes, color. Films for the Humanities and Sciences, 800/257-5126.

Caring for the Terminally Ill. This program emphasizes that the goal of care for the terminally ill is not to conquer the patient's disease but to provide support, ease pain and anxiety, and enhance what time remains. The program shows the role of the spouse, visiting nurses, and hospice personnel in caring for patients; a social worker explains how terminally ill patients often feel abandoned by family members because of emotional and financial stress. 19 minutes, color. Films for the Humanities and Sciences, 800/257-5126.

New Living Wills. This program examines the concept of living wills and advance directives. Host Jamie Guth spends time with families in intensive care units, where they are forced to make decisions about life-saving care; their experience may serve as a guide to viewers who may want to decide before the event whether they wish to be maintained on ventilators, fluids, and drugs. Patients, their families, and doctors also present their views of the situation. 30 minutes, color. Films for the Humanities and Sciences, 800/257-5126.

Dying Wish. This documentary looks at some of the decisions family and caregivers may have to make: to pull the plug that keeps a brain-dead patient's heart beating? to take extraordinary measures to resuscitate a seriously ill patient who will live in great pain? Can society afford to keep one incurable patient alive while dozens die because they lack access to the procedures that would cure them? 52 minutes, color. Films for the Humanities and Sciences, 800/257-5126.

"Doctor Death": Medical Ethics and Doctor-Assisted Suicide. Dr. Jack Kevorkian is surely not the first physician to assist his patients in committing suicide, but he is certainly the first to publicize his work. In this specially adapted Phil Donahue program, the man dubbed "Dr. Death" offers an in-depth explanation of his beliefs about incurable illness and the ethics of doctor-assisted suicide. 28 minutes, color. Films for the Humanities and Sciences, 800/257-5126.

Mercy Killing. Who is to make the choice between prolonging unendurable pain or ending life? What are the obligations of love and of law? These are some of the questions addressed in this specially adapted Phil Donahue program by people who have made hard decisions about their loved ones. 28 minutes, color. Films for the Humanities and Sciences, 800/257-5126.

REFERENCES

Anspaugh, D. J., & Hamrick, M. H. (1983). *Activities for health decisions.* Winston-Salem, NC: Hunter.

Bee, H. L. (1987). *The journey of adulthood.* New York: Macmillan.

Brodsky, D., & Ezell, G. (1985). *Impact of availability of health care information on the market behavior of providers and consumers.* Unpublished research report submitted to the AARP/Andrus Foundation, December 1985, Washington, DC.

Burdman, G. (1986). *Healthful aging.* Englewood Cliffs, NJ: Prentice-Hall.

Butler, R. & Lewis, M. (1982). *Aging & mental health.* St. Louis: Mosby.

DeSpelder, L. A., & Strickland, A. L. (1992). *The last dance* (3rd ed.). Mountain View, CA: Mayfield.

Ebersole, P., & Hess, P. (1990). *Toward healthy aging: Human needs and nursing response* (3rd ed.). St. Louis: Mosby.

Ferrini, A. F., & Ferrini, R. L. (1993). *Health in the later years* (2nd ed.). Dubuque, IA: Wm. C. Brown.

Greene, W. H. & Read, D. S. (1980). *Creative teaching in health.* Prospect Heights, IL: Waveland Press, Inc.

Humphry, D., & Wickett, A. (1987). *The right to die: Understanding euthanasia.* New York: Harper & Row.

Kalish, R. (1985). *Death, grief, and caring relationships* (2nd ed.). Monterey, CA: Brooks/Cole.

Kearl, M. (1989). *Endings: A sociology of death and dying.* New York: Oxford University Press.

Kubler-Ross, E. (1975). *Death: The final stage of growth*. Englewood Cliffs, NJ: Prentice-Hall.

Leviton, D. (1985). Counseling the bereaved or dying: An aspect of health education. *Health Education, 16,* 35–40.

Loya, R. (1983). *Health education teaching ideas*. Reston, VA: AAHPERD.

MacNeil, R. D., & Teague, M. L. (1987). *Aging and leisure: Vitality in later life*. Englewood Cliffs, NJ: Prentice-Hall.

Molnar-Stickles, L. (1985). Effect of a brief instructional unit in death education on the death attitudes of prospective elementary school teachers. *Journal of School Health, 55,* 234–236.

Oaks, J., & Ezell, G. (1993). *Dying and death* (2nd ed.). Scottsdale, AZ: Gorsuch Scarisbrick.

Spence, A. P. (1989). *Biology of human aging*. Englewood Cliffs, NJ: Prentice-Hall.

Teague, M. L. (1987). *Health promotion programs: Achieving high-level wellness in the later years*. Indianapolis: Benchmark.

Tillman, K. G., & Toner, P. R. (1990). *How to survive teaching health*. West Nyack, NY: Parker.

Wass, H., Berardo, F. M., & Neimeyer, R. A. (1988). *Dying: Facing the facts* (2nd ed.). Washington, DC: Hemisphere.

Zipprich, K. G. (1977). *Health education puzzles and puzzlers*. Portland, ME: J. Weston Walch.

Epilogue

The teacher is the critical attribute to a successful comprehensive K-12 Health Education Program. The skill with which the teacher coordinates and adapts the continuous, multifaceted information from the ever increasing health and social resources through the professional network to the school and community and faculty to the classroom is vital for the continuous evolution of a quality program.

Rebecca Gibson Laemel

It is hoped that this textbook provides the framework for providing a comprehensive health education program. The emphasis has been on the instructional component which seeks to provide a solid cognitive base complemented by opportunities to assess and formulate a value system. The intent is that all teaching be directed toward the formation of positive health attitudes which will be manifested in behavior conducive to the highest quality life possible for each student.

The Nation's Health Objective for the year 2000 are clearly indicative of moving Americans toward the ideal of high-level wellness and the acceptance of personal responsibility for individual, family, and community well-being. To accomplish the nation's objectives, there is no more important site than that of school. Each state and community must strive to develop a comprehensive school health program. This requires an effort which begins in kindergarten and continues through grade 12. Each step in the educational process must be predicated in what has previously occurred in the learning situation. However, instruction is only one component of a comprehensive school health program; health services, healthful environment, and administration coordination are all necessary.

Health education can be viewed as a planned service of experiences that promote disease prevention behavior and reinforce positive health experiences for each individual. These experiences must aid students in learning how to live and make adjustments to the society in which they live. Health is essential to all that occurs within the educational experience. Without good health, pupils will have difficulty reading, writing, and performing the necessary activities for learning.

The content areas of health education are many and varied. Health education is neither family life, drug, spiritual, nor physical education. Although each one is an important component, a truly health-educated person is one who is physically and psychologically fit and who is capable of making positive heath decisions concerning drugs, lifestyles, and the environment. Each year new crises arise that require health educators to modify, add to, or change curricular effort. New challenges exist in the areas of HIV education, nutrition, and environmental issues. The one constant in all this is the classroom teacher. The professional dedication and love for the student must always be present if health education is to be successful. What students learn about themselves, their peers, and their society begins with the teacher.

Many professional organizations, including private and federal agencies, are striving to promote health education within the schools. For example, the Association for the Advancement of Health Education (AAHE), the American School Health Association (ASHA), the American Public Health Association (APHA), the American Medical Association (AMA), the American Heart Association, the American Lung Association, and the American Cancer Society are some of the groups that support health education. In addition, there are several agencies within the federal government that seek to support health education programs. Despite the efforts of these and other groups, heath education still does not receive the necessary priority by school districts or school boards to have a significant impact. Some schools do offer comprehensive and sequential health education for students. Unfortunately, too many provide very little and only then to meet what is considered necessary to combat crises. The health program described in this text will enable teachers to plan effective health education programs. More importantly, the authors hope it will motivate teachers to seek the support of local and state officials to establish comprehensive school health educators for their schools and school districts so that health education can truly impact in a positive fashion on the schools' most important product—the students it serves.

Index

ISBN 0-02-303562-5